The Psychology of Criminal and Antisocial Behavior

To Natalie. The love of my life: friend, wife, lover, and muse. Partner in all things but my own folly, from which you rescue me often. To paraphrase the immortal words of Robert Burns: "To know you is to love you, love but you, and love forever."

— Grant Sinnamon

The Psychology of Criminal and Antisocial Behavior

Victim and Offender Perspectives

Edited By

Wayne Petherick

Grant Sinnamon

AMSTERDAM • BOSTON • HEIDELBERG • LONDON
NEW YORK • OXFORD • PARIS • SAN DIEGO
SAN FRANCISCO • SINGAPORE • SYDNEY • TOKYO

Academic Press is an imprint of Elsevier

Academic Press is an imprint of Elsevier
125 London Wall, London EC2Y 5AS, United Kingdom
525 B Street, Suite 1800, San Diego, CA 92101-4495, United States
50 Hampshire Street, 5th Floor, Cambridge, MA 02139, United States
The Boulevard, Langford Lane, Kidlington, Oxford OX5 1GB, United Kingdom

Notices
Knowledge and best practice in this field are constantly changing. As new research and experience
broaden our understanding, changes in research methods, professional practices, or medical treatment
may become necessary.

Practitioners and researchers must always rely on their own experience and knowledge in evaluating
and using any information, methods, compounds, or experiments described herein. In using such
information or methods they should be mindful of their own safety and the safety of others, including
parties for whom they have a professional responsibility.

To the fullest extent of the law, neither the Publisher nor the authors, contributors, or editors, assume
any liability for any injury and/or damage to persons or property as a matter of products liability,
negligence or otherwise, or from any use or operation of any methods, products, instructions, or ideas
contained in the material herein.

Library of Congress Cataloging-in-Publication Data
A catalog record for this book is available from the Library of Congress

British Library Cataloguing-in-Publication Data
A catalogue record for this book is available from the British Library

ISBN: 978-0-12-809287-3

For information on all Academic Press publications
visit our website at https://www.elsevier.com/

Working together
to grow libraries in
developing countries

www.elsevier.com • www.bookaid.org

Publisher: Sara Tenney
Acquisition Editor: Elizabeth Brown
Editorial Project Manager: Joslyn Chaiprasert-Paguio
Production Project Manager: Lisa Jones
Designer: Matthew Limbert

Typeset by TNQ Books and Journals

Contents

CHAPTER 3   Victimology and Predicting Victims of Personal Violence **79**

GAELLE L.M. BROTTO, GRANT SINNAMON AND WAYNE PETHERICK

**CHAPTER 4   Threat and Violence Intervention: Influenced
by Victim and Offender Perspectives 145**

JAMES S. CAWOOD

**CHAPTER 5   Profiling in Violent Crimes: The Perpetrator
and the Victim in Cases of Filicide 167**

FÁTIMA ALMEIDA AND DUARTE N. VIEIRA

CHAPTER 6   Risk Assessment in Youth Justice: A Child-Centered Approach to Managing Interventions..211

GARETH NORRIS, GWYN GRIFFITH AND HEATHER NORRIS

CHAPTER 11   **Domestic Violence: Psychological Issues Related to the Victim and Offender** **343**

MAURO PAULINO

CHAPTER 12   **Honor Killings and Domestic Violence: The Same or Different?** **361**

CARLETTA XAVIER, WAYNE PETHERICK AND GRANT SINNAMON

**CHAPTER 15   Child Sexual Offenders: The Psychology
of Offending** **439**

LARISSA CHRISTENSEN

**CHAPTER 16   The Psychology of Adult Sexual Grooming:
Sinnamon's Seven-Stage Model of Adult
Sexual Grooming** **459**

GRANT SINNAMON

CHAPTER 17 **Searching for the Spectrum of the Querulous......489**

GRANT LESTER

CHAPTER 18 **A Multidisciplinary Approach to Understanding
Internet Love Scams: Implications for Law
Enforcement..523**

MAJEED KHADER AND POH SHU YUN

About the Authors

Fatima Almeida

Fatima holds a master's degree in forensic psychology from the Faculty of Psychology and Educational Sciences of the University of Coimbra, Portugal. She also has a master's in legal medicine and forensic sciences from the Faculty of Medicine of the University of Coimbra, Portugal, where her thesis was about profiling in violent crimes. Fatima is currently a PhD student of forensic sciences at the Faculty of Medicine of the University of Oporto (where she studies serial sexual offenders, serial killers, and filicide). She is currently associate professor of forensic psychology at Instituto de Educação e Cidadania and is also the Psychology Branch Coordinator of the ICATE project as well as a member of the Psychological Assessment and Psychometrics Laboratory (Faculty of Psychology and Educational Sciences of the University of Coimbra, Portugal). Fatima has authored numerous books and articles about criminal profiling and forensic psychology.

Gaelle Brotto

Gaelle Brotto has a bachelor's of psychology degree from the University of Lille 3 in France and a master's of criminology degree from Bond University in Australia. Her research interests are in the areas of victimology, criminal motivations, and the utility and application of typologies. She is a doctoral scholar in the Faculty of Society and Design at Bond University and is about to submit her PhD thesis, which has developed a victim motivational typology based on behaviors, motivations, and personality traits in order to better understand victimization.

James S. Cawood

Dr. James S. Cawood is president of Factor One, a California-based corporation specializing in threat assessment and management, violence risk assessment, behavioral analysis, security consulting, and investigations.

He currently serves on the editorial board of the *Journal of Threat Assessment and Management* (American Psychological Association) and is the former president of the Association of Threat Assessment Professionals (ATAP). He has also served as the association's second vice president and president of the Northern California Chapter of ATAP; on the ASIS International Foundation Board and was secretary of the board; as the chairman of the board of the California Association of Licensed Investigators and has served as chairman of their Legislative Committee; and as a board member for the Association of Workplace Investigators.

Dr. Cawood is a graduate of UC Berkeley, holds a master's degree in forensic psychology from Argosy University, and a PhD in psychology from Northcentral University. He has served on the faculties of Golden Gate University, in their security management degree program and the University of California, Santa Cruz extension, teaching threat management. He is a Certified Protection Professional, Professional Certified Investigator, Physical Security Professional, Certified Fraud Examiner,

Certified Security Professional, Certified Professional Investigator, Certified International Investigator, and Certified Threat Manager. He has also written articles and book chapters for various professional publications.

Larissa Christensen
Larissa S. Christensen has recently submitted her PhD (psychology) at Deakin University, Melbourne. Her main research/academic interest is the attrition of child sexual abuse cases from the criminal justice process, in particular, exploring the case characteristics associated with the attrition of child sexual abuse cases in the early stages of the criminal justice process. Her work has led to the identification of a number of recommendations to prevent the unnecessary attrition of child sexual abuse cases. She is currently a sessional academic in the School of Criminology and Criminal Justice at Griffith University, Queensland, and has been awarded for her teaching excellence. She is currently working on a range of projects for the Queensland Police Service. Her recent work has been published in Psychiatry, Psychology, and Law and is currently in press with the International Journal of Police Science and Management.

Therese Ellis-Smith
Therese Ellis-Smith is a forensic psychologist who has worked in correctional services for over 25 years. She has developed criminogenic programs and correctional policy, in addition to holding senior management roles, in several Australian jurisdictions. Therese is currently completing a doctor of philosophy program at Bond University. Her current research interests include arson profiling and the assessment and treatment of arsonists, particularly those from indigenous communities. Therese is also a member of the Australian Psychological Society College of Forensic Psychologists national committee. She supervises provisional psychologists, operates a private practice, presents at local and international conferences, and is an adjunct teaching fellow at Bond University.

Gwyn Griffith
Dr. Gwyn Griffith is the service manager of a Youth Offending Team based in Aberystwyth, United Kingdom. He originally trained as a mathematical biologist gaining a PhD from the University of Wales, Cardiff, in 1989. He then worked as a research scientist up to 2001 when he retrained as a probation officer. From 2001 to 2008 he worked for the National Probation Service delivering rehabilitation programs to adult offenders. He then switched over to youth justice. He has an interest in applying research findings in actual practice with young people.

Majeed Khader
Majeed Khader is the director of the Home Team Behavioural Sciences Centre under the Ministry of Home Affairs, Singapore. Dr. Majeed is also the chief psychologist of the Singapore Police Force. A trained hostage negotiator, his previous operational duties include being the ex-deputy commander of the crisis negotiation unit and a trainer with the negotiation unit. He teaches criminal psychology part time as an assistant professor

(adjunct) at the School of Humanities and Social Sciences at Nanyang Technology University. For the past 23 years, Dr. Majeed has overseen the development of psychological services in the areas of stress, resilience, employee selection, deception psychology, leadership, crisis negotiations, crime profiling, and crisis psychology. For his work, he was awarded the National Day Public Administration Award (Bronze) in 2006 by the President of Singapore and once again the Public Administration Award (Silver) in 2014. Majeed holds a master's degree (with distinction) in forensic psychology from the University of Leicester, United Kingdom, and a PhD in psychology (specializing in personality and crisis leadership) from the University of Aberdeen, Scotland. He also holds a degree in Economics and Sociology from the University of London. Majeed has been invited as a speaker to organizations in Indonesia, Malaysia, Japan, Canada, Hong Kong, and the United States to share information on crime psychology, terrorism, and leadership. He has also presented at the FBI, NCIS, and the RCMP. He has been the chairman of three major international conferences held in Singapore titled the "Asian Conference of Criminal and Operations Psychology." He has been the Asian director and sits on the board of the US-based Society of Police and Criminal Psychology. He is a registered psychologist with the Singapore Psychological Society, and a member of the British and American psychological societies.

Andrea Lee
Andrea is a postgraduate scholar in the Faculty of Society and Design and the Faculty of Law at Bond University, Gold Coast, Australia. Her research interests address issues facing male victims of partner violence and the assessment and management of partner violence risk. Contact: andrea.lee@student.bond.edu.au.

Grant Lester
Dr. Lester is a consultant forensic psychiatrist whose public practice is with the Victorian Institute of Forensic Mental Health, Victoria. His public practice has been in high-security mental health facilities and prisons. He is also a sitting member of Victoria's Mental Health Tribunal.

His private work and research interest has been into querulent and vexatious complainants and litigants and he has researched with Ombudsman's Offices and Courts throughout Australia. He currently presents and trains staff of courts, government and private organizations in the management of unreasonable complainant or litigant behavior including both administrative techniques as well as risk assessment and management of aggressive and violent behaviors.

Robyn Lincoln
Robyn Lincoln is assistant professor in criminology at Bond University, Gold Coast, Australia. Her research and publications have centered on violence in Aboriginal communities, forensic interviewing techniques, and wrongful convictions. She recently completed two federally funded research projects on the consequences of naming indigenous youth involved in justice proceedings and a year-long industry-partnered study to examine violence against urban bus drivers. Contact: rlincoln@bond.edu.au.

Amber McKinley
Dr. Amber McKinley is an applied victimologist and subject coordinator for JST311 Evidence and Investigation and JST345 Police and Victims at Charles Sturt University's Australian Graduate School of Policing and Security. She holds bachelor of liberal studies, master's of criminal justice, and doctor of philosophy degrees. Her thesis investigated Homicide Solvability Factors and Applied Victimology in New South Wales from 1994 to 2013. Amber is also a squadron leader (specialist reserve) in the Royal Australian Air Force and consults with the Australia Defense Force Investigative Service. She teaches and researches an array of topics, including applied and forensic victimology, homicide, solvability and clearance rates, criminal behaviors, police investigations of serious crimes, and the changing typologies of Australian homicide. Amber's current research projects are focused on aspects of multiagency and trauma-informed victim care in police investigations.

Gareth Norris
Dr. Gareth Norris is a senior lecturer in the Department of Psychology at Aberystwyth University, United Kingdom. He is a graduate of the MSc Investigative Psychology course from Liverpool University and was awarded his PhD from Bond University, Australia, on the topic of the authoritarian personality. Gareth has a general interest in the application of psychology in legal contexts and in particular the use of technology in the courtroom. He has published in a number of high-profile journals and presented at international conferences, including the American Bar Association and National Association of Criminal Defense Lawyers. One of the main areas of his research focus is in the interpretation and application of statistical evidence, and the use of such information, such as risk assessment inventories, in guiding legal decision-making.

Heather Norris
Heather Norris is a teaching fellow in the Department of Law and Criminology at Aberystwyth University, United Kingdom. After graduating from Dartmouth College, New Hampshire, United States, she studied criminology in Australia, where she found her interest in youth justice. She is particularly interested in the psychological impact of restorative justice (RJ) on participants in the youth justice system, and her doctoral thesis is an interdisciplinary approach evaluating the impact of RJ on happiness, school engagement, and self-esteem in young people. Further interests include mental health and the criminal justice system, as well as pedagogical research.

Michele Pathé
Michele is a senior forensic psychiatrist with the Queensland Forensic Mental Health Service and an adjunct professor at the Key Centre for Ethics, Law, Justice and Governance at Queensland's Griffith University. She was formerly a consultant psychiatrist and assistant clinical director at the Victorian Institute of Forensic Mental Health and the director of Threat Management, a private clinic for victims of stalking. Dr. Pathé is currently the consulting psychiatrist to the Queensland Fixated Threat Assessment Centre (QFTAC), a joint police-mental health intelligence agency for high-risk, often

mentally ill, fixated persons. She is a member of the Fixated Research Group, whose original studies commissioned by the British Home Office gave rise to the foundational FTAC in London in 2006.

For the past 25 years, Dr Pathé has had a clinical and research interest in stalking, threats, and public figure fixation and has collaborated with local, interstate, and international law enforcement and intelligence agencies to develop risk mitigation strategies in these areas. She has lectured extensively in this field, authoring and coauthoring three books, over 70 research articles, book chapters, a doctoral thesis, and risk assessment tools.

Mauro Paulino

Mauro Paulino is currently a coordinator at Mind, Institute of Clinical and Forensic Psychology (Lisbon, Portugal). He is also a forensic psychologist consultant at the Instituto Nacional de Medicina Legal e Ciências Forenses, IP (Gabinete Médico-Legal e Forense Península Setúbal) and a clinical director of Pelo Sonho - Cooperativa de Solidariedade Social, supervising shelter and care center for victims of spousal violence. Mauro received his master's degree in legal medicine and forensic sciences at the University of Lisbon, School of Medicine, completing his research in the field of spousal violence. He is an author and coordinator of several books, namely Abusadores Sexuais de Crianças: A Verdade Escondida (Child Sexual Offender: The Hidden Truth edited by Prime Books), Profiling, Vitimologia & Ciências Forenses: Perspetivas Atuais (Profiling, Victimology & Forensic Sciences: Today's Perspectives, 2nd ed., edited by Pactor), O Inimigo Em Casa: Dar Voz Aos Silêncios da Violência Doméstica (The Enemy at Home: Giving Voice to the Silence of Domestic Violence, 2nd edition, edited by Prime Books), Psicologia, Justiça & Ciências Forenses: Perspetivas Atuais (Psychology, Justice & Forensic Sciences: Current Perspectives edited by Pactor), and Forensic Psychology of Spousal Violence: Psychodynamics, Forensic Mental Health Issues and Research (edited by Elsevier Academic Press). He is a guest lecturer at various national and international universities and training sessions on spousal violence.

Wayne Petherick

Wayne is associate professor of criminology in the Faculty of Society and Design at Bond University, Queensland, Australia. He is author or editor of *Profiling and Serial Crime (3rd ed.)*, *Applied Crime Analysis*, and *Forensic Criminology*. At Bond, Wayne teaches in the subjects Criminal Profiling, Applied Crime Analysis, Criminal Motivations, Crime and Deviance, and Profiling and Crime Analysis (postgraduate), and Forensic Criminology (postgraduate). Wayne's research interests include statement analysis and the detection of deception, case linkage analysis, risky online behaviors for children and adolescents, and victim and offender motivation.

Wayne is also principal of Forensic Analytic, offering training and consultancy on applied crime analysis, an area he has pioneered, stalking, risk assessment and threat management, homicide, arson, stalking, sexual assaults, and false reports. He has lectured in Australia and in the United States, also consulting on cases in both countries. He is a frequent commentator in both the print and electronic media on stalking, violent crime, risk and threat, and other areas of criminological interest.

Wayne can be contacted on wayne@forensicanalytic.com or wpetheri@staff. bond.edu.au.

Yolande Robinson

Yolande's research is being overseen by esteemed criminologist professor Ross Homel, AO, Foundation Professor of Criminology and Criminal Justice, Griffith University. The intention of Yolande's PhD is to improve outcomes for children and youth at risk in disadvantaged communities, with specific focus on current and best practices for including community members in the dissemination of evidenced-based, quality crime prevention programs and initiatives. Yolande has recently informed a major project for the Department of Justice and Attorney General (Youth Justice), and regularly addresses a wide range of groups and organizations on issues related to her research interests, which include community mechanisms for crime prevention, social control and community development, reducing youth delinquency and antisocial behavior, and improving outcomes for children and families in disadvantaged areas, online sexual predation of children, and bullying and harassment.

Poh Shu Yun

Poh Shu Yun graduated from Nanyang Technological University in 2015 with an honors degree in psychology. She is currently working as a child protection officer with the Ministry of Social and Family Development in Singapore.

Grant Sinnamon

Grant Sinnamon, BPsych (Hons), MCouns, MPsych (Clinical), PhD (Medicine: Psychiatry and Psychiatric Neuroscience). Grant is married to Natalie and together they have four children. Grant is the creator of the REPAIR Model: a six-step intervention model for working with children and adults with complex needs. The model is an evidence-based intervention platform that emphasizes the need to recognize, manage, and address the systemic neurofunctional challenges associated with complex trauma, mental illness, and developmental disorders. With an interest in regenerational and translational mental and neurophysiological health, Grant is involved in clinical practice and teaching, and has a number of active research projects in the areas of clinical, neuro, and developmental psychology, criminology, and the emerging field of clinical psychoneuroimmunology. Grant's work encompasses two great passions: the psychoneuroimmunology of childhood onset autoimmune diseases and their complications; and developmental neurobiology and the structural, systemic, and functional impact of early life experiences on the growing brain and on later-life health and well-being. Grant's interest in criminology stems from an interest in the impact of early life adversity on neurodevelopmental trajectory and personality formation, and the consequences for adult neuropsychological, behavioral, and physiological function. In his clinical research, Grant was among the first researchers to characterize the extent and nature of clinical affective disorders in children with type 1 diabetes, and to quantify and report the impact of depression on cognitive function in youth. Grant is also the cofounder of the HART-BEAT research alliance, which is a collaborative group established to create translational research links between the basic, social, and clinical sciences, and clinical, community, and educational practice. As well as authoring a number of scientific papers in peer-reviewed journals, Grant has contributed psychological content chapters to books in the areas of serial crime and criminal profiling, and applied crime analysis.

Duarte Nuno Vieira

Duarte is the dean and a full professor at the Faculty of Medicine of the University of Coimbra (Portugal) and a visiting professor in several other European and South American universities. He is president of the European Council of Legal Medicine, of the Forensic Advisory Board of the Prosecutor of the International Criminal Court, of the Ibero-American Network of Forensic Medicine and Forensic Science Institutions, of the Portuguese Association for Bodily Injury Assessment, and vice president of the European Confederation of Experts on Evaluation and Repair of Bodily Injury. He is chairman of the Thematic Federation on Legal and Forensic Medicine of the European Union of Medical Specialists and a member of the Executive Committee of the Working Group in Forensic Pathology and Forensic Anthropology of the Permanent Committee of INTERPOL on Disaster Victim Identification. He is also a member of the Advisory Board of the Portuguese National Mechanism for the Prevention of Torture. He has been president of the International Academy of Legal Medicine, of the International Association of Forensic Sciences, of the World Association of Police Medical Officers, of the Mediterranean Academy of Forensic Sciences, and of the Latin American Association of Medical Law. Duarte has also been president of the Portuguese National Institute of Legal Medicine and Forensic Sciences and of the Portuguese Medico-Legal Council. He works on a regular basis as forensic consultant for the United Nations High Commissioner for Human Rights, and he is a member of the Forensic Advisory Board of the International Committee of the Red Cross and a member of the Forensic Expert Group of the International Rehabilitation Council for Torture Victims. He has published over 250 scientific papers, he is editor or coeditor of nine books, and serves on the editorial boards of several international leading scientific publications of his area of medical expertise, as well as on the editorial boards of national forensic scientific journals from 18 different European, American, Asian, Middle Eastern, and African countries. He is chief executive editor of the Journal of Forensic Research (edited by Taylor & Francis), international associate editor of the Spanish Journal of Legal Medicine (edited by Elsevier), and chief editor of the Portuguese Journal of Personal Injury. He received honorary fellowships from 18 universities, scientific associations and academies from Europe, Central and South America, Africa, and Asia, and also has been awarded with distinctions from different governments and municipalities, and received 15 scientific prizes. He was awarded by the American Academy of Forensic Sciences, in 2014, with the Douglas Lucas Medal Award, the most prestigious international award in the area of legal and forensic medicine. Professor Vieira also participated in more than 35 international missions promoted by the International Amnesty, European Commission, International Red Cross, United Nations, USAID, and others, especially in the field of human rights in countries from Europe, Latin America, the Middle East, Africa, Australasia, and Asia, and intervened as expert witness in legal proceedings in countries from Europe, American, African, and Asian continents (one of his main fields of work is the investigation and documentation of torture and ill-treatment).

Carletta Xavier

Carletta Xavier is a graduate of the University of Tasmania (2014) and has a master's of criminology from Bond University (2016). Growing up, she was captivated by crime shows such as Criminal Minds, and Crime Scene Investigation (CSI). Whilst understanding that TV portrayals remain unrealistic, forensic examinations and looking into the criminal's psyche intrigued her. This naturally led her studies to involve psychology and criminology, and influenced her research interests to predominately consider perpetrators of crime and criminal behavior. In the future, Carletta wishes to work within the area of human intelligence gathering and analysis.

When not studying, she can be found enjoying time spent with friends and family, including social functions and adventuring.

Foreword

Traditionally the foreword of a book is written by a subject matter expert or someone else who may be in a position to extol the virtues of the editor(s), author(s), and book. This is done to help with the promotion of the book and to lend credibility to the title.

But a foreword doesn't always have to be written by a third party, and the author or editor will sometimes write their own piece for a variety of reasons, as we have done here. Our reason for doing so began nearly 30 years ago.

We first met at Immanuel Lutheran College on the Queensland's Sunshine Coast. Grant was a year ahead but was known through mutual friends and a cousin. He was sporty and academic (while Wayne was neither!). We progressed through our school years with no idea or understanding that we would part company in the postschool years, only to have sporadic contact, until our paths would once again cross a decade into the new millennium leading to new collaborations and partnerships.

Thanks to a fortuitous "people you may know" notification on Facebook, we renewed contact once again around 2011, and as luck would have it, Grant had recently taken up a teaching/research position at a university in South Australia where Wayne was traveling in the not-too-distant future for a marketing trip. We met up for a bike ride from where Grant was working in the lobby bar of the hotel where Wayne was staying.

We began discussing something herein referred to as "the event," which had happened in recent history. This event led to research into the origins of disordered personalities and antisocial behavior, which was to form the basis of something we have elsewhere called the pathways model. After reading hundreds of articles and dozens of books, Wayne had failed to find a single logical or holistic explanation as to how someone progresses from critical developmental periods into adult criminal and antisocial behavior. Discussing the findings of this research, Wayne was to present his ideas, while Grant (based on his education, background, and research) provided the neurodevelopmental backdrop to these. As it happens, the preliminary ideas about developmental pathways to maladaptive behaviors were supported by neurological literature and functional neuroanatomy.

An agreement was made to put the model onto paper, giving it life and form.

Since this time we have worked on numerous publications together, either as contributors or coauthors. We have presented and taught together, and now work together teaching in the criminology program at Bond University while also supporting our side ventures.

It was this research and the development of the pathways model that led to further research into various crime types and the biological, psychological, and environmental factors that lead to crime and antisocial behaviors. Beyond a few works that focused more on the practice of forensic psychology, there didn't seem to be that many works that covered the breadth of topics we wanted to canvass. They were out there for sure, including one published in the mid-2000s, with another published in 2010. While similar, none examined the sheer spectrum of behaviors and crimes, and none covered these in the ways we wanted to cover them. We also wanted to utilize the wealth of experience that existed in a variety of fields including forensic psychology and psychiatry, (forensic) criminology, and sociology. We approached a number of industry leaders as well as students doing research in areas we wanted to include, and were pleased with the warm and welcome reception we received from them.

So one day we sat at a café and formulated a plan for this book. We started out big and whittled down the topics to avoid or reduce overlap. We set about finding authors that we knew, and approached a few that we didn't, further refining the topic and chapter list. Once we had this, we approached Elsevier with a proposal that was promptly accepted, and from here we were given deadlines and time frames (many of which we "renegotiated," sorry Joslyn and Liz!). Chapters started to come in, and owing to other commitments some authors were replaced with others. Further writing and refinement took place over the coming months, and you are now holding the end product of that process in your hands. For this, we thank you.

While we have both written a number of works, this one has been the most personal because of the relationships involved and the sheer amount of time represented by these.

While popular concepts view criminality/victimity as a binary state (you are either a criminal/victim or you are not), the reality is far more complex. While either status may be conferred by the law, once an appropriate set of conditions have been met, the lead up into and through this status involves a great many preconditions and contributions from different sources that make it difficult if not impossible to identify a single moment in time at which someone becomes a criminal or a victim. For example, is a domestic violence victim "made" at that moment they are struck by an intimate partner or at that moment in their development where they vicariously learned that being a victim was a normal part of life? Was the domestic abuser created in the instant when they struck their partner or when they learned through a role model that physical violence was an acceptable conflict resolution strategy?

We teach our students that, despite media sound bites, behavior is multidetermined and multifaceted. To borrow from science, criminal and victim behavior is best thought of as a complex system. More specifically, they are part of a complex adaptive system in that they are part of a dynamic set of relationships and interactions, that they are *gestalt* (more than the sum of the parts), and can adapt to a variety of events or collections of events. To add to this complexity, the individual parts and the collective whole will differ between individuals and environments but also between crime types.

We have tried to keep much of this theme running throughout the chapters in this work such that the complex nature of the crime or behavior covered is revealed. While we could not provide a panacea to the question that has plagued criminology since its inception (Why does crime occur?), we hope that we and authors have gone some way to addressing the "big questions" as represented by those things between these covers. We apologize in advance for anything we may have omitted herein, but rest assured we will take all suggestions for subsequent editions!

With these things in mind, we developed a best fit for the layout of this work. Given the breadth and depth of the chapters covered, it was difficult to find only a few main themes that ran throughout each work to arrange this work into a cohesive whole. But we have done our best in this regard, and therefore we present the content as follows.

In the opening chapter, Grant discusses psychopathology as a mediator of antisocial and criminal behavior. The relationship between crime and mental disorder is often overstated, and in this chapter the relationship between crime and disorder is discussed as well as the disorders with the greatest prevalence in this context. The author provides a link between disorder and the motivational context in which crime and antisocial conduct occur based on other works we have presented.

The next chapter, written by Petherick and Sinnamon, discusses catathymic violence in its various permutations including the chronic and acute types. This chapter provides both a historic and contemporary view of catathymia going back over a century to the works of Wertham and Maier. This is followed by a discussion of compulsive homicides and the ways in which these may differ from catathymia. The chapter ends with sadism, looking also at the historical context for sadistic behavior including the Marquis de Sade and the seminal work of Krafft-Ebbing. A further discussion about the possible confusion between catathymia and sadism rounds out this chapter.

Chapter 3 presents the research of Gaelle Brotto in examining victims of personal violence. This research was based on the earlier suggestion of Petherick and the subsequent work of Petherick and Ferguson and Petherick and Sinnamon, that the motivational typologies we use to describe criminal behavior are also adequate motivations for victim behavior (and, in fact, also noncriminal behavior). The research presented in this chapter demonstrates that these typologies, with some modification, are effective in describing victim motivations to behave in ways that place them in a situation in which they can be harmed. Further, this research showed that you can predict the type of victimization from the type of motivation.

Jim Cawood, a world-renowned expert in violence assessment and intervention, has provided Chapter 4 of this book. Jim's chapter examines the backdrop to violence and the various ways that the risk of violence can be assessed, and in some ways, predicted. He then goes on to discuss the different influences introduced into the process by victim and offender factors. Throughout the chapter the nature and efficacy of various interventions are discussed.

In compiling a list of authors for this work, we truly wanted to recruit an international group of contributors that could provide a sense not only of their area but of how these things operate in their country and culture. We truly had authors from the four corners of the globe. In this fifth chapter, Fátima Almeida and Duarte Nuno Vieira from Portugal look into the perpetrators and victims in cases of filicide. This chapter examines the historical aspects of filicide, followed by filicide and mental illness, also providing a systematic overview of the different classifications. Demographic, historical, situational, clinical, and offense characteristics including methods and motives close the chapter.

From the United Kingdom, Gareth Norris, Gwyn Griffith, and Heather Norris provide "Risk Assessment in Youth Justice: A Child-Centered Approach to Managing Interventions." This chapter opens with definitions for risk assessment and youth justice, and canvasses the variety of issues present when conducting risk assessments within the sphere of youth criminal and antisocial behaviors. As with any modern discussion of risk assessment, there is a question of what should be done once an at-risk individual has been identified. This is discussed here, along with the importance and role of restorative approaches within youth problem behavior.

Petherick provides a general overview of stalking in Chapter 7. This includes a history of stalking legislation and behavior, a look at some of the individual behaviors involved in stalking, as well as a detailed examination of some of the systems used to classify stalking behavior. This chapter closes with a discussion of stalking among special populations including university students and forensic psychologists among others before finishing with stalking as a serial crime.

Following this and providing a more detailed examination of stalkers of public figures, renowned forensic psychiatrist Michele Pathé examines the fixated loner. Michele discusses the difference between public and private figure stalkers and the assessment of risk among the fixated loner. Research into stalkers of the British royal family is presented and the role of mental illness in the stalking of celebrities and public figures discussed. A variety of intervention services aimed specifically at high-profile targets are also provided.

At the halfway point, Huntingdon and Petherick provide an overview and suggested definition and characterization of cyberbullying and online aggression. The problems with a universal definition thus far as well as the problems these present are discussed. Key and core characteristics of aggression, harassment, and bullying are provided before suggesting a unifying definition for these. The importance of a working and viable definition for academics, researchers, and detection or prevention are also given.

Also from Portugal, Mauro Paulino of the *Instituto de Psicologia Clinica e Forense* in Portugal provides insight into the psychological issues related to victims and offenders in domestic violence (DV). The background topic of domestic violence begins the discussion before moving onto risk factors for the victim, offender, and context. This chapter also discusses problem aspects of domestic violence, including under-reporting.

In Chapter 11, Andrea Lee and Robyn Lincoln look specifically at male victims of domestic violence. This chapter presents what may be considered a controversial aspect of domestic violence—that men are perpetrated against at similar rates to women. Other aspects include LGBT violence and the gender paradigm as related to DV before looking into the forms of violence and abuse perpetrated against men. This chapter closes with precipitating factors, reporting factors, and the impacts of DV.

Having once been presented with the possibility that an honor killing was simply a racist way to label domestic violence, Petherick began exploring the similarities and differences between these two events. In this chapter, Xavier, Petherick, and Sinnamon provide a historical and contemporary account of honor killings and domestic violence with a view to determining whether they are the same or different. This is done through an examination of the victims, offenders, and offenses in domestic violence and honor killings. Results suggest that while an honor killing is a type of DV, there are enough differences to indicate that they should be considered separate entities with unique and distinct features and characteristics.

In many jurisdictions around the world, the rate at which homicides remain unsolved is around 12%. This means that for about one in eight homicides an offender will never be brought to justice. In Chapter 13, McKinley looks at homicide in Australia to "illustrate trends, patterns, and specific behavioural aspects relevant to these events." This chapter highlights the reasons why people kill, homicide trends, and the features of homicides.

In Chapters 14 and 15, Lara Christensen of Griffith University examines victims and offenders in child sexual abuse. The features of victims and offenders are discussed, along with common misconceptions surrounding victims, offenders, and the offenses. Reasons for not reporting are also provided along with characteristics and prevalence. Also included are aspects related to the milieu of offending and the psychology of parties involved.

In the last decade we have been able to establish a much better understand of the grooming of children online. This includes no shortage of media attention, right through to movies and documentaries made about specific cases and instances. In Chapter 16, Grant goes outside of the grooming of children and offers a somewhat unique view of the grooming of adults for sexual purposes. This chapter examines the various reasons why this has largely been unexplored to date, including victim blaming, stigmatization, and the reluctance to report among others. In this chapter, Grant goes on to present a new model of adult sexual grooming in an attempt to fill a significant gap in the literature, which has hitherto tended to place adult and child sexual grooming into the same box.

WP was fortunate enough to attend a conference in Melbourne many years ago where he saw a presentation on an area that was not well known or researched. Fortunately this presentation was given by someone who had contributed to this literature in this field, who was also one of the most engaging presenters seen in 18 years of tertiary education. When we conceived this title, this speaker was one of the first to be proposed to contribute, and we were delighted when he accepted the offer to write a chapter for us. In Chapter 17, Grant Lester, forensic psychiatrist, is "Searching for the Spectrum of Querulous" in which he details the attempt to understand and cope with persistent complainers. In legal circles these are known as vexatious litigants, who in clinical terms suffer from querulous paranoia. This chapter, like the presentation, is informative and enlightening and we are happy to have been able to include it in this work.

One of the final chapters is provided by Majeed Khader and his colleague Poh Shu Yun from Singapore. This chapter is written from the point of view of the implications of Internet love scams for law enforcement, and discusses the evolution and development of these online scams through the discussion of their features and perpetration. The psychological factors of victims and offenders are also included here before closing with intervention strategies. As with many other chapters in this work, this is a relatively new and emerging area, and this chapter is a valuable contribution to this book.

One of the more pervasive and destructive crimes is discussed in the penultimate chapter by Therese Ellis-Smith. Ellis-Smith provides "Firesetters: A Review of Theory, Facts, and Treatment." The theories are the current corpus used to explain arson and firesetting behavior, coupled with the typologies that have been developed to explain this behavior. The prevalence, impact, and cost of arson are discussed along with the clearance rates. The chapter ends with the programs developed for arsonist treatment.

In this final chapter, Wayne Petherick discusses cults. While researching this chapter, the author was struck by the lack of rigorous academic research on cults even though they are so destructive and relatively pervasive. This chapter was written to provide the reader with a background to cults, the differences between cults and religion, the attraction to cults, and the features of a cult as identified by Lifton after his study of thought reform used by the Nazis in World War II.

So, there you have it—how we, the authors, grew up, put on big-boy pants, and added colleagues and coauthors to our existing friends status. We have also explained the foundations of the chapter contents of this text and the rationale for their inclusion. What remains is the final word, which perhaps ironically is to say that, on these topics there is no "final" word. Crime and (by its very definition) antisocial behaviors, take place in a social space. As such they are constructed elements of a dynamic environment. This ever-changing, interactive world is subject to alteration, advancement, evolution, integration, and separation of ideas and practices, and at times, regression to periods of a "future past." This means there is unlikely to ever be a "final" or definitive word on the topics explored in this text, or indeed any factor that is determined by the ethics, morality, and social will of the day. This said, we hope you enjoy and are challenged by the topics herein. They, at least for this moment in time, represent the socially constructed phenomena that constitute the cultural journey of crime, deviance, and antisocial behaviors.

Acknowledgments

Another book project down and the same lesson reinforced—choose good and capable people who can do what you ask in the time frame you ask it, and life will be infinitely easier.

My experience from this project, which we chose to title *The Psychology of Crime and Antisocial Conduct*, has been warm and positive. It has at times been stressful (when dealing with authors who initially agree then later withdraw for whatever reason), fulfilling (when approaching authors who, with little to go on, agreed to be a part of our work), and enlightening (when reading through chapters not directly within my areas of expertise). I can safely say that through this project I have grown and developed, cultivated new skills, and more finely tuned old ones.

There are of course the usual suspects to thank—My own children for being orphaned at various (but brief) points, and of course my boss, professor Raoul Mortley, for being accommodating and giving me the time to work on things such as this.

And of course I could not forget my encouraging, loving, and gracious partner, Natasha. Tash is about the biggest bibliophile you could ever come across, and her love and encouragement go further than the eye can see—although, I do occasionally suspect she is just looking to add another book to her collection! She has both offered editorial and motivational support throughout and gotten me back behind the keyboard when and as needed. Always willing to down her own tools and give me useful advice, I couldn't, and wouldn't want to, do it without her.

A huge thanks also to all of the contributors. Many experts in their own right, while others are "growing into their professional skin," an edited volume such as this would be nothing without them. I sincerely hope I am not missing any names, and if I am, I will humbly apologize right now: Grant Sinnamon, Lara Christensen, Mauro Paulino, Fatima Almeida, Yolande Robinson, Carletta Xavier, Gareth Norris, Heather Norris, Gwyn Griffith, Duarte Nuno Vieira, Grant lester, Michele Pathé, Majeed Khader, Poh Shu Yun, Grant Lester, Andrea Lee, Robyn Lincoln, Therese Ellis-Smith, and Amber McKinley.

A huge thanks, as always, goes out to the expert and professional team at Elsevier, most notably Liz and Joslyn, for their ongoing support and encouragement (and oft times tolerance). You are always a pleasure to work with, and I always enjoy the process of putting a project together with you. Here's cheers until the next one if you will have me/us!

Last, but by no means least, there is Grant and his wonderful family. Like mine, they encourage and support his many projects and they always make Grant available for loan when I have a wacky idea, this one included. Thanks go to Grant's wife, Natalie, for helping with the editorial and other duties, too. You're definitely part of the team Nat, and we wouldn't be here without you! I first met Grant as a high school student where he was one grade ahead of me. Post school we lost contact for a while, but thanks to the wonders of social networking met again over a glass of merlot and have been working on projects ever since. While we have cowritten before, this is our first coedited volume together and hopefully one of many to come. Thanks mate, you are an unstoppable force and a pleasure to work with—"Take us out of the world, Wash…got us some crime to be done."

–Wayne Petherick

Any work of this nature does not happen in a vacuum. Indeed, I liken the experience of writing this, my first collection of edited works, to that of Bill and Ted embarking on their first excellent adventure. We have crossed generations, crossed cultures and languages, have dodged and weaved and made monumental promises of deferred service to family, friends, and colleagues, and have put together a melting pot of ideas, expertise, and personalities into a collective experience—all for educational purposes. We even managed to take out the garbage on a few occasions. Ultimately, like Bill and Ted, Wayne and I hope the result is most excellent, and that it inspires its readers to appreciate that understanding and dealing with deviant behavior is an adventure into the shades of gray, in which so much of the human experience finds its richness, excitement, fear, and loathing, and in the end, for better or worse, where culture stimulates its relentless evolution.

So, having undertaken this excellent adventure, there are, as always, many who helped us on the journey. First of all, the team at Anderson Publishing have been amazing. Thank you. The back room is where the action happens, and they are always in the thick of it.

This work is a collaboration, and there are a number of incredibly smart people who have given their time and knowledge to create the end product. Clinical, legal, and academic professionals alike typically suffer from a decided lack of spare time, and yet all of the authors have given freely of their time to share their knowledge and experience in their respective fields of expertise. Thank you for your commitment and your generosity.

To my children, Charlotte, Dillon, Mackenzie, and Indiana. Thanks for putting up with my long work hours and short playtime. Here's to fewer "goodbyes" by the car, and more "goodnight" kisses and cuddles by the bedside. You are my greatest creation, my greatest joy, and a gift without equal. Thank you for choosing me as your Dad, I love you all so very much.

To Natalie, my wife, my queen, my everything. My beautiful Sparky, no words can express my gratitude and my appreciation for your support, your patience, and your love. So with all I am, I say thank you my love.

Finally, thanks go to Wayne Petherick, my partner in this project, ironically, one of the more antisocial activities in which I have engaged. Known by many names: doctor, associate professor, criminologist, colleague, fellow time traveler, and Browncoat; but above all else, you are an outstanding human being, and I am proud to call you friend. You are the reason my name appears on this dust cover, and I thank you for the "excellent adventure."

–Grant Sinnamon

Psychopathology as a Mediator of Antisocial and Criminal Behavior

1

Grant Sinnamon

Bond University, Gold Coast, QLD, Australia; Bela Menso Brain and Behaviour Centre,
Varsity Lakes, QLD, Australia

CHAPTER OUTLINE

The Psychology of Criminal and Antisocial Behavior. http://dx.doi.org/10.1016/B978-0-12-809287-3.00001-8

INTRODUCTION

Many psychopathologies result in the significant manifestation of antisocial behaviors. Some of these are antisocial in the context of the sufferer withdrawing from social interaction and isolating himself or herself as a defensive mechanism to help avoid the unpleasant thoughts, feelings, behaviors, and physiological reactions that are a feature of the disorder. Anxiety disorders, depression, trauma, and conditions that affect communication and/or socialization, such as autism, are examples of conditions that fit this description. The use of immersive technologies, nonsuicidal self-injury, and alcohol may also be seen in this light as they are often used as means of avoiding, attenuating, treating, or self-medicating these symptoms. Generally speaking, avoidant behavior of this nature is unlikely to result in criminal behavior. The exception is when self-medicating with alcohol is undertaken by a minor or if an adult exchanges alcohol for illicit substances. At other times, psychopathology influences the manifestation of behaviors that are more expressive in nature. That is to say, these behaviors are focused outward at other people, animals, or objects. When this occurs, the behavior necessarily impinges on others, whether directly, such as in the case of an assault, or indirectly, such as when the behavior involves property theft or damage. It is in this context that psychopathology is likely to result in criminal behaviors. Expressive behaviors can be volitional, nonvolitional, or incidental.

- Volitional: A volitional behavior is a deliberate act that is committed to achieve a specific end. The end may or may not be a legitimate endeavor. A legitimate endeavor can include acts such as sexual or physical assault, theft, or other behavior that is undertaken as a direct means to achieve a desired outcome. An illegitimate endeavor may include speeding, illicit drug use, or other high-risk behavior undertaken while in a manic or psychotic episode, or other state that distorts the offender's capacity for insight or judgment.
- Nonvolitional: A nonvolitional behavior is an act committed as a result of delusional or hallucinogenic cognitions that establish a false presumption on the part of the offender. Command hallucinations (e.g., "the Seagull told me that man was evil, and it was my duty to stab him before he hurt anyone else") and delusional thoughts of cause and effect (e.g., "if I kill his wife then he will love me, and we can be together forever") are examples of this form of criminal act.
- Incidental: Incidental behaviors are illegal acts that occur incidentally to another objective. An example of this may be someone who has a pathology that presents as generally avoidant but finds himself in a highly anxiety-provoking situation that triggers a panic attack. As a result, the individual may "lash out" to try and escape (avoid) the fear-provoking stimuli. He may assault someone, destroy property, or steal a bike, car, or other means of transportation to flee.

Although mental illness may contribute to antisocial and criminal behaviors, it is imperative that we appreciate that psychopathology and criminal behavior are not ubiquitous. The reality is that individuals with a mental illness are at an exponentially greater risk of being a victim of crime than they are of becoming an offender.

This being said, there are certain psychopathologies, as well as cognitive, affective, motivational, and behavioral manifestations, that, when present, may collude with environmental circumstances to increase the risk that an individual will engage in antisocial and/or deviant behaviors. It is also true that many of these antisocial or deviant acts may well cross the line and also be criminal. However, to reiterate, it is far more common that these emotional, cognitive, and psychobehavioral manifestations collude with environmental circumstances to increase the risk of a mentally ill person becoming a victim of crime. For the mentally ill, as with all individuals; the socioenvironmental circumstances are of paramount importance in mediating the ultimate outcome. It is perhaps the first rule to keep in the forefront of your mind when immersing yourself in the world of crime and the individual—no one lives in a vacuum, and it is the interaction between the individual and the external mechanics of his ecology (family, peers, education, socioeconomic status, society and culture, etc.) that ultimately determines the outcome (Bronfenbrenner & Ceci, 1994). Indeed, the corporate world is full of psychopathic personalities who have never committed a murder but have ruthlessly used their psychological make-up to allow them to pursue financial goals and objectives despite the potential impact on others. In fact, the study of what has become known as *corporate psychopathy* is a burgeoning field within the arena of organizational psychology (Babiak, Neumann, & Hare, 2010; Mathieu, Neumann, Babiak, & Hare, 2015; Yamagishi, Li, Takagishi, Matsumoto, & Kiyonari, 2014).

In this chapter, we will explore how psychopathology can mediate antisocial and criminal behaviors. We will explore some of the mainstream diagnosed psychopathologies that are associated with crime and criminal behaviors, and we will explore the expression of our constituent thoughts, emotions, motivations, and other psychological components of our psyche that influence the risk for criminal behavior. While mainstream mental illness and crime are popular topics in the media and a common "go-to" for politicians and lobbyists looking for a convenient scapegoat when terrible events occur; it is the constituent parts that are potentially of the greatest value to the justice system, as they provide a direct insight into the mind and motivation of the individual and, therefore, provide the greatest value when trying to (a) understand the factors contributing to a crime and (b) the inherent characteristics of a standing crime, or crime scene and, importantly, (c) to predict future criminal acts.

WHAT IS PSYCHOPATHOLOGY?

Psychopathology refers to our understanding, study, or knowledge of any illness, disorder, dysfunction, or dysregulation of the mental processes that govern an individual's cognition, affect, and behavior (Sinnamon, 2015). The word itself comes from three Ancient Greek roots. *Psyche* means "mind" or "soul," *pathos* means "suffering, feeling, emotion, calamity" or literally translated as "what befalls one," and; *logia* means "to speak." Over time, suffixes derived from *logia* such as "-logy"/"-ology" have come to mean "study of," "science of," or "branch of knowledge [of]" (Harper, 2013).

Therefore, for our purposes in this chapter, we will define *psychopathology* as "the branch of knowledge and collective body of conditions relative to the suffering of the mind" (Sinnamon, 2015).

Clinically, the diagnosis of a psychopathology requires the individual to meet several diagnostic criteria that relate to a variety of general and disorder-specific guidelines. Generally, the symptoms of a clinically remarkable psychopathology must (a) originate within the individual as opposed to being a situational reaction and (b) be outside of the individual's physical and/or mental control (American Psychiatric Association, 2013; Sinnamon, 2015). According to Sinnamon (2015), clinicians will often disagree about whether a reaction is a situationally driven response or a pathological condition. Conditions will often move from being an externally derived reaction to an internal state, at which time the condition is pathologized. Psychopathology associated with traumatic events and bereavement are two such examples where this can be a difficult distinction to make. Depression, anxiety, fear, cognitive distortion, behavioral dysfunction, and significantly disordered affect are all contextually appropriate responses to an acute experience of a major trauma or grief. If, however, these presentations are still a primary feature of the individual's life several months after the experience, then the reactions are considered abnormal and may be identified as pathological. If these physical and mental reactions are unable to be controlled by the individual, they would meet the general criteria for psychopathology symptoms.

Disorder-specific criteria are dependent on the characteristic symptomatology of each disorder. These disorder-specific criteria are set out in the American Psychiatric Association's *Diagnostic and Statistical Manual of Mental Disorders*, currently in its fifth edition (DSM-5; American Psychiatric Association, 2013), and in the World Health Organization's *International Statistical Classification of Diseases and Related Health Problems*, currently in its 10th revision (ICD-10; World Health Organisation, 1992, 2010). For example, to be diagnosed with major depressive disorder (MDD or unipolar depression), an individual must meet several diagnostic criteria that relate to the known key characteristics and symptoms of the disorder, such as increased negative affect, anhedonia, lassitude, changes to sleep and dietary practices, psychomotor changes, cognitive impairment, feelings of guilt and worthlessness, and suicide ideation (American Psychiatric Association, 2013; Sinnamon, 2015; World Health Organisation, 2010).

When assessing an individual for psychopathology, there are four factors or themes that form the lens through which the "abnormality" of symptoms should be interrogated. Also known as *the 4Ds of Abnormality*, these are deviance, distress, dysfunction, and danger (Comer, 2005). Using the 4Ds, the clinician is able to assess deviance and abnormality based on the potential for the symptom presentation to negatively impact the individual, her family and peers, and the wider community. Ultimately, it is potential for harm or serious dysfunction that dictates whether a cluster of symptoms will be labeled as pathological (Table 1.1).

Any thoughts, emotions, and behaviors that are "different" and/or "inconvenient" have been increasingly pathologized by the developed world. As the world

Table 1.1 The Four Key Themes (4Ds) of Abnormality Used in the Consideration of Psychopathological Symptomology

Factor	Description
Deviance:	Refers to the extent to which an individual's specific cognitions, affect, and behaviors are considered to be outside of what is "acceptable" and/or "normal" within his or her common social environment. When making this consideration, it is important to recognize that there are many subcultural groups whose thoughts, beliefs, emotional responses, and behaviors bear little resemblance to the wider cultural norms of a society. Therefore, the measure of deviance must be considered in the appropriate context of the individual and not simply by a predefined mainstream cultural normative set.
Distress:	Refers to the extent to which the presenting symptoms cause emotional distress to the individual experiencing them.
Dysfunction:	Refers to the extent to which the presenting symptoms impair the individual from engaging in his or her "normal" daily activities such as work, study, self-care, or engaging in general activities of daily living like washing, preparing a meal, or dressing appropriately. Additionally, dysfunction is increasingly used to refer to systemic neurophysiological deficits that are known (or thought) to be complicit in the presenting psychological impairments. It is important to be aware that not all dysfunctional behavior has a pathological origin. Some individuals may choose to engage in dysfunctional behaviors such as self-harm, hunger strikes, or sadomasochistic sexual endeavors (although certain sexually deviant behaviors may qualify as pathological).
Danger:	Refers to the inherent risk of harm either to the individual or others, usually by the individual, as a result of presenting symptoms. Examples of high-risk symptomology include aggressive paranoia, delusions or hallucinations involving persecution or directives to harm self or others, and suicide ideation.

Adapted from Comer, R. 2005. Fundamentals of abnormal psychology (4th ed.). New York: Worth.

shrinks through a combination of advances in technology, global media sharing, and increased corporate multinationalism, there appears to be a corresponding trend toward social homogeneity, in which ways of thinking, experiencing, and interacting with the world that do not readily "fit" are being pathologized and labeled as deviant and, in some cases, this deviance has included a pathologizing of some "states and ways of being," while others have been ostracized to the point of criminality. I have previously lamented the loss of individuation, social choice, and the celebration of difference and the alternative experience (Sinnamon, 2015), a point that many social commentators and academics are making in a small but vociferous contrary discourse (Blažič & Vojinovič, 2002; Brown, 2012; Butler, 2013; Lelandais, 2013).

As I have previously stated (Sinnamon, 2015, p. 210):

This phenomenon is reflected in the evolution of psychopathology where many personal characteristics and behaviours long experienced by individuals have now become recognised pathologies. Some of these, such as those characterising the attention deficit disorders, have progressed in this fashion amidst considerable controversy. This is perhaps one of the differentiating factors of psychiatry over many, if not most, other areas of medicine. That is the reality that diagnosing psychopathology is often an arbitrary process in which individual opinion and experience, as much as any "hard" evidence, plays a large role in the diagnostic outcome proffered by the attending mental health professional.

Therefore, and as always, I caution all those who are engaged in fields of endeavor that involve the confluence of individual human characteristics and society (Sinnamon, 2015, p. 211):

The differential, evanescent and heterogeneous nature of many psychopathologies mean that collectivist and generalistic processes should be avoided at every opportunity. Instead one should always maintain the awareness that there is potential for considerable individual difference in every situation. Therefore, in the case of crime analysis; there is little to be gained from thinking along lines of "this person is schizophrenic" or "is an alcoholic." Rather, it will serve you much more effectively to think in terms of specific factors that can be individuated. For example, "this person is paranoid" or "this person does not empathise." Individuating symptoms of psychopathology or deviant cognition, affect and behaviour (or behaviour management) will allow you to create far more accurate representations, profiles, and predictive models than any singular psychopathology label will.

WHAT IS FORENSIC PSYCHOPATHOLOGY?

Forensic psychopathology can be defined as (Sinnamon, 2015, pp. 212–213):

A specialized area in which the focus rests on those psychological maladies and their symptoms and consequences that, for one reason or another, intersect with the legal system. Simply put, forensic psychopathology is interested in clinical psychopathologies with criminal implications. This includes any psychological or neuropsychological condition that impacts the perpetrators of criminal acts as well as their victims.

When psychology and criminology meet, there is a shared space in which human factors are examined and compiled in an attempt to understand and predict likely future human behaviors. In this space, people are investigated within the context of specific characteristics, states, traits, and other unique circumstances. This is a scientific approach and, as such, is grounded in the principles of change and emergent knowledge, in which historical "knowledge" is continually being superseded, reconsidered, and discarded in the face of the emerging evidence. This updating of knowledge, and individuating of people and circumstances, is fundamentally at odds with the legal system in which precedent and the generalization of the application (of law) provide the basis for decision making, strategy, legal argument, and judicial ruling.

The challenge for forensic psychology is being exacerbated in the wake of a resurgence in an increasingly vengeful and punitive justice system. In many Western countries, prevention projects are on the decline, prisons and their populations are growing markedly, and prison life is becoming punitive rather than rehabilitative. Rational conversation about crime and criminality is being replaced by moral panic, and "fundamental attribution error-laden rationale that places blame and responsibility squarely on the individual and their personal 'weaknesses' or 'personality flaws" (Sinnamon, 2015, p. 213). This is happening despite the well-established data and the emergent research highlighting that offender and victim risk is associated with a complex interplay between a range of environmentally shaped, biopsychosocially derived factors.

MENTAL ILLNESS AND CRIMINALITY

The debate about the relationship between mental illness and criminality has a long history. Indeed, the scientific literature on the topic dates back more than 100 years (Gross, 1911; Healy & Tenney-Healy, 1915; Lombroso & Ferrero, 1895; Maudsley, 1876; McDonald, 1905). While these debates continue, by the later part of the twentieth century, researchers had largely reached consensus that any apparent relationship between psychopathology and crime was more likely due to a confluence of the social corollaries that accompany mental illness than to clinical mental illness or an underlying unique criminal personality (Cohen, 1996; Cullen, 1994; McKenzie & Harpham, 2006; Paterson & Stark, 2001; Wallace, Mullen, & Burgess, 2014). The statistical data of recent decades, particularly in the period postdeinstitutionalization (the 1980s saw a process of large-scale deinstitutionalization of people with mental illness into community-based care services across several Western jurisdictions), have again opened this debate. The contemporary data do show identified associations between some mental disorders and the risk of offending (Fazel & Grann, 2006; Hodgins, 1992; Marzuk, 1996). However, there continues to be good evidence that the overall population risk of criminal offending by the mentally ill remains relatively low and is primarily associated with criminality when combined with other extant factors linked to risk of offending such as substance abuse and social dislocation (Elbogen & Johnson, 2009; S Fazel & Grann, 2006). Perhaps the best way to describe the relationship is that while people with mental illness and criminality are not ubiquitous, there are characteristics of some disordered mental states that can contribute to the risk of offending if the circumstances are favorable (or perhaps it is more appropriate to say if the circumstances are unfavorable).

PERSONALITY DISORDERS AND CRIMINALITY

Personality disorders (PDs) are multifactorial syndromes that occur in the face of a confluence of biopsychosocial factors including heritability (genetics and epigenetics), developmental experiences (abuse, trauma, health, attachment, education, and environmental exposure during core brain development), general social and environmental characteristics, personal anatomical and physiological dynamics, and innate character qualities. According to Petherick and Sinnamon (2013, p. 21), the symptoms of personality disorders generically include:

> *Emotional dysregulation, inability to maintain positive relationships, social isolation, anger outbursts, suspicion and lack of trust, inability to delay gratification, poor impulse control, and often there is a history of alcohol and/or substance abuse. The thoughts and behaviours of those with a personality disorders are characteristically considered odd, eccentric, melodramatic, overly emotional, anxious, and/or fearful. Many signs and symptoms of specific personality disorders "bleed" into one another and it is often difficult to proffer an accurate diagnosis that could not be differentially provided by another clinician."*

Many of us have personality traits that are considered by ourselves or others as somewhat "annoying," "quirky," "strange," or just plain "weird." Whether endearing or bothersome, quirky and weird in and of themselves does not necessarily qualify as a disorder. PDs are considered to be a manifestation of a pathology with very deep roots, with a variety of characteristic presentations that are difficult to modify, and are listed along those disorders that are among the most difficult to manage, treat, and remit.

There are 10 separate disorders of personality that are classified into three categories (clusters) of associated characteristics and symptoms—clusters A, B, and C (see Table 1.2).

Personality disorders are commonly left out of the crime–mental illness equation as it is a complex and somewhat contentious area. Given that PDs are characterized by fundamental personality properties that require deviant perspectives, insights, and

Table 1.2 Personality Disorder: Clusters and Characteristics

Cluster	Personality Disorders	Characteristics
A	Paranoid PD Schizotypal PD Schizoid PD	Personality underpinned by characteristics that are considered to be **odd** or **eccentric**
B	Antisocial PD Borderline PD Histrionic PD Narcissistic PD	Personality underpinned by characteristics that are considered to be **dramatic, emotional, or erratic**
C	Avoidant PD Dependent PD Obsessive–compulsive PD	Personality underpinned by characteristics that are considered to be essentially **anxious** or **fearful**

Sinnamon, G. (2015). Psychopathology and Criminal Behavior. In W. Petherick (Ed.), Applied Crime Analysis: A social science approach to understanding crime, criminals, and victims. *Boston: Anderson Publishing.*

associated behaviors, some might argue that substantial types of criminal behaviors have some form of disordered personality as a prerequisite to the commission of that offense. This point notwithstanding, clinical PDs do have a place in the conversation. Individuals with PDs are at increased risk for offending primarily as a result of deviant perceptions, dysfunctional affect regulation, disordered cognitions, and the consequent effect these have on emotion, motivation, and behavior. For example, borderline PD is characterized by inconsistent, self-defeating, and defensive cognitions that drive codependent, approval-seeking, and self-preservation behaviors in a circular process involving relational attraction followed by often violent and destructive relational breakdown; paranoid PD by thoughts of paranoia and persecution that drive a behavioral combination of self-preservation and "get them before they get you"; narcissistic PD by an inflated but fragile self-worth that drives behaviors designed to preserve self-esteem and keep the focus of attention fixed on self; and antisocial PD by a lack of empathy and social awareness and a focus on self-interest that drive behaviors intended to obtain self-serving outcomes, both physical and emotional, with little or no regard to the welfare of others. Further, a common characteristic to all PDs is extreme affective reactivity, which is often accompanied by an underlying comorbid mood disorder.

According to Petherick and Sinnamon (2013), there are five common elements that are associated with personality disordered perpetrators of crime:

1. Poor self-esteem: either very low or high but fragile
2. Emotional negativity bias and lack of capacity to modulate emotional expression
3. High-risk, antisocial, self-serving, or differentially reinforced behavioral tendencies
4. An unwillingness or incapacity to accurately assess and mitigate risk
5. An unwillingness or incapacity to modulate behavior responses

Criminal psychology requires an understanding of the foundational importance of the strong concordance between the dimensions of personality, emotion, motivation, and behavior. PDs influence criminality through the inextricable link between personality and motivation, and the role that motivation plays in mediating behavior (Brown & Pluck, 2000; Sinnamon, 2015). Motivation is the primer of our behaviors as it establishes the direction in which we will assert our efforts as well as the degree to which this direction is held as an attractive or a desirable objective. Motivation also combines the determinants that establish the nature and intent of the chosen course of action—toward or away from a stimulus, friendly or oppositional, calm or aggressive, peaceful or violent, defensive or offensive, flight or fight, etc. So, our personality characteristics are central to the way in which we perceive and interpret our experiences, and our motivation is the means by which we create the impetus to pursue those items we deem necessary to protect, build, or maintain elements of our personality that are perceived and interpreted to be threatened by those experiences. In this way, distorted, dysregulated, and deviant internal mechanisms, such as disordered cognition and hyperdysregulated/hypodysregulated emotionality, build and direct motivation to behave in a manner that (it is believed) will resolve the fractured element of self that has been compromised.

There is a strong positive relationship between PD and violent crime and, in particular, violent recidivism (Fountoulakis, Leucht, & Kaprinis, 2008; Grann, Långström, Tengström, & Kullgren, 1999). Antisocial and borderline PDs are among the most common associated with violent offending (Fountoulakis et al., 2008). These PDs are often linked to violence because they are (Sinnamon, 2015, p. 240):

> *Characterised by an inability or unwillingness to assess risk and adhere to established and elementary social norms. Instead, offenders with [these type of] PD pursue self-serving and/or self-preservation motives with little reflection on morality, social acceptance, or the impact on those around them.*

In these subcategories of PD, the socially deviant and violent behaviors are essentially possible because internal mechanisms, desires, and personal behavior are not subject to the same empathic modulation as they are in the wider population (Raposo, Vicens, Clithero, Dobbins, & Huettel, 2011; Seitz, Nickel, & Azari, 2006).

The link among PD, motivation, and criminal behavior is described next and is derived from the work of Petherick and Sinnamon (2013), and Sinnamon (2015) on the motivational role of PDs within victim and perpetrator typologies (Petherick & Sinnamon, 2013) and criminal psychopathology associated with PDs (Sinnamon, 2015).

REASSURANCE-DRIVEN PD AND CRIMINALITY

When a need for reassurance drives behavior, the motivation comes from a deep-seated need for approval and acceptance from others. There are four PDs that fit within this form of criminal motivation: borderline, histrionic, avoidant, and dependent.

The borderline and histrionic personalities are typically possessed of thought processes and emotions that are reactive, melodramatic, and hyperresponsive. These two PDs are at risk for criminal behaviors due to very low self-esteem, high levels of impulsivity, a strong need for attention and approval, and excessive emotionality and extremely volatile and reactionary behavioral responses. Borderline and histrionic personalities have very poor predictive capacity and are therefore unable to interpret their surroundings and assess the risks that may be present. In the case of borderline and histrionic PDs, the propensity for impulsiveness, volatility, reactive aggression, and lack of capacity to mitigate the hyperemotionality and negative cognitions that are associated with an intense fear of rejection all combine to increase the risk of aggressive outbursts and violent reactions toward others when they feel emotionally or physically threatened. The resulting crimes are generally person-to-person violence, destruction of property, and arson. These individuals are also unlikely to learn from their experiences and therefore have a very high rate of recidivism.

Table 1.3 shows how the borderline PD can be described using the mnemonic "AM SUICIDE" and the histrionic PD by the mnemonic "PRAISE ME" (Pinkofsky, 1997).

The avoidant and dependent personalities symptomatically experience disordered thinking that is extremely anxious, in turn resulting in strong negative emotions that are

Table 1.3 Mnemonic for Borderline Personality Disorder

A	(1)	Abandonment
M	(6)	Mood instability (marked reactivity of mood)
S	(5)	Suicidal (or self-mutilating) behavior
U	(2)	Unstable and intense relationships
I	(4)	Impulsivity (in two potentially self-damaging areas)
C	(8)	Control of anger
I	(3)	Identity disturbance
D	(9)	Dissociative (or paranoid) symptoms that are transient and stress related
E	(7)	Emptiness (chronic feelings of)

Notes: 1. Numbers in brackets correspond to the diagnostic criteria set out in the DSM5 (American Psychiatric Association, 2013); 2. Diagnosis requires the presence of any five of the nine diagnostic criteria.
Pinkofsky, H. B. (1997). Mnemonics for DSM-IV personality disorders. Psychiatric Services, 48(9), 1197–1198.

Table 1.4 Mnemonic for Histrionic Personality Disorder

P	(2)	Provocative (or seductive) behavior
R	(8)	Relationships are considered more intimate than they actually are
A	(1)	Attention-seeking
I	(7)	Influenced easily
S	(5)	Speech (style) wants to impress; lacks detail
E	(3)	Emotional lability; shallowness
M	(4)	Make-up; physical appearance is used to draw attention to self
E	(6)	Exaggerated emotions; theatrical

Notes: 1. Numbers in brackets correspond to the diagnostic criteria set out in the DSM5 (American Psychiatric Association, 2013); 2. Diagnosis requires the presence of any five of the eight diagnostic criteria.
Pinkofsky, H. B. (1997). Mnemonics for DSM-IV personality disorders. Psychiatric Services, 48(9), 1197–1198.

characterized by high levels of fear. Offenders who fall into these PD types often find themselves in codependent relationships. They will submit themselves to the other person and remain in the relationship, even in the face of extreme demands, adversity, and abuse. With deep-seated feelings of inadequacy, these individuals often need to obtain self-esteem by proxy. That is, they need to gain approval from others in order to feel good about themselves. These feelings of inadequacy and the need for acceptance from others combined with other characteristics such as timidity, shyness, submissiveness, and high tolerance for abuse mean that these individuals often place themselves in situations where they are at high risk for personal violence. Table 1.4 and 1.5 shows how the avoidant PD can be described using the mnemonic "CRINGES" (Pinkofsky, 1997).

Reassurance-driven criminal behaviors that are perpetrated by offenders with avoidant and/or dependent PDs are usually motivated out of a desire to retain, or

Table 1.5 Mnemonic for Avoidant Personality Disorder

C	(2)	Certainty (of being liked required before willing to get involved with others)
R	(4)	Rejection (or criticism) preoccupies ones' thoughts in social situations
I	(3)	Intimate relationships (restraint in intimate relationships due to fear of being shamed)
N	(5)	New interpersonal relationships (is inhibited in)
G	(1)	Gets around occupational activity (involving significant interpersonal contact)
E	(7)	Embarrassment (potential) prevents new activity or taking personal risks
S	(6)	Self-viewed (as unappealing, inept, or inferior)

Notes: 1. Numbers in brackets correspond to the diagnostic criteria set out in the DSM5 (American Psychiatric Association, 2013); 2. Diagnosis requires the presence of any four of the seven diagnostic criteria.
Pinkofsky, H. B. (1997). Mnemonics for DSM-IV personality disorders. Psychiatric Services, 48(9), 1197–1198.

obtain, the acceptance and/or approval of others. Commonly these two personality types will become involved in criminal behavior such as theft, prostitution, or participation in a gang-rape or assault or with the manufacture or distribution of drugs or other illegal goods in order to gain entry to, or acceptance by, an individual or group (e.g., codependent relationship or gang membership). As violence is not a natural behavior for this group, for violence against people or property to occur, the individual would need to believe that the target of their approval warrants such an act. This may be either through harm/risk of harm (real or perceived) to an individual with whom they are codependent or through their being rejected in some way (real or perceived) by a person with whom they are codependent. Table 1.6 shows how the dependent PD can be described using the mnemonic "RELIANCE" (Pinkofsky, 1997).

ASSERTIVE-DRIVEN PD AND CRIMINALITY

PD offenders who are assertive-driven are similarly motivated by the need to obtain or restore self-esteem through other people (just like the reassurance-driven PD types). The two groups, however, differ in the emotional content that drives their motivation. Rather than fear driving motivation and subsequent behavior, the assertive-driven PD persons are primarily motivated by anger. PD persons with this orientation tend to have an underlying belief that they are superior to others and therefore deserve more than they already have and, further, are owed something by others (or society).

This group are angry because they believe that they, whether clear or unclear to them, are not getting everything they deserve. Paradoxically, this group tends to have very low self-esteem or a high self-esteem that is very fragile. Motivation, therefore,

Table 1.6 Mnemonic for Dependent Personality Disorder

R	(1)	Reassurance (required for decisions)
E	(3)	Expressing disagreement difficult (due to fear of loss of support or approval)
L	(2)	Life responsibilities (needs to have these assumed by others)
I	(4)	Initiating projects difficult (due to lack of self-confidence)
A	(6)	Alone (feels helpless and discomfort when alone)
N	(5)	Nurturance (goes to excessive lengths to obtain nurturance and support)
C	(7)	Companionship (another relationship) sought urgently when close relationship ends
E	(8)	Exaggerated fears of being left to care for self

Notes: *1. Numbers in brackets correspond to the diagnostic criteria set out in the DSM5 (American Psychiatric Association, 2013); 2. Diagnosis requires the presence of any five of the eight diagnostic criteria.*
Pinkofsky, H. B. (1997). Mnemonics for DSM-IV personality disorders. *Psychiatric Services, 48(9), 1197–1198.*

comes from the desire to restore their self-esteem through obtaining accolades from others. Alternatively, they will attempt to restore self-esteem by emotionally dominating others. They do this by deliberately setting out to make other people feel inferior and in turn make themselves feel more superior. This type of personality is hyperemotional, melodramatic, and extremely intense and is characteristic of the cluster B PDs, such as the antisocial, borderline, histrionic, and narcissistic personality types. Narcissism and histrionic are likely to be the primary personality characteristics associated with this group.

Narcissistic and histrionic PD offenders express these flamboyancies in a highly aggressive and dominating "look at me" manner that is ultimately compensatory in nature. The attitude and behaviorally expressed belief that they are superior are not underpinned by substance but are constantly undermined by their low or high but fragile self-esteem. In this way, their behaviors are motivated by the need to repair the incongruence. They do this through a variety of mechanics including fantasies about success, power, and their attractiveness in the eyes of others. The result is a blurred reality in which exaggerations of personal achievements, successes, and talents are made, resulting in increased need for external praise and recognition to "prop-up" their assertions. The self-absorption means that they usually make ongoing, high-maintenance demands, without the ability to recognize or acknowledge the feelings of those around them.

In the histrionic PD person, behaviors can be overly sexualized or provocative and flirtatious, and these individuals are most commonly egocentric, self-indulgent, and manipulative. The need for continuous appreciation from others means that this group of individuals are also easily manipulated and influenced by others.

The selfish, aggressive, and "I deserve more" personal agenda–driven attitudes of narcissistic PD persons often results in criminal behaviors aimed at obtaining what is believed to be rightfully theirs (for example, financial gain through

Table 1.7 Mnemonic for Narcissistic Personality Disorder

S	(3)	Special (believes he or she is special and unique)
P	(2)	Preoccupied with fantasies (of unlimited success, power, brilliance, beauty, or ideal love)
E	(8)	Envious (of others, or believes others are envious of him or her)
E	(5)	Entitlement
E	(4)	Excess admiration required
C	(1)	Conceited (grandiose sense of self-importance)
I	(6)	Interpersonal exploitation
A	(9)	Arrogant (haughty)
L	(7)	Lacks empathy

Notes: 1. Numbers in brackets correspond to the diagnostic criteria set out in the DSM5 (American Psychiatric Association, 2013); 2. Diagnosis requires the presence of any five of the nine diagnostic criteria.
Pinkofsky, H. B. (1997). Mnemonics for DSM-IV personality disorders. Psychiatric Services, 48(9), 1197–1198.

fraud, theft, or embezzlement in an attempt to obtain material items that they perceive will make them more respected by others). Often the criminal behavior will be purposefully directed at specific individuals in an attempt to take what is theirs as both a means of gaining material possessions and as an act of domination over a rival (whether or not that person is aware of an existing rivalry or even aware of the offender in any personal sense). This could be an employer, sibling, teammate, neighbor, or other person whom the offender has identified as a rival. Further, the aggressive and volatile elements of their personality can lead to violence if their fragile self-esteem is threatened (for example, someone belittles them or embarrasses them in some way, particularly if there is an audience). Any perceived threat to their need for dominance can result in retaliatory aggression. Table 1.7 shows how the narcissistic PD person can be described by using the mnemonic "SPEEECIAL," while histrionic PD persons are represented in Table 1.4 (Pinkofsky, 1997).

ANGER RETALIATORY-DRIVEN PD AND CRIMINALITY

PD offenders driven by retaliatory anger are motivated as a result of some exaggeration and distorted interpretation of the circumstances surrounding an event or events—whether real or perceived. Two groups of personality disordered offenders fall into this group. The first includes offenders with paranoid PD. Paranoid PD offenders act because of a belief that they have been wronged in some way. A very low self-esteem coupled with paranoid disordered thoughts results in a self-preservational process of the externalization of their strong angry emotions onto another. Disordered thinking provides a plausible, though likely untrue, rationale that allows the offender to lay blame elsewhere (for example, the government,

Table 1.8 Mnemonic for Paranoid Personality Disorder

S	(7)	Spouse fidelity suspected
U	(5)	Unforgiving (bears grudges)
S	(1)	Suspicious of others
P	(6)	Perceives attacks (and reacts quickly)
E	(2)	"Enemy or friend" (suspects associates and friends)
C	(3)	Confiding in others feared
T	(4)	Threats perceived in benign events

Notes: *1. Numbers in brackets correspond to the diagnostic criteria set out in the DSM5 (American Psychiatric Association, 2013); 2. Diagnosis requires the presence of any four of the eight diagnostic criteria.*
Pinkofsky, H. B. (1997). Mnemonics for DSM-IV personality disorders. Psychiatric Services, *48(9), 1197–1198.*

a spouse, sibling, employer, or workmate). Events are interpreted with a paranoid negativity bias, and therefore the offender begins to see conspiracy in the actions of those around them, further increasing the level of anger. The lack of capacity to modulate anger responses and inhibit impulsive urges ultimately leads to acts of "retaliation," which can include extreme violence and homicide. Table 1.8 shows how the paranoid PD can be described by using the mnemonic "SUSPECT" (Pinkofsky, 1997).

The second group of retaliatory anger offenders are likely to fall within the sphere of either borderline or narcissistic PD (Tables 1.3 and 1.7). Just like offenders with paranoid PD, these offenders also have very poor capacity to modulate hyperemotional anger responses, assess risk, or manage impulsive behavior. These individuals are usually found to be in existing volatile relationships that when combined with their unstable mood, fear of rejection, and impulsiveness, provide a high-risk environment for violence. These personality types become offenders when they feel threatened and react with a "shoot first" mentality in retaliation for the wrong that they believe is going to be done to them. In the event that a wrong is actually done to them, they are likely to retaliate impulsively and with extreme violence without regard to risk.

Interestingly, paranoid and narcissistic offenders will have characteristically externalised blame onto others and then set about to seek retaliation accordingly however; borderline offenders are more likely to have internalised blame creating an intense self-loathing. The borderline offender seeks to harm the "other" in retaliation, because they blame the other person for "making" them feel the intense negative emotions.

PERVASIVE ANGER-DRIVEN PD AND CRIMINALITY

Pervasive anger is a primary motivating feature of paranoid (Table 1.8), antisocial (Table 1.9), borderline (Table 1.3), histrionic (Table 1.4), and narcissistic offenders (Table 1.7). The key that drives this pervasive hyperresponsive anger is that the

Table 1.9 Mnemonic for Antisocial Personality Disorder

C	(1)	Conformity to law lacking
O	(6)	Obligations ignored
R	(5)	Reckless disregard for safety of self or others
R	(7)	Remorse lacking
U	(2)	Underhanded (deceitful, lies, cons others)
P	(3)	Planning insufficient (impulsive)
T	(4)	Temper (irritable and aggressive)

Notes: *1. Numbers in brackets correspond to the diagnostic criteria set out in the DSM5 (American Psychiatric Association, 2013); 2. Diagnosis requires the presence of any three of the seven diagnostic criteria.*
Pinkofsky, H. B. (1997). Mnemonics for DSM-IV personality disorders. Psychiatric Services, *48(9), 1197–1198.*

disordered personality appears to develop with a schema that generalizes the negativity bias inherent in all PDs, in an aggressive manner. This means that offenders with these PDs are able to find fault everywhere and an "other" is used as a convenient displacement for the internal hyperemotionality that the sufferer cannot modulate or rationalize using internal mechanisms. Any externalized factor can become the lightning rod for the sufferer's anger. These personality types often become offenders when they initiate violent exchanges as a means of exerting control and reestablishing self-esteem. Alternatively, they may damage property if it is a contextually appropriate displacement of their anger. Table 1.9 shows how the antisocial PD can be described by using the mnemonic "CORRUPT" (Pinkofsky, 1997).

EXCITATION-DRIVEN PD AND CRIMINALITY

A complex and challenging offender type, excitation-driven offenders are most likely to have either antisocial (Table 1.9) or dependent (Table 1.6) personality characteristics. The antisocial personality often fits this motivational type as the lack of empathy and social affiliation toward others allows these offenders the emotional space to be able to place themselves in situations where the pain or suffering of others is irrelevant compared to the pleasure obtained for themselves. Sadistic aggression behaviors (described earlier in the chapter), whether consensual or nonconsensual, may therefore appeal.

The strong desire for approval from others is the motivating factor that often results in the dependent personality placing himself or herself in relationships of unequal power in which they are subservient to others. A sadistic partner may entice a dependent personality into increasingly sadistic "play," and the dependent personality may acquiesce due to fear of being rejected and a desire to be accepted. Increasingly violent "play" may move into abuse if the dependent personality cannot (by fear or physical incapacity) extricate himself or herself from the escalation. The greatest risk occurs when the dependent personality encounters the antisocial personality. In this case, the victim–perpetrator relationship is epitomised.

Table 1.10 Mnemonic for Schizoid Personality Disorder

D	(7)	Detached (or flattened) affect
I	(6)	Indifferent to criticism and praise
S	(3)	Sexual experiences of little interest
T		Tasks (activities) done solitarily
A	(5)	Absence of close friends
N	(1)	Neither desires nor enjoys close relations
T	(4)	Takes pleasure in few activities

Notes: 1. Numbers in brackets correspond to the diagnostic criteria set out in the DSM5 (American Psychiatric Association, 2013); 2. Diagnosis requires the presence of any four of the seven diagnostic criteria. Pinkofsky, H. B. (1997). Mnemonics for DSM-IV personality disorders. Psychiatric Services, 48(9), 1197–1198.

While more likely to be a victim than an offender in this form of criminal motivation, dependent personalities may become offenders if they finally "crack" in the face of ongoing abuse and retaliate reflexively. There have been numerous cases in which placid, dependent personality types react aggressively in the face of chronic provocation. This can happen because, although they are largely fear-driven, they also have impaired impulse control, and when provoked, even the mildest mannered of individual or animal may resort to a reflexive fight response and engage in highly aggressive survival behavior. Dependent PD offenders may also be prime candidates for violent crime within an acute catathymic crisis.

In addition, schizoid or schizotypal PD types can be high risk for excitation-driven offending. These personality types have characteristically low levels of emotionality and reward stimulation. In these individuals, altered perceptions and distorted reality may combine with limited emotional expression to motivate a desire to experience greater affect. This can lead to self-harming behaviors as well as thrill-seeking encounters with others. A lack of capacity to assess and mitigate risk makes these personality subtypes potentially at high risk to inflict significant harm on others (offender) as well as become the unwitting victim of others. Table 1.10 shows how the schizoid PD can be described using the mnemonic "DISTANT," and Table 1.11 shows how the mnemonic "ME PECULIAR" can be used for schizotypal PD (Pinkofsky, 1997):

MATERIALLY DRIVEN PD AND CRIMINALITY

All PDs are at risk for offending through this form of criminal motivation. Low or fragile self-esteem, distorted perceptions, paranoia, fear, a need for instant gratification, poor impulse control, needs arising from alcohol and/or substance abuse, anger, and feelings of missing out—or that others are preventing you from obtaining objects or outcomes, fear of rejection and need for approval—can all bring about this motivation. An offender may use criminal means to obtain material gain whether through violence, theft, or illicit commercial activity (drug dealing, gambling, prostitution, fraud).

Table 1.11 Mnemonic for Schizotypal Personality Disorder

M	(2)	Magical thinking or odd beliefs
E	(3)	Experiences unusual perceptions
P	(5)	Paranoid ideation
E	(7)	Eccentric behavior or appearance
C	(6)	Constricted (or inappropriate) affect
U	(4)	Unusual (odd) thinking and speech
L	(8)	Lacks close friends
I	(1)	Ideas of reference
A	(9)	Anxiety in social situations
R	✍	R rule out psychotic disorders and pervasive developmental disorder

Notes: 1. Numbers in brackets correspond to the diagnostic criteria set out in the DSM5 (American Psychiatric Association, 2013); 2. Diagnosis requires the presence of any five of the nine diagnostic criteria, and the ruling out of psychotic or pervasive developmental disorders. Pinkofsky, H. B. (1997). Mnemonics for DSM-IV personality disorders. Psychiatric Services, 48(9), 1197–1198.

SELF-PRESERVATION–DRIVEN PD AND CRIMINALITY

As with materially driven PD offenders, all PDs may be driven by self-preservation motives to commit crime. Self-preservation is a fundamental survival instinct and, in cases where an individual is impaired in their capacity for social reasoning and risk assessment, the natural desire for self-preservation can result in a variety of scenarios in which behavior may become criminal in nature. The desire for self-preservation can lead to the commission of a variety of criminal behaviors aimed at restoring some kind of injustice (real or perceived) or protecting the well-being of self or others (again, whether real or perceived). These forms of motivations are particularly high risk for those who perceive the world through the thick lens of paranoia, through the distorted and delusional schizotypal perceptions, through the "cover my tracks" manipulations of the antisocial personality, or through the myopic view of narcissism whereby elevated beliefs about self-worth, right to have, and expectations of praise, admiration, and material reward may promote aggressive pursuit of these goals.

PSYCHOTIC DISORDERS AND CRIMINALITY

Despite the popular belief perpetrated by significant media bias and the ensuing moral panic after a publicized criminal act that is perpetrated by an individual suffering from a psychotic episode; it is not "marauding hordes of psychotics" who are our biggest threat to life and limb. The reality is that we are far more likely to become a victim of a violent person-to-person crime at the hands of a perpetrator who is already known to us and is not suffering from a current psychotic episode. In the general population, far more people are assaulted and murdered by their intimate partners or ex-intimate partners than any other group. For example, US and Australian intimate partner violence (IPV) is a far greater concern than violence from the mentally ill (Shackelford & Mouzos, 2005). In the United States and many other countries around the world from North America and Europe to the Pacific Islands and Africa, one of the greatest causes of death in pregnant women is uxoricide (Adinkrah, 1999, 2008; Borges & Léveillée, 2005; Di Girolamo & Nesci, 1981; Shackelford & Mouzos, 2005; Williams, 2010).

The research in this area can be somewhat confusing. It is true that individuals suffering an acute psychotic episode have a higher statistical probability of committing an offense than the population average. While a controversial area of social debate, the statistics have been consistent for a prolonged period. Several previous large-scale epidemiological studies have shown this trend. For example, Swanson, Holzer, Ganja, and Jono (1990) and (Swanson, 1994) reported on a large-scale population study in which a random community sample of 10,000 individuals were selected from the Epidemiological Catchment Area Study. The study was undertaken to gain an understanding of the mental health of those living in the United States. The results indicated that 12% of respondents with schizophrenia had committed a violent act in the previous year, compared with 2.4% of the respondents without a mental illness. Similar results have been obtained in which researchers found significantly higher rates of violent offending, between 6% and 33% of those with psychotic disorders (estimated to be about 0.4–0.8% for the period relating to the various studies), compared with overall rates in the nondisordered population of around 2–3%. These studies have used a variety of methods to obtain data (mental health court records cross-matching, longitudinal birth cohorts, prison/presentencing assessment cohorts, survey) and come from across numerous countries, including Australia (Wallace et al., 1998, 2014), New Zealand (Arseneault, Moffitt, Caspi, Taylor, & Silva, 2000), Denmark (Brennan, Mednick, & Hodgins, 2000; Gottlieb, Gabrielsen, & Kramp, 1987), Sweden (Lindqvist & Allebeck, 1990), Finland (Eronen, Tiihonen, & Hakola, 1996), Iceland (Petursson & Gudjonsson, 1981), Spain (Vicens et al., 2011), and the United States (Peterson, Skeem, Hart, Vidal, & Keith, 2010; Wilcox, 1985).

More recently, studies have continued to support these findings; however, the "real-world" facts are more complex than a comparison of within-group incidences would perhaps indicate. Indeed, the evidence certainly supports the position that, as a group, individuals suffering from a psychotic episode—through either organic disease, drug inducement, comorbidity with other disorders, or other factors—have a much higher risk for committing a violent person-to-person crime than do nondisordered individuals in the general population (Appelbaum, Robbins, & Monahan, 2000; Nestor, 2002; Rezansoff, Moniruzzaman, Gress, & Somers, 2013; Tiihonen, Isohanni, Rasanen, Koiranen, & Moring, 1997; Whittington et al., 2013). However, while the risk of an individual committing a violent crime increases several-fold during a psychotic episode, the overall number of violent crimes committed by people with a psychotic disorder as a percentage of all violent crime and homicide is very small (about 5%; Fazel & Grann, 2006). Therefore, although in the big picture, psychotic individuals do not commit a significant proportion of the violent crimes committed, they do commit more than their "fair share" when compared with the general population and other subgroups. The research is clear, however, that other mental illnesses, such as alcohol and substance abuse (Beck, 1994; Vaughn et al., 2010; Wallace et al., 2014), and other major mental illnesses with their foundations in a personality disorder and/or adjustment disorder (Monahan et al., 2000; Steadman et al., 1998) are more predictive of violent offending risk than psychotic disorders and other major mental disorders associated with psychotic presentation such as major depression.

A "catch-22" in forensic psychology is that the mental illnesses most associated with increased offending risk are also those with the greatest treatment adherence challenges (Caligor, Levy, & Yeomans, 2015; Haddad, Brain, & Scott, 2014; Hengartner, 2015; Kane, Kishimoto, & Correll, 2013). Offending risk in psychotic disorders is closely linked to the unique cognitive symptomatology that characterizes presentation such as delusions, hallucinations, and fantasy thinking, and the associated impairments to affect regulation, and to executive functions such as inhibition. Therefore, treatment adherence is a vital element in mitigating risk in this group. Given treatment adherence is a major problem in this mental health group, particularly among younger sufferers; psychopathology with psychotic features are likely to continue to feature regularly in the offender statistics.

DISORDERED THINKING AS FOUNDATION TO ANTISOCIAL AND CRIMINAL BEHAVIOR IN PSYCHOTIC DISORDERS

Disordered thinking in severe psychosis often extends from nonbizarre to bizarre delusions in which the delusions are of a kind that are implausible and fantastic in nature and are often reinforced by hallucinations that provide validation for the delusions (Sinnamon, 2015). For example, paranoid delusions of severe persecution or delusions of grandeur may be reinforced by hallucinations in which the sufferer believes he or she is "being instructed" or is "receiving" secret auditory messages through the toaster or the bird perched on the back fence. Alternatively, the sufferer may "see" secret messages directed to him or her and encrypted in newspaper articles, advertising billboards, or in the television or radio signal. These may be information based—that is, they are providing information about a topic—or they may be command hallucinations, in which instructions are being given to carry out a specific act. In these situations, the delusions and hallucinations drive increasingly obsessional thoughts, which, in turn, drive ever-stronger affective reactions. This produces a feedback loop that further increases the disordered thought processes and ultimately increases the motivation to act on the disordered thoughts and the phantom instructions being "received" in the hallucinations. Eventually, this progresses the internal psychological maelstrom until the desire to act (motivation) becomes a compulsion and the behavioral outcome ensues. Alternatively, sufferers may fight hard to resist the delusions and the hallucinations and fight against the increasing compulsion to act. As previously reported (Sinnamon, 2015, p. 239):

> *In either event, the neurological deficits associated with these conditions prevent any long-term concerted capacity to resist. These neurological deficits are complex and include increased activation of sub-cortical activity in areas such as the brainstem and reticular activating system accompanied by impaired higher-order neural activity in areas of limbic and frontal lobe function resulting in retarded impulse control, increased reflexive responses to stimuli—particularly threatening or perceived-to-be threatening stimuli—increased aggression responses, and reduced capacity for empathy, social affiliation, information processing, and rationality.*

Psychosis and disordered thought processes are a foundational component of forensic psychology as violent, threatening, and offensive antisocial behaviors are often perpetrated in the face of factors associated with obsessions, delusions, paranoias, hallucinations, and fantasies. While the "classic" psychotic disorders such as schizophrenia are not the sole domain of these forms of thought processes, the symptoms themselves are considered to be of a psychotic nature and, therefore, we will explore them more fully in this section. It should be noted, however, that disordered thinking is, to some extent, a characteristic of a relatively substantial number of recognized psychopathologies that have been associated with an increased risk of criminal offending including personality disorders, anxiety disorders, major depression and bipolar depression disorders, conduct disorders, adjustment disorders, substance abuse disorders, trauma-related disorders, and, of course, the psychotic disorders themselves such as schizophrenia. With this in mind, the following sections explore elements of these key disordered thought processes that are associated with criminal behavior.

Obsession

In the criminal framework, obsession has been most associated with the idea of obsessional following or stalking (Sinnamon, 2015)—that is, the obsessional and unwanted following of another person. Miller (2012, p. 495), defines *stalking* as "an intentional pattern of repeated intrusive and intimidating behaviors toward a specific person that causes the target to feel harassed, threatened, and fearful, or that a reasonable person would regard as being so." The act of obsessional following is seemingly as old as humanity itself and has been put into story, song, verse, social commentary, and religious context for several thousands of years, across almost all cultures and historical epochs. Indeed, what we have come to consider the criminal act of stalking has previously been regarded in the context of romantic, though obsessive, advances.

Legislation making obsessional following or stalking a criminal act has only become commonplace in the past 25 years. For example, the first state in the United States to criminalize stalking was California in 1990; however, it did take just an additional 6 years for the remaining 49 states to pass similar antistalking laws (Davis & Chipman, 1997). Other countries have largely undertaken similar legislative programs and established legal protections from unwanted attentions. This has progressed, and stalking has now been widely recognized as a forensic psychopathology. However, the ability to stereotypically "pigeonhole" the act is somewhat more difficult.

While obsessional thinking is a major characteristic of many forms of forensic psychopathology, it is also often an identifiable pathological feature of criminal activity even in the absence of diagnosable psychopathology. Stalking is a good example of where this is often the case. Clinical research has provided extensive detail on psychopathologies related to stalking (Davis & Chipman, 1997; McEwan & Strand, 2013; Thompson, Dennison, & Stewart, 2013). However, the research has also shown that stalkers come from a variety of backgrounds and psychological profiles, many of which do not readily include full syndrome psychopathology. In this instance, there is evidence that the individual characteristics of stalkers still include pathological characteristics such as obsessional thinking, maladaptive social capacity, and codependent or controlling personality traits.

Stalking and its obsessional components are unique to each individual offender. This is because it is a confluence of the individual psychodynamics of thoughts, emotions, and motivations that ultimately go to create, drive, and maintain the stalker's behavioral manifestations. Essentially, the macro-motivation is to control the victim; however, the micro-motivations are driven by disordered thoughts and associated emotions that result from individual histories and mental health derivations. What is known is that, if left unchecked and unrequited, the obsessional thoughts will lead to progressive behaviors that all too often end in tragedy.

The nature and extent of obsessional thoughts will generally determine the salience of the associated emotional responses that are directed at the target of the obsession. Emotional responses in turn mediate the strength of the motivation to act on the obsessions and ultimately on the progression and direction of any behavioral responses. The emotional response also feeds back into the obsessive thought process, providing additional impetus to stimulate a strengthening and progression of the obsessive thoughts (Sinnamon, 2015). Fig. 1.1 shows the basic character of this process.

Stalking behaviors are most commonly analyzed for their potential threat to the target of the obsession. According to Davis and Chipman (1997), the degree of obsession (disordered thinking) can be linked to the severity of the associated mental disorder and the nature and extent of the potential injury to the target of the obsession. Therefore, stalking behaviors are best seen as a spectrum or continuum in which the extent of obsession associated with the behaviors can be used as a yardstick to assess the potential risk of the behaviors escalating to violence.

While the popular view is that continued rejection in the face of clinical erotomania (also known as de Clerambault syndrome)—the irrational belief that an essentially unattainable stranger is passionately in love with you—is the most common cause of violence in stalking cases; the reality is that obsessional following of a stranger leading to violence is relatively rare. Instead, it is far more common that stalking that results in violence or homicide is a case of IPV (Miller, 2012; Norris, Huss, & Palarea, 2011). Stalking is most common when a relationship has soured, usually in the face of some form of domestic violence. This form of stalking is known as simple obsessional stalking and is the most common form of stalking, right across the socioeconomic and cultural spectrum and accounting for as much as half of all stalking cases. It is often difficult to identify unless the victim asks for help as the

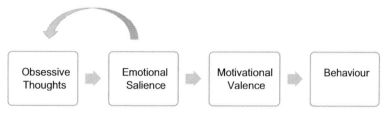

FIGURE 1.1

Important foundational role of thoughts in obsessional following (stalking). Fig. 1.1 shows the direction and causal relationship between internal psychodynamics and behavior.

Sinnamon, G.C.B. (2015). Psychopathology and Criminal Behavior. In W. Petherick (Ed.), Applied Crime Analysis: A social science approach to understanding crime, criminals, and victims. *Boston: Anderson Publishing.*

stalker may not present any outward symptoms of abnormality and can usually maintain an otherwise "normal" existence.

A third form of stalking takes the middle ground between erotomania and simple obsessional stalking. Known as love obsessional stalking, this obsession takes the form of an offender engaging in an ongoing campaign to make the target of their obsession aware of him or her (Sinnamon, 2015). According to Sinnamon (2015), the two parties are most often known to one another. The two may work together, they may interact through a service relationship (for example, local shop staff and customer), they may know each other through a local club or service organization, or they may have a mutual friend through whom they are acquainted. The stalker's obsessive thoughts are often accompanied by creative, though irrational, plans to get the target to notice them. These plans are often bizarre and, as such, are not able to be understood by the victim. When attempts to be noticed are unsuccessful, the stalker will escalate his or her efforts and behaviors will become increasingly irrational and bizarre until the obsessive thoughts and associated emotions move into compulsions. At this time, the risk of violence by the stalker against the target of their obsession (victim) becomes extreme. These basic types of obsessive following can be further broken down and dissected; however, the characteristics of these three remain steadfastly consistent throughout.

The research shows that the level of obsession and relational access to the target are the two key factors that can assist in predicting stalking risk and the risk of behavioral escalation to violence and homicide. Essentially, the greater the obsession and the greater the degree of accessibility by the stalker to their target, the greater is the risk of physical violence (Appelbaum et al., 2000). In contrast, the lower the level of relational access the stalker has to the target of their obsession and the greater the delusional characteristics of the accompanying psychopathology, the lower is the risk of physical violence by the stalker against the target (Appelbaum et al., 2000). According to Appelbaum et al. (2000), this is an interesting finding given that delusional thinking generally increases the risk of aggression. Within the area of stalking behaviors, the only exception to these rules appears to be in cases where the stalking is associated with delusional jealousy in IPV (Carabellese, Rocca, Candelli, & Catanesi, 2014; Silva, Derecho, Leong, & Ferrari, 2000) and in cases of erotomania (Carabellese et al., 2013; McGuire & Wraith, 2000).

Delusion and Paranoia

Delusional thinking has long been considered to be associated with an increased risk of violent behavior, and the past two decades have seen an increase in the empirical evidence supporting this assertion (Appelbaum et al., 2000; Carabellese et al., 2014; Spencer & Tie, 2013; van Dongen, Buck, & van Marle, 2012a,b). Delusional thinking can be characterized by the presence of recurring and persistent delusions that are nonbizarre in nature (Sinnamon, 2015). A delusion is an irrational belief that is held with strong conviction even in the face of contradictory evidence. Delusional thinking must involve nonbizarre delusional thoughts, which means that the delusions must be plausible—they must be of a kind that could possibly be true. An example is a belief that you are being spied on by government agents. This form of paranoia is a good and common example of nonbizarre delusional thinking. This differs from more severe psychosis in which delusions held are often bizarre in nature—that is, they involve beliefs that it would be impossible to be true. An example is a belief that you could fly (Sinnamon, 2015).

People who experience delusional thinking often organize these disordered thoughts into a logical and consistent (although improbable and untrue) schema or view of the world. This means that delusional thinking can often be challenging to identify early enough to mitigate the risk of criminal aggression against another person. This is because the person suffering from the delusions will often appear "normal" even when he or she is in the middle of a delusional episode. The obvious signs may include the individual making odd behavioral choices or they may reflect their delusional beliefs in their comments. For example, if an individual had delusions about being spied on by government agents, they might always use cash when making purchases or they may refuse to use a telephone or computer for fear of being compromised in some way. They may make comments such as "I always use cash because it makes it harder for them to keep track of me." These individuals will often pass unnoticed for an extended period until their delusional thoughts either progress to include a paranoia that they believe is physically threatening to them and so they start to react in more unusual (including potentially aggressive) ways to "protect" themselves, or they either seek help themselves or are identified by an astute family member or friend. Hallucinations are not a common characteristic of delusional thinking and may only occur infrequently or may not occur at all.

Delusional Subtypes With Forensic Association
Jealousy

Jealousy delusions are the form of delusional thinking most commonly associated with violence, usually IPV. When delusional disorder is featured in court cases involving instances of person-to-person violence, it is most often associated with this subtype. In the forensic pathology of this form, the offender usually becomes convinced that his or her intimate partner is having an affair. The delusion is fed by very circumstantial evidence—such as the partner not answering the phone when they call—and they will still hold to the delusion even in the face of evidence to the contrary. The jealous delusional individual will become focused on gathering "proof" and often become increasingly controlling of their partner's movements and contact with others, often to the point of trying to confine them to the home (Sinnamon, 2015).

Paranoid or Persecutory

While the jealousy subtype is the most common forensic form of delusional thinking, the most common form of delusional thought disorders overall is paranoid delusions or persecution-type delusions. In these conditions, individuals are under the delusion that others are conspiring to harm them in some way. This form of the disorder is also a high risk for escalation to aggression and violence if the individual identifies a specific person or persons as the conspirators. If the delusion becomes fixated on a target, then the individual has the potential to progress to "self-defense" against those they perceive as wanting to harm them. Self-defense in this instance often includes a preemptive strike against the perceived aggressors or a heightened threat sense that may misinterpret some interaction between the delusional individual and their apparent aggressors as a threat (to their life) and overreact with extreme violence (Sinnamon, 2015).

Erotomania

Erotomania has been described briefly under obsessional thinking; however, erotomania also includes significant elements of delusional thinking in which the sufferer is under the delusion that some individual—often a stranger or an important person or celebrity—is in love with them. This form of delusion is more common in females and often results in stalking (Carabellese et al., 2013). While rare, this form of delusion does result in both nonfatal violence and homicide against the love interest or other/s who may be perceived as potential rivals or who the stalker believes may have some other irrationally derived role to play in bringing the stalker and their target together (Sinnamon, 2015).

Delusion as a Feature of Other Forensic Psychopathology

As mentioned earlier in the chapter, delusions often occur as a feature of other psychopathologies. Psychotic disorders such as schizoaffective disorder and schizophrenia often have delusional thinking as a prominent characteristic, as can some PDs and mood disorders (both unipolar and bipolar depression) with psychotic features. Moreover, delusions often appear comorbid with neurological conditions such as brain tumor, stroke, acquired brain injury, and some neurodegenerative disorders such as dementia and Alzheimer disease (Crail-Melendez, Atriano-Mendieta, Carrillo-Meza, & Ramirez-Bermudez, 2013; Echávarri et al., 2013; Pareés et al., 2013; Zugman et al., 2013). Alzheimer and dementia conditions are often associated with increased levels of aggression, and therefore any expression of atypical aggression—even physical assault against loved ones—is often an indicator of neurodegenerative disease in an aging or otherwise high-risk (for neurodegenerative disorder) offender. Finally, delusions are a common side effect of a number of drugs—both illicit and prescription (Aggarwal, Banerjee, Singh, Mattoo, & Basu, 2012; Cameron, Block, & Lee, 2013; Signorelli, Battaglia, Costanzo, & Cannavò, 2013). In a forensic setting, drug-induced or medically derived delusional thinking should always be considered and either confirmed or ruled out before moving to other psychopathological explanations.

Ultimately, because disordered thinking such as delusions is a high-prevalence feature in so many psychopathologies, there is little to be gained in focusing on the diagnosis of the full-syndrome psychiatric condition; rather, it is the delusion, obsession, paranoia, etc., that is the characteristic important to understanding the criminal act or the risk for perpetration of a criminal act by a potential offender.

AFFECTIVE DISORDERS AND CRIMINALITY

Mood and anxiety disorders together make up a large collective of conditions generically called affective disorders. These conditions are varied in the nature and character of their presentations, but the common denominator for all affective conditions is that they have as a primary feature a substantial deleterious impact on emotions in those suffering from them. While much of the risk for offending in these conditions comes from one, or a combination of, (a) their potential to present with psychotic features, (b) their significant association with alcohol and substance abuse, and (c) their associated impairments to cognitive function—all of which are discussed in other sections of this chapter; there remains some discourse of value in other areas associated with offending risk in mood and anxiety disorders.

Major Depression

Being diagnosed with depression carries a threefold increase in the risk of committing a violent crime (Fazel et al., 2015). According to Fazel et al. (2015), the rates at which individuals with major depression commit violent crimes is roughly equivalent to the rates at which they self-harm or commit suicide. While the risk remains higher than that of the general population, even when other factors are controlled; the primary crime risk in major depression is associated with alcohol and substance abuse and when the condition presents with psychotic features. Alcohol and other substances may be abused as a form of self-medication and can lead to increased loss of inhibition and uncontrolled anger outbursts that combine to result in violence against others. Violence may occur in the absence of alcohol or other drugs; however, as these act as disinhibitors of behavior, the risk increases markedly when they are introduced. In addition, major depression can present with psychotic features, which substantially increases the risk of offending via the same mechanisms described earlier in the psychotic disorder section of the chapter. Major depression is also associated with neuropsychological impairment in areas such as executive function, learning and memory, and social cognition. These impairments can impact the ability to inhibit behavior, make appropriate decisions, assess risk, and interpret social cues from others. Challenges in these areas may, in turn, contribute to offending behaviors.

Postnatal Depression and Women Who Kill Their Children

Women who kill their children present a profoundly disturbing challenge to the stereotypical perceptions of a mother's protective instincts toward her offspring. This group of offenders is a thankfully small number in the overall crime statistics; nevertheless, when it happens, the impact on the associated community is substantial. The potentially devastating effects of depression in the postnatal environment are brought home in stark reality in the face of infanticide. In the contemporary space, the number of countries legislating to provide reduced penalties for infanticide when a mother is suffering from postnatal depression has increased substantially. These laws generally limit the extent of legal recognition to (a) child-bearing mothers (an important distinction in the postlegalization of same-sex marriage era), (b) mothers who are diagnosed as suffering from hormonally derived depression associated with lactation and/or pregnancy when the offense occurs, and (c) the provisions usually only extend mitigation for the first year postpartum (Friedman, Cavney, & Resnick, 2012b). While infanticide laws have been largely welcomed as an important part of recognizing the existence and impact of postnatal depression, Friedman et al. (2012b) reported that these laws have also come under some criticism. Critics have argued that infanticide legislation is gender-biased and is drafted on inherent misunderstanding of the hormonal basis of postpartum psychiatric disorders and the way in which these disorders might mediate offending behaviors as this relates to the notion of culpability and appropriate sentencing. A major criticism of infanticide laws has also come from the 1-year postpartum limitation applied when recognizing postnatal depression as a mitigating factor. It is argued that this is a significant flaw in the legislation and is based on a misunderstanding of the role and character of motherhood-specific biologically derived psychiatric illness (Friedman et al., 2012b).

Most often, the argument for the legitimacy of the infanticide defense centers around the position that biochemical and hormonal alterations of childbirth result in perinatal, and particularly postpartum, psychiatric episodes (usually depression and/or psychosis, but dissociative and adjustment/denial features are also implicated) that are claimed to be at least in part exculpatory for the murder. The argument against this blanket assumption is that the research indicates substantial variation in the presentation of these features in women who kill their children that are mediated by the age of both the mother and the child victim. According to Friedman, Cavney, and Resnick (2012a), younger mothers who kill their children in the short period immediately postpartum have significantly lower rates of mental illness than do older mothers who kill their older children. This in and of itself has far-reaching implications given that the infanticide defense is, in most jurisdictions, limited to maternal homicide of children within their first year of life. Therefore, older women with psychiatric illness who kill older children may be denied a legitimate defense, and mothers without a legitimate claim to psychiatric mitigation may be able to benefit from such an exculpatory claim.

In Australia, one in every seven mothers are estimated to experience postnatal depression (Deloitte Access Economics, 2012). Worldwide estimates have previously estimated an incidence of between 10% and 15%; however, research has indicated that the incidence may, in fact, be much higher (Almond, 2009). Moreover, indications are that around 10% of fathers may also experience postnatal depression and that mothers' and fathers' experiences of depression in the postpartum period are positively correlated (Paulson & Bazemore, 2010).

Postnatal depression is commonly experienced comorbid with anxiety (Deloitte Access Economics, 2012; Paulson & Bazemore, 2010). The general symptoms of postnatal depression are ubiquitous to those of depression and anxiety in general buy carry additional disordered thinking associated with guilt, worthlessness, paranoia, and harm to self and infant. In some cases, again, as with general depression and anxiety disorders, sufferers can experience psychosis, known as postpartum psychosis or puerperal psychosis. Most often, this is known to occur in the first few weeks postpartum, but it can occur anytime throughout the first few months after giving birth. The incidence is considered rare at around one to two women in every 1000, however, due to the environment, is a serious pathology. Puerperal psychosis has an acute onset and has a high risk of associated violent offending in which both the mother and infant are at risk for suicide, infanticide, and infanticide-suicide. As a psychotic episode, puerperal psychosis is often an extreme presentation that includes aggression and possibly violence, delusions, hallucinations, and other changes in sensory perception, paranoia, grandiosity, irrational and disconnected reactions to stimuli (particularly responses to infant, and incoherence of speech. Any one or combination of these presentations can lead to behavior that results in the death of the infant, mother, proximally close person/s such as older children, intimate partner, adult family member, friend, or neighbor. In cases where postnatal depression is "treated" with self-medication using alcohol or other substances, the risk of puerperal psychosis increases, as does the risk for violent offending during the depressive or psychotic state.

Bipolar Disorder
Bipolar is characterized by a cycling from the emotional lows of major depression to manic episodes associated with extreme emotionality that is either hypermanic or hypomanic. The risk of offending during the lows are the same as those described in the major depression and postnatal depression sections. The risk of offending while in a manic episode is significantly greater than when in a depressed episode (Quanbeck et al., 2004). Bipolar disorder can present with psychotic features and has an increased risk for alcohol and substance abuse and the pursuit of physical and emotional sensory experience, all of which increase the risk of offending behavior (Daff & Thomas, 2014). A study in the United Kingdom that followed patients after release from psychiatric facilities found that patients with bipolar disorder were more likely to commit sexual offences after release than any other identified group in the study (Coid et al., 2015).

Hypermania
Hypermanic episodes are the stereotypical episodes popularly associated with bipolar, or what was once called manic depression. Hypermania is characterized by

hyperactivity, grandiosity, poor insight and judgment, extreme risk-taking, and generally extreme emotionality associated with excitement and risk-taking and thoughts and feelings of grandeur. In this state, individuals are less able to make context appropriate judgments about their behaviors and abilities. They are often hyposensitized to both sensory and emotional stimuli and therefore are at risk of engaging in extreme behaviors in pursuit of these sensations. Hypersexuality, gambling, drug and alcohol use, speeding, extreme spending, thoughts of grandeur, and being able to "take on the world" are the commonplace experiences of a hypermanic episode. In this state, any number of behaviors may lead to a crossing the line into offending behaviors. This can range from speeding in a car and the use of illicit substances, property damage, theft, fraud, and various expressions of public nuisance, through to sexual and/or physical assault.

Hypomania

In hypomania, the manic expression is aggressive in nature and is usually directed in a manner that is antagonistic to others. Hypomanic individuals are likely to pick arguments and/or fights and direct their hyperactivity and other elevated and grandiose thoughts and emotions into antagonistic actions. In this way, the hypomanic individual is at risk of offending due to extreme agitation and the pursuit of conflict. They may become an offender through similar behaviors to that of the hypermanic person; however, their emotional state is likely to be far more aggressive and uncompromising and lead to seeking control and domination over others–power-oriented sexual assault, aggravated robbery, and other violent crimes are commonplace with those whose presentation leads to offending behaviors.

Anxiety

Historically, it was thought that anxiety had a moderating effect on potential criminal behaviors. However, recent evidence indicates that the heightened threat sensitivity associated with anxiety disorders may lead to persistent violent behavior in some individuals (Hodgins, De Brito, Chhabra, & Cote, 2010). Moreover, about 50% of male prisoners with antisocial personality disorder have a comorbid anxiety disorder. Those with this comorbidity present with a significantly higher number of antisocial PD symptoms than those without, and are more likely to have commenced their criminal careers before age 15, to have an alcohol and/or drug abuse disorder, and to have been convicted for a serious crime involving IPV.

Based on the research, the risk of criminal behavior that is associated with anxiety disorders appears to be mediated by the fight-or-flight response and the heightened threat sensitivity that is associated with anxiety. In some individuals, this sensitivity may result in the conditioning of an aggressive coping behavioral style in which threats are "neutralized" using "fight" rather than "flight" strategies. In others, responses may be "flight" oriented and behaviors are motivated by a need to get away from the situation or to avoid a situation in the first place. The need to avoid or resolve a situation of fear can lead to a pathological worry reaction. Worry is a natural and highly beneficial response to circumstances in which a solution is required.

Getting worried generates motivation to solve a problem and therefore is an important emotional function. However, when worry becomes pathological and is triggered for even pedestrian events, worry is no longer as beneficial. Some individuals may, through experience or natural temperament, react to this amplified worry state by going onto the attack. This would explain the relationship between violence and anxiety in a small subgroup of individuals. A second mediator appears to be alcohol and substance abuse. Anxiety disorders are highly related to alcohol and substance abuse comorbidity as these substances are often used to self-medicate (Nicholls, Staiger, Williams, Richardson, & Kambouropoulos, 2014; Vorspan, Mehtelli, Dupuy, Bloch, & Lepine, 2015), in turn increasing disinhibition in users and increasing the risk of impulsive and aggressive behaviors.

INTELLECTUAL IMPAIRMENTS, ACQUIRED BRAIN INJURIES, AND CRIMINALITY

The idea that much of the criminal population is somehow mentally deficient has been a long-standing position reaching back for more than a century (Brock, 1917; Maudsley, 1876; McDonald, 1905). In the contemporary era, numerous studies have found higher rates of lower intelligence and cognitive impairment in offender groups compared with the general population (Cockram, 2005; Glaser, 1996; Glaser & Deane, 1999; Hayes & McIllwain, 1988; Hirschi & Hindelang, 1977; Jones & Coombes, 1990). In Australia, a decade after the push for deinstitutionalization that had begun in the mid-1980s, the New South Wales (NSW) Law Reform Commission, released a report into the level of people with intellectual disability in the legal system (New South Wales Law Reform Commission, 1996). The report found that among the NSW prisoner population, the rates of intellectual disability were "at least 12–13%" (p. 25). This was compared with an estimated rate of 2–3% in the population from which the prisoners were drawn. The report further stated that the rates in those arrested, those charged, and those appearing before the courts were substantially higher again (New South Wales Law Reform Commission, 1996). More recent studies from around the world have supported the high rates of intellectually disabled offenders in the criminal justice system (Crocker, Côté, Toupin, & St-Onge, 2007; Fazel, Xenitidis, & Powell, 2008; Hayes, Shackell, Mottram, & Lancaster, 2007; Hodgins, 1992; Hogue et al., 2006; Holland & Persson, 2011). In Canada, Crocker et al. (2007) found that an estimated 19% of the males being held in pretrial custody were intellectually disabled and a further 30% were in the borderline intelligence range. Moreover, Crocker et al. (2007) found that of those with intellectual disability or intelligence in the borderline range, more than 60% had a substance abuse disorder, and most of the 281 individuals assessed had a history of violent offending. Similarly, Hayes et al. (2007) found that just over 7% of a random sample of prisoners in the United Kingdom had impaired intelligence and a further 24% were in the borderline range. In Sweden, it was found that individuals with a diagnosed intellectual disability but no comorbid mental illness were 3.1 times (males) and 3.7 times (females) more likely to receive a criminal conviction (Hodgins, De Brito, Chhabra, &

Cote, 2010). In the case of violent offenses, Hodgins (1992) found that in those with a mental disability, men were 5.5 times more likely to receive a criminal conviction, while for women the rate was 24.7 times greater.

Certain types of brain injury can cause increased risk for offending (McKinlay et al., 2014; W. H. Williams et al., 2015). There are numerous force trauma and organic injury mechanisms that can produce damage to the brain in areas, and in sufficient scope, so as to cause offending behaviors (Chevignard & Lind, 2014; Fazel, Philipson, Gardiner, Merritt, & Grann, 2009). This is particularly true for individuals with frontal lobe injury as a result of the impact this injury can have on executive functions such as impulse control, risk assessment, and higher-order planning and decision-making (Batts, 2009; DelBello et al., 1999; Grafman et al., 1996; Muller, Schuierer, Marienhagen, Putzhammer, & Klein, 2003; Romero-Martinez & Moya-Albiol, 2013; Vogenthaler, 1987). Organic degenerative conditions such as dementia syndromes associated with Alzheimer disease and other neurodegenerative disorders are also associated with an increase in risk for offending behaviors. Aggressive and, in some cases violent, behaviors are common precursors to institutionalization in the elderly and in others afflicted with such conditions (Chase, 2015; Cipriani, Lucetti, Danti, Carlesi, & Nuti, 2015; Jha et al., 2015; Liljegren et al., 2015). Similarly, individuals with epilepsy have long been overrepresented in the prison system; however, there is debate over whether they have a higher rate of violent offending (Every-Palmer & Norris, 2013; Gauffin & Landtblom, 2014; Volavka, 2011; Whitman et al., 1984). As with almost all areas of psychopathology and offending, alcohol and substance abuse appear to play some role in offending risk with these groups of individuals as well. It is unclear the extent to which this is the case, but it is clear that of all the acquired and organic origins of brain and mind pathology, and the variations in transient and chronic presentations, the use of alcohol and other substances comorbid presents a significantly elevated risk profile for the commission of criminal behaviors, particularly violence.

ADDICTION, ALCOHOL AND SUBSTANCE ABUSE, AND CRIMINALITY

Addictions take many forms, and research has shown a wide pattern of offending behaviors by individuals who have disorders of addiction. Of all the forms that addiction can take, it is addiction behaviors associated with the abuse of alcohol and other substances and gambling that are most associated with criminal offending. Notwithstanding that, depending on age and jurisdiction, the use of alcohol or other substances, or the act of gambling, may be offenses in and of themselves; the issue is whether addiction and alcohol/substance abuse presents a criminal risk by itself, or whether it is the confluence of addiction/abuse with other comorbid psychopathology that presents the risk. There are three circumstances in which addiction/abuse may be associated with an increased risk of offending:

1. Offenses committed in the course of trying to obtain more access to the object of the addiction (more alcohol, more drugs, more money to gamble);

2. Offences committed as a result of being under the influence of the object of addiction (being drunk or under the influence of other substances, or being obsessed/compelled to engage with the gambling process in some way)
3. Offences committed when the addiction occurs comorbid with other psychopathologies and each condition serves to amplify the offending risk factors of the other.

It is common for more than one of these three factors to occur simultaneously, thereby amplifying the offending risk. It is very common for crimes to be commissioned in the efforts to obtain more of the item to which an offender is addicted. While the nature of the crime can vary, they commonly include fraud and theft related activities such as check forgery, embezzlement, theft, larceny, armed robbery, and loan fraud, as well as a variety of offences related to illegal prostitution, drug production and distribution, and a range of cons and scams. In short, anything that can provide quick cash flow or direct product to feed their habit. In this process, violence or other assault of a physically interpersonal nature, generally occurs as a secondary factor. Violence may occur if the addict assaults another person in order to obtain cash or product to fuel his or her addiction. This is a means to an end and the violence remains a secondary motivation, though it is a primary component to the crime.

Often violence may occur because an addict is not thinking clearly, is desperate, and may be suffering severe withdrawal effects or compulsions. These effects can cause significant physical and mental distress. This combination and its accompanying irrationality form a recipe for disaster, and if the addict has a weapon, then there is a high risk of it being used either accidentally (e.g., accidental discharge of a firearm), or in the case of desperation or drug-induced delusion or paranoia, as an uncontrolled and impulsive threat-response. Alcohol and/or substance use is a feature in a significant percentage of almost all IPV crime types. For example, alcohol and/or substance abuse is a significant feature in both offenders and victims of domestic violence and assault in almost every location where statistics have been recorded (Mouzos & Makkai, 2011).

Many addictions are recognized as independent clinical pathologies, including alcohol and other substances, gambling, and sex addiction (American Psychiatric Association, 2013). An exploration of the origins of addiction within the realm of psychopathology can quickly turn into a case of "what came first: the chicken or the egg?" This is because addiction and addictive traits are commonly comorbid with other psychopathologies and the initial directionality of the relationship is not always clear. Alcohol and substance addiction may arise due to a process of self-medication by an individual already suffering from any number of disorders including mood disorders (depression, bipolar, hypomania), anxiety disorders (generalized anxiety disorder, panic disorder, social or other phobia), posttraumatic stress disorder, schizophrenia or other psychotic conditions, and a raft of PDs. Alternatively, the high use of alcohol and other drugs as well as the neurological alterations associated with addictions, such as gambling, sex, and even video game addiction, are associated with the onset of a range of other psychopathologies including mood and anxiety disorders, eating disorders, cognitive impairment, learning and behavioral disorders, and psychotic disorders.

The pressures of "need" that are fueled in addiction present strong criminal motivations in themselves if an addict lacks the legitimate means to fund their addiction. It is also true that when addiction presents comorbid with other mental illness, the individual offending risk factors of both conditions serve to amplify each other and exacerbate the risk of offending even further. Therefore, while psychological comorbidities have characteristics that, under the right circumstances, present them with a propensity toward potentially criminal behaviors, the addition of alcohol or other substance abuse may exacerbate this propensity through a removal of inhibition and rational thought and an increased inclination toward higher-risk behavior.

Psychopathology with characteristics including impulsivity, obsession, compulsion, cognitive impairment, social-moral impairment, lack of empathy, narcissism, and other antisocial elements may collude with increased disinhibition and addictive need to result in significant risk for criminal behavior. Similar pathological symptoms have been linked to other addictions including those that do not involve the ingestion of exogenous chemicals such as gambling, sex, and video game addictions. Finally, in both addiction-related and many of the other connected comorbid psychopathologies, a number of associations have been made with a host of neurostructural, neurochemical, and neurofunctional correlates such as dopamine dysregulation, with the increased psychological symptoms and behavioral risks.

Addiction as a psychopathology then has several possible mechanisms by which it may influence criminal behavior. It may have a direct influence through higher cortical factors such as disinhibition, social-moral judgment, and executive control impairments and via other subcortical neurophysiology alterations affecting behavior, emotion, and motivational mechanics. Addictions may affect criminal behaviors through their mediating role on other comorbid psychopathologies by amplifying associated characteristics. Finally, addictive psychopathology may increase criminality through the need of the addict to acquire resources to help feed the addiction. It is unusual for any of these factors to exist in isolation and, therefore, addictive psychopathology tends to have a number of factors influencing the risk of criminal behavior that combine to exacerbate the risk and further increase the likelihood of offending.

CONCLUSION

No single book chapter or article can ever fully describe the vast richness and controversy that are the domain of criminal psychopathology. What is clear from the research is that certain mental illnesses do increase the risk of engaging in antisocial and criminal behavior. Moreover, mental illness is on the rise, and therefore we can deduce that crime associated with mental illness of all sorts will also increase. It is thus important that the relationship between mental illness and the risk of offending is well understood and that progress is made toward mitigating this risk through appropriate preventative programs and intervention strategies. As I have stated previously:

> *It is only through improvements in our knowledge and the careful and considered application of evidence-based principles that we can ever hope to make inroads to improving the welfare of the mentally ill, reduce the risk of them becoming offenders and ultimately improve our capacity to protect society from what should be preventable criminal behaviour.*

Sinnamon(2015, p. 245)

The psychopathology that is most commonly associated with increased crime risk comes from four discernible, though often comorbid, areas: psychosis, affective disorders, intellectual impairment, and the area of addiction and alcohol/substance abuse disorders. The risk of these disorders influencing criminal behavior is closely mediated by socioenvironmental factors of the individual and in many cases can be readily prevented. Indeed, humans do not live in a vacuum and, at the end of the day, it is the interaction between the individual and the external mechanics of their ecology that determines behavioral outcomes. Although mental illness may contribute to antisocial and criminal behaviors, we must recognize that psychopathology and criminal behavior are not ubiquitous and ultimately realize that the burden of psychological illness, while a risk factor for offending behaviors, creates an exponentially greater risk of being a victim of crime than an offender.

SUMMARY

- Psychopathology refers to our understanding, study, or knowledge of any illness, disorder, dysfunction, or dysregulation of the mental processes that govern an individual's cognition, affect, and behavior (Sinnamon, 2015). Clinically, the diagnosis of a psychopathology requires the individual to meet several diagnostic criteria that relate to a variety of general and disorder-specific guidelines. Generally, the symptoms of a clinically remarkable psychopathology must (a) originate within the individual as opposed to being a situational reactionand (b) be outside of the individual's physical and/or mental control (American Psychiatric Association, 2013; Sinnamon, 2015). Disorder-specific criteria are dependent on the characteristic symptomology of each disorder. These disorder-specific criteria are set out in the American Psychiatric Association's DSM-5 (American Psychiatric Association, 2013) and in the World Health Organization's ICD-10 (World Health Organisation, 1992, 2010).
- When assessing an individual for psychopathology, there are four factors or themes that form the lens through which the "abnormality" of symptoms should be interrogated. Also known as the 4Ds of Abnormality, these are deviance, distress, dysfunction, and danger (Comer, 2005). Using the 4Ds, the clinician is

able to assess deviance and abnormality based on the potential for the symptom presentation to negatively impact the individual, their family and peers, and the wider community. Ultimately, it is potential for harm or serious dysfunction that dictates whether a cluster of symptoms will be labeled as pathological.

- Forensic psychopathology can be defined as "a specialised area in which the focus rests on those psychological maladies and their symptoms and consequences that, for one reason or another, intersect with the legal system. Simply put, forensic psychopathology is interested in clinical psychopathologies with criminal implications. This includes any psychological or neuropsychological condition that impacts the perpetrators of criminal acts as well as their victims" (Sinnamon, 2015, pp. 212–213).

- Psychopathology and forensic psychopathology are scientific approaches and, as such, are grounded in the principles of change and emergent knowledge, in which historical "knowledge" is continually being superseded, reconsidered, and discarded in the face of the emerging evidence. This updating of knowledge, and individuating of people and circumstances, is fundamentally at odds with the legal system in which precedent and the generalization of application (of law) provide the basis for decision-making, strategy, legal argument, and judicial ruling.

- The scientific literature on crime and mental illness dates back more than 100 years with the contemporary view largely holding to the belief that the relationship between psychopathology and crime is complex and more likely due to a confluence of the social corollaries that accompany mental illness rather than any inherent criminality being associated with mental illness or the existence of an underlying unique criminal personality. The contemporary data do show an association between some mental disorders and the risk of offending; however, there continues to be good evidence that the overall population risk of criminal offending by the mentally ill remains relatively low and is primarily associated with criminality when combined with other extant factors linked to risk of offending such as substance abuse and social dislocation.

- PDs are multifactorial syndromes that occur in the face of a confluence of biopsychosocial factors including heritability (genetics and epigenetics), developmental experiences (abuse, trauma, health, attachment, education, and environmental exposure during core brain development), general social and environmental characteristics, personal anatomical and physiological dynamics, and innate character qualities.

- The generic symptomology of PDs includes "emotional dysregulation, inability to maintain positive relationships, social isolation, anger outbursts, suspicion and lack of trust, inability to delay gratification, poor impulse control, and often there is a history of alcohol and/or substance abuse. The thoughts and behaviors of those with a personality disorders are characteristically considered odd, eccentric, melodramatic, overly emotional, anxious, and/or fearful. Many signs and symptoms of specific personality disorders 'bleed' into one another and it is often difficult to proffer an accurate diagnosis that could not be differentially provided by another clinician." The criminal risk from PD stems largely from the disorder that is inherent in cognition and affect regulation, and the impact that these have on motivation (desires, compulsions, perceived needs and threats) and consequent behavior. Extreme affective reactivity, often with underlying comorbid mood disorder, is a hallmark common to all PDs. PDs are of particular relevance to criminality as motivation and personality are inextricably linked, and it is ultimately the characteristics of motivation that determine behavior.

- According to Petherick and Sinnamon (2013), there are five common elements that are associated with personality disordered perpetrators of crime: (1) poor self-esteem: either very low or high but fragile, (2) emotional negativity bias and lack of capacity to modulate emotional expression, (3) high-risk, antisocial, self-serving, or differentially reinforced behavioral tendencies, (4) an unwillingness or incapacity to accurately assess and mitigate risk, and (5) an unwillingness or incapacity to modulate behavior responses.

- There is strong positive relationship between PD and violent crime, and in particular, violent recidivism. Antisocial and borderline PDs are among the most common associated with violent offending. These PDs are often linked to violence because they are "characterised by an inability or unwillingness to assess risk and adhere to established and elementary social norms. Instead, offenders with [these type of] PD pursue self-serving and/or self-preservation motives with little reflection on morality, social acceptance, or the impact on those around them" (Sinnamon, 2015, p. 240).

- Reassurance-driven PD and criminality: When a need for reassurance drives behavior, the motivation comes from a deep-seated need for approval and acceptance from others. There are four PDs that fit within this form of criminal motivation: borderline, histrionic, avoidant, and dependent.

- Assertive-driven PD and criminality: PD pffenders who are assertive-driven are similarly motivated by the need to obtain or restore self esteem through other people (just like the reassurance-driven PD types). The two groups however, differ in the emotional content that drives their motivation. Rather than fear driving motivation and subsequent behavior, the assertive-driven PDs are primarily motivated by anger. PDs with this orientation tend to have an underlying belief that they are superior to others and therefore deserve more than they already have and, further, are owed something by others (or society). This type of personality is hyperemotional, melodramatic, and extremely intense and is characteristic of the cluster B PDs, such as the antisocial, borderline, histrionic, and narcissistic personality types. Narcissism and histrionic are likely to be the primary personality characteristics associated with this group. Narcissistic and histrionic PD offenders express these flamboyancies in a highly aggressive and dominating "look at me" manner that is ultimately compensatory in nature.

- Anger retaliatory-driven PD and criminality: PD offenders driven by retaliatory anger are motivated as a result of some exaggeration and distorted interpretation of the circumstances surrounding an event or events—whether real or perceived.

Two groups of PD offenders fall into this group. The first includes offenders with paranoid PD. Paranoid PD offenders act because of a belief that they have been wronged in some way. A very low self-esteem coupled with paranoid disordered thoughts result in a self-preservational process of the externalization of their strong angry emotions onto another. Disordered thinking provides a plausible, though likely untrue, rationale that allows the offender to lay blame elsewhere (e.g., the government, a spouse, sibling, employer, or workmate). The second group of retaliatory anger offenders are likely to fall within the sphere of either borderline or narcissistic PD. Just like offenders with paranoid PD, these offenders also have very poor capacity to modulate hyperemotional anger responses, assess risk, or manage impulsive behavior. These individuals are usually found to be in existing volatile relationships that, when combined with their unstable mood, fear of rejection, and impulsiveness, provide a high-risk environment for violence. These personality types become offenders when they feel threatened and react with a "shoot first" mentality in retaliation for the wrong that they believe is going to be done to them. In the event that a wrong is actually done to them, they are likely to retaliate impulsively and with extreme violence without regard to risk.

- Pervasive anger-driven PD and criminality: Pervasive anger is a primary motivating feature of paranoid, antisocial, borderline, histrionic, and narcissistic offenders. The key that drives this pervasive hyperresponsive anger is that the disordered personality appears to develop with a schema that generalizes the negativity bias inherent in all PDs, in an aggressive manner. This means that offenders with these PDs are able to find fault everywhere and an "other" is used as a convenient displacement for the internal hyperemotionality that the sufferer cannot modulate or rationalize by using internal mechanisms. Any externalized factor can become the lightning rod for the sufferer's anger. These personality types often become offenders when they initiate violent exchanges as a means of exerting control and reestablishing self-esteem. Alternatively, they may damage property if it is a contextually appropriate displacement of their anger.
- Excitation-driven PD and criminality: A complex and challenging offender type, excitation-driven offenders are most likely to have either antisocial or dependent personality characteristics. The antisocial personality often fits this motivational type as the lack of empathy and social affiliation toward others allow these offenders the emotional space to be able to place themselves in situations where the pain or suffering of others is irrelevant compared with the pleasure obtained for themselves. The strong desire for approval from others is the motivating factor that often results in the dependent personality placing himself or herself in relationships of unequal power in which they are subservient to others. While more likely to be a victim than an offender in this form of criminal motivation, dependent personalities may become offenders if they finally "crack" in the face of ongoing abuse and retaliate reflexively. Dependent PD offenders may also be prime candidates for violent crime within an acute catathymic crisis. Schizoid

or schizotypal PD types can be high risk for excitation-driven offending. These personality types have characteristically low levels of emotionality and reward stimulation, and altered perceptions and distorted reality may combine with limited emotional expression to motivate a desire to experience greater affect. This can lead to self-harming behaviors as well as thrill-seeking encounters with others. A lack of capacity to assess and mitigate risk makes these personality subtypes potentially at high risk to inflict significant harm on others (offender) as well as become the unwitting victim of others.

- Materially driven PD and criminality: All PDs are at risk for offending through this form of criminal motivation. Low or fragile self-esteem, distorted perceptions, paranoia, fear, a need for instant gratification, poor impulse control, needs arising from alcohol and/or substance abuse, anger and feelings of missing out, or that others are preventing you from obtaining objects or outcomes, fear of rejection and need for approval, can all bring about this motivation. An offender may use criminal means to obtain material gain whether through violence, theft, or illicit commercial activity (drug dealing, gambling, prostitution, fraud).

- Self-preservation–driven PD and criminality: As with materially driven PD offenders, all PDs may be driven by self-preservation motives to commit crime. Self-preservation is a fundamental survival instinct and, in cases where an individual is impaired in their capacity for social reasoning and risk assessment, the natural desire for self-preservation can result in a variety of scenarios in which behavior may become criminal in nature. The desire for self-preservation can lead to the commission of a variety of criminal behaviors aimed at restoring some kind of injustice (real or perceived), or protecting the well-being of self or others (again whether real or perceived). These forms of motivations are particularly high risk for those who perceive the world through the thick lens of paranoia, through the distorted and delusional schizotypal perceptions, through the "cover my tracks" manipulations of the antisocial personality, or through the myopic view of narcissism whereby elevated beliefs about self-worth, right to have, and expectations of praise, admiration, and material reward may promote aggressive pursuit of these goals.

- Psychosis and disordered thought processes are a foundational component of forensic psychology as violent, threatening, and offensive antisocial behaviors are often perpetrated in the face of factors associated with obsessions, delusions, paranoias, hallucinations, and fantasies. While popular belief holds that individuals with psychotic disorders are to be feared; the reality is that we are far more likely to become a victim of a violent person-to-person crime at the hands of a perpetrator who is already known to us and is not suffering from a current psychotic episode. In the general population, far more people are assaulted and murdered by their intimate partners or ex-intimate partners than any other group. However, it true that individuals suffering an acute psychotic episode have a higher statistical probability of committing an offense than the population average. While a controversial area of social debate, the statistics have been consistent for a prolonged period. Several large-scale epidemiological studies have shown this trend across diverse populations. Offending risk in psychotic disorders is closely linked to the unique cognitive symptomology such as delusions, hallucinations, and fantasy thinking, and the associated impairments to affect regulation and executive functions such as inhibition. Treatment adherence is a vital element in mitigating risk in this group and is a major challenge, particularly among younger sufferers.

- Disordered thinking in severe psychosis often extends from nonbizarre to bizarre delusions in which the delusions are implausible and fantastic in nature and are often reinforced by hallucinations that provide validation for the delusions.

- In the criminal framework, obsession has been most associated with the idea of obsessional following or stalking (Sinnamon, 2015). That is, the obsessional and unwanted following of another person. While obsessional thinking is a major characteristic of many forms of forensic psychopathology, it is also often an identifiable pathological feature of criminal activity even in the absence of diagnosable psychopathology. Stalking is a good example of where this is often the case. Stalking and its obsessional components are unique to each individual offender. This is because it is a confluence of the individual psychodynamics of thoughts, emotions, and motivations that ultimately go to create, drive, and maintain the stalker's behavioral manifestations. The research shows that the level of obsession and relational access to the target are the two key factors that can assist in predicting stalking risk and the risk of behavioral escalation to violence and homicide. Essentially, the greater the obsession and the greater the degree of accessibility by the stalker to their target, the greater is the risk of physical violence.

- Delusional thinking can be characterized by the presence of reoccurring and persistent delusions that are nonbizarre in nature. Delusional thinking has long been considered to be associated with an increased risk of violent behavior and the past two decades have seen an increase in the empirical evidence supporting this assertion. A delusion is an irrational belief that is held with strong conviction even in the face of contradictory evidence. Delusional thinking must involve nonbizarre delusional thoughts, which means that the delusions must be plausible—they must of a kind that could possibly be true. An example is a belief that you are being spied on by government agents. The most common delusional subtypes include jealousy, paranoid or persecutory, and erotomania.

- Delusions often occur as a feature of other psychopathologies. Psychotic disorders such as schizoaffective disorder and schizophrenia often have delusional thinking as a prominent characteristic, as can some personality disorders and mood disorders with psychotic features. Delusions often appear comorbid with neurological conditions such as brain tumor, stroke, acquired brain injury, and some neurodegenerative disorders such as dementia and Alzheimer disease. Delusions are also a common side effect of a number drugs – both illicit and prescription. In a forensic setting, drug-induced, or medically derived delusional thinking should always be considered and either confirmed or ruled out before moving to other psychopathological explanations.

- The risk of offending in mood and anxiety disorders comes from one, or a combination of, (a) their potential to present with psychotic features, (b) their significant association with alcohol and substance abuse, and (c) their associated impairments to cognitive function.
- Women who kill their own children present a profoundly disturbing challenge to the stereotypical perceptions of a mother's protective instincts toward her offspring. Most often, the argument for the legitimacy of the infanticide defense centers around the position that biochemical and hormonal alterations of child-birth result in perinatal, and particularly postpartum, psychiatric episodes (usually depression and/or psychosis, but dissociative and adjustment/denial features are also implicated), that are claimed to be at least in part exculpatory for the murder. The argument against this blanket assumption is that the research indicates substantial variation in the presentation of these features in women who kill their children that are mediated by the age of both the mother and the child victim. Younger mothers who kill their children in the short period immediately postpartum have significantly lower rates of mental illness than older mothers who kill their older children.
- In bipolar disorder, the risk of offending while in a manic episode is significantly greater than when in a depressed episode. Bipolar disorder can present with psychotic features and has an increased risk for alcohol and substance abuse and the pursuit of physical and emotional sensory experience, all of which increase the risk of offending behavior. Studies have indicated that psychiatric patients with bipolar disorder are more likely to commit sexual offences than any other identified psychiatric patient group. In hypomanic episodes, hypersexuality, gambling, drug and alcohol use, speeding, extreme spending, thoughts of grandeur, and being able to "take on the world," are the commonplace experiences. In this state, any number of behaviors may lead to a crossing the line into offending behaviors. This can range from speeding in a car and the use of illicit substances, property damage, theft, fraud, and various expressions of public nuisance, through to sexual and/or physical assault. In hypomania, the manic expression is aggressive in nature and is usually directed in a manner that is antagonistic to others. In a hypomanic episode, the individual is at risk of offending due to extreme agitation and the pursuit of conflict. Individuals may become an offender through similar behaviors to that of the hypermanic person however, their emotional state is likely to be far more aggressive and uncompromising, and lead to seeking control and domination over others – power-oriented sexual assault, aggravated robbery, and other violent crimes are commonplace with those whose presentation leads to offending behaviors.
- Historically, it was thought that anxiety had a moderating effect on potential criminal behaviors; however, recent evidence indicates that the heightened threat sensitivity associated with anxiety disorders may lead to persistent violent behavior in some individuals. Moreover, about 50% of male prisoners with antisocial personality disorder have a comorbid anxiety disorder. The risk of criminal behavior that is associated with anxiety disorders appears to be

mediated by the fight-or-flight response, and the heightened threat sensitivity that is associated with anxiety. In some individuals this sensitivity may result in the conditioning of an aggressive coping behavioral style in which threats are "neutralized" using "fight" rather than "flight" strategies. In others, responses may be "flight" oriented and behaviors are motivated by a need to get away from the situation or to avoid a situation in the first place. This accounts for the relationship between violence and anxiety in a small subgroup of individuals. A second mediator appears to be alcohol and substance abuse. Anxiety disorders are highly related to alcohol and substance abuse comorbidity as these substances are often used to self-medicate, in turn increasing disinhibition in users and increasing the risk of impulsive and aggressive behaviors.

- Addictions take many forms, and research has shown a wide pattern of offending behaviors by individuals who have disorders of addiction. Of all the forms that addiction can take, it is addiction behaviors associated with the abuse of alcohol and other substances, and gambling, that are most associated with criminal offending. There are three circumstances in which addiction/abuse may be associated with an increased risk of offending: (1) offenses committed in the course of trying to obtain more access to the object of the addiction (more alcohol, more drugs, more money to gamble), (2) offences committed as a result of being under the influence of the object of addiction (being drunk or under the influence of other substances, or being obsessed/compelled to engage with the gambling process in some way), and (3) Offences committed when the addiction occurs comorbid with other psychopathologies and each condition serves to amplify the offending risk factors of the other. Addiction as a psychopathology may have a direct influence on criminal behavior through higher cortical factors such as disinhibition, social-moral judgment, and executive control impairments, and via other subcortical neurophysiology alterations impacting behavior, emotion, and motivational mechanics. Addictions may impact criminal behaviors through their mediating role on other comorbid psychopathologies by amplifying associated characteristics. Finally, addictive psychopathology may increase criminality through the need of the addict to acquire resources to help feed their addiction. It is unusual for any of these factors to exist in isolation and therefore, addictive psychopathology tends to have a number of factors influencing the risk of criminal behavior that combine to exacerbate the risk and further increase the likelihood of offending.

QUESTIONS

1. Define forensic psychopathology, and describe how it fundamentally differs from psychopathology in general.
2. What are the four key dimensions of psychological abnormality?
3. What is the general belief as to the underlying relationship between crime and mental illness?

4. What are the five common elements that Petherick and Sinnamon suggest are associated with personality disordered perpetrators of crime?
5. What are the seven personality orientations associated with criminal behavior in personality disorders, and what are the associated personality disorder types associated with each?
6. What are the key factors and criticisms associated with postnatal depression and infanticide laws?
7. Why are psychotic disorders associated with an increased risk of offending behaviors?
8. What are the key features of disordered thinking, and how do they relate to risk of offending?
9. What are the key features of obsessional thinking, and how do they increase the risk of offending behavior?
10. Detail the characteristics of stalking and the risk factors associated with an escalation of behaviors toward violence.
11. What are the factors associated with anxiety disorders that may result in offending behaviors?
12. How do hypermanic and hypomanic bipolar episodes differ in offending risk?
13. What are the main factors behind depression being associated with criminal behavior?
14. What are the main addictive conditions associated with criminal behaviors?
15. What are the three types of relational interactions between addiction and risk of offending behaviors?

REFERENCES

American Psychiatric Association. (2013). *Diagnostic and statistical manual of mental disorders* (5th ed.). Arlington, VA: American Psychiatric Publishing.

Adinkrah, M. (1999). Uxoricide in Fiji: the sociocultural context of husband-wife killings. *Violence Against Women*, 5(11), 1294–1320. http://dx.doi.org/10.1177/10778019922183381.

Adinkrah, M. (2008). Spousal homicides in contemporary Ghana. *Journal of Criminal Justice*, 36(3), 209–216. http://dx.doi.org/10.1016/j.jcrimjus.2008.04.002.

Aggarwal, M., Banerjee, A., Singh, S. M., Mattoo, S. K., & Basu, D. (2012). Substance-induced psychotic disorders: 13-Year data from a de-addiction centre and their clinical implications. *Asian Journal of Psychiatry*, 5(3), 220–224. Retrieved from http://www.scopus.com/inward/record.url?eid=2-s2.0-84866163600&partnerID=40&md5=a264bba7 3e83deb6045820148afb3d30.

Almond, P. (2009). Postnatal depression: a global public health perspective. *Perspectives in Public Health*, 129(5), 221–227. Retrieved from http://www.ncbi.nlm.nih.gov/pubmed/19788165.

Appelbaum, P. S., Robbins, P. C., & Monahan, J. (2000). Violence and delusions: data from the MacArthur violence risk assessment study. *American Journal of Psychiatry*, 157(4), 566–572. Retrieved from http://www.scopus.com/inward/record.url?eid=2-s2.0-0034025773&partn erID=40&md5=02f6da6470dfb8ef32d9170a459b06ce.

Arseneault, L., Moffitt, T. E., Caspi, A., Taylor, P. J., & Silva, P. A. (2000). Mental disorders and violence in a total birth cohort: results from the Dunedin Study. *Archives of General Psychiatry*, *57*(10), 979–986. Retrieved from http://www.ncbi.nlm.nih.gov/pubmed/11015816.

Babiak, P., Neumann, C. S., & Hare, R. D. (2010). Corporate psychopathy: talking the walk. *Behavioral Sciences & the Law*, *28*(2), 174–193. http://dx.doi.org/10.1002/bsl.925.

Batts, S. (2009). Brain lesions and their implications in criminal responsibility. *Behavioral Sciences & the Law*, *27*(2), 261–272. http://dx.doi.org/10.1002/bsl.857.

Beck, J. C. (1994). Epidemiology of mental disorder and violence: beliefs and Research findings. *Harvard Review of Psychiatry*, *2*(1), 1–6. http://dx.doi.org/10.3109/10673229409017107.

Blažič, M., & Vojinovič, B. (2002). Globalisation and the media. *Informatologia*, *35*(3), 187–192. Retrieved from http://www.scopus.com/inward/record.url?eid=2-s2.0-43749093071&partnerID=40&md5=b3112a91c2445395835541ece50ae40a.

Borges, L. M., & Léveillée, S. (2005). Sex differences in conjugal homicide in Quebec: preliminary observations. *Pratiques Psychologiques*, *11*(1), 47–54. http://dx.doi.org/10.1016/j.prps.2005.01.003.

Brennan, P. A., Mednick, S. A., & Hodgins, S. (2000). Major mental disorders and criminal violence in a Danish birth cohort. *Archives of General Psychiatry*, *57*(5), 494–500. Retrieved from http://www.scopus.com/inward/record.url?eid=2-s2.0-0034055785&partnerID=40&md5=e4d1c53a9f0275e356950d8a0e51befe.

Brock, G. W. (1917). Insanity in American prisons and the prison psychosis. *Journal of Abnormal Psychology*, *12*(4), 232–239. http://dx.doi.org/10.1037/h0071559.

Bronfenbrenner, U., & Ceci, S. J. (1994). Nature-nurture reconceptualized in developmental perspective: a bioecological model. *Psychological Review*, *101*(4), 568–586. Retrieved from http://www.ncbi.nlm.nih.gov/pubmed/7984707.

Brown, M. (2012). Suppressing ideological diversity: John Reed and the threat of injustice. *International Journal of Diversity in Organisations, Communities and Nations*, *11*(4), 99–104. Retrieved from http://www.scopus.com/inward/record.url?eid=2-s2.0-84871510579&partnerID=40&md5=a4a7f6942768521b2409cb730571debe.

Brown, R. G., & Pluck, G. (2000). Negative symptoms: the 'pathology' of motivation and goal-directed behaviour. *Trends in Neurosciences*, *23*(9), 412–417. http://dx.doi.org/10.1016/S0166-2236(00)01626-X.

Butler, J. C. (2013). Authoritarianism and fear responses to pictures: the role of social differences. *International Journal of Psychology*, *48*(1), 18–24. Retrieved from http://www.scopus.com/inward/record.url?eid=2-s2.0-84873920382&partnerID=40&md5=dcd98f62c654ec3dc58a76e106012605.

Caligor, E., Levy, K. N., & Yeomans, F. E. (2015). Narcissistic personality disorder: diagnostic and clinical challenges. *The American Journal of Psychiatry*, *172*(5), 415–422. http://dx.doi.org/10.1176/appi.ajp.2014.14060723.

Cameron, R. E., Block, J., & Lee, N. R. (2013). Psychiatric side effects of mefloquine: applications to forensic psychiatry. *Journal of the American Academy of Psychiatry and the Law*, *41*(2), 224–235. Retrieved from http://www.scopus.com/inward/record.url?eid=2-s2.0-84879173053&partnerID=40&md5=df90232717ba13ed3c7f0c55fabeb90a.

Carabellese, F., La Tegola, D., Alfarano, E., Tamma, M., Candelli, C., & Catanesi, R. (2013). Stalking by females. *Medicine, Science and the Law*, *53*(3), 123–131. Retrieved from http://www.scopus.com/inward/record.url?eid=2-s2.0-84890218013&partnerID=40&md5=354a19d65b6390ebc94045ebf5738257.

Carabellese, F., Rocca, G., Candelli, C., & Catanesi, R. (2014). Mental illness, violence and delusional misidentifications: the role of Capgras' syndrome in matricide. *Journal of Forensic and Legal Medicine, 21*, 9–13. Retrieved from http://www.scopus.com/inward/record.url?eid=2-s2.0-84887930476&partnerID=40&md5=b8b2e3df6b81048a31111aa0262c97fd.

Chase, A. (2015). Dementia. Criminality can be an early sign of frontotemporal dementia. *Nature Reviews. Neurology, 11*(2), 67. http://dx.doi.org/10.1038/nrneurol.2015.1.

Chevignard, M. P., & Lind, K. (2014). Long-term outcome of abusive head trauma. *Pediatric Radiology, 44*(Suppl. 4), S548–S558. http://dx.doi.org/10.1007/s00247-014-3169-8.

Cipriani, G., Lucetti, C., Danti, S., Carlesi, C., & Nuti, A. (2015). Violent and criminal manifestations in dementia patients. *Geriatrics & Gerontology International.* http://dx.doi.org/10.1111/ggi.12608.

Cockram, J. (2005). Justice or differential treatment? Sentencing of offenders with an intellectual disability. *Journal of Intellectual & Developmental Disability, 30*(1), 3–13.

Cohen, S. (1996). Crime and politics: spot the difference. *British Journal of Sociology*, 1–21.

Coid, J. W., Yang, M., Ullrich, S., Hickey, N., Kahtan, N., & Freestone, M. (2015). Psychiatric diagnosis and differential risks of offending following discharge. *International Journal of Law and Psychiatry, 38*, 68–74. http://dx.doi.org/10.1016/j.ijlp.2015.01.009.

Comer, R. (2005). *Fundamentals of abnormal psychology* (4th ed.). New York: Worth.

Crail-Melendez, D., Atriano-Mendieta, C., Carrillo-Meza, R., & Ramirez-Bermudez, J. (2013). Schizophrenia-like psychosis associated with right lacunar thalamic infarct. *Neurocase, 19*(1), 22–26. Retrieved from http://www.scopus.com/inward/record.url?eid=2-s2.0-84872403552&partnerID=40&md5=ab9c3ad6270f1e213ebe59e46a223b4b.

Crocker, A. G., Côté, G., Toupin, J., & St-Onge, B. (2007). Rate and characteristics of men with an intellectual disability in pre-trial detention. *Journal of Intellectual & Developmental Disability, 32*(2), 143–152.

Cullen, F. T. (1994). Social support as an organizing concept for criminology: presidential address to the academy of criminal justice sciences. *Justice Quarterly, 11*(4), 527–559.

Daff, E., & Thomas, S. D. (2014). Bipolar disorder and criminal offending: a data linkage study. *Social Psychiatry and Psychiatric Epidemiology, 49*(12), 1985–1991. http://dx.doi.org/10.1007/s00127-014-0882-4.

Davis, J. A., & Chipman, M. A. (1997). Stalkers and other obsessional types: a review and forensic psychological typology of those who stalk. *Journal of Clinical Forensic Medicine, 4*(4), 166–172. Retrieved from http://www.scopus.com/inward/record.url?eid=2-s2.0-0031392660&partnerID=40&md5=2a2aff2d02045ce715cee854db07e6ad.

DelBello, M. P., Soutullo, C. A., Zimmerman, M. E., Sax, K. W., Williams, J. R., McElroy, S. L., et al. (1999). Traumatic brain injury in individuals convicted of sexual offenses with and without bipolar disorder. *Psychiatry Research, 89*(3), 281–286. Retrieved from http://www.ncbi.nlm.nih.gov/pubmed/10708275.

Deloitte Access Economics. (2012). *The cost of perinatal depression in Australia: Report for post and antenatal depression association.* Melbourne: Deloitte Access Economics. Available online from http://www.panda.org.au/.

Di Girolamo, F., & Nesci, D. A. (1981). Uxoricide in Italy. *Rassegna Penitenziaria e Criminologica, 3*(3–4), 481–497. Retrieved from http://www.scopus.com/inward/record.url?eid=2-s2.0-0019593325&partnerID=40&md5=1316b7ca4c5f98a4c541623acda6f097.

van Dongen, J. D. M., Buck, N. M. L., & van Marle, H. J. C. (2012a). Delusional distress partly explains the relation between persecutory ideations and inpatient aggression on the ward. *Psychiatry Research, 200*(2–3), 779–783. Retrieved from http://www.scopus.com/inward/record.url?eid=2-s2.0-84872418404&partnerID=40&md5=69661d7caa88404421d1abe2cf8be17e.

van Dongen, J. D. M., Buck, N. M. L., & van Marle, H. J. C. (2012b). The role of ideational distress in the relation between persecutory ideations and reactive aggression. *Criminal Behaviour and Mental Health, 22*(5), 350–359. Retrieved from http://www.scopus.com/inward/record.url?eid=2-s2.0-84870554114&partnerID=40&md5=1620d987da6f484d7b97432646562c4e.

Echávarri, C., Burgmans, S., Uylings, H., Cuesta, M. J., Peralta, V., Kamphorst, W., et al. (2013). Neuropsychiatric symptoms in Alzheimer's disease and vascular dementia. *Journal of Alzheimer's Disease, 33*(3), 715–721. Retrieved from http://www.scopus.com/inward/record.url?eid=2-s2.0-84872463391&partnerID=40&md5=b7a88cdd9954039393ddfbe47ebc70f2.

Elbogen, E. B., & Johnson, S. C. (2009). The intricate link between violence and mental disorder: results from the national epidemiologic survey on alcohol and related conditions. *Archives of General Psychiatry, 66*(2), 152–161. http://dx.doi.org/10.1001/archgenpsychiatry.2008.537.

Eronen, M., Tiihonen, J., & Hakola, P. (1996). Schizophrenia and homicidal behavior. *Schizophrenia Bulletin, 22*, 83–89.

Every-Palmer, S., & Norris, J. (2013). Not guilty by reason of epilepsy. Post-ictal delirium and psychosis resulting in violent offending. *The Australian and New Zealand Journal of Psychiatry, 47*(10), 961–962. http://dx.doi.org/10.1177/0004867413479409.

Fazel, S., & Grann, M. (2006). The population impact of severe mental illness on violent crime. *American Journal of Psychiatry, 163*(8), 1397–1403.

Fazel, S., Philipson, J., Gardiner, L., Merritt, R., & Grann, M. (2009). Neurological disorders and violence: a systematic review and meta-analysis with a focus on epilepsy and traumatic brain injury. *Journal of Neurology, 256*(10), 1591–1602. http://dx.doi.org/10.1007/s00415-009-5134-2.

Fazel, S., Wolf, A., Chang, Z., Larsson, H., Goodwin, G. M., & Lichtenstein, P. (2015). Depression and violence: a Swedish population study. *The Lancet Psychiatry, 2*(3), 224–232. http://dx.doi.org/10.1016/S2215-0366(14)00128-X.

Fazel, S., Xenitidis, K., & Powell, J. (2008). The prevalence of intellectual disabilities among 12000 prisoners—A systematic review. *International Journal of Law and Psychiatry, 31*(4), 369–373.

Fountoulakis, K. N., Leucht, S., & Kaprinis, G. S. (2008). Personality disorders and violence. *Current Opinion in Psychiatry, 21*(1), 84–92. http://dx.doi.org/10.1097/YCO.0b013e3282f31137.

Friedman, S. H., Cavney, J., & Resnick, P. J. (2012a). Child murder by parents and evolutionary psychology. *Psychiatric Clinics of North America, 35*(4), 781–795. http://dx.doi.org/10.1016/j.psc.2012.08.002.

Friedman, S. H., Cavney, J., & Resnick, P. J. (2012b). Mothers who kill: evolutionary underpinnings and infanticide law. *Behavioral Sciences & the Law, 30*(5), 585–597. http://dx.doi.org/10.1002/bsl.2034.

Gauffin, H., & Landtblom, A. M. (2014). Epilepsy and violence: case series concerning physical trauma in children of persons with epilepsy. *Neuropsychiatric Disease and Treatment, 10*, 2183–2189. http://dx.doi.org/10.2147/NDT.S68438.

Glaser, B. (1996). Offenders with an intellectual disability. In W. Brookbanks (Ed.), *Psychiatry and the law* (pp. 194–237). Wellington: Brookers.

Glaser, W., & Deane, K. (1999). Normalisation in an abnormal world: a study of prisoners with an intellectual disability. *International Journal of Offender Therapy and Comparative Criminology, 43*, 338–356.

Gottlieb, P., Gabrielsen, G., & Kramp, P. (1987). Psychotic homicides in Copenhagen from 1959 to 1983. *Acta Psychiatrica Scandinavica, 76*(3), 285–292. Retrieved from http://www.scopus.com/inward/record.url?eid=2-s2.0-0023409128&partnerID=40&md5=3de046bc071126a7531fc97c7b221dea.

Grafman, J., Schwab, K., Warden, D., Pridgen, A., Brown, H. R., & Salazar, A. M. (1996). Frontal lobe injuries, violence, and aggression: a report of the Vietnam head injury study. *Neurology, 46*(5), 1231–1238. Retrieved from http://www.ncbi.nlm.nih.gov/pubmed/8628458.

Grann, M., Långström, N., Tengström, A., & Kullgren, G. (1999). Psychopathy (PCL-R) predicts violent recidivism among criminal offenders with personality disorders in Sweden. *Law and Human Behavior, 23*(2), 205–217.

Gross, H. (1911). *Criminal psychology: A manual for Judges, Practitioners, and Students.* Translated from the Fourth German Edition, by H. M. Kallen. Boston: Little, Brown, and Company.

Haddad, P. M., Brain, C., & Scott, J. (2014). Nonadherence with antipsychotic medication in schizophrenia: challenges and management strategies. *Patient Related Outcome Measures, 5*, 43–62. http://dx.doi.org/10.2147/PROM.S42735.

Harper, D. (2013). *Online etymology dictionary. Electronic Edition: Douglas Harper.* Available from http://www.etymonline.com/.

Hayes, S., & McIllwain, D. (1988). *The prevalence of intellectual disability in the NSW prison population.* Report to the Criminology Research Council. Canberra, Australia: Criminology Research Council.

Hayes, S., Shackell, P., Mottram, P., & Lancaster, R. (2007). The prevalence of intellectual disability in a major UK prison. *British Journal of Learning Disabilities, 35*(3), 162–167.

Healy, W., & Tenney-Healy, M. (1915). *Pathological lying, accusation, and swindling: A study in forensic psychology.* Boston: Little, Brown, and Company.

Hengartner, M. P. (2015). The detrimental impact of maladaptive personality on public mental health: a challenge for psychiatric practice. *Front Psychiatry, 6*, 87. http://dx.doi.org/10.3389/fpsyt.2015.00087.

Hirschi, T., & Hindelang, M. J. (1977). Intelligence and delinquency: a revisionist review. *American Sociological Review, 42*(4), 571–587. Retrieved from http://www.ncbi.nlm.nih.gov/pubmed/900659.

Hodgins, S. (1992). Mental disorder, intellectual deficiency, and crime: evidence from a birth cohort. *Archives of General Psychiatry, 49*(6), 476–483. http://dx.doi.org/10.1001/archpsyc.1992.01820060056009.

Hodgins, S., De Brito, S. A., Chhabra, P., & Cote, G. (2010). Anxiety disorders among offenders with antisocial personality disorders: a distinct subtype? *Canadian Journal of Psychiatry, 55*(12), 784–791. Retrieved from http://www.ncbi.nlm.nih.gov/pubmed/21172099.

Hogue, T., Steptoe, L., Taylor, J. L., Lindsay, W. R., Mooney, P., Pinkney, L., et al. (2006). A comparison of offenders with intellectual disability across three levels of security. *Criminal Behaviour and Mental Health, 16*(1), 13–28.

Holland, S., & Persson, P. (2011). Intellectual disability in the Victorian prison system: characteristics of prisoners with an intellectual disability released from prison in 2003–2006. *Psychology, Crime & Law, 17*(1), 25–41.

Jha, M. K., Lambert, E. S., Beadles, B. A., Spradling, B., Martinez, R., Renfro, N., et al. (2015). A case of frontotemporal dementia presenting with treatment-refractory psychosis and extreme violence: response to combination of clozapine, medroxyprogesterone, and sertraline. *Journal of Clinical Psychopharmacology*, *35*(6), 732–733. http://dx.doi.org/10.1097/JCP.0000000000000414.

Jones, G. P., & Coombes, K. (1990). *The prevalence of intellectual deficit among the Western Australian prisoner population.* Perth, Australia: Western Australia Department of Corrective Services.

Kane, J. M., Kishimoto, T., & Correll, C. U. (2013). Non-adherence to medication in patients with psychotic disorders: epidemiology, contributing factors and management strategies. *World Psychiatry*, *12*(3), 216–226. http://dx.doi.org/10.1002/wps.20060.

Lelandais, G. E. (2013). Citizenship, minorities and the struggle for a right to the city in Istanbul. *Citizenship Studies*, *17*(6–7), 817–836. Retrieved from http://www.scopus.com/inward/record.url?eid=2-s2.0-84887986737&partnerID=40&md5=0073f3fad362a9b29945337580564854.

Liljegren, M., Naasan, G., Temlett, J., Perry, D. C., Rankin, K. P., Merrilees, J., et al. (2015). Criminal behavior in frontotemporal dementia and Alzheimer disease. *JAMA Neurology*, *72*(3), 295–300. http://dx.doi.org/10.1001/jamaneurol.2014.3781.

Lindqvist, P., & Allebeck, P. (1990). Schizophrenia and crime: a longitudinal follow-up of 644 schizophrenics in Stockholm. *British Journal of Psychiatry*, *157*, 345–350.

Lombroso, C., & Ferrero, W. (1895). *The female offender.* New York: D. Appleton & Co.

Marzuk, P. M. (1996). Violence, crime, and mental illness: how strong a link? *Archives of General Psychiatry*, *53*(6), 481–486.

Mathieu, C., Neumann, C., Babiak, P., & Hare, R. D. (2015). Corporate psychopathy and the full-range leadership model. *Assessment*, *22*(3), 267–278. http://dx.doi.org/10.1177/1073191114545490.

Maudsley, H. (1876). *Responsibility in mental disease.* London: King & Co.

McDonald, A. (1905). *Man and abnormal man: Including a study of children in connection with bills to establish laboratories under federal and state governments for the study of the criminal, pauper, and defective classes.* Washington: Government Printing Office.

McEwan, T. E., & Strand, S. (2013). The role of psychopathology in stalking by adult strangers and acquaintances. *Australian and New Zealand Journal of Psychiatry*, *47*(6), 546–555. Retrieved from http://www.scopus.com/inward/record.url?eid=2-s2.0-84880517458&partnerID=40&md5=af423cc1de88bd6629f6ec1bd93e7b79.

McGuire, B., & Wraith, A. (2000). Legal and psychological aspects of stalking: a review. *Journal of Forensic Psychiatry*, *11*(2), 316–327. Retrieved from http://www.scopus.com/inward/record.url?eid=2-s2.0-0033771686&partnerID=40&md5=53b575716ad7658b885b3975c541db62.

McKenzie, K., & Harpham, T. (2006). *Social capital and mental health.* Jessica Kingsley Publishers.

McKinlay, A., Grace, R. C., McLellan, T., Roger, D., Clarbour, J., & MacFarlane, M. R. (2014). Predicting adult offending behavior for individuals who experienced a traumatic brain injury during childhood. *The Journal of Head Trauma Rehabilitation*, *29*(6), 507–513. http://dx.doi.org/10.1097/HTR.0000000000000000.

Miller, L. (2012). Stalking: patterns, motives, and intervention strategies. *Aggression and Violent Behavior*, *17*(6), 495–506. Retrieved from http://www.scopus.com/inward/record.url?eid=2-s2.0-84866906991&partnerID=40&md5=de8bad2066d3534415fdfd1220186ff7.

Monahan, J., Steadman, H. J., Appelbaum, P. S., Robbins, P. C., Mulvey, E. P., Silver, E., et al. (2000). Developing a clinically useful actuarial tool for assessing violence risk. *The British Journal of Psychiatry, 176*, 312–319. Retrieved from http://www.ncbi.nlm.nih.gov/pubmed/10827877.

Mouzos, J., & Makkai, T. (2011). *Women's experiences of male violence: Findings from the Australian component of the international violence against women survey. Research and public policy series, no. 56.* Canberra: AIC. Available at http://www.aic.gov.au/publications/current%20series/rpp/41-60/rpp56.aspx.

Muller, J. L., Schuierer, G., Marienhagen, J., Putzhammer, A., & Klein, H. E. (2003). "Acquired psychopathy" and the neurobiology of emotion and violence. *Psychiatrische Praxis, 30*(Suppl. 2), S221–S225. Retrieved from http://www.ncbi.nlm.nih.gov/pubmed/14509082.

Nestor, P. G. (2002). Mental disorder and violence: personality dimensions and clinical features. *American Journal of Psychiatry, 159*(12), 1973–1978. http://dx.doi.org/10.1176/appi.ajp.159.12.1973.

New South Wales Law Reform Commission. (1996). *People with an intellectual disability and the criminal justice system.* Sydney: Government Printing Office.

Nicholls, J., Staiger, P. K., Williams, J. S., Richardson, B., & Kambouropoulos, N. (2014). When social anxiety co-occurs with substance use: does an impulsive social anxiety subtype explain this unexpected relationship? *Psychiatry Research, 220*(3), 909–914. http://dx.doi.org/10.1016/j.psychres.2014.08.040.

Norris, S. M., Huss, M. T., & Palarea, R. E. (2011). A pattern of violence: analyzing the relationship between intimate partner violence and stalking. *Violence and Victims, 26*(1), 103–115. Retrieved from http://www.scopus.com/inward/record.url?eid=2-s2.0-80052082862&partnerID=40&md5=3199a6f7b9de52189c1aa1b2c06a715b.

Pareés, I., Saifee, T. A., Kojovic, M., Kassavetis, P., Rubio-Agusti, I., Sadnicka, A., et al. (2013). Functional (psychogenic) symptoms in Parkinson's disease. *Movement Disorders, 28*(12), 1622–1627. Retrieved from http://www.scopus.com/inward/record.url?eid=2-s2.0-84886410016&partnerID=40&md5=e9a51923d4fbe663b40a9e83f2dd717f.

Paterson, B., & Stark, C. (2001). Social policy and mental illness in England in the 1990s: violence, moral panic and critical discourse. *Journal of Psychiatric and Mental Health Nursing, 8*(3), 257–267.

Paulson, J. F., & Bazemore, S. D. (2010). Prenatal and postpartum depression in fathers and its association with maternal depression: a meta-analysis. *JAMA, 303*(19), 1961–1969. http://dx.doi.org/10.1001/jama.2010.605.

Peterson, J., Skeem, J. L., Hart, E., Vidal, S., & Keith, F. (2010). Analyzing offense patterns as a function of mental illness to test the criminalization hypothesis. *Psychiatric Services, 61*(12), 1217–1222. http://dx.doi.org/10.1176/appi.ps.61.12.1217.

Petherick, W., & Sinnamon, G. (2013). *Motivations: Offender and victim perspectives profiling and serial crime: Theoretical and practical issues* (3rd ed.). , 393–430.

Petursson, H., & Gudjonsson, G. H. (1981). Psychiatric aspects of homicide. *Acta Psychiatrica Scandinavica, 64*, 363–372.

Pinkofsky, H. B. (1997). Mnemonics for DSM-IV personality disorders. *Psychiatric Services, 48*(9), 1197–1198.

Quanbeck, C. D., Stone, D. C., Scott, C. L., McDermott, B. E., Altshuler, L. L., & Frye, M. A. (2004). Clinical and legal correlates of inmates with bipolar disorder at time of criminal arrest. *Journal of Clinical Psychiatry, 65*(2), 198–203. Retrieved from http://www.ncbi.nlm.nih.gov/pubmed/15003073.

Raposo, A., Vicens, L., Clithero, J. A., Dobbins, I. G., & Huettel, S. A. (2011). Contributions of frontopolar cortex to judgments about self, others and relations. *Social Cognitive and Affective Neuroscience, 6*(3), 260–269.

Rezansoff, S. N., Moniruzzaman, A., Gress, C., & Somers, J. M. (2013). Psychiatric diagnoses and multi-year recidivism in a Canadian provincial population. *Psychology, Public Policy, and Law*, *19*(4), 443–543. http://dx.doi.org/10.1037/a0033907.

Romero-Martinez, A., & Moya-Albiol, L. (2013). Neuropsychology of perpetrators of domestic violence: the role of traumatic brain injury and alcohol abuse and/or dependence. *Revista de Neurologia*, *57*(11), 515–522. Retrieved from http://www.ncbi.nlm.nih.gov/pubmed/24265146.

Seitz, R. J., Nickel, J., & Azari, N. P. (2006). Functional modularity of the medial prefrontal cortex: involvement in human empathy. *Neuropsychology*, *20*(6), 743–751. http://dx.doi.org/10.1037/0894-4105.20.6.743.

Shackelford, T. K., & Mouzos, J. (2005). Partner killing by men in cohabiting and marital relationships: a comparative, cross-national analysis of data from Australia and the United States. *Journal of Interpersonal Violence*, *20*(10), 1310–1324. http://dx.doi.org/10.1177/0886260505278606.

Signorelli, M. S., Battaglia, E., Costanzo, M. C., & Cannavò, D. (2013). Pramipexole induced psychosis in a patient with restless legs syndrome. *BMJ Case Reports*. Retrieved from http://www.scopus.com/inward/record.url?eid=2-s2.0-84885669762&partnerID=40&md5=488f5eda0c3a06075b38ba2e602bbe00.

Silva, J. A., Derecho, D. V., Leong, G. B., & Ferrari, M. M. (2000). Stalking behavior in delusional jealousy. *Journal of Forensic Sciences*, *45*(1), 77–82. Retrieved from http://www.scopus.com/inward/record.url?eid=2-s2.0-0033989017&partnerID=40&md5=a3d112ea7a82bb4c7a74beb151b7f504.

Sinnamon, G. (2015). Psychopathology and criminal behaviour. In W. Petherick (Ed.), *Applied crime analysis: A social science approach to understanding crime, criminals, and victims*. Boston: Anderson Publishing.

Spencer, J., & Tie, A. (2013). Psychiatric symptoms associated with the mental health defence for serious violent offences in Queensland. *Australasian Psychiatry*, *21*(2), 147–152. Retrieved from http://www.scopus.com/inward/record.url?eid=2-s2.0-84879225423&partnerID=40&md5=77182816e0fcfef49fcc7350528044b6.

Steadman, H. J., Mulvey, E. P., Monahan, J., Robbins, P. C., Appelbaum, P. S., Grisso, T., et al. (1998). Violence by people discharged from acute psychiatric inpatient facilities and by others in the same neighborhoods. *Archives of General Psychiatry*, *55*(5), 393–401. Retrieved from http://www.ncbi.nlm.nih.gov/pubmed/9596041.

Swanson, J. W. (1994). Mental disorder, substance abuse and community violence: an epidemiological approach. In J. Monahan, & J. H. Steadman (Eds.), *Violence and mental disorder*. Chicago: University of Chicago Press.

Swanson, J. W., Holzer, C., Ganja, V., & Jono, R. (1990). Violence and psychiatric disorder in the community: evidence from the epidemiologic catchment area surveys. *Hospital and Community Psychiatry*, *41*, 761–770.

Thompson, C. M., Dennison, S. M., & Stewart, A. L. (2013). Are different risk factors associated with moderate and severe stalking violence? Examining factors from the integrated theoretical model of stalking violence. *Criminal Justice and Behavior*, *40*(8), 850–880. Retrieved from http://www.scopus.com/inward/record.url?eid=2-s2.0-84880721443&partnerID=40&md5=e4a22b5d8a1aeca763a7fa2cc43c2d88.

Tiihonen, J., Isohanni, M., Rasanen, P., Koiranen, M., & Moring, J. (1997). Specific major mental disorders and criminality: a 26-year prospective study of the 1966 northern Finland birth cohort. *American Journal of Psychiatry*, *154*(6), 840–845. http://dx.doi.org/10.1176/ajp.154.6.840.

Vaughn, M. G., Fu, Q., Delisi, M., Beaver, K. M., Perron, B. E., & Howard, M. O. (2010). Criminal victimization and comorbid substance use and psychiatric disorders in the United States: results from the NESARC. *Annals of Epidemiology*, *20*(4), 281–288. http://dx.doi.org/10.1016/j.annepidem.2009.11.011.

Vicens, E., Tort, V., Duenas, R. M., Muro, A., Perez-Arnau, F., Arroyo, J. M., et al. (2011). The prevalence of mental disorders in Spanish prisons. *Criminal Behaviour and Mental Health*, *21*(5), 321–332. http://dx.doi.org/10.1002/cbm.815.

Vogenthaler, D. R. (1987). An overview of head injury: its consequences and rehabilitation. *Brain Injury*, *1*(1), 113–127. Retrieved from http://www.ncbi.nlm.nih.gov/pubmed/3331550.

Volavka, J. (2011). Violent crime, epilepsy, and traumatic brain injury. *PLoS Medicine*, *8*(12), e1001148. http://dx.doi.org/10.1371/journal.pmed.1001148.

Vorspan, F., Mehtelli, W., Dupuy, G., Bloch, V., & Lepine, J. P. (2015). Anxiety and substance use disorders: co-occurrence and clinical issues. *Current Psychiatry Reports*, *17*(2), 4. http://dx.doi.org/10.1007/s11920-014-0544-y.

Wallace, C., Mullen, P., & Burgess, P. (2014). Criminal offending in schizophrenia over a 25-year period marked by deinstitutionalization and increasing prevalence of comorbid substance use disorders. *American Journal of Psychiatry*, *161*(4), 716–727.

Wallace, C., Mullen, P., Burgess, P., Palmer, S., Ruschena, D., & Browne, C. (1998). Serious criminal offending and mental disorder. Case linkage study. *The British Journal of Psychiatry*, *172*, 477–484. Retrieved from http://www.ncbi.nlm.nih.gov/pubmed/9828986.

Whitman, S., Coleman, T. E., Patmon, C., Desai, B. T., Cohen, R., & King, L. N. (1984). Epilepsy in prison: elevated prevalence and no relationship to violence. *Neurology*, *34*(6), 775–782. Retrieved from http://www.ncbi.nlm.nih.gov/pubmed/6539441.

Whittington, R., Hockenhull, J. C., McGuire, J., Leitner, M., Barr, W., Cherry, M. G., et al. (2013). A systematic review of risk assessment strategies for populations at high risk of engaging in violent behaviour: Update 2002–8. *Health Technology Assessment*, *17*(50), i–xiv+1–128.

Wilcox, D. E. (1985). The relationship of mental illness to homicide. *American Journal of Forensic Psychiatry*, *vi*, 3–15.

Williams, M. (2010). Imagining uxoricide: reading the scene of the crime. *Australian Feminist Studies*, *25*(65), 281–294. http://dx.doi.org/10.1080/08164649.2010.504293.

Williams, W. H., McAuliffe, K. A., Cohen, M. H., Parsonage, M., Ramsbotham, J., & General The Lord, D. (2015). Traumatic brain injury and juvenile offending: complex causal links offer multiple targets to reduce crime. *The Journal of Head Trauma Rehabilitation*, *30*(2), 69–74. http://dx.doi.org/10.1097/HTR.0000000000000134.

World Health Organisation. (1992). *International statistical classification of diseases and related health problems* version: 2010 (ICD-10) [online edition] (10th Revision). Geneva: World Health Organisation. Available at. http://apps.who.int/classifications/icd10/browse/2010/en.

World Health Organisation. (2010). *ICD-10 classifications of mental and behavioural disorder: Clinical descriptions and diagnostic guidelines* (2nd ed.). Geneva: World Health Organisation.

Yamagishi, T., Li, Y., Takagishi, H., Matsumoto, Y., & Kiyonari, T. (2014). In search of *Homo economicus*. *Psychological Science*, *25*(9), 1699–1711. http://dx.doi.org/10.1177/0956797614538065.

Zugman, A., Pan, P. M., Gadelha, A., Mansur, R. B., Asevedo, E., Cunha, G. R., et al. (2013). Brain tumor in a patient with attenuated psychosis syndrome. *Schizophrenia Research*, *144*(1–3), 151–152. Retrieved from http://www.scopus.com/inward/record.url?eid=2-s2.0-84873525600&partnerID=40&md5=dd1b411b5e09b08cef5ea14f4935b9f2.

Catathymia and Compulsive Homicide: A Psychological Perspective

2

Grant Sinnamon[1,2], Wayne Petherick[1]

[1]Bond University, Gold Coast, QLD, Australia; [2]Bela Menso Brain and Behaviour Centre, Varsity Lakes, QLD, Australia

CHAPTER OUTLINE

INTRODUCTION

The motivation and psychological characteristics that underpin the behaviors resulting in homicide can differ substantially. Some behaviors may be associated with episodic psychopathology that skews thinking and emotion and therefore drives homicidal behaviors via psychotic delusion, obsession, and paranoia, or through reduced capacity for self-awareness, reflection, impulse control, risk assessment, or social cognition. Others may be a result of more pervasive features that produce narcissistic, antisocial, and other personality characteristics that mediate motivation and behavior. Catathymic crisis, compulsive homicide, and sadism are three areas in which these pathological and personality mediators result in both impulsive as well as premeditated murder. They each represent a challenging offending space in which considerable investment has been made in trying to understand, predict, and prevent these crimes—often with little success.

CATATHYMIC CRISIS

According to Sinnamon (2015, p. 219), a catathymic crisis is *an unexpected, impulsive, and explosive violent outburst that is not readily understandable from the situation in which it occurred but rather is only able to be understood in the context of individual unconscious (or outside of conscious awareness) motivations.* The term *catathymia* originates from the Greek roots *kata* and *thymos*, which is translated as *in accordance with emotion/s*. A catathymic behavioral reaction occurs when emotions are so overwhelming that they take over psychological rationality, compromising impulse control, and resulting in a reflexive outburst of excessive violence. The term catathymia was first used by Maier in 1912. According to Maier (1912), the catathymic process (*Katathyme*) was a visceral and violent behavioral response brought about by a powerful, reflexive psychological response to a strong and inflexible emotional attachment to an underlying schema(s). The schemas associated with this reaction do not necessarily represent their subject matter with any accuracy or, for that matter, reality. In this way, some psychotic presentations could be catathymic in nature (such as paranoid delusions) if they originate from underlying psychological phenomena such as maladaptive cognitions to trauma. However, others such as drug-induced psychoses are not catathymic because they are the product of chemically altered brain function rather than a process of psychogenesis.

The original idea of catathymia forwarded by Maier (1912), Wertham (1937), and their contemporaries was that the condition was its own clinical identity. However, within the current diagnostic framework, catathymia, catathymic process, and catathymic crisis are not directly translatable to a single unique pathology. Catathymia was recognized in earlier versions of the *Diagnostic and Statistical Manual of Mental Disorders* (DSM), however, it was excluded in the DSM-IV (American Psychiatric Association, 2000) and remains absent from the most recent DSM incarnation (DSM5; American Psychiatric Association, 2013), and from the *International Classification of Disease* (World Health Organization, 1992). In contemporary diagnostic protocols, catathymia is considered to be a secondary event, resulting from circumstances found in multiple psychopathologies. Therefore, in its modern incarnation (Sinnamon, 2015, p. 220):

> *Catathymia is more likely to be considered as a syndrome, symptom or consequence within the confines of other mental disorders such as post-traumatic stress disorder, psychotic disorders (particularly those with delusional characteristics), mood disorders (and mood disorders with psychotic features), and several of the personality disorders.*

In contemporary circles catathymia is used to describe any explosive or impulsively violent behavior that appears to have its roots in heightened emotionality and

that is charged by irrational thought processes or beliefs. The manner in which catathymia is represented within the criminal sphere can be quite varied. For example,
violent serial crime, familial homicide, stalking-related violence, and sudden (often)
inexplicable interpersonal violence perpetrated against a stranger or casual acquaintance are all often laced with catathymic crisis.

A catathymic crisis has been described in many ways. Sinnamon (2015) has previously used three subcategories to describe the variation in catathymic expression that
may occur. The first is delusional catathymic process (DCP) and is, in essence, a general description of the original catathymic crisis espoused by early proponents such as
Maier (1912) and Wertham (1937). The second and third are the dual categorizations
suggested by Revitch and Schlesinger (1978), in which catathymic crisis may occur
within either a chronic catathymic crisis (CCC) or an acute catathymic crisis (ACC).

DELUSIONAL CATATHYMIC PROCESS

DCP aligns closely with Maier's original ideas of catathymia and with the ideas put
forward by Frederic Wertham in the 1930s (Wertham, 1937). According to Wertham
(1937), a (delusional) catathymia results when the highly emotion-charged content of
underlying cognitions, beliefs, and ideas transform the character of the emergent flow
of thoughts in a way that results in irrational wishes, desires, fears, and ambivalent
striving. Wertham argued that through this process the prospective offender develops
a delusional belief that they must commit a specific violent act against another person
or against themselves in order to achieve or resolve the situation to its conclusion. This
idea manifests in the mind as a definite plan with an accompanying strong motivation
to see it through, however, the plan may be resisted at some level within the individual's
mind and therefore meet with behavioral hesitation or delay. According to Wertham
(1937, p. 974) "the violent act usually has some symbolic significance over and above
its obvious meaning. … [and the cognitive processes of the individual] may have an
almost delusional character in its rigidity and inaccessibility to logical reasoning."

Wertham suggested that the pathogenesis of the psychological conditions required
for a catathymic crisis to manifest was entrenched in an environmental etiology. It
was Wertham's belief that traumatic experience manifested extreme emotional turmoil that ultimately resulted in an unresolvable inner conflict. This experience and its
subsequent inner conflict creates an associated hyperemotionality. In the individual's
mind, the experience, the unresolvable conflict, and the associated hyperemotionality are all blamed on external influences, and the individual's thought processes
become increasingly self-absorbed, disturbing, and irrational, until they suddenly
come to a decision (generally embedded within a delusion) that some violent act
is the only solution (Wertham, 1937). This decision becomes increasingly obsessional with related thought processes becoming increasingly irrational, reinforcing
the delusional thoughts and validating the obsession. The person becomes convinced
that this violent act is the only solution to their internal conflict.

Although the individual may resist the urge to act, eventually they will commit (or
attempt to commit) the offense. Wertham asserted that committing the act produces a

(usually) temporary catharsis during which the offender will feel relief from the inner conflict and emotional turmoil, and during which they may experience a sense of normality. The individual may even achieve some form of insight into their condition. For some, psychological recovery may ensue while in others the relief is temporary and they are eventually "recalled" to violence to relieve the inner tension again. This form of catathymic process is often seen in serial crime, and Wertham believed that the associated violence was not limited to violence against another person but could also extend to lighting fires, arson, self-harm such as self-castration or other genital mutilation, self-blinding, and other forms of significant nongenital self-mutilation; and suicide (which, in this context, may be construed as a form of intrinsically engaged homicide).

Wertham suggests that there are five stages within this form of catathymic process (Wertham, 1978):

1. the initial disordered thinking
2. development of a plan and increased emotional turmoil
3. heightened emotional turmoil resulting in the committal of the violent act
4. a sense of superficial calm and normality
5. (re)establishment of an inner calm

According to Sinnamon (2015), in the most common event of a resolution that is only temporary, a sixth stage occurs in which the individual comes full circle and the same psychological and emotional turmoil that they could not resolve previously once again begins to emerge. This is then followed by the reexperiencing of the previous five stages.

CHRONIC CATATHYMIC CRISIS

Revitch and Schlesinger (1978) proposed a model that considered catathymia as a psychological phenomenon that takes either a chronic or acute form, and did not consider catathymic crisis to be a construct that exists as a single clinical entity. In this way, both chronic (CCC) and acute (ACC) catathymic crises are therefore elements of the motivational processes and behavioral presentation that occur within the psychodynamics of broader psychopathology.

The construct of CCC is essentially the same as that forwarded within DCP and espoused by Maier (1912), Wertham (1937), and their contemporaries. In essence, the primary difference between CCC and DCP is the structural differentiation of their stages, in that Revitch and Schlesinger have reduced Wertham's five stages down to just three (Revitch & Schlesinger, 1978):

1. the incubation period
2. the committal of violence
3. the achievement of relief

According to Revitch and Schlesinger (1989), the incubation period may be quite short (a few days), or it may be quite long (several years). During this period, the (future) offender becomes progressively more emotionally disturbed, irrational (and possibly delusional) in their thoughts. Once a target of their irrationality has been identified, they also become progressively obsessive about their (future) victim. It is during this phase that the individual links an act of violence with a resolution to their inner turmoil and everything they have associated with it. If the (future) victim has a relationship with the (future) offender, then it is often the case that as the inner turmoil and intense emotional instability increase and start to push toward the surface, then disturbed, irrational, and obsessional thought processes will be noticed by the victim and they will withdraw from the offender. This in turn often exacerbates the irrationality, tension, anger, and conflict within the offender, hastening the progression toward the inevitable violence. In the instance of stalking, this relationship may not be real but rather may be a delusion on the part of the offender. The psychological characteristics of this period include depression and what Schlesinger (2007) refers to as schizophrenic-like thinking. Suicidal and homicidal thoughts are prevalent and, if the offender does not receive relief from the violent act, suicide is often a further outcome.

CCC can manifest over a prolonged period in one of three ways. As in the previous example, CCC may occur in the confines of a long-term relationship in which the future perpetrator and future victim are known to each other, often intimately. Various incarnations of familial homicide and familial murder-suicide are prime examples of this form of CCC. CCC may also occur within the confines of a one-way obsessional–delusional interaction in which the future perpetrator forms an irrational attachment to another person (most often it is a male offender and a female victim except in cases where the delusional thinking is erotomanic) and delusional thought processes conspire to evolve a belief that violence either against the individual or against another on behalf of the individual will resolve the perpetrator's internal conflict. Myriad stalking cases can be seen in this light, perhaps one of the more famous being that of John Hinckley Jr's obsession with actress Jodie Foster and his attempted assassination of then-president of the United States, Ronald Regan. Finally, CCC may occur as a result of obsessional or delusional thinking by the future offender that, at least in the early stages of the process, are not targeted to a specific individual. Instead, the future offender is fixated on the act of violence itself rather than on a specific "victim." Alternatively, the future offender may be fixated on both the act and a victim "type," which then assists them to eventually progress to the selection of a specific victim. Some serial killers could be seen within this manifestation of CCC.

ACUTE CATATHYMIC CRISIS

In contrast to the progressive buildup to violence that occurs in CCC, ACC takes place as a sudden outburst that is triggered by an often pedestrian interaction with an individual who is either a casual acquaintance (for example, the girl behind the counter at the local coffee shop) or a stranger that the perpetrator has just met. In the case of ACC, the offender is triggered into a violent reaction as a result of some action or perceived action by the stranger. An example of this form of catathymic crisis is when a "spontaneous" violent act is perpetrated against a stranger in an unlikely situation such as when a chance sexual encounter results in homicide. A stereotypical situation could be where a young male with underlying sexual issues (for example, latent or conflicted homosexual feelings, or early life abuse or attachment factors that, while not contributing to an obvious psychological abnormality, are creating significant emotional conflict) is confronted by a woman (or man) with a sexually assertive personality. The (about-to-be) victim may behave or make a comment that triggers the underlying aggressive response (think of it as a maladaptive fight–flight defense mechanism) with the end result being homicide.

Schlesinger (2007, p. 11) states that "the acute catathymic process taps deeper levels of emotional tension and is triggered by an overwhelming emotion attached to an underlying conflict." Although the offender may sometimes be able to provide an explanation for their behavior and a detailed account of what transpired, it is often the case that they have no or only partial recollection of the violent act itself. According to Schlesinger, there are several similarities between chronic and acute catathymic events that result in homicide (for Schlesinger's original list of similarities, see Schlesinger, 2004, p. 138). Sinnamon (2015, p. 223) previously presented a description of Schlesinger's original similarities, characterizing the similarities between CCC and ACC in the following manner:

1. With a few exceptions, cases primarily involve men killing women.
    a. The main instance where females become offenders against a male victim is in cases of domestic violence between intimate partners, although less than 3% of all men who are murdered are killed by their female intimate partner (Schlesinger, 2004).
    b. Male-to-male catathymic homicide is most likely to occur in the context of acute catathymic crisis.
    c. Female-to-female catathymic homicide is extremely rare with most cases occurring between incarcerated women.
2. The victim is generally symbolic or representative of deeper-seated conflicts. The victim is not the "real" issue.
3. The victim's behavior (or perceived or imagined behavior) triggers the highly volatile existing emotion-laden internal conflict(s).
4. Internal conflicts are generally egocentric in that they are focused on thoughts and emotions around real or imagined personal inadequacies. These are often relational in nature (often stemming from early life–generated attachment issues) and in adult circumstances tend to extend to the sexual arena.
5. The homicidal act works to redact the internal turmoil and emotional tension.
6. In the immediate posthomicide period, the offender will generally experience a time of psychological balance or homeostasis. This generally includes feelings of relief and a stabilizing (or flattening) of affect.
7. The offender does not generally try to avoid capture for very long. They will often give themselves up to police or tell a friend or trusted authority such as a priest.

8. Mental health professionals are generally very poor at recognizing the risk that is inherent in the offender's conflicted emotionality during the prehomicide incubation period.
9. Investigation and crime analysis may miss the sexually derived offender motivations because they are often relatively obscure. The act may not present in any way like a sex crime, and the scene may be more indicative of a more general violent crime. Indeed, the sexual motivations may not become apparent until the analysis can include direct contact with the (cooperative) offender.

Similarly, Schlesinger has identified a number of differentiating characteristics between acute and chronic catathymic crisis. Table 2.1 presents the differentiating characteristics of the two catathymic forms.

Table 2.1 Differentiating Characteristics of Acute and Chronic Catathymic Processes (Schlesinger, 2004, p. 162)

Characteristic	Acute	Chronic
Activation of process	Triggered by a sudden overwhelming emotion attached to underlying sexual conflicts of symbolic significance	Triggered by a buildup of tension, a feeling of frustration, helplessness, and inadequacy sometimes extending into the sexual area
Relationship to the victim	Usually a stranger	Usually a close relation such as an intimate or former intimate partner
Victim symbolization	Often a displaced matricide	Rarely a displaced matriarch but the victim may have symbolic significance
Incubation period	Several seconds	One day to one year, or more; may involve stalking
Level of planning	Unplanned	Planned, frequently in the form of an obsessive rumination
Method of attack	Sudden, violent; often overkill	Violent but not sudden
Crime scene	Very disorganized, reflecting a lack of planning	Less disorganized
Sexual activity	Occasional sexual activity just before the attack; impotency common	Sexual activity rare at time of homicide
Postmortem behavior	Sometimes necrophilia and occasionally dismemberment	Rarely necrophilia or dismemberment
Feeling following the attack	Usually flattening of emotions	Usually a feeling of relief
Memory of the event	Usually poor	Usually preserved

Schlesinger, L. B. (2004). Sexual murder: Catathymic and compulsive homicides. Boca Raton, Fl: CRC Press p. 162.

COMPULSIVE HOMICIDE

Compulsive homicide differs from catathymic homicide in that the event is not an attempt to resolve some internal cognitive-emotional conflict but is a manifestation of a long-standing deep-seated compulsion to kill. The offender is not attempting to use homicide to relieve some inner turmoil but rather is using homicide to satisfy a long-running (possibly sexually sadistic) fantasy. Compulsive homicide can be either "unplanned," in which the offender murders in a crime of opportunity, or it can be "planned," in which the offender takes significant time to plan, prepare, and execute the murder, often with substantial symbolism and ritualistic behavior.

UNPLANNED COMPULSIVE HOMICIDE

Like ACC, unplanned compulsive homicide (UCH) is a behavioral outcome resulting from disordered internal thought processes and motivations. However, unlike ACC offenders whose emotionality is charged by internal conflict (the combination of which results in the motivational trigger for violent behavior), offenders in cases of UCH have no such internal "conflict" driving their emotion and motivation. Rather, UCH offenders have an internal desire to kill, often associated with a fusion of violence and sexual arousal, which they may use within the confines of fantasy for a number of years before finally acting on their desires. As the name implies, unplanned compulsive homicide is generally a crime of opportunity and, therefore, the ultimate enactment of their homicidal desires is often due to a confluence of opportunity and some situation that reduces self-control sufficient to allow the impulsive explosion of violence to ensue. This may be environmental factors such as being alone with a vulnerable victim candidate while intoxicated (thereby reducing their behavioral inhibitions), or it may involve opportunity concurrent with endogenous factors such as comorbid mental illness.

PLANNED COMPULSIVE HOMICIDE

Just like CCC, planned compulsive homicidal (PCH) behavior is the culmination of an extended period of obsessive rumination involving the killing of another person. This is, however, where the similarities stop. PCH involves an intense desire or compulsion to kill in order to emulate a sexually sadistic fantasy construction. The killing of another person is not motivated by a belief that it is a means of resolving a problem (internal conflict), but rather the act of killing, usually in some ritualistic manner, is the motivation in itself. In this way PCH is (usually) a sexually motivated compulsive homicidal act perpetrated because of a deep inner desire to kill and not because the murder will achieve any purpose (whether logical, irrational, or delusional). Offenders who commit PCH may be classically psychopathic and often show severe traits of personality disorders, particularly narcissistic and antisocial. Rare females who commit PCH may also present with borderline, paranoid, or histrionic personality traits.

SADISTIC AGGRESSION

Sadism is a term that has lost some of its literal meaning as a result of casual use where it is employed to describe a vast array of behaviors others perceive as punishing. For example, one may be accused of being a sadist for working too many hours, for exercising too long, for studying too hard, or encouraging or prompting the same in another person. As a clinical disorder, it has one of the lowest diagnostic thresholds though it does require behaviors that are extreme and not believed to be all that common. However, the true prevalence of all variants of sadism is not known (Fedoroff, 2008). This section will discuss sadism, and the sexual satisfaction obtained from victim pain and suffering, starting with a history of the term and the disorder itself.

Sadism is believed to be a psychosexual disorder where the individual has a preferred or exclusive sexual gratification that is deviant (Geberth, 2006). While it is not the purpose of this section, or indeed this chapter, to provide an extensive discussion on the etiology of sadism, a number of hypotheses have been put forth as to cause. They include psychiatric disorders such as schizophrenia (Myers, Burket, & Hustead, 2006) and Chuang (2011) proposes that sadists suffer from a psychiatric disease in which there is an abnormal threshold for pain whereby inflicting pain upon another produces synesthesia, which activates the mirror system. The mirror system, or mirror neuron system, fires when an animal acts or observes the same act in another as though the observer were the one doing or experiencing the act (Rizzolatti & Craighero, 2004; Rockelein, 2006).

While there are both explicit and implied links between sadism and catathymia, it is possible that sadistic behavior may be incorrectly identified in a catathymic event. This is possible because the violent and explosive emotional purge that characterizes catathymia may indeed appear to be an act of sadism simply because of the level of violence involved. This may also occur because of the coupling of observations in a chronic catathymic crisis such as evidence of sexual behavior that preceded the violent incident. A *cum hoc fallacy* ("with this [therefore], because of this") may occur when something like semen is used to bolster an assessment of sexual satisfaction that accompanied the violence. Such a case of diagnostic confusion may be made more possible by the idiosyncratic way in which the diagnostic criteria are applied. For example, Marshall, Kennedy, Yates, and Serran (2002) suggest that few experts followed the DSM of the day (DSM-IV-TR), with Marshall and Hucker (2006, p. 2) noting that:

> *We found that while most authors indicated they used the criteria specified by either the American Psychiatric Association's Diagnostic and Statistical Manual of Mental Disorders (DSM), or the World Health Organization's International Classification of Disease (ICD), to diagnose their subjects, in fact the criteria they actually specified did not comply with either of these systems. Each researcher chose an idiosyncratic list of criteria which typically included some features from both DSM and ICD, but also included other features not mentioned in either of these texts.*

An earlier study of that first author and colleagues found similar results (Marshall et al., 2002)—that there was not much diagnostic agreement between psychiatrists in assessing the potential for sadism in 12 dangerous sexual offenders.

SADISM: BACKGROUND AND POTTED HISTORY

Sadism was named after a French aristocrat and revolutionary Donatien Alphonse Francois de Sade, who lived between 1740 and 1814. Better known as the Marquis de Sade, he fought against the ruling elite at the time arguing for greater general freedoms for the citizenry. He is perhaps best known for his arguments for greater sexual freedoms, demanding less intrusion from the government for such behaviors. This went against the political grain, and as a result, de Sade spent a great deal of his adult life in prisons and asylums. Over his lifetime, including during periods of incarcerations, de Sade wrote a number of works with one of the most famous being *Justine* and another titled *Juliette*. Though many of these were destroyed in an effort to kill his message, a number of his works are available through reprint today such as *Justine: Philosophy in the Bedroom and Other Writings* (de Sade, 1965).

While there was seemingly great personal enjoyment of his beliefs as represented by his stories, he also dedicated his works to those of a similar bent (de Sade, 1795, p. 3):

> *To Libertines,*
>
> *Voluptuaries of all ages, of every sex, it is to you that I offer this work; nourish yourselves upon its principles: they favour your passions, and these passions, whereof godly insipid moralists put you in fear, are naught but the means Nature employs to bring man to the ends she prescribes to him; hearken only to these delicious promptings, for no voice save that of the passions can conduct you to happiness.*
>
> *Lewd women, let the voluptuous Saint-Ange be your model; after her example, be heedless of all that contradicts pleasure's divine laws, by which all he life she was enchained.*
>
> *Young maidens, too long constrained by a fanciful Virtue's absurd and dangerous bonds and by those of a disgusting religion, imitate the fiery Eugenie; be as quick as she to destroy, to spurn all those ridiculous precepts inculcated in your by imbecile parents.*
>
> *And you, amiable debauchees, you who since birth have known no limits but those of your desires and who have been governed by your caprices alone, study the cynical Dolmancé, proceed like him as far as he is you would travel the length of those flowered ways your lechery prepares for you; in Dolmancé's academy be at last convinced it is only by exploring and enlarging the sphere of his tastes and whims, it is only by sacrificing everything to the senses' pleasure that this individual, who never asked to be cast into this universe of woe, that this poor*

creature who goes under the nature of Man, may be able to sow a smattering of
roses atop the thorny path of life.

Sadism was first accepted as a topic for scientific study by Richard Kraft-Ebing and
Stekel (Frances & Wollert, 2012), an Austro-German psychiatrist, and Kraft-Ebing
was also one of the first to discuss sadism as a clinical entity (Aggrawal, 2009;
Marshall & Kennedy, 2003). In *Psychopathia Sexualis*, Krafft-Ebing (1965, p. 87)
notes:

Sadism, especially in its rudimentary manifestations, seems to be of common
occurrence in the domain of sexual perversion. Sadism is the experience of sexual
pleasurable sensations (including orgasm) produced by acts of cruelty, bodily
punishment afflicted on one's own person or witnessed in others, be they animals
or human beings. It may also consist of an innate desire to humiliate, hurt, wound
or even destroy others in order thereby to create sexual pleasure in one's self.

While this was the first formal and systematic study of sadism by a clinician,
there can be no doubt that the behavior existed, in one form or another, prior to this.
For example, the Kama Sutra first released in the 4th century contains a reference
to sadism including the practice of pinching, biting, and flogging erotic body parts
(Aggrawal, 2009). Gilles de Rais (1404–1440), a French nobleman and compatriot
of Joan of Arc, was a well-known sadist and is suspected of killing between approximately 140 and 800 peasant children, mostly males (Leyton, 1986). It is alleged that
he took more pleasure from witnessing the torture than he did from having sex with
the children (Schlesinger, 2000). A Hungarian noblewoman, the Countess Elizabeth
Bathory (1560–1614), was accused of torturing and killing young girls and women,
and is identified as one of the most infamous serial killers and sadists in Hungarian
and Slovak history (Aggrawal, 2009).

In *The Mask of Sanity*, Cleckley (1941) gives some treatment to sadism in the
context of comorbidity with psychopathy. Here, he states (p. 290–291):

In a broader sense it might be said that the apparently wilful persistence with
which they bring humiliation and emotional suffering upon those who love them,
as well as failure and unpleasant circumstances upon themselves, marks all psy-
chopaths as both sadists and masochists. Only in this sense, however, are these
impulses common or consistent, and the gratification is probably not the directly
erotic sensation enjoyed by perverts who literally whip others or have themselves
whipped. I get the impression that a great many of the people who have attracted
attention primarily as sadists have many characteristics of the classic psychopath.

Cleckley also goes on to warn of the dangers of sadists, in that (p. 291):

The real psychopath who is a real (persistently organized) sadist, of course, ranks
as an extremely dangerous person. Like all psychopaths, he is unlikely to be
greatly altered by punishment or training or treatment, and he constitutes a grave
problem. People of this type are often responsible for perverse and murderous
attacks on children frequently noticed in the newspapers.

Of course, this risk is not presented solely and only by the psychopath-sadist, and any sadistic behavior is going to be a risky undertaking. We must also be cautious in interpreting or inferring the degree to which these two disorders are or will be comorbid. One can be a psychopath without being a sadist, and thus the opposite must also be possible. Notably absent from Cleckley's discussion is the paring of the victim's suffering with the sexual arousal of the offender. Having said this, his work focuses primarily on the psychopath and is not a treatise on sadism in its own right. In short, such an omission may be accounted for in a way other than a lack of attention to diagnostic detail.

In 1977 Groth, Burgess, and Holmstrom published *Rape: Power, Anger, and Sexuality* in which they provide an expanded typology from that proposed later by Groth (1979) in *Men Who Rape*. This typology included two power types and two anger types, the latter of which was the anger-excitation rapist (p. 1242):

> *The* anger-excitation rapist *finds pleasure, thrills, and excitation in the suffering of his victim. He is sadistic and his aim is to punish, hurt, and torture his victim. His anger is eroticized.*
>
> …
>
> *Rape, then, rather than being an expression of sexual desire, in fact is the use of sexuality to express issues of power and anger. In every case of rape all three factors coexist but their relative intensities and interrelationships vary.*

In their study of the prevalence of each type of rapist, these authors found that of 133 offenders in the total sample, only 6% (N = 8) were sadists.

Historically, permutations of the DSM have included sadism in one form or another, and Sexual Sadism is the term used from DSM-III through to DSM-IV-TR. In the latest incarnation of the DSM (fifth edition; American Psychiatric Association, 2013), sadism is classified under Paraphilic Disorders as Sexual Sadism Disorder, 302.84. In this work, sadism has one of the lowest diagnostic thresholds, having only two diagnostic criteria, though the behavior needed to meet both criteria must occur in extremis. These criteria are that (p. 695):

1. Over a period of at least 6 months, recurrent and intense sexual arousal from the physical or psychological suffering of another person, as manifested by fantasies, urges, or behaviors.
2. The individual has acted on these sexual urges with a nonconsenting person, or the sexual urges or fantasies cause clinically significant distress or impairment in social, occupational, or other important area of functioning.

Earlier versions of the DSM required that the acts were real and not simulated, though this language was removed in the fifth edition. Consistent throughout all versions is the requirement that the physical and psychological suffering of the victim must be linked to the offender's sexual gratification. As with most disorders, the experience must occur for a period longer than 6 months to ensure that such urges or fantasies are not experimental, transient, or episodic. In most editions, the individual can be said to meet the diagnostic threshold should "the sexual fantasies or urges cause marked distress or interpersonal difficulty." This "nonexpressed" type (our term) is similar to the muted sadism type proposed as part of the Massachusetts Treatment Center: Revision 3 (MTC:R3) typology. In this typology, sadism falls under the "sexual" motivation and has two subtypes. The first (Type 4) is overt sadism, which fits more with the stereotypical sadistic offense, that is, the aggression is sexualized (Knight, Warren, Reboussin, & Soley, 1998; Knight, 1999). In the second (Type 5, muted sadistic) the binding of aggression and sexuality are only fantasized (Knight et al., 1998; Knight, 1999).

This typology, and specific parts thereof, are not without criticism, however. Specifically, it could be said that sadism is and always has been the pairing of sexual excitement or satisfaction through the pain and suffering of another. As such, it cannot be "muted" as this would involve mental elements only and would no more make someone a sadist than fantasizing about killing someone would make them a murderer. Gannon, Collie, Ward, and Thakker (2008) note that no actual evidence exists that supports the muted sadistic type, while the vindictive type appears more similar to the sadistic type than previously thought. As a result of these findings, Knight and Cerce (2001) recently revised the MTC:R3.

As an alternative diagnostic instrument to the DSM, the World Health Organization provides the *International Classification of Diseases* (ICD), now in its 10th edition. Unlike the DSM, the ICD covers physical ailments such as disease and parasitic infection, as well as those involving psychological dysfunction. In the ICD, sadism is listed under F60–F69 Disorders of Adult Personality and Behavior, Disorder of Sexual Preference, F65.5 Sadomasochism. As the name implies, this classification includes both sadism and masochism, while also acknowledging that both disorders can coexist (World Health Organization, 2016, p. 172):

F65.5 Sadomasochism

A preference for sexual activity which involves the infliction of pain or humiliation, or bondage. If the subject prefers to be the recipient of such stimulation this is called masochism; if the provider, sadism. Often an individual obtains sexual excitement from both sadistic and masochistic activities.

SADISTIC AGGRESSION

Sadistic behavior in the psychological sense and sadistic behavior in the criminal sense are two quite different entities. Psychopathologically, sadistic aggression or sadistic behavior is defined clearly in the DSM5 (American Psychiatric Association, 2013) and the ICD-10 (World Health Organization, 1992) as a paraphilia or atypical sexually arousing deviance as discussed before. In this way, sadism has been, psychologically speaking, placed firmly into the realm of the sexual; it is not about the enjoyment of inflicting pain on others but rather it is about the sexual pleasure derived from doing so. In this situation, a diagnosis or label requires only that a person receives sexual gratification from engaging in behavior that inflicts physical or psychological pain on another person—whether or not the other person is consenting.

In a forensic sense however, this is not the case. Sadistic aggression refers to the process of inflicting physical pain on another person, or by restricting the freedom of another person, for one's own pleasure (not necessarily sexual) in the absence of consent. In general terms, the courts are not interested in what two consenting adults do in the privacy of their own home (there are exceptions if the activities progress toward the endangerment of life, a minor is involved, or the "consent" given by the receiving party is suspect due to their having a reduced cognitive capacity to do so either organically or as a result of ingestion of a substance, or through the use of coercion, intimidation, or fraud). Therefore, criminally speaking, sadistic aggression occurs when, for their own pleasure, one person restrains the liberty of or inflicts physical pain upon another individual who is an unwilling partner or on a partner for whom there are reasonable doubts as to their legal and/or functional capacity to provide an informed consent, whether or not the offender receives or is motivated by the potential to receive sexual gratification.

The crossover of psychopathological sadistic aggressor and criminally sadistic aggression then exists somewhere within a very wide and significantly gray line. As forensic psychopathology must, by definition, include the existent quality of a criminal act, forensically psychopathological sadistic aggression must therefore contain the qualities ascribed it by law more rigidly than those ascribed to sadistic aggression under mental health diagnostic criteria. The essential element of criminal pathological sadistic aggression then is that an offender receives pleasure (which may or may not be sexual in nature) from inflicting physical pain or restraint (of freedom) on a nonconsenting individual (now a victim). The secondary component that must also be satisfied is the notion of the behavior being pathological in nature. That is, the condition must adhere to guidelines for classification as a mental disorder. That is to say, in general terms the symptoms being experienced must originate within the individual and not be a situational reaction, and they must be outside of the individual's physical or mental control (American Psychiatric Association, 2013).

Therefore, the first hurdle sadistic aggression must meet to be considered a pathological entity is the desire to victimize another person by inflicting physical pain, and the pleasure derived from engaging in such an act must be generated internally (a craving of sorts) and not be a reaction to a situational stimulus. For example, wanting to punch someone for crashing into the back of your car and then feeling really good about doing it afterward does not qualify you as a sadistic aggressor (no matter what the onlookers may yell at you). Secondly, the internally generated desire must be motivating to the point of compulsion such that the desire is uncontrollable. Again, really wanting to punch the other driver but instead taking a deep breath and driving away after exchanging details does not constitute an uncontrollable compulsive desire. The desire must be so strong as to become obsessive and almost painful to withhold from enacting.

The second general hurdle for our version of sadistic aggression is the question of how it fairs against the 4Ds of abnormality: deviance, distress, dysfunction, and danger (Table 2.2; Comer, 2005). To make a determination that our definition of sadistic aggression can meet the general criteria for a psychopathology and therefore

Table 2.2 Characteristics of Behavior and Motivations Associated With Acute Catathymic Crisis, Chronic Catathymic Crisis, Unplanned Compulsive Homicide, and Planned Compulsive Homicide, as Tabled by Sinnamon (2015, p. 226)

| Characteristic | Impulsive Homicidal Behavior | | Planned Homicidal Behavior | |
	ACC	UCH	CCC	PCH
Desires and motivations	No clear conscious desires, but motivated by intense feelings of inadequacy. May be derived from early life attachment issues and often extend to become sexually oriented	Strong (compulsive) desire to kill that present, usually for an extended period of years. Motivated by sexual fantasy involving sadistic violence	No clear conscious desires, but motivated by intense and pro-gressive emotion-fueled internal conflicts resulting in increased feelings of helplessness and inadequacy. May be derived from early life attachment issues and often extend to become sexually oriented. Has increasingly obses-sive thoughts about killing that are victim specific. Believes that killing the proposed victim is a solution to their problem (internal conflicts and emotional turmoil)	Strong (compulsive) desire to kill that becomes progressively stronger, usually for an extended period of years. Motivated by sexual fantasy involving elaborate (but not victim-specific) sadistic violence
Relationship with victim	Victim is most often a stranger or very casual acquaintance who inadvertently taps the underly-ing cognitive-emotional conflict triggering a catathymic response	Often known to the offender. The victim does not tap any internal conflict but rather becomes a victim because they have a vulnerability that provides the opportunity for the offender to murder	Victim is most often either an inti-mate partner or (relatively) recent former intimate partner, or a stranger with whom the offender has developed an obsession. The offender links the victim to their internal cognitive-emotional conflict through increasingly obsessional, irrational, and (often) delusional thought processes. The offender progresses to the belief that murdering the victim is the solution to their problem	Victim is most often a stranger, but may occasionally be an acquain-tance. It is extremely rare for the victim to be in, or have formerly been in, an intimate relationship with the offender for any extended period of time. However, given the highly sexualized construction of the fantasy and offense, some element of sexuality may be present in the manner in which the offender and victim become acquainted. For example, the offender may lure the victim through a sexual liaison (or the promise/possibility of one)

Continued

Table 2.2 Characteristics of Behavior and Motivations Associated With Acute Catathymic Crisis, Chronic Catathymic Crisis, Unplanned Compulsive Homicide, and Planned Compulsive Homicide, as Tabled by Sinnamon (2015, p. 226)—cont'd

Characteristic	Impulsive Homicidal Behavior		Planned Homicidal Behavior	
	ACC	**UCH**	**CCC**	**PCH**
Behavioral/visible indications of risk	No significantly obvious indicators. The offender is often introverted or withdrawn although they may sometimes make threats that they will be violent or "explode." These are usually ignored by those who witness them	Does not make overt threats, however, there are often a number of indicators in the background. These include sadistic sexual fantasy with a compulsion to act on them, outbursts of anger, disordered mood (e.g., depression and anxiety), environmental factors that increase personal stress levels (relationship breakdown, job loss, financial problems), pathological dishonesty, manipulative, animal cruelty, high levels of voyeurism and possibly fetish sm and sexually motivated burglary, previous DV or (if male) other physical acts against women, general attitude of misogyny, compulsive or ritualistic behaviors, early life adversity such as childhood abuse and childhood sexual abuse (often at the hands of a maternal figure).	Generally, the offender makes no threats or show obvious external indicators if intent however, the offender may confide in a friend or respected authority figure such as priest. Disclosures are often ignored or underestimated by those who are confided in	Offender will rarely, if ever, make threats or provide an overt warning of intent, however, as with UCH, there are myriad behavioral indicators in the background (see UCH "behavioral/visible indicators of risk" in this table). Cruelty to animals may extend to using animals as "practice" for the "real event." Indicators may therefore include a succession of pets that meet with untimely "accidents" or "illnesses" and a string of missing pets within an extended neighborhood area near the offender (although killers who fit into this group are often very good at planning and therefore may take precautions to ensure they abduct or obtain animals in locations appropriately distant to their own neighborhood)

Sexual behavior at time/scene of the crime	Necrophilia and/or body mutilation is relatively common—offender may dismember the victim postmortem	Offender may sexually assault the victim during the attack or postmortem either personally penetrating the victim or by inserting various objects into the victim	Overtly sexual behaviors while committing the offense are rare	Sexual behaviors are a hallmark of this form of homicide and are therefore commonly associated with the offense. Behaviors may include those similar to UCH, however, they are likely to include more ritualistic or symbolic characteristics. Remember, this is usually a planned-in-detail fulfillment of a long-term sexually sadistic fantasy
Postcrime behavior	Does not generally attempt to escape from the police. Will often turn themselves in to police or confide in a friend or trusted authority figure who will assist them to do so	Makes a concerted effort to escape the police, however, the unplanned and disorganized nature of the offender and the crime usually mean they are unsuccessful and are apprehended relatively quickly	Generally, makes no attempt to escape the police. Will often attempt suicide in concert with (murder-suicide is often a distinguishing feature of intimate spouse homicide events), or in the immediate aftermath of the offense (offender will be found dead in their home or other favorite location, or will suicide while in prison)	Offender plans well and works hard to avoid personal detection. Careful planning often results in successful evasion of authorities resulting in repeat offending and multiple victims. Offender is often caught through serendipity rather than meticulous police work

Note (Schlesinger, 2004), provides a good additional source of information in this area.

qualify as a forensic psychopathology, it must be evaluated for its extant levels of deviance, distress, dysfunction, and danger.

Certainly, the notion of receiving pleasure from inflicting physical pain on another is antagonistic to the prevailing broad cultural social norms of the vast majority of the known world and is therefore deviant. There is some argument that activities such as sadism, while certainly deviant to the wider cultural norms, is in fact an accepted normalcy for the subculture in which it thrives and therefore should not be summarily categorized as it is. There is certainly some sympathy for this position in the context of sadism as a sexual paraphilia within the confines of general psychopathology. If indeed we were exploring sadism in the pure context of psychopathology, then we could distinguish between sadism perpetrated upon a consensual partner (a masochist) versus that perpetrated on an unwilling partner who, by the defining elements of sadistic behavior, can be readily characterized as a victim. However, here in the context of forensic psychopathology, we are limited to considering the deviance inherent in the act of receiving pleasure from inflicting pain on a victim and not on a willing confederate. In that context, there is little doubt as to the significantly deviant nature of the behavior and its underlying psychological machinations.

The second of the 4Ds is distress. In most cases, the extent to which the offender is distressed by their sadistic desires and behaviors appears limited. In this element of the test then sadistic aggression fails the psychopathology test. However, the extent to which the offender's behavior produces distress in their victims and the broader community is significant, and this distress is also an element of the evaluation process. We can therefore surmise that forensically defined sadistic aggression can and does certainly produce significant distress to those impacted by its behavioral manifestation. It is an aspect of a significant number of forensic psychopathologies that offenders are less distressed by the behavioral characteristics of their pathology than are their victims and others around them in general. Certainly, psychopathy, antisocial personality disorder, and planned compulsive homicide, to name a few, are all examples of psychopathologies with the potential for significant forensic implications in which the individuals with the pathology appear far less distressed about their characteristics than do those with whom they interact.

The third of the 4Ds is dysfunction and refers to the extent to which the syndrome results in dysfunction in one or more important areas of the offender's life. Sadistic aggression has the potential to create significant dysfunction, particularly within the social sphere of an offender's life. In the context of sexually sadistic aggression, the sadistic behavior often becomes an overwhelming element of sexual gratification for the sufferer. This need for sadistic engagement for sexual fulfillment represents a high degree of sexual dysfunction in the context of our forensic definition as any sadistic behavior must be nonconsensual. In the more general forensic definition of sadistic aggression, the offender may engage in other compulsive acts of sadistic aggression to obtain pleasurable feedback such as assault and battery. In this context an individual may be a regular antagonist in local pubs and bars, or they may actively prowl the streets looking for unwitting (and unwilling) victims. This again represents a high degree of social dysfunction and, as such, illustrates that sadistic aggression certainly has the potential to produce extensive dysfunction.

The final element of the 4Ds is danger and refers to the extent to which the condition represents an active danger to the sufferer/offender and/or others. Given the very nature of the act of sadistic aggression in the forensically defined context, there is a clear danger of significant harm to others as a result of the offender's behaviors. Therefore, forensically defined sadistic aggression meets the danger to self or others test of psychopathology. Given the assessment performed previously, it is clear that sadistic aggression, as it is defined by criminal law, has the capacity to also meet the criteria to establish it as a pathological entity.

The reader should note that this process has not only been an exercise to assess sadistic aggression but it has provided us an opportunity to undertake a practical evaluation of a criminally defined act in respect to its pathological identity. This form of assessment can be undertaken on any number of specific behaviors, symptoms, characteristics, or criminally defined behavioral conditions. While not always of use in and of itself, unless for some academic perspective, it is useful as a means of linking criminal elements and psychopathological characteristics when analyzing crimes, criminals, and predictive models. This is particularly true when there is no directly corresponding pathological entity under the constraints of either the DSM or ICD.

The psychopathological form of sadistic aggression does not correlate with psychopathy but is more akin to a social deviance. It has been argued that sadistic aggression as a paraphilia in which engagement is consensual should not be considered a mental illness at all (Laws & O'Donohue, 2008). However, forensically defined sadistic aggression has several correlates with the psychopathic personality. The diagnostic criteria for antisocial personality disorder (ASPD) in the DSM-5 (American Psychiatric Association, 2013) are shown in Table 2.3 with primary correlates of criminally defined sadistic aggression shaded. Other elements of ASPD may correlate depending on individual circumstances.

Crime statistics show that the majority of sadistic crimes are not overtly sexual in nature and so perhaps there is an argument for the establishment of two distinct groups of criminally sadistic aggression—sexually sadistic crime and nonsexually sadistic crime—the common thread being that both groups are sadistic aggression that is not consensual. From the criteria set out in Table 2.3, it is clear that individuals who engage in criminal sadistic aggression have several elements of psychopathy. Therefore any crime analysis could possibly view a criminally sadistic act—whether sexual or nonsexual—as a behavioral manifestation of psychopathy.

At this juncture it is also necessary to consider instances in which behavior may appear to be sadistic in nature but may fulfill wholly functional purposes. As discussed earlier, sadism may be overidentified because the link between the infliction of pain and associated sexual arousal may be overstated, oversimplified, or misidentified, and there is certainly a casual adoption of the term where it may be used to describe any punishing act (of the self or others). As also discussed earlier, the identification of actual sadism requires both a mental element and a behavioral expression.

Table 2.3 General List of Diagnostic Criteria for ASPD Based on the Diagnostic Criteria Established in the DSM-5 (American Psychiatric Association, 2013)

General Diagnostic Criteria for Antisocial Personality Disorder

The essential features of a personality disorder are impairments in personality (self and interpersonal) functioning and the presence of pathological personality traits. To diagnose antisocial personality disorder, the following criteria must be met:

1. Significant impairments in **personality functioning** manifest by:
   a. Impairments in **self-functioning** (a or b):
      i. **Identity:** Egocentrism; self-esteem derived from personal gain, power, or pleasure.
      ii. **Self-direction:** Goal setting based on personal gratification; absence of prosocial internal standards associated with failure to conform to lawful or culturally normative ethical behavior.

AND

   b. Impairments in **interpersonal functioning** (a or b):
      i. **Empathy:** Lack of concern for feelings, needs, or suffering of others; lack of remorse after hurting or mistreating another.
      ii. **Intimacy:** Incapacity for mutually intimate relationships, as exploitation is a primary means of relating to others, including by deceit and coercion; use of dominance or intimidation to control others.

2. Pathological **personality traits** in the following domains:
   a. **Antagonism**, characterized by:
      i. **Manipulativeness:** Frequent use of subterfuge to influence or control others; use of seduction, charm, glibness, or ingratiation to achieve one's ends.
      ii. **Deceitfulness:** Dishonesty and fraudulence; misrepresentation of self; embellishment or fabrication when relating events.
      iii. **Callousness:** Lack of concern for feelings or problems of others; lack of guilt or remorse about the negative or harmful effects of one's actions on others; aggression; sadism.
      iv. **Hostility:** Persistent or frequent angry feelings; anger or irritability in response to minor slights and insults; mean, nasty, or vengeful behavior.
   b. Disinhibition, characterized by:
      i. **Irresponsibility:** Disregard for—and failure to honor—financial and other obligations or commitments; lack of respect for—and lack of follow through on—agreements and promises.
      ii. **Impulsivity:** Acting on the spur of the moment in response to immediate stimuli; acting on a momentary basis without a plan or consideration of outcomes; difficulty establishing and following plans.
      iii. **Risk taking:** Engagement in dangerous, risky, and potentially self-damaging activities, unnecessarily and without regard for consequences; boredom proneness and thoughtless initiation of activities to counter boredom; lack of concern for one's limitations and denial of the reality of personal danger.

1. The impairments in personality functioning and the individual's personality trait expression are relatively stable across time and consistent across situations.
2. The impairments in personality functioning and the individual's personality trait expression are not better understood as normative for the individual's developmental stage or sociocultural environment.
3. The impairments in personality functioning and the individual's personality trait expression are not solely due to the direct physiological effects of a substance (e.g., a drug of abuse, medication) or a general medical condition (e.g., severe head trauma).
4. The individual is at least age 18 years.

American Psychiatric Association. (2013). Diagnostic and statistical manual of mental disorders (5th ed.). Arlington, VA: American Psychiatric Publishing.

When analyzing any situation in which there are extremes of behavior, such as torture or mutilation, we must ensure that we are using the appropriate thresholds for inclusion and exclusion so that we are not inappropriately identifying sadism, as the index behavior may indeed be something entirely different. At the very least, such a call requires considerable conservatism; if we do not have *both* the physical and psychological suffering and evidence of sexual arousal, then the assessment of sadism must be put on hold until such a time as that evidence presents. Put another way, torture is clearly evident in sexual sadism (Hickey, 2005) but it may also exist outside of this diagnostic construct.

Numerous media examples exist depicting the existence of torture without the concomitant sexual arousal. These include cases where the victim is tortured for their money or the location of valuables (first example, Achong (2011)), or cases where the victim is tortured for their PIN number (second example, please note that we are treating the following reports at face value so as to not reduce the argument to the accuracy of media accounts):

A Central businessman has become the nation's second murder victim since the end of the state of emergency last Monday. Joshua Henry, 72, of Paria Avenue, Lange Park, Chaguanas, was killed during a robbery at his home on Saturday afternoon. Police said Henry was beaten to death by three unmasked bandits who stormed his home in search of cash and valuables. His killing has raised the murder toll for the year to 312. According to police reports, at around 5.30 pm, Henry, who operated a car rental company at his home, was summoned to his front gate by three men. Police said the men then ordered Henry into the house where they tied him up, using a bedspread and other pieces of fabric.

Four of Henry's relatives who were also at home were taken into separate bedrooms where they were bound and gagged. After some time, Henry's daughter Coleen, managed to free herself, after which she freed her relatives. Police said Henry's lifeless body was discovered by his relatives in a room at the lower level of the house. Investigators said Henry was bound to a chair and bore marks of violence to the face and upper body. Police said that Henry was also found with a sheet tied tightly around his neck and might have been strangled by the men. Paramedics who responded to the scene shortly after were unable to revive Henry. He was pronounced dead by a District Medical Officer (DMO) who visited the scene. His body was taken to the Forensic Sciences Centre, St James, where a post-mortem is expected to be conducted later today.

Investigators said they believed that Henry might have been tortured by the men to reveal the location of cash and valuables. Relatives told investigators that a television, two computers, cellphones, cash and jewelry were missing from the house. Police said they believed that the men fled the scene in a waiting vehicle. On Friday, the body of Lenny Slinger, 58, of Sahadeen Trace, Vega de Oropouche, was found in a gravel pit in Sangre Grande. Police said they believed Slinger, who was employed as a watchman, died after being hit on the head with a blunt object at a quarry site on Gordon Trace, Turure, Sangre Grande. The scene was visited by Snr Supt Edward Castillo, Supt Johnny Abraham, Inspector Wayne

Lawrence and officers of the Chaguanas CID and Task Force. Abraham is continuing investigations.

In the following example, a man was tortured for his PIN number (CBS46, 2013):

Gwinnett County Police said that a man was walking from his car after coming home from work early Wednesday morning, when two men approached him and held him up at gun point. And the night didn't end there.

Police said the men made that victim get back in his car and drive them on I-85 toward Atlanta, eventually making him pull over and get in the back seat, where authorities say the men pistol-whipped him and burned him with a cigarette lighter until he gave them his PIN number.

Police have a picture of one of the men, believed to be shown driving the victim's car, withdrawing money from a Wells Fargo ATM on Cheshire Bridge Road.

Police said the men eventually left that man in his car at an Atlanta apartment complex and fled, after keeping him captive for five hours.

Police also said the victim's brother got a phone call from the men demanding a ransom for his brother's return.

The victim was visibly injured, police said, but did not want to go to the hospital.

It should be obvious then that, while this report has features of sadistic behavior, that torture and like acts may occur for reasons that have nothing to do with sexual satisfaction. The important thing to consider is the context, not only the content.

CONCLUSIONS

Catathymia and compulsive homicide can be both unplanned or planned, however, they each represent a unique homicide category and have similarly unique offender profiles. Sadistic aggression may coexist as motivation or partial motivation within either chronic catathymia or compulsive homicidal offending, or be a unique act in itself. For any act of violence to be considered sadistic, the offender's motivation must be a powerful, internally derived desire to seek pleasure from inflicting pain on another. Ultimately, catathymia, compulsive homicide, and sadistic aggression all represent seriously deviant behaviors that are complex, difficult to understand and predict, and therefore, extremely challenging to prevent.

SUMMARY

- The motivation and psychological characteristics that underpin the behaviors resulting in homicide can differ substantially. Some behaviors may be associated with episodic psychopathology that skews thinking and emotion and therefore drives homicidal behaviors via psychotic delusion, obsession, and paranoia, or through reduced capacity for self-awareness, reflection, impulse control, risk assessment, or social cognition. Others may be a result of more pervasive features that produce narcissistic, antisocial, and other personality characteristics that mediate motivation and behavior. Catathymic crisis, compulsive homicide, and sadism are three areas in which these pathological and personality mediators result in both impulsive as well as premeditated murder.

- According to (Sinnamon, 2015, p. 219), a catathymic crisis is "an unexpected, impulsive, and explosive violent outburst that is not readily understandable from the situation in which it occurred but rather is only able to be understood in the context of individual unconscious (or outside of conscious awareness) motivations."
- In contemporary circles, catathymia is used to describe any explosive or impulsively violent behavior that appears to have its roots in heightened emotionality and that is charged by irrational thought processes or beliefs.
- Sinnamon (2015) has previously used three subcategories to describe the variation in catathymic expression that may occur: delusional catathymic process (DCP), chronic catathymic crisis (CCC), and acute catathymic crisis (ACC).
- DCP results when the highly emotion-charged content of underlying cognitions, beliefs, and ideas transform the character of the emergent flow of thoughts in a way that results in irrational wishes, desires, fears, and ambivalent striving. Through this process the prospective offender develops a delusional belief that they must commit a specific violent act against another person or against themselves in order to achieve or resolve the situation to its conclusion. This idea manifests in the mind as a definite plan with an accompanying strong motivation to see it through, however, the plan may be resisted at some level within the individual's mind and therefore meet with behavioral hesitation or delay. The violent act may have some symbolic significance over and above its obvious meaning, and they may have a somewhat delusional character in its rigidity and inaccessibility to logical reasoning.
- While Wertham (1978) suggested that there are five stages within DCP, Sinnamon (2015), has extended this to include a sixth stage. These six stages are: (1) The initial disordered thinking; (2) Development of a plan and increased emotional turmoil; (3) Heightened emotional turmoil resulting in the committal of the violent act; (4) A sense of superficial calm and normality; (5) (Re)establishment of an inner calm; and (6) a sixth stage occurs in which the individual comes full circle and the same psychological and emotional turmoil that they could not resolve previously once again begins to emerge. This is then followed by the reexperiencing of the first five stages above.
- Chronic catathymic crisis is essentially the same as DCP with the primary difference being a structural differentiation of the stages. In CCC, Revitch and Schlesinger (1978), have reduced Wertham's (1978) five stages down to just three: (1) The incubation period; (2) The committal of violence; and (3) The achievement of relief.

- In contrast to the progressive buildup to violence that occurs in DCP and CCC, acute catathymic crisis takes place as a sudden outburst that is triggered by an often pedestrian interaction with an individual who is either a casual acquaintance or a stranger that the perpetrator has just met. In ACC the offender is triggered into a violent reaction as a result of some action or perceived action by the victim.
- The ACC taps deep levels of emotional tension and is generally triggered by the stimulation of an overwhelming emotion that is attached to an underlying psychological conflict. The offender may sometimes be able to provide an explanation for their behavior and a detailed account of what transpired, however, it is more often the case that they have no or only partial recollection of the violent act itself.
- Sinnamon (2015, p. 223) has characterized the similarities between CCC and ACC in the following manner: (1) With a few exceptions, cases primarily involve men killing women; (2) The victim is generally symbolic or representative of the deeper-seated conflicts. The victim is not the "real" issue; (3) The victim's behavior (or perceived or imagined behavior) triggers the highly volatile existing emotion-laden internal conflict(s); (4) Internal conflicts are generally egocentric in that they are focused on thoughts and emotions around real or imagined personal inadequacies. These are often relational in nature (often stemming from early life–generated attachment issues) and in adult circumstances tend to extend to the sexual arena; (5) The homicidal act works to redact the internal turmoil and emotional tension; (6) In the immediate posthomicide period, the offender will generally experience a time of psychological balance or homeostasis; (7) The offender does not generally try to avoid capture for very long. They will often give themselves up to police or tell a friend or trusted authority such as a priest; (8) Mental health professionals are generally very poor at recognizing the risk that is inherent in the offender's conflict's emotionality during the prehomicide incubation period; and (9) Investigation and crime analysis may miss the sexually derived offender motivations due to them often being relatively obscure.
- Compulsive homicide differs from catathymic homicide in that the event is not an attempt to resolve some internal cognitive-emotional conflict but is a manifestation of a long-standing deep-seated compulsion to kill.
- Like ACC, unplanned compulsive homicide (UCH) is a behavioral outcome resulting from disordered internal thought processes and motivations. However, unlike ACC offenders whose emotionality is charged by internal conflict (the combination of which result in the motivational trigger for violent behavior), offenders in cases of UCH have no such internal "conflict" driving their emotion and motivation.
- UCH offenders have an internal desire to kill, often associated with a fusion of violence and sexual arousal, which they may use within the confines of fantasy for a number of years before finally acting on their desires. UCH is generally a crime of opportunity and, therefore, the ultimate enactment of their homicidal desires is often due to a confluence of opportunity and some situation that reduces self-control sufficiently to allow the impulsive explosion of violence to ensue.
- Just like CCC, planned compulsive homicidal (PCH) behavior is the culmination of an extended period of obsessive rumination involving the killing of another person. This is, however, where the similarities stop.

- PCH involves an intense desire or compulsion to kill in order to emulate a sexually sadistic fantasy construction. The killing of another person is not motivated by a belief that it is a means of resolving a problem (internal conflict) but rather the act of killing, usually in some ritualistic manner, is the motivation in itself. In this way PCH is a (usually) sexually motivated compulsive homicidal act perpetrated because of a deep inner desire to kill and not because the murder will achieve any purpose (whether logical, irrational, or delusional).
- Offenders who commit PCH may be classically psychopathic and often show severe traits of personality disorders, particularly narcissistic and antisocial. Rare females who commit PCH may also present with borderline, paranoid, or histrionic personality traits.
- Sadism is believed to be a psychosexual disorder where the individual has a preferred or exclusive sexual gratification that is deviant.
- While there are both explicit and implied links between sadism and catathymia, it is possible that sadistic behavior may be incorrectly identified in a catathymic event. This is possible because the violent and explosive emotional purge that will characterize catathymia may indeed appear to be an act of sadism simply because of the level of violence involved. This may also occur because of the coupling of observations in a chronic catathymic crisis such as evidence of sexual behavior that preceded the violent incident.
- Sadism and psychopathology have been known to be comorbid. However, we must be cautious in interpreting or inferring the degree to which these two disorders are, or will be, comorbid. One can be a psychopath without being a sadist, and thus the opposite must also be possible.
- Sadism is essentially the pairing of sexual excitement or satisfaction through the pain and suffering of another. As such, it cannot be "muted" as this would involve only mental elements and would no more make someone a sadist than fantasizing about killing someone would make them a murderer.
- Sadistic behavior in the psychological sense and sadistic behavior in the criminal sense are two quite different entities.
- Psychopathologically, sadistic aggression or sadistic behavior is defined clearly in the DSM5 (American Psychiatric Association, 2013) and the ICD-10 (World Health Organization, 1992) as a paraphilia or atypical sexually arousing deviance. In this way, sadism has been, psychologically speaking, placed firmly into the realm of the sexual; it is not about the enjoyment of inflicting pain on others, but rather it is about the sexual pleasure derived from doing so. In this situation, a diagnosis or label requires only that a person receives sexual gratification from engaging in behavior that inflicts physical or psychological pain on another person—whether or not the other person is consenting.
- In a forensic sense, however, this is not the case. Sadistic aggression, in the legal sense, refers to the process of inflicting physical pain on another person, or by restricting the freedom of another person, for one's own pleasure (not necessarily sexual) in the absence of consent. In general terms, the courts are not interested in what two consenting adults do in the privacy of their own home (there are exceptions if the activities progress toward the endangerment of life,

a minor is involved, or the "consent" given by the receiving party is suspect due to their having a reduced cognitive capacity to do so either organically or as a result of ingestion of a substance, or through the use of coercion, intimidation, or fraud). Therefore, criminally speaking, sadistic aggression occurs when, for their own pleasure, one person restrains the liberty or inflicts physical pain upon another individual who is an unwilling partner or on a partner for whom there are reasonable doubts as to their legal and/or functional capacity to provide an informed consent, whether or not the offender receives or is motivated by the potential to receive sexual gratification.

- The first hurdle sadistic aggression must meet to be considered a pathological entity is that the desire to victimize another person by inflicting physical pain, and the pleasure derived from engaging in such an act, must be generated internally (a craving of sorts) and not be a reaction to a situational stimulus. Secondly, the internally generated desire must be motivating to the point of compulsion such that the desire is uncontrollable.
- When analyzing any situation in which there are extremes of behavior, such as torture or mutilation, we must ensure that we are using the appropriate thresholds for inclusion and exclusion so that we are not inappropriately identifying sadism, as the index behavior may indeed be something entirely different. At the very least, such a call requires considerable conservatism: if we do not have *both* the physical and psychological suffering and evidence of sexual arousal, then the assessment of sadism must be put on hold until such a time as that evidence presents.
- Ultimately, catathymia, compulsive homicide, and sadistic aggression all represent seriously deviant behaviors that are complex, difficult to understand and predict, and, therefore, extremely challenging to prevent.

QUESTIONS

1. Briefly define catathymia.
2. What are the different types of catathymia?
3. It is possible for someone experiencing a catathymic crisis to not remember the violence that ensues. True or false?
4. A person who doesn't experience sexual satisfaction from the pain and suffering of another can still be classified as a sadist. True or false?
5. According to the authors, a catathymic act could be misinterpreted as sadistic. True or false?
6. Describe the six stages of the delusional catathymic process set out in the chapter and posited by Wertham (original five stages; 1978), and extended by Sinnamon (2015) to include a sixth stage.
7. Revitch and Schlesinger (1989), present a three-stage model of chronic catathymia. Describe these three stages and their characteristics.
8. Chronic and acute catathymia have a number of similarities. Describe the nine similarities as they have been outlined by Sinnamon (2015).

9. What are the key defining characteristics of catathymia, compulsive homicide, and sadistic aggression that help to differentiate each from the others?
10. If you were to attend a homicide crime scene, explain what factors (evidence) might present at the scene that could assist you to establish whether the offense was an impulsive or planned homicide.

REFERENCES

American Psychiatric Association. (2000). *Diagnostic and statistical manual of mental disorders* (4th ed., text revised). Arlington, VA: American Psychiatric Publishing.

American Psychiatric Association. (2013). *Diagnostic and statistical manual of mental disorders* (5th ed.). Arlington, VA: American Psychiatric Publishing.

Achong, D. (December 12, 2011). Robbers hit Lange Park home. *The Guardian*. Available from http://www.guardian.co.tt/news/2011/12/11/businessman-72-tortured-and-killed.

Aggrawal, A. (2009). Sexual sadism. In A. Aggrawal (Ed.), *Forensic and medico-legal aspects of sexual crimes and unusual sexual practices*. Boca Raton: CRC Press.

CBS46. (2013). *Police search for men who kidnapped, tortured man for PIN number*. Available from http://www.cbs46.com/story/23409368/police-search-for-men-who-kidnapped-tortured-man-for-pin-number#ixzz494JK1CqR.

Chuang, J. (2011). A possible mechanism of sadism. *Medical Hypotheses, 76*, 32–33.

Cleckley, H. M. (1941). *The mask of sanity: an attempt to clarify some issues about the so-called psychopathic personality*. St. Louis: C. V. Mosby Co.

Comer, R. (2005). *Fundamentals of abnormal psychology* (4th ed.). New York: Worth.

de Sade, D. A. (1795). *Philosophy in the bedroom. Electronic Edition*.

de Sade, D. A. F. (1965). *Justine: Philosophy in the bedroom and other writings*. London: Arrow Books.

Fedoroff, J. P. (2008). Sadism, sadomasochism, sex, and violence. *The Canadian Journal of Psychiatry, 53*, 637–646.

Frances, A., & Wollert, R. (2012). Sexual sadism: avoiding its misuse in sexually violent predator evaluations. *The Journal of the American Academy of Psychiatry and the Law, 40*(3), 409–416.

Gannon, T. A., Collie, R. M., Ward, T., & Thakker, J. (2008). Rape: psychopathology, theory, and treatment. *Clinical Psychology Review, 28*, 982–1008.

Geberth, V. J. (2006). *Practical homicide investigation: tactics, procedures, and forensic techniques* (4th ed.). Boca Raton: CRC Press.

Groth, A. N. (1979). *Men who rape: The psychology of the offender*. New York: Plenum Press.

Groth, N., Burgess, A. W., & Holmstrom, L. L. (1977). Rape: power, anger, and sexuality. *The American Journal of Psychiatry, 134*(11), 1239–1243.

Hickey, E. (2005). *Sex crimes and paraphilia*. New Jersey: Prentice Hall.

Knight, R. A. (1999). Validation of a typology for rapists. *Journal of Interpersonal Violence, 14*(3), 303–330.

Knight, R. A., & Cerce, D. D. (2001). *Validation and revision of the multidimensional assessment of sex and aggression*. National Criminal Justice Reference Service Award Number 94-IJ-CX-0049.

Knight, R. A., Warren, J. I., Reboussin, R., & Soley, B. J. (1998). Predicting rapist type from crime-scene variables. *Criminal Justice and Behaviour, 25*(1), 46–80.

Krafft-Ebing, R. (1965). *Psychopathia sexualis: a medico-forensic study*. New York: G. Putnam and Sons.

Laws, D. R., & O'Donohue, W. T. (2008). Introduction. In D. R. Laws, & W. T. O'Donohue (Eds.), *Sexual deviance: theory, assessment, and treatment* (2nd ed.) (pp. 1–20). New York: Guilford Press.

Leyton, E. (1986). *Hunting humans:The rise of the modern multiple murderer*. Toronto: McClelland and Stewart.

Maier, H. W. (1912). Katathyme Wahnbildung und Paranoia [Catathymic delusions and paranoia]. *Zeitschrift fur die gesamte Neurologie und Psychiatrie, 5,* 545.

Marshall, W. L., & Hucker, S. J. (2006). Issues in the diagnosis of sexual sadism. *Sexual Offender Treatment, 1*(2).

Marshall, W. L., & Kennedy, P. (2003). Sexual sadism in sexual offenders: an elusive diagnosis. *Aggression and Violent Behaviour, 8,* 1–22.

Marshall, W. L., Kennedy, P., Yates, P., & Serran, G. (2002). Diagnosing sexual sadism in sexual offenders: reliability across diagnosticians. *International Journal of Offender Therapy and Comparative Criminology, 46*(6), 668–677.

Myers, W. C., Burket, R. C., & Hustead, D. S. (2006). Sadistic personality disorder and comorbid mental illness in adolescent psychiatric inpatients. *The Journal of the American Academy of Psychiatry and Law, 34*(1), 61–71.

Revitch, E., & Schlesinger, L. B. (1978). Murder: evaluation, classification, and prediction. In I. L. Kutash, S. B. Kutash, & L. B. Schlesinger (Eds.), *Violence: Perspectives on murder and aggression* (pp. 138–164). San Francisco: Jossey-Bass.

Revitch, E., & Schlesinger, L. B. (1989). *Sex murder and sex aggression*. Springfield, Il: Charles C Thomas.

Rizzolatti, G., & Craighero, L. (2004). The mirror neuron system. *Annual Review of Neuroscience, 27*(1), 169–192, http://dx.doi.org/10.1146/annurev.neuro.27.070203.144320.

Rockelein, J. E. (2006). *Elseviers dictionary of psychological theories*. Amsterdam: Elsevier Science.

Schlesinger, L. B. (2000). Serial homicide: sadism, fantasy, and a compulsion to kill. In L. B. Schlesinger (Ed.), *Serial offenders: Current thought, recent findings*. Boca Raton: CRC Press.

Schlesinger, L. B. (2004). *Sexual murder: Catathymic and compulsive homicides*. Boca Raton, Fl: CRC Press.

Schlesinger, L. B. (2007). The Catathymic process: psychopathology and psychodynamics of extreme interpersonal violence. In L. B. Schlesinger (Ed.), *Explorations in criminal psychopathology: Clinical syndromes with forensic implications, second edition*. Springfield, Il: Charles C Thomas Publisher Ltd.

Sinnamon, G. (2015). Psychopathology and criminal behaviour. In W. Petherick (Ed.), *Applied crime analysis: A social science approach to understanding crime, criminals, and victims*. Boston: Anderson Publishing.

Wertham, F. (1937). The catathymic crisis: a clinical entity. *Archives of Neurology and Psychiatry, 37*(4), 974–978. http://dx.doi.org/10.1001/archneurpsyc.1937.022601602740.

Wertham, F. (1978). A catathymic crisis. In I. L. Kutash, S. B. Kutash, & L. B. Schlesinger (Eds.), *Violence: Perspectives on murder and aggression* (pp. 165–170). San Franscisco: Jossey-Bass.

World Health Organization. (1992). *International statistical classification of diseases and related health problems*. 10th Revision, version: 2010 (ICD-10) [online edition] Geneva: World Health Organization. Available at http://apps.who.int/classifications/icd10/browse/2010/en.

World Health Organization. (2016). *International classification of diseases*. Available from http://www.who.int/classifications/icd/en/.

Victimology and Predicting Victims of Personal Violence

3

Gaelle L.M. Brotto[1], Grant Sinnamon[1,2], Wayne Petherick[1]

[1]Bond University, Gold Coast, QLD, Australia; [2]Bela Menso Brain and Behaviour Centre,
Varsity Lakes, QLD, Australia

CHAPTER OUTLINE

The Psychology of Criminal and Antisocial Behavior. http://dx.doi.org/10.1016/B978-0-12-809287-3.00003-1

INTRODUCTION

Victim comes for the Latin word *victima* and historically referred to any living being (human or animal) that was to be slaughtered or used in sacrifice (Burgess & Regehr, 2010; Ferguson & Turvey, 2009; Royal Spanish Academy, 2008). From a contemporary point of view, a victim is someone who suffers from harm or loss. There are then two different standpoints when defining the term *victim*: general and penal. From a general point of view, the term includes all people who suffer harm or loss by accident, natural disasters, or war (Ferguson & Turvey, 2009). On the other hand, from a legal perspective, the definition includes any harm or loss attributable to the action of an individual, group, or organization that can affect a person (Petherick & Sinnamon, 2014). According to Jerin and Moriarty (1998, p. 1), a crime victim is "anyone who is injured or killed due to a violation of the criminal law." Thus anyone can suffer from one form of crime or another. Therefore, we are all potential victims. This chapter presents the historical antecedents of modern victimology, outlines the main concepts at the genesis of the field, and presents an evidence-based model of victim typologies associated with risk of becoming a victim of personal violence.

THE EMERGENCE OF VICTIMOLOGY AND ITS PIONEERS

According to Jerin and Moriarty (1998), there are three distinct historical eras in which there were distinct differences in the manner in which victims were treated: the Golden Age, the Dark Age, and the Age of the Reemergence of the Victim.

THE GOLDEN AGE

The Golden Age or "victim justice system" was a period of time, according to Shichor and Tibbetts (2002, p. 3) in which "the individual made the law, and he was the victim, the prosecutor, and the judge." The victims had to deal with the offenders because there were no authorities to enforce the law (Doerner & Lab, 2011; Ferguson & Turvey, 2009; Jerin & Moriarty, 1998). The victim was presumed to be innocent and passive (Shichor & Tibbetts, 2002). At this time, there was a basic social system of retribution and restitution that helped protect victims who had to generally fend for themselves (Doerner & Lab, 2011). According to Doerner and Lab (2011, p. 2) retribution meant that "the offender would suffer in proportion to the degree of harm caused by his or her actions," while restitution involved the offender making "payment in an amount sufficient to render the victim whole again." In the simplest terms, the principle of "an eye for an eye" epitomizes the character of the Golden Age (Doerner & Lab, 2011).

THE DARK AGE

The Golden Age of dealing with offenses persisted until the Middle Ages, and then drastic changes were observed (Jerin & Moriarty, 1998). In contrast to the Golden Age, the Dark Age has been described as a "criminal-oriented justice system," where offenses were not considered as being perpetrated against the victims or their relatives but against the law of the king or state (Ferguson & Turvey, 2009; Shichor & Tibbetts, 2002). As stated by Shichor and Tibbetts (2002, p. 9) the "focus shifted toward offender punishments and rights as opposed to victim rights and restoration." Reasons for such changes were the emergence of local governments, the acceleration and spread of urbanization, the industrial revolution, and the rise in power of the Roman Catholic Church (Ferguson & Turvey, 2009). The victim, who had an important role in the past, was, in the Dark Age, nothing more than a piece of evidence who was largely not considered in the decision process (Jerin & Moriarty, 1998). As explained by Doerner and Lab (2011, p. 3):

> The development of formal law enforcements, courts, and correctional systems in the past few centuries have reflected an interest in protecting the state. For the most part, the criminal justice system simply forgot about victims and their best interests. Instead, the focus shifted to protecting the rights of the accused.

REEMERGENCE OF THE VICTIM

The early part of the mid-20th century (1940s) saw the "rediscovery" of victims and victims' rights being initiated by an emerging scholarly interest in the victim–offender relationship (Petherick & Sinnamon, 2014). After being focused for so long on the criminal, people started to study the dyad of the victim–offender to better understand the role of the victim during the criminal act. The term *victimology* first appeared in the literature in 1949. Indeed, according to Karmen (2010, p. 32), it seemed obvious to many that "victims were forgotten figures in the criminal justice process whose best interests had been systematically overlooked, but merited attention," as those within the criminal justice system began to realize that the greatest impact of a criminal act was felt by those who were the direct victims of the offense. This increasing realization, combined with the emerging interest in the victim–offender relationship, led to the development of the field of victimology in which the role of the victim within the criminal act became the central focus (Ferguson & Turvey, 2009). While criminology is defined as the study of crime and criminals, victimology, a subdiscipline of criminology, focuses on the study of people harmed by criminals (Ferguson & Turvey, 2009). Ferguson and Turvey (2009, p. 2) explicitly defined victimology as "the scientific study of victims and victimization, including the relationships between victims and offender, investigators, courts, corrections, media and social movements." Victimology and some related fields of study have been expanded since the middle of the 20th century by the work of some scholars including individuals such as Hans von Hentig, Benjamin Mendelsohn, Stephen Schafer, and Marvin Wolfgang (Doerner & Lab, 2011; Ferguson & Turvey, 2009). In order to better understand the circumstances of victimization and the relationship between victim and offender, criminologists started to categorize victims according to types; it was the debut of victim typologies. Those early typologies are based on different factors: biological, psychological, sociological, demographic, and even psychiatric (Burgess & Roberts, 2010).

Key Figures
Hans von Hentig

One of the pioneers in the study of crime victims, German criminologist Hans von Hentig first studied the characteristics that may contribute to predispose a person to become a criminal (Jerin & Moriarty, 1998; Wilson, 2009). Later, based on his previous research he started to try to understand what predisposes some people to become victims of crime (Doerner & Lab, 2011; Ferguson & Turvey, 2009). Specifically, and as stated by Ferguson and Turvey (2009, p. 12), von Hentig believed "that some victims contributed to their own victimisation by virtue of many converging factors, not all of which were in their control." Crime occurs between two persons, a perpetrator and a victim who interact together. As specified by Wilson (2009, p. 308), "the criminal and the victim may come from two different worlds, but the perpetrator and the victim often bring equal weight to the mechanics of the crime." Similar to a criminal, a victim's behavior can be classified according to three factors: psychological, sociological, and biological (Wilson, 2009). This suggests that victims' characteristics can contribute to victimization, and that victims are born victims and not made victims. Von Hentig classified the victims of crime in a 13 categories typology where the victims were either fully responsible, completely innocent, or somewhere in the middle. Each category describes a characteristic that increases the vulnerability of someone to become a victim of crime (Table 3.1).

Table 3.1 Hans von Hentig's Victim Typology

Characteristics	Description
1. The young	Children and infants: physically weaker, less mental prowess, fewer legal rights, economically dependent on their caretakers.
2. The female	All women: physically weaker than men, culturally conditioned to accept men's authority, financially dependent, conditioned to believe that their value is associated with their bodies, therefore their sexuality.
3. The old	The elderly: many of the same vulnerabilities as children.
4. The mentally defective and deranged	The feeble-minded, the "insane," drug addicts, and alcoholics: have an altered perception of reality.
5. Immigrants	Foreigners unfamiliar with the culture: gaps in communication and comprehension.
6. Minorities	The racially disadvantaged: groups against which there is some amount of bias and prejudice.
7. Dull normals	The simple-minded persons: same type of exposure as the mentally defective and deranged.
8. The depressed	Persons with various psychological maladies: they can expose themselves to all manner of danger.
9. The acquisitive	The greedy, those looking for quick gains: may suspend their judgment or put themselves in dangerous situations in order to achieve their goals.
10. The wanton	The promiscuous persons: they engage themselves in indiscriminate sexual activity with different partners.
11. The lonesome or heartbroken	The widows, widowers, those in mourning: they are prone to substance abuse and become easy prey.
12. The tormentor	The abusive parents: they expose themselves to the harm they inflict, the resulting angst, and the degree to which their victims fight back.
13. The blocked, exempted, or fighting	Victims of blackmail, extortion, and confidence scams: they are exposed to continual financial loss or physical harm, or must suffer the consequences that come from bringing the police in to assist.

Adapted from Doerner, W. G., & Lab, S. P. (2011). Victimology, (6th ed.). Cincinnati, OH: Lexis Nexis/Anderson Publishing Company; Ferguson, C., & Turvey, B. E. (2009). Victimology: a brief history with an introduction to forensic victimology. In B. E. Turvey & W. A. Petherick (Eds.), Forensic victimology: examining violent crime, victims in investigative and legal contexts (pp. 13–14). San Diego, CA: Elsevier Science.

This typology operated on the assumption of "victim proneness" and posited that a normal person or nonvictim is characteristically a white, heterosexual male (Walklate, 2007). In a similar vein to Lombroso's assertions of the "born criminal," this assumption calls to mind the idea of a "born victim," an idea with little in the way of empirical merit.

Benjamin Mendelsohn

Another instigator on the study of crime victims is the French-Israeli attorney Benjamin Mendelsohn, who created the term *victimology*. He is, in the literature, considered to be the father of victimology (Doerner & Lab, 2011; Ferguson & Turvey, 2009; Wilson, 2009). While working on cases and interviews with victims and witnesses, Mendelsohn found that usually there were preexisting interpersonal relationships between the offenders and their victims and that some victims play a role in their own victimization (Jerin & Moriarty, 1998; Wilson, 2009). This was discussed under the term *victim precipitation* that is defined by Ferguson and Turvey (2009, p. 15) as a "crime caused or partially facilitated by the victim." In a similar way to von Hentig, in 1956, Mendelsohn developed a typology (see Table 3.2), which combines victims' levels of culpability and legal issues (Jerin & Moriarty, 1998). Nevertheless, Mendelsohn's typology is based on situational factors while von Hentig's was based on personal characteristics (Ferguson & Turvey, 2009).

Stephen Schafer

In 1968 Dr. Stephen Schafer, professor of sociology, published a significant book for the advance of victimology: *The Victim and His Criminal: A Study in Functional Responsibility* (Ferguson & Turvey, 2009). After interviewing criminals, he developed a typology, relatively close to the one proposed by Mendelsohn, based on the degree of responsibility of victims in crimes (Petherick & Sinnamon, 2014). Schafer's typology contained seven levels of victim responsibility and is described in Table 3.3.

Table 3.2 Mendelsohn's Victim Typology

Level of Culpability	Description
Completely innocent victim	No provocative or facilitative behaviors.
Victim with minor guilt	Inadvertently places him/herself in a compromising situation.
Victim as guilty as offender	Engages in vice crimes and is hurt; Includes victim of suicide.
Victim guiltier than offender	Provokes or instigates the causal act.
Most guilty victim	Starts off as the offender and in turn is hurt.
Imaginary victim	Pretends to be a victim.

Adapted from Doerner, W. G., & Lab, S. P. (2011). Victimology, p. 5. (6th ed.). Cincinnati, OH: Lexis Nexis/Anderson Publishing Company.

Table 3.3 Schafer's Victim Typology

Type	Victim Responsibility	Description
1. Unrelated victims	Entirely innocent	All unfortunate targets of offenders.
2. Provocative victims	Shares responsibility	All situations where the offender is reacting to some action or behavior of the victim.
3. Precipitative victims	Some degree of responsibility	People who place themselves in dangerous situations by the way they dress, where they go and at what time, and what they say for instance.
4. Biologically weak victims	Not responsible	Young, elderly, physically or mentally weak people who become easy targets for offenders.
5. Socially weak victims	Not responsible	The immigrants, minorities, or isolated who become easy targets for offenders.
6. Self-victimizing victims	Total responsibility	Prostitutes, drug users, gamblers, and other people who voluntarily interact with criminals.
7. Political victims	Not responsible	People who oppose those in power or people who are kept in subservient social positions.

Adapted from Doerner, W. G., & Lab, S. P. (2011). Victimology, p. 6. (6th ed.). Cincinnati, OH: Lexis Nexis/Anderson Publishing Company; Wilson, J. K. (2009). The Praeger handbook of victimology. Santa Barbara, CA: ABC-Clio.

Marvin E. Wolfgang and the Concept of Victim Precipitation

It was in 1967 that the term *victim precipitated* first appeared in Patterns in Criminal Homicide (Muftic, Bouffard, & Bouffard, 2007). Its author, Dr. Marvin E. Wolfgang, a professor of crime, legal studies, and law, is considered the first person who provided empirical support for his argument by analyzing homicide records in Philadelphia between 1948 and 1952 (Doerner & Lab, 2011; Pesta, 2011). In his study, he discovered that over 25% of all cleared homicides were victim precipitated, with males being more likely to precipitate homicide than females (Curtis, 1974; Doerner & Lab, 2011; Pesta, 2011). Wolfgang recognized that in each homicide there were at least two factors, the offender and the victim, and that they shared similarities as well as having their own unique points of difference (Pesta, 2011). Wolfgang suggested that "some victims precipitate criminal homicide by striking the first blow, brandishing a weapon, or initiating violence in some other way with the intention of settling a dispute" (Wilson, 2009, p. 27). Wolfgang asserts that often it is the victim behavior that precipitates the events, and therefore always seeing a victim as weak and passive and a perpetrator as brutal, aggressive, and overpowering is not necessarily accurate. Many crime victims "contribute to their own victimisation either by inciting or provoking the criminal or by creating or fostering a situation likely to lead to the commission of the crime" (Fattah, 2000, p. 23). The role of the victim can either be motivational such as by using attracting, arousing, or inducing behaviors, or functional by using provoking, facilitating, or even precipitating behaviors.

Inspired by Wolfgang's work, the concept of victim precipitation inspired many studies to emerge. Menachem Amir, Wolfgang's student, examined whether victim precipitation could be applied in rape cases. Similar to Wolfgang's work, Amir, in his book *Patterns in Forcible Rape* (1971), which is considered to be a controversial analysis of rape, gathered data from Philadelphia's police records between 1958 and 1960 (Doerner & Lab, 2011). He found that less than 20% of rape cases were victim precipitated (Curtis, 1974; Doerner & Lab, 2011). According to Wilson (2009, p. 15), and based on Amir's definition, an "act was victim precipitated when the victim actually agreed or was perceived by the offender to have agreed and did not protest strongly enough to change that perception." Some factors such as the consumption of alcohol, the seductive attitude of the victim, the fact that the victim was wearing revealing clothing, the use of inappropriate language, the victim's reputation, and being at the wrong place at the wrong time helped to precipitate the rape (Doerner & Lab, 2011; Pesta, 2011). Amir's work was, and still is, strongly criticized because it is considered to promote victim blaming. Indeed, Amir's study focused on the offender's interpretation of the victim's behavior rather than commentary from the victim or any form of attempted objective evaluation of the behavioral evidence (Fattah, 1980).

THE CONCEPTS OF VICTIM PRECIPITATION AND VICTIM BLAMING

VICTIM PRECIPITATION

As stated previously, it is through the concept of victim precipitation that the idea of a victim's role in his/her own victimization has been expanded. There are, according to Siegel (2010), two different levels in the provocative acts: active precipitation and passive precipitation. Passive precipitation occurs when victims "unknowingly threaten their attacker" by, for instance, dressing in a provocative way or accepting a promotion that can lead to a feeling of frustration or threat to the attacker's reputation (Siegel, 2010, p. 81). On the other hand, active precipitation is observed in a situation where it is the victim who initiates threatening behaviors and/or the actual use of physical force (Siegel, 2010). However, this later concept has been largely criticized because of the victim-blaming character of the approach (Eigenberg & Garland, 2008; Siegel, 2010; Timmer & Norman, 1984). For instance, according to Timmer and Norman (1984, p. 65):

> *Potential victims are seen as inviting or provoking the offender's behavior, thus sharing responsibility for the crime (p.63). […] Wherever victim precipitation is offered as an explanation, it serves to place responsibility on the victim, you cause, or help to cause, your own victimization; you deserve what you get.*

VICTIM BLAMING

We are not likely to blame the victim of a burglary, of a drunk driver, or of a mass shooting, however, we do often place some form of responsibility on the victims of other crimes such as domestic violence, stalking, or sexual assault. We will often make statements or ask questions of/about victims of these crimes such as "Why do victims stay in abusive relationships?" or "Why was she alone late that night wearing those provocative clothes?" or by making statements such as "Dressed like that she was just asking for it."

It is important to consider that "regardless of any situational or lifestyle choices that might increase risk, victims are not responsible for the acts of rapists" (Turvey, 2011, p. 213). This concept can be generalized to any crime victims. However, "blaming the victims of negative events for their own fate is a phenomenon that has found a substantial empirical niche in social psychology in the last four decades" (Pauwels, 2002, p. 1). There are two theories in the literature that help to explain victim blaming: defensive attribution theory (DAT) and the just world hypothesis (JWH).

DAT was posited by Shaver in 1970 and argues that when an individual is confronted with the seemingly whimsical victimization of another person, they become threatened by the realization that such random misfortunes could also happen to them. The forced acknowledgment of the potential for such an experience then results in a negative emotional response that initiates a cognitive coping strategy to meet the need for self-preservation, and a sense of security, predictability, and personal control. Shaver (1970) argues that the cognitive coping strategies include defensive attribution mechanisms that influence the perceptions of other people's misfortunes, such as victimization, in such a way that provides a predictive explanatory platform. The central tenet of DAT is that people can protect themselves against unfortunate and unpredictable occurrences by perceiving the event as avoidable. We tend to do this by making defensive attribution distortions of the victim's role in his or her own victimization, through increased attribution of responsibility to him or her. Therefore, in the DAT, blaming victims is a self-serving motivational bias created by the observer to cope with a distressing event. It protects the observer from the possibility of random misfortune by attributing personal responsibility to the victim of a criminal act.

The JWH is a form of DAT that was first introduced by Lerner in 1965. According to Lerner and Miller (1978, p. 1030), the JWT argues that:

Individuals have a need to believe that they live in a world where people generally get what they deserve. The belief that the world is just enables the individual to confront his physical and social environment as though they were stable and orderly. Without such a belief it would be difficult for the individual to commit himself to the pursuit of long-range goals or even to the socially regulated behavior of day-to-day life. Since the belief that the world is just serves such an important adaptive function for the individual, people are very reluctant to give up this belief, and they can be greatly troubled if they encounter evidence that suggests that the world is not really just or orderly after all.

Therefore, under a just world belief, there are two possible ways to be appeased that justice has been restored in the face of a criminal action. The first is to see that the victim is suitably compensated, and the second is to be convinced that the victim deserves to suffer.

VICTIM BLAMING IN HOMICIDE

The homicide literature is the first place in which the notion of victim blaming appears when Wolfgang (1958) introduced the term *victim-precipitated homicide*. According to Wolfgang (1958, p. 252):

> *The term victim-precipitated homicide is applied to those criminal homicides in which the victim is direct, positive precipitator in the crime. The role of the victim is characterized by his having been the first in the homicide drama to use physical violence directed against his subsequent slayer. The victim-precipitated cases are those in which the victim was the first to show and use a deadly weapon, to strike a blow in an altercation—in short, the first to commence the interplay or resort to physical violence.*

Victim precipitation is cited as a major contributing factor to homicide with between 25% and 50% of homicides being victim identified as possessing substantial elements of victim precipitation (Timmer & Norman, 1984). In this way, a victim-precipitated homicide, or indeed any crime, includes all offenses that would not occur without the precipitating actions or omission of the victim (Gobert, 1977).

VICTIM BLAMING IN SEXUAL ASSAULT

Rape myths are prominent in the literature. Plenty of myths about victims' culpability and theories have been developed to blame the victims. Common myths regarding victims of sexual assault include beliefs such as:

1. Men cannot be raped. This is a myth long held despite the evidence indicating that across developed countries men account for around 10% of victims (Patel, 2009). According to the myth, "a man should be able to fight back or escape the attacker, and is therefore more to blame if raped" (Strömwall, Alfredsson, & Landström, 2013, p. 208).
2. There is no rape if the victim did not resist (Patel, 2009; Turvey, 2011). According to Turvey (2011, p. 217):

> *Belief in this myth belies an utter ignorance of the common responses to rape that may be exhibited by the victim. Indeed, some victims may choose to fight back violently, even to the point of their own death. That is one end of the spectrum. Other victims may choose to simply acquiesce, whereas other may be incapable of any deliberate response. It all depends on the victim's individual personality, capability, and experiences.*

3. The victim has been in some way seductive or provocative (Turvey, 2011). Zur (1994, p. 7) states:

Women victims are too often blamed for being provocative, seductive, sugges-tive, for proposing, teasing, or just plain "asking for it" (Eg: Brownmiller, 1975; Keen, 1991; Russel, 1984). Men in this myth are seen as helplessly lusty, sexually frustrated beings, responding to sexually provocative women.

4. The victim could have prevented the attack if she wanted to (Turvey, 2011).

5. "Evidence of oral sex is a proof that the victim must have given consent" (Turvey, 2011, p. 213).

6. The "unrapeable" victims. They include, according to Turvey (2011), women or men who cannot be raped because of their lifestyle or because of their relation-ship with the accused. According to the myth (Turvey, 2011, p. 216):

Because of who they are or because of how they live, they have somehow given up the right to refuse sexual access to themselves—or they are somehow deserving of rape and therefore do not require the benefit of justice. These include prostitutes (and other sex industry workers), those who live or dress promiscuously, and the intimate partners of the accused, especially their wives.

These myths have been substantial contributors to the cultural tolerance of rape and the ongoing nature of apologetics that is regularly applied to perpetrators. This not only increases the potential for rape as elements of a society see these myths as a form of tacit approval for forced sexual engagement with another; it also impacts the victim's ability to receive appropriate levels of assistance, can increase the stigma and trauma associated with being raped, and significantly increase the risk of revic-timization. Patel (2009, p. 21) states that:

Beyond rape's direct effects on psychological and physical health, blaming a victim for the rape may further complicate several outcomes. Particularly, find-ings show that blaming a victim for the rape may adversely affect the victim's psychological response to the assault, over and above the immediate sequelae of the assault itself (Davis, Brickman, & Baker, 1991; Ullman, 1996). Victim blame has also been associated with negatively impacting a victim's self-reported rate of recovery following a rape (Ullman, 1996). Not surprisingly, victim blame has also been found to be predictive of whether or not victims blame themselves for their assaults (Wyatt, 1992). In some reports, such perceptions of blame have been considered secondary victimization particularly when victims receive nega-tive attributions of blame from social support groups or authorities (Frese, Moya, & Megias, 2004). In summary, victim blame can have a strong adverse impact on the victim.

The counterargument is simply that the rapist is responsible for rape and not the victim. According to Turvey (2011, p. 213), "regardless of any situational or lifestyle choices that might increase risk, victims are not responsible for the acts of rapists."

VICTIM BLAMING IN STALKING

Victims of stalking, particularly those of stalkers who were, at one time, an intimate partner, are routinely held responsible, judged, and not taken seriously (Weller, Hope, & Sheridan, 2013). For instance, according to research conducted by Pearce and Easteal (1999), Australian police officers are less likely to use the available stalking legislations in cases of stalking involving ex-partners. This is problematic because for instance in the United-States 59% (Weller et al., 2013) and in Australia 40% (Pearce & Easteal, 1999) of the victims are stalked by an intimate, or ex-intimate partner. Despite the fact that stalking behaviors by an offender that knows his/her victim are more common, more likely to involve violence and physical threat, and will persist over a longer duration of time, they are less likely to result in conviction (Weller et al., 2013). According to Sheridan, Gillett, Davies, Blaauw, and Patel (2003), the "just world" hypothesis would explain the attribution of blame to the victim. Indeed, according to Sheridan et al. (2003, p. 88), a "man who assaults his wife may be perceived as more 'entitled' to do so due to her past transgressions, but a stranger who makes a similar attack on a woman has no just entitlement because no history exists between the two." For others, being stalked is not even considered as being victimized in the way that they see stalking as a form of flattery toward victims (Family Service Regina, 2014).

VICTIM BLAMING IN DOMESTIC VIOLENCE

Until relatively recent history, a wife was subject to patria potestas in Romana (Ring, 1998). This was a legal state under which the patriarch of the family had absolute sovereignty (including the power of life and death) over the other family members including, wife, children, and grandchildren (Merriam-Webster, 2016). Female children were only subjected to this authority until they were married, at which time they became a part of the family into which they were married and therefore became subject to the patriarch of this familial group. In Roman society, women were considered intellectually and physically inferior and in need of protection, therefore the law was applied to women with the intention of proffering protection rather than dominion over wives. This provision became blurred over the last two millennia and women were ultimately folded into the general structure of patria potestas throughout the era of the Holy Roman Empire and the Western social "spin-off" social systems. Various legal and social systems have slowly changed some of tenets of patria potestas. For example, the permission to control life and death was revoked in many countries by the 18th or 19th century (Ring, 1998). However, other provisions remained such as "The Rule of Thumb" in which a man could beat his wife and children provided the stick used was no bigger than the width of his thumb (Ring, 1998).

It was not until Pope John Paul II released his apostolic letter on the dignity of women in 1988, titled *Mulieris Dignitatem* (Isanga, 2010), that the Catholic

Church altered this patriarchal position of sovereignty and overtly advocated for what is known as "Christian complementarianism." This position forwarded the view that men and women hold complementary and equal roles within a marriage. This declaration by the Roam Catholic Church came at a time when many countries around the world were in the midst of a social and legal revolution, in which women were being increasingly provided protections and rights under both changing social norms and formal legislative provisions. Unfortunately, and despite the vast improvements in the social and legal protections provided to women within the marriage/relational space, women continue to experience significant levels of domestic violence at the hands of intimate partners. Moreover, despite these improvements, society continues to allow the perpetuation of several myths about victims of domestic violence.

Myths of domestic violence often stereotype the victim as the "battered woman" who is small, fragile, and haggard. Victims are perceived as having limited options, no external skills or personal attributes that can relay control and choice, and are therefore economically dependent on the perpetrator. Additionally, domestic violence is often considered to be an issue that poor people and minorities experience, in environments where residents are accustomed to violence in all forms, and the fearfulness and passivity of the victims are emphasized as a resignation to the status quo. As victims of domestic violence come from all walks of life, there are undoubtedly some who may reflect this stereotypical perception, however, the research shows very clearly that age, sex, race, religion, background, socioeconomic status, geography, education, and many other of the stereotyped characteristics of victims of domestic violence are false (Bellack, Hersen, Morrison, & Van Hasselt, 2013; Drijber, Reijnders, & Ceelen, 2013; Smith, Fowler, & Niolon, 2014).

Many of the myths of domestic violence have been circulating for decades, with Walker (1979) identifying 21 myths of domestic violence. Many have remained in the social psyche relating to domestic violence and include battered victims are masochistic; they are asking for it; men cannot be victimized by their partners; victims deserved to get beaten; and victims can leave the relationship if they really wanted to (Feather, 1996; Sundberg, Barbaree, & Marshall, 1991; Walker, 1979; Yollo & Bogard, 1988; Zur, 1994). Ultimately, the myths surrounding domestic violence have served to perpetuate the belief that the victim's own behavior has somehow been a precipitating factor in their own assault.

CONTEMPORARY CONCEPTS

Around the 1970s, two "opportunity theories," lifestyle-exposure theory and routine activity theory, were created to explain criminal victimization in other ways. These theories imply that the lifestyle of people can influence victimization because different authors find that there is a link between victims' lifestyles and criminal events

(Miethe & Meier, 1990; Robinson, 1997). Globally, and according to Miethe and Meier (1990, p. 244), these theories "presume that the habits, lifestyles, and behavioral patterns of potential crime victims enhance their contact with offenders and thereby increase the chances that crime will occur."

THE LIFESTYLE-EXPOSURE THEORY

Hindelang, Gottfredson, and Garofalo (1978) developed lifestyle-exposure theory, which is considered one of the first systematic theories to explain criminal victimization (Fattah, 2000; Meier & Miethe, 1993; Wilson, 2009). According to Siegel (2010, p. 77), "the basis of lifestyle exposure is that crime is not a random occurrence but rather a function of the victim's lifestyle." Lifestyle theory implies that demographic characteristics, such as age, gender or income, role expectations, and structural constraints have an influence on daily activities and increase the likelihood of victimization (Averdijk, 2011; Miethe, Stafford, & Long, 1987). According to lifestyle-exposure theory, lifestyle involves "daily activities done on a routine basis (e.g., daily work or school routines) or leisure activities" (Wilson, 2009, p. 158). Therefore, behaviors including alcohol consumption or going out at night in public places, for instance, are considered as increasing the risk of being victimized. The following is a perfunctory list of high-risk lifestyles that lead to a greater chance of victimization: consuming alcohol and taking drugs, getting involved in crime, being a young runaway living on the street, being a teenage male, carrying a weapon, or being involved in a criminal career, to name a few (Siegel, 2010).

ROUTINE ACTIVITY THEORY

Inspired by the lifestyle theory, Cohen and Felson (1979) developed routine activity theory after observing an increase in crime rates, such as robbery, aggravated assault, forcible rape, and homicide, while the social trends and economic conditions in the United States were generally stable (Cohen & Felson, 1979). According to Cohen and Felson (1979, p. 589) for a crime to occur these are the three minimal elements: "(1) motivated offenders, (2) suitable targets, and (3) the absence of capable guardians against a violation." In other words, for a crime to occur, there is contact between a motivated offender and one or more targets isolated from the protection of somebody. These three minimal elements can be explained as follows (Robinson, 1997):

1. A "likely [or motivated] offender" includes anyone with an inclination to commit a crime.
2. A "suitable target" includes any person or thing that may evoke criminal inclinations, and may include the target item's actual or realizable monetary value; symbolic desirability; visibility to offenders or their informants; accessibility; and portability. Suitability may also be determined by the ease of escape from the target site.

3. A "guardian" includes any person who can protect a target, including friends; formal authorities (e.g., police and security personnel); "intimate handlers" (e.g., parents, teachers, coaches, friends, employers); and "place managers" (e.g., janitors or apartment managers).

Based on this, an explanation for the changes of crime rates and trends is a variation in the victims' behavior that increases criminal opportunities. For instance, and as explained by Cohen and Felson (1979), one of the reasons that could explain the growth in the crime rate between 1960 and 1980 in the United States is related to the expansion of female employment, which resulted in more people being away from home during the day and has led therefore to more burglaries.

Even though some of these theories have been subject to controversies or criticized, they do in some way give explanation to why some people become victims of crime while others do not. It is important to understand the patterns of victimization. According to Wilcox (2010, p. 985):

> *Theories of victimization are varied. They include those that focus on victimization as a function of opportunity (at various levels of analysis), those that focus on victimization as a function of social interactional dynamics between victim and offender, and those that focus on victimization as a function of deep social division in terms of power and control. All such varied perspectives have received empirical support in the research literature. As such, victimization is clearly a complex phenomenon, which results from a multitude of broad social and microsituational influences. Although these theories tend to be viewed as "competing" and studied in isolation, there is little doubt that all have merit and assist in providing a comprehensive understanding of victimization.*

VICTIM CHARACTERISTICS AND MOTIVATIONS

Historically, the literature and empirical research was focused heavily on offender risk and motivations. A number of models have been created to explain offender characteristics and offending risk. More recently, there is emerging evidence that indicates that the presence of certain individual characteristics also increases the risk of becoming a victim of crime. Several models have now been developed to also articulate this risk. This notion of offender and victim individual characteristics differs from the traditional demographic risk profiles that have been used to identify risk factors for crime. A number of demographic factors have been identified as being associated with crime risk, and this continues to the present to be an important element in crime prevention, investigations, and resource allocation. These demographic factors include such things as socioeconomics, residential location, familial constitution, age, social status, gender, and race (Burgess & Roberts, 2010; Siegel, 2010).Some of the key findings in this regard are shown in Table 3.4

Table 3.4 Demographic Characteristics of Victims

Gender	Males and females are not subjected to the same crimes. Men are more likely to become victims of homicide, robbery, and blackmail, while females are at a greater risk of sexual assault and kidnapping (ABS, 2012b; Australian Institute of Criminology, 2010, Chapter 4). Men are twice as likely as women to be victimized by a stranger, while women are at greatest risk of personal assault (including assault resulting in murder) from an intimate partner (Lauritsen & Rezey, 2013).
Age	Age has a substantial impact on the risk of being a victim of crime. People over 35 years of age have substantially lower rates of victimization those aged 15 to 24 (Lauritsen & Rezey, 2013). For example, in Australia, age also significantly reflects the type of crime you are likely to be a victim of (ABS, 2012b): • Around 60% of all murder victims are aged 25 to 54 • Almost half of all victims of sexual assault are aged 10 to 19 • Around half of all robbery victims are aged 20 to 34
Social status	Those living in poverty are the most likely to be victims of violent and property crime (Siegel, 2010).
Marital status	Those who have never been married are more likely to be victims of a crime than those who are married. Widows and widowers have the lowest rates of victimization (ABS, 2007a; Australian Institute of Criminology, 2010, Chapter 4). According to Siegel (2010), this marital status-victimization risk association is secondary via the influences of age, gender, and lifestyle. For example: • Adolescents and teens, who have the highest victimization risk, are too young to have been married • Young single people go out in public more often and sometimes interact with high-risk peers, increasing their exposure to victimization • Widows and widowers suffer much lower victimization rates because they are older, interact with older people, and are more likely to stay home at night and avoid public places. (p. 76)
Race and ethnicity	In the United States, African Americans are more likely than Caucasians to become victims of crime even though the gap between black and white people in victimization rates is narrowing (Siegel, 2010). According to Siegel (2010, p. 76) this difference is because "… income inequality, racial and minority group members are often forced to live in deteriorated urban areas beset by alcohol and drug abuse, poverty, racial discrimination, and violence. Consequently, their lifestyle places them in the most at-risk population group." In English-speaking countries, migrant populations are either equally or less likely to experience personal crime than those born in the country (ABS, 2007b; Brzozowski & Mihorean, 2002; Jansson, 2006; Johnson, 2005). However, Jansson (2006) found that mixed-ethnicity populations were at an increased risk of victimization. First Nations people have been identified at a significantly higher risk of victimization. For example, in Australia, it is the aboriginal and Torres Strait Islander populations that are highly victimized (Fitzgerald & Weatherburn, 2001). According to Fitzgerald and Weatherburn (2001), aboriginal people are heavily overrepresented among victims who report crimes to the police despite being far less likely to report being victims of crime than nonaboriginals. Crime tends to be intraracial. In the United States, African Americans tend to victimize African Americans; white Americans victimize white Americans (Siegel, 2010). Similarly, in Australia, if the victim was aboriginal, the offender was usually aboriginal. According to Fitzgerald and Weatherburn (2001, p. 2): • In 4 out of 7 murder cases • 73% of sexual assault • 72% of children sexual assault • 80% of assault • 85% of domestic violence • 86% of assault occasioning grievous bodily harm

Table 3.4 Demographic Characteristics of Victims—cont'd

Prior victimization	According to Siegel (2010, p. 76) "… individuals who have been crime victims have a significantly higher chance of future victimisation than people who have not been victims." There are three factors or characteristics that seems to explain chronic victimization: 1. **Target vulnerability:** The victims' physical weakness or psychological distress renders them incapable of resisting or deterring crime and makes them easy targets. 2. **Target gratifiability:** Some victims have some quality, possession, skill, or attribute that an offender wants to obtain, use, have access to, or manipulate. Having attractive possessions such as leather coat, may make one vulnerable to predatory crime. 3. **Target antagonism:** Some characteristics increase risk because they arouse anger, jealousy, or destructive impulses in potential offenders. Being gay or effeminate, for example, may bring on undeserved attacks in the street; being argumentative and alcoholic may provoke barroom assaults.
Relationship to offender	According to Siegel (2010, p. 76): *Although many violent crimes are committed by strangers, a surprising number of violent crimes are committed by relatives or acquaintances of the victims. In fact, more than half of all nonfatal personal crimes are committed by people who are described as being known to the victim.* When it comes to nonpersonal crime such as robbery, the offender is most commonly unknown to the victim. However, this is reversed in cases of personal violence. For victims of personal violence, including murder, sexual assault, and physical assault, the offender is far more likely to be known by the victim, with the greatest risk coming from an intimate partner (ABS, 2009; Lauritsen & Rezey, 2013; Queensland Police Service, 2012). According to Doerner and Lab (2011, p. 64):*Most acts of homicide and assault occur between individuals who know each other, rather than between strangers. Victim precipitation and alcohol consumption appear to be almost essential ingredients in any serious confrontation.*

VICTIMS OF INTERPERSONAL VIOLENCE: EXPLAINING VICTIM CHARACTERISTICS AND MOTIVATIONS

The World Health Organization (WHO) defines violence as:

> … *the intentional use of physical force, or power, threatened or actual, against oneself, another person, or against a group or community, that either results in, or has a likelihood of resulting in injury, death, psychological harm, mal-development or deprivation*
>
> **Krug, Dahlberg, Mercy, Zwi, and Lozano (2002, p. 5).**

Krug et al. (2002), divide violence into three categories that differ according to who is committing the violent act:

1. Self-directed violence, that includes any violence that a person inflicts to him/herself;
2. Interpersonal violence that is inflected by another individual or small group of individual;
3. Collective violence that is inflicted by a larger group such as states, terrorist organizations, political groups.

Interpersonal violence refers to any violent act by a person or persons against another including physical assault, sexual assault, stalking, and domestic violence.

Physical Assault: The ABS (2009, para.1) defines assault as "the direct infliction of force, injury or violence upon a person, including attempts or threats." Aggravated assault is a widespread crime around the world. For example, in 2010, there were around 780,000 victims of assault in the United States (FBI, 2010). Similarly, in Canada assault is the most prevalent crime with around 250,000 assault convictions in 2011 (Brennan, 2013). Assault is also the most widespread crimes in Australia with more than 170,000 convictions for assault being recorded in 2011 (ABS, 2009). Assault has a seasonal effect, with more assaults occurring during the summer months than in the colder seasons (ABS, 2009). The victim–offender relationship is significantly different in male victims compared to female victims. For example, in Australia, more than 80% of female victims know the offender, while more than half of male victims are assaulted by strangers.

Sexual Assault: It is very difficult to find similar definitions of sexual assault because it means different things to different people (Savino & Turvey, 2005). Firstly, it is possible to find authors that use the words *rape* and *sexual assault* interchangeably. Indeed, Douglas, Burgess, Burgess, and Ressler (2006, p. 295) define rape and sexual assault as "criminal offenses in which victims are forced or coerced to participate in sexual activity." However, others do not use the terms rape and sexual assault interchangeably. For instance, the Rights of Women (2006, para. 6) defines sexual assault as a situation where an offender "intentionally touches the victim, and the touching is sexual, and the victim does not consent to the touching, and the offender does not reasonably believe that the victim consents." A rape is considered a serious violent sexual assault. This definition is, however, not specific enough in the distinction between rape and sexual assault, and a better distinction between both can be found in Savino and

Turvey (2005). They define rape as a "non-consensual sexual penetration," while sexual assault is defined as a "non-consensual sexual contact" (Savino & Turvey, p. 1). It is important to take into consideration that both rape and sexual assault can be committed by men and women toward either men or women.

According to the Advocates for Human Rights (2006a), 10–15% of women around the world reported being forced to have sex at least one time in their life. Moreover, despite the high reported prevalence of sexual assault, it remains a largely unreported crime and therefore statistics are likely to be far more severe than the statistics demonstrate (Advocates for Human Rights, 2006a).

Stalking: As defined by Pathé (2002, p. 8) stalking refers to a "constellation of behaviors involving repeated and persistent attempts to impose on another person unwanted communication and/or contact." It can include phone calls, emails, and letters, as well as behaviors such as harassment, threats, following, and surveillance, and may lead to assault and homicide (Mullen, Pathé, Purcell, & Stuart, 1999; Petherick, 2009). In the United States, Basile, Swahn, Chen, and Saltzman (2006) found that 4.5% of adults aged 18 or older reported having being stalked in their lives. Basile et al. (2006, para. 7) concluded that "lifetime stalking affects 1 of 22 adults (almost 10 million people) in the United States; that is, 1 of 50 men and 1 of 14 women." This figure appears to be much lower than other Western countries. This is because stalking in America is limited to those people who feel in danger or feel their life is threatened (Basile et al., 2006; Petherick, 2009). In other countries such as Australia, where stalking involves a broader definition of behaviors, research indicates that as many as 1:4 women, and about 1:8 men, report having been stalked (Purcell, Pathé, & Mullen, 2002).

Domestic Violence: Contrary to the popular belief that danger comes from outside of the social group, numerous studies show that one's intimate partner is a far greater source of violence risk (Phillips, 2006). Turvey (2008b, p. 299) defines domestic violence as "physical aggression between family members, household members, or intimates." The research suggests that between one quarter and one half of all women in the world have been abused by intimate partners" in their life (Advocates for Human Rights, 2006b, para. 2). Domestic violence is closely associated with homicide risk. For example, in the United States, three women per day are victims of domestic homicide by their intimate partners (Turvey, 2008a). In Australia the statistics are similarly horrific with an average of two women being murdered by their intimate partners each week. If the Australian statistics are extrapolated to an equal population to that of the United States, this statistic would be equal to around 3.7 homicides per day.

According to the Australian Injury Prevention Network (2012, p. 1):

> *Interpersonal violence is a cause of suffering and trauma, which has devastating consequences for the mental, physical and sexual health of the victim. It affects us as individuals, parents, spouses, educators, researchers and citizens. The breadth of the problem is staggering with public health officials identifying interpersonal violence as a public health issue of epidemic proportions.*

This type of violence occurs in a wide range of contexts and includes, for instance, domestic violence, violent crime, sexual assault, child and elder abuse, and neglect

(Australian Injury Prevention Network, 2012). Interpersonal violence can be divided into two subcategories according to Krug et al. (2002):

- **Family and intimate partner violence:** Violence largely between family members and intimate partners, usually, though not exclusively, taking place in the home. The former group includes forms of violence such as child abuse, intimate partner violence, and abuse of the elderly.
- **Community violence:** Violence between individuals who are unrelated, and who may or may not know each other, generally taking place outside the home. The latter includes youth violence, random acts of violence, rape or sexual assault by strangers, and violence in institutional settings such as schools, workplaces, prisons, and nursing homes.

Interpersonal violence is a widespread crime around the world. For example, Walby and Allen (2004, p. V), stated that interpersonal violence in England is "widely dispersed in that some experience of domestic violence (abuse, threats or force), sexual victimisation, or stalking, is reported by over one third (36%) of people." Rosenberg et al. (2006) stated that in 2001, 1.6 million people around the world died as a result of non-militaristic violence, of which 34% were due to interpersonal violence. In Australia, sexual and physical assault and domestic violence are among the most prevalent form of violence (ABS, 2012a).

Ultimately, when exploring crime and criminality, as it has been stated by Petherick and Sinnamon (2014, p. 409): "… the victim's role in the criminal event cannot be understated, and without the ability to account for their emotions, actions, and the subsequent consequences, any understanding of the crime will be incomplete."

Understanding the motives and behaviors of victims is the purpose behind developing models of victim typologies.

UNDERSTANDING VICTIM MOTIVATIONS AND BEHAVIOR THROUGH TYPOLOGIES

A number of attempts have been made to understand the causes of criminal behaviors and the motivational forces behind crimes such as the work of Groth (1979), Groth, Burgess, and Holmstrom (1977), Hazelwood (2009), and Petherick and Turvey (2008). Informed by this work, there has been a recent effort to apply typology modeling to victims as well as the offender. Two such models have been developed by Petherick and Ferguson (2012), and more recently Petherick and Sinnamon (2014).

DEFINING TYPOLOGIES AND THEIR UTILITY

Comparing and classifying is a central facet of the criminological enterprise as "without classification, there could be no advances in conceptualization, reasoning, language, data analysis or, for that matter, social science research" (Bailey, 1994, p. 1). Classification, or "the ordering of entities into groups" (Bailey, 1994, p. 1), can either be unidimensional, based on a single characteristic, or multidimensional, based on a number of characteristics (Doty & Glick, 1994). The terms *classification* and *typology* have been used interchangeably; however, typologies tend to be multidimensional and conceptual (Collier, Laporte, & Seawright, 2012; Doty & Glick, 1994), and generally "produced by the intersection of two or more variables to create a set of categories or types" (Maxfield & Babbie, 2012, p. 99). Typologies provide a descriptive tool that allows scholars to present "an exhaustive and perhaps even definitive array of types" (Bailey, 1994, p. 12) that permit ease of understanding of complex social problems and concepts (Neuman & Wiegand, 2000). They are parsimonious because they have the potential to reduce thousands or even millions of individual cases down to a few main types (Bailey, 1994), thus yielding simplicity and order. In addition, they can offer direction for both theorizing and empirical research.

Typologies, if well constructed, can do more than just place a nominal label on a group or concept; they assist in comprehensiveness by highlighting the relevant dimensions of a type (Bailey, 1994; Collier et al., 2012; Doty & Glick, 1994). Indeed, a robust typology exhibits a complete set of dimensions on which the types are based in order to be more exhaustive. Thus, while they are simple on the one hand, they are also designed to provide "completeness" of understanding. Furthermore, they present the relationship between the types and the dimensions in order to enhance comparisons that yield ease of "appraisal of the similarities and variation in the typology" (Bailey, 1994, p. 13). In summary, the merits of conceptual typologies are that:

> *A well-constructed typology can be very effective in bringing order out of chaos. It can transform the complexity of apparently eclectic congeries of diverse cases into well-ordered sets of a few rather homogeneous types, clearly situated in a property space of a few important dimensions [...]. Perhaps no other tool has such power to simplify life for the social scientist.*
>
> **Bailey (1994, p. 33).**

Being able to develop appropriate typologies can be very useful in many areas of research including criminology. In the past, criminals were classified as part of a homogeneous group, however, more recent research has demonstrated that there are several criminal types, and understanding these types provides for a clearer understanding of offender motivations and behavior. For example, rapists, stalkers, and batterers, to name a few, are all a part of a subclassification of offending that is often seen as relatively heterogeneous (Boon & Sheridan, 2001; Knight & Prentky, 1987; Saunders, 1992). Groups such as this receive a description as being heterogeneous because, at face value, the motives and/or pattern of behaviors that characterize within-group offenders appear dissimilar. The appearance of uniqueness comes from the surface examination of the variables such as individual physical differences, attraction preferences, contemporary and developmental environmental differences, and the vast differences in offenders' personal competencies and capacity to explain and/or justify their behaviors to investigators. While the notion of heterogeneity has substantial face validity, research has begun to illustrate that, despite offenders having a number of individual differences, there are collective factors that can be used to classify offenders into homogenous typologies based on underlying motivation, personality, and other psychological characteristics. These offender typologies have formed the foundations of contemporary efforts to produce similar victim classifications.

OFFENDER TYPOLOGIES
Groth's Typology
In 1977 Groth, in collaboration with Ann Burgess and Lynda Holmstrom, proposed a typology of rape based on two main axes: power and anger (see Table 3.5). Their clinical typology of rape is based on the analysis of offenders' and victims' accounts. According to Groth et al. (1977), all rapes had three different components: power, anger, and sexuality in *Men Who Rape: The psychology of the offender*, Groth (1979, p. 13), and he described rape as an act where both "aggression and sexuality are involved, but it is clear that sexuality becomes the means of expressing the aggressive needs and feelings that operate in the offender and underlie his assault." As explained in Petherick and Sinnamon (2014, p. 403), "in a power offense, sexuality is an expression of conquest, while in anger rape sexuality is a hostile act. In sadistic rape, anger and sexuality become fused and the offender receives sexual gratification from pain and suffering." According to the hierarchy and relationships among these factors, the rapists' motivations were characterized as power assertive, power reassurance, anger retaliation, and anger excitation. Groth and his colleagues found that offenders were more likely to be power oriented (65%) rather than anger oriented (35%) (Groth et al., 1977).

The Hazelwood Typology
Inspired by Groth (1979), Hazelwood's typology (2009) (see Table 3.6) represents the first significant adaptation of the typology developed by Groth et al. (1977).

In *Practical Aspects of Rape Investigation*, Hazelwood and Burgess (2009) were the first ones who actually modified the previous typology in a significant way, by adding two additional types and categorizing the verbal, sexual, and physical behavior of the offender (Petherick & Sinnamon, 2014).

The opportunistic and gang rapist subtypes differ from the other subtypes as they are not motivational in nature but rather are offending modus operandi. For example, a power assertive or power reassurance rapist can decide to rape an opportunistic victim in order to restore his self-confidence. Here, the victim is chosen in a contextual situation.

Despite the fact that these typologies were created to specifically describe the motivation of sexual offenders, Petherick and Turvey (2008) recognized that this form of typology could also be used to describe other offenses such as stalking, domestic violence, assault, or fraud, and to explain more complex behavior such as that of gang members or crime victims. According to Petherick and Turvey (2008, p. 280): "The needs, or motives, that impel human criminal behaviors remain essentially the same for all offenders, despite behavioral expression that may involve kidnapping, child molestation, terrorism, sexual assault, homicide, or arson."

The Behavioral-Motivational Typology
Using Groth's typology as the foundational framework, Petherick and Turvey (2008) developed the behavioral-motivational typology (see Table 3.7).

Table 3.5 Groth's Rapist Typology

The Power Rapist

The power rapist is seeking control and power over its victim. The purpose of any physical aggression is to achieve submission. The offenders are described as having few skills in interpersonal relationships, a feeling of inadequacy in everyday and sexual life. They are characterized as having a problem with self-image and self-esteem and use sexuality in an effort to restore them. The power rapist uses rape to reassure himself, and to test his competency, however, because he will often experience impotency and/or premature ejaculation, he never feels reassured, and therefore looks for another victim. The level of aggression used by these offenders varies though there is usually no real intention to hurt or degrade the victim. As Groth et al. (1977, p. 1240) states: [The rape is] "the way in which this type of person asserts his identity, potency, mastery, strength, and dominance and denies his feelings of worthlessness, rejection, helplessness, inadequacy, and vulnerability." Groth divided the power rapist into two subtypes:

> **The Power Reassurance Rapist**
>
> The power reassurance rapist uses the rape in order "to resolve disturbing doubts about his sexual adequacy and masculinity. He wants to place a woman in a helpless, controlled position in which she cannot refuse or reject him, thereby shoring up his failing sense of worth and adequacy" (Groth et al., 1977, p. 1241). The offender has low self-esteem and uses the rape to restore his masculinity and adequacy. Because the power reassurance rapist created a fantasy scenario of a "consenting" victim, he is the less likely to use physical force.
>
> **The Power Assertive Rapist**
>
> The power assertive rapist also has low self-esteem but uses the rape to express his virility, mastery, and dominance. The rape is a reflection of the inadequacy he experiences in terms of his sense of identity and effectiveness. This offender does not care much about the victim's well-being because the rape is his way to express his virility.

The Anger Rapist

The anger rape is characterized by an expressed anger, rage, contempt, and hatred for the victim. The offender is likely to beat, sexually assault, and force the victim to perform or submit to degrading acts. The level of force used to subdue the victim is often far in excess of what is required and is intended to hurt the victim. The motive is revenge and punishment. As stated by Groth et al. (1977, p. 1241), the aim of this type of rapist is "to vent his rage on his victim and to retaliate for perceived wrongs or rejections he has suffered at the hands of women." This type of rapist displays a great deal of anger toward women. There is often no sexual satisfaction in the rape and the offender is likely to experience difficulty achieving erection or ejaculation. The relationships with the women of his life are conflicted, irrational, contain extreme jealousy and suspicion, and are likely to have included physical assault. The offender is likely to use alcohol and drugs during the assault. Victims describe the attack as being preceded by a sudden and dramatic change in the offender's behavior that results in a "blitz-style" assault. The anger rapist has also been divided in two subtypes:

> **The Anger Retaliation Rapist**
>
> The anger retaliation rapist "commits rape as an expression of his hostility and rage towards women. His motive is revenge and his aim is degradation and humiliation" (Groth et al., 1977, p. 1242).
>
> **The Anger Excitation Rapist**
>
> The anger excitation rapist rapes because he "finds pleasure, thrills and excitation in the suffering of his victim. He is sadistic and his aim is to punish, hurt, and torture his victim. His aggression is eroticized" (Groth et al., 1977, p. 1242).

Table 3.6 Hazelwood's Rapist Typology

The Power Reassurance Rapist

The power reassurance rapist is driven by a relational fantasy with his victims even though he does not know them. He is less likely to harm his victims and if he does there was no intent of punishing or degrading them because it will ruin the illusion of a consensual relationship. The purpose of his attack is to restore his masculinity and reassure himself by overpowering his victims through forced sexual acts. Again, even though he does degrade or traumatize his victims, he is not conscious of it. He uses minimal or moderate level of force and he is well known for his pseudo-unselfish verbal and sexual behavior. He chooses his victim in a "comfort zone" where he can in advance target several vulnerable victims to increase his chance of success in case of an unsuccessful attack. The victims are either alone, with small children, or aged because they will pose the least threat. Consistent with the pseudo-unselfish behavior of the reassurance rapist, he is most likely to apologize for the attack and ask for forgiveness and may even try to later contact the victim.

The Power Assertive Rapist

The assertive offender feels inadequate and has a low self-worth. However, for the assertive offender, fantasy plays a minor role in the rape and he has no doubt of his masculinity. He uses rape to express his dominance and virility, and making his victims feel bad makes himself feels better. Consequently, the assertive rapist does not exhibit any empathy for his victims and he has no concern about their well-being, distress, or pain. Victims are seen as objects to be used for gratification. He usually assaults victims of opportunity and uses moderate to excessive force to control the victim. He does rip or tear the victims' clothing and may be subject to sexual dysfunction such as impotence or anorgasmia.

The Anger Retaliatory Rapist

The anger retaliatory rapist is driven by anger and retaliation. This subtype seems to be less observed and the crime more violent. They use sex to punish and degrade the victims that they literally hate because they either did something wrong or the offender believes that they did something wrong. The retaliatory offender is sexually and verbally selfish and uses high to excessive level of force to gain control. The level of force is usually unnecessary and beyond what would be needed to control his victim. He uses a blitz attack to subdue his victim and to inflict immediate injury, to be sure that the victim cannot resist. The attacks are not usually premeditated and can therefore take place at any time, in any place, subject to the emotional reactivity of the offender. The victims are opportunistically selected and are commonly described as being in the wrong place at the wrong time and possessing some simulacrum characteristic that triggers hatred and aggression in the offender.

The Anger Excitation Rapist

This type of offender can be classified as a sexual sadist who is "psychosexually aroused by the suffering of his victims" (Hazelwood, 2009, p. 107). His attacks are highly ritualistic and fantasy plays a major role in his crime. This type of rapist is the most violent, and paraphilia such as sadism, voyeurism, or sexual bondage, which is part of his complex fantasy life, is a common component. This offender is excited by the suffering, humiliation, and degradation of the victim. The purpose of the attack is to inflict the most physical and emotional pain to the victim. Contrary to the other types of rapist, this offender is often characterized as methodical and sophisticated. The rape is well planned, rehearsed, and methodically executed. Everything is preplanned such as the weapon, the transport used, the travel routes, and so on. He uses an excessive to brutal level of force, which will often result in the serious injury or death of the victim.

Table 3.6 Hazelwood's Rapist Typology—cont'd

Opportunistic Rapist

The opportunistic rapist is described as an "impulsive type of sexual offender but that is not to say he lacks proficiency as a burglar or a robber. He simply had not anticipated committing a sexual assault because he was originally at the assault location to commit a robbery or burglary" (Hazelwood, 2009, p. 108). Contrary to the other types of rapists, the primary motive of an opportunistic offender is truly sexual. This opportunist sexually assaults while committing another crime such as burglary, or robbery, which is the reason why he will spend a relatively short period with the victim and use minimal level of force. He can be described as sexually and verbally selfish.

The Gang Rapist

The gang rape is described as a situation where "the victim is attacked by a group of three or more males who are operating with a pack mentality. The crime is committed in an impulsive manner" (Hazelwood, 2009, p. 109). It is a very frightening situation for the victim who is generally weak, vulnerable, or "deserving" the attack. Because of the group impact, the males that have to prove something to the others will be extremely physically and sexually violent.

UNDERSTANDING VICTIM BEHAVIOR THROUGH OFFENDER TYPOLOGIES

In any criminal event there is interaction between two persons: an offender and his or her victim. Understanding offender behavior has been the primary focus for decades, and behavioral typologies such as Groth's (1979) or Hazelwood's (2009) typologies have been widely used in criminology and are the basis for understanding the motivation behind rape and other criminal behavior. As stated by Petherick and Sinnamon (2014, p. 409):

> While those typologies relate to offender behaviour, it should be noted that they are a fitting representation of general motivational dynamics, and as such they apply not only equally to victims but also as descriptors of more common everyday behaviours. This is because criminal (and victims) experience the same depth and breadth of emotions and needs as all others, and so it should be not surprising that their behaviour serves many of the same needs. It is usually in the execution of these behaviours and the choices they make that they differ.

Therefore, it seems possible to classify victims' behaviors, according to their needs and wants, in the same way that motivational typologies classify offenders.

The Victim-Motivational Typology

The victim-motivational typology was created by Petherick and Ferguson (2012) to understand the emotional and psychological milieu of victimization. This typology, inspired mainly by the work of Groth (1979) and Hazelwood (2009), reflects the characteristics of offender typologies onto victims' behaviors.

Table 3.7 Petherick and Turvey's Behavioral-Motivational Typology

The Behavioral-Motivational Typology (Petherick & Turvey, 2008)

Power Reassurance (aka compensatory).

Recognized by crime scene behaviors, which evidence restoration of their self-confidence by a use of low level of violence. Characteristics include a lack of self-confidence, extreme shyness, feelings of personal and social inadequacy, and sensitivity to rejection. Likely to take care about the welfare of their victims. They will reassure and compliment them. They will use a minimal level of violence either by threats or use of a weapon, to get the victim's compliance. They choose stranger victims who live in an area where the offender feels comfortable. They are more likely to engage in surveillance of their potential victims before the attack and are likely to try to contact the victim after the attack.

Power Assertive (aka entitlement).

The power assertive or entitlement offender, similar to the power reassurance offender, evidences intention of restoring their self-confidence. However, they intend to restore their self-worth through the use of moderate to high level of violence. Demeans and humiliates the victim in order to restore his level of self-confidence. According to Petherick and Turvey (2008, p. 283), these behaviors suggest an "underlying lack of confidence and a sense of personal inadequacy, which are expressed through control, mastery, and humiliation of the victim, while demonstrating the offender's sense of authority." The purpose of their offense is to make others feel bad in order to make themselves feel better. The level of force, used against the victim, increases with the victim resistance during the offense. If the offenders do not used a weapon during the attack, they are susceptible to use a higher level of violence to overpower the victim. Victims are usually unknown to the offender but may be either preselected or opportunistic because the power assertive offenders chose them by availability, accessibility, and vulnerability.

Anger Retaliatory (aka anger or displaced).

The anger retaliatory or displaced anger type is evidenced by crime scene behavior where a great deal of rage and anger is observable. Offenders' behaviors are driven by anger or revenge, which can lead them to attack impulsively. The offender's characteristics are verbally and sexually selfish, they use projection in order to blame the victim for what happened, and will use humiliating behaviors. The attack is generally the result of an emotional reaction against victims, who share the offender's life such as relatives, girlfriends or coworkers, or anyone who symbolizes one of these people to the offender. However, in some situations, anger retaliatory offenders can plan their attack and attack a specific victim or group of victims. It is expected in the crime scene to observe a great amount of anger through the use of a high level of violence. Offenders are likely to be engaged in risky and antisocial behaviors.

Sadistic (aka anger excitation).

The sadistic or anger excitation offender is evidenced by a crime scene where sexual gratification from victim pain and suffering is observed. The primary motive is sexual gratification but it is obtained through brutal physical aggression, torture, and degradation of the victim. All aspects of the offense are planned and executed methodically. The victim, usually unknown to the offender, is chosen carefully based on their vulnerability. The sadistic offender eroticizes physical aggression, which is used as the tool to provoke fear and submission in the victim. During the attack the offender is likely to use sadistic behaviors, bondage, torture, and a brutal or high level of force in specific sexual areas of the victim's body to inflict significant pain.

Profit (aka material gain).

Profit or material gain–oriented offenders include all behaviors that serve for personal gain. The attack is committed in order to provide personal or material gain for the offender. The offense is generally very short, well planned or opportunistic, profit oriented, and perpetrated toward unknown victims though the use of moderate force. Profit-motivated behaviors do not necessarily satisfy psychological or emotional needs unless the material gain is associated with a psychological need or compulsion.

It is important to take into consideration that, as with the offenders' typologies, the following types are not unique categorizations (Petherick & Sinnamon, 2014, p. 414):

> *There are no absolute boundaries between each type, and it is possible for one victim to exhibit characteristics of more than one type. It is also possible for a victim to start as one type, and through a process of experience, adaptation, and change, move between types as dictated by their experiences and their willingness (or ability) to learn from past mistakes that placed them in risky situations.*

The victim typology developed by Petherick and Ferguson (2012), and further described by Petherick and Sinnamon (2014) (see Table 3.8), comprises seven different victim motivations:

Table 3.9 summarizes the typologies espoused by each of the main models just described.

EMPIRICAL EVIDENCE OF A SEVEN-FACTOR VICTIM TYPOLOGY

Based on the work of Petherick and Ferguson (2012) and Petherick and Sinnamon (2014), the authors used a model of 24 variables of motivation and personality characteristics (Table 3.10), in a group of 160 male and female victims of personal violence (specifically: domestic violence, sexual assault, physical assault, and stalking), to test the utility of the theory of a victim typology. A unique seven-factor typology model was identified though a principle components analysis (PCA) of the 24 motivation and personality characteristics. The final section of this chapter describes a new *Seven-Factor Typology of Victim Characteristics*.

When the results of these 24 variables from the 160 victims were subjected to a PCA, seven factors were identified that correspond to a unique victim type. Table 3.13 shows the resulting seven-factor typology of victim characteristics derived from the PCA.

THE "REASSURANCE-ORIENTED TYPE"

According to the research results, the reassurance-oriented victim was most highly associated with a low level of self-esteem, poor self-efficacy, feelings of inadequacy, poor social skills and antisocial behaviors, and to use projection as a defense mechanism. These victims were also characteristically high in fear of rejection and abandonment, feelings of failure, and a high need for reassurance. Reassurance-oriented victims also indicated a higher likelihood of engaging in self-harming behaviors, and scored very low on domination and authoritarian characteristics.

A Comparison With Existing Typologies

This reassurance-oriented victim type is consistent with typologies forwarded by other victim and offender models, for example, the power-reassurance rapist described

Table 3.8 The Victim-Motivational Typology

The Behavioral-Motivational Typology (Petherick & Ferguson, 2012; Petherick & Sinnamon, 2014)

Reassurance-Oriented Victims

The reassurance-oriented victim, like the power-reassurance offender, strives to restore or reinforce their level of self-esteem or self-worth through different behaviors. They are prone to a lack of self-confidence, feelings of inadequacy, and have trouble in social interactions. They can, for example, decide to stay in an abusive relationship because they may feel gratitude toward their abuser. Buel (1999, p. 21), states:

> A victim who is overweight or has mental health, medical, or other serious problems often appreciates that the abuser professes his love, despite the victim's perceived faults. Many batterers tell a victim, 'You are so lucky I put up with you; certainly nobody else would,' fueling the victim's low self-esteem and reinforcing her belief that she deserves no better than an abusive partner.

The reassurance-oriented victim may also be victimized because they believe that it is somehow what they deserve and because of that have been subjected or will be subjected to repeated victimization. For these victims, the psychological and physical cost of the abuse is less important than the emotional cost of being alone (Petherick & Sinnamon, 2014). Reassurance-oriented victims are often party to victim-precipitated offenses as a result of the combination of their poor social skills, need for approval from others, and their inherent passive and introspective nature. These kinds of victims have such low level of self-esteem and are so unaware of the environmental and social cues around them that they desperately seek to establish new relationships despite the evidence of the high risk for violence and abuse.

Assertive-Oriented Victims

Assertive-oriented victims are also driven by low self-esteem but focus their efforts to restore their self-worth through the derogation of others. In short, they improve their own feeling of worth by making people around them feel bad. Using a dominating personality, they will try to dominate, control, and humiliate others. This is generally not well received by those around them and ultimately leads to stress, frustration, anxiety, and anger in those on the receiving end of these behaviors. In this way, these victims precipitate their own victimization by behaving aggressively toward others who may be less inclined to accept these actions.

Anger Retaliatory Oriented Victims

Retaliatory-oriented victims harbor a "great deal of rage, either toward a specific person, group, institution, or a symbol of one of these" (Petherick & Turvey, 2008, p. 285). This anger comes from a feeling of inadequacy or failure and, as a result, they often blame others for their problems, whether real or perceived. Reasons for blaming others can be an emotional immaturity or an inability to take blame or responsibility for their own action, and therefore, the blame is projected onto others. Roeckelein (2006, p. 252) defines the mechanism of "projection" as "attributing unacceptable impulses, feelings, or thoughts to other individuals." To summarize, the victim's behaviors are driven by anger or revenge, which leads them to act impulsively and will bring about anxiousness, stress, and aggressive responses from others, which will increase the chance of being victimized.

Pervasively Oriented Victims

The pervasive anger type, absent from early typologies, is found in the Massachusetts Treatment Center: Revision 3 (MTC:R3) developed by Knight, Warren, Reboussin, and Soley (1998). According to Petherick and Ferguson (2012, p. 7), in some instances, "the anger is the result of a generalized state that is pervasive." It will include people whom "anger permeates many, if not all, aspects of life" (Petherick, Sinnamon, & Jenkins, 2012). Anybody can be the target of the anger because the anger is global and undifferentiated.

Table 3.8 The Victim-Motivational Typology—cont'd

Excitation-Oriented Victims

The excitation-oriented type is the most difficult to adapt from the offenders' typologies. In the offender typologies, the offender is classified as sadistic, and refers to "an individual who experiences sexual gratification from the pain and suffering of another" (Petherick & Sinnamon, 2014, p. 417). As sadism is a motivational construct involving at least two people, the sadist and the victim, this subtype requires slight modification to be applied to victim behaviors. Therefore, to explain victim motivations, the excitation can take two different forms: the sadism and the masochism. In this context sadism could mean either actual sadism (directed at another) or masochism (directed at the self).

According to the DSM-IV (American Psychiatric Association, 1994) sexual sadism involves:

> *Acts (real, not simulated) in which the individual derives sexual excitement from the psychological or physical suffering (including humiliation of the victim) ... Others act on the sadistic urges with a consenting partner (who may have Sexual Masochism) who willingly suffers pain or humiliation. Still others with Sexual Sadism act on their sadistic sexual urges with nonconsenting victims. In all of these cases, it is the suffering of the victim that is sexually arousing. When Sexual Sadism is severe, and especially when it is associated with Antisocial Personality Disorder, individuals with Sexual Sadism may seriously injure or kill their victims (p. 530).*

In sadistic cases, victim precipitation occurs when the victim is engaged in sadistic acts and then fights back after realizing the danger of the situation.

Sexual masochism is defined in the DSM-IV (American Psychiatric Association, 1994) as:

> *Acts (real, not simulated) of being humiliated, beaten, bound, or otherwise made to suffer...Others acts on the masochistic sexual urges by themselves (e.g. binding themselves, sticking themselves with pins, shocking themselves electrically, or self-mutilation) or with a partner. One particularly dangerous form of Sexual Masochism, called "hypoxyphilia", involves sexual arousal by oxygen deprivation obtained by means of chest compression, noose, ligature, plastic bag, mask, or chemical (often a volatile nitrite that produces temporary decrease in brain oxygenation by peripheral vasodilatation) (p. 529).*

In masochistic situations, victims expose themselves to harm or loss either alone or with a partner. It can include, as stated before, cases of hypoxyphilia or cases where victims are engaged in other forms of self-harm such as scarification or cutting (Petherick & Ferguson, 2012).

It is important to take into consideration that the number of excitation-oriented victims is low (Hazelwood & Burgess, 2009; Petherick & Ferguson, 2012). Moreover, victims can also, in some cases, engage in self-harm in order to regulate negative affect. In this case, the behavior could also be categorized as preservation-oriented behavior (see following) (Petherick & Ferguson, 2012).

Materially Oriented Victims

The materially oriented victim is engaged in behaviors that serve material or personal gain, such as monetary or through the acquisition of goods. They can precipitate their own victimization because of a lack of financial resources, which can, for instance, lead them to stay with an abusive but wealthy partner or a financially controlling one. To illustrate this point, Buel (1999, p. 20), states:

> *Financial despair quickly takes hold when the victim realizes that she cannot provide for her children without the batterer's assistance. ... A comprehensive*

Continued

Table 3.8 The Victim-Motivational Typology—cont'd

Texas study found that 85 percent of the victims calling hotlines, emergency rooms, and shelters had left their abusers a minimum of five times previously, with the number one reason cited for returning to the batterer being financial despair. These victims were simply unable to provide for themselves and their children without emergency assistance, and many who had such assistance were still in financial trouble.

They can also increase their risk of becoming a victim by getting into dangerous situations such as prostitution, drug dealing, or other forms of exploitation at the hands of people who know they are seeking money. Moreover, situations that put victims in demanding situations such as gambling troubles, drug addiction, controlling partners, or unprofitable employment can result in depression, stress, and frustration, and further aggravate their situation (Buel, 1999). In cases where the behaviors create dissonance, they will minimize or rationalize the situation, thinking that it is necessary because the short-term costs that are generated are smaller than the long-term beneficial gains. However, such feelings will lead them to engage in increasingly risky behaviors, increasing their chance of getting hurt and victimized.

Preservation-Oriented Victims

Preservation-oriented victims are those that engage in "strike back" behaviors against a real or perceived oppressor, or source of psychological stress and torment. This preservation behavior can result in precipitating events in which they are unable to physically back up their actions, thereby becoming the victim rather than the "successful" aggressor. Alternatively, some preservation-oriented victims seek to preserve themselves and others (such as children) by remaining in an abusive relationship. Indeed, research shows that one of the high-risk factors of domestic homicide is the attempt to leave the abusive relationship (Johnson, Lutz, & Websdale, 2000; Turvey, 2008b).

Table 3.9 The Different Subtypes of the Main Offenders' and Victims' Typologies

Groth's Typology	Hazelwood's Typology	Behavioral and Motivational Typology	Victim-Motivational Typology
The power reassurance	The power reassurance	Power reassurance (compensatory)	Reassurance oriented
The power reassurance	The power reassurance	Power assertive (entitlement)	Assertive oriented
The anger retaliation	The anger retaliation	Anger retaliatory (anger or displaced)	Anger retaliatory
The anger excitation	The anger excitation	Sadistic (anger excitation)	Pervasively oriented
	The opportunistic rapist	Profit (material gain)	Excitation oriented
	The gang rape		Materially oriented
			Preservation oriented

Table 3.10 Min Score, Max Score, Mean, Standard Deviation, Median, Mode and Cronbach α Values of the 24 Variables Used in the Development of the Seven-Factor Typology of Victim Characteristics

Variable	Name of Measure	# of Items	Method of Response	References	Cronbach's α for Sample
Self-esteem[a]	Rosenberg's self-esteem scale (RSES)	10	4-pt Likert scale	Rosenberg (1965)	0.925
Self-efficacy[a]	General self-efficacy scale (GSE)	10	4-pt Likert scale	Schwarzer and Jerusalem (1995)	0.888
Social interaction	Social interaction anxiety scale (SIAS)	20	5-pt Likert scale	Mattick and Clarke (1998)	0.962
Rejection/abandonment	Anxiety subscale of the experience in close relationship scale	18	7-pt Likert scale	Brennan, Clark, and Shaver (1998)	0.963
Domination	Henceforth Mark VI	14	Yes/no/?	Ray and Lovejoy (1988)	0.869
Humiliation	Cumulative humiliation subscale (CHS) of the humiliation inventory	12	5-pt Likert scale	Hartling and Luchetta (1999)	0.915
Aggression	Aggression questionnaire (AQ)	29	5-pt Likert scale	Buss and Perry (1992)	0.931
Anger	Anger self-report questionnaire (30 items) (ASR)	30	6-pt Likert scale	Reynolds, Walkey, and Green (1994)	0.898
Empathy[a]	Multidimensional Emotional empathy scale	30	5-pt Likert scale	Caruso and Mayer (1998)	0.906
Reassurance	Threat-related reassurance seeking scale (TRSS)	8	7-pt Likert scale	Cougle et al. (2012)	0.948
Narcissism	Narcissistic personality inventory-16 (NPI-16)	16	Dichotomous	Ames, Rose, and Anderson (2006)	0.788
Rage/revenge	Revenge planning subscale of the displaced aggression questionnaire (DAQ)	11	7-pt Likert scale	Denson, Pedersen, and Miller (2006)	0.969
Impulsivity	Revised Dickman impulsivity inventory-short version (DII-short)	23	5-pt Likert scale	Dickman (1990); Adan, Natale, Caci, and Prat (2010)	0.814
Inadequacy[a]	Revised Janis-Field feelings of inadequacy scale (R-JFFIS)	18	5-pt Likert scale	Crawford (2005)	0.949
Failure	Subscales of the performance failure appraisal inventory revised form (PFAI-Revised)	11	5-pt Likert scale	Conroy, Willow, and Metzler (2002)	0.904

Continued

Table 3.10 Min Score, Max Score, Mean, Standard Deviation, Median, Mode and Cronbach α Values of the 24 Variables Used in the Development of the Seven-Factor Typology of Victim Characteristics—cont'd

Variable	Name of Measure	# of Items	Method of Response	References	Cronbach's α for Sample
Projection	Projection questionnaire	18	5-pt Likert scale	Bilić, Buzov, Gruden, and Jokić-Begić (1998)	0.923
Antisocial	Subtypes of antisocial behavior questionnaire (STAB)	32	5-pt Likert scale	Burt and Donnellan (2009)	0.956
Sadism	Sadism scale	20	Yes/no/?	Freund, Steiner, and Chan (1982)	0.89
Masochism	Masochism scale	11	Yes/no	Freund et al. (1982)	0.916
Self-harm	Self-harm inventory (SHI)	22	Yes/no	Sansone and Sansone (2010)	0.903
Finance	Scale of economic abuse (SEA)	28	7-pt Likert scale	Adams, Sullivan, Bybee, and Greeson (2008)	0.908
Risky	Risk-attitude scale	15	5-pt Likert scale	Weber, Blais, and Betz (2002)	0.879
Strike-back	Items have been created	11	Yes/no	See Table 3.11	0.765
Self-defense	Items have been created	23	Yes/no	See Table 3.12	0.788

[a]Reverse scale score—the lower the scores are, the more the respondent is dysfunctional for this characteristic.

Table 3.11 Items of the Strike-back Measure

Item#	Strike Back Items
1.	Have you ever been scared about your safety or somebody else's safety?
2.	Have you ever been scared about your survival or somebody else's survival?
3.	Have you ever thought about engaging yourself in strike-back behavior (leaving an abusive partner, fighting back, or killing an abusive partner) to protect yourself?
4.	Have you ever thought about engaging yourself in strike-back behavior (leaving an abusive partner, fighting back, or killing an abusive partner) to protect one of your friend?
5.	Have you ever thought about engaging yourself in strike-back behavior (leaving an abusive partner, fighting back, or killing an abusive partner) to protect a family member?
6.	Have you ever thought about engaging yourself in strike-back behavior (leaving an abusive partner, fighting back, or killing an abusive partner) to protect your kid(s)?
7.	Have you ever been engaged in strike-back behavior (leaving an abusive partner, fighting back, or killing an abusive partner) to protect yourself?
8.	Have you ever been engaged in strike-back behavior (leaving an abusive partner, fighting back, or killing an abusive partner) to protect one of your friends?
9.	Have you ever been engaged in strike-back behavior (leaving an abusive partner, fighting back, or killing an abusive partner) to protect a family member?
10.	Have you ever been engaged in strike-back behavior (leaving an abusive partner, fighting back, or killing an abusive partner) to protect your kids?
11.	Have you ever been scared of leaving an abusive partner by fear of the consequences?

Notes: Instructions to respondents: Listed below are a number of statements concerning your personal feelings. Read each item and decide whether the answer is positive ("yes") or negative ("no") for you.

by Groth et al. (1977), and Hazelwood and Burgess (2009); the power-reassurance type described by Petherick and Turvey (2008); and the reassurance-oriented victim type described by Petherick and Ferguson (2012). A common key component of all of those "reassurance-oriented" type is self-esteem. All models agree that the main reason behind the behaviors of the reassurance-oriented victims and offenders is to restore or reinforce their self-worth. People characterized as reassurance oriented will feel inadequate, need reassurance, and have little idea of appropriate social interactions. Another characteristic, which is common in the literature to the reassurance-oriented type, is the fear of rejection. Indeed, reassurance-oriented offenders engage with their victims in such a way as to remove the possibility of rejection (Groth et al., 1977; Petherick & Turvey, 2008; Petherick & Ferguson, 2012), while reassurance-oriented victims are willing to accept any abuse because the personal physical cost is less than the emotional cost of being rejected (Petherick & Ferguson, 2012; Petherick & Sinnamon, 2014).

Table 3.12 Items of the Self-Defense Measure

Item#	Self-Defense Items
1. Have you ever used **rationalization** to explain, leave, or deal with some situations?	
Explanation:	Involves explaining an unacceptable behavior or feeling in a rational or logical manner, avoiding the true reasons for the behavior. For example, a person who is turned down for a date might rationalize the situation by saying they were not attracted to the other person anyway, or a student might blame a poor exam score on the instructor rather than his or her lack of preparation. When confronted by success or failure, people tend to attribute achievement to their own qualities and skills while failures are blamed on other people or outside forces.
2. Have you ever used **projection** to explain, leave, or deal with some situations?	
Explanation:	Involves taking our own unacceptable qualities or feelings and ascribing them to other people. For example, consider a person in a couple who has thoughts of infidelity. Instead of dealing with these undesirable thoughts consciously, he or she subconsciously projects these feelings onto the other person, and begins to think that the other has thoughts of infidelity and may be having an affair. Projection works by allowing the expression of the desire or impulse, but in a way that the ego cannot recognize, therefore reducing anxiety.
3. Have you ever used **introjection** to explain, leave, or deal with some situations?	
Explanation:	Involves subconsciously "takes in" to imprint of another person including all their attitudes, messages, prejudices, expressions, even the sound of their voice, etc. This often is observed in children as they introject aspects of the parent into themselves. For instance, a child has a parent who is very spiritual. The child incorporates spirituality into himself.
4. Have you ever used **identification** to explain, leave, or deal with some situations?	
Explanation:	Modeling one's behavior and/or character after someone else. For instance, Sally is only four years old but she tries to look and act exactly like her mother. Last week, Sally went into her mother's bedroom and decorated herself with lipstick, face cream, and mascara.
5. Have you ever used **isolation of affect** to explain, leave, or deal with some situations?	
Explanation:	It is the separation of memory from emotion... The person can remember and talk about the trauma but feels no emotion. For instance, a person who talks about a car accident where he lost family members as if it is someone else's story.
6. Have you ever used **sublimation** to explain, leave, or deal with some situations?	
Explanation:	It is the redirection of impulses into socially acceptable activities—normal and healthy. For example, a man who is dissatisfied with his sex life but who has not stepped out on his wife becomes very busy repairing his house while his wife is out of town.
7. Have you ever used **displacement** to explain, leave, or deal with some situations?	
Explanation:	This defense reduces anxiety or pressure by transferring feelings toward one person to another. For instance, a salesman is angered by his superior but suppresses his anger; later, on return to his home, he punishes one of his children for misbehavior that would usually be tolerated or ignored.
8. Have you ever used **repression** to explain, leave, or deal with some situations?	
Explanation:	Painful, frightening or threatening emotions, memories, impulses, or drives that are subconsciously pushed or "stuffed" inside. For instance, soldiers exposed to traumatic experiences in concentration camps during wartime sometimes had amnesia and were unable to recall any part of their ordeal, or an adult who was molested as a child has no recollection of the event and believes the parent who molested her was wonderful.

9. Have you ever used **suppression** to explain, leave, or deal with some situations?

   Explanation: Painful, frightening, or threatening emotions, memories, impulses, or drives that are consciously pushed or "stuffed" inside. For instance, a young man at work finds that he is letting thoughts about a date that evening interfere with his duties; he decides not to think about plans for the evening until he leaves work. Or a student goes on vacation worried that she may be failing; she decides not to spoil her holiday by thinking of school.

10. Have you ever used **conversion** to explain, leave, or deal with some situations?

    Explanation: Mental conflict converted to a physical symptom. For example, a woman witnesses her spouse engaging in an affair and converts the anxiety of seeing that into blindness. The blindness alleviates the anxiety.

11. Have you ever used **regression** to explain, leave, or deal with some situations?

    Explanation: Giving up current level of development and going back to a prior level. For instance, a child who has been potty-trained for 5 years begins wetting the bed when her parents are arguing.

12. Have you ever used **reaction formation** to explain, leave, or deal with some situations?

    Explanation: Believing or behaving the opposite of the way one actually does. This is commonly seen in individuals recovering from addiction. For example, a man suffers from alcoholism and has entered rehabilitation. What he really wants is to drink, but he expresses that he hates alcohol; or a married woman who is disturbed by feeling attracted to one of her husband's friends treats him rudely.

13. Have you ever used **simple denial** to explain, leave, or deal with some situations?

    Explanation: Unconsciously refusing to accept what has happened that is too difficult to bear. For instance, a father witnesses his child being killed in a car accident, but repeatedly says, "That wasn't my son. No, no, it couldn't have been my son. He was at soccer practice."

14. Have you ever used **splitting** to explain, leave, or deal with some situations?

    Explanation: The inability to see gray areas. A person who uses splitting sees things as all good or all bad. This often is seen in borderline personality disorder. For instance, a woman enters a new relationship and believes her partner to be "perfect." When the partner does something wrong, the same woman immediately believes the partner to be horrible. She is unable to see that sometimes good people make mistakes.

15. I have thought of or already kicked back at an abusive person

16. I have thought of or already punched back at an abusive person

17. I have thought of or already shoved an abusive person

18. I have thought of or already slapped an abusive person

19. I have thought of or already pushed an abusive person

20. I have thought of or already burnt an abusive person

21. I have thought of or already bit an abusive person

22. I have thought of or already stabbed an abusive person

23. I have thought of or already chocked an abusive person

Notes: *Instructions to respondents: Please answer the following questions by checking either, "Yes" or "No." Check "Yes" only to those items that you have done intentionally, or on purpose, to defend yourself, a friend, a family member or your kid(s). Have you ever intentionally, or on purpose, done any of the following.*

Table 3.13 The Seven-factor Typology of Victim Characteristics With PCA Loadings

Factor and Name of Victim Type	Factor #1 Reassurance Type	Factor #2 Anger Type	Factor #3 Excitation Type	Factor #4 Submissive Type	Factor #5 Self-Preservation, Externally Oriented Type	Factor #6 Self-Preservation Internally Oriented Type	Factor #7 Domination Type
Motivation and Personality Characteristics of Victims of Personal Violence	Self-esteem (−0.851)	Anger (0.848)	Masochism (0.927)	Empathy (0.859)	Strive-back (0.807)	Risky (−0.505)	Narcissism (0.884)
	Reject/Abandon (0.785)	Aggression (0.802)	Sadism (0.908)	Humiliation (−0.704)	Self-defense (0.692)	Projection (−0.460)	Dom/Authority (0.738)
	Failure (0.783)	Impulsivity (0.785)	Risky (0.635)	Reassurance (0.451)	Finance (0.598)	Self-Harm (−0.453)	Self-Efficacy (0.562)
	Social (0.751)	Rage/Revenge (0.755)	Self-harm (0.581)	Reject/Abandon (0.332)		Finance (0.339)	Inadequacy (−0.533)
	Projection (0.727)	Antisocial (0.617)	Antisocial (0.565)	Impulsivity (−0.324)		Self-defence (−0.336)	Social (−0.528)
	Inadequacy (0.721)	Risky (0.476)		Dom/Authority (−0.318)		Anti-Social (−0.325)	Reassurance (−0.443)
	Self-efficacy (−0.694)	Self-defense (0.443)					Self-Esteem (0.438)
	Self-harm (0.621)	Humiliation (0.391)					Failure (−0.367)
	Reassurance (0.586)	Finance (−0.351)					
	Dom/Authority (−0.454)	Narcissism (0.322)					
	Antisocial (0.302)						

Notes: A positive loading means a positive association, while a negative loading means a negative association.

Comparatively, this type is most similar to Petherick and Ferguson's (2012), reassurance-oriented type. The present type and the reassurance type posited by Petherick and Ferguson (2012) share all of the described characteristics as well as two additional characteristics: fear of failure and submissiveness. The passive and submissive nature of this type is likely to underscore the motivations that lead to precipitative behaviors. Table 3.14 shows the comparison of the reassurance-oriented type across the victim/offender typology models.

The reassurance-oriented type identified in the PCA of the seven-factor model of victim characteristics is also associated with three variables not identified in the corresponding types of other models: increased risk of self-harm, characteristic antisocial behaviors, and the use of projection as a defense mechanism. This is not unexpected as all three are characteristically expressed as maladaptive

Table 3.14 Between-Models Comparison of the Reassurance-Oriented Type Characteristics of the "Seven-Factor Typology of Victim Characteristics"

	Victim Typology		Offender Typology		
	Brotto (2016)	Petherick and Ferguson (2012)	Groth et al. (1977)	Hazelwood and Burgess (2009)	Petherick and Turvey (2008)
Low self-esteem	✓	✓	✓	✓	✓
Fear of rejection/ abandon	✓	✓	✓		✓
Fear of failure	✓	✓			
Social inadequacy	✓	✓	✓	✓	✓
Use of Projection	✓				
Feeling of Inadequacy	✓	✓	✓		✓
Low self-efficacy	✓	✓	✓		✓
Self-harm	✓				
Need of reassurance	✓	✓	✓	✓	✓
Submissive-ness	✓	✓			
Use of Antisocial behaviors	✓				

coping mechanisms to reinforce, protect, or restore an individual's self-esteem, or to mitigate the negative emotional reactions associated with low self-worth (Dombeck, 2004; Grohol, 2013).

Ultimately, the reassurance-oriented victim is, according to Petherick and Sinnamon (2014, p. 422):

> At high risk for co-dependent relationships in which they will submit themselves to another and remain even in the face of extreme adversity and abuse. Feelings of inadequacy and the need to obtain esteem through others combined with timidity, shyness, submissiveness, and high tolerance for abuse means these individuals often place themselves in situations where they are at high risk for personal violence.

THE "ANGER-ORIENTED TYPE"

Anger-oriented victims are characterized by a high level of anger and aggression. They are likely to be very impulsive, driven by rage and revenge, be characteristically antisocial, and to actively engage in high-risk behaviors. The anger-oriented victim is also likely to score high in self-defensiveness and narcissism, and is likely to actively seek to humiliate others as a means of restoring their own self-esteem. The self-absorbed and aggressive focus of these victims means that they are substantially less likely to suffer from financially abusive circumstances.

A Comparison With Existing Typologies

As the name suggests, the results showed anger as a key component of this victim typology, which is a characteristic that is consistent with existing typologies such as the "anger retaliatory rapist" described by Groth et al. (1977) and Hazelwood and Burgess (2009); the "anger retaliatory" type described by Petherick and Turvey (2008); and the "anger retaliatory victim" type described by Petherick and Ferguson (2012) (see Table 3.15). All models were consistent to say that victim and offender behaviors are driven by anger either toward individuals, groups or organization as a result of cumulative real or perceived wrongs. All anger types described in all models are also consistent in their assertion that because this type is driven by anger, they are likely to act impulsively and aggressively and to seek revenge when wronged—whether actual or perceived. In this type, victim precipitation often occurs as their overt aggressiveness results in anxiety and aggression in others, which creates a never-ending cycle of power struggles (Petherick & Ferguson, 2012).

While all models show the anger type characterized by anger, aggression, and a tendency to use humiliation of others as an ego-restoring tactic, the anger type in this model is perhaps most similar to that espoused by Petherick and Turvey (2008), as these two models uniquely highlight the additional likelihood of this type engaging in antisocial and high-risk behaviors.

Table 3.15 Between-Models Comparison of the Anger-Oriented Type Characteristics of the "Seven-Factor Typology of Victim Characteristics"

	Victim Typology		Offender Typology		
	Brotto (2016)	**Petherick and Ferguson (2012)**	**Groth et al. (1977)**	**Hazelwood and Burgess (2009)**	**Petherick and Turvey (2008)**
Anger	✓	✓	✓	✓	✓
Aggression	✓	✓	✓	✓	✓
Impulsivity	✓	✓	✓	✓	✓
Rage/revenge	✓	✓	✓	✓	✓
Antisocial	✓		✓		✓
Risky behaviors	✓				✓
Self-defense	✓				
Humiliation	✓		✓	✓	✓
Narcissism	✓				
Negative correlation with financial abuse	✓				
Projection		✓			✓
Feelings of inadequacy		✓			
Fear of failure		✓			

The "anger-oriented type" identified in the present model includes two variables not previously identified in any of the previous models: self-defense behaviors and narcissism. In any situation where self-integrity is threatened, people are motivated to repair it, and this motivation can lead to defensive responses (Sherman & Cohen, 2006). These defense mechanisms can be automatic and unconscious in nature, and when they are characterized by "fight" rather than "flight" responses, are often linked with impulsivity and aggression. This, in turn, can result in precipitative behaviors. For instance, an individual can be harmed as a result of a conflict where he/she impulsively attacks another individual without considering all the variables such as size difference, the presence of a weapon, or some other environmental variable. When anger, narcissism, and a low self-esteem combine, the result can be narcissistic rage that becomes directed at others (Krizan & Johar, 2015). This narcissistic vulnerability is strongly linked to poor self-esteem as low self-esteem is a core driver of aggressive behaviors due to its relationship with shame, hostility, and anger (Krizan & Johar, 2015).

As summarized by Petherick and Ferguson (2012, p. 105), individuals or victims that are classified as anger oriented become victims because:

> *Their overt aggressiveness may bring about stress, anxiety, and aggression in others. For example, they may inhibit the opportunities of significant others out of hatred and anger resulting from perceived or imagined wrongs. This may begin a never ending cycle of power struggles, creating tumultuous relationships.*

THE "EXCITATION-ORIENTED TYPE"

The excitation-oriented victim scores highly in masochistic and sadistic traits, and is very likely to engage in high-risk, antisocial, and self-harming behaviors.

A Comparison With Existing Typologies

The "excitation-oriented type" of the current model is consistent with the "excitation type" found in the literature. This includes the "anger excitation rapist" described by Groth et al. (1977) and Hazelwood and Burgess (2009); the "sadistic" type described by Petherick and Turvey (2008); and the "excitation-oriented" type described by Petherick and Ferguson (2012). In all of these models, the key component is sadism (Table 3.16).

However, it is very difficult to compare the "excitation-oriented type" of the present model with the offender types of other models. Indeed, offenders and victims are not driven by the same motivation (Petherick & Ferguson, 2012). Offenders are often described as sadists, which is "an individual who experiences sexual gratification from the pain and suffering of another" (Petherick & Sinnamon, 2014, p. 417),

Table 3.16 Between-Models Comparison of the Excitation-Oriented Type Characteristics of the "Seven-Factor Typology of Victim Characteristics"

	Victim Typology		Offender Typology		
	Brotto (2016)	Petherick and Ferguson (2012)	Groth et al. (1977)	Hazelwood and Burgess (2009)	Petherick and Turvey (2008)
Masochism	✓	✓			
Sadism	✓	✓	✓	✓	✓
Risky behaviors	✓				
Self-harm	✓	✓			
Antisocial	✓				
High level of aggression			✓	✓	✓
Domination			✓	✓	✓
Humiliation			✓	✓	

are sexually driven, while victims who can engage in sadistic behaviors are not only driven by sexual gratification, therefore, and as stated by Petherick and Sinnamon (2014) a slight adjustment has to be made in order to apply the type to victims' behaviors. According to Petherick and Sinnamon (2014, p. 417):

> *While engaging in this behaviour may increase the chance for victimization, charac-terizing this type only as one where sexual gratification is at play may be problem-atic. To be able to adapt this victim behaviour, it is therefore necessary to slightly modify the main theme of the behaviour in terms of the needs served.*

The excitation-oriented victim type of the present model is consistent with the "excitation-oriented victim type" described by Petherick and Sinnamon (2014). Indeed, both typologies include masochism, sadism, and self-harm as the main vari-ables that characterize this type. Adopting one of two forms, sadism in this context could mean actual sadism (directed at another) or masochism (directed at the self).

According to the DSM-V (American Psychiatric Association, 2013, p. 530), sexual sadism involves:

> *Acts (real, not simulated) in which the individual derives sexual excitement from the psychological or physical suffering (including humiliation of the victim) .... Others act on the sadistic urges with a consenting partner (who may have Sexual Masochism) who willingly suffers pain or humiliation. Still others with Sexual Sadism act on their sadistic sexual urges with nonconsenting victims. In all of these cases, it is the suffering of the victim that is sexually arousing. When Sexual Sadism is severe, and especially when it is associated with Antisocial Personal-ity Disorder, individuals with Sexual Sadism may seriously injure or kill their victims.*

In sadistic cases, victim precipitation occurs when the victim is engaged in sadistic acts and then fights back after realizing the danger of the situation.

Sexual masochism is defined in the DSM-V (American Psychiatric Association, 2013, p. 529) as:

> *Acts (real, not simulated) of being humiliated, beaten, bound, or otherwise made to suffer...Others acts on the masochistic sexual urges by themselves (e.g. binding themselves, sticking themselves with pins, shocking themselves electrically, or self-mutilation) or with a partner. One particularly dangerous form of Sexual Masochism, called "hypoxyphilia", involves sexual arousal by oxygen depriva-tion obtained by means of chest compression, noose, ligature, plastic bag, mask, or chemical (often a volatile nitrite that produces temporary decrease in brain oxygenation by peripheral vasodilatation).*

In masochistic situations, victims expose themselves to harm or loss either alone or with a partner. It can include, as stated before, cases of hypoxyphilia or cases where victims are engaged in other forms of self-harm such as scarification or cutting (Petherick & Ferguson, 2012; Petherick & Sinnamon, 2014).

Although it has been argued that sadomasochism should be removed from the official classification of mental disorders (Moser & Kleinplatz, 2006; Reiersol & Skeid, 2006), it is important to recognize the fact that victim precipitation can occur as a result of sadomasochistic behaviors with a number of situations where masochistic behavior has caused serious physical harm or been life-threatening (Hucker, 2008).

Unique to the present model, risky and antisocial behaviors were identified as characteristics of the "excitation-oriented type." This could be explained by the link that exists between extreme paraphilic sadomasochism and both antisocial and risky behaviors (Meston & Frohlich, 2013). For instance, victims may engage in a sado-masochistic activity in which whipping, burning, stabbing, or other behavior is taken too far and turns to victimization. Another example of masochistic practice that can be precipitative is hypoxyphilia, which is described as a dangerous and fatal practice that consists of deliberately cutting off the airflow supply, through mechanical or chemical means, to induce mild cerebral hypoxia for sexual gratification (Medical Dictionary, 2009).

The proportion of excitation-oriented offenders and victims has been described as comparatively small (Hazelwood & Burgess, 2009; Petherick & Ferguson, 2012; Petherick & Sinnamon, 2014). However, the prevalence of sexually sadistic crimes is open to contention. According to Canter and Youngs (2009, p. 346):

> DSM-IV (American Psychiatric Association, 1994) proposes 10% of rapists will be sexual sadists. Other studies give estimates of the number of sexual offenders who are sadists ranging from 5-10% (Groth, 1979), 45% (Fedora et al., 1992) to 80% (MacCulloch et al., 1983). Allnutt et al. (1996) state that only 5.6% of the 728 sexual offenders they studied met DSM-III-R (American Psychiatric Association, 1987) Criteria for sexual sadism; Langevin and Langevin (in Marshall and Kennedy, 2002) claim that 45% of 91 sexual aggressives were sadists (using Clarke Sex History questionnaire). The variety of prevalence rates suggests that the definition and recognition of sexual sadism in practice is very variable and probably rather confused.

The "excitation-oriented type" was identified in 15% of the sample used to develop the seven-factor model. This is a substantial subgroup of the sample.

THE "SUBMISSIVE-ORIENTED TYPE"

The "submissive-oriented type" of the seven-factor model is characterized by a high level of empathy, a need for reassurance, and a high level of fear of rejection and abandonment. These victims also score very low on behaviors associated with a need for humiliating others, impulsivity, and domination and authority.

This type is the only one that is not directly comparable to other types within existing models. However, this type accounted for 7.5% of the sample group used to identify the seven-factor model. The characteristics of this type are comparable to the diagnostic criteria set out for dependent personality disorder (DPD) (American Psychiatric Association, 2013), and, therefore, victims who display these characteristics will have a high likelihood of having a DPD (Kilgus, Maxmen, & Ward, 2016). The symptoms of DPD illustrate a clear set of risks for precipitative actions (or inactions) by these victims (Sinnamon, 2016): For example:

1. Permitting others, or even going so far as to actively encourage others, to make important life decisions for you;
2. Subordinating your own needs for the needs of others, particularly those on whom you are dependent. This includes unreasonable compliance to the wants and demands of others;
3. Lack of will to make reasonable demands upon those you are dependent upon;
4. Extreme discomfort and helplessness when alone, including an exaggerated fear of being unable to care for yourself;
5. Ruminations about being abandoned by intimate and/or dependent relations. Fear of being left alone to care for yourself;
6. Inability to make even rudimentary or pedestrian decisions without excessive advice and reassurance from others.

Overwhelming empathy could also result in codependency (Vaknin, 2015). Codependents are often described as needy, demanding, submissive, and suffering from abandonment anxiety (Malloy & Berkery, 1993; Vaknin, 2015). Victim precipitation occurs because no matter how badly they can be mistreated, they will remain committed. The overwhelming empathy will make the victim feel guilt either because they believe that their own behaviors and/or attitudes were responsible for driving the abuser to mistreat them, or because of the concern over the negative impact ending a relationship may have on the abuser.

THE "SELF-PRESERVATION, EXTERNALLY ORIENTED TYPE"

The main characteristic of these victims is a high degree to which they engage in strive-back behaviors. Self-preservation, externally oriented victim types characteristically strive to regain control and/or balance. These victims also showed a substantial level of engagement in high-risk behaviors, experiences of financial abuse, and dependence.

A Comparison With Existing Typologies

This current type is not comparable with any of the offenders' typologies as none described a self-preservation form of motivation that applied to offenders. However, it is comparable with the "self-preservation-oriented type" as well as some characteristics of the "materially oriented type" described by Petherick and Ferguson (2012). Indeed, as described by Petherick and Sinnamon (2014, p. 418), victims who fit in this cluster are more likely to use strive-back and self-defense behaviors in order to "restore some kind of imbalance of power, especially in

Table 3.17 Between-Models Comparison of the Self-Preservation, Externally Oriented Type Characteristics of the "Seven-Factor Typology of Victim Characteristics"

	Victim Typology		
	Brotto (2016)	**Petherick and Ferguson (2012)**	
		Materially-Oriented	**Self-Preservation Oriented**
Strive-back behaviors	✓		✓
Self-defense behaviors	✓		✓
Financial abuse	✓	✓	

situations where their own lives, or the life of another (usually in their care) is threatened" (see Table 3.17). Fear and desperation are prevalent responses of victims who strive-back against their abuser (Mackenzie & Colvin, 2009). Indeed, fear and desperation do lead to self-preservation behaviors for people fearing for their own safety or the safety of their relatives (Mackenzie & Colvin, 2009). Moreover, acts of desperation can be committed when no alternative means of escape from danger/risk can be seen, for example, a fear of leaving the relationship due to the risk of retaliation, a fear of leaving the relationship due to concerns over the well-being of children involved, or a fear of leaving because there is nowhere to go (Mackenzie & Colvin, 2009).

THE "SELF-PRESERVATION, INTERNALLY ORIENTED TYPE"

Like the previous type, the self-preservation, internally oriented type is characterized by engaging in behaviors designed to protect the self or other loved ones (e.g., children). The difference between the two is that this group focuses behaviors on restoring balance in internal mechanisms rather than through external factors. The internally oriented type therefore engages in behaviors associated with regulation/mediation of physiological arousal and psychological malaise including numerous forms of high-risk behaviors (drugs, sex, etc.), self-harming behaviors, and social isolation or other antisocial behavioral practices. They are also likely to have a dependent personality and commonly find themselves in financially abusive relationships. Correspondingly, these victims show an aversion to projection, physical self-defense behaviors.

A Comparison With Existing Typologies

This current type is not comparable with any of the offenders' typologies as none described a self-preservation form of motivation that applied to offenders. However, the "self-preservation, internally oriented type" of the current model seems to be

Table 3.18 Between-Models Comparison of the Self-Preservation, Internally Oriented Type Characteristics of the "Seven-Factor Typology of Victim Characteristics"

	Victim Typology		
	Brotto (2016)	Petherick and Ferguson (2012)	
		Materially-Oriented	Self-Preservation Oriented
Negative correlation with risky behaviors	✓		✓
Negative correlation with use of rrojection	✓		
Negative correlation with self-harm	✓		✓
Negative correlation with use of self-defense behaviors	✓		✓
Negative correlation with antisocial behaviors	✓		✓
Financial abuse	✓	✓	
Risky behaviors		✓	
Antisocial behaviors		✓	

a combination of two types of the typology developed by Petherick and Ferguson (2012): "materially oriented" and "self-preservation-oriented" types (see Table 3.18).

Contrary to the "self-preservation, externally oriented type" that includes strive-back and the use of self-defense behavior to keep the homeostasis, the "self-preservation, internally oriented type" is characterized by passive behaviors in order to protect this homeostasis. In this case the preservation-oriented victim will remain in the abusive or threatening situation because it is safer than fighting back or leaving, which almost guarantees harm or loss.

The victims that fit into this cluster were also likely to suffer from financial abuse and are compatible with the description of the "materially oriented victims" type described by Petherick and Sinnamon (2014, p. 418) as it describes the victim that "stays with a controlling partner because they cannot afford to survive on their own, among others."

This type is characterized by victims who internally self-preserve by not taking any risks and acting passively. This type would include dependent personalities and avoidant personalities as described by Petherick and Sinnamon (2014). For instance, dependent personalities by their characteristics will allow the abuse while avoidant personalities might isolate themselves and therefore precipitate the assault (Petherick & Sinnamon, 2014).

THE "DOMINATION-ORIENTED TYPE"

Victims who fit into the domination-oriented type are highly narcissistic, have a high level of self-esteem and self-efficacy, and are highly dominating and authoritarian. These victims are also correspondingly low in feelings of inadequacy, need for reassurance, fear of failure, and need for social interaction. Overall, this type presents as arrogant, self-absorbed, and extremely confident in their own abilities. The risk of victimization comes when their own abilities do not measure up to this self-assurance, and when their own attitudes of self-importance, upset, anger, or offend others who may take offense and retaliate with physical force or other criminal responses.

A Comparison With Existing Typologies

Despite some rearrangement, the "domination-oriented type" of the current model is in some points consistent with the "assertive type" found in the literature. This includes the "power assertive rapist" described by Groth et al. (1977) and Hazelwood and Burgess (2009); the "power assertive" offender described by Petherick and Turvey (2008); and the "assertive-oriented" victim type described by Petherick and Ferguson (2012). In all of these models a key component is domination and authority.

First, it should be acknowledged that this typology uses the term *domination* instead of *assertiveness*. It is the authors' opinion that "assertive type" has been misapplied in previous typology models. Assertiveness is the quality of "being able to make overtures to other people, and to stand up for oneself in a nonaggressive way" (Marano, 2014, para. 4). However, in all typologies that comprise an assertive type, aggressive and impulsive behaviors are also present, which is inconsistent with the definition of assertiveness. Indeed, the difference between aggression and assertion is essentially the use of domination.

In a similar vein to Petherick and Turvey's (2008), and Petherick and Ferguson's (2012) "assertive type," the "domination-oriented type" of this typology is characterized by a high degree of narcissism. Narcissistic individuals are characterized by a "grandiose self-concept, feelings of superiority, self-centeredness, and sense of entitlement" (Orth, Robins, Meier, & Conger, 2015, p. 134). It is not surprising that narcissism is found to be negatively correlated with feelings of inadequacy, a need for reassurance, social interactivity, and a fear of failure. Moreover, the link between narcissism and domination/authority found in the principal components analysis during the evaluation of this typology is supported in the extant literature. For example, Johnson, Leedom, and Muhtadie (2012), assert that narcissistic personality disorder is associated with extremely high dominance motivation and self-perceived power (Table 3.19).

Individuals, offenders or victims, with a high degree of narcissistic personality characteristics will attempt to dominate others in order to protect their self-esteem (Kohut, 1977; Morf & Rhodewalt, 2001; Petherick & Sinnamon, 2014; Raskin, Novacek, & Hogan, 1991). It is likely that individuals fitting this type will possess either a low self-esteem or a high but unstable self-esteem. Indeed, Wink (1991) described two forms of narcissism: overt and covert. The overt type is characterized by exhibitionism,

Table 3.19 Between-Models Comparison of the Domination-Oriented Type Characteristics of the "Seven-Factor Typology of Victim Characteristics"

	Victim Typology		Offender Typology		
	Brotto (2016)	Petherick and Ferguson (2012)	Groth et al. (1977)	Hazelwood and Burgess (2009)	Petherick and Turvey (2008)
Narcissism	✓	✓			✓
Dom/authority	✓	✓	✓	✓	✓
High self-efficacy	✓				
High self-esteem	✓				
Negative correlation with feeling of inadequacy	✓				
Negative correlation with problems in social interactions	✓				
Negative correlation with need of reassurance	✓				
Negative correlation with fear of failure	✓				
Low self-esteem		✓			✓
Feeling of inadequacy			✓		
Social inadequacy			✓		
Fear of rejection			✓		
Moderate to high level of aggression		✓	✓	✓	✓
Lack of empathy				✓	✓
Impulsivity		✓		✓	✓

exaggerated sense of self-importance, grandiosity and desire for attention, and is associated with a high self-esteem. The covert type is characterized by hypersensibility to criticism, lack of self-confidence, social withdrawal, and grandiosity, and is associated with low or high-fragile self-esteem (Brookes, 2015; Miller et al., 2011; Pincus et al., 2009; Rohmann, Neumann, Herner, & Bierhoff, 2012; Rose, 2002). The covert type or "dark side" of narcissism commonly leads to maladaptive personality patterns and psychopathy (Baumeister, Smart, & Boden, 1996). The high self-esteem of this type is likely to be unstable and therefore increases the chance of victimization as it is linked to higher tendencies toward hostility and anger (Kernis, Grannemann, & Barclay, 1989). Indeed, high but unstable self-esteem "would produce heightened sensitivity to ego threats, because the individual has much to lose and is vulnerable to the miserable feeling of a brief drop in self-esteem, and so his or her sensitivity may lead to maximal hostility" (Bushman & Baumeister, 1998, p. 219).

PREDICTING THE CRIME RISK USING THE SEVEN-FACTOR MODEL OF VICTIM CHARACTERISTICS

Using the same sample that was used for the development of the model, the authors evaluated the relationship between each of the seven victim types of the identified model, and the four interpersonal violence crimes that the victims had experienced. A fifth crime type was also investigated, that being a multiple crime type in which victims had experienced more than one of the four types of interpersonal violence crimes. When victim subtypes of the seven-factor model were analyzed based on their experiences of interpersonal violent crime, a clear relationship was identified between crime type and victim type.

Self-Preservation, Internally Oriented Victim Type Is Significantly Associated With Risk for Domestic Violence

Individuals who possess the characteristics of the self-preservation, internally oriented victim type have the highest risk of becoming a victim of domestic violence. One of the most prominent characteristics of the self-preservation, internally oriented victim type is financial abuse. Financial abuse and financial despair are often described as reasons for victims to stay in an abusive relationship (Buel, 1999; Gharaibeh & Oweis, 2009; Petherick & Ferguson, 2012). Economic abuse is defined by Morgan and Chadwick (2009, para. 8) as "exerting control over household or family income by preventing the other person's access to finances and financial independence." Financial abuse is a significant issue that primarily impacts women. It crosses socioeconomic and geographic locations, and is closely associated with domestic violence (Corrie & McGuire, 2013). Financial abuse is considered to be an underreported crime, however; the statistics still show it to be a major issue. For example, it affects a reported 1.86 million Australians, which represents about 50% of all women who report an abusive relationship (Corrie & McGuire, 2013). Economic abuse often leads to the victim being "trapped" in a violent relationship because of financial despair (Buel, 1999; Corrie & McGuire, 2013).

Another characteristic of the "self-preservation, internally oriented type" is the use of self-protective behaviors in order to reduce the likeliness of harm or loss; it includes, for example, reducing risky situations or the use of submissive behaviors. In the literature, there are some frightening statistics about leaving abusive relationships. For instance, in Australia two in five women experience violence at the hands of their (ex) intimate partner after separation (Ross, 2015) and 50–75% of domestic violence homicides happen at the time of separation or in the immediate period after separation from an abusive intimate partner (Kasperkevic, 2014). Therefore, the decision to stay is, for some victims, a self-preservative action with an evidentiary basis. The self-preservation instinct of some victims leads them to stay because the cost of being victimized is smaller within the abusive relationship than it is in the face of a retaliatory action from an abusive partner, or the real or perceived risk of financial hardships once removed from the relationship. Indeed, there is a correlation between financial abuse and poverty and the combination of abuse and poverty may force a victim to remain in an abusive relationship for internal self-preservation reasons (Morgan & Chadwick, 2009).

Anger Victim Type Is Significantly Associated With Risk of Sexual Assault and Physical Assault

Individuals who possess the characteristics of the anger-oriented victim type are at a significantly higher risk of becoming a victim of sexual and physical assault. Regarding the link between anger and the chance of being a victim of physical assault, it does make direct sense as anger and aggressive behaviors toward others will bring aggressive retaliatory responses in return, and therefore increase the chance of victimization (Petherick & Sinnamon, 2014). Moreover, "anger types" are characterized by a greater risk of engaging in antisocial and high-risk behaviors, which may further exacerbate the risk of victimization.

The link between the anger type and the risk of being sexual assaulted once again centers largely around the anger-type characteristics of high-risk and antisocial behaviors. The extant literature provides evidence of a clear relationship between high-risk behaviors, such as alcohol and substance abuse, and sexual promiscuity, and vulnerability to sexual victimization. For instance, alcohol is a factor in 50–70% of all reported sexual assaults (Abbey, 1991; Pernanen, 1991).

Reassurance Victim Type Is Significantly Associated With Risk of Being Stalked

Individuals who possess the characteristics of the reassurance-oriented victim type are at a significantly higher risk of being stalked. In this case, it is very likely that the stalker will be a partner or ex-partner whose motivation is the continuation or reestablishment of a domestic relationship. This kind of stalking behavior called domestic violence/stalking represents 75–80% of reported stalking behavior (Roberts & Dziegielewski, 1996). The motive behind the stalker behavior is to maintain control over a weak victim with the idea that "If I can't have him/her, no one else can either" (Roberts & Dziegielewski, 1996). In this case the victim is afraid of ending the relationship and afraid of retaliation. Those stalking victims exhibit behavioral and emotional reaction comparable to hostages who suffered from the "Stockholm syndrome." As with all victims of interpersonal violence, stalking victims are likely to be influenced by a low self-esteem, a denial of the seriousness of the stalking behaviors, an inability to trust, and an unhealthy sense of dependency on the stalker (Bolton & Bolton, 1987; Roberts & Dziegielewski, 1996).

Anger, Excitation, and Self-Preservation, Externally Oriented Victim Types are Significantly Associated With Risk of Being a Victim of Multiple Violent Crime Types

Individuals who possess the characteristics of the anger-oriented, excitation-oriented, or the self-preservation-oriented victim types are at a significantly higher risk of becoming a victim of multiple crimes of interpersonal violence. There is a broad range of research literature that clearly evidences the relationship between increased victimization risk and personal characteristics associated with higher engagement with violent behavior, lower self-control, anger, aggression, masochism, sadism, fear, and desperation (Daday, Broidy, Crandall, & Sklar, 2005; Hucker, 2008; Jennings, Higgins, Tewksbury, Gover, & Piquero, 2010; Piquero, MacDonald, Dobrin, Daigle, & Cullen, 2005; Petherick & Sinnamon, 2014; Silver, 2002; Sinnamon, 2016; Wittebrood & Nieuwbeerta, 1999). Moreover, "anger" and "excitation" types are characterized by a characteristic engagement with antisocial and high-risk behavior, which again, increase victimization risk.

CONCLUSIONS

Ultimately, crimes involve both offenders and victims. While the historical focus has been on exploring offender characteristics in order to understand the circumstances, motivations, and behavioral factors that lead to the perpetration of a criminal act, contemporary discourse has also begun to recognize the value in improving our knowledge of victims and their unique role in the criminal process. Several models have been proposed to help explain the characteristics of both offenders and victims, and the way in which these characteristics influence the risk of offending and/or becoming a victim of a criminal act. The seven-factor model of victim characteristics is the latest iteration of these typological models and represents an empirically founded culmination of several previous victim typologies.

While there is now evidence to indicate that victim typologies may provide a predictive capability to identify potential victims of crime before they occur, it is essential to temper victimology with a sensitivity to the ever-present risk of the pendulum swinging from victim characteristics and victim precipitation to a more sinister position in which victim blaming and victim "victimization" becomes commonplace. Used with compassion and awareness of this risk, the process of victimology is a powerful tool to identify victim risk and to inform programs and policies to educate and protect those most at risk.

SUMMARY

- Victim, comes for the Latin word *victima*, and historically referred to any living being (human or animal) that was to be slaughtered or used in sacrifice (Burgess & Regehr, 2010; Ferguson & Turvey, 2009; Royal Spanish Academy, 2008). From a contemporary point of view, a victim is someone who suffers from harm or loss.
- Ferguson and Turvey (2009, p. 2) define victimology as "the scientific study of victims and victimization, including the relationships between victims and offender, investigators, courts, corrections, media and social movements." Victimology and some related fields of study have been expanded since the middle of the 20th century by the work of some scholars including individuals such as Hans von Hentig, Benjamin Mendelsohn, Stephen Schafer, and Marvin Wolfgang. In order to better understand the circumstances of victimization and the relationship between victim and offender, these individuals and others have developed different victim typologies, based either on biological, psychological, or sociological factors.
- There are two different standpoints: general and penal/legal.
- Generally, victim refers to all people who suffer harm or loss by accident, natural disasters, or war (Ferguson & Turvey, 2009).
- Legally, the definition includes any harm or loss attributable to the action of an individual, group, or organization that can affect a person (Petherick & Sinnamon, 2014). According to Jerin and Moriarty (1998, p. 1), a crime victim is "anyone who is injured or killed due to a violation of the criminal law."
- There are three distinct historical eras in which there were distinct differences in the manner in which victims were treated: the Golden Age, the Dark Age, and the Age of the Reemergence of the Victim.
- The Golden Age: In the simplest terms, the principle of "an eye for an eye" epitomizes the character of the Golden Age. The Golden Age or "victim justice system" was a period in which individuals made the law and personally enacted the role of the victim, prosecutor, and judiciary. There was a basic social system of retribution and restitution that helped protect victims who had to generally fend for themselves. Retribution meant that the perpetrator would be made to suffer in proportion to the degree of harm caused by the offense. Restitution involved the offender restoring the victim through a proportionate payment sufficient to return the victim to their preoffense state (or as close as possible).
- The Dark Age: Drastic changes occurred in the middle (or dark) age, and the focus moved to a criminally oriented justice system. Criminality was concerned with offenses not perpetrated against the victims or their relatives but against the law of the king or state. The focus shifted toward offender punishments and rights rather than victim rights and restoration. Reasons for these changes included the emergence of local governments, the beginning of urbanization, the industrial revolution, and the rise in power of the Roman Catholic Church. In this system, the victim was no longer seen as important and was relegated to

nothing more than a piece of evidence who was largely not considered in the decision process.

- Reemergence of the Victim: The early part of the mid-20th century (1940s) saw the "rediscovery" of victims and victims' rights being initiated by an emerging scholarly interest in the victim–offender relationship (Petherick & Sinnamon, 2014). After being focused for so long on the criminal offender, people started to study the dyad of the victim–offender to better understand the role of the victim during the criminal act. The term *victimology* first appeared in the literature in 1949, as those within the criminal justice system began to realize that the greatest impact of a criminal act was felt by those who were the direct victims of the offense. This increasing realization, combined with the emerging interest in the victim–offender relationship, led to the development of the field of victimology in which the role of the victim within the criminal act became the central focus. While criminology is defined as the study of crime and criminals, victimology, a subdiscipline of criminology, focuses on the study of people harmed by criminals.

- It is through the concept of victim precipitation that the idea of a victim's role in his/her own victimization has been expanded. There are two different forms of precipitation: active precipitation and passive precipitation. Passive precipitation occurs when victims unknowingly threaten their attacker, while active precipitation occurs when the ultimate victim initiates threatening behaviors and/or the actual use of physical force. The idea of active precipitation has been criticized because of the victim-blaming character of the approach.

- There are two concepts in the literature that help to explain victim blaming: defensive attribution theory (DAT), and the just world hypothesis (JWH).

- DAT was posited by Shaver in 1970, and argues that when an individual is confronted with the seemingly whimsical victimization of another person, they become threatened by the realization that such random misfortunes could also happen them. The forced acknowledgment of the potential for such an experience then results in a negative emotional response that initiates a cognitive coping strategy to meet the need for self-preservation, and a sense of security, predictability, and personal control. The cognitive coping strategies include defensive attribution mechanisms that influence the perceptions of other people's misfortunes, such as victimization, in such a way that provides a predictive explanatory platform. The central tenet of DAT is that people can protect themselves against unfortunate and unpredictable occurrences by perceiving the event as avoidable. We tend to do this by making defensive attribution distortions of the victim's role in his or her own victimization, through increased attribution of responsibility to him or her. Therefore, in the DAT, blaming victims is a self-serving motivational bias created by the observer to cope with a distressing event. It protects the observer of the possibility of random misfortune by attributing personal responsibility to the victim of a criminal act.

- The JWT is a form of DAT that was first introduced by Lerner in 1965. The JWT argues that individuals have a need to believe that they live in a world where people generally get what they deserve. The belief that the world is just enables the individual to confront his physical and social environment as though they were stable and orderly. Without such a belief it would be difficult for the individual to commit himself to the pursuit of long-range goals or even to the socially regulated behavior of day-to-day life. Therefore, under a just world belief, there are two possible ways to be appeased that justice has been restored in the face of a criminal action. The first is to see that the victim is suitably compensated, and the second is to be convinced that the victim deserves to suffer.
- Two opportunity theories, the lifestyle-exposure theory and the routine activity theory (RAT), were created to explain criminal victimization in another way. These theories imply that the lifestyle of people can influence victimization because there is a link between victims' lifestyle and criminal events. These theories presume that the habits, lifestyles, and behavioral patterns of potential crime victims enhance their contact with offenders and thereby increase the chances that crime will occur.
- The lifestyle-exposure theory: Hindelang, Gottfredson, and Garofolo (1978) developed the lifestyle-exposure theory, which is considered one of the first systematic theories to explain criminal victimization. The essence of lifestyle exposure is that crime is not a random occurrence but rather a function of the victim's lifestyle including demographic features and behavioral characteristics. The lifestyle theory implies that demographic characteristics, such as age, gender, or income, role expectations, and structural constraints have an influence on daily activities and increase the likelihood of victimization. Behaviors including alcohol consumption or going out at night in public places are considered as lifestyle factors that increase the risk of being victimized.
- The routine activity theory: RAT was developed after the observation was made that there had been an increase in crime rates of offenses such as robbery, aggravated assault, forcible rape, and homicide, while the social trends and economic conditions in the United States had remained generally stable. According to RAT, for a crime to occur three conditions need to be present: (1) motivated offenders; (2) suitable targets; and (3) the absence of capable guardians against a violation. In other words, for a crime to occur, there is a contact between a motivated offender and one or more targets isolated from sufficient protection to prevent the crime. A "likely [or motivated] offender" includes anyone with an inclination to commit a crime. A "suitable target" includes any person or thing that may evoke criminal inclinations, which would include the actual value of the target and the monetary and symbolic desirability of it for offenders, the visibility to offenders or their informants, the access to it, the ease of escape from the site, as well as the portability or mobility of objects sought by offenders. A "guardian" is a person who can protect a target, including friends and formal

authorities such as police and security personnel, "intimate handlers" such as parents, teachers, coaches, friends, employers, and "place managers" such as janitors, and apartment managers.

- Historically, the literature and empirical research was focused heavily on offender risk and motivations. A number of models have been created to explain offender characteristics and offending risk. More recently, there is emerging evidence that indicates that the presence of certain individual characteristics also increases the risk of becoming a victim of crime. Several models have now been developed to also articulate this risk. This notion of offender and victim individual characteristics differs from the traditional demographic risk profiles that have been used to identify risk factors for crime. A number of demographic factors have been identified as being associated with crime risk, and this continues to the present to be an important element in crime prevention, investigations, and resource allocation. These demographic factors include such things as socioeconomics, residential location, familial constitution, age, social status, gender, and race.

- The World Health Organization defines violence as: "… the intentional use of physical force, or power, threatened or actual, against oneself, another person, or against a group or community, that either results in, or has a likelihood of resulting in injury, death, psychological harm, mal-development or deprivation" (Krug et al., 2002, p. 5).

- Violence can be divided into three categories that differ according to who is committing the violent act: *self-directed violence*, that includes any violence that a person inflicts to him/herself; *interpersonal violence* that is inflected by another individual or small group of individuals; and, *collective violence* that is inflicted by a larger group such as states, terrorist organizations, and political groups.

- According to the Australian Injury Prevention Network (2012, p. 1), "Interpersonal violence is a cause of suffering and trauma, which has devastating consequences for the mental, physical and sexual health of the victim. It affects us as individuals, parents, spouses, educators, researchers and citizens. The breadth of the problem is staggering with public health officials identifying interpersonal violence as a public health issue of epidemic proportions." Interpersonal violence refers to any violent act by a person or persons against another including physical assault, sexual assault, stalking, and domestic violence.

- Physical assault is the direct infliction of force, injury, or violence upon a person, including attempts or threats.

- Sexual assault is defined differently in various jurisdictions. However, the Rights of Women (2006, para. 6) defines sexual assault as any situation in which the perpetrator "… intentionally touches the victim, and the touching is sexual, and the victim does not consent to the touching … ."

- Stalking can be defined as a set of behaviors involving repeated and persistent attempts to impose unwanted communication and/or contact on another person. It can include phone calls, emails, and letters, as well as behaviors such as harassment, threats, following, and surveillance, and may lead to assault and homicide.

- Domestic violence is defined as physical aggression between family members, household members, or intimates.
- This type of violence occurs in a wide range of contexts and includes, for instance, domestic violence, violent crime, sexual assault, child and elder abuse, and neglect (Australian Injury Prevention Network, 2012). Interpersonal violence can be divided into two subcategories: family and intimate partner violence and community violence.
- Family and intimate partner violence: Violence largely between family members and intimate partners, usually, though not exclusively, taking place in the home. The former group includes forms of violence such as child abuse, intimate partner violence, and abuse of the elderly.
- Community violence: Violence between individuals who are unrelated, and who may or may not know each other, generally taking place outside the home. The latter includes youth violence, random acts of violence, rape or sexual assault by strangers, and violence in institutional settings such as schools, workplaces, prisons, and nursing homes.
- Understanding the motives and behaviors of victims is the purpose behind developing models of victim typologies. Being able to develop appropriate typologies can be very useful in many areas of research including criminology. In the past, criminals were classified as part of a homogeneous group, however, more recent research has demonstrated that there are several criminal types, and understanding these types provides for a clearer understanding of offender motivations and behavior.
- Groth's typology: In 1977 Groth, in collaboration with Ann Burgess and Lynda Holmstrom, proposed a typology of rape based on two main axes: power and anger. Their clinical typology of rape is based on the analysis of offenders' and victims' accounts. According to Groth and colleagues, all rapes have three different components: power, anger, and sexuality. Rape is described as an act where both aggression and sexuality are involved, but it is sexuality that is used as the means of expressing the aggressive needs and feelings that operate in the offender and underlie his assault. According to Petherick and Sinnamon (2014, p. 403), "… in a power offense, sexuality is an expression of conquest, while in anger rape sexuality is a hostile act. In sadistic rape, anger and sexuality become fused and the offender receives sexual gratification from pain and suffering." According to the hierarchy and relationships among these factors, the rapist's motivations are characterized as power assertive, power reassurance, anger retaliation, and anger excitation.
- Hazelwood adapted Groth's typology model by adding two additional types: the opportunistic and the gang rapist. The opportunistic and gang rapist subtypes differ from the other subtypes as they are not motivational in nature but rather are offending modus operandi. For example, a power assertive or power reassurance rapist can decide to rape an opportunistic victim in order

to restore his self-confidence. Here, the victim is chosen in a contextual situation.

- Despite the fact that Groth's and Hazelwood's typologies were created to specifically describe the motivation of sexual offenders, Petherick and Turvey (2008) recognized that this form of typology could also be used to describe other offenses such as stalking, domestic violence, assault, or fraud, and to explain more complex behavior such as that of gang members or crime victims. According to Petherick and Turvey (2008, p. 280): "The needs, or motives, that impel human criminal behaviors remain essentially the same for all offenders, despite behavioral expression that may involve kidnapping, child molestation, terrorism, sexual assault, homicide, or arson."

- The victim typology developed by Petherick and Ferguson (2012), and further described by Petherick and Sinnamon (2014), comprises seven different victim motivations: reassurance-oriented victims; assertive-oriented victims; anger retaliatory-oriented victims; pervasively oriented victims; excitation-oriented victims; materially oriented victims; preservation-oriented victims.

- An empirical evaluation of victim typologies by Brotto (2016) revealed evidence for a seven-factor model of victim characteristics as presented in this chapter: reassurance type; anger type; excitation type; submissive type; self-preservation, externally oriented type; self-preservation, internally oriented type; domination type. This new evidence-based typology has both commonalities with previous typology models as well as identified unique victim types not previously described.

- The seven-factor model of victim characteristics has shown to have a strong capacity to predict the type of crime those identified as having specific victim characteristics are likely to experience. This is the first model to illustrate predictive utility for victimization risk.

QUESTIONS

1. Define victim and victim precipitation: provide an example.
2. Describe the three historical periods of victim treatment.
3. Describe the key figures in the emergence of victimology.
4. Describe the key components of victim precipitation.
5. Describe the four theories developed to explain victim blaming.
6. Describe Groth's and Hazelwood's typologies. Explain how they differ and how they are similar.
7. What are the key components of the behavioral-motivational typology?
8. What are the key components of the victim-motivational typology?
9. Describe the seven-factor model of victim characteristics and how each factor is similar and how it differs to other victim and offender models.
10. How do the factors of the seven-factor model of victim characteristics relate to crime of interpersonal violence?

REFERENCES

Abbey, A. (1991). Acquaintance rape and alcohol consumption on college campuses: how are they linked? *American Journal of College Health, 39*(4), 165–170.

Adams, A. E., Sullivan, C. M., Bybee, D., & Greeson, M. R. (2008). Development of the scale of economic abuse. *Violence Against Women, 14*(5), 563–588. http://dx.doi.org/10.1177/1077801208315529.

Adan, A., Natale, V., Caci, H., & Prat, G. (2010). Relationship between circadian typology and functional and dysfunctional impulsivity. *Chronobiology International, 27*(3), 606–619. http://dx.doi.org/10.3109/07420521003663827.

Advocates for Human Rights. (2006a). *Prevalence of sexual assault.* Retrieved from http://stopvaw.org/Prevalence_of_Sexual_Assault.html.

Advocates for Human Rights. (2006b). *Prevalence of domestic violence.* Retrieved from http://stopvaw.org/Prevalence_of_Domestic_Violence.html.

American Psychiatric Association. (1994). *Diagnostic and statistical manual of mental disorders* (4th ed.). Washington, DC: American Psychiatric Association.

American Psychiatric Association. (2013). *Diagnostic and statistical manual of mental disorders* (5th ed.). Arlington, VA: American Psychiatric Publishing.

Ames, D. R., Rose, P., & Anderson, C. P. (2006). The NPI-16 as a short measure of narcissism. *Journal of Research in Personality, 40*(4), 440–450. http://dx.doi.org/10.1016/j.jrp.2005.03.002.

Amir, M. (1971). *Patterns in forcible rape.* Chicago, IL: University of Chicago Press.

Australian Bureau of Statistics. (2007b). *Perspectives on migrants, 2007. Article: Migrants' experiences of crime victimization.* ABS cat no. 3416.0 Canberra: Australian Commonwealth Government. Retrieved from http://www.abs.gov.au/ausstats/abs@.nsf/Lookup/3416.0Main%20Features32007opendocument&tabname=Summary&prodno=3416.0&issue=2007&num&view.

Australian Bureau of Statistics. (2012a). *Crime and Safety, Australia, Apr 2005. Article: The crime and safety survey.* ABS cat no. 4509.0 Canberra: Australian Commonwealth Government. Retrieved from http://www.abs.gov.au/AUSSTATS/abs@.nsf/productsbyCatalogue/669C5A997EAED891CA2568A900139405/.

Australian Bureau of Statistics. (2012b). *Recorded crime – Victims, Australia, 2012. Article: Person victim characteristics.* ABS cat no. 4510.0 Canberra: Australian Commonwealth Government. Retrieved from http://www.abs.gov.au/ausstats/abs@.nsf/Lookup/E850B8189D9F2A44CA257B88001295CF?opendocument.

Australian Bureau of Statistics (ABS). (2007a). *Australian social trends 2007, Article: Interpersonal violence.* ABS cat no. 4102.0 Canberra: Australian Commonwealth Government. Retrieved from http://www.abs.gov.au/AUSSTATS/abs@.nsf/Latestproducts/4B2A703C9CB10C90CA25732C00207D2C?opendocument.

Australian Bureau of Statistics (ABS). (2009). *Recorded crime – Victims, Australia, 2009, Article: Relationship of offender to victim.* ABS cat no. 4510.0 Canberra: Australian Commonwealth Government. Retrieved from http://www.abs.gov.au/ausstats/abs@.nsf/0/54BB4F6E9D0FF658CA2577360017A76C?opendocument.

Australian Injury Prevention Network. (2012). *Interpersonal violence position paper.* Retrieved from http://www.aipn.com.au/documents/AIPNviolence_Sept12forcomment.pdf.

Australian Institute of Criminology. (2010). *Selected offender profiles.* Retrieved from http://www.aic.gov.au/publications/current%20series/facts/1-20/2010/4_selected_offender_profiles.html.

Averdijk, M. (2011). Reciprocal effects of victimization and routine activities. *Journal of Quantitative Criminology*, *27*(2), 125–149. http://dx.doi.org/10.1007/s10940-010-9106-6.

Bailey, K. D. (1994). *Typologies and Taxonomies: An introduction to classification techniques.* Thousand Oaks, CA: Sage Publications, Inc.

Basile, K. C., Swahn, M. H., Chen, J. C., & Saltzman, L. E. (2006). Stalking in the United States: recent national prevalence estimates. *American Journal of Preventive Medicine*, *31*(2), 172–175. http://dx.doi.org/10.1016/j.amepre.2006.03.028.

Baumeister, R. E., Smart, L., & Boden, J. M. (1996). Relation of threatened egotism to violence and aggression: the dark side of high self-esteem. *Psychological Review*, *103*(1), 5–33. http://dx.doi.org/10.1037/0033-295X/96/s3.00.

Bellack, A. S., Hersen, M., Morrison, R., & Van Hasselt, V. B. (2013). *Handbook of family violence.* Springer Science & Business Media.

Bilić, V., Buzov, I., Gruden, V., & Jokić-Begić, N. (1998). The projection questionnaire: design, use and utility. *Collegium Antropologicum*, *22*(1), 277–289.

Bolton, E., & Bolton, S. (1987). *Working with violent families: A guide for clinical and legal practitioners.* Newbury Park, CA: Sage Publications, Inc.

Boon, J. C. W., & Sheridan, L. (2001). Stalker typologies: a law enforcement perspective. *Journal of Threat Assessment*, *1*(2), 75–97. http://dx.doi.org/10.1300/J177v01n02_05.

Brennan, S. (2013). *Police-reported crime statistics in Canada, 2011.* Statistics Canada. Retrieved from http://www.statcan.gc.ca/pub/85-002-x/2012001/article/11692-eng.htm#a6.

Brennan, K. A., Clark, C. L., & Shaver, P. R. (1998). Self-report measurement of adult attachment: an integrative overview. In J. A. Simpson, & W. S. Rholes (Eds.), *Attachment theory and close relationships* (pp. 46–76). NY: The Guilford Press.

Brookes, J. (2015). The effect of overt and covert narcissism on self-esteem and self-efficacy beyond self-esteem. *Personality and Individual Differences*, *85*(1), 172–175. http://dx.doi.org/10.1016/j.paid.2015.05.013.

Brotto, G.L.M. (2016). *Crime victims and criminals: the same needs or different? An analysis of victims motivations based on existing offenders.* (Unpublished doctoral thesis). Bond University, QLD, Australia.

Brzozowski, J. A., & Mihorean, K. (2002). *Technical report on the analysis of small groups in the 1999 general social survey.* cat. No. 85F0036XIE Index of downloadable statistics Canada publications. Retrieved from http://publications.gc.ca/Collection/Statcan/index-e.html.

Buel, S. M. (1999). Fifty obstacles to leaving, a.k.a, Why abuse victims stay. *The Colorado Lawyer*, *28*(10), 19–28.

Burgess, A. W., & Regehr, C. (2010). Victimology concepts and theories. In A. W. Burgess, C. Regehr, & A. R. Roberts (Eds.), *Victimology: Theories and applications* (pp. 31–65). Sudbury, MA: Jones & Bartlett Publishers.

Burgess, A. W., & Roberts, A. R. (2010). Crime and victimology. In A. W. Burgess, C. Regehr, & A. R. Roberts (Eds.), *Victimology: Theories and applications* (pp. 1–30). Sudbury, MA: Jones and Bartlett Publishers.

Burt, S. A., & Donnellan, M. B. (2009). Development and validation of the subtypes of antisocial behavior questionnaire. *Aggressive Behavior*, *35*(5), 376–398.

Bushman, B. J., & Baumeister, R. E. (1998). Threatened egotism, narcissism, self-esteem, and direct and displaced aggression: does self-love or self-hate lead to violence. *Journal of Personality and Social Psychology*, *75*(1), 219–229. http://dx.doi.org/10.1037/0022-3514/98/53.00.

Buss, A. H., & Perry, M. (1992). The Aggression questionnaire. *Journal of Personality and Social Psychology*, *63*(3), 452–459.

Canter, D., & Youngs, D. (2009). *Investigative Psychology: Offender profiling and the analysis of criminal action*. West Sussex, UK: John Wiley & Sons Ltd.

Caruso, D. R., & Mayer, J. D. (1998). *A measure of emotional empathy for adolescents and adults* (Unpublished Manuscript). Retrieved from http://www.unh.edu/emotional_intelligence/ei%20Measuring%20Mood/mm%20Measuring%20empathy.htm.

Cohen, L. E., & Felson, M. (1979). Social change and crime rate trends: a routine activity approach. *American Sociological Review*, *44*(4), 588–608.

Collier, D., Laporte, J., & Seawright, J. (2012). Putting typologies to work: concept formation, measurement, and analytic rigor. *Political Research Quaterly*, *65*(1), 217–232. http://dx.doi.org/10.1177/1065912912437162.

Conroy, D. E., Willow, J. P., & Metzler, J. N. (2002). Multidimensional fear of failure Measurement: the performance failure appraisal inventory. *Journal of Applied Sport Psychology*, *14*(2), 76–90. http://dx.doi.org/10.1080/10413200252907752.

Corrie, T., & McGuire, M. (2013). *Sharing solutions across sectors: A spotlight on economic abuse research report*. North Collingwood, VictoriaGood: Shepherd Youth & Family Service and Kildonan UnitingCare.

Cougle, J. R., Fitch, K. E., Fincham, F. D., Riccardi, C. J., Keough, M. E., & Tiampano, K. R. (2012). Excessive reassurance seeking and anxiety pathology: test of incremental associations and directionality. *Journal of Anxiety Disorders*, *26*(1), 117–125. http://dx.doi.org/10.1016/j.janxdis.2011.10.001.

Crawford, D. C. B. (2005). *Self-esteem and depression of employed versus male homosexuals in long-term monogamous partnerships* (Master's thesis) University of the Witwatersrand, Johannesburg, South Africa. Retrieved from http://wiredspace.wits.ac.za/bitstream/handle/10539/177/Masters_Dissertation.pdf?sequence=2.

Curtis, L. A. (1974). Victim precipitation and violent crime. *Social Problems*, *21*(4), 594–605.

Daday, J. K., Broidy, L. M., Crandall, C. S., & Sklar, D. P. (2005). Individual, neighborhood, and situational factors associated with violent victimization and offending. *Criminal Justice Studies*, *18*(3), 215–235. http://dx.doi.org/10.1080/14786010500287347.

Denson, T. F., Pedersen, W. C., & Miller, N. (2006). The displaced aggression questionnaire. *Journal of Personality and Social Psychology*, *90*(6), 1032–1051. http://dx.doi.org/10.1037/0022-3514.90.6.1032.

Dickman, S. J. (1990). Functional and dysfunctional impulsivity: personality and cognitive correlates. *Journal of Personality and Social Psychology*, *58*(1), 95–102. http://dx.doi.org/10.1037/0022-3514.58.1.95.

Doerner, W. G., & Lab, S. P. (2011). *Victimology* (6th ed.). Cincinnati, OH: Lexis Nexis/Anderson Publishing Company.

Dombeck, M. (2004). *Defense mechanisms. MentalHelp.net*. Retrieved from https://www.mentalhelp.net/articles/defense-mechanisms/.

Doty, D. H., & Glick, W. H. (1994). Typologies as a unique form of theory building: toward improved understanding and modeling. *The Academy of Management Review*, *19*(2), 230–251.

Douglas, J. E., Burgess, A. W., Burgess, A. G., & Ressler, R. K. (2006). Rape and sexual assault. In J. E. Douglas, A. W. Burgess, A. G. Burgess, & R. K. Ressler (Eds.), *Crime classification manual: A standard system for investigating and classifying violent crimes* (2nd ed.) (pp. 293–353). San Francisco, CA: Josey-Bass.

Drijber, B. C., Reijnders, U. J., & Ceelen, M. (2013). Male victims of domestic violence. *Journal of Family Violence*, 28(2), 173–178.

Eigenberg, H., & Garland, T. (2008). Victim blaming. In L. J. Moriarty (Ed.), *Controversies in victimology* (2nd ed.) (pp. 21–36). Newark, NJ: Matthew Bender & Company.

Family Service Regina. (2014). *Stalking and the crime of criminal harassment: victim impact* Retrieved from. http://familyserviceregina.com/+pub/document/stalking/Web%20 Victim%20Impact.pdf.

Fattah, E. A. (1980). Victimologie: tendances récentes. *Criminologie*, 13(1), 6–36.

Fattah, E. A. (2000). Victimology: past, present and future. *Criminologie*, 33(1), 17–46. http:// dx.doi.org/10.7202/004720ar.

FBI's Uniform Crime Reporting (UCR) Program. (2010). *Crime in the United States 2010. Article: Aggravated assault.* Washington, DC: U.S. Government Printing Office. Retrieved from http://www.fbi.gov/about-us/cjis/ucr/crime-in-the-u.s/2010/crime-in-the-u.s.-2010/ violent-crime/aggravatedassaultmain.

Feather, N. T. (1996). Domestic violence, gender and perceptions of justice. *Sex Roles*, 35(7–8), 507–519. http://dx.doi.org/10.1007/bf01544134.

Ferguson, C., & Turvey, B. E. (2009). Victimology: a brief history with an introduction to forensic victimology. In B. E. Turvey, & W. A. Petherick (Eds.), *Forensic victimology: examining violent crime, victims in investigative and legal contexts* (pp. 1–32). San Diego, CA: Elsevier Science.

Fitzgerald, J., & Weatherburn, D. (December 2001). *Aboriginal victimization and offending: The picture from police records.* Crime and Justice Statistics Bureau Brief. Retrieved from http://www.lawlink.nsw.gov.au/lawlink/bocsar/ll_bocsar.nsf/vwfiles/bb17. pdf/$file/bb17.pdf.

Freund, K., Steiner, B. W., & Chan, S. (1982). Two types of cross-gender identity. *Archives of Sexual Behavior*, 11(1), 49–63.

Gharaibeh, M., & Oweis, A. (2009). Why do Jordanian women stay in an abusive relationship: implications for health and social well-being. *Journal of Nursing Scholarship*, 41(4), 376–384. http://dx.doi.org/10.1111/j.1547-5069.2009.01305.x.

Gobert, J. J. (1977). Victim precipitation. *Columbia Law Review*, 77(4), 511–553.

Grohol, J. (2013). 15 common defense mechanisms. *Psych Central*. Retrieved from http:// psychcentral.com/lib/15-common-defense-mechanisms/.

Groth, A. N. (1979). *Men who rape: The psychology of the offender.* New York, NY: Plenum Press.

Groth, A. N., Burgess, A. W., & Holmstrom, L. L. (1977). Rape: power, anger and sexuality. *American Journal of Psychiatry*, 134(11), 1239–1243.

Hartling, L. M., & Luchetta, T. (1999). Humiliation: assessing the impact of derision, degradation and debasement. *The Journal of Primary Prevention*, 19(4), 259–278.

Hazelwood, R. R. (2009). Analyzing the rape and profiling the offender. In R. R. Hazelwood, & A. W. Burgess (Eds.), *Practical Aspects of rape investigation: A multidisciplinary approach* (4th ed.) (pp. 97–122). Boca Raton, FL: CRC Press.

Hazelwood, R. R., & Burgess, A. W. (2009). *Practical aspects of rape investigation: A multidisciplinary approach* (4th ed.). Boca Raton, FL: CRC Press.

Hindelang, M. J., Gottfredson, M. R., & Garofalo, J. (1978). *Victims of personal Crime: An empirical foundation for a theory of personal victimization.* Cambridge, MA: Ballinger Publishing Co.

Hucker, S. J. (2008). Sexual masochism: assessment and treatment. In D. R. Laws, & W. T. O'Donohue (Eds.), *Sexual Deviance: Theory, assessment and treatment* (2nd ed.) (pp. 264–271). New York: The Guilford Press.

Isanga, J. (2010). Mulieris Dignitatem, Ephesians 5, and domestic violence: grounding international women's human rights. *Ave Maria Law Review, 8*(2), 405–429.

Jansson, K. (2006). *Black and minority ethnic groups' experiences and perceptions of crime, racially motivated crime and the police: Findings from the 2004/05 British Crime Survey, Home Office Online Report 25/06*. Retrieved from http://webarchive.nationalarchives. gov.uk/20110218135832/http:/rds.homeoffice.gov.uk/rds/pdfs06/rdsolr2506.pdf.

Jennings, W. G., Higgins, G. E., Tewksbury, R., Gover, A. R., & Piquero, A. R. (2010). A longitudinal assessment of the victim–offender overlap. *Journal of Interpersonal Violence, 25*(12), 2147–2174. http://dx.doi.org/10.1177/0886260509354888.

Jerin, R. A., & Moriarty, L. J. (1998). *Victims of crime*. Chicago, IL: Nelson-Hall Publishers.

Johnson, H. (2005). *Experiences of crime in two selected migrant communities*. Trends and Issues in Crime and Criminal Justice (No. 302) Canberra: Australian Institute of Criminology. Retrieved from http://www.aic.gov.au/publications/current%20series/ tandi/301-320/tandi302.html.

Johnson, J. A., Lutz, V. L., & Websdale, N. (2000). Death by intimacy: risk factors for domestic violence. *Pace Law Review, 20*(1), 263–296.

Johnson, S. L., Leedom, L. J., & Muhtadie, L. (2012). The dominance behavioral system and psychopathology: evidence from self-report, observational, and biological studies. *Psychological Bulletin, 138*(4), 692–743. http://dx.doi.org/10.1037/a0027503.

Karmen, A. (2010). *Crime victims: An introduction to victimology* (7th ed.). Belmont, CA: Wadsworth Cengage Learning.

Kasperkevic, J. (2014). Private violence: up to 75% of abused women who are murdered are killed after they leave their partners. *The Guardian*. Retrieved from http://www. theguardian.com/money/us-money-blog/2014/oct/20/domestic-private-violence- women-men-abuse-hbo-ray-rice.

Kernis, M. H., Grannemann, B. D., & Barclay, L. C. (1989). Stability and level of self-esteem as predictors of anger arousal and hostility. *Journal of Personality and Social Psychology, 56*(6), 1013–1022.

Kilgus, M. D., Maxmen, J. S., & Ward, N. G. (2016). *Essential psychopathology and its treatment* (4th ed.). New York, NY: W.W. Norton & Company.

Knight, R. A., & Prentky, R. A. (1987). The developmental antecedents and adult adaptations of rapist subtypes. *Criminal Justice and Behavior, 14*(4), 403–426. http://dx.doi.org/10.1 177/0093854887014004001.

Knight, R. A., Warren, J. I., Reboussin, R., & Soley, B. J. (1998). Predicting rapist type from crime-scene variables. *Criminal Justice and Behavior, 25*(1), 46–80. http://dx.doi.org/10. 1177/0093854898025001004.

Kohut, H. (1977). *The restoration of the self*. New York, NY: International Universities Press.

Krizan, Z., & Johar, O. (2015). Narcissistic rage revisited. *Journal of Personality and Social Psychology, 108*(5), 784–801. http://dx.doi.org/10.1037/pspp0000013.

Krug, E. G., Dahlberg, L. L., Mercy, J. A., Zwi, A. B., & Lozano, R. (2002). *World report on violence and health*. Geneva: World Health Organization.

Lauritsen, J. L., & Rezey, M. L. (2013). *Measuring the prevalence of crime with the national crime victimization survey* (Technical report) Bureau of Justice Statistics. Retrieved from http://www.bjs.gov/content/pub/pdf/mpcncvs.pdf.

Lerner, M. J., & Miller, D. T. (1978). Just world research and the attribution process: looking back and ahead. *Psychological Bulletin, 85*(5), 1030–1051.

Mackenzie, G., & Colvin, E. (2009). *Victims who kill their abusers: A discussion paper on defences* (report prepared for the Attorney-General and Minister for Industrial Relations). Queensland Government.

Malloy, G. B., & Berkery, A. C. (1993). Codependency: a feminist perspective. *Journal of Psychological Nursing & Mental Health Services*, *31*(4), 15–19. http://dx.doi.org/10.3928/0279-3695-19930401-08.

Marano, H. E. (2014). Assertiveness, not aggressiveness. *Psychology Today*. Retrieved from https://www.psychologytoday.com/articles/200402/assertiveness-not-aggressiveness.

Mattick, R. P., & Clarke, J. C. (1998). Development and validation of measures of social phobia scrutiny fear and social interaction anxiety. *Behaviour Research and Therapy*, *36*(4), 455–470.

Maxfield, M. G., & Babbie, E. (2012). *Basics of research methods* (3rd ed.). Belmont, CA: Wadsworth.

Medical Dictionary. (2009). *Sexual asphyxia (redirected from hypoxyphilia)*. Retrieved from http://medical-dictionary.thefreedictionary.com/Hypoxyphilia.

Meier, R. F., & Miethe, T. D., (1993). Understanding theories of criminal victimisation. In Tonry, M. H. (Eds.), *Crime and justice*, (Vol. 17) (pp. 459–499). Chicago, IL: University of Chicago Press.

Merriam-Webster. (2016). *Patria potestas*. Published by Merriam-Webster Online. At http://www.merriam-webster.com/dictionary/patria%20potestas.

Meston, C., & Frohlich, P. (2013). *Sexual paraphilias*. Retrieved from http://homepage.psy.utexas.edu/homepage/group/MestonLAB/HTML%20files/Resources_msd_para.htm.

Miethe, T. D., & Meier, R. F. (1990). Opportunity, choice, and criminal victimization: a test of a theoretical model. *Journal of Research in Crime and Delinquency*, *27*(3), 243–266. http://dx.doi.org/10.1177/0022427890027003003.

Miethe, T. D., Stafford, M. C., & Long, J. S. (1987). Social differentiation in criminal victimization: a test of routine activities/lifestyle theories. *American Sociological Review*, *52*(2), 184–194.

Miller, J. D., Hoffman, B. J., Gaughan, E. T., Gentile, B., Maples, J., & Campbell, W. K. (2011). Grandiose and vulnerable narcissism: a nomological network analysis. *Journal of Personality*, *79*(5), 1013–1042. http://dx.doi.org/10.1111/j.1467-6494.2010.00711.x.

Morf, C. C., & Rhodewalt, F. (2001). Unraveling the paradoxes of narcissism: a dynamic self-regulatory processing model. *Psychological Inquiry*, *12*(4), 177–196.

Morgan, A., & Chadwick, H. (2009). *Key issues in domestic violence*. Canberra: Australian Institute of Criminology. Retrieved from http://www.aic.gov.au/publications/current%20series/rip/1-10/07.html.

Moser, C., & Kleinplatz, P. J. (2006). DSM-IV-TR and the paraphilias: an argument for removal. *Journal of Psychology and Human Sexuality*, *17*(3–4), 91–109. http://dx.doi.org/10.1300/J056v17n03_05.

Muftic, L. R., Bouffard, L. A., & Bouffard, J. A. (2007). An exploratory analysis of victim precipitation among men and women arrested for intimate partner violence. *Feminist Criminology*, *2*(4), 327–346. http://dx.doi.org/10.1177/1557085107306429.

Mullen, P. E., Pathé, M., Purcell, R., & Stuart, G. W. (1999). Study of stalkers. *The American Journal of Psychiatry*, *156*(8), 1244–1249. Retrieved from http://proquest.umi.com.ezproxy.bond.edu.au/pqdweb?RQT=318&pmid=2864.

Neuman, W. L., & Wiegand, B. (2000). *Criminal justice research methods: Qualitative and quantitative approaches*. Boston, MA: Allyn and Bacon.

Orth, U., Robins, R. W., Meier, L. L., & Conger, R. D. (2015). Refining the vulnerability model of low self-esteem and depression: disentangling the effects of genuine self-esteem and narcissism. *Journal of Personality and Social Psychology*, *110*(1), 133–149. http://dx.doi.org/10.1037/pspp0000038.

Patel, M. N. (2009). *Why do we blame victims of sexual assault?* (Doctoral dissertation). Available from ProQuest Dissertations & Theses database. (UMI No. 3381962).

Pathé, M. (2002). *Surviving stalking.* Cambridge, UK: Cambridge University Press. Retrieved from http://catdir.loc.gov/catdir/samples/cam033/2001052720.pdf.

Pauwels, B. G. (2002). *Blaming the victim of rape: The culpable control model perspective* (Doctoral dissertation). Available from ProQuest Dissertations & Theses database. (UMI No. 3052448).

Pearce, A., & Easteal, P. (1999). The "domestic" in stalking. *Alternative Law Journal, 24*(4), 165–170.

Pernanen, K. (1991). *Alcohol and human violence.* New York, NY: Guilford.

Pesta, R. (July 2011). *Provocation and the point of no return: An analysis of victim-precipitated homicide* (Thesis submitted in partial fulfillment of the degree of Master of Science in the Criminal Justice Program). Younstown State Univeristy.

Petherick, W. A. (2009). Serial stalking: looking for love in all the wrong place? In W. A. Petherick (Ed.), *Serial crime: Theoretical and practical issues in behavioral profiling* (2nd ed.) (pp. 257–281). San Diego, CA: Elsevier Science.

Petherick, W. A., & Ferguson, C. (2012). Understanding victim behaviour through offender behaviour typologies. In G. Coventry, & M. Shircore (Eds.), *Proceedings of the 5th Annual Australian and New Zealand Critical Criminology Conference.* Cairns North Queensland: Rydges Esplanade Resort.

Petherick, W., & Sinnamon, G. (2014b). Motivations: offender and victim perspectives. In W. Petherick (Ed.), *Profiling and serial crime: Theoretical and practical issues* (3rd ed.) (pp. 393–430). Waltham, MA: Anderson publishing.

Petherick, W. A., Sinnamon, G., & Jenkins, A. (2012). *Self-esteem, personality disorder, victim motivation, and neuropsychological correlates* (Unpublished manuscript).

Petherick, W. A., & Turvey, B. E. (2008). Criminal motivation. In B. E. Turvey (Ed.), *Criminal profiling: An introduction to behavioural evidence analysis* (3rd ed.) (pp. 273–307). San Diego, CA: Elsevier Science.

Phillips, J. (2006). *Domestic violence in Australia: An overview of the issues.* Retrieved from http://www.aph.gov.au/library/intguide/sp/Dom_violence.htm.

Pincus, A. L., Ansell, E. B., Pimentel, C. A., Cain, N. M., Wright, A. G., & Levy, K. N. (2009). Initial construction and validation of the pathological narcissism inventory. *Psychological Assessment, 21*(3), 365. http://dx.doi.org/10.1037/a0016530.

Piquero, A. R., MacDonald, J. M., Dobrin, A., Daigle, L., & Cullen, F. T. (2005). Self-control, violent offending, and homicide victimization: assessing the general theory of crime. *Journal of Quantitative Criminology, 21*(1), 55–71. http://dx.doi.org/10.1007/s10940-004-1787-2.

Purcell, R., Pathé, M., & Mullen, P. E. (2002). The prevalence and nature of stalking in the Australian community. *Australian and New Zealand Journal of Psychiatry, 36*(1), 114–120. http://dx.doi.org/10.1046/j.1440-1614.2002.00985.x.

Queensland Police Service. (2012). *Offender/Victim relationships.* Retrieved from http://www.police.qld.gov.au/Resources/Internet/services/reportsPublications/statisticalReview/1112/documents/OffenderVictimRel.pdf.

Raskin, R., Novacek, J., & Hogan, R. (1991). Narcissism, self-esteem, and defensive self-enhancement. *Journal of Personality,, 59*(1), 19–38.

Ray, J. J., & Lovejoy, F. H. (1988). An improved directiveness scale. *Australian Journal of Psychology, 40*(3), 299–302. Retrieved from http://jonjayray.tripod.com/mk6dir.html.

Reiersol, O., & Skeid, S. (2006). The ICD diagnoses of fetishism and sadomasochism. *Journal of Homosexuality, 50*(2–3), 243–262. http://dx.doi.org/10.1300/J082v50n02_12.

Reynolds, N. S., Walkey, F. H., & Green, D. E. (1994). The anger self-report: a psychometrically sound (30 item) version. *New Zealand Journal of Psychology, 23*(2), 64–70.

Right of women. (March 2006). *What is sexual assault*. Retrieved from http://www.rightsofwomen.org.uk/pdfs/sexual_assault.pdf.

Ring, R. B. A. (1998). *Blame attributions of domestic violence victims by police officers* (Master's thesis, University of Houston Clear Lake, Houston, United States). Retrieved from http://search.proquest.com.ezproxy.bond.edu.au/docview/304571919/previewPDF?accountid=26503 (UMI: 1395160).

Roberts, A. R., & Dziegielewski, S. F. (1996). Assessement typology and intervention with the survivors of stalking. *Aggression and Violent Behavior, 1*(4), 359–368.

Robinson, M. B. (1997). Lifestyles, routine activities, and residential burglary victimization. *Journal of Crime and Justice*. Retrieved from http://www.pscj.appstate.edu/vitalifestyles.html.

Roeckelein, J. E. (2006). *Elsevier's dictionary of psychological theories*. San Diego: Elsevier Science.

Rohmann, E., Neumann, E., Herner, M., & Bierhoff, H. (2012). Grandiose and vulnerable narcissism: self-construal, attachment, and love in romantic relationships. *European Psychologist, 17*(4), 279–290. http://dx.doi.org/10.1027/1016-9040/a000100. http://dx.doi.org/.

Rose, P. (2002). The happy and unhappy faces of narcissism. *Personality and Individual Differences, 33*(3), 379–392. http://dx.doi.org/10.1016/S0191-8869(01)00162-3.

Rosenberg, M. (1965). *Society and the adolescent self-image*. Princeton, NJ: Princeton University Press.

Rosenberg, M. L., Butchart, A., Mercy, J., Narasimham, V., Waters, H., & Marshall, M. S. (2006). *Interpersonal violence*. Retrieved from http://files.dcp2.org/pdf/DCP/DCP40.pdf.

Ross, M. (2015). *One in four Australian women a victim of intimate partner violence ANROWS report finds*. Retrieved from http://www.abc.net.au/news/2015-10-22/one-in-four-women-a-victim-of-intimate-partner-violence/6875092.

Royal Spanish Academy. (2008). *Dictionary of the Royal Spanish Academy*. Madrid: Royal Spanish Academy.

Sansone, R. A., & Sansone, L. A. (2010). Measuring self-harm behavior with the self-harm inventory. *Psychiatry, 7*(4), 16–20.

Saunders, D. G. (1992). A typology of men who batter: three derived from cluster analysis. *American Journal of Orthopsychiatry, 62*(2), 264–275. http://dx.doi.org/10.1037/h0079333.

Savino, J. O., & Turvey, B. E. (2005). Defining rape and sexual assault. In J. O. Savino, & B. E. Turvey (Eds.), *Rape investigation handbook* (pp. 1–22). San Diego, CA: Elsevier Science.

Schwarzer, R., & Jerusalem, M. (1995). Generalized self-efficacy scale. In J. Weinman, S. Wright, & M. Johnston (Eds.), *Measures in health psychology: A user's portfolio. Casual and control beliefs* (pp. 35–37). Windsor, UK: NFER-NELSON.

Shaver, K. G. (1970). Defensive attribution: effects of severity and relevance of the responsibility assigned for an accident. *Journal of Personality and Social Psychology, 14*(2), 101–113. http://dx.doi.org/10.1037/h0028777.

Sheridan, L., Gillett, R., Davies, G. M., Blaauw, E., & Patel, D. (2003). 'There's no smoke without fire': are male ex-partners perceived as more 'entitled' to stalk than acquaintance or stranger stalkers? *British Journal of Psychology, 94*(1), 87–98. http://dx.doi.org/10.1348/000712603762842129.

Sherman, D. K., & Cohen, G. L. (2006). The psychology of self-defense: self-affirmation theory. In M. P. Zanna (Ed.), *Advances in experimental social psychology* (Vol. 38) (pp. 183–242). San Diego, CA: Academic Press.

Shichor, D., & Tibbetts, S. G. (2002). *Victims and victimization: Essential readings.* Prospect Heights, IL: Waveland Press.

Siegel, L. J. (2010). *Criminology: Theories, patterns, and typologies* (10th ed.). Belmont, CA: Wadsworth.

Silver, E. (2002). Mental disorder and violent victimization: the mediating role of involvement in conflicted social relationships. *Criminology, 40*(1), 191–212. http://dx.doi.org/10.1111/j.1745-9125.2002.tb00954.x.

Sinnamon, G. C. B. (2016). Psychopathology of antisocial and criminal behaviours. In W. Petherick, & G. C. B. Sinnamon (Eds.), *The psychology of antisocial and criminal behaviour.* Boston, MA: Anderson Publishing.

Smith, S. G., Fowler, K. A., & Niolon, P. H. (2014). Intimate partner homicide and corollary victims in 16 states: national violent death reporting system, 2003–2009. *American Journal of Public Health, 104*(3), 461–466.

Strömwall, L. A., Alfredsson, H., & Landström, S. (2013). Rape victim and perpetrator blame and the Just World hypothesis: the influence of victim gender and age. *Journal of Sexual Aggression: An international, interdisciplinary forum for research, theory and practice, 19*(2), 207–217. http://dx.doi.org/10.1080/13552600.2012.683455.

Sundberg, S. L., Barbaree, H. E., & Marshall, W. L. (1991). Victim blame and the disinhibition of sexual arousal to rape vignettes. *Violence and Victims, 6*(2), 103–120.

Timmer, D. A., & Norman, W. H. (1984). The ideology of victim precipitation. *Criminal Justice Review, 9*(2), 63–68. http://dx.doi.org/10.1177/073401688400900209.

Turvey, B. E. (2008a). Domestic homicide. In B. E. Turvey (Ed.), *Criminal Profiling: An introduction to behavioural evidence analysis* (3rd ed.) (pp. 483–506). San Diego, CA: Elsevier Science.

Turvey, B. E. (2008b). Intimate violence. In B. E. Turvey, & W. A. Petherick (Eds.), *Forensic victimology: Examining violent crime victims in investigative and legal contexts* (pp. 299–327). San Diego, CA: Elsevier Science.

Turvey, B. E. (2011). Forensic victimology in cases of sexual assault. In J. O. Savino, & B. E. Turvey (Eds.), *Rape investigation handbook* (2nd ed.) (pp. 209–229). San Diego, CA: Elsevier Science.

Vaknin, S. (2015). *Malignant self-love: Narcissism revisited.* Czech Republic: Narcissus Publications.

Walby, S., & Allen, J. (2004). *Domestic violence, sexual assault and stalking: Findings from the British crime survey.* Retrieved from http://www.broken-rainbow.org.uk/research/Dv%20crime%20survey.pdf.

Walker, E. (1979). *The battered woman.* New York, NY: Harper & Row.

Walklate, S. (2007). *Imagining the victim of crime.* Maidenhead, UK: Open University Press.

Weber, E. U., Blais, A., & Betz, N. E. (2002). A domain-specific risk attitude scale: measuring risk perceptions and risk behaviors. *Journal of Behavioral Decision Making, 15*(4), 263–290. http://dx.doi.org/10.1002/bdm.414.

Weller, M., Hope, L., & Sheridan, L. (2013). Police and public perceptions of stalking: the role of prior victim-offender relationship. *Journal of Interpersonal Violence, 28*(2), 320–339. http://dx.doi.org/10.1177/0886260512454718.

Wilcox, P. (2010). Victimization, theories of. In B. Fisher, & S. Lab (Eds.), *Encyclopedia of victimology and crime prevention* (pp. 978–986). Thousand Oaks, CA: SAGE Publications, Inc.

Wilson, J. K. (2009). *The Praeger handbook of victimology.* Santa Barbara, CA: ABC-Clio.

Wink, P. (1991). Two faces of narcissism. *Journal of Personality and Social Psychology*, *61*(4), 590–597. http://dx.doi.org/10.1037/0022-3514.61.4.590.

Wittebrood, K., & Nieuwbeerta, P. (1999). Wages of sin? the link between offending, lifestyle and violent victimization. *European Journal of Criminal Policy and Research*, *7*(1), 63–80.

Wolfgang, M. (1958). *Patterns in criminal homicide*. Philadelphia, PA: University of Pennsylvania Press.

Yollo, K., & Bogard, M. (Eds.). (1988). *Feminist perspectives in wife abuse*. Beverly Hills, CA: Sage Publications, Inc.

Zur, O. (1994). Rethinking 'Don't blame the victim': the psychology of victimhood. *Journal of Couple Therapy*, *4*(3/4), 15–36. Retrieved from http://www.zurinstitute.com/victimhood.html.

Threat and Violence Intervention: Influenced by Victim and Offender Perspectives

4

James S. Cawood

Factor One, Inc., San Leandro, CA, United States

CHAPTER OUTLINE

INTRODUCTION

The topic of interventions for violence could easily stretch to a multivolume work, so given this is a chapter work, the coverage intentionally covers large topics, with references that lead to further exploration of the topics covered. This chapter is not meant to address every intervention or permutation of interventions—just those that are the most frequently used. The presentation of different possible perceptions of the victims and the perpetrators to the interventions, drawn from over 30 years of casework, is meant to illuminate and illustrate the central concept leading to successful interventions for violence: that violence does not occur when the perpetrator perceives that violence will not accomplish their goal(s), as that person defines them at the time. In other words, for violence intervention to be effective in reducing future violence, similar to other psychological and behavioral interventions, the intervention must introduce a stimulus into the environment of the perpetrator (e.g., ideas, concepts, awareness, psychological or physical restrictions, etc.), which the perpetrator incorporates into their perception of the world, which in turn causes the perpetrator to alter their perception of what behaviors will achieve their needs or goals, while devaluing the continued use of violent behaviors. Perceptions are the foundations of behavioral actions, so changes in perception change actions (Hart & Logan, 2011). As we explore this central concept, it will become clear why some of the current interventions have not worked as successfully as they could, due to both conceptual and methodological problems, and also why victims may misunderstand, and therefore not follow-through on, the use of interventions that could be successful in their individual case. We will see this particularly in the use of restraining orders and court proceedings as interventions.

It should be recognized at the outset that violence in any particular case may not have been stoppable by any available intervention, other than the perpetrator not being alive to commit the act. However, just as physical violence is a low-base rate behavior (Skeem & Monahan, 2011), the confluence of elements that lead to the point where all available interventions would be unsuccessful is even rarer. So, though it is acknowledged that some cases have tragic outcomes that may not have been prevented in that specific circumstance, that is not the norm; it is the "black swan" (International Handbook of Threat Assessment, 2014).

This chapter will first briefly discuss violence as a human behavior and violence risk assessment as a practice. The purpose of this is to establish a theoretical and practical framework that will anchor the discussion regarding interventions. As each intervention is discussed, different possible interpretations of that intervention will be provided from both the victim and perpetrator perspectives. In the case of incarceration as an intervention, it will be assumed that the perpetrator might be released from incarceration at some point, because if that is not the case, then the potential victim pool is limited to those inside the institution of incarceration and that discussion is outside the scope of this chapter.

THE CONSTRUCT OF HUMAN VIOLENT BEHAVIOR AND ITS ASSESSMENT AND LINK TO INTERVENTIONS

The current implicit theory of human violence is that each act of violence is a construct of biological, psychological, sociological, contextual, and environmental elements that coalesces at a particular point in time for a violent act to occur (Accomazzo, 2012; Cavanaugh, 2012). We can call this the BPSCE theory of human violence. This theory is implicit in that the biological, psychological, sociological, contextual, and environmental elements of violence have a sound foundation in the empirical literature related to human violence however, this information is rarely discussed as an explicit holistic theory. The practical recognition of this theory is found in the choice of behavioral cues tied to at least one, if not all, of these elements that serve as the risk factors to be assessed by every current violence risk assessment instrument or tool including the VRAG (Quinsey, Harris, Rice, & Cormier, 1998), all versions of the HCR-20 (Douglas, Hart, Webster, & Belfrage, 2013), and the Cawood Assessment and Response Grids (Cawood & Corcoran, 2009).

One behavioral cue can serve as an example of this connection between violence theory, empirical research, and practical assessment of violence risk: substance use and its documented link to human violence. Substance use has been empirically linked to violence in a broad range of studies with diverse samples of the human population (e.g., people with delusional disorders, students, soccer fans, domestic abusers, etc.) (Heilbrun, 2009). Substance use has also been linked to biological factors (e.g., dopamine), psychological factors (e.g., anxiety reduction), sociological factors (e.g., family history), contextual factors (e.g., situational social conformity/peer pressure), and environmental factors (e.g., accessibility, general use by a large portion of many human societies or cultures). Because of these linkages between violence and substance use, each of the violence risk assessment tools given as examples, which represent both the actuarial and structured professional judgment sides of the violence risk assessment community, have substance use as a risk factor that needs to be evaluated as a part of the violence risk assessment processes. So, theory leads to empirical testing, which leads to both theory refinement and practical application of theory for better outcomes.

This theory of human violence also links assessment to interventions for violence, because during the assessment of violence, first the biological, psychological, sociological, contextual, and environmental factors and influences that could be involved with violence for that individual are identified. This starts with their exhibited behavior and works back to those elements from that point. Then, these elements and influences for the individual are assessed for their contribution to driving that individual's behavior at a particular point in time with a particular individual or group of individuals. From this assessment and analysis, a primary behavioral hypothesis is formed regarding what may motivate this person to commit future violent acts, only then can an effective intervention strategy be developed that will lead to reducing the risk of violence, hopefully for a long duration. Once again with substance use as an example, imagine that an individual has committed a series of violent acts while under the influence of alcohol and has not committed any violent acts when sober. It would seem reasonable then, as a working hypothesis, that lowering the frequency and/or quantity of alcohol use would reduce the potential for violence to occur. So what interventions could be considered? From a biological perspective, changing the neurochemical reaction to alcohol is difficult, though pharmacological treatments such as disulfiram (aka: Antabuse) have been shown to have some efficacy. The practical answer about whether to use this intervention is centered on the likelihood of medication adherence by the individual of concern.

From a psychological perspective, motivational interviewing (Miller & Rollnick, 2002) has shown good efficacy; however, as with pharmacotherapy, the question of treatment adherence is paramount. From a sociological perspective, it is impossible to change the past, but it is possible to help a person understand that history is not destiny. Does the person have the cognitive and emotional intelligence to engage in self-reflection? From a contextual perspective, one can reduce the number of relationships or situations that can influence the future decision to use substances. Would this person be willing or able to limit his interactions with others in which drinking is a normal part of the relationship dynamic?

Last, from an environmental perspective, it might be possible to limit the availability of substances in the environment for a period of time until other factors can become a positive influence. Are there legal means or financial resources to place this person in some form of rehabilitation center environment until he could develop other methods to control his drinking? From a practical perspective, long-term change comes from this person making the decision that using the substance does not meet their ongoing needs/goals. So how do we provide interactions (i.e. interventions) that maximize the likelihood of this individual changing his perspective, which then changes their behavior in a direction that decreases the potential risk of violence? In some cases, the process of perspective change could be accelerated by a good interview, while in other cases it might be a voluntary or forced involvement with a psychological assessment and intervention, civil or criminal court actions, and/or a short-term incarceration. This leads us into the discussion about the range of interventions that currently exist for decreasing violence risk and violent behavior.

INTERVENTIONS

Successful interventions are about the individual changing some perceptions or reactions to the world around them, which then changes their behavior in a positive (nonviolent) direction. Interventions are most effective when they are selected and presented in such a way that the subject of the intervention is less likely to reject or deflect the attempt to influence them and more likely to allow the intervention to activate different thoughts, emotions, or perceptions that then lead to more constructive behavioral outcomes. Therefore, we will explore general categories of interventions, recognizing that within these categories the actual interventions would be most effective when individualized for each person, through something as simple as how it is explained, to something more complex like the terms and conditions of a restraining order.

The range of legal interventions in most countries of the world are fairly limited in reality. They include interviews, voluntary mental health evaluations, voluntary medical or mental treatments of various types, civil administrative or disciplinary actions of some type; formal requests to cease or desist from certain actions, no trespass orders, restraining orders, protective orders, involuntary mental health evaluations, arrest, criminal prosecution, and probation and/or parole, which is behavioral monitoring with consequences.

THE INTERVIEW

Interviewing is the most common intervention that is used in most violence-related cases, yet it is not often perceived as an intervention but seen only as an information-gathering tool. This means that the opportunity to use it intentionally as an intervention is lost. From the very start of the interaction in which an interview occurs, information is being transmitted and received by both parties (Shepherd & Griffiths, 2013). This includes the perceived reason for the interview, the environment where the interview is conducted, facial expressions and body movements of both parties, the types of materials being carried, how the person is dressed, how they are groomed, and what they smell like, among others. All of these elements can make the subject of the interview more or less engaged in the process, thereby affecting the ability of the interviewer, or the process, to positively influence their perceptions. During the interview, each party continually assesses each other, and beyond the interview when they reflect on what occurred. Therefore, the ability for this interview process to influence behavior begins when the subject of the interview becomes aware that an interview is going to take place and extends beyond the interview until both parties cease to experience thoughts, emotions, or perceptions stimulated by the interview.

So, to maximize the overall value of the interview, as the interviewer begins to prepare for the interaction, the question is not only what information would the interviewer like to learn during the encounter (e.g., behavioral, factual, emotional, psychological, etc.), but also what perceptions might the subject of the interview have of the interviewer or this situation? How might those perceptions influence the subject's willingness to engage in meaningful ways? What can the interviewer do to minimize negative reactions that are avoidable? To this end, the interviewer has a number of factors to consider that may assist in enhancing their ability to engage with the interviewee and therefore facilitate effective attitude and behavior change. These include dressing in a manner that does not highlight the differences between the interviewer and interviewee, creating unintentional emotional reactions, or disturbing the interviewee's attention (e.g., bright colors, bold stripes or plaids, provocative/revealing clothing, etc.). Other factors may include a casual rather than authoritarian demeanor, deliberate and cautious physical motion, and using plain/simple language that intones sincerity and interest. Language should not be "jargonistic" or include statements that are ambiguous, confusing, or patronizing, such as "I understand," "Right," "I get you," and "I want to hear your side of the story," among others.

Remember, if you are the interviewer, you already have actual control over the process because you have initiated the process and they are engaging with you. Therefore, the person may feel that he has little or no control over whether they talk to you—though they still have control over what they choose to communicate to you. Hence, my suggestion is that the interviewer do all they can, from the very beginning of the interview, to have the subject of the interview not be reminded that they have a lesser degree of control. This is true if the person is an employee or in custody, or at their home or in public space. People interact when they perceive it is in their best interest to do so and do not interact when they perceive it is not, so removing as many perceptual cues that interacting is not valuable for them, maximizes opportunities for engagement. Using the enhanced cognitive interviewing style (Shepherd & Griffiths, 2013) has been shown to be a fast and effective way to stimulate topic-relevant discussions during the interpersonal interview process. This style of interviewing is designed to communicate that the interviewer does not have a set agenda, other than learning how the subject of the interview perceives the situation.

Using an example of a domestic violence interview with a subject of concern, the interview might start like this:

> *Interviewer*: "I have been asked to understand the dynamic between you and your spouse with the hope of finding a path forward so everyone can feel safer. What is your sense of what is going on?"

Note that the interviewer is quickly explaining their role, is not implying who is at fault, and is using plain-language, non-accusatory statements, and open questions to allow for a broad range of potential starting places. The subject of the interview is in control of where they start any narrative and what they talk about, hopefully perceiving that the interviewer is trying to understand the whole situation, rather than just taking sides and casting them as the wrong-doer. The experience of this author using this approach is that even when the results of the assessment or investigation do not ultimately align with what the parties initially wanted to occur, they are less likely to blame an unfair process and therefore less likely to feel justified to resort to extralegal means of resolution (i.e., violence). This is because they believe they have been fairly heard, but the decision-makers just did not agree with them on balance. This is particularly true in domestic violence situations in which the main perpetrator believes the whole system is stacked against them and never appreciates their perspective, which can be a means to minimize and rationalize their use of violence in the first place but which also can be a perspective that is accurate (Dutton, 2006).

Continuing with domestic violence as an example, it is important that this approach is also used with the victims as they often feel conflicted about what they tell an interviewer about what has occurred, due to embarrassment, shame, their own minimization and rationalization of what has occurred, their mixed concerns about what will happen to the perpetrator, and their uncertainty or fear regarding the civil and criminal court processes. Certainly, the interviewer does not want to communicate with the perceived victim that the interviewer is skeptical of what they are being told, or not supportive of the perspective of the victim, in the same way they do not want to be perceived like that by the identified perpetrator. However, the interviewer does have to remain open to new information and also understand that a safer, less violent, resolution of the situation between the parties requires that both of them perceive the process to be fair. This will ensure that they participate in future behaviors that de-escalate the potential for violence versus seeking ways to escalate it.

Building on the information gleaned from the interview process, along with all the other collateral information gathered during the threat assessment, additional interventions could be considered and plans developed for implementation. The preferred pathways for intervention are less intrusive and externally controlled as they have a greater likelihood of long-term success than externally controlled and intrusive interventions (Miller & Rollnick, 2002). In other words, going back to the alcohol example, an alcoholic who decides on their own that drinking is not good for them and actively engages in a process of change, based on their own internally generated motives, has a much stronger probability of achieving lasting sobriety than is someone who is ordered by the court to seek alcohol rehabilitation for a proscribed period of time. This can be illustrated by the number of individuals who have multiple driving under the influence (DUI) charges, though each time it has been mandated that they seek and engage in treatment.

This rationale is the basis of why the next types of interventions discussed involve voluntary agreement to seek further support or treatment. To the degree that the subject of concern is willing to participate in seeking additional help, and then follows through to go to the appointments and participates in any treatments, their behavior is self-reinforcing in that they are working toward a goal and participating. They are providing themselves positive behavioral feedback that they value the effort being made, which can provide the necessary motivation to continue in a more positive direction. As stated previously, this positive progress is perceived as self-directed, therefore of more value, than doing something simply to satisfy the needs of others. However, if the person of concern has a history of agreeing to voluntary evaluations or treatments and not following through on their commitments, then it will be important for the threat assessor/manager to bring this information into the dialogue with the person of concern and seek to understand how this individual sees this situation differently than he has in the past.

The assessor/manager might say something like this, again using the domestic violence example:

> *Interviewer/Assessor*: "I heard you suggest that you think that an anger management program would be helpful to you to provide you more tools to deal with your emotions that have led you to act violently. As I was gathering information on this situation, I noted that you have completed a prior anger management program a year ago and that after that there were several more times that a violent assault happened with your spouse. What is your sense of that? What additional information or tools do you think would help at this time to make this training more effective for you?"

Notice that there is no implication that this suggestion might not work, just an attempt to explore how this next time might be different, while also alerting the person of concern that the assessor/manager is aware that the prior effort to use this intervention was not effective. This provides an opportunity for the assessor to also gain insight into whether, this time, this type of intervention or program would have an improved likelihood of lowering violence, or whether this is just an attempt to placate the assessor or have the subject feel better about themselves with no authentic commitment to any real change.

Asking these additional questions about voluntary interventions is also important for the ongoing relationship with the victim. If the victim believes that the assessor is naïve or "being fooled" by the person of concern, because the assessor cannot demonstrate that they have a thorough knowledge of the subject's prior behavior and lack of follow-through on their commitments to voluntary interventions, then the victim will lose confidence in the assessor and may not follow through on the various suggestions that the assessor makes to increase the victim's safety, such as documenting all attempts at interaction by the subject of concern, being more aware of their surroundings, increasing security at their residence, notifying the assessor or law enforcement of any new behaviors of concern, etc. This lack of trust and the resulting behavior can also make any attempted future interventions less effective, thus decreasing safety because there may be a weakened commitment to change their behavior, due to a loss of belief in the possibility of change, engendered by prior failed attempts.

ADMINISTRATIVE OR DISCIPLINARY ACTIONS

Another intervention type is an array of administrative or disciplinary actions. In relation to threat or violence risk assessment and management cases, these interventions usually fall under some type of employment, mental health, or correctional relationship. In other words, these can be used when the subject of concern is connected to an organization that has an established relationship with the individual, so that actions can be taken to influence their employment or other privileges in an effort to have the person of concern decide not to continue the behavior of concern. An example of this, in an employment setting, might be to place the person on administrative leave, with or without pay, until certain activities have been completed (e.g., an investigation has been conducted, they have participated in an interview, taken a drug test, etc.). In an inpatient mental health setting, it might be that they have agreed to participate in group therapy for a full week and until they do so, they would not be allowed to be in the activities room during free recreation periods. In a correctional setting, it could be that they would be confined to their cell for a week, or not allowed to work at their prison job to earn canteen credits until they agree to not harass another prisoner during yard time.

The key to these types of intervention, like all interventions, is that before they are initiated careful consideration be given to how this person will most likely perceive the intervention. If it is believed they will comply and their reaction to compliance will not further their need to establish control by escalating problematic behavior, the next step is to determine how to communicate the start of the intervention so that this process itself does not cause the escalation we are trying to avoid. An example of this would be a workplace violence assessment where a preliminary assessment of the person of concern has been done. In cases where the client wants to place a person on administrative leave for a period of time while the client conducts an investigation, this author has suggested the way to communicate this would be something like the following:

> *Manager*: "This situation has raised some concerns that we want to investigate. In conducting this investigation, we are concerned that people might mistake an innocent action you might make as an attempt to intimidate them or influence the investigation, such as you just passing by them during the normal course of work and looking at them. To protect you from these possibly unfounded claims

of inappropriate conduct, we believe that assigning you to home for a few days, while we investigate, is the best way to proceed. So we are placing you on leave, effective immediately, and will call you two days from now at 2pm to check in with you and let you know where we are in the process."

In approaching the communication in this way, it accomplishes what we want in the workplace, removing a person of concern while we gather more information, while presenting the request in a way that it is perceived as protecting that person from additional claims that could be false, rather than we are doing it because they are a "mad dog" and cannot be trusted to maintain their composure around other workers. This may appear to be a disingenuous approach, however, those that have conducted workplace threat assessments will have experienced emotionally charged environments where, as the case assessment proceeds, allegations of new intimidating or threatening behavior are being reported because people are primed to interpret any behavior from this individual that way, even normal business interactions. These ongoing reports can cause the assessment process to get slowed down, when steps could have been taken, like administrative leave, to mitigate the possibility of this happening.

My philosophy, applied to all aspects of threat and violence risk assessment and management, is that one should always tell the truth, just not always tell the *whole* truth, unless it will move the case in a positive (non-violent) direction. This philosophy and practice is not only driven by a strong belief in truthful and ethical conduct, but because if someone tells a lie to manipulate someone else and the person who was lied to learns about the lie at a later date, the basis for trust is broken. As a threat manager, if either the victim or person of concern no longer trusts you, you have limited or lost your ability to have information you present be accepted by them, effectively losing your ability to positively influence their behavior. In the worst case scenario, both the victim and person of concern may react so negatively to learning of the lie that it substantially increases the risk of violence in the situation, as well as the risk of harm to the assessor. As a result, this author suggests that assessors make every effort to not lie to anyone during either the assessment or intervention process. This will ultimately improve long-term outcomes, legally and behaviorally, and substantially lower risk of potential harm rather than escalate it.

WORKING WITH VICTIMS

We have explored potential concerns or reactions to administrative or disciplinary actions focused on the individual of concern's perspective, but what about the victim? The victim also may have a range of perceptions on this. They may believe that any action that we take is less than what is deserved — a "give them the maximum hurt" perspective. Alternatively, they may be concerned that any action that is taken will "just make the situation worse" and therefore not want any action taken that will raise the risk to himself, as they see it. Last, they may feel that no administrative or disciplinary action is going to work, so it is just a waste of time and resources to use these interventions at all and we should move immediately to stronger interventions like a restraining order, involuntary mental health commitment, or criminal arrest. The key to working with a victim is the same as working with the person of concern; first, we need to understand how they view this situation and what their focus and emotional sensitivities are, and then consider those perspectives in what interventions we contemplate and how we communicate our reasoning regarding the suggested interventions. Remember that if the victim is not supportive of the interventions you are suggesting, or at least will tolerate the use of them, they can both unintentionally and intentionally make them less effective or disrupt them.

An example of intentional disruption would be a victim who is unhappy that the person of concern "gets a vacation" by not having to do his job or getting to be away from others, so he begins to stir up people in the workplace, demanding that he lobby the organization for stronger measures. He also could conduct his own investigation to gather more evidence to support stronger measures, not understanding that this actually may create more workplace disruption and fear. So the choice of interventions needs to consider the victim's possible perception of the selected interventions and how that perception may impact the efficacy of the chosen intervention. The victim's perception can also influence how and when to communicate what the interventions might be. Using an extension of the example we have just developed with the employment example, prior to going into the interview with the person of concern, a meeting is held with the identified victim, having already determined that the victim is very anxious. The interaction might go something like this: "We have done some initial information gathering, including our interview with you, and have reached the point where we need to interview Johnny. Our sense right now is that after the interview, one of the likely outcomes is that we will place Johnny on leave so that we can complete the process without having him be in a position to influence the inquiry or having others be concerned that he is around and could cause harm easily. What is your sense of how he might act?"

"I am terrified that he will just get even angrier at me and that it will just make the situation worse. So, can't you just let him alone after the interview and let him go back to work?"

"We did consider that option, but we are concerned that he will be upset as this process moves along, that could mean that he might act out to you and also to others. We also considered that we could place you on leave with pay, so that you could feel safer – being away from work. But from what you had said before, you felt safe at work and less safe at home. So it seems like asking him to spend a few days away, without trying to contact anyone, including you, would give us an opportunity to minimize risk to you and others, and also give us a chance to see if Johnny can manage his behavior appropriately, given some boundaries."

"Well, I guess we can try that, but I want an escort to my car in the parking lot for a while and want to be told how he reacts to the interview."

"Okay, we will be sure both of these requests are honored."

So, to summarize, we interviewed the victim to understand how they connected to the world and when we came back to talk about next steps, we provided information related to what we thought the initial intervention might be, what we had considered in regard to that choice, and then responded to the victim's request for some additional steps, which lessened the chance that she would act out of anxiety or anger disrupting the effectiveness of this initial intervention.

You will notice that I used the term *initial intervention*. So far it has been implied that interventions are layered events, which are interwoven as the process moves forward, but let me explicitly state that this is the case. It will be a very rare case in which several interventions are not activated (e.g., interview and voluntary evaluation; interview and administrative or disciplinary action; interview and request to direct all further communication to a particular party; interview, police report, and request for a protective order, etc.). In some cases, these will happen sequentially and in some cases they may happen in parallel. We want to use the right intervention or interventions, at the right time, correctly tailored to the perception of the recipient of intervention(s) so it has the maximum ability to influence the recipient to move away from violence. But, like psychotropic medications, interventions sometimes have to be used in combination to alleviate the complex needs of a recipient of the intervention(s).

CEASE AND DESIST REQUESTS

Formal requests to cease and desist behaviors of concern, which can be in the form of either verbal and/or written requests, are another possible intervention to use when the behavior is inappropriate and concerning, but there is reason to believe, based on prior behavior and/or stated priorities, that the individual of concern will be receptive to an attempt to create a behavioral boundary without making the situation "public." This intervention allows the person of concern to not be exposed to a wider audience regarding their behavior, with the attendant potential consequences, which is assessed as likely to matter to them. Generally, a verbal request is considered less powerful than a written request, as a written request creates a document that remains available as evidence of the request, while a verbal request does not leave "proof," other than the testimony of the parties involved regarding what was communicated. Verbal "proof" is less valuable to rely on as a foundation for any escalated future actions such as a restraining order or criminal case report, as it can be contested more easily (for example, a "he said, she said" situation). This request to cease or desist actions of concern can be coupled with a suggestion of redirection, which allows the individual to still communicate what they wish to, just not to the concerned recipient of that contact.

An example of this might be a former employee who has begun to repeatedly harass his former supervisor, and the number of contacts have now raised concerns of harassment and potential stalking. After assessment of the behavior, it might be determined that corporate counsel will make a phone call to the former employee and state that she is "aware that he has been attempting to contact his former supervisor concerning his belief that he was treated unfairly. The number and tone of the contacts have reached the point that this behavior was brought to my attention and appears to be bordering on harassment. If you would like to discuss the situation with me, I will conduct a full review to understand the circumstances of the situation and to see if further action needs to be taken. However, further attempts to contact your former supervisor, rather than contacting me with your concerns, may require that I consider legal actions to stop this harassing behavior. Would you like to talk to me now or set up a time later this week?" The contact by the corporate counsel notifies the person of concern that the supervisor has sought help within the organization and now that the person of concern is engaging the full power of the business, not just relying on their own ideas or instincts.

Also, having corporate counsel make this notification, signifies that this is a "formal" legal request to cease the behavior or additional consequences could be triggered. However, the recipient of this message is also provided with the choice to engage with corporate counsel and have the grievance heard and potentially acted on, so they have to decide if they are really trying to resolve the grievance or are just angry and wanting to "get back at" the former supervisor. Often in these circumstances, the decision is made to engage with corporate counsel and see how it goes and the harassing behavior pattern is disrupted. It needs to be explicitly stated here that, as with all interventions, there is no bluffing. In other words, if you state to someone that there may be consequences for further behaviors, then before that is stated, there needs to be planning in place regarding the consequences and consideration given to what will be the likely outcome of initiating those consequences.

As previously stated, if the threat manager or entity does not tell the truth about the type and certainty of the consequences, then the person of concern learns that the manager or other communicator cannot be trusted, and by breaking that trust, the ability to further influence the person of concern is weakened. This makes further effective intervention more difficult and safety more tenuous. So one needs to "measure twice and cut once," meaning they need to think through the chain of events of potential interventions and further consequences, before they communicate those plans or set plans in motion. Restraining orders are another example of this, as will be seen next.

RESTRAINING ORDERS

For the purposes of this chapter, we are going to group no trespass orders, restraining orders, and protective orders into the same group. No trespass orders, depending on the jurisdictional rules related to the party who seeks the order, can range from a formal written request, similar to a written cease and desist request but directing the person away from a particular geographic location, to a formal request by law enforcement to stay away from a particular geographic location with a resulting criminal offense if the person does not. Restraining orders are generally civil orders in which a court is petitioned to stop a particular type of harassing or threatening behavior. The consequences for failing to follow the restraining order are either civil in nature (e.g., loss of privileges or fines) or criminal (e.g., probation, jail time, or prison time). Protective orders are similar to restraining orders, except they are issued in conjunction with reported behavior that is deemed initially to be criminal, and therefore failing to follow the order will have a criminal justice system consequence, meaning arrest or jail time, among others.

The vast majority of these actions is public in nature, meaning that in most countries in which the "rule of law" is the foundation of that country's operational structure, these orders can become known by a wide variety of parties. This can have an impact on both the community reputation of the person subject to the order, as well as their legal rights, which may matter to that individual. The important thing to remember about orders is to be effective they have to be enforceable. If an order is not enforced, it is not a neutral event. In threat management cases, if an order is not enforced effectively when it is violated, meaning in a timely and appropriate manner, it provides a form of proof (i.e., "actions speak louder than words") to the recipient of that order that the issuer of the order (i.e., society) was not serious about them stopping their behavior, so they can continue their behavior as they please. This is often the same message that the victim (protectee) of the order gets as well when the order is not enforced effectively. They learn they are on their own to protect themselves and cannot expect that community resources will help them. These perceptions are harmful to safe resolution of these cases. If the person of concern continues their behavior, it can escalate to more serious behaviors that can lead to their eventual incarceration, injury, or death or and further injury and death of the victim.

Society experiences increased costs for prosecution and incarceration, while also feeling a weakened belief in the ability for the legal system to address his concerns. At a minimum this weakening of belief in the legal system can affect funding for the legal system, but a more serious reaction is disengaging from the system and considering the use of extra-legal means to manage situations, which leads to vigilantism and lawlessness. So with that as context, what does this mean? It means that when considering seeking these types of orders, a competent threat manager needs to consider several factors before they seek such an order or suggest that someone do so. The first factor is whether it is likely that if the threat manager got such an order, they believe that the person who will receive it will be positively influenced to stop their behavior; in other words, is the opinion of the behavioral assessment that the order will be effective in changing behavior? If the answer is no or that it might make the person more likely to act negatively to "prove they are serious," then seeking the order is ill advised.

Past problematic behavior by the person of concern in the face of negative consequences can be an indicator that can provide insight into this analysis. The second factor that needs to be considered, if it is believed that the order can serve as a positive influence, is whether the behavior exhibited to date meets the criteria for issuance of the order in the jurisdiction in which it is being sought. This means understanding not just what the letter of the law is, but its actual application in that particular jurisdiction, with that particular judiciary. Seeking an order and failing to get it has several negative consequences. One is that it can empower the subject of the potential order to believe they are more powerful than the seeker of the order. Another concern is that failure to get the order can enrage the person of concern because it may appear to them that the seeker of the order has attempted to "harm" them in an "illegal way" (i.e., the court did not support the order), affecting their reputation or legal rights, as there are legal consequences to such orders including limiting freedom of movement, association, and potentially limiting employment. Regarding the limitation of employment, who is going to hire someone subject to a restraining or protective order, given the liability that could be engendered if they hurt someone while an employee? As mentioned previously, failure to get an order can also disenfranchise the seeker of the order (i.e., the victim) to trust and believe that the legal system can protect them.

The next factor to consider, if it is believed that an order will be granted with the evidence at hand, is whether there be timely enforcement if there is a violation of the order. A study by the California Department of Justice in 2005 revealed the average number of restraining order violations that needed to occur before district attorneys in several counties would enforce the order was four. In one county the district attorney did not enforce any orders that had been issued (Task Force on Local Criminal Justice Response to Domestic Violence, 2005). These actions rendered the orders not only useless for managing the behavior of individuals subject to the orders, but worse—most likely empowered the persons subject to these orders to believe they were "above the law." So will the police arrest, the prosecuting attorney prosecute, and the judge agree and enforce?

The lack of certainty of this has led this author to seldom advise the seeking of a restraining or protective order, unless there is evidence of personal commitment on the part of local law enforcement to enforce the order, and the case assessment shows that seeking the order, and not having it enforced, will not significantly escalate the seriousness of the risk, as the risk has already been shown to be extremely high. An example of this would be cases where the victim has been hospitalized with injuries already or there is reason to believe that the person of concern is beyond having their conduct influenced by a court order. In these cases, the order might be sought solely to protect the victim, or seeking party, from being seen as uncooperative or negligent by the legal system, rather than as being seen as a means to influence the subject of concern. Remember that if law enforcement or the legal system comes to the conclusion that victims are not cooperative, this can easily result in them withdrawing their attention and resources, effectively decreasing victim safety, while raising the risk of harm. To summarize, trespass orders, restraining orders, and protective orders, like all interventions, need to be considered after careful analysis of the individual perspective of the person of concern, the impact on the victim's perspective, and the ability to have the intervention provide a positive influence for changing the person of concern's behavior away from escalating risk of violence.

INVOLUNTARY MENTAL HEALTH EVALUATIONS AND TREATMENT ORDERS

Involuntary mental health evaluations and involuntary treatments are possible in those cases where the laws support the involuntary detention of individuals that may pose a significant danger to themselves or others or are deemed to be gravely disabled (Melton et al., 2007). The purpose of this detention is to allow mental health professionals to evaluate the level of danger and determine if the person needs to be held in some type of mental health facility for treatment to reduce his level of danger. In some cases, the law allows for involuntary psychotropic medications or other treatments to be administered to the person, with or without a hearing process of some type. In most jurisdictions, the initial detention is conducted by law enforcement personnel in the field and then the individual is transported to a mental health facility for further evaluation by a mental health professional. The decision to report the individual to law enforcement and request a "welfare check," or other form of assessment, because of a concern of "dangerousness," has the same considerations, risks, and rewards as mentioned regarding protective and restraining orders: Will this make the situation safer? Does the behavior meet the required criteria for that jurisdiction to make a detention? Does the person meet the required criteria for a continued hold at the mental health facility to which they will be transported? Will the treatment there be adequate to lower the risk? If the answer to any of these questions is not supportive of initiating the process, then the process probably should not be initiated, as it will, most likely, just elevate the level of emotional energy and behavioral volatility in the situation. After all, who wants to be detained by law enforcement and taken to a mental health facility and questioned against their will, only to be released quickly, because it seems they do not meet the criteria for being held? The person of concern then will most likely conclude that this was just an attempt to "persecute them" unfairly and give them additional justification for acting against the parties who initiated this sequence of events. Psychiatric bed space in mental health facilities all over the world is very limited, even in the face of greater need, so only the most serious cases are held in the facility for involuntary treatment and many people that would benefit from treatment do not get it (Melton et al., 2007).

ARREST, PROSECUTION, AND PROBATION

The final form of interventions available are criminal arrest, criminal prosecution, and probation and/or parole with behavioral conditions may be available. This section alone could fill another entire book or series of books. The first consideration for using these types of interventions are whether the ongoing imprint made on the person of concern's life (e.g., having a criminal record, impact on employment, possible limitation of certain rights for life, etc.) are necessary to achieve the goal of diversion from violence and safety of the victim. Using a hammer to achieve a result that could be accomplished with a feather, is not only an abuse of power but also can engender the type of emotional and situational escalation and negative outcome that we have been continually reminding you that we are trying to stop with our interventions. Remember that if criminal charges are filed and prosecuted, the victim is most likely going to have to provide testimony (i.e., the accused gets to face his accuser in court) and that victim, and any one supporting them, will be indelibly imprinted on the memory of the person of concern as having been involved in achieving this result and any negative consequences that come out of this process, including injuries in custody and other bad outcomes (e.g., loss of a job, divorce, loss of child custody, loss of a home, loss of friends and support of family, etc.). If it is the only means that seems reasonably matched with the assessment of risk level to achieve safety, then so be it, proceed.

The next questions are who can file charges for this situation? What are their resources, ability, and willingness to arrest the person of concern and get the prosecutor to file charges? What are the minimum and maximum sentences for the charges? What has the prosecutor's office pled similar charges down to? How effective are the parole (prison related) or probation (jail related) offices that would be responsible for this person when they are released? Do these entities have special monitoring programs for charges of this type? What has their track record been in monitoring cases of this type? How many failures have occurred during their supervision? Are there effective victim advocates in the applicable court system that can help the victim and effectively monitor the case? In addition to these questions we could discuss the efficacy of some of the specialized programs that individuals are required to participate in as a part of their sentencing, such as batterer's programs for domestic violence and anger management programs. I will let the readers research the outcomes of these programs on their own, in their own jurisdictions, but I will tell you that in the United States these types of programs currently have little empirical science to support their efficacy for reducing violent outcomes when the methodology of the studies has been adequate to allow for appropriate control of other moderating variables. Much money is being spent with little or no value returned in reduction of violence. As you can see from the list of questions that need to be answered and the variety of answers that may be forthcoming, the analysis of whether to initiate a process of criminal arrest and prosecution is not a simple analysis to make, but in some cases, this level of intervention is the only hope that the victim has to take control of the situation and attempt to reduce the level of violence they may experience, both currently and in the future.

CONCLUSION

In this chapter, the wide variety of potential interventions that can be used for cases involving threats and violence have been reviewed. It has been stressed that interventions are only effective when they are applied in thoughtful and strategic ways that influence the person of concern to change their behavior away from inappropriate behavior, because they perceive, from their own perspective, that is in their own best interest, as they define it. Absent that choice on the part of the person of concern, any intervention is only temporary at best and may actually provide the fuel to escalate the situation and make the victim even less safe from harm. Victims also have their own perception on the value of interventions and consideration should be made in the choice of interventions to be sensitive to how the victim perceives the value of the intervention and to educate them in the process of their use and the possible outcomes that can occur, both good and bad. If the victim does not agree to the use of an intervention and participate willingly in the implementation of the intervention, then the potential of that intervention for a positive outcome is weakened, if not eliminated. Even though the results of an ineffective intervention may be most directly felt by the victim, a threat manager who is committed to their work will also be affected when cases they are managing result in bad outcomes. So use thorough threat and violence risk assessments and thoughtful, individually focused interventions, for increasing safety of victims and reducing the number and severity of future violent acts.

SUMMARY

- The central concept leading to successful interventions for violence is that violence does not occur when the perpetrator perceives that violence will not accomplish his goal(s), as he defines them at the time.
- For violence intervention to be effective in reducing future violence, the intervention must introduce a stimulus into the environment of the perpetrator (e.g., ideas, concepts, awareness, psychological or physical restrictions, etc.), which the perpetrator incorporates into his perception of the world, which in turn causes the perpetrator to alter his perception of what behaviors will achieve his needs or goals while devaluing the continued use of violent behaviors. Perceptions are the foundations of actions, so changes in perception change actions.
- It should be recognized that violence in any particular case may not have been stoppable by any available intervention, other than the perpetrator not being alive to commit the act. However, just as physical violence is a low-base rate behavior, the confluence of elements that lead to the point where all available interventions would be unsuccessful is even rarer. So, though it is acknowledged that some cases have tragic outcomes that may not have been prevented in that specific circumstance, that is not the norm, it is the "black swan."
- The current implicit theory of human violence is that each act of violence is a construct of biological, psychological, sociological, contextual, and environmental elements that coalesces at a particular point in time for a violent act to occur. We can call this the BPSCE theory of human violence. This theory is implicit in that the biological, psychological, sociological, contextual, and environmental elements of violence have a sound foundation in the empirical literature related to human violence however, this information is rarely discussed as an explicit holistic theory.
- This theory of human violence also links assessment to interventions for violence, because during the assessment of violence, first the biological, psychological, sociological, contextual, and environmental factors and influences that could be involved with violence for that individual are identified. This starts with his exhibited behavior and works back to those elements from that point. Then these elements and influences for the individual are assessed for his contribution to driving that individual's behavior at a particular point in time with a particular individual or group of individuals. From this assessment and analysis and a primary behavioral hypothesis is formed regarding what may motivate this person to commit future violent acts, only then can an effective intervention strategy be developed that will lead to reducing the risk of violence, hopefully for a long duration.

- Successful interventions are about the individual changing some perceptions or reactions to the world around him, which then changes his behavior in a positive (non-violent) direction. Interventions are most effective when they are selected and presented in such a way that the subject of the intervention is less likely to reject or deflect the attempt to influence them and more likely to allow the intervention to activate different thoughts, emotions, or perceptions that then lead to more constructive behavioral outcomes.
- Interviewing is the most common intervention that is used in most violence related cases, yet it is not often perceived as an intervention but seen only as an information gathering tool. This means that the opportunity to use it intentionally as an intervention is lost. When appropriately planned and executed, the interview is an integral element of successful intervention.
- Another intervention type is an array of administrative or disciplinary actions. In relation to threat or violence risk assessment and management cases, these interventions usually fall under some type of employment, mental health, or correctional relationship. In other words, these can be used when the subject of concern is connected to an organization that has an established relationship with the individual, so that they can take actions to influence his employment or other privileges in an effort to have the person of concern decide not to continue the behavior of concern.
- The key to working with a victim is the same as working with the person of concern; first, we need to understand how they view this situation and their focus and emotional sensitivities, and then consider those perspectives in what interventions we contemplate and how we communicate our reasoning regarding the suggested interventions. Remember that if the victim is not supportive of the interventions you are suggesting, or at least will tolerate the use of them, they can both unintentionally and intentionally make them less effective or disrupt them.
- Formal requests to cease and desist behaviors of concern, which can be in the form of either verbal and/or written requests, are another possible intervention to use when the behavior is inappropriate and concerning, but there is reason to believe, based on prior behavior and/or stated priorities, that the individual of concern will be receptive to an attempt to create a behavioral boundary without making the situation "public." This intervention allows the person of concern to not be exposed to a wider audience regarding his behavior, with the attendant potential consequences, which is assessed as likely to matter to them. Generally, a verbal request is considered less powerful than a written request, as a written request creates a document that remains available as evidence of the request, while a verbal request does not leave "proof," other than the testimony of the parties involved regarding what was communicated.
- Restraining orders are generally civil orders in which a court is petitioned to stop a particular type of harassing or threatening behavior. The consequences for failing to follow the restraining order are either civil in nature (e.g., loss of privileges or fines.) or criminal (e.g., probation, jail time, or prison time).

Protective orders are similar to restraining orders, except they are issued in conjunction with reported behavior that is deemed initially to be criminal, and therefore failing to follow the order will have a criminal justice system consequence, meaning arrest or jail time, among others.

- The vast majority of actions relating to "orders" of some form or another are public in nature, meaning that in most countries in which the "rule of law" is the foundation of that country's operational structure, these orders can become known by a wide variety of parties. This can have an impact on both the community reputation of the person subject to the order, as well as their legal rights, which may matter to that individual. The important thing to remember about orders is to be effective they have to be enforceable. If an order is not enforced, it is not a neutral event and could escalate the risk in the situation.

- Involuntary mental health evaluations and possible involuntary treatments are possible in those cases where the laws support the involuntary detention of individuals that may pose a significant danger to themselves, others, or are deemed to be gravely disabled. The purpose of this detention is to allow mental health professionals to evaluate the level of danger and determine if the person needs to be held in some type of mental health facility for treatment to reduce their level of danger. In some cases, the law allows for involuntary psychotropic medications or other treatments to be administered to the person, with or without a hearing process of some type. In most jurisdictions, the initial detention is conducted by law enforcement personnel in the field and then the individual is transported to a mental health facility for further evaluation by a mental health professional.

- The final form of interventions available are criminal arrest, criminal prosecution, and probation and/or parole with behavioral conditions. The first consideration for using these types of interventions are whether the ongoing imprint made on the person of concern's life (e.g., having a criminal record, impact on employment, possible limitation of certain rights for life, etc.) are necessary to achieve the goal of diversion from violence and safety of the victim. Using a hammer to achieve a result that could be accomplished with a feather, is not only an abuse of power, but also can engender the type of emotional and situational escalation and negative outcome that we are trying to stop with our interventions. Remember that if criminal charges are filed and prosecuted, the victim is most likely going to have to provide testimony (i.e., the accused gets to face his accuser in court) and that victim, and any one supporting them, will be indelibly imprinted on the memory of the person of concern as having been involved in achieving this result and any negative consequences that come out of this process, including injuries in custody and other bad outcomes (e.g., loss of a job, divorce, loss of child custody, loss of a home, loss of friends and support of family, etc.).

- Interventions are only effective when they are applied in thoughtful and strategic ways that influence the person of concern to change their behavior away from inappropriate behavior, because they perceive, from their own perspective, that it is in their own best interest as they define it. Absent that choice on the part of the person

of concern, any intervention is only temporary at best and may actually provide the fuel to escalate the situation and make the victim even less safe from harm.
- Victims also have their own perception on the value of interventions and consideration should be made in the choice of interventions to be sensitive to how the victim perceives the value of the intervention and to educate them in the process of their use and the possible outcomes that can occur, both good and bad. If the victim does not agree to the use of an intervention and participates willingly in the implementation of the intervention, then the potential of that intervention for a positive outcome is weakened, if not eliminated.

QUESTIONS

1. Define *threat* and *threat assessment*.
2. What is the implicit or BPSCE theory of human violence? Describe its components.
3. Describe what is meant by "intervention" in the context of the threat of violence.
4. Provide a detailed description of the interview process in threat intervention.
5. Provide a detailed explanation of the administrative and disciplinary processes that may be used in threat intervention.
6. How are cease and desist actions used in threat intervention?
7. Describe the use of restraining orders and similar actions in threat intervention. Provide details about the issues that must be considered when deciding to make use of this option.
8. How are involuntary mental health assessments and treatment orders used in threat interventions?
9. Criminal prosecution and its associated elements are used in threat assessment as a last resort. Describe this process and the various considerations when deciding to use this course of action as an intervention strategy.
10. Threat intervention also entails addressing issues related to the victim. Discuss the factors associated with working with victims and outline the factors that should be considered when doing so.

REFERENCES

Accomazzo, S. (2012). Anthropology of violence: historical and current theories, concepts, debates in physical and socio-cultural anthropology. *Journal of Human Behavior in the Social Environment*, 22(5), 535–552. http://dx.doi.org/10.1080/10911359.2011.598727.

Cavanaugh, M. M. (2012). Theories of violence: social science perspectives. *Journal of Human Behavior in the Social Environment*, 22(5), 607–618. http://dx.doi.org/10.1080/10911359.2011.598757.

Cawood, J. S., & Corcoran, M. H. (2009). *Violence assessment and intervention: The practitioner's handbook* (2nd ed.). Boca Raton, FL: CRC Press.

Douglas, K. S., Hart, S. D., Webster, C. D., & Belfrage, H. (2013). *HCR-20V3: Assessing risk for violence user guide*. Vancouver, British Columbia, Canada: Mental Health, Law, and Public Policy Institute, Simon Fraser University.

Dutton, D. G. (2006). *Rethinking domestic violence*. Vancouver, British Columbia, Canada: University of British Columbia Press.

Hart, S. D., & Logan, C. (2011). Formulation of violence risk using evidence-based assessments: the structured professional judgment approach. In P. Sturmey, & M. McMurran (Eds.), *Forensic case formulation* (pp. 83–105). Malden, MA: John Wiley & Sons, Ltd.

Heilbrun, K. (2009). *Evaluation for risk of violence in adults*. New York, NY: Oxford University Press.

Meloy, J. R., & Hoffmann, J. (Eds.). (2014). *International handbook of threat assessment*. New York, NY: Oxford University Press.

Melton, G. B., Petrila, J., Poythress, N. G., Slobogin, C., Lyons, P. M., & Otto, R. K. (2007). *Psychological evaluations for the courts* (3rd ed.). New York, NY: The Guilford Press.

Miller, W. R., & Rollnick, S. (2002). *Motivational interviewing: Preparing people for change (2)*. New York, NY: The Guilford Press.

Quinsey, V. L., Harris, G. T., Rice, M. E., & Cormier, C. A. (1998). *Violent offenders: Appraising and managing risk*. Washington, DC: American Psychological Association.

Shepherd, E., & Griffiths, A. (2013). *Investigative interviewing: The conversation management approach* (2nd ed.). Oxford University Press.

Skeem, J. L., & Monahan, J. (2011). Current directions in violence risk assessment. *Current Directions in Psychological Science*, 20(1), 38–42. http://dx.doi.org/10.11 77/0963721410397271.

Task Force on Local Criminal Justice Response to Domestic Violence. (June 2005). *Keeping the promise: Victim safety and batterer accountability*. Retrieved from http://www. ncdsv.org/images/CA-AG_DVKeepingThePromiseVictimSafetyAndBattererAccountabil ity_6-2005.pdf.

Profiling in Violent Crimes: The Perpetrator and the Victim in Cases of Filicide

Fátima Almeida[1], Duarte N. Vieira[2]

[1]University of Oporto, Porto, Portugal; [2]University of Coimbra, Coimbra, Portugal

CHAPTER OUTLINE

INTRODUCTION

Filicide, infanticide, and neonaticide are distinct concepts of the same reality and, despite our unified cries of love for our children, occur daily in contemporary society. These acts have existed since the dawn of humanity and have been in the literature from the earliest eras of recorded history. These crimes can be perpetrated by the mother, the father, or by both and include stepparents and other parental figures.

Despite the evolution of scientific knowledge on this type of crime, in some countries filicide is a verdict that applies only to the killings carried out by mothers (Liam & Koenraadt, 2008). However, in Western countries, men have become increasingly likely to be convicted of killing their child.

The legal framework of filicide varies from country to country and can be regarded as having two opposing aspects: treatment and punishment (Freire & Figueiredo, 2006). In many cases when the crime is committed by mothers in the first year of a child's life, the law reduces the penalties based on the principle that a woman who commits this kind of crime finds the balance of her mind disturbed for biological and/or psychological reasons or because she has not fully recovered from having given birth (Friedman & Resnick, 2007).

Insight into motivations, causes, circumstances, and risk factors associated with this crime are still insufficient, thus making prevention difficult (Friedman, Horwitz & Resnick, 2005). In addition, problems related to the determination of medicolegal ethology constrain knowledge on the prevalence of filicide, as many child deaths (especially those who are aged less than 1 year) are classified as unknown/undetermined, making real causes unclear and whether in fact there was a crime committed by parents.

Several studies have suggested, among other causes, child maltreatment (which turns out to be fatal), altruistic reasons, psychotic symptoms, spouse revenge, social factors (e.g., socioeconomic conditions), or the existence of diseases or malformations in children as causal factors for the crime.

This chapter frames filicide in historical and conceptual terms, to make an extensive review of literature about protective and risk factors to the perpetration of the crime by one or both parents, to examine the gender differences in filicidal offense characteristics and associated variables in order to establish a common profile of filicidal offenders and victims, and to suggest some strategies to prevent this crime.

BACKGROUND HISTORY

The killing of a child by his or her biological parents has been an occurrence in human history since its origins in every culture and every population. We can divide the background history of filicide into three distinct periods:

1. As a legitimate practice
2. As a criminal practice
3. As an act possibly related to mental illness

FILICIDE AS A LEGITIMATE PRACTICE

Although little is known about filicide practice in ancient civilizations (i.e., the way parents killed their children and under what circumstances), archaeological findings suggest that this type of crime was regarded as a legitimate practice in some periods of history, and it may occur:

- If children are born out of wedlock (i.e., if they were illegitimate or unwanted)
- As a mean of population control (being sacrificed in resource-poor heights)
- As a way to limit the number of female children (Liam & Koenraadt, 2008)
- To control the family size (Liam & Koenraadt, 2008)
- To exterminate the weak and abnormal children (i.e., those with defects or deficiencies) (Liam & Koenraadt, 2008)
- By the desire for power or money
- Due to disability (e.g., mental, economic) of the mother affecting her ability to treat the child (West, 2007)
- By superstition (Freire & Figueiredo, 2006)
- For a ritual sacrifice (Freire & Figueiredo, 2006)

As early as 7000 BC, there is evidence of the existence of child sacrifice, suggesting that primitive man sought to control population growth and minimize defects within the social group.

The first historical reference to filicide comes to us from Babylon, 4000–2000 BC. Abrahamic religious writings also bear witness to ancient filicide. For example, in around 1400 BC, Moses reportedly wrote the first manuscript of a collection of oral histories of the Jewish people and condensed them into what was to become known as the *Book of Genesis*, although the contemporary versions of Genesis are derived from an edited version of these writings that have their origins in about the sixth century BC, after the Israelites return from Babylonian exile (Mazar, 1969). In it he tells the story of Abraham who, at the request of God, prepared to sacrifice his son Isaac as a sign of obedience, but an Angel appeared at the last minute to grant him a reprieve in return for his demonstrated preparedness to acquiesce to God's authority (King James Bible, 1611). Old Testament Biblical Texts further tell of filicide and the cannibalism of young children in times of food shortage: "So we boiled my son, and did eat him: and I said unto her on the next day, Give thy son, that we may eat him: and she hath hid her son" (King James Bible, 1611, 2 Kings, 6:29).

However, the richest historical accounts reach us from Roman and Greek antiquity. In ancient Roman civilization, the patriarch (as owner) had, in certain circumstances, the legal right to kill his children (*patria potestas*) (Stroud, 2005). Similarly, in ancient Greece, it was permitted, indeed expected, for parents to kill their children if they exhibited defects that could be considered as unfit for military service. In Sparta, each newborn was submitted to the assembly of the elders' judgment: if he or she was judged as "unfit," they would send the infant to the Taigeto lot, where they were killed or abandoned as feed for the animals (Cruz, 1994). In 431 BC, Greek mythology also describes the story of Medea, who, having been betrayed by her husband, Jason, killed her two daughters and her rival.

In Carthage, the systematic practice of child sacrifice was interrupted only when there was a population decrease and then taken up again for economic reasons related to the distribution of familial inheritance.

In ancient Indian civilization, higher-caste families were required to provide a reasonable-sized dowry as an accompaniment to the bride when she was married, providing a powerful incentive for the killing of female babies who may have been "surplus" to the needs of marriage for political and social affiliation or commercial alliance. In lower-caste and poorer families, a dowry was payable in return for the female bride, and therefore, female children without prospects for marriage became a burden to the family rather than an economic asset, and for this reason, filicide of these female children was also commonplace. This dowry pressure continues in a number of social spheres, and if a family does not have the means to arranging for it, female children are submitted to social ostracism. Among the poorest rural households, the persistence of female filicide and selective abortions is therefore attributed to this dowry pressure and the economic burden that it presents when there is a failure to either provide or procure it.

The Chinese culture also presents a long history of female child filicide, as they are considered to have a lower value than male children. The doctrine of Confucius (551–479 BC) did not even allow a woman to possess the name of the family or the honor of their ancestors, which put them in an extremely vulnerable position.

Further, practices related to the killing of newborns with congenital anomalies have long been reported in African and Inuit societies. The explanation for these deaths has an evolutionary basis, since filicide of those with undesired characteristics ensured the survival of the fittest. Filicide has, therefore, been a universal practice across cultures and historical epochs throughout recorded human history.

FILICIDE AS A CRIMINAL PRACTICE

With the spread of Christianity in AD 300, Emperor Constantine opposed the killing of children by their parents and criminalized filicide across the Holy Roman Empire in AD 374. This decision had a strong influence from Jewish law, which penalized infanticide and despised abortion. Consequently, from this time forward, a woman who killed a newborn or attempted an abortion would be excommunicated, although, depending on the circumstances, a priest may have reduced the punishment and imposed a penance for a period of time (Assis, 1994). However, there is evidence of the renewed prevalence of filicide throughout the Middle Ages, associated with factors such as poverty and a lack of economic resources. In addition, the spread of

Christianity promoted a religious and cultural hostility toward nonmarital sex and the consequent birth of a child out of wedlock. As a result of this conviction, women were stigmatized and illegitimate children were deprived of legal human rights. This presented additional pressures and added to the renewed "popularity" of filicide as an option in these circumstances.

Among the Muslims, the death of a female children was very common until the 17th century. Researchers attribute these crimes to women's status, which was regarded as a man's property. For children to be spared a life of misery, mothers often dismissed their babies.

European society of the 16th and 17th centuries condemned sexual offenses such as fornication and bastardy. The penalties for these crimes were especially tough in England, condemning mothers who refused to identify the father of their child to flogging in public or to imprisonment. The connection between illegitimacy and infanticide resulted in the crime being considered as something only perpetrated by unmarried women (Schwartz & Isser, 2000). At the same time there was a drastic change in opinion about the murder of children, and in 1647, Russia became the first country to adopt more severe punitive sentencing for women who killed their children. Punishments were extreme and include being buried alive, drowning, and decapitation.

More than a century later, in 1783, William Hunt proposed the differentiation between the crime of neonaticide from other types of homicide. Despite the intention to condemn the female offenders for the perpetration of the crime and to dissuade them from killing their children, the so-called Poor Law, created in 1834 in England and Wales to make girls realize the severe consequences of sexual crime and thus preserve their chastity, reducing the bastardy (Schwartz & Isser, 2000), only contributed to increase the number of neonaticides. Single mothers stopped receiving assistance from their parishes and now had to live in a Poor House, in extremely precarious conditions (Schwartz & Isser, 2000).

Legal distinctions between manslaughter and infanticide were adopted across Europe from around 1888. First in France and then in England, laws were created that considered filicide as a crime punishable by death. In contrast to the foundational legal tenet of "presumed innocence," both countries enacted the legal assumption that mothers would be guilty until they proved their innocence, meaning that they were responsible for proving in court that their child was not a victim of murder.

FILICIDE AND ITS RELATION TO MENTAL ILLNESS

In England, this scenario changed with the establishment of the Infanticide Acts, dated 1922 and 1938. These laws recognized the effect that the birth and care of a child could have on the mental health of the mother, up to 12 months' postpartum. Subsequently, several countries have adopted similar laws, with the exception of the United States.

The 20th century brought a new perspective to crime, linking it to mental illness. Two French psychiatrists, Jean-Etienne Esquirol and Victor Marcé, were the first to postulate the existence of a causal relationship among pregnancy, birth, and maternal mental illness (Oberman, 2002). Other investigators quickly adopted this perspective and almost immediately began, worldwide, to associate filicide with mental illness.

The reasons for the commission of contemporary filicide vary according to culture and can be categorized as (Schwartz & Isser, 2000):

- A form of postpartum abortion (i.e., to dispose of an unwanted child because of denial, fear, illegitimacy, religious beliefs, birth defects, altruism, mercy, gender, parental or financial disability, retaliation, or revenge);
- The unintended result of child abuse (Munchausen syndrome by proxy);
- The result of a diminished parental ability resulting from postpartum psychosis or depression.

As we can see, the emphasis remains on maternal filicide, partly because some legal systems in Europe have infanticide laws, which hold women less accountable for their filicidal actions due to maternal stress factors (Mariano, Chan, & Myers, 2014).

Currently, a child's murder causes public reactions of anger, horror, and disgust (Freire & Figueiredo, 2006; Stroud, 2005), although in some cultures the practice of selective filicide continues. For example, China's one-child law, designed to curb its rapid population growth, resulted in government-enforced abortion up to full-term, as well as systemic child abandonment, neglect, and neonaticide. As in historical contexts, it is disproportionately the female children who bear the brunt of the negative fallout from these laws and their consequences as families who can only have one child strive to ensure that they have a son.

In summary, the reaction of community to filicide has moved like a rollercoaster over the past 450 years, beginning with indulgence, rising to severity, to returning to indulgence again.

Current stands indicate that the appraisal is changing once again toward a more severe stance, partly due to the studies showing the rise in paternally committed filicide. Historically, fathers were either not considered to commit acts of filicide, or were legally protected when doing so as a result of legal statutes such as Patria Potestas Romana, under which holder of patriarchal authority held absolute dominion over his household, including that of life and death. Contemporary views, in Western legal systems, are seen to be taking an increasingly hard line against men who abuse and kill children, and this is reflected in the increased prosecution and harsher punitive measures.

DEFINITION OF FILICIDE

Filicide (*filia/filius* means own daughter/son and *occidere* is a homicide or manslaughter in Latin) is a cross-cultural phenomenon defined as the killing of a child/young person (or more), under the age of 18, by one or both parents (Freire & Figueiredo,

| Filicide (children's age < 18 years) |
| Infanticide (children's age < 1 year) |
| Neonaticide (children's age < 24 hours) |
| Feticide (intrauterine death) |

FIGURE 5.1

Definitions of filicide.

Adapted from West, S. (2007). An overview of filicide. Psychiatry, 2, 48–57.

2006; West, 2007), or even by stepparents or other parental figures (Mariano et al., 2014). This type of murder is divided into two categories, according to the victim's age: infanticide (killing of a child less than 1 year) and neonaticide (when the victim does not survive the first 24 hours of life) (Kauppi, Kumpulainen, Karkola, Vanamo, & Merikanto, 2010; Liam & Koenraadt, 2008; Putkonen, Weizmann-Henelius, Lindberg, & Eronen, Hakkanen, 2009; Resnick, 1969).

The literature also considers the existence of the crime of feticide[1], when a fetus has intrauterine death due to a criminal act by one of the parents (cf., Fig. 5.1).

It should be noted that the term "filicide" does not exclude the death of adult children (i.e., older than 18 years) or crimes committed by nonbiological parents of the children (i.e., stepfathers or stepmothers). However, studies carried out to date tend to focus on underage victims (Mariano et al., 2014) and crimes committed by biological parents, and we have chosen to follow this categorization.

THE LEGAL CONCEPT OF FILICIDE

Regarding the evolution of the legal treatment of filicide, we may find that there are three distinct periods throughout history: (1) a period of permission or indifference, between the seventh century BC and the fifth century AC, (2) a period of reaction in favor of a newborn child, between the fifth century and the 18th century AC, and (3) a period of reaction in favor of the guilty woman, from the 18th century to the present.

The legal processes have generally tended to deal leniently with female filicide offenders. For example, juries are often unwilling to convict a woman for neonaticide, possibly because of the failure for the accused woman to fit the societal stereotype of a murderer. They might also consider that she has enough guilt over the act to feel sufficiently punished. Even when they commit the same offense, men are much

---

[1]Some countries (e.g., India) consider this act as a form of sex selective abortion (that is, as a crime), while others (e.g., England) consider it as a **medical practice** that should be performed before medical abortion (which legitimates it as a practise).

more likely than women to be sent to prison. Whatever the reason, for no other crime is there such a lack of conviction.

Currently, the legal definition of filicide varies from country to country and two opposite lines in the framework of this phenomenon may be considered, bringing together the various existing positions: the treatment and the punishment of offenders (Freire & Figueiredo, 2006).

For example, England's Infanticide Act (1938) was based on the concepts of puerperal and lactational insanity (Friedman, Horwitz, & Resnick, 2005, p. 1582). The act reduced the charge from murder to manslaughter for women who killed their infant aged less than 1 year "if the balance of her mind was disturbed by reason of her not having fully recovered from the effect of lactation" (Marks, 2003). More than 20 countries (e.g., England, Australia, Canada, Germany, New Zealand) have such legislation that can assert that mothers who kill their children may suffer from a serious mental disorder. Conversely, in the United States, there is no special status of filicidal woman in the legal statutes, and the act is considered within the standard forms of homicide (Freire & Figueiredo, 2006).

Inconsistency is the hallmark of these filicide laws across the world, and a woman may receive leniency and funded social and psychological support in one instance, while elsewhere the same crime may be treated with extreme disdain and result in life imprisonment or, in some jurisdictions, the death penalty.

It should be noted that current criminal justice scholars have suggested a strong influence of gender in the treatment of offenders within all levels of the criminal justice system (Wiest & Duffy, 2012), this is:

- Female offenders are much more likely to be successful in using the insanity defense to avoid criminal responsibility than are male offenders (Mariano et al., 2014);
- Male offenders are more likely to receive harsh sentences than are female offenders (Frazier, Bock, & Henretta, 1983);

Female offenders are much more likely to receive a nonincarceration sentence for similar offences than are male offenders (Frazier et al., 1983);

- Heterosexual female defendants are judged to be less guilty than the other defendant types (homosexual females, heterosexual males, and homosexual males) and to deserve shorter sentences (Ragatz & Russell, 2010);
- Within prisons, the administrators' treatment of female and male offenders are very different: for example, when female and male inmates commit violent acts, women are frequently labeled *mentally ill* and placed in treatment, while men are labeled *criminal* and punished (Wiest & Duffy, 2012).

CLASSIFICATION SYSTEMS OF FILICIDE

According to the literature, parents kill their children for various reasons, under a variety of circumstances. The reports presented by the media, the study of clinical cases, and the crime statistics have shown that filicide cannot be explained by a single construct, as if the deaths were homogeneous events (Mckee, 2006). However, scientific research has shown common standards in this type of crime over the past decades, both in relation to perpetrators and victims and to the crime itself.

Thus, several attempts have been made to determine the motive that leads parents to kill their children (Bourget, Grace, & Whitehurst, 2007; Putkonen et al., 2011). The first classifications (e.g., D'Orban, 1979; Resnick, 1969; Scott, 1973) relied exclusively on maternal filicide, while newer types (e.g., Bourget & Bradford, 1990; Bourget & Gagné, 2002; Guileyardo, Prahlow, & Barnar, 1999) also emphasize the paternal filicide.

The first and most influential classification of filicide was developed by Resnick in 1969, through the revision of 131 cases, in the time period between 1751 and 1967. The author classified the crime into five categories, according to the apparent motives (i.e., altruism, acute psychosis, unwanted child, accident, revenge) that led to its commission and concluded that most filicides occur for altruistic reasons (49%), while neonaticides are perpetrated particularly because the child is not desired. In addition to the presentation of this definition, Resnick described two types of neonaticide: active (i.e., the death of the newborn is a direct result of violence, usually followed by intense panic) and passive (i.e., the death of the newborn is a direct result of neglect after birth).[2]

In 1973, Scott investigated 46 parents who committed filicide, developing a categorization system based on the impulse to kill. Thus, death could be a consequence of (1) the elimination of an unwanted child (for assault or neglect), (2) a compassionate attitude, (3) a severe mental disease, or (4) an external stimulus or (5) the very stimulation from the victim.

In 1979, D'Orban studied 89 cases of women convicted of filicide, infanticide, and attempted murder in a 6-year period and, also based on the impulse to kill, he identified five types of maternal filicide: (1) by beating (the more frequent), (2) by retaliation, (3) by mental illness, (4) of an unwanted child, and (5) for mercy.

In 1990, Bourget and Bradford were the first authors to recognize the importance of the gender of the perpetrator of the crime, noting that filicide is not a practice carried out only by the mothers. Through the analysis of 13 cases, they also concluded that it is of great importance to study the attributes of both parents (especially current psychopathology) as well as that of the child that may have precipitated the crime.

In 1999, Guileyardo et al. identified 16 subtypes of filicide, based on the primary motive or cause that led to the perpetration of the crime. The authors concluded that each of these subtypes is sufficiently distinctive to warrant a separate categorization and described each of them in detail. Four subtypes are noted as being based on Resnick system (1969) and in particular altruistic filicide, filicide by acute psychosis, filicide of an unwanted child, and filicide for revenge.

In 2001, through the analysis of 219 cases of child murder, Meyer and Oberman created a system to identify the causes of crime perpetrated by the progenitor, identifying five categories: (1) neonaticide (for denial/dissociation or deliberately concealed pregnancy) (2) assisted/coercive (women are forced by their partners), (3) negligence (children die from lack of food, health or safety care), (4) related to abuse

---

[2]E.g., putting the newborn in the toilet, not take any action to prevent his drowning or abandon him to death in outdoor locations.

(there is no history of aggression, but the crime is committed by accident), and (5) purposeful filicide (due to severe mental illness, emotional distress or personality disorder).

Alder and Polk (2001) analyzed 32 cases of filicide and found three primary categories: (1) filicide-suicide (mothers who kill their children and then commit suicide because they were devastated by family circumstances), (2) fatal assault (the mothers have a history of abuse toward the child but had no intention of committing the crime), and (3) neonaticide (the mothers have never psychologically adjusted to the pregnancy and fear the consequences arising from the birth of the baby).

In 2002, Bourget and Gagné developed a classification system taking into account various characteristics and circumstances associated with filicide, including the motive, the intention to kill, and psychiatric illness of the perpetrator. All kinds of filicide (i.e., by mental illness, by fatal abuse, by retaliation, for mercy, or for other causes) take into account the fact that the act may or may not be intentional and the desire to kill the child may or not be conscious.

In 2006, McKee grouped the filicide mothers into five categories: (1) detached mothers (category that reflects the underlying motivation to commit the crime, and is subdivided into four types: denial, ambivalent, resentful, and exhausted), (2) abusive/neglectful mothers (category that reflects the nature of the mothers' parental failure, subdivided into recurrent, reactive and inadequate), (3) depressed/psychotic mothers (category that reflects the mothers' most descriptive diagnoses or symptom patterns of mental illness, which is subdivided into delusional, impulsive, and suicidal), (4) retaliatory mothers (single category without subcategories that highlights the mother's wish to punish others' interference in her relationship with her child through the perpetration of filicide), and (5) psychopathic mothers (category that describes mothers whose relationships with their children are categorized by maternal exploitation and self-indulgence, which is subdivided into financial, addicted, and narcissistic, according to the primary reasons for their self-serving use of their child). This model was developed taking into account relational, contextual, and developmental dimensions that explain the maternal motivations to committing the crime. The name of each category describes the nature and the quality of the relationship between the mother and the child(ren).

In 2015, Mariano, Chan, and Myers proposed three transdisciplinary, empirically informed filicide categories primarily defined by effects of (1) psychopathology associated with neurotransmitter disturbances (i.e., a portion of filicides are associated with affective, psychotic, and personality disorders influenced in part by central nervous system serotonergic disturbances), (2) gender and sex hormones (defending that sex hormones exert direct effects on brain development soon after birth and on the expression of aggression, they consider the sexual dimorphism and hormonal influences in filicide, namely the elevated adrenocorticotropic hormone levels and an increase in testosterone levels), and (3) evolutionary motives (killing one's biological children or stepchildren can confer certain evolutionary advantages; e.g., selectivism, resource competition). Table 5.1 presents the summary of the common characteristics to several filicide classification systems.

Table 5.1 Comparison of Maternal Filicide Classification Systems

Author(s), Data	Rejection	Unintended	Mental/Illness	Emphasis Retaliation	Antisocial	Other
Resnick (1969)	Unwanted	Accidental	Acute psychosis	Spouse revenge	None	Altruism
Scott (1973)	Unwanted	None	Gross mental pathology	None	None	Mercy
D'Orban (1979)	Unwanted	Battering	Mentally ill	Retaliating	None	Mercy
Bourget and Bradford (1990)	Neonaticide	Accidental	Altruism Psychotic silicide/suicide	Retaliating	None	Paternal filicide
Guileyardo et al. (1999)	Unwanted	Accidental Negligence and neglect Sexual abuse	Acute psychosis MSBP Substance abuse Seizure disorder	Spouse revenge	Sadism	Altruism
Alder and Polk (2001)	Neonaticide	Fatal assault	Filicide-suicide	None	None	None
Meyer and Oberman (2001)	Neonaticide	Abuse/neglect	Purposeful	None	Assisted	None
Bourget and Gagné (2002)	None	Fatal abuse	Mentally ill	Retaliating	None	Mercy
Mckee (2006)	Detached	Accidental/ neglectful	Psychotic/depressed	Retaliatory	Psychopathic	None
Mariano et al. (2014)	Evolutionary effects	None	Associated with neurotransmitter disturbances	None	None	Gender and sex hormonal influences

Adapted from Mckee, G. (2006). Why mothers kill. Oxford: Oxford University Press.

According to the literature (c.f., Bourget & Gagné, 2005), there are several limitations found in the various classification systems presented:

- The absence of a standardized data organization system for the classification of filicide
- The absence of a strict criteria, which leads to an overlap between categories, resulting in difficulties in assigning a case to a specific category
- The exclusion of potential factors and variables predictive of filicide
- The absence of clarity about the role of the sex differences of the perpetrator in the committing of the crime

However, the analysis of the multiple classification systems also shows some similarities between them, namely (Mckee, 2006):

- The emphasis on the importance of mental illness at the time of commission of the crime
- The failure in the establishment of emotional bonds with the child
- The inadequate parenting practices

In addition, the researchers found similar frequencies for the cases within similar categories.

In short, being a multifaceted and a multidimensional concept, there has been difficulty in constructing a classification covering all the variables involved, which facilitates the identification of subgroups and allows a more precise analysis of filicide perpetrators. Moreover, the differences in the results found in the studies of various countries make the universalization of classification systems difficult.

INCIDENCE, PREVALENCE AND STATISTICAL PROBLEMS

Over the past 50 years, the studies to determine statistical data on filicide have multiplied in several countries, including its incidence, prevalence, and risk factors (Mckee, 2006). Although rates of filicide have declined in developed countries, it remains a leading cause of child death (Koenen & Thompson, 2008).

In 2015, Mariano, Chan, and Myers presented the first comprehensive analysis of US filicide, tabulated over a 32-year period in the US Federal Bureau of Investigation's Supplementary Homicide Reports (SHR). They analyzed a total of 632,017 individuals arrested—but not convicted—for homicides during the period of 1976–2007, finding that 94,146 (14.9% of cases) were able to be classified as filicides. They also concluded that one-third of victims were under 1 year of age, that fathers were as likely as mothers to kill infants, and that, over time, the total number of cases in the country has remained relatively stable at around 500 a year.

Also, in Finland, the homicide rate is higher than that in other developed countries: 7.31 of female babies and 6.54 of male babies under 1 year of age per 100,000 births died from homicide, according to a study by Gartner between 1965 and 1980 (Kauppi et al., 2010).

The lowest rates of child homicide occur in countries such as Spain, Netherlands, Italy, and Greece, while rates in England and Wales have remained stable in recent years (Freire & Figueiredo, 2006). In Sweden, there has been a decrease in the number of victims over time, which may indeed be related to the legalization of abortion (which leads to reduction in the number of neonaticides) and debate about the ill treatment and the legal prohibition of corporal punishment to the child (Somander & Rammer, 1991).

In Table 5.2 is further information about the number of homicides of children, according to a review of studies conducted in several countries.

In countries where the birth rate is low, isolated cases of filicide can generate high crime rates, as in Luxembourg. Therefore, extreme caution should be taken when comparing the data in countries with a small number of inhabitants (Almeida, 2012).

In 2009, Portugal media reported unofficial data on 15 children who died at the hands of their parents, six of whom were babies suffocated by their mothers soon after birth. The same sources indicated that in 2010, 12 children were killed in these circumstances (Almeida, 2012). In addition to these data, no official epidemiological

Table 5.2 Prevalence of Filicide Determined in the Various Countries

Country	Year/Period	Number of Filicides	Sources
Australia	1996	25	Strang (1996)
Austria	1995–2005	86	Putkonen et al. (2009)
Canada	2001	69	Yarwood (2004)
Croatia	1980–2004	24	Marcikić et al. (2006)
England and Wales	1997–2006	314	Flynn, Shaw, and Abel (2013)
Finland	1995–2005	66	Putkonen et al. (2009)
Japan	1994–2005	615	Yasumi and Kageyama (2009)
Netherlands	2007	9	Nieuwbeerta and Leistra (2007)
Northern Ireland	2002–2007	14	Hall (2007)
Portugal	2004–2013	42	Almeida (2014)
Québec	1991–1998	34	Bourget and Gagné (2002)
Scotland	2002	10	Yarwood (2004)
Spain	2010	20	Dados não oficiais
USA	1976–2007	94,146	Mariano et al. (2014)
Sweden	1973–2008	151	Lysell, Runeson, Lichtenstein, and Långström (2014)
Turkey	1995–2000	96	Karakus, Ince, Ince, Arican, and Sozen (2003)

Adapted from Almeida, F. (2012). Mães filicidas: Contextualização e fundamentação. In F. Almeida, & M. Paulino (Coords.), Profiling, vitimologia e ciências forenses: Perspetivas atuais (pp. 315–343). Lisboa: Pactor).

tudy of this crime in our population exists until the time of our study in 2014 (Almeida & Vieira, 2014).

The literature review shows that most victims are killed by their biological parents and only a minority are victims of other types of perpetrators (usually a man with a sexual motive) (Freire & Figueiredo, 2006). Moreover, it emphasizes the fact that the values shown in these studies are underestimated and could be inaccurate, which limits the knowledge of the nature of death and the relationship between perpetrators (Putkonen et al., 2011). These biases are, for this reason, various aspects:

- Varying the source, vary the measured data.
- In statistical terms, children who survived the attempts of filicide do not count.
- It is unknown whether the number of concealed pregnancies or babies that have been abandoned, whose bodies were placed in garbage containers, buried in remote places, or left in unoccupied housing sites.

It should also be added that:

- Some studies included the killing of a child of any age (e.g., United States) by a parent, given that filicide and parent–child relationships do not end when offspring reach age 18, while others focused on victims under age 18 (e.g., England and Wales) or age 15 (e.g., Japan).
- Some studies included crimes committed only by mothers, while others included crimes committed by both parents, or even by stepparents or other parental figures.
- Some studies include crimes where the parents were convicted, while others do not.
- Studies often focus on types of filicide separately using different sample parameters.

The cases involving medical and legal factors are added (Mckee, 2006). To establish the true prevalence of this crime, at least four conditions should be known:

1. All deceased children's bodies must be discovered and examined.
2. The exact cause of each death must be determined.
3. The circumstances of the death must be specified (i.e., accidental or intentional).
4. The parent must be convicted of killing his or her child.

Since the research about filicide is typically based on official reports (i.e., death certificates and police data), it is often difficult to establish the true causes of death, even for experienced professionals, since (Mckee, 2006):

- A significant percentage (between one-fifth and one-tenth) of deaths (by exclusion) attributed to sudden infant death syndrome (SIDS) are cases of filicide.
- Parents can induce diseases in children that may culminate in death (Munchausen's syndrome by proxy).
- Investigation may be compromised by the fact that the death of the child was accidental or intentional, even if the cause of death can be established.
- Considered accidental deaths are rarely reported or prosecuted as a result of abuse.

Also, the reluctance to pin the responsibility for the crime on a suffering parent should be taken into account (Friedman & Friedman, 2010). Further, many judges assert that guilt for killing one's child is punishment enough (Marcikić et al., 2006).

Despite the prevalence and consequent statistical problems presented, filicide seems to be declining. The reasons for this decline appear to result from the combination of several factors, including religion, the (re)moralization of society, a more humanistic vision of life, the existence of better social conditions, the legalization of abortion, and the adoption of policies related to the use and accessibility to contraceptive methods (Smith, 2006).

CRIMINAL AND FORENSIC CHARACTERISTICS OF FILICIDE

Filicide can be associated with characteristics of the perpetrator, the victim, and the relationship between them. However, it is noted that currently paternal filicide is not yet well understood, due to the small number of studies in this area and little consistency about the variables that should or should not be described and quantitatively or qualitatively measured (Mckee, 2006).

Contrary to current Western thinking, filicide is not always an unpredictable crime committed by mentally ill parents. For example, Oberman (2002) showed that parents who commit filicide often cannot raise children under the circumstances dictated by their specific position in place and time.

The first year of the child's life is a critical period for the perpetration of this crime with an increased risk of death within the first 24 hours after birth (Freire & Figueiredo, 2006). This may be due to the fact that, in most cases, the children do not attend day care, spending a great amount of time in the parent company (Friedman & Friedman, 2010).

THE PERPETRATOR

Most parts of research conclude that the risk of a child's homicide is greatest within their own family, and the crime is committed, in most cases, by one or both parents (Strang, 1996). Until now, various features of filicide perpetrators have been the subject of study and risk factors related to demographic characteristics (e.g., age, sex, marital status, ancestry, educational level, place of residence, employment status, socioeconomic status, and intellectual functioning), historical characteristics (e.g., family relationships, parental divorce, abuse in childhood and adulthood, history of prior arrests), situational characteristics (e.g., state of the marital relationship, financial condition, condition to care, parent–child relationship and child temperament), and clinics (i.e., previous history of mental illness, psychiatric problems in the family, results in psychological assessment tests, psychiatric diagnosis) have been found (Mckee, 2006).

DEMOGRAPHIC CHARACTERISTICS

Age. Women who commit neonaticide are usually teenagers (or younger than 20 years) and unmarried, who deny or conceal their pregnancies, had no prenatal care, did not undergo childbirth at the hospital and have no plans to take care of their children (Bourget et al., 2007; Friedman & Friedman, 2010; West, 2007). Subsequent psychiatric evaluation reveals that many of these girls suffer from severe dissociative states, associated with a history of abuse and a chaotic family life. Due to various reasons (e.g., religion, culture, money, ambivalence and immaturity), they are not willing to look for alternatives such as abortion or the transfer of children for adoption (Oberman, 2002). After exclusion of cases of neonaticide, most studies conclude that mothers are in the age group of 20 years when the crime occurs (Mckee, 2006), being younger than men, who normally have the age of 30.

Sex. The literature does not agree on the reasons for the differences between filicide rates by mothers and fathers. There is some admission of the possibility that the differences between the male and female perpetrators may be found in the factors related to the characteristics of the victim, method of homicide, and the background leading up to the crime (Putkonen et al., 2011). While some studies report a higher incidence of maternal filicide (Kauppi et al., 2010), others concluded that fathers are as likely as mothers to kill their children (Mariano et al.,2014). The fact that most studies focus on female samples (because neonaticides are almost exclusively committed by the mother as well as infanticides) means that women are identified as major and unique perpetrators (Freire & Figueiredo, 2006). Contradictory results have also been reported indicating that filicides perpetrated one week after the child's birth are often committed by fathers or stepfathers (Kauppi et al., 2010).

Marital status. The literature also has no consensus regarding the marital status of filicides, with research showing opposing results that women are mostly married, or in a married-like relationship on the one hand, and other studies showing that female offenders are mostly single on the other (Mckee, 2006). However, in cases of neonaticide it is unlikely that mothers are married (because they are younger). As for men, several studies conclude they are married or are in divorce proceedings at the time of the crime (Oberman & Meyer, 2008). Most studies show that single mothers are more prone to perpetrating filicide than are single fathers (Dawson, 2015).

Ancestry. While some studies suggest that the incidence of child homicide is higher among black populations, others conclude that it is higher among whites. However, when taking into account the socioeconomic status, there is no statistically significant difference between the various population groups (Craig, 2004).

Educational level. Specifically, with regard to neonaticidal mothers, some researchers indicate poor education (lower secondary education) and dropping out of school before age 16 as risk factors (Marcikić et al., 2006). However, the relationship between the mother's level of education and child murder may not be so linear, since many mothers younger than 17 have not yet had the opportunity to complete 12 years of schooling (Marcikić et al., 2006; Overpeck, 2002). The literature also emphasizes that men tend to be unskilled or semi-skilled, pointing to their low education as a risk factor for the perpetration of the crime (Smith, 2006).

Residence area. The few investigations that have studied this feature suggest that neonaticide is more common in rural areas where abortion is not socially accepted. However, the literature is sparse with regard to this variable and its relation to the crime of filicide (Craig, 2004).

Professional situation. According to the literature, a feature which distinguishes filicides from other homicides is the fact that they are employed at the time(s) of the offense(s) (Putkonen et al., 2011). However, and once again, there is no consensus on this aspect as several studies show the unemployment situation of the parent (and the subsequent degradation of living conditions) as a factor that encourages the commission of the crime (Freire & Figueiredo, 2006; West, 2007).

Socioeconomic status. Most studies emphasize that the perpetrators are from disadvantaged backgrounds and several researchers refer to the lack of financial resources as a common characteristic to women and men who commit the crime or to women who abandon their newborns (Mckee, 2006).

Intellectual functioning. The literature cites as a characteristic of mothers who commit filicide that intellectual functioning is generally below average (Mckee, 2006; Oberman & Meyer, 2008). However, much of the research literature concerning filicide is decades old and, there is little or no attention paid to intellectual functioning of perpetrators. A research conducted by Farooque and Ernst (2003) revealed that more than 40% of the parents who kill their children were diagnosed with mental retardation or borderline intellectual functioning. Although their sample was small their findings may suggest that the level of intellectual function of the parent plays an important role in the safety of their children. Parenting and stress management skills are probably deficient in persons with impaired intellectual functioning, acting as triggers for the perpetration of the crime.

HISTORICAL CHARACTERISTICS

Many filicidal women come from large families and have severe parental conflict and chaotic family history that is sometimes even violent (Freire & Figueiredo, 2006). They had, therefore, weak family ties (i.e., history of abandonment, maternal loss in childhood, absent mother or perpetrator of abuse, negligent father with history of substance abuse or mental illness), with frequent parental separations and financial instability (Mckee, 2006). Also, the history of victimization has been reported as a risk factor, in particular physical or sexual abuse and domestic violence (Oberman, 2002).

According to the literature, the family of the neonaticidal woman is characterized by role confusion, emotional neglect, violation of limits, and bizarre parental relationships. The father is often intrusive and jealous, while the mother is cold, hostile, or absent (due to physical or mental illness or substance abuse). The fact that the family did not notice the typical physical changes of pregnancy in women illustrates the isolation that she feels and the relationship that she has with the members of their family or other significant elements (Oberman & Meyer, 2008).

The few studies that exist indicate that mothers living alone at the time of the crime have few social contacts and lack of family and community support and the child is the one person who establishes a relationship with her. This aspect usually results from a history of violent abuse by perpetrators in childhood.

It should also be noted that filicide mothers are often in violent and abusive relationships at the time their children were killed. Also, belonging to families with religious or cultural biases against sexual intercourse (mainly outside of marriage) or the fact that women are illegal immigrants who fear that their pregnancy threatens their residency is often cited (Oberman & Meyer, 2008).

Usually, filicide mothers have no history of prior arrests at the time of the crime (Oberman & Meyer, 2008). The low percentage of women who have committed crimes have a history of theft, robbery, or prostitution.

The few studies about paternal filicide usually emphasize that these parents are living a situation of despair or marital stress, have been the subject of infidelity by the partner, or are going through a case of contentious divorce. A history of domestic violence, multiple sibling victims (Kauppi et al., 2010), physical child abuse, social isolation, or lack of support cut across both perpetrators. The majority of research has shown that fathers who kill their children are more likely to have a criminal record than filicidal mothers (Dawson, 2015).

SITUATIONAL CHARACTERISTICS

During pregnancy, there may be various situational risk factors for filicide directly related to the mother's companion:

- His unwillingness to use contraception (which can lead to unwanted pregnancies)
- Maintaining relationships with other women (that increase the likelihood of contracting sexually transmitted diseases passing to the fetus and can compromise the stability of the relationship)
- His unwillingness to provide care and support measures (which accentuate the woman's emotional burden that will have to take care of the child alone)
- The use of reactive violence, predatory or coercive intimidation, and subjugation of women to his wishes

After delivery, separation or infidelity can also contribute to the increased risk of filicide.

The mother's financial status is defined in terms of economic self-sufficiency, that is, their ability to provide care to children without resorting to the biological father or his family. The risk arises when the mother lives in poverty (without possibility to access to prenatal and postnatal care) and depends on public support measures or any third party for their livelihood (which therefore increases the risk of domestic violence and exploitation). Such situations lead to depression and despair, increasing the risk of filicide-suicide (Mckee, 2006).

The mother's ability to care is defined in terms of her obligations to the infant or child. Several studies indicate that the situations in which mothers have one or more children (below 17 years) diminish their resilience and ability to provide them adequate care (Bourget et al., 2007). Single mothers who are the sole caregiver of several children are more vulnerable to exhaustion and stress due to maternal responsibilities, which puts them at high risk of negligent supervision and impulsive or reactive abuse that can lead to accidental filicide. Also, the fact that the mother had a history of abuse as a child can be an indicator of the tendency to apply physical disciplinary measures to their baby.

Religion, environment, ambivalence (e.g., emotional, situational), immaturity, and a culture that promotes self-destructive impulses are also often cited as risk factors, and circumstances such as inadequate or overcrowded accommodation, the possibility of eviction, and cohabitation with stepchildren are very common sources of stress among filicidal mothers.

With regard to the parent–child relationship, parents whose experience of intimacy in childhood was marked by discord and violence are more likely to relate to their children through violence. In many cases of filicide, the offender demonstrates an exaggerated sense of connection with the child before the crime, which can be a result of a reactive attachment formation: the primary rejection is camouflaged by an excessive attention on children. This troubled relationship can still be characterized by a reversal in roles: the father relies on the child, while considering that parenting it entails too many responsibilities (Freire & Figueiredo, 2006). Research on this area is scarce.

CLINICAL CHARACTERISTICS

Numerous studies have reported an association between filicide and psychiatric illness of the perpetrator, especially when this person suffers from major depression with psychotic features. Also, personality disorders, especially borderline personality, have been found in both filicidal women and men. Psychotic disorders, schizophrenia, bipolar disorder, adjustment disorders, abuse or substance dependence, and suicidal ideation are also cited. Regarding women, a history of psychiatric problems in their family is more frequent in cases of filicide than in the general population (e.g., mental illness, alcoholism, and substance abuse) (Mckee & Shea, 1998).

Although the influence of serious mental disorders such as depressive and psychotic disorders has been noted in both genders, these disorders are found to be more pronounced among female perpetrators compared with male perpetrators (Liam & Koenraadt, 2008).

Mental illness can be classified as one of two types, taking into account its inception: acute (i.e., beginning after the child's birth) and chronic (i.e., prior to the birth of the child) (Smith, 2006).

Hiding of pregnancy. Specifically regarding the neonaticide, hiding or denial of the pregnancy and subsequent birth outside hospital facilities is an additional risk factor (Friedman & Friedman, 2010). Among the risk factors for denial of pregnancy are youth (is most common in adolescence), passive behavior (usually women are coerced into having sex), substance abuse (in case of emotional denial), social isolation (for cases of covert denial), schizophrenia (in case of psychotic denial), eating disorders, and irregular menstruation (Miller, 2002). When mothers are teenagers or young adults (i.e., under the age of 20 years), the pregnancy can result from illicit or incestuous relations, that are unknown and/or not supported by parents or carers. In some countries (e.g., Croatia), for mothers living with the terror, shame, and guilt that accompanies a pregnancy without marriage, fear has been identified as a primary motivating factor for committing infanticide (Marcikić et al., 2006).

Postpartum psychosis. Factors increasing the risk of postpartum psychosis (De Bortoli, Coles, & Dolan, 2012, p. 3):

> *Include sleep deprivation, hormonal shifts after birth, psychological stressors (e.g., marital problems, older age, single parent, financial pressures), bipolar disorder or schizoaffective disorder, past or family history of postpartum psychosis, previous psychiatric hospitalisations, menstruation or cessation of lactation, as well as obstetric factors that increase the risk marginally (primiparity, complicate delivery, premature delivery, acute Caesarean section and long duration of labour.*

However, the relationship between postpartum disorders and filicide is unclear and has been the subject of debate in medical and legal literature. What we know is that compared with nonpsychotic women at the time of the crime, postpartum psychotic women tend to be older and divorced or separated and to have higher levels of education, history of substance abuse, hospitalizations for psychiatric reasons, ongoing treatment of mental illness, and previous suicide attempts (Lewis & Bunce, 2003). Therefore, if left untreated, they have a high risk of committing suicide or filicide. This particularly happens when the illusory beliefs are focused on the child (e.g., they may hear voices telling them to sacrifice the child in the name of God, or that it is half human and half alien). Some authors believe that filicide is a psychotic act, which is partly the result of a severe personality disturbance in which there is marked regression in ego control, making it possible to open the primitive expression of violence that had long ago been suppressed from conscience. Moreover, for these individuals (in themselves vulnerable to stress due to disease characteristics), the accumulation of emotional and physical stress associated with parenting plays an important role in sudden and catastrophic failure in the psyche of an already weakened self. For each of these patients, as part of their personality disorder is the repressed rage that is violently released by his psychosis (Papapietro & Barbo, 2005).

Postpartum depression. During the first year after the birth of the child, 10–25% of mothers develop postpartum depression. The beginning of this symptomatology seems to be related to personal factors and vulnerabilities such as poverty or marital conflict (De Bortoli et al., 2012). Symptoms develop gradually and include depressed mood (often accompanied by anxiety), markedly diminished interest or pleasure in daily activities, loss of appetite accompanied by weight loss after delivery, insomnia and even frequent awakenings when the baby is sleeping, physical agitation or motor retardation, excessive and inappropriate feelings of guilt, worry, diminished concentration and ability to make decisions, and recurrent thoughts of death or suicidal ideation. Also, psychotic symptoms, such as delusions, may be present. Some mothers may neglect the child because of these deficits or hide the symptoms for fear of being stigmatized or lose custody (Mckee & Shea, 1998). Apparently they kill the child without great violence and tend to be impulsive and reactive before a stressful event. These mothers have low self-esteem and a poor impulse control and may display anxiety and antisocial behavior. Since parenting requires patience, maturity, durability, and energy, it is not surprising that depressed mothers kill their children in very energetic conditions (Smith, 2006). Women who experience postpartum depression are predisposed to developing depressive disorders in other periods not associated with child birth (De Bortoli et al., 2012).

Schizophrenia or severe bipolar disorder. Women with these mental disorders are often the victims of unplanned and unprotected pregnancy. Although the literature about pregnancy in women with schizophrenia is scarce, it is known that the increase of stressor agents contributes to decompensation after delivery (Meyer & Spinelli, 2002). Mothers with schizophrenia are more violent compared to mothers who have a psychotic bipolar disorder. There are few reported cases of schizophrenic mothers who commit filicide, perhaps due to the fact that they are highly vulnerable to child custody loss due to their inability to take care of their baby, or have an increased risk of spontaneous abortions, stillbirths, and induced abortions.

Depressive disorders with psychotic features, psychosis or schizophrenia, major depressive disorder, and acute substance intoxication seem to be common in men who commit filicide (West, 2007). Male perpetrators were also noted for their antisocial behavior in adolescence and adulthood, which, in combination with adverse life experiences, may lead to homicidal acts (Debowska, Boduszek, & Dhingra, 2015). Over half of fathers identified in filicide cases had contact with others regarding a mental health problem (e.g., medical or psychiatric staff, police staff, family) (Bourget & Gagné, 2005).

However, although the international psychiatric literature on filicide refers to some kind of mental illness among parents who commit filicide (Friedman, Horwitz & Resnick, 2005) and the general public links filicide to mental illness; the rate of parents who commit filicide are diagnosed with mental illness is actually low (Amon et al., 2012). Clearly, most parents who have mental illness do not kill or assault their children. However, acute symptoms of mental illness may elevate risk (Friedman & Friedman, 2010).

OFFENSE CHARACTERISTICS

Differences have been reported between filicides committed by mothers and those committed by fathers (Mariano et al., 2014). Let us consider some characteristics quoted in the literature.

Triggers. Substance abuse, desperation, and a lack of interest in parenting are often quoted (Putkonen et al., 2011).

Vulnerabilities. A predisposition to mental illness and an unfavorable social environment are often quoted (Putkonen et al., 2011).

Precipitating factors. The family and marital stress (e.g., rejection, distrust, separation, or divorce) is quoted by various authors as factors that lead to the perpetrating of the crime. More than half of crimes are immediately precipitated by the child's crying (Fujiwara, Barber, Schaechter, & Hemenway, 2009). In paternal filicide, a father may misinterpret a child's behavior as threatening and overreact, perhaps impulsively (Mariano et al., 2014).

The type of crime. Neonaticide is almost exclusively committed by mothers. Infanticide is usually committed by mothers, while fathers are more often perpetrators of filicide in late childhood (Liam & Koenraadt, 2008).

Time of the crime. Usually, the crime occurs around noon on any day of the week, more often in the winter. Compared to male perpetrators, crimes occur in the morning or evening, usually at the weekend, no reference being found regarding other relevant criminal characteristics.

Location of crime. In cases of infanticide and filicide, crimes are usually committed at home. In the case of filicidal mothers, they are usually found alone with the victim.

The behavior after the crime. Usually mothers clean the crime scene and try to hide the child's body more often than fathers. This is because the male perpetrators have no fear of being caught and female perpetrators seek to distance themselves emotionally from the victim. Moreover, they can be embarrassed by the perpetrating of the crime creating an assumption that this does not fit their self-image (Häkkänen-Nyholmemail et al., 2009).

Suicide. Suicide is often associated with filicide, both attempted (filicide-parasuicide) and consummated (filicide-suicide) (Liem, de Vet, & Koenraadt, 2010; Putkonen et al., 2009). The filicide perpetrators have high rates of suicide attempts and these are, in most cases, serious and successful. However, filicide-suicide is a less-studied category due to the difficulty in collecting information after the death of the perpetrator (Kauppi et al., 2010). The results found in the literature are contradictory with regard to those who commit filicide-suicide more often, whether the mothers or the fathers. The greatest agreement among researchers refers to the fact that desperate or depressed parents can take the life of their children before attempting or committing suicide (Hon, 2011). Also mental illness, especially depression, is a significant finding in cases of filicide-suicide (Bourget et al., 2007). Normally, the suicide does not follow the neonaticide, the filicide of unwanted children, the filicide by retaliation and filicide by fatal abuse (Bourget et al., 2007). Research revealed that paternal filicide-suicide can occur in conjunction with uxoricide (i.e., killing one's wife). These acts are referred to as familicide and appear to be motivated by vengeful anger. Risk factors for such killings include marital disharmony or separation and sexual jealousy (Debowska et al., 2015).

Protective factors. In addition to the risk factors for maternal filicide, it is also important to note the existence of protective factors, namely (Mckee, 2006):

- Be older than 25 years
- Have an average or above average IQ

- Have completed upper secondary education
- No diagnosis of mental disorder
- Have no history of previous trauma
- Planned pregnancy, positive attitude to pregnancy and prenatal and postnatal
- Positive bounds with the mother
- Non-violent father who provides adequate support
- Good family relationship
- Marital relationship free of violence
- The absence of substance abuse
- Provision of resources and proper care to your baby
- Have a healthy, calm, and quiet child

THE VICTIM

Most studies on filicide focus only on the characteristics of the perpetrator, making no reference to the characteristics of the child that put them at risk of filicide. The scarce literature on this aspect highlights the importance of factors such as gender, age, ancestry, birth circumstances, the number of victims, the history of prior victimization, the presence of persistent cramps, feeding difficulties, and temperament (De Bortoli et al., 2012).

Sex. Several studies indicate that the children victims of filicide are not predominantly boys or girls (Somander & Rammer, 1991). Others conclude there are predominantly male victims (Liam & Koenraadt, 2008). This may be due to the fact that boys are more physically vulnerable than girls (placing them at increased risk of death, regardless of the cause), due to the fact that they are perceived to be more aggressive (and required a more serious discipline), the way they interact with the environment (they are more active, more assertive, and more prone to vocalizing), and due to the parental beliefs that boys are more robust, require less protection, and are more demanding and more difficult to handle (and may enhance aggression as a response) (Marleau & Laporte, 1999). Other studies also suggests the possibility of a relationship between maternal motivation for filicide and the sex of the victim, that is, daughters are at high risk in the case of selfless situations while boys are at high risk for retaliatory situations against the companion (Marleau & Laporte, 1999). Findings are also contradictory as to whether the victim's sex varies by gender of the perpetrator. For example, some research shows fathers were more likely to kill male children compared to mothers, whereas other work found mothers killed a higher proportion of male victims (Dawson, 2015). Furthermore, there appears to be a relationship between the age and sex of the victim. For example, from 10 to 18 years old, it is more likely for boys to be killed by their parents during family disputes.

Age. Generally, it is considered that the younger the child, the greater is the risk of filicide, with the first day of life being a higher risk. This risk decreases with the increasing of the woman's age (Freire & Figueiredo, 2006; Strang, 1996). According to the literature, most dead children are younger than 6, and the first 6 months of life is the period of greatest vulnerability, since it is conducive to the period for postpartum psychosis (Resnick, 1969). Also, the younger the child, the more likely the mother is to perceive it as her personal property, to feel inseparable from it and subsequently culminate in filicide-suicide situation. There are significant statistic differences in the age of the children killed by different groups of mothers: mothers who suffer from mental illness tend to victimize older children, while abusive mothers tend to kill younger children (D'Orban, 1979). Victims of filicide by fatal abuse are usually younger and unwanted (Bourget et al., 2007). Fathers rarely commit neonaticide, more often killing older children compared to mothers who more often kill infants (Dawson, 2015).

Ancestry. Some studies point out that minorities are disproportionately affected, with more than half the victims being black (Finkelhor & Ormrod, 2001). Others point to higher percentages of white victims, followed by black victims and other minorities (Mariano et al., 2014).

The circumstances of birth. Children with low birth weight, low gestational age (or prematurity), and low Apgar scores (Kilsztajn, Lopes, Carmo, & Reyes, 2007) are at greater risk of filicide. Moreover, the risk of morbidity increases due to the lack of prenatal care and the consequences of giving birth without assistance (Friedman & Friedman, 2010).

The number of victims. Many filicides involve the death of an only child, mainly because neonaticide and infanticide are committed by women who are first-time mothers. However, some women kill more than a child when they commit filicide. The literature suggests that men predominated as perpetrators of familicides, involving both spouse (the primary target) and child(ren) (the collateral victim/s). This may be related to the concepts of women and children being considered as a man's property and the lethal violence is an attempt to re-establish his patriarchal rights under threat (Liam & Koenraadt, 2008).

The history of prior victimization. Children who have been victims of previous abuse or continued abuse are at greater risk of filicide, since at any time they can suffer fatal abuse (Freire & Figueiredo, 2006). The literature emphasizes the fact that one in every two children who die from beatings has a documented history of prior abuse. However, it is extremely rare for a parent to kill a sexually abused child, regardless of age, although this may be more common with older girls for the purpose of the silence.

The presence of persistent cramps. A study carried out in this area indicates that 70% of mothers have thoughts and explicit aggressive fantasies, and 26% have infanticide thoughts during episodes of cramp (Levitzky & Cooper, 2000). With limited judgment, the decrease in impulse control, sleep deprivation, and despair to keep the baby quiet, the mother may have recurring thoughts to silence the crying child, even violently. Many mothers of children with these symptoms do not try to hurt or kill, but these findings suggest that such violence is considered (Friedman & Friedman, 2010).

Temperament. Temperament is defined in terms of behavior, mood, attitude, and behavior that may precipitate filicide by the mother. Difficult children to care for, disobedient, with avoidant or resistant attachment styles or affective blunting, may precipitate physical abuse culminating in its death (Mckee, 2006). Attention is called upon the fact that this risk factor does not decrease the mother's guilt for the crime, acknowledging only that there are more easy-going children than others.

The literature also emphasizes the association between filicide and the presence of severe disabilities in children (e.g., mental retardation, autism) (Palermo, 2003). In some cases, this deficiency can be an increased risk factor for suicide-filicide cases, because the parent feels unable to change the situation that causes pain. Also children who are developmentally challenged have a high risk of being abused (Friedman & Friedman, 2010).

THE METHODS USED TO KILL

Methods used by parents to kill their children differ from the usual methods of homicide. The literature also emphasizes the existence of gender differences in methods to commit the crime, namely the presence of deception/lying after the act (i.e., trying to hide the crime or the shame) that is more common in women, and attempted suicide is more frequent in fathers. In addition, fathers usually employ more violent methods (e.g., beatings, use of a firearm or weapon, fall from a ravine, or crushed by a train), while mothers use less violent methods (e.g., asphyxia by suffocation, drowning or strangulation, exposure to toxic agents, poisoning).

These findings are in line with the social imagery of gender differences: the methods used by men tend to be more violent, aggressive, and impersonal, while the methods used by women are more passive, less violent, and more personal. However, once there is a greater likelihood that the male parent kills older children, more power will have to be employed because they tend to resist attack (Putkonen et al., 2011).

The most common methods of neonaticide include asphyxia, drowning, strangulation, head trauma, exposure to extreme conditions (hypothermia or hyperthermia), and stabbing (Friedman & Friedman, 2010).

Cases in which children die as a result of fire, are thrown to ravenous animals (e.g., pigs), or are buried alive are also cited. Less usual methods such as inserting needles into the skull are also reported. The mothers normally use their own hands to strangle/suffocate or drown the baby, because they are unable to cause any physical damage (Mckee, 2006). Neonaticidal mothers typically act on their own. The suffocation may be related to an attempt at silencing the child's persistent crying and avoiding the detection of crime.

As the child's age increases, so does the degree of violence associated with crime. In cases of infanticide or filicide associated with negligence, almost 60% of children are shaken, assaulted, abused, or thrown to their deaths. Weapons (e.g., guns or knives) are rarely used by filicidal mothers, while poisoning is frequent (Liam & Koenraadt, 2008).

CIRCUMSTANCES OF DEATH

There is no universal way to classify the circumstances of deaths by filicide. However, as mentioned above, it is possible to draw five main scenarios that meet the circumstances for the perpetration of the crime (Strang, 1996):

1. Death subsequent to family disputes, usually by retaliation due to the end of a relationship between the parents
2. Death subsequent to fatal abuse

3. Death due to parent's mental illness (which have a bizarre character)
4. Death of children victims of fatal sexual abuse
5. Death of newborn children, who are abandoned without information about them, the perpetrator, or the crime

The knowledge of the place of delivery, especially in cases of neonaticide, is an important criminal and forensic characteristic. Women who commit neonaticide usually give birth alone at home and postpone notifying the authorities about the occurrence (when they do it). During childbirth they make little or no noise and experience feelings of exhaustion and panic. They often tend to hide the body by putting it into a plastic bag, keeping it in a closet or a plastic bag, or putting it in a trash container. Almost all neonaticide mothers kill their children in bathrooms, rooms, or other nonhospital environments. When they deliver on their own, the probability of not detecting neonaticide through a direct action or through negligence (leaving it in a remote location) increases significantly. Large amounts of blood present on the bed or in the bathroom indicate the place where the birth took place and the child's corpse concealment can be an indicator of no premeditation when a cabinet or a container is used (Byard, 2004).

Regarding the body disposal site, the most likely is for it to be left in the garbage (e.g., in public restrooms), abandoned in bed or elsewhere in the house (e.g., attics, hatches, and flowerbeds), or left in landfills, containers, forests, woods, road borders, or barns, which are readily accessible (Fujiwara et al., 2009). Occasionally, mother's clothes are arranged with the body to facilitate their identification. The further way the body is dropped and the less personal items there are next to it, the harder it is to relate the child with a particular woman, unless of problems associated with childbirth result in the need for medical care and treatment (Byard, 2004).

THE MOTIVE

The reasons for killing children are varied and have differed among communities and over time (Byard, 2004). Like other violent crimes, the reason that apparently led to the perpetration of the crime varies in cases of filicide. However, the most commonly cited reasons include jealousy, suspicion of infidelity on the part of the partner, poor economic conditions, stress, lack of emotional or social support, mental illness, unwanted pregnancy, and neglect. Several researchers found that younger women who commit infanticide or neonaticide do it through fatal abuse, while the crimes for mercy, retaliation, or psychosis are committed by older women.

In more recent times, infanticide may be rooted on fears of shame or rejection by family members, particularly when pregnancy has occurred in young, unmarried women. Infanticide may also occur if a pregnancy has been the result of an extramarital affair, in an attempt to hide the event from a spouse, or if there are financial concerns regarding the cost of another child, or the loss or restriction of employment (Byard, 2004).

But when we are examining the reasons that lead to the committing of filicide, the two most common scenarios emerging from police reports are related to family disputes and fatal abuse (Strang, 1996).

Family disputes. Most children are killed following the end of the relationship between their parents. In the case of male perpetrators, the wife/mother is usually the primary victim and the child is caught in the middle of this deadly violence. Other times it may succumb in the period in which the parent has its temporary custody. This type of incident is one of the factors responsible for the high rate of suicide/attempted suicide among offenders.

Fatal abuse. The attacks to the child are sudden and impulsive; the offender is the caregiver of the child at the time of the crime and seems to express anger and frustration by imposing a punishment or discipline. This abuse can take the form of battered child syndrome (the abusive behavior results from the stress of the moment). Other children die after being inflicted offenses over a long period of time. Sick or premature babies are particularly vulnerable to these situations, especially when the parents are young and live in isolation.

THE CAUSE OF DEATH AND MEDICOLEGAL PROBLEMS

The causes of death to be recorded on the death certificate are all diseases, morbid conditions, or injuries that caused the death or contributed to it, as well as the circumstances of the accident or violent act which produced such injuries. They can be classified as natural, violent, or unknown/undetermined.

Violent deaths include homicides (e.g., asphyxia, burns, poisoning, fatal injuries, neglect, exposure to extreme conditions, etc.), suicides, or accidents. In deaths resulting from external causes, the coroner may also try to ascertain whether they were intentional, unintentional, or due to undetermined cause (Overpeck, 2002).

Usually, the death of a child creates challenges to the pathologist in what concerns the cause of death. The cases are particularly complicated when they involve the death of a fetus or a newborn.

In cases of neonaticide, pathological findings tend to be nonspecific, particularly when the deaths were caused by suffocation, drowning, or failure in the support and provision of appropriate care for newborns. The questions to be answered by the pathologist dealing with a suspected case of neonaticide include (Byard, 2004):

1. The estimation of the gestational age of the child
2. The determination of indicators of extrauterine life or death in utero
3. The presence or absence of underlying organic lethal diseases
4. The document of lethal and nonlethal lesions
5. The assistance in the establishment of the mother's identity
6. The determination of cause, mechanism, and circumstances of death, if possible

It is essential that the pathologist has access to the crime scene details, the circumstances of death, to the resuscitation maneuvers performed on the victim, to the medical and obstetric history of the mother, and all the details that emerge along the criminal investigation before starting the autopsy (Howatson, 2006). This can be an asset to the expert's ruling on the medicolegal etiology of the case.

Moreover, the neonaticide may be premeditated: women can plan to keep the concealment of pregnancy and childbirth, or passivity and denial may have characterized their condition, with surprise upon delivery. This premeditation is not always easy to determine.

Cases of violent deaths, and in any type of crime, add to the difficulties in distinguishing between a death by murder or by accident and, as mentioned, a significant percentage of deaths that are attributed by exclusion to SIDS and that may be ultimately filicide cases (Mckee, 2006). Several factors have been associated with increased risk of child's sudden death, including early motherhood, large families, smoking and drug abuse by mothers, prematurity, low birth weight, and multiple births. The diagnosis of SIDS requires a negative history as well as a negative autopsy result. Also, the induction of illness in children may result in its death, and this not be attributed to a violent cause (Mckee, 2006).

When observing the deaths of more than a child for no apparent reason or in cases that the death is assigned (by exclusion) to SIDS, suspicions are raised among professionals who deal with these cases, making it vital to set up a research protocol (national or even international) to investigate sudden and unexpected children's deaths.

For example, in this context, in 2004 a protocol by The Royal College of Pathologists and The Royal College of Pediatrics and Child Health was created to investigate the sudden and unexpected deaths in infancy. According to this protocol (p. 1):

> In the absence of any eye-witness evidence of harmful conduct, the police investigations relied upon medical expertise, particularly that of paediatrics and pathologists. That evidence, when placed under careful scrutiny, raised serious concerns about the role of the expert witness in the courts, about the standard of proof and the quality of evidence, and about the procedures adopted for the investigation of sudden unexpected deaths of children.

Among other things, this protocol emphasizes the need:

- To establish the cause of death of the child as far as possible
- For specialized trained individuals to carry out the death investigation, involving multi-agency working, close collaboration and the sharing of information among all the institutions and professionals involved
- To protect the parents who are unjustly accused of a crime when this did not happen (for innocent parents to have a child taken from them, or to be prosecuted and convicted of killing a child who actually died of natural causes, is the stuff of nightmares)

- To protect the child when there is evidence that it is at risk (in a small percentage of cases, mothers and fathers do induce illness on their children and sometimes fatally harm them)
- To expand the number of pediatric pathologists experienced in infant autopsies
- To establish a specific qualification in forensic pediatric pathology to cover deaths in infancy
- To concentrate the investigation just on the child, but considering the family history, past events and the circumstances in which it lived
- To take a standard set of investigative samples immediately upon arrival to accident and emergency department staff and after death is confirmed
- To visit the local where the child died and to talk to parents preferably within 24 h of the death
- To order a postmortem examination to be carried out as soon as possible, preferably within 48 h by the most appropriate pathologist

CONCLUSION

Contrary to popular belief, filicide is not a new or rare phenomenon. It is best described as ubiquitous, culturally, and economically transversal throughout history (Smith, 2006).

The opinion of society about filicidal mothers is usually firm, but ambivalent. On one hand, it is considered that justice should punish the loss of innocent lives, on the other, although it is not known the complexity of mental illness, it is believed that something should be very wrong with a parent who murders their own child. This presents some explanation for society's mixed emotions regarding the use of the insanity plea in filicide cases (West, 2007).

Filicide is a complex crime, multifactorial, and disproportionate in terms of magnitude and whose circumstances are different from other types of homicide. Given the nature of this crime, it is difficult to find traits that consistently apply to both the perpetrators and the victims (West, 2007), due to the different populations studied, the place where the information was obtained (i.e., in the general population, in the psychiatric population or in prison environment). The lack of national and international research, the methodological issues raised in the investigations already carried out, the existence of few studies that includes filicidal fathers and the lack of theoretical progress are some of the barriers to successfully understand filicide. In addition, some studies are mostly retrospective and based on small samples and the child's age changes the potential risk of filicide (i.e., the younger, the greater the risk) (West, 2007).

However, this chapter demonstrated that individuals who committed neonaticide should be studied separately from infanticide and filicide offenders due to significant motivational differences underpinning their crimes. A careful review of literature helps us to identify some trends (cf., Table 5.3) and therefore some action plans.

Usually the neonaticidal mothers are characterized on the basis of demographic and social variables (i.e., they are typically young, single, with low education and low

Table 5.3 Profile of the Filicide

	Filicidal Mother	Filicidal Father
Age	Under 25	Above 30
Ancestry	Of all population groups	Of all population groups
Marital status	Single (with no relation with the father of the child) or in an abusive relationship	Married or in divorce proceedings
Educational level	Low	Low
Residence area	Predominantly rural	Predominantly rural
Professional situation	Usually unemployed	Usually employed
Socioeconomic status	Low	Low
Intellectual functioning	Above average	Above average
Mental disorders	Less pronounced Personality disorders, schizophrenia, psychosis, depression	More pronounced Personality disorders, substance abuse, major depression, schizophrenia, psychosis, dysthymia
Historic characteristics	From large families, with severe parental conflicts, weak family ties, and financial instability.	Physical child abuse, social isolation, and lack of support
Situational characteristics	Poverty, exhaustion, stress, immaturity	Marital stress
Vulnerabilities	Social isolation, lack of support	Social isolation, lack of support, unemployment
Precipitating factors	Despair, lack of interest in parenting	Abuse and the influence of substances, despair, betrayal
Suicide	No prior attempt	Prior attempts
Type of crime	Neonaticide and infanticide	Infanticide and filicide
Method	Passive and personal	Violent and impersonal
Motive	Fatal abuse, unwanted child, altruism, revenge, acute psychosis, lack of support, fear	Retaliation, revenge, anger, fatal abuse, coercion, acute mental disease
Victim characteristics	Younger and females	Older and males
Number of victims	Usually one	Usually more than one victim (familicide)
Criminal record	No history or prior arrests	Prior criminal record or arrests
Time of the crime	During the day	In the morning or at night

socioeconomic status, and living with their parents) and according to characteristics related to pregnancy (i.e., undesired and unsupervised pregnancy, denial of pregnancy, concealment of the physical manifestations of pregnancy). Although neonaticide is usually related with the presence of mental illness, the rate of mothers who are actually diagnosed with mental illness is very low (Häkkänen-Nyholmemail et al., 2009). When present, personality disorders are the most common. Moreover, it is suggested that these mothers may find it difficult to communicate with their families due to the presence of a strict fundamentalist education or deep religious convictions (Craig, 2004).

The infanticidal and filicidal mothers are usually older (aged between 25 and 34 years), married, or in a marital relationship (but without a strong relationship with the husband or partner or entirely fulfilled). Although they may not be victims of abuse, they do not feel emotional or financial support (or both) from the partner. In general, it seems there is no relationship between infanticide and low economic status or the presence of defects in the child (Craig, 2004). The presence of psychiatric disorders in infanticidal and filicidal mothers seems to be more relevant than in neonaticidal mothers (Craig, 2004) and includes postpartum psychosis, chronic mental disorders (e.g., schizophrenia), affective disorder with postpartum onset, and substance abuse. The infanticide or filicide is often an extension of a suicidal act.

The filicidal fathers tend to be in their late 20s when the crime occurred, and on average, the children are typically older than those killed by mothers (West, 2007). They tend to use more violent methods and tend to kill more than one victim, and the motive for the perpetration of the crime includes jealousy or revenge. Psychosis, depression, and alcohol or substance abuse seems to be common in men who commit filicide.

First, and specifically in the field of criminal and forensic investigations, the fact that a child dies mostly at the hands of a parent is an important statistic data for the framing of suspects of the practice of child homicide (Almeida, 2014).

Second, given all the variables involved in a parent's decision to kill a child, no specific treatment plan can be proposed. Although there are exceptions, most filicidal women are not recurring or chronic offenders. In fact, because most filicidal mothers kill only once, research on treatment may be irrelevant. Filicide is an irreversible act, and this is why the prevention is so crucial (Smith, 2006; West, 2007).

Third, to prevent filicide, it is important to know both the characteristics of the perpetrator and the circumstances of the crime (West, 2007).

Primary interventions[3] performed before women who do not show immediate signs or indicators of being presently at risk, serve to (Friedman & Resnick, 2007):

- Inform about future risks and consequences derived from crime
- Clarify about the risks of sex without using contraception
- Provide knowledge about sexual practice
- Provide access to contraception
- Create a safe environment (i.e., at home, at school, or at the facility) and conducive to discussion about sexuality

Secondary interventions[4] in maternal filicide should include programs for adolescents and young adults who become pregnant or have recently given birth (should therefore be implemented during pregnancy, immediately before or after birth, or during childhood) (Friedman & Resnick, 2007). For example, in the

---

[3] A primary intervention program should be implemented in individuals (or groups) in which it is possible to express a certain type of behavior (e.g., committing filicide) at some point in their lives.

[4] A secondary intervention program should be implemented before the occurrence of a particular behavior, so it is centered on people who are at imminent risk of committing a crime.

United States, these measures go from encouraging the mothers of newborns who will abandon or discard up their babies to do so in hospitals or similar public agencies without legal punishment, if there are no signs of neglect or abuse. They may also include:

- The education and counseling (school and community) in helping mothers postpone a second pregnancy
- The treatment of mood disorders developed postpartum (e.g., psychotherapy, antidepressant medication, support groups)
- To help the establishment of emotional bonds with the child

Tertiary interventions[5] may serve to (Friedman & Resnick, 2007):

- Temporarily remove the vulnerable child, combined with the frequency of parental education sessions ordered by the court
- Compulsory counsel in mental health
- Protect and develop family reunification plans

The prevention, in cases of neonaticide, is seriously compromised by the fact that many women rarely seek any avenues of help (Bourget et al., 2007). Moreover, psychiatrists should evaluate the risk of filicide in a systematic way, as they do for suicide (Friedman & Resnick, 2007). It would, therefore, be important to determine the role of mental illness in this context.

When the pregnant woman goes to the medical appointment, her mood should be assessed so as to detect depression or psychosis and, if so, to admit the possibility of internment in a mental facility. The interview with a pregnant woman is useful to get a general idea about her thoughts regarding the pregnancy and the baby. It is necessary to specifically question her about the plans she has upon the arrival of the child, trying to discover feelings of ambivalence, anger, or resentment.

Without proper support, many young women who are at risk of denial of pregnancy do not have the adequate prenatal support. When the contractions begin and childbirth occurs, they can no longer hide or deny their status. Some are admitted to the hospital to give birth or, in some cases, to complain of abdominal pains (contractions); others are giving birth at home, to avoid their detection. The risks to the child include not only the neonaticide but the morbidity associated with lack of prenatal care, leading to the increase in premature births. The sooner the denial of pregnancy is detected, the more opportunities there are to prevent complications. Support for young mothers should include education about their options, including adoption and abortion, the importance of prenatal care; how they should approach the subject with their parents; and the ability to attend classes on parenting. In hospital emergency, it is important to include pregnancy in the differential diagnosis when there are abdominal and pelvic symptoms. Pharmacotherapy may relieve a denial although in most cases it is not sufficient.

---

[5] A tertiary intervention program should be implemented to rehabilitate, to prevent the recurrence of a certain behavior and to reinsert the person in society.

The intervention is still necessary to take into account:

- To keep an open mind, without judgment
- To try to understand the psychological condition for the denial
- To listen attentively
- To prepare a guide for addressing the mother–infant relationship after birth
- The prenatal care and follow-up and support visits (outreach)
- To discourage the use of ultrasound (may increase the emotional impact, anxiety levels and the risk of trauma)
- To assess parental behavior and provide for the possibility of rehabilitation (e.g., parental coaching, classes on parenting and support groups)
- In face of risk of abuse to notify the child protection agencies (to protect the child) and support to the mother
- To realistically assess the social support of women (family, friends, community support structures)
- The combination of psychoeducation (of sexuality) and psychotherapy can help some women overcome earlier losses and to feel able to make active choices about family planning

Women with **postpartum depression** have significantly more obsessive and aggressive thoughts than usual. These women have violent thoughts (e.g., put the baby in the microwave, drown him, or stab him) that they consider an abomination. The intervention in postpartum depression should include:

- The medical history (to look for possible organic contributions for depression)
- The research about prescribed medications (particularly for pain), excessive medication, and substance abuse (drugs and alcohol)
- A thyroid count after delivery
- An hemoglobin count and screening hypercalcemia
- The application of Edinburgh Postnatal Depression Scale (Cox, Holden, & Sagovsky, 1987)
- The interpersonal psychotherapy
- The prescription of antidepressants (e.g., fluoxetine, paroxetine), bearing in mind that infants will be exposed to the medication

Women with **suicidal thoughts** should be referred for emergency mental health services, and assisted immediately. All threats to hurt the child should be taken seriously, and the child protection services and psychiatric services should be notified.

In case the woman has **postpartum psychosis** (Friedman & Friedman, 2010):

- A psychiatric emergency must be considered (such as suicidality), so that the mother must be immediately evaluated
- Hospitalization for treatment and monitoring may be appropriate
- The mother–baby bond should be evaluated
- Must address education about symptoms of mental disorder and available treatments
- The decision to contact Child Protection Services may be taken in conjunction with the psychiatrist

It is important that women feel they are in a safe environment, which is not stigmatized, which can reveal all their symptoms and will have available help.

Mothers with **obsessive-compulsive postpartum disorder** may experience intense fears and constant worries about hurting their child (Friedman & Friedman, 2010). Mental health services should be notified, since the symptoms are disruptive and psychiatric treatment can lead to improvement of symptoms.

With regard to **babies with colic**, it is important (Friedman & Friedman, 2010):

- To assess the impact that the cramps have on the mother
- To work strategies "to deal with the crying child," rather than on "what not to do"
- To intervene in order to normalize the crying
- To seek support/family support

As for the mothers of **children with developmental disorders**, and in order to prevent the child's death, it is necessary (Friedman & Friedman, 2010):

- To discuss the possibility of providing palliative care or hospitalization
- To evaluate the existence of parental problems such as the feeling of overload in care
- To identify relational, financial and social problems
- To promote increased coping strategies

Fourth, most intervention programs target only the mothers. Fathers and stepfathers should also be targets of interventions. For example, community-based interventions that educate parents of newborns on behavior that may trigger rage, such as crying or hard-to-soothe behavior, have shown some success (Fujiwara et al., 2009).

Fifth, while suggestions have been made for prevention of certain types of filicide, little is known to date about prevention of filicide-suicide. Assuming that the parents who commit filicide showed evidence of psychiatric symptoms prior to their death, we suggest enhancing recognition, diagnosis, and treatment of mental illness symptoms among parents and educating community about these symptoms. Doing so could help to further the goal of prevention of filicide-suicide. Clinicians should also be alert to the possibility of filicide in depressed and psychotic parents. They should screen for psychiatric symptoms and directly question the parents regarding the fate of their children in the event of their suicide. Appropriate treatment should be initiated and safety measures should be taken. The clinician should also determine whether any child is overloved, considered an extended part of the self, or the focus of paranoid delusions (Friedman, Horwitz & Resnick, 2005).

At last, psychopathy is an important construct in explaining criminal behavior and has especially been linked to violent criminality (Putkonen et al., 2009). Therefore, we suggest for future research, the application of the Hare Psychopathy Checklist, a commonly used instrument for the operationalization of psychopathy, in order to establish a comparison between the filicide mothers and control groups regarding the presence of mental disorders (Crighton, 2009). Although there is not yet a study about the relationship between the psychopathy and the filicide, the presence of psychopathic traits (e.g., egocentricity, impulsivity, lack of empathy, remorse as well as shallow and labile affects) is already documented on the perpetrators of this crime (Putkonen et al., 2009).

SUMMARY

- Filicide, infanticide, and neonaticide are distinct concepts of the same reality, and despite our unified cries of love for our children, they occur daily in contemporary society. These acts have existed since the dawn of humanity and have been in the literature from the earliest eras of recorded history. These crimes can be perpetrated by the mother, the father, or by both and include stepparents or other parental figures.
- Despite the evolution of scientific knowledge on this type of crime, in some countries filicide is a verdict that applies only to the killings carried out by mothers (Liam & Koenraadt, 2008). However, nowadays, in Western countries, men have become increasingly likely to be convicted of killing their child.
- The legal framework of filicide varies from country to country and can be regarded as having two opposing aspects: treatment and punishment. In many cases when the crime is committed by mothers in the first year of a child's life, the law reduces the penalties based on the principle that a woman who commits this kind of crime finds the balance of her mind disturbed for biological and/or psychological reasons, or because she has not fully recovered from having given birth.
- We can divide the background history of filicide into three distinct periods: (1) as a legitimate practice, (2) as a criminal practice, and (3) as an act possibly related with mental illness.
- **Filicide as a Legitimate Practice:** Although little is known about filicide practice in ancient civilizations (i.e., the way parents killed their children and under what circumstances), archaeological findings suggest that this type of crime was regarded as a legitimate practice in some periods of history, and it may occur for the following reasons: (1) children are born out of wedlock; (2) as a means of population control; to limit the number of female children; (3) to control the family size; (4) to exterminate the weak and abnormal children; (5) desire for power or money; (6) disability of the mother affecting her ability to care for the child; (7) superstition; (8) ritual sacrifice; (9) as early as 7000 BC there is evidence of the existence of child sacrifice, suggesting that primitive man sought to control population growth and minimize defects within the social group.
- **Filicide as a Criminal Practice:** With the spread of Christianity in AD 300, Emperor Constantine opposed the killing of children by their parents, and criminalized filicide across the Holy Roman Empire in AD 374. This decision had a strong influence from Jewish law, which penalized infanticide and despised abortion. Consequently, from this time forward, a woman who killed a newborn or attempted an abortion would be excommunicated, although, depending upon the circumstances, a priest may have reduced the punishment and imposed a penance for a period of time.

- There is evidence of the renewed prevalence of filicide throughout the Middle Ages, associated with factors such as poverty and a lack of economic resources. The spread of Christianity promoted a religious and cultural hostility toward nonmarital sex and any consequent birth of a child out of wedlock. As a result of this conviction, women were stigmatized and illegitimate children were deprived of legal human rights. This presented additional pressures and added to the renewed "popularity" of filicide as an option in these circumstances.

- European society of the 16th and 17th centuries condemned sexual offenses such as fornication and bastardy. The penalties for these crimes were especially tough in England, condemning mothers who refused to identify the father of their child to flogging in public or to imprisonment. The connection between illegitimacy and infanticide resulted in the crime being considered as something only perpetrated by unmarried. At the same time there was a drastic change in opinion about the murder of children, and in 1647, Russia became the first country to adopt more severe punitive sentencing for women who killed their children. Punishments were extreme and include being buried alive, drowning, and decapitation.

- More than a century later, in 1783, William Hunt proposed the differentiation between the crime of neonaticide from other types of homicide. Despite the intention to condemn the female offenders for the perpetration of the crime, and to dissuade them from killing their children, the so-called Poor Law, created in 1834 in England and Wales to make girls realize the severe consequences of sexual crime and thus preserve their chastity, reducing the bastardy, only contributed to increase the number of neonaticides. Single mothers stopped receiving assistance from their parishes and now had to live in a poor house, in extremely precarious conditions.

- Legal distinctions between manslaughter and infanticide were adopted across Europe from around 1888. First in France and then in England, laws were created that considered filicide as a crime punishable by death. In contrast to the foundational legal tenet of "presumed innocence," both countries enacted the legal assumption that, mothers would be guilty until they proved their innocence, meaning that they were responsible for proving in court that their child was not a victim of murder.

- **Filicide and its Relation to Mental Illness:** In England, this scenario changed with the establishment of the Infanticide Acts, dated 1922 and 1938. These laws recognized the effect that the birth and care of a child could have on the mental health of the mother, up to 12 months postpartum. The 20th century brought a new perspective to crime, linking it to mental illness. Two French psychiatrists, Jean-Etienne Esquirol and Victor Marcé, were the first to postulate the existence of a causal relationship between pregnancy, birth, and maternal mental illness. Other investigators quickly adopted this perspective and almost immediately began, worldwide, to associate filicide to mental illness.

- The reasons for the commission of contemporary filicide vary according to culture and can be categorized as: (1) a form of postpartum abortion (i.e., to dispose of an unwanted child because of denial, fear, illegitimacy, religious beliefs, birth defects, altruism, mercy, gender, parental or financial disability, retaliation or revenge); (2) the unintended result of child abuse (Munchausen syndrome by proxy); and (3) the result of a diminished parental ability resulting from postpartum psychosis or depression.

- Filicide (*filia/filius* means own daughter/son and *occidere* is a homicide or manslaughter in Latin) is a cross-cultural phenomenon defined as the killing of a child/young person (or more), under the age of 18, by one or both parents, or by stepparents or other parental figure. This type of murder is divided into two categories, according to the victim's age: infanticide (killing of a child less than 1 year) and neonaticide (when the victim does not survive the first 24 h of life). The literature also considers the existence of the crime of feticide, when a fetus has intrauterine death due to a criminal act by one of the parents.
- The evolution of the legal treatment of filicide, has traveled through three distinct periods in history: (1) a period of permission or indifference, between the seventh century BC and the fifth century AD, (2) a period of reaction in favor of a newborn child, between the fifth century and the 18th century AD, and (3) a period of reaction in favor of the guilty woman, from the 18th century to the present.
- Inconsistency is the hallmark of these filicide laws across the world, and a woman may receive leniency and funded social and psychological support in one instance, while elsewhere the same crime may be treated with extreme disdain and result in life imprisonment or, in some jurisdictions, the death penalty.
- Guileyardo et al. (1999), identified 16 subtypes of filicide, based on the primary motive or cause that led to the perpetration of the crime. The authors concluded that each of these subtypes is sufficiently distinctive to warrant a separate categorization and described each of them in detail. Four subtypes are noted as being based on Resnick system (1969) and in particular altruistic filicide, filicide by acute psychosis, filicide of an unwanted child, and filicide for revenge.
- Risk factors for the perpetration of filicide have been identified across characteristics related to demographics, personal history, situation/environment, and clinical features.
- Many filicidal women come from large families, have severe parental conflict and chaotic family history, that is sometimes even violent. They had, therefore, weak family ties (i.e., history of abandonment, maternal loss in childhood, absent mother or perpetrator of abuse, negligent father with history of substance abuse or mental illness), with frequent parental separations and financial instability. Also the history of victimization has been reported as a risk factor, in particular physical or sexual abuse and domestic violence.
- According to the literature, the family of the neonaticidal woman is characterized by role confusion, emotional neglect, violation of limits, and bizarre parental relationships. The father is often intrusive and jealous, while the mother is cold, hostile, or absent (due to physical or mental illness or substance abuse). The fact that the family did not notice the typical physical changes of pregnancy

in women illustrates the isolation that she feels and the relationship that she has with the members of their family or other significant elements.

- The few studies that exist indicate that mothers living alone at the time of the crime have few social contacts and lack of family and community support, and the child is the one person who establishes a relationship with her. This aspect usually results from a history of violent abuse by perpetrators in childhood. Filicide mothers are often in violent and abusive relationships at the time they kill their child. Also belonging to families with religious or cultural biases against sexual intercourse (mainly outside of marriage) or the fact that women are illegal immigrants who fear that their pregnancy threatens their residency are often cited.

- The few studies about paternal filicide usually emphasize that these parents are living in a situation of despair or marital stress, have been the subject of infidelity by the partner or are going through a case of contentious divorce. A history of domestic violence, multiple sibling victims, physical child abuse, social isolation, or lack of support cut across both perpetrators. The majority of research has shown that fathers who kill their children are more likely to have a criminal record than filicidal mothers.

- Numerous studies have reported an association between filicide and psychiatric illness of the perpetrator, especially when this person suffers from major depression with psychotic features. Also, personality disorders, especially borderline personality, have been found in both filicidal women and men. Psychotic disorders, schizophrenia, bipolar disorder, adjustment disorders, abuse or substance dependence, and suicidal ideation are also cited. Regarding women, a history of psychiatric problems in their family is more frequent in cases of filicide than in the general population (e.g., mental illness, alcoholism, and substance abuse).

- Mental illness can be characterized as either being acute (i.e., beginning after the child's birth) or chronic (i.e., prior to the birth of the child). Although the influence of serious mental disorders such as depressive and psychotic disorders has been noted in both genders, these disorders are found to be more pronounced among female perpetrators when compared to male perpetrators.

- The most common methods of neonaticide include asphyxia, drowning, strangulation, head trauma, exposure to extreme conditions (hypothermia or hyperthermia), and stabbing (Friedman & Friedman, 2010).

- There is no universal way to classify the circumstances of deaths by filicide. However, it is possible to draw five main scenarios in which they occur: (1) death subsequent to family disputes, usually by retaliation due to the end of a relationship between the parents; (2) death subsequent to fatal abuse; (3) death due to parent's mental illness (which have a bizarre character); (4) death of children victims of fatal sexual abuse; and (5) death of newborn children, who are abandoned without information about them.

- Filicide is a complex crime, multifactorial, and disproportionate in terms of magnitude and whose circumstances are different from other types of homicide.

Given the nature of this crime, it is difficult to find traits that consistently apply to both the perpetrators and the victims, due to the different populations studied, the place where the information was obtained (i.e., in the general population, in the psychiatric population, or in prison environment). The lack of national and international research, the methodological issues raised in the investigations already carried out, the existence of few studies that includes filicidal fathers and the lack of theoretical progress are some of the barriers to successfully understand filicide. In addition, some studies are mostly retrospective and based on small samples and the child's age changes the potential risk of filicide (i.e., the younger, the greater is the risk).

QUESTIONS

1. Define *filicide, neonaticide, infanticide*, and *feticide*.
2. Describe the three historical periods of filicide and their characteristics.
3. Describe the issues surrounding the legal concepts of filicide.
4. Describe the characteristics of female filicide offenders.
5. Describe the characteristics of male filicide offenders.
6. Describe the systems of filicide classification and the issues surrounding establishing a universal classification system.
7. Describe Guileyardo et al.' 16 motive-cause subtypes of filicide.
8. Describe and provide details of the Resnick system of filicide characteristics.
9. There are numerous statistics around incidence, prevalence, and other statistics of filicide. Examining these statistics, discuss the commonalities and differences between jurisdictions and offender types and the various factors influencing these differences.
10. Describe the offense characteristics of filicide.
11. Discuss some of the interventions – primary, secondary, and tertiary – for filicide and the various issues that are relevant to these interventions.

REFERENCES

Alder, C., & Polk, K. (2001). *Child victims of homicide*. Cambridge: Cambridge University Press.

Almeida, F. (2012). Mães filicidas: Contextualização e fundamentação. In F. Almeida, & M. Paulino (Eds.), *Profiling, vitimologia e ciências forenses: Perspetivas atuais* (pp. 315–343). Lisboa: Pactor.

Almeida, F. (2014). *Profiling em crimes violentos: O perpetrador e a vítima em casos de filicídio*. Tese de mestrado não publicada em Medicina Legal e Ciências Forenses, apresentada à Faculdade de Medicina da Universidade de Coimbra.

Almeida, F., & Vieira, D. N. (2014). Profiling em crimes violentos, o perpetrador e a vítima em casos de filicídio. *Peritia – Revista Portuguesa de Psicologia, 22*, 2–16.

Amon, S., Putkonen, H., Weizmann-Henelius, G., Almiron, M. P., Formann, A., Voracek, M., et al. (2012). Potential predictors in neonaticide: the impact of the circunstances of pregnancy. *Archives of Women's Mental Health, 15,* 167–174. http://dx.doi.org/10.1007/s00737-012-0268-0.

Assis, S. (1994). Crianças e adolescentes violentados: Passado, presente e perspectivas para o futuro. *Cadernos de Saúde Pública, 10*(1), 126–134.

Bourget, D., & Bradford, J. M. (1990). Homicidal parents. *Canadian Journal of Psychiatry, 35*(3), 233–238.

Bourget, D., & Gagné, P. (2002). Maternal filicide in Québec. *The Journal of the American Academy of Psychiatry and the Law, 30,* 345–351.

Bourget, D., & Gagné, P. (2005). Paternal filicide in Québec. *The Journal of the American Academy of Psychiatry and the Law, 33,* 354–360.

Bourget, D., Grace, J., & Whitehurst, L. (2007). A review of maternal and paternal filicide. *The Journal of the American Academy of Psychiatry and the Law, 35,* 74–82.

Byard, R. W. (2004). Medicolegal problems with neonaticide. In M. Tsokos (Ed.), *Forensic pathology reviews* (Vol. 1) (pp. 171–185). New York: Humana Press.

Cox, J. L., Holden, J. M., & Sagovsky, R. (1987). Detection of postnatal depression: development of the 10-item edinburgh postnatal depression scale. *British Journal of Psychiatry, 150,* 782–786.

Craig, M. (2004). Perinatal risk factors for neonaticide and infant homicide: can we identify those at risk? *Journal of the Royal Society of Medicine, 97,* 57–61.

Crighton, D. (2009). Offender profiling. In D. Canter, & D. Youngs (Eds.), *Investigative psychology: Offender profiling and the analysis of criminal action* (3rd ed.) (pp. 148–159). Chichester: John Wiley & Sons, Ltd.

Cruz, A. (1994). *Maus tratos à criança.* Porto: Porto Editora.

Dawson, M. (2015). Canadian trends in filicide by gender of the accused, 1961–2011. *Child Abuse & Neglect, 47,* 162–174.

De Bortoli, L., Coles, J., & Dolan, M. (2012). Maternal infanticide in Australia: mental disturbance during the postpartum period. *Psychiatry, Psycology and Law,* 1–11 First article.

Debowska, A., Boduszek, D., & Dhingra, K. (2015). Victim, perpetrator, and offense characteristics in filicide and filicide-suicide. *Aggression and Violent Behavior, 21,* 113–124.

D'Orban, P. T. (1979). Women who kill their children. *British Journal of Psychiatry, 134,* 560–571.

Farooque, R., & Ernst, A. (2003). Filicide: a review of eight years of clinical experience. *Journal of the National Medical Association, 95*(1), 90–94.

Finkelhor, D. & Ormrod, R. K. (2001). The homicides of children & youth. Juvenile Justice Bulletin – NCJ187239, (pp. 1–12). Washington, DC: US Government Printing Office.

Flynn, S. M., Shaw, J. J., & Abel, K. M. (2013). Filicide: mental illness in those who kill their children. *PLoS One, 8*(4), 1–8. http://dx.doi.org/10.1371/journal.pone.0058981.

Frazier, C. E., Bock, E. W., & Henretta, J. C. (1983). The role of probation officers in determining gender differences in sentencing severity. *The Sociological Quarterly, 24*(2), 305–318.

Freire, A., & Figueiredo, B. (2006). Filicídio: incidência e factores associados. *Análise Psicológica, 4*(XXIV), 437–446.

Friedman, S. H., & Friedman, J. B. (2010). Parents who kill their children. *Pediatrics in Review, 31*(2), e10–e16. http://dx.doi.org/10.1542/pir.31-2-e10.

Friedman, S. H., Horwitz, S. M., & Resnick, P. J. (2005). Child murder by mothers: a critical analysis of the current state of knowledge and research agenda. *American Journal of Psychiatry, 162,* 1578–1587.

Friedman, S. H., & Resnick, P. J (2007). Child murder by mothers: patterns and prevention. *World Psychiatry, 6,* 137–141.

Fujiwara, T., Barber, C., Schaechter, J., & Hemenway, D. (2009). Characteristics of infant homicides: findings from a us multisite reporting system. *Pediatrics, 124*(2), 210–217.

Guileyardo, J. M., Prahlow, J. A., & Barnar, J. J. (1999). Familial filicide and filicide classification. *The American Journal of Forensic Medicine and Pathology, 20*(3), 286–292.

Häkkänen-Nyholmemail, H., Putkonen, H., Lindberg, N., Holi, M., Rovamo, T., & Weizmann-Henelius, G. (2009). Gender differences in finnish homicide offence characteristics. *Forensic Science International, 186*(1–3), 75–80.

Hall, M., (2007). Key child protection statistics in Northern Ireland. NSPCC NI Policy and Research Unit.

Hon, K. L. (2011). Dying with parents: an extreme form of child abuse. *World Journal of Pediatrics, 7*(3), 266–268.

Howatson, A. G. (2006). The autopsy for sudden unexpected death in infancy. *Current Diagnostic Pathology, 12,* 173–183.

Karakus, M., Ince, H., Ince, N., Arican, N., & Sozen, S. (2003). Filicide cases in Turkey, 1995–2000. *Croatian Medical Journal, 44,* 592–595.

Kauppi, A., Kumpulainen, K., Karkola, K., Vanamo, T., & Merikanto, J. (2010). Maternal and paternal filicides: a retrospective review of filicides in Finland. *The Journal of the American Academy of Psychiatry and the Law, 38,* 229–238.

Kilsztajn, S., Lopes, E., Carmo, M., & Reyes, A. M. (2007). Vitalidade do recém-nascido por tipo de parto no Estado de São Paulo, Brasil. *Cadernos de Saúde Pública, 23*(8), 1886–1892.

King James Bible. (1611). *The bible, king James version [1611], Book of Genesis* (electronic ed.). Accessed May 5, 2016, from. http://www.kingjamesbibleonline.org/.

Koenen, M. A., & Thompson, J. W., Jr. (2008). Filicide: historical review and prevention of child death by parent. *Infant Mental Health Journal, 29*(1), 61–75. http://dx.doi.org/10.1002/imhj.20166.

Levitzky, S., & Cooper, R. (2000). Infant colic syndrome: maternal fantasies of aggression and infanticide. *Clinical Pediatrics, 39,* 395–400.

Lewis, C., & Bunce, S. (2003). Filicidal mothers and the impact of psychosis on maternal filicide. *The Journal of the American Academy of Psychiatry and the Law, 31,* 459–470.

Liam, M., & Koenraadt, F. (2008). Filicide: a comparative study of maternal versus paternal child homicide. *Criminal Behavior and Mental Health, 18,* 166–176. http://dx.doi.org/10.1002/cbm.695.

Liem, M., de Vet, R., & Koenraadt, F. (2010). Filicide followed by parasuicide: a comparison of suicidal and non-suicidal child homicide. *Child Abuse & Neglect: The International Journal, 34*(8), 558–562.

Lysell, H., Runeson, B., Lichtenstein, P., & Långström, N. (2014). Risk factors for filicide and homicide: 36-year national matched cohort study. *Journal of Clinical Psychiatry, 75*(2), 127–132. http://dx.doi.org/10.4088/JCP.13m08372.

Marcikić, M., Dumencić, B., Matuzalem, E., Marjanović, K., Pozgain, I., & Ugljarević, M. (2006). Infanticide in eastern Croatia. *Collegium Antropologicum, 30*(2), 437–442.

Mariano, T. Y., Chan, H. C., & Myers, W. C. (2014). Toward a more holistic understanding of filicide: a multidisciplinary analysis of 32 years of U.S. arrest data. *Forensic Science International, 236,* 46–53.

Marks, M. N. (2003). Infanticide in Britain. In M. G. Spinelly (Ed.), *Infanticide: Psychosocial and legal perspectives on mothers who kill* (pp. 185–197). Washington, DC: American Psychiatric Publishing.

Marleau, J., & Laporte, L. (1999). Gender of victims and motivation of filicidal parents: is there a relationship? *Canadian Journal of Psychiatry, 44*, 924–925.

Mazar, B. (1969). The historical background of the Book of Genesis. *The Journal of Near Eastern Studies, 28*(2), 73–83.

Mckee, G. (2006). *Why mothers kill.* Oxford: Oxford University Press.

Mckee, G., & Shea, S. (1998). Maternal filicide: a crossnational comparison. *Journal of Clinical Psychology, 54*(5), 679–687.

Meyer, C. L., & Oberman, M. (2001). *Mothers who kill their children: Understanding the acts of moms from Susan Smith to the "Prom Mom".* New York: Johns Hopkins University Press.

Meyer, C., & Spinelli, M. (2002). Medical and legal dilemas of postpartum psychiatric disorders. In M. Spinelli (Ed.), *Infanticide: Psychological and legal perspectives on mothers who kill* (pp. 167–183). Washington: Washington DC American Psychiatric Publishing.

Miller, L. (2002). Denial of pregnancy. In M. Spinelli (Ed.), *Infanticide: Psychological and legal perspectives on mothers who kill* (pp. 81–102). Washington: Washington DC American Psychiatric Publishing.

Nieuwbeerta, P., & Leistra, G. (2007). *Fatal violence.* Amsterdam: Prometheus.

Oberman, M. (2002). A brief history of infanticide and the law. In M. Spinelli (Ed.), *Infanticide: Psychological and legal perspectives on mothers who kill* (pp. 03–18). Washington: Washington DC American Psychiatric Publishing.

Oberman, M., & Meyer, C. L. (2008). *When mothers kill: Interviews from prison.* New York: NYU Press.

Overpeck, M. (2002). Epidemiology of infanticide. In M. Spinelli (Ed.), *Infanticide: Psychological and legal perspectives on mothers who kill* (pp. 19–30). Washington, DC: American Psychiatric Publishing.

Palermo, M. (2003). Preventing filicide with autistic children. *International Journal of Offender Therapy and Comparative Criminology, 47*, 47–57.

Papapietro, D., & Barbo, I. (2005). Commentary: toward a psychodynamic understanding of filicide – beyond psychosis and into the heart of darkness. *The Journal of the American Academy of Psychiatry and the Law, 33*(4), 505–508.

Putkonen, H., Anos, S., Eronen, M., Klier, C., Almiron, M., Cederwall, J., et al. (2011). Gender diferences in filicide offense characteristics: a comprehensive register-based study of child murder in two European countries. *Child, Abuse & Neglect, 35*, 319–328.

Putkonen, H., Weizmann-Henelius, G., Lindberg, N., Eronen, M., & Häkkänen, H. (2009). Differences between homicide and filicide offenders: Results of a nationwide register-based case-control study. *BMC Psychiatry, 9*(27). http://dx.doi.org/10.1186/471-244X-9-27.

Ragatz, L. L., & Russell, B. (2010). Sex, sexual orientation, and sexism: what influence do these factors have on verdicts in a crime-of-passion case? *The Journal of Social Psychology, 150*(4), 341–360. http://dx.doi.org/10.1080/00224540903366677.

Resnick, P. J. (1969). Child murder by parents: a psychiatric review of filicide. *The American Journal of Psychiatry, 126*, 325–334.

Schwartz, L., & Isser, N. (2000). *Child homicide: Parents who kill.* Florida: CRC Press.

Scott, P. D. (1973). Parents who kill their children. *Medicine, Science and the Law, 13*, 120–126.

Smith, J. (2006). Infanticide. In D. Mackenzie, L. O'Neill, W. Povitsky, & S. Acevedo (Eds.), *Different crimes, different criminals: Understanding, treating and preventing criminal behavior* (pp. 11–32). Maryland: Matthew Bender & Company.

Somander, L., & Rammer, L. (1991). Intra and extrafamilial child homicide in Sweden 1971–1980. *Child Abuse & Neglect, 15*, 45–55.

Strang, H. (1996). Children as victims of homicide. *Australian Institute of Criminology, 53*, 1–6.

Stroud, J. (2005). European child homicide studies: quantitative studies and a preliminary report on a complementary qualitative research approach. *Social Work in Europe, 7*(3), 31–37.

West, S. (2007). An overview of filicide. *Psychiatry, 2*, 48–57.

Wiest, J. B., & Duffy, M. (2012). The impact of gender roles on verdicts and sentences in cases of filicide. *Criminal Justice Studies*, 1–19.

Yarwood, D. (2004). Child homicide: reviewed of statistics and studies. *Dewar Research, 6*, 1–22.

Yasumi, K., & Kageyama, J. (2009). Filicide and fatal abuse in Japan, 1997–2005: temporal trends and regional distribution. *Journal of Forensic and Legal Medicine, 16*, 70–75. http://dx.doi.org/10.1016/j.jflm.2008.07.007.

Risk Assessment in Youth Justice: A Child-Centered Approach to Managing Interventions

Gareth Norris[1], Gwyn Griffith[2], Heather Norris[1]

[1]Aberystwyth University, Aberystwyth, Ceredigion, United Kingdom; [2]Ceredigion Youth Justice and Prevention Service, Aberystwyth, Ceredigion, United Kingdom

CHAPTER OUTLINE

INTRODUCTION

Risk assessment is a complex term to both define and operationalize; by its very nature, "risk" is a dynamic and fluid concept that is context, culturally, and personally defined (Beck, 1992). While risk extends to a range of situations, for example, most recently discussed in relation to business and financial markets, one area where it has also grown in prominence is in relation to understanding, predicting, and preventing criminal behavior (Bonta, Law, & Hanson, 1998). Risk of "dangerousness," for example, is never far from the political and media agenda; violent and extreme criminal events are nearly always followed by intense scrutiny of the predictive information held about individuals, for instance, their mental state and previous offending history (see Michael Stone inquiry; Francis, 2007 for review). Similarly, reoffending/recidivism is predicted by a range of measures that combine static risk factors (e.g., age at first offense, age, gender, etc.) with dynamic indicators (e.g., drug use, homelessness, significant relationships, etc.) to produce composite "scores," which are then used in targeting interventions and/or sentencing options. In essence, whether the risk is dangerousness, self-harm, offending, absconding, or

The Psychology of Criminal and Antisocial Behavior. http://dx.doi.org/10.1016/B978-0-12-809287-3.00006-7

otherwise, the techniques operate on broadly similar principles: we seek to predict the likelihood of behavior "*a*" from background characteristics and previous behaviors "*b*," "*c*," ... "*z*." The validity of which – despite many decades of criminological and psychological research – is complex and often contradictory (Blackburn, 2000; Kroner, Mills, & Reddon, 2005).

Youth justice is one area where the issue of risk and the limitations of criminological/psychological theory and the associated assessment tools are critically debated (Haines & Case, 2012). Young people have specific human rights and minimum standards of care, as defined by *United Nations Convention on the Rights of the Child* (UNICEF, 1999). Somewhat in contrast to their adult counterparts, young "offenders" are seen as deserved of "protection from harm" and provided with more lenient and constructive sanctions in relation to offending behavior (Youth Justice Board, 2003). Lower limits of age of criminal responsibility are an example of this tiered justice provision. The Youth Justice System has traditionally been governed by the interrelated concepts of punishment and welfare (Hendrick, 2015). The welfare model of youth justice was developed late in the 19th century, when it was acknowledged that child offenders were a vulnerable population in need of care and protection. However, this system of managing youth offenders soon grew out of favor; it was seen as largely ineffectual, and by the 1970s, punitive disposals were on the rise (Newburn, 2007) and the development of new actuarial methods of risk assessment began to dominate Youth Justice Systems from this time forward. The new focus on risk factors, such as parental practices, IQ, and social economic status, began a campaign that concentrated on early prevention within the target population, thus resulting in the early criminalization of many young people. These actuarial models largely neglected the importance of context and community as important factors in any young person's life. By the 1980s, crime rates had continued to rise despite increased punitive measures, and as a result, the criminal justice system – and youth justice in particular – came under attack for its ineffectual practices (Newburn, 2007). During this period a number of advances, including the growth of the victims' rights movement, the body of evidence supporting the inadequacy of the current punitive state, and the rise of community-based problem solving, all contributed to the burgeoning interest in new methods, such as restorative justice (Cunneen & Goldson, 2015). This new system of justice was viewed as an alternative to the existing adversarial model currently in place.

RISK ASSESSMENT: HOW DOES IT WORK?

The psychological assessment of offenders has been a prominent aspect of criminology and forensic psychology/psychiatry for many decades. While debates continue on the nature of clinical versus actuarial prediction (Dawes, Faust, & Meehl, 1989), requirements for more transparent, structured, and measurable assessments in court, along with the apparent increased validity of such instruments, have favored the latter method (Cunningham & Reidy, 1999). Whereas clinical methods rely on the training and skills of the practitioner(s), actuarial assessments of risk involve the use of previous incidents and/or individual background features to predict future outcomes (Douglas, Cox, & Webster, 1999). Where no previous precedent exists, for example, in the case of new, novel, or low base-rate events, then risk can be assessed by the creation of hypothetical scenarios that seek to model a range of possible outcomes. In the context of criminal behavior, the risk assessment generally follows a kind of "matching" process that seeks to align the current individual to a "typical" offender or set of lifestyle indicators. These then provide statistical probabilities as to the *likelihood* of the current person behaving in a *similar* fashion to the modeled individual. In its most simple form, we may wish to know the chance of any particular person "x" committing crime "y" if they present with characteristic "z." For example, if we want to know "Mary" (subject variable "x") is likely to be caught shoplifting (outcome variable "y"), then we know there is a significant chance of this occurring if they currently have substance dependence problems (predictor variable "z"). Clearly, more complex sets of variables are examined in modern risk assessment tools; often the interactions between specific predictors (e.g., "substance dependence" and "homelessness") may be even more illustrative of higher levels of risk. Hence, risk assessment can somewhat become a double-edged sword; the more complex the model, the greater is the prediction reliability, but lower validity as the model becomes more specific. Conversely, the simple model has high validity (is likely to predict outcomes reasonably well), but lower validity resulting from a "wider net" cast among the target group – the false-positive/false-negative paradox (see later). In a nutshell, risk assessment concerns itself with identifying those whom are most likely to be dangerous/offend/reoffend and minimize the impact on those for whom crime and antisocial behavior is less likely to be a repeat and/or continual lifestyle choice (i.e., the low-risk group).

How these factors are actually identified, measured and weighted in a risk assessment measure is therefore open to considerable debate and extensive research has spanned over four decades. Early studies such as Monahan (1981) identified age and offense type, for example, as variables that could be used to predict later behavior (e.g., reconviction). The presence of these two and other variables can be used to develop decision-making tools that aim to understand the way background factors and previous behavior can influence future actions. Many of these variables are developed theoretically as well as being observed and recorded. For example, diversionary practices that seek to avoid criminalizing individuals caught for their first offense are linked to ideas of labeling (Becker, 1963). However, despite the relative acceptance of labeling as a theoretical explanation of deviancy, there is no one measure or experimental manipulation to conclusively endorse its existence. Instead, we may initiate various proxy measures in order to operationalize these predictive factors, for instance, age at first offense or number of previous convictions. In trying to predict complex human behaviors, we seemingly require more intricate instruments with which to guide decisions. Criminal and antisocial behavior is a reaction to a multifaceted environment, which interacts with the individual; hence, assessment inventories require knowledge and evaluation of personality, family environment, work/school history, peer interaction, and neighborhood characteristics. Some of these variables might appear fairly illustrative; previous contact with the police, for example, *could* be highly predictive of future offending but may also appear in a large number of the target population (i.e., young offenders). Hence, previous contact with the police may have high predictive ability, but low discriminant capacity in being able to differentiate between *actual* future offenders. Similarly, some variables might be low in frequency, but be positively discriminant between high- and low-risk offenders, in the case of truancy from elementary school, for example (Loeber & Dishion, 1983). In the youth justice context, considerable research has been extended to the identification of individual and social factors, which can then be used to identify those young people whom are at most at risk of later offending. While reducing reoffending among adults is also a priority, in the youth justice sector this becomes more prominent in that there is an emphasis on recognizing those young people who will become "tomorrow's criminals" (Loeber, Slot, van der Laan, & Hoeve, 2008). This is most often achieved by aggregating longitudinal data to statistically isolate variables that can model prototypical young offenders. Evidence for the efficacy of this approach is mixed; for example, a meta-analytical study by Lipsey and Derzon (1998) provided evidence for some variables associated with later adult offending in samples of young offenders, such as poor academic performance and separation from parents. More-complex multivariate analyses have been less conclusive and largely unable to concur on the most significant predictors (Farrington, 2005). Alongside the risk factors are so-called protective factors that serve to limit the development of delinquent behavior (Tremblay & LeMarquand, 2001). Protective factors essentially are characteristics of the individual and their social situation, which reduce the propensity for negative behavior(s). For example, low impulsivity (the protective factor) may reduce engagement in criminal activity between two individuals in similar situations. Similarly, closeness of family bonds may limit delinquency between peers in similar neighborhoods. Some of these elements are relatively simple to measure, whereas others are more subjective and/or esoteric in nature, relying on practitioner expertise and access to reliable confirmatory evidence.

Access to reliable information is a key feature of any risk assessment; decisions made without the full support of accurate data, run the risk of increasing the error rate – false-positive/-negative – exponentially. Data will come from a number of sources; as we will discuss in the case study, the referral process has a number of layers that seek to establish the veracity of any instances of antisocial and criminal behavior. Reports will be collected from a range of agencies, including schools, social services, the police, and youth justice themselves. Verification of these sources of information for legitimacy and accuracy is also required. Increasingly practitioners are using social media in order to verify and even initiate necessary interventions (Zastany, 2013). Ethical, legal, and practical considerations notwithstanding, the material gleaned from such sources might be open to interpretation and contextual clarification; it is likely that material posted on social media could be inflamed and/or fabricated for a variety of reasons. Similarly, self-report data are also likely to be misreported; Sawyer, Meldrum, Tonge, and Clark (1992); in

Van Domburgh, Vermeiron, and Doreleijers (2008, p. 167) suggest that: "children tend to underreport their externalising problem behaviors, while parents tend to underreport their child's internalising behaviors." A similar parallel to the attribution error in psychological decision-making literature, which has also been explored in relation to offenders' justifications for their behavior (Blumenthal, Gudjonsson, & Burns, 1999). The consequences for the outcome of any information gathering exercise conducted with the individual and/or anyone with a vested interest in their welfare should proceed with caution so as to preserve the validity of the information gathering process. Children and/or adults likely to be taken into care or returned to secure units may have a vested interest in "playing down" (or "up") certain aspects of their behavior/situation. Corroboration is vital as is the reliance on the most valid form of information available, for example, in respects to mental health issues and associated behavioral states such as self-harm. In these instances, the boundaries of expertise and overall competency to diagnose must be respected. Where information is missing, it should be recorded and attempts made to rectify absent data. The assessment and gathering of information and verifying the quality is where the experience and skill of criminal justice professionals become of paramount importance. In contrast to clinical prediction, the assessment tools guide decision-making and provide a framework to base interventions within.

CONSEQUENCES OF RISK ASSESSMENT: THE FALSE-POSITIVE/FALSE-NEGATIVE PARADOX

With any risk assessment tool, there will always be a margin of error; no human behavior is perfectly linear and predictable and arguably less so criminal and antisocial behavior by young people. This error can be broken down into two key elements: a *false-positive* is where an assessment tool has incorrectly identified an individual as belonging to a particular class as defined by the instrument (e.g., high risk of violence), when in fact there is no further example of this behavior within the specified time-frame. Conversely, the *false-negative* is where an assessment fails to identify the risk (say of future offending) and the individual in question goes on to actually commit further crimes. In both scenarios, the sensitivity of the assessment tool is compromised by its inability to identify the two outcomes successfully. While it is unreasonable to expect 100% concordance rates between the risk prediction and actual future behavior, the validity and reliability of the tool needs to be empirically evaluated. By way of an example, consider a metal screening machine at an airport security check. Set the tolerance too high and it will detect any piece of metal on an individual. Such a scenario will lead to searches of many individuals suspected of carrying weapons onto an aircraft, when in fact most (if not all) are completely "innocent" – a *false-positive* (we have identified a risk when none is actually present). Alternatively, set the tolerance too low and the risk then shifts to potentially allowing dangerous individuals onto an airplane carrying weapons or explosives – a *false-negative* (we have failed to identify a risk when one is actually present).

Tolerances – whether at an airport or in youth justice practice – can be altered up or down according to the prevailing situations and resources.

Such issues are more than a moot point; the consequences for aviation security of false-positives are relatively minor (increased waiting at checkpoints, for example), but disastrous for a false-negative (terrorist incidents, for example). In respect to youth justice risk assessment, what we experience when an assessment tool is oversensitive - and produces too many false-positives – is an increase in interventions and possibly even preventative detention of young people whom pose little or no risk (see Case Study). False-negatives on the other hand, could lead to criminal events and impact on victims through the failure to identify those likely to be dangerous or at risk of future offending for instance. No tool possesses perfect accuracy (or anywhere near); hence, these instruments are validated on samples and opened up to empirical examination in order to establish their actual predictive capacity. Where things become even more complicated are through the identification of moderating and mediating variables, which exert influence on predictor variables to produce some quite sophisticated models of delinquency pathways. For example, high levels of impulsivity may not in themselves predict later delinquency, and neither does living in an economically marginalized neighborhood. However, in combination, these two variables have an interaction effect that seeks to increase the likelihood of later antisocial and criminal behavior (Loeber, Slot, Stouthamer-Loeber, 2008). Deciding on which variables are important and the *weights* assigned to these are likely to have an important bearing on the outcomes for individuals. In order to identify the level of risk, we need to make an informed decision as to what level is reasonable to take (see Towl & Crighton, 2000). In some cases, such as very violent and/or sexually dangerous offenders, the bar may be set extremely high. For example, those offenders identified as having dangerous and severe personality disorder (DSPD), then their level of risk may be mean that they are detained indefinitely in a secure unit under the Mental Health Act (Jones, 2007). Similarly, young people identified as at risk of victimization can be taken into protective care by Social Services. However, these extreme cases – while still informed by risk assessment practices – are less commonplace.

Base rates of offending also have significant influence over whether assessment of risk is optimal or even possible. Some crimes occur at such a low frequency that prediction is futile if not impossible. For example, crimes such as homicide and some sexual offending occur in such low frequencies that their occurrence is largely the result of "random" factors that could not be predicted (see Needs & Towl, 1997). In these cases, Van Domburgh et al. (2008) suggest that: "the best prediction is that nobody will meet the criterion because the inherent "margin of error" for prediction of the outcome hampers actual prediction of such a rare outcome" (p. 166). For example, a recent review of young people involved in school shootings was able to identify a range of potential risk factors associated with school and street "rampage" shootings (Bushman et al., 2016). While a number of factors are identified worthy of additional attention (e.g., alcohol/substance misuse, social isolation, mental illness, access to firearms, etc.), the authors nonetheless concede that "individual-based surveillance to predict rampage shootings is inherently much more difficult than place-based surveillance" (p. 30). The article cites three main reasons: first, the rarity of the events (the low base-rate), second, discrepancies in information availability and access, and, finally, the ethical and legal considerations facing wide-ranging surveillance of young people: "because of these concerns and the likelihood of an unacceptably high false-positive rate, mining of social network data should be used to provide secondary rather than primary evidence for deciding whether and how to intervene in the event of received threats or warnings related to a specific individual" (p. 30). Hence, we can see that despite some promising areas for concern in relation to the "triggers" involved in mass acts of violence of this type, existing attempts to provide alerts to schools have been largely futile and in fact can "dissuade students who hear threats from coming forward to report their concerns out of fear of overreaction in a climate of a high level of false-positives" (p. 31). While the presence of some predictors may be present in already identified "at-risk" populations (e.g., social isolation), it is not possible to extrapolate these predictive criteria to more general populations.

Conversely, some predictor variables may have very low prevalence rates but are highly correlated with certain problem behaviors. These factors generally are not used in general population screening instruments (see Loeber & Dishion, 1983). Deciding *what* to include in screening tools and more-focused risk assessments can sometimes become more art than science; it is here that trained and experienced practitioners need to make active and informed decisions over and above any risk "score" in the management of problem behaviors. In some respects, risk assessment is conducted as an aid memoir to active decision-making; the identified risk then informs interventions and consequences for the individual under assessment. Monahan and Steadman (1996) use meteorological predictions as an illustration of the way in which decisions are reached in mental health cases. In particular, Monahan and Steadman point to the fact that very minor and seemingly inconsequential changes to various weather patterns can and do have catastrophic effects; weather systems are argued to be analogous to human behavior: prone to influence from random and/or unidentified elements that act in an arbitrary rather than linear fashion as assumed in many of the instruments we use to predict these outcomes (weather or human behavior). The important issue in regards to predicting children and young people's later offending is that any risk assessment needs to be tied to the developmental stage which the individual may be at, between or developing into, which may be further complicated by the fact that age may not be a reliable predictor of this (Smith, 2007). Furthermore, while some indicators may be reliable predictors in older populations, the presence of these factors in younger people does not necessarily correlate with *current* behavior(s) patterns. The prevalence of hindsight biases can mean that reliable indicators of risk in adult populations (e.g., previous history of violence and particularly age at first offense) can be retrospectively applied to young people when there is no specific evidence to suggest that they will go on to offend in the short to medium term (Loeber, Slot, Stouthamer-Loeber, 2008). Using predictors of adult offending with young people runs the risk of ignoring the developmental stages of the adolescent personality; many childhood behaviors are variations of otherwise normal behaviors, which themselves are often reactions to difficult life circumstances (Case & Haines, 2014). Whereas the adult personality is more stable, the disposition of the younger age group is more malleable and open to change.

RISK IN YOUTH JUSTICE: WHAT ARE WE ASSESSING AND WHAT DO WE DO WITH IT?

Risk assessment can take many forms. Risk can be used to identify risk of future offending, responsivity to treatment, risk of violence, risk of suicide and self-harm, risk of drug abuse, risk of vulnerability, and a multitude of other behaviors/characteristics, for example, dangerousness. The majority of these risks are measured using structured actuarial measurement and provide "scores" that are then used to compare across individuals or identify those above and below predefined thresholds. The primary tool used in Youth Justice in England and Wales is Asset/AssetPlus - a structured risk assessment tool that evaluates the individual across a number of domains (family, school, etc.) and factors (dynamic and static) (Wilson & Hinks, 2011). The more recently introduced AssetPlus (see Baker, 2014) introduces contextual information that encompasses the varying life events and temporal interactions that may increase the risk or inhibit antisocial and criminal tendencies. The data from Asset/AssetPlus are used in a variety of ways by youth justice practitioners, but mostly it is an instrument with which to target interventions and make decisions as to child welfare provisions.

Youth Offending Teams (YOTs) were established by all local authorities in England and Wales under the requirements of the 1998 Crime and Disorder Act. The act specifies that the primary aim of YOTs is to "reduce offending by young people." The structure of and processes and methodologies followed by all YOTs are broadly similar. Referrals come into the team via three main routes:

1. Referrals for prevention services from social workers, teachers/schools, parents/carers, police, and young people themselves (known as "preventions referrals"). These referrals account for around two-thirds of all referrals, and the subjects of these referrals are considered by the referrers to be at risk of coming into contact with the police through antisocial and/or criminal behavior.

2. Formal bureau referrals from the police force are part of the agreed criminal justice processes for young people. Bureau referrals account for approximately a quarter of all referrals. Since 2014, all young people aged 10–17 years who admit responsibility for an offense that has been reported to, and investigated by the police, are referred to the bureau system (provided they have not committed a serious specified offense and there is sufficient evidence to ensure realistic chance of conviction if the matter was referred to the criminal courts). The bureau system was put in place following the implementation of in the 2012 Legal Aid and Sentence Planning Act. One of the key

aims of this act was to reform the way in which authorities could deal with criminal offenses outside of the formal court system. The act seeks to promote the use of noncriminal methods in appropriate cases by the use of noncriminal community disposals.

3. Referrals from the criminal courts (youth courts) account for less than one-tenth of all referrals. The subjects of these referrals have been formally charged with criminal offenses and referred to the criminal courts by the Crown Prosecution Service.

All prevention and bureau cases screened (see Case Study) as being at medium or high risk of offending and/or having medium or high safeguarding concerns, are then allocated to qualified staff for further assessment along with all court referrals (YOTs have a statutory duty to complete full assessments on all court referrals) and are subject to further in-depth risk assessment. These evaluations typically take around 12 h to complete. Further assessment is undertaken using the ASSET Risk and Needs Assessment System. This is structured actuarial risk assessment tool, combining static and dynamic risk factors to estimate risks of reoffending and prompts clinical assessments to assess risk of serious harm to others and safeguarding risks. The ability of this tool to predict reoffending of cohorts of young people has been validated and has been shown to have good discriminatory power (Wilson & Hinks, 2011). Later than planned, in April 2016 the ASSET system will be superseded by an updated version called ASSETplus. This version of the system uses a new static risk predictor called Youth Offender Group Reconviction Score (YOGRS). The ability of YOGRS to predict reoffending rates of cohorts of young people has been validated (Baker, 2014). It is based on a similar risk predictor (Offender Group Reconviction Score) that has been used by probation services in England and Wales for many years (Fitzgibbon, 2007).

Currently, where further assessment indicates that the risk levels are lower than those indicated by the screening tool, the young people are either signposted to third sector organizations (nongovernment, often charities) that offer more generic services to young people and their families or they are offered minimal interventions by YJPS as per statutory requirements. Around 86% of full assessments of bureau and prevention referrals indicate medium risk of reoffending with 4% indicating high risk of reoffending. For court referrals 60% of full assessments indicate medium risk of reoffending and 40% indicate high risk of reoffending. Where further assessment indicates medium or high risk, young people are offered a tailored intervention package aimed at reducing risks. The intervention package is directly based on the ASSET assessment and targets specific dynamic risk factors that have been identified. The top three dynamic risk factor that are consistently identified in ASSET assessments are *cognitive factors* (attitudes, opinions, beliefs and thinking that support and justify offending behavior), *family, personal relationships and lifestyles* (the young person's interpersonal relationships with family and friends), and *substance misuse* (alcohol and drug use). Risk assessment (predominantly ASSET) is used at several stages of the youth justice process, from initial contact through to sentencing in severe cases. Other risk assessment and evaluative inventories, such as the Psychopathy Checklist: Youth Version (PCL: YV; Forth, Kosson, & Hare, 2003), Antisocial Process Screening Device (APSD; Frick & Hare, 2001), and Structured Assessment of Violence Risk in Youth (SAVRY; Borum, 2000) are also used on a more ad hoc basis, particularly with more rare and/or serious cases in the United Kingdom and further afield.

CASE STUDY: CEREDIGION YOUTH JUSTICE AND PREVENTION SERVICE

One of the key ethical concerns when screening young people is the duty of care so as not to stigmatize young people by applying "adult" evaluations to their behavior – a process known as labeling, which may then go on to create a "self-fulfilling prophecy" of further deviance (Rock, 2007). Formal interventions with young people have shown mixed evidence for labeling per se, but nonetheless a strong correlation exists with regards to the link between criminalizing young people and later persistent and serious offending. Ceredigion YJPS screens all preventions and bureau referrals to assess the risk of offending, by trained youth justice practitioners (either a qualified social worker or probation officer or other staff that have completed the YJB Professional Certificate in Effective Practice in Youth Justice). They use a screening tool that has been developed by, and subject to preliminary validation by, Ceredigion YJPS and Aberystwyth University. The tool identifies referrals that involve young people that are unlikely to enter the youth criminal justice in the 1-year period subsequent to referral (low risk cases). To enter the youth criminal justice system a young person must either be referred to the bureau (i.e., have admitted to an offense under investigation by the police) or be charged with an offense and referred to the criminal court. Analysis of the criminal Justice system in England and Wales suggests that currently only around 1 in 20 offenses committed by young people are actually reported to the police and proven (MOJ, 2016). This is important to bear this in mind as it means that the screening tool is set up to identify young people who are not offending at a sufficient frequency to make it likely that they will enter the criminal justice system; being screened as low risk by the tool does not indicate that a young person is unlikely to offend in the next 12 months. Rather, it indicates that they are not offending sufficiently frequently to make it likely that they will come to the attention of the police for at least one of the offenses they have committed.

As well as assessing risk of contact with the criminal justice system, the screening tool also acts as a screen for potential safeguarding issues. To date, this aspect of the tool has not been validated against hard safeguarding outcomes. However, the screening questions that relate to safeguarding issues are based on concerns that should trigger further more in-depth assessments by practitioners in order to safeguard young people. Safeguarding concerns by the tool are rated as low, medium, or high. The screening process requires the practitioner to access the YJPS and Ceredigion Social Services databases. They also have to work with partners to carry out checks on the local education authority, police, Careers Wales, and CAMHS systems. Screening one referral takes around 30 min compared to 12 h for a full ASSET assessment (Wilson & Hinks, 2011).

The rationale for using the preliminary screening of all prevention and Bureau referrals is as follows:

- Ceredigion YJPS only has the capacity to undertake full detailed assessments and offer interventions to, a limited number of young people. Limited resources need to be targeted effectively.
- Research indicates that interventions to reduce risks of offending are only effective if they target only those people who are assessed at being at medium or high risk of offending (proven offending as indicated by conviction and formal disposal data) by a validated risk assessment process. Interventions that do not take into account this "risk principle" (which is one of the key effective practice principles) tend to either have no effect or to actually increase risks. The increase in risk may be because peer influences and "labeling" effects can be important factors in youth offending and mixing young people who may be actively offending at high rates with those who are not may increase the impact of these factors.

CASE STUDY: CEREDIGION YOUTH JUSTICE AND PREVENTION SERVICE—CONT'D

- Evidence suggests that most young people who enter the criminal justice system do not go on to reoffend within 12 months whether or not they receive a formal intervention to try to reduce their risk of offending. Prior to the introduction of the bureau system in 2014, 70% of young people entering the criminal justice system for the first time received no intervention. Despite this only around 20% of first-time entrants went on to commit a proven reoffense within 12 months.
- All services that work with young people have a duty to safeguard (All Wales Child Protection, 2008). YJPS, therefore, needs a process to ensure that if any potential safeguarding concerns in relation to young people referred into the service these are followed up and acted on if necessary.

  Preventions and bureau referrals that are screened as low risk of offending and low safeguarding concerns are not assessed further. As of April 2016, this group of young people will not be offered a targeted intervention aimed at reducing their risks by YJPS. They will instead be signposted to third sector organizations that offer more generic services to young people and their families. Around 60% of preventions and bureau referrals are screened as low risk with no safeguarding concerns.

TOWARD A MORE-INCLUSIVE SYSTEM OF YOUTH JUSTICE: RISK ASSESSMENT AND RESTORATIVE APPROACHES

One emerging movement in youth justice concerns the notion of "child first-offender second" (CFOS; Case & Hanes, 2014). The notion of *positive youth justice* is not necessarily new and has been presented as the Positives Futures initiative in the United Kingdom and similarly in the United States as the Positive Youth Development Program (Catalano, Berglund, Ryan, Lonczak, & Hawkins, 2004); rather, it draws from recognition of the limitations of the risk-led approach to youth justice, which is overly punitive and adult-centric. In essence, rather than seeing children and young people as part of the problem, it flips the emphasis on resolution to seeing the juvenile stakeholders as part of – if not the central pivot – the solution (see Drakeford, 2010). Previously, youth justice practice in England and Wales (and overseas) has been: "[…] irrevocably linked to *risk*, driven by assessment and intervention focused on identifying and responding to measured 'risk factors' for a host of negative behaviors […] and negative outcomes" (Case & Haines, 2014, p. 2). These approaches – developed and adopted across most Western countries – seek to address the issue of youth crime and deviancy through targeting individual defects present in the young person (Kelly, 2012), rather than working toward promoting social inclusion and the re-establishment of healthy relationships with family, peers, school, and the wider community (Hart & Thompson, 2009).

Research also supports the notion of a more holistic approach to assessment and intervention. For example, Loeber, Slot, Stouthamer-Loeber (2008) put forward a cumulative model of risk, which adds more emphasis on contextual elements of the equation in order to understand the development of severe juvenile and later adult antisocial and criminal behavior. In particular, they emphasize "although theories of disruptive behavior and delinquency often have several factors in common (e.g., juveniles' relationship with parents and peers), they differ in their relative emphasis on domains, settings and details of explanatory factors, and the ways these factors are interrelated" (p.133). In essence, the way in which risk of delinquency manifests itself in the individual is domain specific; that is each factor (family, peers, neighborhood, etc.) can have an impact on later delinquency at a range of times. The "salience" or priority of these domains has been relatively underexplored from a developmental perspective (i.e., do family problems precede school disruption?). Loeber et al. suggest that risk factors should be thought of as a nested model, with varying levels of risk and mobility between domains a critical factor: "risk factors from all domains (individual, family and peers) and the two contexts (schools and neighbourhoods) contribute to the explanation of delinquency escalation processes" (p. 141). However, it is important to note that Loeber et al. are also keen to stress that alongside risk of delinquency, "promotive" factors (those that seek to lead to positive outcomes) are also present within these domains. These differ conceptually from protective factors, which seek to limit engagement with negative domains, through for example, increased self-esteem or locus of control. Promotive factors are themselves positive aspects of the individual and their situation.

Hence, work with young offenders requires not just the recognition of different domains but also that these environments can and do have positive as well as negative influences on the behavior and risk associated with the individual. McCold and Wachtel (2002, p. 112) use the social discipline window to illustrate the differences in support and accountability between different models of justice. Fig. 6.1 illustrates the high support/high control values found in restorative processes used widely in youth justice across the world. In essence, processes are done "with" the participants rather than "for" (rehabilitation) or "to" (adversarial):

Three broad differences can further be distinguished between traditional adversarial justice and restorative justice. First, the traditional model of justice views crime as a violation against the state, rather than the victim; hence, the harm experienced by the victim is viewed as a transgression of the law rather than a personal

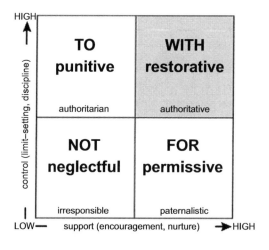

FIGURE 6.1

Social discipline window (McCold & Wachtel, 2002).

harm experienced by an individual. The victim's role largely includes acting as a witness on behalf of the state prosecution, whereas within restorative justice the victim plays a central role in all matters, including decision-making (Van Ness and Strong, 2010).

The second difference between these types of justice models is the role of the community. Crime does not occur in insolation but transpires within a physical or social group who all share a number of social bonds (Loeber, Slot, Stouthamer-Loeber (2008)). The importance of community is paramount to perhaps the most well-known restorative theory. Reintegrative shaming (Braithwaite, 1989) was developed to explain the underlying mechanisms of restorative justice. The theory states that the use of group disapproval and shame, followed by the reintegration of the offender back into their original community, is the cornerstone of effective restorative practices. Braithwaite (1989, p. 100) defines *shaming* as "all societal processes of expressing social disapproval which have the intention or effect of invoking remorse in the person being shamed." This broad definition allows many practices to be considered restorative in nature as there are not currently any specific guidelines as to what is considered a restorative shaming method or how best to produce the feelings of shame in the offender. However, this pivotal theory does stress the importance of a productive outcome and the essential component of reacceptance of the offender by key community stakeholders. This reacceptance eliminates the feelings of shame felt during the restorative justice proceedings. Crime not only is a direct infliction of some type of harm but also damages the social bonds of a community. Therefore, restorative advocates support the need for community involvement to help mend the broken social bonds between the offender and victim but also the offender and community. The community itself may be the family member and friends of the victim and offender but importantly can include local community members.

The final main difference is the focus on punishment. Restorative justice largely works outside the use of punishment and instead views crime as a source of harm which must be repaired. This may take the form of financial or some other material compensation but most importantly also includes emotional reparations. Victims experience different types of harm due to the behavior of an offender. The CJS may have some ability to repair broken items and offer compensation to the victim; however, it does little to repair the emotional harm done to the victim. Victims report "emotional reconciliation to be far more important than material or financial reparation" (Strang & Sherman, 2003; p. 22). Furthermore, Zehr (1985) states that accepting an apology is the most healing act after being victimized. The ability of an apology to repair emotional damage of the victim is apparent, although unlikely within the CJS, is one of the central components within restorative practices (Doak & O'Mahony, 2010). The link with the CFOS and positive youth justice (see Case & Haines, 2014) is most prominent here in respects to punishment, which have been demonstrated to have negative outcomes including further offending and escalation of seriousness of criminal behaviors.

Restorative justice has been largely a success in the youth justice sector, as compared to the adult criminal justice system. It has many advantages, including empowering victims, supporting the needs of young offenders, and limiting the number of young offenders who enter the criminal justice system. Restorative justice can include diverse practices at different stages within a juvenile justice system. For example, the typical victim–offender conference involves a formal meeting between the victim and the offender. This is mediated by a trained restorative facilitator and close family members are often in attendance. Bazemore and Umbreit (2001, p. 1) define *restorative conferencing* encompassing "a range of strategies for bringing together victims, offenders, and community members in non-adversarial community-based processes aimed at responding to crime by holding offenders accountable and repairing the harm caused to victims and communities." This type of practice was largely developed in New Zealand where family-group conferencing began in 1989 under the Children-Young Persons and Families Act, which addressed both welfare and criminal matters of young people. This model was adopted in Wagga–Wagga Australia by the New South Wales Police Service. In 1991, the Police Service offered victim–offender conferences similar to those in New Zealand but was facilitated by the police service. Due to successful introduction of restorative conferencing in Wagga–Wagga, New South Wales, later a law passed (the Young Offenders Act) that made conferencing a statutory requirement for all eligible youth offenders.[1] The influence of the Wagga–Wagga spread worldwide, including Canada (sentencing circles), the United States (community reparations boards, Vermont), and the United Kingdom (referral orders).

Recently, many countries have used strategies to deliver restorative justice at an earlier stage as a method of diverting offenders from formal criminal justice proceedings and is where risk assessment and priority screening methods come to the fore. For example, Thames Valley Police advocated a restorative caution in an effort to make their police warnings more meaningful by encouraging young people to take responsibility and to ensure they understand the implications of their actions. This may take place immediately following an arrest of after a young person has been charged. A second common intervention point is after conventional prosecution and conviction but as a substitute to sentencing. Most countries using restorative justice in a youth justice context have options to refer young offenders to some type of restorative justice practice, as opposed to formal sentencing procedures. In New South Wales, half of all referrals for restorative justice conferencing come from the court as a sentencing option.[2] In the United Kingdom, restorative justice as a substitute for traditional sentencing is generally referred to as a "referral order" (see earlier). These orders include a youth offending panel, where two trained members of the community and one youth offending team member facilitates a restorative succession with the young person and their families (and possibly the victim). Outcomes

---

[1] Eligible offenses include assault, robbery, break, enter and steal, motor vehicle theft, theft, receiving, property damage and disorderly conduct. Offences excluded are sexual offenses, offenses causing a death, certain drug offenses, offenses relating to apprehended violence orders.

[2] The other half comes from the police pre-court.

are agreed by the panel members and offender, such as reparative or rehabilitative measures; after the outcomes have been met the conviction is considered "spent."

Restorative justice measures may also be included in conjunction with traditional sentencing. In these instances, certain sentences are given with restorative intentions such as reparation or restitution orders. In many countries specific sentencing disposals are available to courts that are actively restorative in nature such as the youth justice reparation order and the action plan order in the United Kingdom. The success of restorative justice in youth justice encouraged many youth offending teams to develop restorative programs in local schools.[3] The implementation of restorative justice in schools by youth justice services rests on the need to end the school to prison pipeline. The recent development of "zero tolerance" education systems increases the number of students already accessing youth justice and adult justice systems before leaving school. The main aims of restorative justice in schools are to reduce offending and victimization in general, in particular in regards to bullying, and increase attendance; therefore, curbing the pipeline to formal justice systems. Within a school setting restorative justice can take many forms which include both preventative and reactionary practices. It is widely accepted that a whole-school approach (Hopkins, 2004), an implementation style that incorporates preventative, as well as reactionary practices is the most successful. This is largely contributed to the positive changes to the culture and overall ethos the school experiences with effective implementation of a restorative justice program. Preventative practices largely include the use of restorative language, such as enquiring questions and positive body language and voice tone are all necessary to a whole school approach. Reactionary practices are used after a conflict or incident and include formal conferencing, but can also take the form of the less formal mini or corridor conferencing. These have the aim of repairing relationships and the social bonds within the school. Evidence suggests the restorative schools have lower incidents of bullying and victimization rates, as well as higher levels of attendance (McCluskey, 2013).

CONCLUSION

This chapter has aimed to provide some insight into the complex and often contentious world of risk assessment in youth justice. Many of the limitations and criticisms apply also to the adult offending population; however, we must recognize that there is a societal – and legal - responsibility to young people to not stigmatize and/or penalize their developing behavior using the criminal justice system. We have outlined a number of issues in the Welfare Model that young people face, which often serves as a precursor to their offending, for example, abuse and neglect in the home, bullying at school, and association of antisocial peers. Many young people offend as a reaction to situations in their lives, which they cannot adequately deal with. Identifying these risks is the problem. Previous generations of risk assessment have

---

[3] This may be referred to as restorative approaches in some literature.

focused on static factors associated with offending, for example, age at first offense, which a young person is unable to change; risk assessment becomes in essence a self-fulfilling prophecy for those that go on to reoffend. For those whom are able to stay outside the criminal justice systems we assign responsibility to the interventions targeted at their behavior and/or personal circumstances and community.

The Children First/Offenders Second and initiatives such as the advanced screening tool and Restorative Approaches go some way to address the shortcomings inherent in the "Risk Factor Prevention Paradigm" (Haines & Case, 2015). These reductionist approaches – including the "scaled approach" – seek to delineate the packages of interventions based not on the offense or reasons for offending, but rather focus almost entirely on the level of "risk" as identified by arguably limited instruments. Similarly, they seek to serve preemptive interventions based on a presumed propensity for future behavior. Again, particularly where young people are concerned, their behavior is both heterogeneous and complex; it remains to be seen whether the recent introduction of AssetPlus, with its emphasis on contextual factors, will be sufficient to adequately address the lack of validity in its predecessor (Asset) and the myriad of other assessment tools also used at various stages with the youth and criminal justice systems. Regardless of the success of AssetPlus, we endorse the agenda of CFOS and the working in partnership with young people to address *their* offending – seeing them as part of the solution rather than the problem. Initiatives in Ceredigion Youth Justice and further afield are tapping into this agenda, for example, using bespoke screening tools and restorative approaches, and while youth crime is still a political and social issue, we should be mindful that crime rates for young people have continued to fall at rates of up to 50% in the last 2 years. Clearly changes in the way we work with young people at risk of entering the CJS are working.

SUMMARY

- "Risk assessment" is a complex term to both define and operationalize. By its very nature, "risk" is a dynamic and fluid concept that is context, culturally, and personally defined.
- Reoffending/recidivism is predicted by a range of measures that combine static risk factors (e.g., age at first offense, age, gender, etc.) with dynamic indicators (e.g., drug use, homelessness, significant relationships, etc.) to produce composite "scores," which are then used in targeting interventions and/or sentencing options.
- Youth justice is one area where the issue of risk and the limitations of criminological/psychological theory and the associated assessment tools, is critically debated. Young people have specific human rights and minimum standards of care, as defined by United Nations Convention on the Rights of the Child (UNICEF, 1999). Somewhat in contrast to their adult counterparts, young "offenders" are seen as deserved of "protection from harm" and are, therefore, provided with more lenient and constructive sanctions in relation to offending behavior

- The psychological assessment of offenders has been a prominent aspect of criminology and forensic psychology/psychiatry for many decades. While debates still continue on the nature of clinical versus actuarial prediction, requirements for more transparent, structured, and measurable assessments in court, along with the apparent increased validity of such instruments, has favored the latter method. Whereas clinical methods rely on the training and skills of the practitioner(s), actuarial assessments of risk involve the use of previous incidents and/or individual background features to predict future outcomes.
- In a nutshell, risk assessment concerns itself with identifying those whom are most likely to be dangerous/offend/reoffend and minimizes the impact on those for whom crime and antisocial behavior is less likely to be a repeat and/or continual lifestyle choice (i.e., the low-risk group). How these factors are actually identified, measured, and weighted in a risk assessment measure is therefore open to considerable debate, and extensive research has spanned over four decades.
- Access to reliable information is a key feature of any risk assessment; decisions made without the full support of accurate data, run the risk of increasing the error rate – false-positive/-negative – exponentially.
- With any risk assessment tool, there will always be a margin of error; no human behavior is perfectly linear and predictable and arguably less so criminal and antisocial behavior by young people. This error can be broken down into two key elements; a false-positive is where an assessment tool has incorrectly identified an individual as belonging to a particular class as defined by the instrument (e.g., high risk of violence), when in fact there is no further example of this behavior within the specified time-frame. Conversely, the false-negative is where an assessment fails to identify the risk (say of future offending) and the individual in question goes on to actually commit further crimes. In both scenarios, the sensitivity of the assessment tool is compromised by its inability to identify the two outcomes successfully. While it is unreasonable to expect 100% concordance rates between the risk prediction and actual future behavior, the validity and reliability of the tool need to be empirically evaluated.
- Risk assessment can take many forms. Risk can be used to identify risk of future offending, responsivity to treatment, risk of violence, risk of suicide and self-harm, risk of drug abuse, risk of vulnerability and a multitude of other behaviors/characteristics, for example, dangerousness. The majority of these risks are measured using structured actuarial measurement and provide "scores" that are then used to compare across individuals or identify those above and below predefined thresholds.
- One emerging movement in youth justice concerns the notion of "child first-offender second." The notion of positive youth justice is not necessarily new and has been presented as the Positives Futures initiative in the United Kingdom and similarly in the United States as the Positive Youth Development Program; rather, it draws from recognition of the limitations of the risk-led approach to youth justice, which is overly punitive and adult-centric. In essence, rather than seeing children

and young people as part of the problem, it flips the emphasis on resolution to seeing the juvenile stakeholders as part of – if not the central pivot – the solution.

- Three broad differences can further be distinguished between traditional adversarial justice and restorative justice. First, the traditional model of justice views crime as a violation against the state, rather than the victim; hence, the harm experienced by the victim is viewed as a transgression of the law rather than a personal harm experienced by an individual. The second difference between these types of justice models is the role of the community. Crime does not occur in insolation but transpires within a physical or social group who all share a number of social bonds. The final main difference is the focus on punishment. Restorative justice largely works outside the use of punishment and instead views crime as a source of harm that must be repaired. This may take the form of financial or some other material compensation but most importantly it also includes emotional reparations.

- Recently, many countries have used strategies to deliver restorative justice at an earlier stage as a method of diverting offenders from formal criminal justice proceedings and is where risk assessment and priority screening methods come to the fore. Restorative justice measures may also be included in conjunction with traditional sentencing. In these instances, certain sentences are given with restorative intentions such as reparation or restitution orders.

- The recent development of "zero tolerance" education systems increases the number of students already accessing youth justice and adult justice systems before leaving school. The main aims of restorative justice in schools are to reduce offending and victimization in general, in particular in regard to bullying and increase attendance; therefore, curbing the pipeline to formal justice systems. Within a school setting restorative justice can take many forms, which include both preventative and reactionary practices. It is widely accepted that a whole-school approach, an implementation style that incorporates preventative, as well as reactionary practices, is the most successful.

QUESTIONS

1. Define and operationalize "risk assessment."
2. In what contexts can youth risk assessment be used? Provide examples.
3. Outline the process of youth risk assessment and include the strengths as well as the challenges inherent in this process.
4. Discuss diversionary practices and their relationship to labeling theory.
5. What is the false-positive/false-negative paradox?
6. The validity of risk assessment is based on the factors surrounding base rates of offending. What is meant by this term? Provide examples?
7. The primary tool used in Youth Justice in England and Wales is Asset/AssetPlus. Describe this model and how it is used.
8. What is the "child first-offender second" model?

9. Name and describe the three main differences between traditional adversarial justice and restorative justice.
10. What strategies have been used to deliver restorative justice programs earlier in proceedings so that offenders are diverted away from formal criminal justice proceedings, including both rehabilitative programs as well as in combination with traditional sentencing?

REFERENCES

All Wales Child Protection. (2008). *All wales child protection procedures.* Available online http://www.childreninwales.org.uk/wp-content/uploads/2015/09/All-Wales-Child-Protection-Procedures-2008.pdf.

Baker, K. (2014). *Assessing the predictive validity of the asset youth risk assessment tool using the Juvenile Cohort Study (JCS).* London: Crown/YJB.

Bazemore, G., & Umbreit, M. (2001). *A comparison of four restorative sentencing models. Juvenile Justice Bulletin.* Washington, D.C: United States Department of Justice, Office of Justice Programs, Office of Juvenile Justice and Delinquency Prevention.

Beck, U. (1992). *Risk society.* London: Sage.

Becker, H. S. (1963). *Outsiders: Studies in the sociology of deviance.* New York: Free Press.

Blackburn, R. (2000). Risk assessment and prediction. In J. McGuire, T. Mason, & A. O. Kane (Eds.), *Behaviour, crime and legal processes: A guide for forensic practitioners* (pp. 177–204). Chichester: John Wiley.

Blumenthal, S., Gudjonsson, G., & Burns, J. (1999). Cognitive distortions and blame attribution in sex offenders against adults and children. *Child Abuse and Neglect, 23*(2), 129–143.

Bonta, J., Law, M., & Hanson, K. (1998). The prediction of criminal and violent recidivism among mentally disordered offenders: a meta-analysis. *Psychological Bulletin, 123,* 123–142.

Borum, R. (2000). Assessing violence risk among youth. *Journal of Clinical Psychology, 56,* 1263–1288.

Braithwaite, J. (1989). *Crime, shame and reintegration.* Cambridge: Cambridge University Press.

Bushman, B. J., Newman, K., Calvert, S. L., Downey, G., Dredze, M., Gottfredson, M., et al. (2016). Youth violence: what we know and what we need to know. *American Psychologist, 71*(1), 17–39.

Case, S., & Haines, K. (2014). *Children first, offenders second. Positive promotion: Reframing the prevention debate.* Youth Justice, 1–14.

Catalano, R. F., Berglund, L. M., Ryan, J. A. M., Lonczak, H. S., & Hawkins, D. J. (2004). Positive youth development in the United States: research findings on evaluations of positive youth development programs. *Prevention and Treatment, 5* Article 15.

Cunneen, C., & Goldson, B. (2015). Restorative justice? A critical analysis. In B. Goldson, & J. Muncie (Eds.), *Youth crime and justice* (pp. 137–156). London: Sage.

Cunningham, M., & Reidy, T. (1999). Don't confuse me with the facts: common errors in violence risk assessment at capital sentencing. *Criminal Justice and Behaviour, 26,* 20–43.

Dawes, R. M., Faust, D., & Meehl, P. E. (1989). Clinical versus actuarial judgment. *Science, 243,* 1668–1674.

Doak, J., & O'Mahony, D. (2010). Developing mediation and restorative justice for young offenders across Europe. In F. Dunkel, J. Grzywa, P. Horsfield, & I. Pruin (Eds.), in collaboration with A. Gensing, M. Burman, & D. O'Mahony, *Juvenile justice systems in Europe* (Vol. 4) (pp. 1691–1720). Germany: Forum Verlag Godesberg. ISBN: 978-3-936999-75-4.

Douglas, K. S., Cox, D. N., & Webster, C. D. (1999). Violence risk assessment: science and practice. *Legal and Criminological Psychology, 4,* 149–184.

Drakeford, M. (2010). Devolution and youth justice in wales. *Criminology and Criminal Justice, 10,* 137–154.

Farrington, D. P. (2005). *Integrated developmental and life-course theories of offending.* New Brunswick, NJ: Transaction.

Fitzgibbon, D. W. M. (2007). Risk analysis and the new practitioner myth or reality? *Punishment & Society, 9*(1), 87–97.

Forth, A., Kosson, D., & Hare, R. (2003). *The hare psychopathy checklist: Youth version.* New York: Multi-Health Systems.

Francis, R. (May 2007). The Michael Stone inquiry: a reflection. *Journal of Mental Health Law,* 41–49.

Frick, P. J., & Hare, R. D. (2001). *Antisocial processes screening device.* Toronto: Mental Health Systems.

Haines, K. R., & Case, S. P. (2012). The failed approach? *Youth Justice, 12*(3), 212–228.

Haines, K., & Case, S. (2015). *Positive youth justice: children first, offenders second.* London: Policy Press.

Hart, D., & Thompson, C. (2009). *Young people's participation in the youth justice system.* London: NCB.

Hendrick, H. (2015). Histories of youth crime and youth justice. In B. Goldson, & J. Muncie (Eds.), *Youth crime and justice* (pp. 3–16). London: Sage.

Hopkins, B. (2004). *Just schools: A whole school approach to restorative justice.* Gateshead: Athenaeum Press.

Jones, R. (November 2007). Deprivations of liberty: mental health act or mental incapacity act? *Journal of Mental Health Law,* 170–173.

Kelly, L. (2012). Representing and preventing youth crime and disorder: intended and unintended consequences of targeted youth programs in England. *Youth Justice: An International Journal, 12,* 101–117.

Kroner, D. G., Mills, J. F., & Reddon, J. R. (2005). A coffee can, factor analysis, and prediction of antisocial behavior: the structure of criminal risk. *International Journal of Law and Psychiatry, 28*(4), 360–374.

Lipsey, M. W., & Derzon, J. H. (1998). Predictors of violent or serious delinquency in adolescence and early adulthood: a synthesis of longitudinal research. In R. Loeber, & D. P. Farrington (Eds.), *Serious and violent juvenile offenders: Risk factors and successful interventions* (pp. 86–105). Thousand Oaks, CA: Sage Publications.

Loeber, R., & Dishion, T. J. (1983). Early predictors of male delinquency: a review. *Psychological Bulletin, 94,* 68–99.

Loeber, R., Slot, W., van der Laan, P. H., & Hoeve, M. (2008). Child delinquents and tomorrow's serious delinquents: key questions addressed in this volume. In R. Loeber, W. Slot, P. van der Laan, & M. Hoeve (Eds.), *Tomorrow's criminals: The development of child delinquency and effective interventions* (pp. 3–20). Surrey: Ashgate.

Loeber, R., Slot, W., & Stouthamer-Loeber, M. (2008). A cumulative developmental model of risk and promotive factors. In R. Loeber, W. Slot, P. van der Laan, & M. Hoeve (Eds.), *Tomorrow's criminals: The development of child delinquency and effective interventions* (pp. 133–164). Surrey: Ashgate.

McCluskey, G. (2013). Challenges to education: restorative approaches as a radical demand on conservative structures of schooling. In H. Cremin, G. McCluskey, & E. Sellman (Eds.), *Restorative approaches to conflict in Schools: Interdisciplinary perspectives on whole school approaches to managing relationships*. London: Routledge.

McCold, P., & Wachtel, T. (2002). Restorative justice theory validation. In E. G. M. Weitekamp, & H.-J. Kerner (Eds.), *Restorative justice: Theoretical foundations*. Devon, UK: Willan Publishing.

MOJ. (2016). *Proven re-offending statistics quarterly bulletin: April 2013 to march 2014 (England and Wales)*. London: ONS/Ministry of Justice.

Monahan, J. (1981). *Predicting violent behaviour: An assessment of clinical techniques*. Beverley Hills: Sage.

Monahan, J., & Steadman, H. J. (1996). Violent storms and violent people: how meteorology can inform risk communication in mental health law. *American Psychologist, 51*, 931–938.

Needs, A., & Towl, G. J. (1997). Reflections on clinical risk assessment with lifers. *Prison Service Journal, 113*, 14–17.

Newburn, T. (2007). Youth crime and youth culture. In M. Maguire, R. Morgan, & R. Reiner (Eds.), *The oxford handbook of criminology* (pp. 575–601). Oxford: Oxford University Press.

Rock, P. (2007). Sociological theories of crime. In M. Maguire, R. Morgan, & R. Reiner (Eds.), *The oxford handbook of criminology* (pp. 3–42). Oxford: Oxford University Press.

Sawyer, M., Meldrum, D., Tonge, B., & Clark, J. (1992). *Young people and mental health*. Melbourne: National Youth Affairs Research Scheme.

Smith, D. J. (2007). Crime and the life course. In M. Maguire, R. Morgan, & R. Reiner (Eds.), *The oxford handbook of criminology* (pp. 641–683). Oxford: Oxford University Press.

Strang, L., & Sherman, H. (2003). *Restorative justice: The evidence*. London: The Smith Institute.

Towl, G. J., & Crighton, D. A. (2000). Risk assessment and management. In G. J. Towl, M. J. McHugh, & L. Snow (Eds.), *Suicide in prisons*. Leicester: BPS Books.

Tremblay, R. E., & LeMarquand, D. (2001). Individual risk and protective factors. In R. Loeber, & D. P. Farrington (Eds.), *Child delinquents: Development, intervention, and service needs* (pp. 137–164). Thousand Oaks, CA: Sage Publications.

UNICEF. (1999). *United Nations convention on the rights of the child*. Geneva: UNICEF.

Van Domburgh, L., Vermeiron, R., & Doreleijers, T. (2008). Screening and assessments. In R. Loeber, W. Slot, P. van der Laan, & M. Hoeve (Eds.), *Tomorrow's Criminals: The development of child delinquency and effective interventions* (pp. 165–178). Surrey: Ashgate.

Van Ness, D., & Strong, K. (2010). *Restorating justice: An introduction to restorative justice*. MA, USA: Elsevier.

Wilson, E., & Hinks, S. (2011). *Assessing the predictive validity of the asset youth risk assessment tool using the Juvenile Cohort Study (JCS)*. London: Ministry of Justice Research Series.

Youth Justice Board. (2003). *Assessment, planning interventions and supervision*. London: YJB.

Zastany, R. A. (2013). *Assessing the utility of social media for adult probation*. Institute for Court Management ICM Fellows Program 2012–2013 Court Project Phase May 2013. Available online at http://citeseerx.ist.psu.edu/viewdoc/download?doi=10.1.1.362.1512&rep=rep1&type=pdf.

Zehr, H. (Semptember 1985). Retributive justice, restorative justice*New perspectives on crime and justice* (Vol. 4).

Reciprocity and Exchange: Perspectives of Male Victims of Family Violence

7

Andrea Lee, Robyn Lincoln
Bond University, Gold Coast, QLD, Australia

CHAPTER OUTLINE

INTRODUCTION

Family violence (FV) is an overarching label for a host of interpersonal behaviors that range from the minor to the mortal. It constitutes a largely "hidden" form of crime because of its dependence on reporting levels and its reliance on limited data sources. The known patterns are skewed because of its politicization, which have rendered some victims invisible. For example, it has been established that males are subject to all forms of domestic abuse and yet their victimization receives scant attention (Archer, 2000; Capaldi, Kim & Short, 2007; Dutton, 2012; Straus, 1993; Straus & Gelles, 1992). The aims of this chapter are to address the gender debate around

The Psychology of Criminal and Antisocial Behavior. http://dx.doi.org/10.1016/B978-0-12-809287-3.00007-9

FV and in particular to examine what is known about male victims by drawing on a recent analysis of narrative accounts of men who have experienced abuse at the hands of their female partners. The chapter presents detail of the forms, frequencies, and motivations where males are victims and then discusses the impacts of female-perpetrated violence. It concludes that a binary (male vs. female and offender vs. victim) framework constrains our understanding of this dynamic, multicausal crime event.

DEFINING VIOLENCE IN FAMILIES

Aggression occurring within the domestic sphere takes many nomenclatures from spousal abuse, wife abuse, and wife bashing to relationship violence or gender-based violence (Morgan & Chadwick, 2009). While domestic violence (DV) describes violence occurring within a familial dynamic (including against children), intimate partner violence (IPV) is specifically between two adults who are, or were, in an intimate relationship (Gelles, 2007). IPV can occur in any intimate partnership, including heterosexual, gay, lesbian, and transgender relationships (Chan, 2005; Renzetti, 1987). In Australia, the term "family violence" (FV) has been invoked, especially in the context of Indigenous interpersonal aggression among extended family members (Morgan & Chadwick, 2009; Stanley, Tomison, & Pocock, 2003). However, in the public and political discourse as well as in the research literature, IPV and DV are used interchangeably, and the all-encompassing term of "FV" tends to be eschewed.

DV is a serious social issue that not only causes physical harm but also contributes to mental ill health, drug and alcohol abuse, self-harm, and suicide (Cook, 2009). It is understood that approximately 46% of Australians know someone involved in FV. This statistic suggests that "the behaviour is widespread, almost to the point of being a normal, expected behaviour pattern in many homes" (AIC, 1990, p. 33). Its impact on children in the home has a profound effect on their well-being and extends to families and communities (Bartels, 2010). Yet, the true extent of the problem is unknown as most incidents go unreported. Aggregate data from the United Kingdom suggest that up to 40% of DV victims are male. This proportion, derived from the Home Office and the British Crime Survey, remains steady despite some annual variations during the last decade (Campbell, 2010). Similarly figures from police sources in New South Wales for 2011 show that there were over 31,000 male victims of FV, which comprises approximately 34% of all those reporting to law enforcement in that jurisdiction.

LESBIAN, GAY, BISEXUAL, AND TRANSGENDER VIOLENCE

Clearly, in same-sex relationships there is evidence of abusive behaviors with 26% of gay men and 44% of lesbian women reporting experiences of aggression at the hands of their partners (Chan, 2005). In the United States, for example, the National Violence Against Women Survey found that 21.5% of men and 35.4% of women living with a same-sex partner experienced physical IPV in their lifetimes, compared with

7.1% and 20.4% for men and women, respectively, with a history of only opposite-sex cohabitation. Transgender respondents had an incidence of 34.6% over a lifetime according to a Massachusetts survey (Glass, 2014). Similarly, the Centers for Disease Control and Prevention 2010 National Intimate Partner and Sexual Violence Survey, released again in 2013 with new analysis, reports in its first-ever study focusing on victimization by sexual orientation that the lifetime prevalence of rape, physical violence, or stalking by an intimate partner was 43.8% for lesbians, 61.1% for bisexual women, and 35% for heterosexual women, while it was 26% for gay men, 37.3% for bisexual men, and 29% for heterosexual men (Glass, 2014).

Statistical data are fundamental to our understanding of victimization, particularly for "hidden" forms of crime (Coleman & Moynihan, 1996). Two key sources are administrative data and personal surveys: the former comprising statistics collected by police departments, hospital emergency departments, and agencies such as shelters and victim support groups, and the latter derived from specialized surveys such as the Personal Safety Survey by the Australian Bureau of Statistics (ABS, 2012) or the International Crime Victims Survey (ICVS, 2011). Generally, the incidents captured by administrative data are more likely to be at the extreme end of the harm continuum where physical injury required some form of police or hospital intervention. Data collection differs across jurisdictions, as do legal terminology, definitions, and legislation. For example, some jurisdictions do not formally record DV matters without victim consent or where an assault is unsubstantiated by police or courts (ABS, 2012). Police statistics reflect only those events that required police intervention (Kaufman-Kantor & Straus, 1990; Straus, 1993), and some have suggested that up to 90% of partner assaults are not official identified (Straus, 2006).

THE GENDER PARADIGM AND GENDER SYMMETRY

The various "waves" of feminist thought have contributed much to the discipline of criminology, and especially to that of victimology (Renzetti, 2013). These multiple strands have provided new theories, highlighted hidden forms of crime, exposed violence in the private sphere, and promoted alternative methods of dealing with offending (Daly, 1998; Renzetti, 2013). Yet there has been scant attention paid to the male victims of DV with few published works and empirical studies (Sarantakos, 2004), and even fewer that address intimate partner violence in lesbian/gay/bisexual/transgender (LGBT) communities (Chan, 2005). This deficit appears antithetical to the fundamental principles of what would be regarded as the inclusivist approach embedded in feminist criminology. While the existence of global gendered violence is undeniable (Carrington, 2015), in the case of modern western democracies in the 21st century the reciprocal or exchange nature of FV begs further investigation.

The gender paradigm is best described as a philosophy that views DV in terms of sexual segregation and patriarchy. It reinforces the notion that DV is a gendered crime that is primarily perpetrated by men against women. Scholars supportive of the gender paradigm explicitly define DV as *violence against women* (Hamberger & Potente, 1994; Pence & Paymar, 1993). This gendered narrative is widely applied and accepted in mainstream media and in the majority of antiviolence policy and discourse. Gender-specific terminology such as "wife bashing" has reinforced a mutually exclusive binary characterization of FV as comprising female victims and male perpetrators. It has been blind to the reality of women's violence against children, of abuse against extended family members, and victimization of those in same-sex relationships. This linguistic framework is underscored by empirical studies that have relied on selective samples. Information about male perpetrators is typically drawn from criminal justice records, and data on male victims are rarely considered (Cook, 2009; DeKeseredy & Schwartz, 2003). The legacy of such biased enquiries is the stereotyping of men's behavior as aggressive and abusive, while women are portrayed as defenseless victims (Dutton, 2012).

This position is now undergoing redress toward a more balanced understanding of female-perpetrated violence (Dutton, Corvo, & Hamel, 2009; Dutton & Nicholls, 2005). Most notably, the works of Straus (1993, 2006, 2011) and Gelles (2007) provided a new perspective by introducing the concept of gender symmetry (Johnson, 2006; Straus, 2011; Straus & Scott, 2007). Symmetry between sexes does not necessarily claim that females and males are equally violent but that the prevalence is similar among genders. The first comprehensive study to use a large representative sample was that of Straus, Gelles, and Steinmetz (1981), which raised concerns about the accuracy of some of the feminist studies. By 1988, there were 40 published studies supporting gender symmetry. By 2010, there were more than 200 peer-reviewed studies endorsing such claims (Anderson, 2005; Archer, 2000; Capaldi, Kim, & Short, 2007; Cook, 2009; Dutton, 2012; Fiebert, 2014; Moffitt, Caspi, Rutter, & Silva, 2001; Straus, 2006, 2007). Despite this paradigm shift, it is important to question "how and why victimhood has come to occupy the kind of position that it does in informing cultural, political and policy responses" including "DV" (Walklate, 2016, p. 5), where, for example, it is imperative to ensure that intersections of race and class are given preeminence, along with broader sociocultural issues (Renzetti, 2013).

Within the DV realm, the perception remains that men are unlikely to be victims and violent women are rare. Straus (2007) wrote about ways researchers concealed and distorted evidence to support the feminist notion of the gender paradigm. Tactics included the suppression of evidence of male victimization, avoiding the use of data that contradicted feminist belief, the obstruction of funding, and the harassment of researchers who produced evidence of gender symmetry (Cook, 2009). This has extended to personal threats and "actions and attempted character assassinations" (Cook, 2009, p. 111). In the face of significant social change, the gender paradigm still holds sway. Even though it is now common for both partners to contribute financially in the majority of marriages (Strachan, 2010) and that younger women are often the most highly educated cohort (ABS, 2015), the feminist framework "remains a closed system, unresponsive to data that would force a more complex view of intimate partner violence" (Dutton, 2012, p. 102).

FORMS OF VIOLENCE AGAINST MEN

It has long been acknowledged that FV can take forms other than physical aggression such as verbal abuse, psychological abuse, damage of personal property, and abuse of power (ABS, 2012). Most often, the general literature, policy documents, and empirical studies tend to focus on physical forms of violence including sexual assault (Strauss, 1993). Additionally, physical abuse is the key subject at the center of the gender controversy, and most statistics on gender-specific perpetration of DV are referring to its physical manifestation.

Violence severity occurs on a spectrum and presents challenges to succinctly classify levels of severity. Most studies examining DV categorize the level of harm as either minor or severe. Examples of minor violent acts are slapping, grabbing, pushing, shoving, and throwing objects at another, while severe acts of violence include kicking, biting, threatening to use a knife or deadly weapon, or using a knife or other deadly weapon (Cook, 2009; Douglas, & Hines, 2011).

The most extreme and rare form of FV is domestic homicide where victims include intimate partners, children, parents, siblings, or other family members such as grandparents and cousins (Davis, 2010). In Australia, domestic homicides account for between 32% and 47% of all homicides annually; 23% of domestic homicide victims are intimate partners (where victim and offender are current or former partners). One-quarter of the victims of intimate partner homicide are men and 75% are women (Bryant & Cussen, 2015).

There has been much attention devoted to the types of aggression that constitute FV against women with a wide range of verbal, physical, and emotional behaviors incorporated into a lengthy catalog (Cook, 2009). This section presents some of the specific manifestations reported by male victims (see Fig. 7.1) aligned with what is known from the extant literature.

FORMS OF ABUSE

Verbal abuse in the form of yelling, screaming, and swearing is common and can lead to harm because it is designed to humiliate, degrade, and intimidate a partner or family member. In some cases, the men in verbally abusive relationships retreat or withdraw from their partner, only to discover it heightens the anger. Physical violence ranges from pushing and shoving to sustained instances of punching and kicking. Weapons and objects are sometimes used such as knives, guns, boiling water, glass, and bricks (McNeely, Cook, & Torres, 2001). Studies consistently show that in domestic conflict, women were significantly more likely to throw an object, slap, kick, bite, and hit with a fist or an object (Straus & Gelles, 1986). Weapon use seems to be higher in female-on-male violence than in male-on-female violence, where in one study it was found that 85% of women used weapons compared to 25% of men (McLeod, 1984). Attacking a partner while the partner is asleep or incapacitated by drugs/alcohol is another neutralizing strategy used by women (McNeely & Mann, 1990). Sexual abuse includes belittling sexual performance, initiating sex then pushing

---

PHYSICAL

Verbal The abuse began verbally at first. I'd be called lazy if I didn't jump to it when my ex wanted me to do something, regardless of how busy I was. Everything I did was scrutinised and criticised without a word of encouragement (Lee).

Physical I woke to her in the house and myself on fire. She had poured kerosene on me and lit me alight. I suffered third degree burns to my face and chest, second degree burns to my genitals and hands (David).

Sexual After the abuse my ex demanded sex, to which I said no ... I kept saying no, and when I couldn't perform, she'd hop off and slap my penis hard with her hand and say I was useless in bed, and "I don't know why you're here" (John).

NON-PHYSICAL

Emotional My girlfriend is regularly emotionally and psychologically abusive towards me ... She tells me everything that is wrong is automatically my fault. I have to ask permission before I do anything and I just can't take any more. It has broken me down so much that I really don't feel like I am worth anything or even care about myself (Alan).

Social She became extremely controlling, taking over my personal affairs such as my email, Facebook, and even my online banking account ... I wasn't allowed to see my family, or friends as I was told if I did she would leave and take our daughter away to where I couldn't find them (Brendan).

Financial Police suggest that I just leave. But I couldn't. My daughter needed me to protect her, and I was in a financial hold by my ex. She used money to keep me at home. I couldn't go out and visit friends for just half an hour (John).

Legal-Admin My ex wife was very aware of the attitudes and practices of society in general and law enforcement and the courts in particular. She would tell me straight to my face that she would make up a story about me accusing her if I ever called the police (Justin).

FIGURE 7.1

Male reports of the types of abuse extracted from their narratives.

the partner away just prior to orgasm, using sexual aggression to intimidate, demanding sex when the partner is unwilling or unable, and forcing sex without consent (Sarantakos, 2004). It has been reported that women use sex as punishment or as a means of manipulation, some demanding sex and then ridiculing their partner if they are unable to perform (Lewis & Sarantakos, 2001). However, it must be noted that this form of aggression is not confined to heterosexual relationships (Chan, 2005).

Other forms of abuse are psychological or emotional and are less overt and subtle yet are purposeful, sustained, or threatening. Often, it manifests in the form of constant fault-finding in the other or not permitting the partner to have a point of view on any topic. Social forms of abuse occur when one partner systematically denies the social connections of the other partner to cause harm and distress. It can be motivated by control or jealousy or as a mean to alienate the recipient from sources of support. Examples include forbidding a partner to socialize with friends, demanding passwords to social media to monitor and control communication, and turning family or friends against a partner with lies and manipulation. Those experiencing financial abuse report that their spouse controls or withholds access to financial resources, such as bank accounts; in other scenarios, there are threats to contact employers that could result in job loss. The final type in this category of nonphysical abuse comes under the heading of legal and administrative ill treatment (Tilbrook, Allan, & Dear, 2010) where partners use "agencies as accomplices in their crimes against their husband" (Sarantakos, 2004, p. 287). The legal/administrative abuse often cited is that of making false reports to the police claiming violence, reporting false allegations of child abuse, and lying about victimization to gain favor in criminal or family court proceedings (Schupe, Stacey, & Hazelwood, 1988). This accords with the widely held belief that women are unlikely to physically abuse their male partners. Yet, in documenting the phenomena of false allegations, women are more likely to be believed when falsely reporting physical abuse, rape, and sexual molestation of their children (Lewis & Sarantakos, 2001).

While it is not the purpose here to provide a detailed description of the manifestations of FV, the present examination of the forms that female-perpetrated violence can take contributes to the gender debate. This is because the divergent findings among FV researchers and feminist researchers could be attributed to the type of violence studied (Cook, 2009; Johnson, 2006). It has been suggested, for example, that FV researchers examine the most common form of FV, which is "situational couple violence" that is likely to be isolated, minor, and mutual in its perpetration; while feminist researchers study "intimate terrorism," which is the form of violence that is largely perpetrated by men to exercise control over their female partners and is repetitive and ongoing with the potential to escalate (Johnson, 1995). It is clear from the narratives subject to analysis in the present research that the range of offensive behaviors experienced by males parallels those experienced by women. They include the gamut of physical attacks from minor verbal taunts to serious violent assaults, including with weapons. They are characterized by escalation, are often bidirectional or reciprocal, and extend to other family members.

PRECIPITATING FACTORS IN FAMILY VIOLENCE

Of particular relevance to the gender debate is the notion of reciprocal violence (Headley, Scott, & de Vaus, 1999), also referred to as common couple violence (Johnson, 1995; Johnson & Ferraro, 2000), situational couple violence (Kelly & Johnson, 2008), or bidirectional violence (Swan & Snow, 2002). This has been found to be common in intimate partnerships, with up to half of all violent couples engaging in mutual conflict (Cook, 2009; Gelles, 2007; Stets & Straus, 1990; Straus, 2011). One typology of female domestic aggression yields three distinct types: the aggressors (who exhibit coercive violence), the victims (who abuse in self-defense), and women who participate in bidirectional violence. The most common form of female violence was bidirectional; when both partners were violent toward each other (Swan & Snow, 2002). Thus, in most cases, the violent conflict is mutual, bidirectional, or an exchange of abuse (Cook, 2009; Sommer, 1994).

It has long been posited that there exists variance in the motivating factors in FV dependent on the sex of the perpetrator (Hamberger, Lohr, Bonge, & Tolin, 1997). Violent women are said to be driven by anger and frustration or motivated to retaliate against provocation (Morgan & Chadwick, 2009) or are expressing a loss of control or a sense of powerlessness (Mulroney & Chan, 2005). One study that examined motivations of 23 violent female partners established that anger and not getting their partner's attention were pervasive themes, followed by self-defense and retaliation (Bair-Merritt et al., 2010). Yet others have found that both men and women use partner violence for coercive control; although it is acknowledged that the notion of control might be interpreted differently or the exercise of it might be for different purposes (Hamby, 2009). This view submits that women use control to gain greater autonomy, whereas men use control to demonstrate authority (Kernsmith, 2005). Alternately, it is claimed that the use of control may be situationally dependent, being that women attempt to exhibit control over immediate situations, whereas men tend to establish "widespread authority" over a longer period of time (Dasgupta, 2002, p. 7).

An examination of male motivations to perpetrate violence found two distinct categories: violence to assert domination or control over a partner or violence that is committed impulsively in response to frustration and anger (James, Seddon, & Brown, 2002). Others have advocated that the motivations common across both female and male abusers are control, anger expression, and coercive communication (Hamberger et al., 1997). In general, the literature suggests that both sexes share a range of motivations but sometimes employ them for different purposes or by applying different techniques. We would concur with the conclusions drawn by Mulroney and Chan (2005), who found that women's motivations for violence were multicausal.

An often-cited reason for dismissing the case of violent females is the assumption that women perpetrating DV are simply defending themselves (Jewkes, 2002). Obvious differences relate to physicality and the acceptance that females are at greater risk of physical harm due to their stature, size, and strength. By contrast, one American study of domestic homicides found that the majority of the 145 female offenders studied did not murder their spouse out of fear or self-defense but because of greed or to conceal an affair or eliminate their partner (Mann, 1998). Almost 60% of the women planned the killing in advance, with 70% acting while their partner was drunk, drugged, restrained, or asleep (Mann, 1998). Another study examining women who were incarcerated for spousal murder found that 60% reported they were not victims of chronic physical abuse (McCormick, 1976).

Self-defense is viewed as rightful conduct (Findlay, Odgers, & Yeo, 2014) when an individual "reasonably perceives he or she is in imminent danger of serious bodily damage or death" (Walker, 1993, p. 208). It is a common mitigating defense in DV court cases, but there are a number of studies to show that the majority of female-initiated assaults are not exclusively a reaction to male aggression (McNeely & Robinson-Simpson, 1987; Mould, 1990; Sarantakos, 1999; Straus, 1993). Ninety percent of the abusive women in a study conducted by Pearson (1997) reported using violence against their partner because they were jealous, angry, or frustrated, not because they were in imminent danger; and other confirmatory research indicated that less than 10% of violent women claimed they acted in self-defense (Sommer, 1994).

The concept of battered woman syndrome (BWS) arose in the United States in the 1970s as a defense strategy to assist women who were charged with killing abusive partners (Bull, 2010). The syndrome attempts to explain reactive aggression by women who have been subject to enduring violence (Easteal, 1992) and sees such behavior as defensive in nature (Dobash, Dobash, Cavanagh, & Lewis, 1998; Henning, Jones, & Holdford, 2003). While there are other defenses that can be applied—diminished responsibility, provocation, lack of intent, self-defense, and insanity (Bradfield, 2002), it is BWS that legitimates the victim status of women who kill (Bradfield, 2002; Cook, 2009; Sarantakos, 2004). In Australia, in only 15% of cases where women were charged with spousal-murder was there an acquittal; 9% result in a murder conviction and almost 70% deliver a conviction for manslaughter (Bradfield, 2002). Despite concerns about its juridical value and utility, the notion of BWS achieved a focus on crimes in the home and highlighted the consequences of serial domestic abuse (Dragiewicz, 2014), and it is noteworthy in the present analysis that evidence of a "battered" syndrome for male victims of FV is revealed.

REPORTABILITY

IPV of all kinds tends to have low levels of official reporting, but this is more pronounced when the victims are in a domestic or familial relationship (Findlay et al., 2014). Victim surveys in Australia report that 80% of women and 95% of men never contact the police about violence by their current partner; and 26% of women and 54% of men had never disclosed the abuse to anyone (ABS, 2012). It has been well documented that violence against a male partner is even less likely to be reported than is violence against a female partner (Daly & Wilson, 1988; Henmann, 1996; Langly & Levy, 1977; Ruback, 1994; Sarantakos, 1999; Stanko & Hobdell, 1993). The Australian statistics—drawn from a variety of sources such as the ABS, AIC, and relevant state bureaus in 2010–12—indicate that "only 5.3% of male victims of current partner violence had contacted police" (Moore, 2015).

There are many reasons for this underreporting that apply to both genders (Morgan & Chadwick, 2009). First, there is the nature of the crime event itself as it can be considered too personal, too minor, or not serious enough to warrant official attention (McGregor & Hopkins, 1991). There are also practical barriers such as the belief that the police could not act, a desire to deal with the issues themselves, being incapacitated through feeling too upset or suffering injuries following an incident, and the difficulties inherent in the reporting processes (ABS, 2012). In addition, emotional and cultural barriers are invoked as the rationale for not reporting. These are bounded by humiliation, shame, or embarrassment; for males in particular there is fear of being teased, being unwilling to discuss such issues (Moore, 2015), a sense that they will not be believed, maintaining silence on the issue, and being seen an unmanly or weak (Campbell, 2010). A significant reason though is borne of fear of retaliation or reprisal from the aggressor, whether female or male (Morgan & Chadwick, 2009).

IMPACTS OF DOMESTIC VIOLENCE

FV has profound effects on indirect victims. As referred to earlier, children are often present during FV incidents with proportions ranging from 27% to 44% (Morgan & Chadwick, 2009). It is increasingly recognized that a child's exposure to DV consti- tutes emotional and psychological abuse (Goddard & Bedi, 2010; Richards, 2011), as it is known to have a profound effect on a child's well-being (Bartels, 2010). Exposure is considered to have occurred if a child witnesses the violence, is forced to participate, told they are to blame, used as a hostage, or feels compelled to inter- vene (Richards, 2011). It constitutes a risk factor for behavioral disorders such as depression, drug use, high-risk sexual activity, self-harm, or suicide and major health problems such as heart disease, obesity, and sexually transmitted disease (Krug, Mercy, Dahlberg, & Zwi, 2002). It is widely accepted that violence either witnessed or directly experienced as a child increases the risk that the behavior will be repli- cated as an adult (Hayes & Prenzler, 2014; Mouzos & Makkai, 2004). Additionally, there is a growing body of work that has established a link between witnessing or experiencing violence as a child and the increased risk of victimization as an adult (Sternberg et al., 1993).

In a large representative study that examined the characteristics of perpetrators in substantiated cases of child abuse and neglect in the United States, neglect was the main type of abuse involving female caregivers (US DHHS, 2005), underscoring the fact that mothers are most likely to abuse their offspring, including in homicide incidents (AIC, 2006; Dutton, 2012; Gaudiosi, 2009).

The impact of FV on victims is similar for both men and women, including con- fusion, betrayal, fear, vulnerability, and damage to self-esteem. The extreme end of victim impact bares itself in the form of self-harm and suicide. The state of Utah is alone in measuring FV-related suicides, so their statistics are noteworthy. Sixty-five domestic deaths were examined, of which 44 were suicides (2 female victims and 42 male victims) and 21 were homicides (11 female victims and 10 male victims). When the number of DV-related homicides and suicides were combined, the majority of victims were men (Davis, 2010).

REPERCUSSIONS OF GENDER BIAS

For male victims of FV, there are few avenues to seek information specific to their needs. One rare resource is the One-in-Three website established in 2009. It is the only site of its kind in Australia that is committed exclusively to the accurate reporting of FV data and the acknowledgment of male victims. It is therefore not surprising that the site's invitation for men to anonymously share stories has attracted a significant number of contributions. From a pool of 150 testimonies, 50 were selected and analyzed to glean the experience of partner violence, its impact on them (and their children), and to what extent these circumstances influenced their willingness to report.

Results suggest that male FV victims suffer further victimization because of the sociopolitical gender bias against them. This bias takes many forms and is entrenched in a strongly held belief that men are the most likely perpetrators of FV and women, the most likely victim. The major factors affecting men's hesitation to disclose violence appear to be fear based. This concept of fear emerged as a significant theme in the men's stories. Men reported fearing not being believed, not being treated fairly, losing their children, and fearing their female partner. A key contributor to their sense of fear was the perception that men are deemed to be unlikely victims of IPV and therefore they would be denied the same support offered to women.

> I know now that the only reason I kept trying to save the relationship was because of the children. I wanted them to have a mum and dad under the one roof. Little did I know the damage being done to them.
>
> **Kyle**

> My wife hits me, pushes me, tries running me down in our car, smashes the house up, throws household objects while my daughter is in the house. We have an 8-month-old daughter [who] has seen the lot.
>
> **James**

> After seeing the psychiatrist several times, I had my plan, I had to leave, no matter how hard it would be to "abandon" my daughter, I just had to go. I felt embarrassed and ashamed and blamed to the point suicide seemed an easier option than leaving. I felt so isolate.
>
> **Brendon**

Men raised concerns about not being believed by police, friends, and magistrates. Even when male victims were believed, they feared they would not be assisted or would be blamed for the abuse. It is generally understood that men would find it easier to seek help and disclose the abuse if there was greater public acknowledgment that males can also be victims of abuse, if there were appropriate services for men, and if they were confident that they will be given effective help.

> She grabbed both children. I tried stopping her from leaving with them. She punched me in the face several times and then rang 000 and told them that I was punching her. The police came – they weren't interested in anything I had to say,

they just wanted to hear what she had to say. Eventually the police let her leave with both children. I couldn't believe it, there were no court orders, nothing, they had no right to let her take them. I was lost, I didn't know what to do.

Kyle

Despite the common belief that only women feel the fear of male-inflicted DV, men reported fearing their partner for a range of reasons. For some, it was a fear of harm from physical violence; for others, it was fear that their partner would physically or emotionally hurt the children. There was no question that men feared the actions of their female partner.

Every time I moved towards the door she'd go for me with the knife. I was terrified the children would be injured. I sat on the couch and she came towards me again. By this time I had no will to fight it. I said "if you're going do it, just do it – just kill me – get it over and done with – I can't handle it any more."

Robert

MEN AND THEIR CHILDREN

Parents experience a profound sense of loss and bewilderment when they lose access to their children. It is not uncommon for one parent to use the children as a bargaining tool or to threaten to deny access if demands are not met. Men reported fear that they would be discriminated against in custodial decisions because of their gender. There was a common perception among the male contributors that their ex-partner would receive favor in family court decisions, even when the mother had a history of violence. A number of men expressed genuine frustration with the court system when access to their children was limited or denied, and this fear was compounded if their former partners lied or made false allegations against them. Fear of losing access to children was a common theme in the men's contributions, and was particularly acute in separations that were marred by conflict and bitterness.

I have been physically assaulted (slapped once and more recently punched several times and slapped). I am afraid to report this to any authority for the fear of ridicule and becoming a social outcast. I don't want to lose my son and want to give him a happy family to grow up in. The thought of not being able to see him every day is depressing.

The testimonies suggested strongly that male victims fear discrimination on the basis of their gender. Their narratives were replete with the theme that "men cannot be victims" and discussion of the stigma that male victims endure.

It is my considered opinion that while we genderise domestic violence there will never be equality within service provision or justice until the focus is on victims. Domestic violence should be in terms of victims.

Mathew

How many men are in the shadows falling apart with no-one there to see, no support and feeling guilt that we failed as a partner and as a father.

Tony

VICTIM PRECIPITATION

FV, from a criminological perspective, has some unique features particularly because of the intimate relational context between victim and offender. Unlike most other forms of violence (e.g., street violence, riots, and hate crimes), there exists a dyadic relationship, a pattern of behavior established through intimacy and a continuum of victimization. Precipitation, not to be conflated with "victim-blaming," refers to the actions or circumstances of a victim that increases the chance of victimization (Felson & Messner, 1998). It is an important area to examine, particularly because of the intimate relationship within which the violence occurs. The overall aim of identifying precipitation is to manage those contributing circumstances or behaviors to avoid or mitigate victimization.

I wasn't allowed to see my family, or friends as I was told if I did she would leave and take our daughter away to where I couldn't find them. Everything was a threat, everything became an ultimatum ... if I did this or that she would beat me, or leave with our daughter, or in some cases she would kill me, and she would describe in great detail how she would do so too. I became terrified of my life, she was so unpredictable I was scared to go home to her.

Brendan

I kept moving from room to room, asking her to leave me alone, telling her that I was tired and didn't want to talk. There's no point in arguing back. She shut the door and put her full body weight up against it and continued to call me every name under the sun. I took that for about 10 minutes, constantly asking her to "please leave me alone." She refused, saying she wouldn't let me go until I understood her point of view. I told her she was restricting my movement, and to let me go. She wouldn't move so I pulled the door in to escape, moving her in the process. She punched me in the back. She then called the police.

Tom

We were bathing the children and she was squirting our daughter with the handheld shower and said to her let's get daddy. So she wet me. Thinking she was in a good mood and wanted to have fun, I turned the shower back on to her, wetting her in the process. Well she went psycho at me, screaming, and she punched me several times in the head. At that moment I realized that I can't keep living like this and told her to get out. I locked myself in the bedroom, she kicked the door in and began assaulting me again. I finally stood up to her and said stop, no more you have hit me for the last time.

Kyle

I got home after 2 months and she was there waiting for me, she said she was so sorry for acting crazy and it was because she had come out of an abusive relationship, and had been waiting for me because she thought I was worth the wait. That's when I made the biggest mistake of my life and felt sorry for her, because I thought everybody deserved a second chance. For the next 3 years she continually abused me ... verbally, physically, and emotionally and I was continually trying to get away from her, but she was an absolute master at forcing me to stay with her.

Tony

After some petty argument, I've had my throat jabbed and choked, my testicles hit, smacked in the head and kicked in the shins, amongst other things. Due to fear of damaging the relationship I'm dependant on, I am reluctant to proceed to take further action to rectify the problem. On confrontation, her liability for such a thing is denied and I fear that I will not be able to resolve this issue in my relationship. I have been warned to be careful, because she might get me into trouble with untrue allegations and will be favoured for being female, especially if she shows her emotions.

Paul

CONCLUSIONS

FV continues to be characterized as a gendered crime against women. This ignores the victimization of men, children, and those with other familial relations to the abuser. As has been demonstrated here, men suffer the same range of abuses as female victims both physical (verbal, assault, and sexual abuse) and nonphysical (emotional, social, financial, and legal). There is also the same range of motivating or situational factors involved (jealousy, control, anger), as it is acknowledged that FV for both genders is multicausal. Further, there is evidence that parallels can be drawn for male victims as escalation characterizes the violence they endure—where verbal abuse eventually becomes routine and then intensifies into pushing and slapping and then, on occasion, into more serious aggravated or premeditated assaults. Similarly, males appear to experience the "battered" syndrome where it is difficult for them to leave abusive relationships because of children, financial ties, and threats of repercussions where their attempts to depart can trigger further violence.

While it is not the remit here to explore specific policies across jurisdictions, it is instructive to note that support services and educational campaigns rarely make provision for male victims. For example, a recent nationwide package of measures by the federal government in Australia allocated only 2% of its $100 million expenditure to males, and this money was allocated for male offenders, not victims (Moore, 2015). This underscores the claims by males who report abuse that they are perceived as "second-class victims" and not treated seriously by police and service providers. They are rendered "invisible to the authorities" and their "plight is largely overlooked by the media, in official reports and in government policy" (Campbell, 2010). Such an imbalance is not only discriminatory for men but also renders invisible members of the LGBT community (Moore, 2015). It also is important to recognize that violence in the home is not confined to criminal justice jurisdictions but is addressed in family court precincts and attention is warranted to the gender bias in that noncriminal realm (Dragiewicz, 2014).

The consideration of the male victims' experiences, as discussed in this chapter, suggests that offender programs and victim support must be gender inclusive. Male victims with children in their care are particularly at risk because of the current lack of gender-neutral support and accommodation services. When child victims are considered, there is no basis for a gendered approach to FV. In fact, a gendered approach is harmful as it further perpetuates a general acceptance that female violence is a myth. The knowledge that a child is as likely to be physically abused by their biological mother as they are by a male suggests strongly that support cannot be exclusively available only for females. Understanding what motivates FV perpetrators is important to formulating effective responses and interventions (Braaf & Meyering, 2013, p.9). Additionally, when female perpetrators are not identified (or acknowledged as perpetrators), they receive little assistance, support, or treatment. The debate about whether male or female victims have primacy only detracts from understanding of the intervention and treatment needs of both genders (Cook, 2009, p. 34).

However, it should be stressed that, in our view, FV is not a binary crime with males exclusively as perpetrators and females solely as victims. There are clearly gendered aspects of violence in the home but to render it in a gendered paradigm is to omit a full picture of the offending patterns. Similarly, the second feature highlighted in this chapter is that DV is rarely a singular crime event and this is where feminist scholarship in terms of its methodological approaches (e.g., narratives and discourse analysis) can make a significant contribution to our understanding of the exchange process and the ongoing nature of intimate partner violence. The third key factor raised here is that violence in the home is intergenerational and extends to other family members; we have borrowed the notion of FV from the excellent work that informs our understanding of aggression in Indigenous communities in Australia (Blagg, Ray, Murray, & Macarthy, 2000). The qualitative data drawn from our exploratory research demonstrate that children and other family members are direct or indirect victims to IPV, and thus a more holistic and inclusive term of FV is a first step in capturing its complexity. This should not be seen as a binary matter where females are pitted against males for there is violence in same-sex relationships, between parents and adult or adolescent children, and across broader generational levels (i.e., grandparents) or wider familial relationships. Thus, it is important to be cognizant of these patterns. Further, when viewed as a crime event or series of events, the complexity of FV in terms of its nature and frequency, along with its precipitating factors is firmly acknowledged.

DV is not solely about gender inequality and patriarchal social structures and processes. The macro societal factors such as socioeconomic pressures, the more meso-level ingredients such as alcohol and drug abuse and mental illness, plus the micro and situational forces are far more implicated as keys to abuse in the home than gender. Australia does appear to have embraced the broader notion of "FV" evidenced by a state royal commission and the appointment of a federal minister under that title (Arndt, 2016, p, 1). Yet the discourse remains one that focuses "only on aggression by men and white-washes women's role in FV" in that it fails to concede that "most families with a history of violence include female as well as male perpetrators" (Arndt, 2016, p. 6). It is claimed that there are in excess of "1700 articles in peer-reviewed journals" to eschew the gendered approach for both "women and men are actively involved in most violence in the home; women often initiate violence, and it isn't simply self-defense" (Arndt, 2016, p. 6). Thus, we concur with Renzetti (2013), who urges a consideration of the repositioning of women as both perpetrators and victims and encourages the funding and publication of research that challenges the gender paradigm (Cook, 2009).

Male victims of abuse in intimate partnerships continue to endure false accusations or arrest by police because of misunderstandings under the prevailing gendered paradigm. They report that the society-wide bias impacts on them additionally to the aggression. They express concern for their children as direct victims or as witnesses and are doubly concerned about legal procedures that will thwart access to their children. They live in a climate of fear as a result of the community perceptions, the potential to be falsely accused, and the threats to their relationships with their offspring. Until a gender-inclusive family approach is adopted, men will continue to feel fearful about reporting or seeking support, violent women will avoid detection and accountability, and children in violent homes will remain at risk.

SUMMARY

- FV is an overarching label for a host of interpersonal behaviors that range from the minor to the mortal. It constitutes a largely "hidden" form of crime because of its dependence on reporting levels and its reliance on limited data sources. The known patterns are skewed because of its politicization, which has rendered some victims invisible.
- Aggression occurring within the domestic sphere takes many nomenclatures from spousal abuse, wife abuse, and wife bashing to relationship violence or gender-based violence. While DV describes violence occurring within a familial dynamic (including against children), IPV is specifically between two adults who are, or were, in an intimate relationship. IPV can occur in any intimate partnership, including heterosexual, gay, lesbian and transgender relationships. In Australia, the term FV has been invoked especially in the context of Indigenous interpersonal aggression among extended family members. However, in the public and political discourse as well as in the research literature, IPV and DV are used interchangeably, and the all-encompassing term of "FV" tends to be eschewed.

- In same-sex relationships, there is evidence of abusive behaviors with 26% of gay men and 44% of lesbian women reporting experiences of aggression at the hands of their partners.
- The various "waves" of feminist thought have contributed much to the discipline of criminology, and especially to that of victimology. These multiple strands have provided new theories, highlighted hidden forms of crime, exposed violence in the private sphere, and promoted alternative methods of dealing with offending. Yet there has been scant attention paid to the male victims of DV with few published works and empirical studies, and even fewer that address intimate partner violence in LGBT communities. This deficit appears antithetical to the fundamental principles of what would be regarded as the inclusivist approach embedded in feminist criminology. While the existence of global gendered violence is undeniable, in the case of modern Western democracies in the 21st century the reciprocal or exchange nature of FV begs further investigation.
- The gender paradigm is best described as a philosophy that views DV in terms of sexual segregation and patriarchy. It reinforces the notion that DV is a gendered crime that is primarily perpetrated by men against women. Scholars supportive of the gender paradigm explicitly define DV as violence against women. This gendered narrative is widely applied and accepted in mainstream media and in the majority of antiviolence policy and discourse. Gender-specific terminology such as "wife bashing" has reinforced a mutually exclusive binary characterization of FV as comprising female victims and male perpetrators. It has been blind to the reality of women's violence against children, of abuse against extended family members, and victimization of those in same-sex relationships. This linguistic framework is underscored by empirical studies that have relied on selective samples. Information about male perpetrators is typically drawn from criminal justice records, and data on male victims are rarely considered
- It has long been acknowledged that FV can take forms other than physical aggression such as verbal abuse, psychological abuse, damage of personal property, and abuse of power. Most often the general literature, policy documents and empirical studies tend to focus on physical forms of violence including sexual assault. Additionally, physical abuse is the key subject at the center of the gender controversy, and most statistics on gender-specific perpetration of DV are referring to its physical manifestation.
- Violence severity occurs on a spectrum and presents challenges to succinctly classify levels of severity. Most studies examining DV categorize the level of harm as either minor or severe. Examples of minor violent acts are slapping, grabbing, pushing, shoving and throwing objects at another while severe acts of violence include kicking, biting, threatening to use a knife or deadly weapon, or using a knife or other deadly weapon.
- The most extreme and rare form of FV is domestic homicide where victims include intimate partners, children, parents, siblings, or other family members

such as grandparents and cousins. In Australia, domestic homicides account for between 32% and 47% of all homicides annually. Twenty-three percent of domestic homicide victims are intimate partners (where victim and offender are current or former partners). One-quarter of the victims of intimate partner homicide are men and 75% are women.

- Of particular relevance to the gender debate is the notion of reciprocal violence, also referred to as common couple violence, situational couple violence, or bidirectional violence. This has been found to be common in intimate partnerships with up to half of all violent couples engaging in mutual conflict. One typology of female domestic aggression yields three distinct types: the aggressors (who exhibit coercive violence), the victims (who abuse in self-defense), and women who participate in bidirectional violence. The most common form of female violence was bidirectional; when both partners were violent toward each other.

- There exists variance in the motivating factors in FV dependent on the sex of the perpetrator. Violent women are said to be driven by anger and frustration or motivated to retaliate against provocation, or are expressing a loss of control or a sense of powerlessness. Male motivations to perpetrate familial violence exist in two distinct categories: violence to assert domination or control over a partner, or violence that is committed impulsively in response to frustration and anger.

- FV has profound effects on indirect victims. As referred to earlier, children are often present during FV incidents with proportions ranging from 27% to 44%. It is increasingly recognized that a child's exposure to DV constitutes emotional and psychological abuse, as it is known to have a profound effect on a child's well-being. Exposure is considered to have occurred if a child witnesses the violence, is forced to participate, told they are to blame, used as a hostage, or feels compelled to intervene. It constitutes a risk factor for behavioral disorders such as depression, drug use, high-risk sexual activity, self-harm, or suicide and major health problems such as heart disease, obesity, and sexually transmitted disease. It is widely accepted that violence either witnessed or directly experienced as a child increases the risk that the behavior will be replicated as an adult. Additionally, there is a growing body of work that has established a link between witnessing or experiencing violence as a child and the increased risk of being victimized as an adult.

- FV, from a criminological perspective, has some unique features particularly because of the intimate relational context between victim and offender. Unlike most other forms of violence (e.g., street violence, riots, and hate crimes) there exists a dyadic relationship, a pattern of behavior established through intimacy and a continuum of victimization. Precipitation, not to be conflated with "victim-blaming," refers to the actions or circumstances of a victim that increases thei chance of victimization. It is an important area to examine, particularly because of the intimate relationship within which the violence occurs. The overall aim of identifying precipitation is to manage those contributing circumstances or behaviors to avoid or mitigate victimization.

QUESTIONS

1. Explain the differences between the concepts of gender symmetry and the gender paradigm.
2. Describe the two main forms of data collection that provide information about the incidence and prevalence of DV.
3. What are the key advantages of each form of data collection?
4. What is legal-administrative form of abuse, and how is it related to gender discrimination, particularly for male victims?
5. Explain the similarities and differences between men's and women's motivational factors in perpetrating DV.
6. Discuss the significance of adopting the notion of bidirectional intimate partner violence to the gender debate.
7. List the challenges male DV victims may face when they contemplate reporting the violence to authorities.
8. Provide an argument for government policy to adopt a "family" view of DV rather than a "gendered" view.
9. Discuss the spectrum of impacts that DV has on victims.
10. Is there an argument for the legitimacy of "battered man syndrome"? Explain.
11. What are the key risks to children who are raised in violent homes?
12. Relevant to your own jurisdiction, investigate the DV support agencies that exist, and to what degree they cater to the needs of DV victims regardless of gender.

REFERENCES

Anderson, K. (2005). Theorizing gender in intimate partner violence research. *Sex Roles, 52*, 853–865.

Archer, J. (2000). Sex differences in aggression between heterosexual partners: a meta-analytic review. *Psychological Bulletin, 126*, 651–680.

Arndt, B. (March 30, 2016). Minster's story fails the gender test. *The Australian*, 1–6.

Australian Bureau of Statistics (ABS). (2012). *The personal safety survey*. Cat. No. 4906.0. Canberra.

Australian Bureau of Statistics (ABS). (2015). *Education and work, Australia*. Cat. No. 6227.0. Canberra.

Australian Institute of Criminology (AIC). (1990). *Violence: Directions for Australia*. Canberra: AIC.

Australian Institute of Criminology (AIC). (2006). *Children present in family violence incidents. Crime Facts Info* No. 137 Canberra: AIC. Available at http://aic.gov.au/publications/current series/cfi/121–140/cfi137.aspx.

Bair-Merritt, M., Crowne, S., Thompson, D. A., Sibinga, E., Trent, M., & Campbell, J. (2010). Why do women use intimate partner violence? A systematic review of women's motivations. *Trauma, Violence, & Abuse, 11*(4), 178–189.

Bartels, L. (2010). *Emerging issues in domestic/family violence research*. Canberra: Australian Institute of Criminology.

Blagg, H., Ray, D., Murray, R., & Macarthy, E. (2000). *Crisis intervention in aboriginal family violence*. Canberra: Department of Prime Minister and Cabinet.

Braaf, R., & Meyering, I. (May, 2013). The gender debate in domestic violence: the role of data. *Australian Domestic and Family Violence Clearing House, Issues Paper 25*. Available at http://www.adfvc.unsw.edu.au/PDF%20files/IssuesPaper_25.pdf.

Bradfield, R. (2002). *The treatment of women who kill their violent male partners within the Australian criminal justice system* (Ph.D. thesis) University of Tasmania. Available at http://eprints.utas.edu.au/1045/.

Bryant, W., & Cussen, T. (2015). *Homicide in Australia: 2010–11 to 2011–12 National Homicide Monitoring Program annual report. Monitoring Report*, No. 23 Canberra: Australian Institute of Criminology. Available at http://www.aic.gov.au/publications/current%20series/mr/21-40/mr23.html.

Bull, M. (2010). *Punishment and sentencing: Risk, rehabilitation and restitution*. Melbourne: Oxford University Press.

Campbell, D. (September 5, 2010). More than 40% of domestic violence victims are male, report reveals. *The Guardian*. Available at http://www.theguardian.com/society/2010/sep/05/men-victims-domestic-violence.

Capaldi, D., Kim, H., & Short, J. (2007). Observed initiation and reciprocity of physical aggression in young at-risk couples. *Journal of Family Violence*, 22(2), 101–111.

Carrington, K. (2015). *Feminism and global justice*. London: Routledge.

Chan, C. (2005). *Domestic violence in gay and lesbian relationships*. Sydney: Australian Domestic and Family Violence Clearinghouse.

Coleman, C., & Moynihan, J. (1996). *Understanding crime data: Haunted by the dark figure*. Buckingham: Open University Press.

Cook, P. (2009). *Abused men: The hidden side of domestic violence*. Westport: Praeger.

Daly, K. (1998). Crossroads and intersections: building from feminist critique. In K. Daly, & L. Maher (Eds.), *Criminology at the crossroads*. Oxford: Oxford University Press.

Daly, M., & Wilson, M. (1988). Parent-offspring homicides in Canada, 1974–1983. *Science*, 242, 519–524.

Dasgupta, S. (2002). A framework for understanding women's use of nonlethal violence in intimate heterosexual relationships. *Violence Against Women*, 8, 1364–1389.

Davis, R. (2010). Domestic violence-related deaths. *Journal of Aggression, Conflict and Peace Research*, 2(2), 44–52.

DeKeseredy, W., & Schwartz, M. (2003). Backlash and whiplash: a critique of Canada's general social science survey on victimization. *Online Journal of Justice Studies*, 1(1). Available at http://sisyphe.org/article.php3?id_article=1689.

Dobash, R., Dobash, R., Cavanagh, K., & Lewis, R. (1998). Separate and intersecting realities: a comparison of men and women's accounts of violence against women. *Violence Against Women*, 4, 382–414.

Douglas, E., & Hines, M. (2011). The helpseeking experiences of men who sustain intimate partner violence: an overlooked population and implications for practice. *Journal of Family Violence*, 26(6), 473–485.

Dragiewicz, M. (2014). Domestic violence and family law: criminological concerns. *International Journal for Crime, Justice and Social Democracy*, 3(1), 121–134.

Dutton, D. (2012). *Rethinking domestic violence*. Vancouver: UBC Press.

Dutton, D., Corvo, K., & Hamel, J. (2009). The gender paradigm in domestic violence research and practice part II: the information website of the American Bar Association. *Aggression and Violent Behavior*, 14, 30–38.

Dutton, D., & Nicholls, T. (2005). The gender paradigm in domestic violence research and theory: the conflict of theory and data. *Aggression and Violent Behavior, 10,* 680–714.

Easteal, P. (1992). Battered woman syndrome: what is "reasonable"? *Alternative Law Journal, 17*(5), 220–223.

Felson, R. B., & Messner, S. F. (1998). Disentangling the effects of gender and intimacy on victim precipitation in homicide. *Criminology, 36,* 405–423.

Fiebert, M. S. (2014). Examining assaults by women on their spouses or male partners: an updated annotated bibliography. *Sexuality & Culture, 18*(2), 405–467. http://dx.doi.org/10.1007/s12119-013-9194-1.

Findlay, M., Odgers, S., & Yeo (2014). *Australian criminal justice.* Melbourne: Oxford University Press.

Gaudiosi, J. (2009). *Child maltreatment.* Washington: U.S. Department of Health and Human Services, Administration for Children and Families. Available at http://www.acf.hhs.gov/sites/default/files/cb/cm2009.pdf.

Gelles, R. (2007). The politics of research: the use, abuse, and misuse of social science data – the case of intimate partner violence. *Family Court Review, 45,* 42–51.

Glass, J. D. (September 4, 2014). Two studies that prove domestic violence is an LGBT issue. *The Advocate.* Available at http://www.advocate.com/crime/2014/09/04/2-studies-prove-domestic-violence-lgbt-issue.

Goddard, C., & Bedi, G. (2010). Intimate partner violence and child abuse: a child centred perspective. *Child Abuse Review, 19,* 5–20.

Hamberger, L., Lohr, J., Bonge, D., & Tolin, D. (1997). An empirical classification of motivations for domestic violence. *Violence Against Women, 3,* 401–423.

Hamberger, L., & Potente, T. (1994). Counseling heterosexual women arrested for domestic violence: implications for theory and practice. *Violence and Victims, 9*(2), 125–137.

Hamby, S. (2009). The gender debate on intimate partner violence: solutions and dead ends. *Psychological Trauma, 1*(1), 24–34.

Hayes, H., & Prenzler, T. (2014). *Introduction to crime and criminology* (4th ed.). Sydney: Pearson.

Headley, B., Scott, D., & de Vaus, D. (1999). Domestic violence in Australia: are women and men equally violent? *Australian Social Monitor, 2*(3), 57–62.

Henmann, M. (1996). Domestic violence: do men under-report? *Forensic Update, 47,* 3–8.

Henning, K., Jones, A., & Holdford, R. (2003). Treatment needs of women arrested for domestic violence: a comparison with male offenders. *Journal of Interpersonal Violence, 18,* 839–856.

International Crime Victims Survey (ICVS). (2011). Directory of family and domestic violence statistics, 2011. *Australian Bureau of Statistics.* Retrieved from http://www.abs.gov.au/ausstats/abs@.nsf/Lookup/4533.0Chapter2002011.

James, K., Seddon, B., & Brown, J. (2002). *"Using it" or "losing it": Men's constructions of their violence towards female partners.* Research paper. Sydney: Australian Domestic and Family Violence Clearinghouse. Available at http://austdvclearinghouse.unsw.edu.au/Occasional/James_et_al_research_paper_final.pdf.

Jewkes, R. (2002). Intimate partner violence: causes and prevention. *Lancet, 359*(9315), 1423–1429.

Johnson, M. (1995). Patriarchal terrorism and common couple violence: two forms of violence against women. *Journal of Marriage and the Family, 57,* 283–294.

Johnson, M. (2006). Gender symmetry and asymmetry in domestic violence. *Violence Against Women, 12,* 1003–1018.

Johnson, M. P., & Ferraro, K. J. (2000). Research on domestic violence in the 1990s: making distinctions. *Journal of Marriage and the Family, 62*(4), 948–963.

Kaufman-Kantor, G., & Straus, M. A. (1990). The "drunken bum" theory of wife beating. In M. A. Straus, & R. J. Gelles (Eds.), *Physical violence in American families: Risk factors and adaptations to violence in 8,145 families*. New Brunswick: Transaction Publishers.

Kelly, J., & Johnson, M. (2008). Differentiation among types of intimate partner violence: research update and implications for interventions. *Family Court Review, 46*(3), 476–499.

Kernsmith, P. (2005). Exerting power or striking back: a gendered comparison of motivations for domestic violence perpetration. *Violence and Victims, 20*, 173–185.

Krug, E. G., Mercy, J. A., Dahlberg, L. L., & Zwi, A. B. (2002). The world report on violence and health. *Lancet, 360*(9339), 1083–1088.

Langly, R., & Levy, R. C. (1977). *Wife beating: The silent crisis*. New York: Pocket Books.

Lewis, A., & Sarantakos, S. (2001). Domestic violence and the malevictim. *Nuance, 3*, 1–15.

Mann, C. (1998). Getting even? Women who kill in domestic encounters. *Justice Quarterly, 5*(1), 33–50.

McCormick, C. (1976). *Battered women: The last report*. Chicago, Cook County: Department of Corrections.

McGregor, H., & Hopkins, A. (1991). *Working for change: The movement against domestic violence*. Sydney: Allen & Unwin.

McLeod, M. (1984). Women against men: an examination of domestic violence based on an analysis of official data and national victimization data. *Justice Quarterly, 1*, 171–193.

McNeely, R., Cook, P., & Torres, J. (2001). Is domestic violence agender issue or a human issue? *Journal of Human Behavior in the Social Environment, 4*(4), 227–251.

McNeely, R., & Mann, C. (1990). Domestic violence is a humanissue. *Journal of Interpersonal Violence, 5*, 129–132.

McNeely, R., & Robinson-Simpson, G. (1987). The truth about domestic violence: a falsely framed issue. *Social Work, 32*, 485–490.

Moffitt, T. E., Caspi, A., Rutter, M., & Silva, P. (2001). *Sorting out differences in antisocial behaviour: Findings from the first two decades of the Dunedin longitudinal study*. Cambridge: Cambridge University Press.

Moore, C. (November 24, 2015). Story of domestic violence against men is hidden, complicated and disputed. *Brisbane Times*. Available at http://www.brisbanetimes.com.au/queensland/story-of-domestic-violence-against-men-is-hidden-complicated-and-disputed-20151122-gl55v7.html.

Morgan, A., & Chadwick, H. (2009). *Key issues in domestic violence. Research in Practice*, No. 7. Canberra: Australian Institute of Criminology.

Mould, D. (1990). Data base or data bias? *American Psychologist, 45*, 676.

Mouzos, J., & Makkai, T. (2004). *Women's experiences of male violence: Findings from the Australian component of the International Violence Against Women Survey (IVAWS). Research and Public Policy Series*, No. 56. Canberra: Australian Institute of Criminology.

Mulroney, J., & Chan, C. (2005). *Men as victims of domestic violence: Report*. Sydney: Australian Domestic and Family Violence Clearinghouse.

New South Wales Auditor-General. (2011). *New South Wales Auditor-General's Report: Performance Audit. Responding to domestic and family violence*. Sydney, NSW: Audit Office of New South Wales.

One in Three Campaign. (2009). *Family violence*. Available at http://www.oneinthree.com.au.

Pearson, P. (1997). *When she was bad: Women and the myth of innocence*. Toronto: Random House.

Pence, A., & Paymar, M. (1993). *Education groups for men who batter: The Duluth model*. New York: Springer.

Renzetti, C. (1987). Intimate violence in lesbian relationships. *Journal of Social Science Research, 15*, 41–59.

Renzetti, C. (2013). *Feminist criminology*. London: Routledge.

Richards, K. (2011). *Children's exposure to domestic violence in Australia. Trends and Issues in Crime and Criminal Justice*, No. 419. Canberra: Australian Institute of Criminology.

Ruback, R. (1994). Advice to crime victims: effects of crime, victim, and adviser factors. *Criminal Justice and Behavior, 21*(4), 423–442.

Sarantakos, S. (1999). Husband abuse: fact or fiction. *Australian Journal of Social Issues, 34*(3), 231–252.

Sarantakos, S. (2004). Deconstructing self-defense in wife-to-husband violence. *The Journal of Men's Studies, 12*(3), 277–296.

Schupe, S., Stacey, W., & Hazelwood, L. (1988). Violent men, violent couples: the dynamics of domestic violence. *Journal of Criminal Justice, 16*(1), 81–82.

Sommer, R. (1994). *Male and female partner abuse: Testing a diathesis-stress model* (Ph.D. dissertation). Winnipeg: University of Manitoba.

Stanko, E., & Hobdell, K. (1993). Assault on men: masculinity and male victimization. *British Journal of Criminology, 33*(3), 400–415.

Stanley, J., Tomison, A. M., & Pocock, J. (2003). *Child abuse and neglect in Indigenous Australian communities. Child Abuse Prevention Issues*, 19 Melbourne: Australian Institute of Family Studies. Available at http://www.aifs.gov.au/nch/pubs/issues/issues19/issues19.pdf.

Sternberg, K., Lamb, M., Greenbaum, C., Cichetti, D., Cortes, R., Krispin, O., et al. (1993). Effects of domestic violence on children's behaviour problems and depression. *Developmental Psychology, 9*(1), 44–52.

Stets, J. E., & Straus, M. A. (1990). Gender differences in reporting marital violence and its medical and psychological consequences. In M. A. Straus, & R. J. Gelles (Eds.), *Physical violence in American families* (pp. 151–165). New Brunswick: Transaction Publishers.

Strachan, G. (2010). Still working for the man? Women's employment experiences in Australia since 1950. *The Australian Journal of Social Issues, 45*(1), 117.

Straus, M. A. (1993). Physical assaults by wives: a major social problem. In R. J. Gelles, & D. R. Loseke (Eds.), *Current controversies on family violence* (pp. 67–87). Newbury Park: Sage.

Straus, M. A. (2006). Future research on gender symmetry in physical assaults on partners. *Violence Against Women, 12*, 1086–1097.

Straus, M. A. (2007). Processes explaining the concealment and distortion of evidence on gender symmetry in partner violence. *European Journal of Criminal Policy Research, 13*, 227–232.

Straus, M. A. (2011). Gender symmetry and mutuality in perpetration of clinical-level partner violence: empirical evidence and implications for prevention and treatment. *Aggression and Violent Behavior, 16*(4), 279–288.

Straus, M. A., & Gelles, R. (1986). Societal change and change in family violence from 1975 to 1985. *Journal of Marriage and the Family, 48*(8), 465–479.

Straus, M. A., & Gelles, R. J. (Eds.). (1992). *Physical violence in American families*. New Brunswick: Transaction Publishing.

Straus, M. A., Gelles, R., & Steinmetz, S. (1981). *Behind closed doors: Violence in the American family*. Garden City: Anchor.

Straus, M. A., & Scott, K. (2007). *Gender symmetry in partner violence: The evidence, the denial and the implications for primary prevention and treatment*. Available at http://pubpages.unh.edu/~mas2/V70%20version%20N3.pdf.

Swan, S., & Snow, D. (2002). A typology of women's use of violence in intimate relationships. *Violence Against Women, 8*(3), 286–319.

Tilbrook, E., Allan, A., & Dear, G. (2010). *Intimate partner abuse of men*. Perth: Men's Advisory Network & Edith Cowan University.

United States Department of Health and Human Services, Administration on Children, Youth, and Families (US DHHS ACF). (2005). *National Survey of Child and Adolescent Well-being (NSCAW): CPS sample component wave 1 data analysis report*. Washington: Government Printing Office.

Walker, L. (1993). Legal self-defence for battered women. In M. Hansen, & M. Harway (Eds.), *Battery and family therapy*. Newbury Park: Sage.

Walklate, S. (2016). The metamorphosis of the victim of crime: from crime to culture and the implications for justice. *International Journal for Crime, Justice and Social Democracy, 5*(4), 4–16. http://dx.doi.org/10.5204/ijcjsd.v5i4.280.

Stalking

8

Wayne Petherick
Bond University, Gold Coast, QLD, Australia

CHAPTER OUTLINE

INTRODUCTION

Stalking legislation is well into its third decade of life since first being introduced in California in 1990. The first Australian state to follow suit was Queensland in 1993, while the United Kingdom didn't introduce specific stalking legislation until 2012 (The Protection of Freedoms Act, 2012). Prior to this, victims in the United Kingdom were covered by the Protection from Harassment Act (1997). Stalking is an offense that originated directly as a result of the effect on victims (Mullen, Pathé, & Purcell, 2009), though various other accounts of the impetus for stalking legislation exist.

The Psychology of Criminal and Antisocial Behavior. http://dx.doi.org/10.1016/B978-0-12-809287-3.00008-0

While the offense and the proscribed behaviors differ by jurisdiction, stalking generally consists of a pattern or course of conduct intentionally directed at another person that would cause a reasonable person fear or apprehension. While media coverage of this crime focuses on celebrities and the most extreme cases, the vast majority of victims are neither famous nor represent the worst-case scenario. In fact, the majority of stalkers seem to be trying to, albeit in a socially unacceptable way, establish a relationship with the victim (see Mullen et al., 2009). In short, most stalkers believe that through their constant intrusions the victim will eventually come to like them and perhaps want to establish an intimate relationship with them.

This chapter will examine various aspects of stalking and begins with a discussion of the various definitions of stalking before briefly examining the legal history of stalking. Following this, the incidence and prevalence of stalking are considered before discussing various typologies designed to classify stalking behavior. From there, special populations of stalking victims such as psychologists, celebrities, and university students are examined, before closing the chapter with recidivism among stalkers. This chapter provides a broader and general focus than that of Pathé (this volume), which focuses more on a particular type of stalker—that of the fixated loner.

WHAT IS STALKING?

Stalking in general involves the predatory pursuit and harassment of one person toward another. While first used to describe the pursuit of celebrities by obsessed fans in the 1980s, the term has a more involved history. In fact, only the focus animal has changed from its original use (game sought by hunters) to that common today (humans).

When the first people spread across the globe, they moved into areas where bipeds were an unusual sight, and therefore one to be feared by local fauna. In this primitive time, ranged weapons were poorly suited to the task of hunting at long distances or high speeds, meaning that hunters had a difficult time getting within range to capture their food. A behavioral adaptation followed, whereby the hunter used familiar indigenous animals that were less likely to incite a fear reaction in the game they were hunting. Crouching down behind these animals allowed the hunter to better close the distance and more effectively utilize their ranged weapons.

An animal commonly employed for this purpose was a horse. This was called the stalking horse.

Stalking presents an interesting conundrum with regard to classification as a socially deviant behavior. Many of the acts that constitute stalking are routine, nonharmful, and may be reflective of many acts that make up typical courting behavior (following, surveilling, and telephoning, among others). This author has given many community talks on stalking, from its origins to its classification as a criminal offense, and has found that inevitably, someone in the audience proudly claims "that is exactly how I met my wife and we have been married 30 years!" While humorous and good natured, these claims do highlight how our view of this behavior has changed over the years.

So then, if stalking behavior is largely reflective of courting behavior, albeit an extreme form, how justified are we in identifying it as deviant, and by extension criminal?

The behavior we have come to define and regard as stalking was, in the past, likely considered normal, typical, and acceptable. From this historical point of view, the lengths stalkers would go to in "proving their love" defined the eligibility of a suitor, not a stalker. As such, recent legal debate regarding stalking has revolved around the criminalization of what are, in many situations, extremes of courting behaviors (see D'arcy, 2000; Dennison & Thompson, 2000; Keenahan & Barlow, 1997). Regardless of how we may have viewed this behavior in the past, the current reality is that it is culturally unacceptable, and in many regions, proscribed by criminal law.

This classification is useful for describing many of the component behaviors of stalking that may be considered objectively deviant (for example, Peeping Tom activity, stealing, and threatening). However, other subjectively viewed behaviors, such as repeated calling and following, are often a necessary part of the formation of healthy consensual relationships, depending on the personal preferences of those involved. From an evolutionary perspective, these behaviors are quite necessary for the development of pair-bonding and the continuation of the species.

This, of course, is not intended to excuse intrusive and maladaptive behavior with a delusional, threatening, or criminal intent. Rather, it acknowledges that many healthy relationships require time and persistence to develop. More subjectively viewed behaviors become stalking when the victim experiences fear, expresses this fear, and the intrusion doesn't stop.

While there is some concordance between "normal" behaviors and stalking behaviors, stalking is typically characterized by the behavior's duration and persistence. "In the spectrum of actions that lie between surveillance and physical harm, it is probably repeated harassment that defines the difference between stalking and unwanted courtship by a stranger, rejected suitor, or former lover" (Miller, 2001, p. 5). Additionally, Kienlen (1998, p. 51) notes that "while stalking behavior may be manifested by seemingly benign gestures (e.g., gifts, letters) meant to be symbols of the stalker's affection, the victim reacts in fear due to the stalker's inability or unwillingness to accept the reality that the victim is uninterested in a relationship." To add to the problem of classification, "the behaviors involved in stalking experiences may be called by many names—advances, approaches, flirting, pursuit, harassment, bothering, annoying, courting and so on. The stalker may see what they are doing as one thing, while the person being stalked has quite another view" (Smoyak, 2000, p. 6).

The key to differentiating between the previous "types" of intrusion is perhaps exemplified by the quoted material. Further explanation is warranted.

First, the behavior must be repetitive. It must occur on a number of occasions over a period of time. Many individuals may see a rejection as a challenge, or as a test of the strength of the commitment to acquiring a relationship with a given person.

There can be no doubt that, at least for some, the receiver may choose to test the desire and will of the pursuer by seeing the lengths they are willing to go to in order to prove their worth. This of course blurs the lines for the pursuer, especially where the object of the affections is flippant or vague in their responses.

Over time, of course, any pursuit behavior may turn from being mild—though persistent—attention, to harassment that brings about fear in the target. The point at which this happens may be hard to identify for one or both parties, and may lead to deviant pursuit wherein the target identifies the behavior as nuisance, though does not yet suffer its ill effects.

And it is as this point that, given more time and unwanted attention, the attentions of the stalker may turn criminal when the victim starts to experience fear or apprehension. As suggested by Kienlen and Smoyak, it is the victim's reaction to the pursuit that will satisfy most legal thresholds and define the act as a crime. It would be a rare instance where such a crime was reported to police without the victim experiencing ill effect. The author was involved in one case of a female being stalked by a male over a period of 20 years. When asked why the victim would finally report the harassment after 20 years, her response was simply "I just cannot take it anymore!"

Another example may be illustrative. The author was involved in a case where a female in her early twenties was the subject of the attractions of a male in his early twenties. Initially, she received a number of telephone calls from him, was approached by him in public, and received many handwritten letters announcing his intentions. This went on for some time, and she reported being initially flattered by the attention. Over time, she expressed her desire to remain friends and clearly communicated that she wanted nothing more from the relationship. However, over time the suitor would not take this as a definitive request to cease romantic interest, and he continued in his pursuit. The target of this attention reported that the behavior continued to be flattering and while she repeated her desire for nothing more between them, she also reported the continued flattery that accompanied his attention. In time, she tired of saying no and decided that, as he was a "nice guy," she considered dating him to see if something could come of the relationship. This followed from his latest habit of bursting into tears in the face of rejection all the while announcing his undying love for her. Eventually, she caved to his demands and the couple dated for a period of approximately 18 months. During this time he would call her at home and at work (calls to her home often ran into the triple digits in a given 24-h period and her work colleagues stopped putting calls through to her), he would visit her at home and at work, he would follow when she went out socially (trying to remain covert but mostly failing), and at one point, he held a knife to her throat on one of many occasions she terminated the relationship. Shortly after this she sought the help of the author and a colleague to try and terminate the relationship and subsequent stalking permanently.

This case effectively highlights all three phases of the evolution of fixation and the evolution of that fixation from romantic attention to stalking. First, a motivated individual sought out the attentions of a suitable partner, this moved from initial flattery to rebuff, which was closely followed by deviant attention and later actual stalking. Luckily, this individual was one of a number of persistent harassers who was able to be warned off simply by demonstrating how their behavior violated the criminal law, and the intrusion desisted soon after.

As a parting comment, it should be noted that this description of stalking as a deviance is in no way intended to excuse pathological persistence or criminal behavior—only to define it and frame it in such a way that contextual differences can be highlighted, and to show the often fine line between the acceptable and the criminal.

STALKING BEHAVIORS

Within any discussion that seeks to define stalking, we must also look toward the range of behaviors that constitute this misfeasance at length. Stalking is not characterized simply by the existence of any or all of these behaviors but by their duration and frequency. Ultimately it is these two criteria by which the following will be judged. Before embarking on a discussion of specific behaviors, it will also be useful to examine a variety of studies on stalking behaviors, and their findings with regard to types and prevalence. A summary of these can be found in Table 8.1.

TELEPHONE CALLS

Telephone calls are widely noted as the most common stalking behavior (Häkkänen et al., 2003; Pathé, 2002; Tjaden, 1997), likely owing to the widespread accessibility and relatively low cost of this medium. Also, the proliferation of cellular technology means that stalkers are no longer prohibited by ties to a single location. As much stalking behavior could be identified as following a pattern of compulsion (a drive to engage in a specific behavior) and reinforcement (a reward experienced for performing a certain behavior or act), the telephone represents both a necessary evil and a tool prone to abuse by the stalker. It is not uncommon for phone calls to be excessive with any given victim with several sources citing call frequencies in the hundreds (Petherick, 2008).

WRITTEN COMMUNICATIONS

In some instances the stalker may turn to the printed word as a means to engage their victim. In these cases, the stalker may send letters in favor of the telephone as a more personal form of communication. Electronic mail and text messages would be included in this category. Both forms can provide rich information about the sender. These should be maintained in as close to original condition as possible in the event that specific analysis or intervention is required at a later date.

SURVEILLANCE

Surveillance is another common tool of stalkers. They like to "keep tabs" on their victims, and to know where they are, what they are doing, and who they are doing it

Table 8.1 Nature and Prevalence of Stalking Behaviors

	Sheridan, Davies, and Boon (2001a)	Tjaden (1997)	Budd, Mattinson, and Myhill (2000)	Mullen, Pathé, Purcell, and Stuart (1999)	Häkkänen, Hagelstam, and Santilla (2003)	McFarlane et al. (1999)
Telephone		78%	Obscene 26% Silent 43%	78%	62%	45% (43%)
Letter writing	82%	62%	Letters or cards 23%	65%	12%	10% (15%)
Following		71%	Outside workplace 14% Followed 16% Victim's house 20%	73%	15%	53% (60%)
Watching	91%					47% (46%)
Intimidation			6%			
Assault	32%	31%	Touched or grabbed 6% Used physical force 8%	36%	62% With weapon 12%	
Sexual assault	3% (on 22 victims)	7%	Forced into a sexual act 2%	1% (included in assault category)	4%	
Attempted murder	25%	3%				
Murder					5%	
Threats	53%	58%	9%	58%	To kill 51% Violence 23% Harm children 13%	Phone 22% (12%)
Third party harassment	59% Threatens friends/family 39% Assault 17%			Threats 39% Assault 6%	Threats 19% Violence 7%	Frightened family 24% (31%)
Abduction		2%				
Received gifts		50%	Unwanted items 6%	48%	2%	
E-mail or electronic	"Bug" 13%			Camera or audio 4 cases		
Gathers intelligence	77%					
Trespass	68%				Visits 10%	
Approaches	66%			86%		
Slander	60%					
Damages property	Car 40% Home/garden 38%	36%		40%	35%	34% (49%)
Other	Abuse 51% Assumes victim status 39% Theft 30%			Stalking by proxy 3 cases Spurious legal action 12 cases	Intrudes home 34% Invades privacy 34% Weapon 25% Steals 12%	Weapon 39% (40%) Threatened children 13% (11%) Threatened suicide 19% (34%) Hurt pet 11% (11%)

with at varying times. For the stalker who is not otherwise gainfully engaged, surveillance can be a full-time activity, and can be time-consuming and costly. If the stalker is employed, this can result in lost productivity, work absences, sleeping at work, or loss of employment. While a knee jerk reaction for many employers may be to terminate the stalker, this can prove to be even more destructive. Firstly, it provides the stalker with more time to engage in pursuit behavior, and secondly the victim may be blamed for the stalker's newfound predicament. The individual responsible for the termination may also become a target for the stalker.

When the stalker employs a third party for the surveillance, it is known as stalking by proxy (see Mullen, Pathé, & Purcell, 2000). This third party may be a private investigator, family, and/or friends. In this capacity, the third party allows the stalker indirect access to the victim, and may be conned into believing that the victim is a cheating spouse, a welfare defaulter, or other unsavory character. In these cases, it may be commonplace to blame the third party for their involvement though they are yet another victim of the stalker's manipulations. Unless complicit, they can be held no more accountable than any other person who unwittingly works in pursuance of the stalker's goals.

CONTACT WITH FAMILY AND FRIENDS

When information is not discernible through other channels, the stalker may turn to the family and friends of the victim in an attempt to fill voids, or they may try to recruit friends or family of the victim to their cause, thus making themselves appear the victim. In the case of former intimates, this may add to the stress on the target, and also the maladaptive nature of the stalking as friends may be common to both parties. Other parties may unwittingly provide the offender with information about the victim, their work and recreational activities, new love interests, and even any actions they have taken against the stalker thus far.

In certain situations the stalker may be able to convince family members and friends that the victim is on drugs or experiencing psychological issues, further pointing out that they only wish to help but the victim is pushing them away. The appearance of the alleged addiction or disorder may be validated by the victim's erratic behavior, including distrust of others, which is brought about by stress, lack of sleep, and hypervigilance. Such claims may be easier to make if the victim has failed to inform others of their situation.

UNWANTED GIFTS

There is unlimited breadth to the range of gifts that may be presented to the stalking victim. These may range from the sublime (chocolates, flowers, music) to the obscure (a lock of the stalker's hair, an article of their clothing) to the morbid (a dead animal, feces, a mutilated doll). Again, these can be of critical importance and carry great evidentiary value should the case require criminal justice intervention. Unwanted gifts may also take the form of deliveries such as pizzas, taxis, landscaping supplies, or other services. The choice of the gift itself may also be a telling feature of the stalker's motivation or intent, and the place of purchase may provide other evidence.

OTHER ELECTRONIC TECHNOLOGIES

While mobile phones are among the latest preferred devices, other electronic mediums are readily employed. Pagers are one example, and with the advent of Internet technologies, stalkers are also turning their interests toward cyberspace. This variant is known as cyberstalking, and it is no doubt one of the most common forms of pursuit. Here, stalkers can acquire victims, gather and post information about a victim's movements and associations, communicate with victims, and in some cases, pretend to be them. While a useful and legitimate tool, it too is prone to misuse and can prove to be a sizable hurdle to the stalking victim and investigator alike because much online behavior can occur covertly until it is found by or brought to the attention of another person.

The following example from Wolff (2008) provides one such misuse of the social networking service Facebook:

> Students had the option in the survey to add their own reasons of why they use Facebook. Multiple students added that they use the Scrabulous application, which allows them to play Scrabble with their online friends. In addition, a surprising number of students anonymously entered that they use the social networking site for "stalking."
>
> Elisa Lopez '11, who reports spending two hours on the site a day, describes common stalker-like behavior as she says "I like to keep track of my friends without them knowing." However, Lopez does say that she will contact her friends if she notices something interesting.
>
> While other students may not be as forthcoming as Lopez, many do spend their time on Facebook looking at the profiles of their friends. Many students report spending their time looking at their friends' pictures or their "walls" to see what others have written to them.
>
> Dean Larimore states he is surprised that people use the site to "stalk" each other but he is aware that people communicate more informally and that humor is hard to communicate in a virtual format. He also cautions that there is always the potential for abuse, which makes it important for students to stay in contact with family and friends offline.
>
> Psychology professor Andrew Ward explains this phenomenon by citing several theories. According to the social comparison theory, "we like to compare ourselves relative to other people." Ward states that people will observe their friends online to "see what the norm is in a particular environment."
>
> A male student, "John," allowed us to witness his typical Facebook activity which could be classified as "stalking.' When, "John," signs on to the site, he generally uses the "home" feature to see what is new in the online lives' of his friends. After the "Home" feature, he then proceeds to the "Friends" section to see which friends recently updated their profiles. If he sees something that catches his eye he will open his friend's profile to discover the new updates.

Then once he is in the profile of a friend, he notices a picture of a "mutual friend" or an attractive person who is in their friend's "Swarthmore Friends" category. He then clicks to this new profile and proceeds to look at this person's pictures. Then, he notices another student, which leads to another profile and then more clicks and another profile. In the end, "John" has visited countless number of pages and viewed information and pictures about friends, acquaintances and strangers. "John" says he does not consider this fun, but rather a distraction from work.

While "John's" web surfing or "stalking" may be more sporadic, others stalk with a specific goal in mind. One student divulged that one of their main reasons for using the site was "to look up people my friends have crushes on."

Another student, Shaun Kelly '10, says he specifically searches through his girlfriend's Facebook account. He says he checks the new friends his girlfriend made but explains that that he and his girlfriend have a mutual understanding that "we will both Facebook stalk each other."

In addition to stalking friends, one student stated that he/she uses the site to stalk old friends and admitted "I don't keep in touch, but I observe them." Ward explains that this could be a result of the self-evaluation maintenance theory. He states that people may be interested in tracking the progress of distant acquaintances in order "to assure themselves that they are not falling behind" (in that the old friend has not accomplished something or achieved something new in an unrelated domain).

The lesson to be learned is to be careful what you put on your profile as there is a good chance your friends, acquaintances or strangers may be Facebook stalking you.

A BRIEF HISTORY OF STALKING AND STALKING LEGISLATION

Stalking is considered a crime in most jurisdictions, whether in North America, or Australia, or in other parts of the world. Given the differences in legal systems, it is difficult to provide one catchall legal construction of stalking as each has different basic requirements of the elements that make up the offense. However, legal examinations of stalking suffers the same problem as most others, and Sheridan et al. (2001a) note that one of the most prominent questions to arise out of the criminalization of stalking behavior is *what exactly constitutes stalking?* Therefore, before any attempt is made to examine stalking as a social problem, it is necessary to consider how it is defined, which presents problems of its own.

Mullen, Pathé, and Purcell (2000) suggest that the term *stalking* has come to describe persistent attempts to impose on another various forms of communication or contact. Cupach and Spitzberg (1998, p. 234–235) use the term obsessive relational intrusion (ORI) to describe a more narrow intrusion, defining ORI as "repeated and unwanted pursuit and invasion of one's sense of physical or symbolic privacy by another person, either stranger or acquaintance, who desires and/or presumes an intimate relationship." This is perhaps more like deviant pursuit discussed later in this chapter.

Should a definition contain some discussion of motive, and should it describe the presence or absence of psychiatric disturbance? Should it provide examples of behavior and exactly how broad should it be? It is clear that the answer to these and other questions will not be easily found but the presentation of the following definition may go some way to alleviating the difficulties in defining this multifaceted behavior.

For the purpose of this work, I shall use the definition I have previously provided where stalking is defined as "a constellation of harassment or pursuit behaviors that may, when considered in isolation seem innocuous, but when viewed collectively and in the context in which they occurred, constitute a maladaptive and proscribed course of conduct." This is useful for a number of reasons.

First, it acknowledges not only the broad range of behaviors that make up stalking but also notes their potential innocence when viewed individually. Second, it makes no attempt to explain motive as any definition would by necessity have to encompass cases born of desperation, revenge, and sexual stimulation, which represent a diverse group of drives. Lastly, it acknowledges the maladaptive nature of stalking behaviors when viewed collectively and in the context in which they have occurred.

More to the focus of this chapter, why is this behavior, which is centuries old, now considered both criminal and deviant? As explained in Finch (2001, p. 83) "the social context of the criminalization of stalking requires exploration in order to understand why stalking was deemed to merit legal intervention at a particular point in time."

The social milieu in which stalking emerged tended to involve a celebrity victim with an obsessed and even deluded fan as the stalker. This high-profile history is reflected in the expectations some have about what they will find when researching the subject as discussed by Perez (1993, p. 264): "When I began researching the topic of stalking...I considered it an interesting subject, but one with limited potential for substantial legal research. I expected to find three or four magazine articles dealing with celebrities and their obsessed fans."

The realization soon follows, however, that this media-fueled expectation is ill informed. "Joe Citizen" is much more likely to be a victim of this crime than are celebrities, though there can be no doubt that celebrity cases are largely responsible for elevating stalking in the social conscience.

To examine stalking as a crime, it is necessary to do two things. The first is to discuss, in a general sense, how something comes to be recognized as a social problem, and how these social problems qualify as being of a sufficiently serious nature to become the subject of criminal law. Secondly, we must identify those features in specific actions or omissions that make them appropriate for criminalization.

The law states a contingency specifying that a particular act (and in many systems, the omission of an act) will be followed by some kind of legal penalty (Blackburn, 1993). While there is some difference in particular laws (for example, not all jurisdictions have stalking laws), most advanced systems penalize conduct described as treason, murder, aggravated assault, theft, robbery, burglary, arson, and rape (Blackburn, 1993). While the nature of these acts falls somewhere along a continuum of severity, they are all generally recognized by the fact that they constitute social harm.

The basis of any legal system is the acceptance of a set of norms or rules that govern practice in a given society at a given time. These norms or rules are dynamic and subject to change, usually as a result of shifting societal standards and mores. Examples include the repeal of laws relating to homosexuality and of course outlawing stalking behavior.

But what exactly makes stalking worthy of prohibition? Victim impact is the most reasonable answer, as the effects on victims are considerable and enduring. It is also likely with each victim that the consequences of the invasion will last far beyond the stalking itself, creating chronic psychological suffering. While some may argue that stalking is not serious[1], is easily tolerable, or may even be flattering, there can be no doubt of its destructive nature. It is therefore not unreasonable to expect the law to provide some protection.

Queensland was the first Australian state to legislate against this behavior, with initial protection in the United Kingdom falling under the Protection from Harassment Act of 1997. Stalking laws were enacted in California, the first American state to have such laws in 1990 (Meloy, 1999; Sheridan et al., 2001a; Sheridan, Davies, & Boon, 2001b). While it is often noted that the catalyst for stalking legislation in the United States was the murder of actress Rebecca Schaeffer by Robert John Bardo (see Holmes, 2001; Morowitz, 2003), the real impetus for the introduction of legislation was a number of domestic violence murders (Lemon, 1994). Municipal Court Judge John Watson of Orange County was disillusioned with the then-current state of the protection-order system, notably repeated breeches of orders, and approached Senator Royce who introduced the bill that became California Penal Code 646.9 (Lemon, 1994). As stated by Watson (1998):

> While I was a Municipal Court Judge in Newport Beach in 1990, five women were murdered by ex-lovers, estranged husbands, or would-be suitors. All the victims had restraining orders and were terrified for their lives. Each told friends that they believed they would be killed by the person named in the orders.
>
> After the killings, there was a feature article about the tragedies. A police officer was interviewed and was asked why their department hadn't taken any steps to protect these innocent victims. He answered that until a crime was committed there was nothing they could do.

---

[1] Anecdotal experience has shown this author that despite the deleterious effects of stalking victimization, many friends, family, colleagues, and even members of the criminal justice system fail to acknowledge this. Some have even gone as far as to suggest the harassment is flattering, or that the focus of the attention should consider themselves lucky to have someone who is interested.

Therefore, I drafted the first anti-stalking law in the United States, Penal Code Section 646.9. This section makes it a felony to cause another, or their family, to be in reasonable fear for their safety and carries a state prison sentence.

I presented my idea to then State Senator Ed Royce (R). We went to Sacramento together and made a presentation to the appropriate Senate and Assembly Committees. The law passed and within three years was copied in every state in the United States.

Many of the difficulties in developing so-called "antistalking" legislation rest in the fact that the offense is often characterized by elements of psychological terror as opposed to being the result of direct physical contact or assault. This makes quantifying the behaviors themselves difficult for the uninitiated, and creates further problems in identifying the extent of harm to the victim. Swanwick (1996, p. 26) has made the following observation:

The offense and its criminality are unusual in that often no physical elements are present, only mental elements, and render liable to criminal sanction activities which on the surface are innocuous and commonplace but which, when constituting a course of conduct and with the necessary intent, form the basis of the criminal offense. It is therefore, a difficult offense for which to legislate. Existing criminal sanctions have not proved adequate to provide redress or protection against the activities which constituted stalking.

Despite the positive move many jurisdictions have made toward enacting viable stalking legislation, there are many who are concerned over specific elements of it. For example, Weiner (1995) and Goode (1995) both highlighted imperfections in the earlier laws. They note that much of the legislation is vague and poorly defined, and suffers from "overbreadth"—the inclusion of much activity that is not in reality stalking. The actual role played by intent is another issue, as are the difficulties faced by miscarriages of justice resulting from any collection of these issues. For example, the behaviors of a particular stalker may not originate from an intent to harm but these behaviors may be just as injurious.

Stalking laws are often framed in response to local preoccupations, whether that be protecting the famous, ex-partners, or in strengthening existing laws when inequities are identified (Mullen, Pathé, & Purcell, 2000). This problem is also framed in part by its connectedness to preexisting social issues. Prominent among many of the first highly publicized stalking cases were instances of murder, rape, or grievous bodily harm, and so part of its recognition is undoubtedly connected to other victim harms that are already within public and legal discourse.

LEGISLATIVE FRAMEWORK

While we now have an adequate understanding of the development of stalking as a problem of social concern, we must now turn to an examination of the legislative context within which stalking laws have developed. This will be done by first detailing those crimes that predated stalking legislation that may have applied in cases of serious harassment.

Barlow and Kauzlarich (2002) identify crime as an act that violates a criminal law. Inherent within this definition is the notion that to violate a law, we must act in some way, that is, some form of behavior must be exhibited that carries a sanction under the criminal law. In the language of the law, this is known as actus reus. I can *think* about doing something as often as I like. I can think about following a love interest 24/7, following her home, surveilling her while she eats at her favorite restaurant, and observing her through the window of her gym. This fantasy can consume me to the point where other aspects of my life will suffer. There is nothing anyone can do about this because we cannot be held legally responsible for what we think of doing (with very exceptions, such as in conspiracy to commit a certain crime). It is not until these thoughts (cognitions, or mens rea under the law) become coupled with behaviors (actions) that they fall within the ambit of the criminal law and become subject to penalty.

It has been noted that the "psychiatric literature on stalking has been hampered by the difficulty arriving at an agreed definition of stalking" (Stocker & Nielssen, 2000, p. 5), and that "there has been much debate over what elements or processes comprise stalking" (Sheridan, Blaauw & Winkel, 2003, p. 148). These authors further note that because of this most commentators borrow from legal discourse in defining this problem, which can be problematic in itself. Sheridan et al. (2003) point out that some legislation describes which behaviors are punishable, whereas other legislation applies only broad terms in defining what constitutes stalking.

Meloy (1998, p. 2) notes that while legislation differs from state to state, stalking provisions generally have three criteria. These are: "(1) a pattern (course of conduct) of behavioral intrusion upon another person that is unwanted; (2) an implicit or explicit threat that is evidenced in the pattern of behavioral intrusion; and (3) as a result of these behavioral intrusions, the person who is threatened experiences reasonable fear." In an earlier paper, Meloy and Gothard (1995) defined stalking as the willful, malicious, and repeated following or harassing of another person that threatens his or her safety. Holmes (2001, p. 20) provides four components of stalking: a deliberate course of actions; a repeated course of action; this action causes a reasonable person to feel threatened, terrorized, harassed, or intimidated; and this action actually causes the victim to feel threatened, terrorized, harassed, or intimidated. Regardless of the jurisdiction, the classification of stalking remains fairly uniform, and it is mainly in specific legal requirements, such as the number of individual acts, that they differ.

As stated, legislators have found it difficult to frame stalking laws because many of the behaviors that constitute stalking are routine, mundane, or harmless (Sheridan & Davies, 2001). In the United Kingdom, it was not deemed appropriate to tightly define stalking because the clustering of a number of seemingly innocuous behaviors when taken together constitute stalking harassment (Sheridan, 2001). This is one reason why "legislatures have experienced great difficulty in framing legal sanctions to effectively outlaw stalking activities" (Sheridan & Davies, 2001, p. 3). When viewed in isolation, stalking behaviors are perceptually nonthreatening, though when you look at the universe of behavior in a given case, and factor in the duration, it is reasonable to see how it constitutes an intrusive and deleterious invasion of private life.

INCIDENCE AND PREVALENCE OF STALKING

While a number of studies indicate the distribution of stalking in the community, the true nature of this crime likely remains hidden. This is because of a number of methodological issues within the research, and a more pervasive criminological phenomenon—the dark figure of crime, which is the difference in official figures between the reported or recorded incidence of a criminal event and its actual incidence (Hagan, 1984; Penney, 2014). Methodological issues range from small samples to the use of poor questionnaires and may include other more problematic aspects such as bias. The truth of the matter with regard to the incidence (the frequency of occurrence) and prevalence (the number of cases in a population at a specific time) is that anything we currently have is a best or educated guess.

In Australia, the first community study was undertaken by the Australian Bureau of Statistics (ABS) in 1996 and titled Women's Safety (McLennan, 1996). The ABS found that 2.4% of women over the age of 18 had been stalked by a man in the last 12 months, with 15% having been stalked by a man at least once in their lifetime. Of those polled, 7.5% were still undergoing victimization at the time of the survey. This study showed that women were more likely to be stalked by strangers than men they knew.

This study is not without its critics, however. Mullen et al. (2009) note that among other things the study did not include in its definition a fear criteria common to many stalking statutes, it did not study the frequency of explicit threats or violence related to the stalking, and it did not include males as victims. Despite these criticisms, the ABS study was one of the first of its kind and illustrated that stalking is a significant social problem in Australia.

Purcell, Pathé, and Mullen (2000) conducted a smaller scale study of their own involving a random selection of 3700 men and women in Victoria. For those who responded positively to those forms of harassment in the definition, further information was sought about the frequency and presence of fear during the harassment. The study found that 23.4% of the respondents had been stalked at some point in their life, with 5.8% being stalked in the 12 months prior to the survey. Approximately 10% were subjected to prolonged harassment involving multiple intrusions that lasted at least four weeks. Females were far more likely to be a victim of stalking in their lifetime. Those who were younger were more likely to be stalked with those aged 18–35 making up 31.8% of the sample, 36–55 making up 27.6%, and only 14.6% of those over 56 years of age reported being stalked.

In the biggest and most widely cited study in the United States, the National Institute of Justice noted that "survey findings indicate that stalking is a bigger problem than previously thought, affecting about 1.4 million victims annually" (Tjaden, 1997, p. 1). Other reports indicate that 8% of women and 2% of men have been stalked at some time in their life, which is over one million women and over a quarter of a million men (Tjaden & Thoennes, 1998). This study (of 8000 men and 8000 women) also found that most victims are female, that 52% of all victims are aged 18–29, and that women are significantly more likely than men (59% vs. 30%) to be stalked by someone with whom they had a prior relationship.

In the United Kingdom the picture is just as grim. The British Home Office produced a report on the nature of stalking from the British Crime Survey, which showed that 11.8% of adults aged 16 to 59 were the subject of unwanted and persistent attention at least one time since age 16 (Budd et al., 2000). They further found that, like their Australian and US counterparts, victims were more likely to be female (73% of the survey). Another similarity is that youth tends to elevate one's risk of victimization, with almost a quarter of women aged 16 to 19 and a fifth of women aged 20 to 29 reporting stalking harassment. This is compared with only one-tenth of women aged 55 to 59.

Perhaps the most widely studied subpopulation are university students. There are a number of potential reasons for this. Firstly, the age at which one leaves for university is generally the age at which many people experience their first "adult" relationship. Secondly, for many people, this is the first time away from home and the social and familial support networks that may have been relied on in previous periods of crisis. This may also mark the first serious period of experimentation with alcohol and/or drugs. Lastly, some sources have indicated that younger females, typically aged between 18 and 35 (Purcell et al., 2000 and Tjaden & Thoennes, 1998, respectively), are the most common victims of stalking.

Fremouw, Westrup, and Pennypacker (1997) conducted a study on stalking among undergraduate college students in West Virginia. This study explored two facets of stalking with the first assessing the behaviors of those who stalk and the second assessing the victims of stalking. Also considered was the relationship of the victim to the stalker. Two actual studies were conducted, with the second using a sample of 299 participants with a revised questionnaire. This second study was designed to replicate the results of the first.

Their findings suggest that stalking among this population is higher than that indicated by most community samples. In this study, 44 of the 165 female respondents (26.6%) and 17 of 129 (14.7%) male respondents reported that they had been stalked. In the second study, the rate was somewhat higher with 35.2% of females and 18.4% of males reporting victimization. Interestingly, this study also inquired as to the number of respondents who had themselves stalked another. Only three of 129 males responded in the positive, meaning that either the participants underreported their own stalking behaviors (a possible, even likely outcome) or that those individuals responsible for the victimization were outside of the study sample. Most females (47% in the first study and 40% in the second) were stalked by someone they had "seriously dated." Males were stalked by someone they had "seriously dated" in about one-quarter of the reported instances, 24%.

In a similar study, Fisher, Cullen, and Turner (2002) conducted a national survey in the United States of stalking among college women. Their sample was considerably larger than the previous study, with some 4446 respondents completing the survey. All told, the response rate was around 85%. Of this sample, 13.1% of females had been stalked at least once since the academic year had begun. Of those who had been stalked, 12.7% has been stalked twice, and 2.3% were stalked three or more times. This rate is also higher than many community samples. Nearly all of the stalkers were male. Coleman (1997) carried out a similar study into the extent of student victimization. With 141 undergraduates as a sample, 29.1% responded positively to being stalked. Furthermore, 9.2% of the students stated that this repeated attention was either malicious, physically threatening, or fear inducing.

In a more recent study, Basile, Swahn, Chen, and Saltzman (2006) gave national prevalence estimates in the United States. This study of 9684 interviews (4877 women and 4807 men) showed that of those aged 18 and older, 4.5% reported being stalked in a way they perceived as threatening. About 7% of women were stalked and about 2% of men were victimized. These findings were in line with the previous findings of the National Institute of Justice.

All of these studies tend to suggest that the picture of stalking in English-speaking countries is fairly universal—young females tend to be victimized more often by males they know or with whom they have had a former relationship.

STALKING TYPOLOGIES AND STALKING RISK ASSESSMENT

Over time there have been numerous typologies developed to understand stalking behavior—far too many to canvass in a single chapter. As such, the focus will be on a number of the main typologies including one of the first to be developed by Zona and colleagues, through to the typology of Mullen and his colleagues in Australia. The focus here will be on the Mullen et al.s' typology as this is also used as the basis for the Stalking Risk Profile (SRP), which is the "gold standard" in stalking risk assessment.

The aim of each typology will differ greatly according to who developed it, coupled with the purpose for its development. Some typologies have been created with law enforcement and investigations in mind (for example, the Sheridan and Boon system), while others are motivational in nature, describing the motivation for the offender and victim (for example, Petherick & Sinnamon, 2014), and others still are mental health or pathology based (Geberth's, 1992 discussion of stalkers is one such example). Others, such as the Mullen et al. system are multiaxial, covering many different facets of the stalking spectrum.

The first formal classification system for stalkers was developed by Zona, Palarea, and Lane (1998) while working for the Los Angeles Police Department (LAPD) Threat Management Unit (TMU). This unit was the first dedicated police unit established specifically to deal with the stalking threat. Their typology was considerably more basic than recent efforts, though this could be understood given the state of the art at the time. The first type was known as the simple obsessional, which was the most common, and involved those cases where the victim and the stalker have some prior relationship. A significant number of these cases are an outgrowth of a prior intimate relationship (Zona et al., 1998), though the relationship can include simple acquaintances or work colleagues.

In the love obsessional type there is a lack of an existing relationship between the stalker and the victim (Zona et al., 1998). This type is likely to victimize celebrities and may be the "obsessed fan" (Racine & Bullock, 2014). Zona et al. suggest that this type may also involve noncelebrities, and provide the following example (p. 78):

> A woman began receiving harassing phone calls for no apparent reason. The male caller would first discuss his interest in dating her, but would then become angry and threaten to harm her. The investigation ultimately revealed that the night prior to the first phone call, the woman was out at a dance club. After exiting the club, she verbally exchanged her phone number with another person. The perpetrator happened to be with earshot of the victim and, while eavesdropping on her conversation, memorized her phone number. He then began a campaign of harassment that lasted for many months.

The final type in the Zona et al. (1998) classification is the erotomanic. In erotomania, the sufferer has a delusional belief that they are loved by another, where the sufferer is usually a female and the object of affections a male, usually of higher social status (Jordan et al., 2006; Mullen, 1997; Pinals, 2007). This is not a common diagnosis in the general population but may not be unusual in stalking (Zona et al., 1998). These authors later added false victimization syndrome to account for those cases that were false reports.

Sheridan and Boon (2002) present a typology that differs in two important ways. First, it is based on information from British crime victims as opposed to being based on literature reviews or mental health or police files. Second, it is aimed explicitly at law enforcement, for "people who require guidance as to patterns in offender motivation and the contingent course of best practice for case management" (p. 69). This classification system has four types: ex-partner harassment/stalking; infatuation harassment; delusional fixation stalking; and sadistic stalking. These will now be discussed at greater length, with the following information being taken from Sheridan and Boon (2002).

The ex-partner type is the most common and represented 50% of their overall sample of 124 cases. This stalker is driven by bitterness and hate that is linked to relationship history, which is likely to have involved domestic violence. Friends and family may be recruited to the cause, and any new relationships will trigger feelings of jealousy and aggression. The relationship may be characterized by high levels of physical violence, threat, and property damage.

The infatuation harassment type represented 18.5% of the total sample and has two subtypes. The first is young love and the second midlife love. Both exhibit similar behaviors and represent the same underlying motivations, though each has different case management implications. The target is beloved and all pervasive in the thoughts of the stalker, and the victim is the focus of intense fantasy. There is an intense yearning with particular attention to what "might be." Because of this, there are usually low levels of danger to the victim.

In delusional fixation stalking (15.3% of the sample), the stalker has a delusional conviction that there is a current and idealized relationship with the target. There is not usually any significant relationship with the victim, and the intrusion is usually not characterized by threats. As they are possessed of a delusional belief of idealized love, the stalker is not usually open to reason with or from the victim. Their perception is that of reciprocity, and where the relationship does not fit within their idealized view, another will be blamed for interfering.

In the last type, the victim is seen as prey of the predatory stalker. This is the sadistic type and represents the smallest group (12.9%). This is typical of sadistic offending subgroups who usually comprise the smaller/est samples of typologies (as with the typologies presented by Hazelwood, 2009 for rape). The victims of these types of stalker are low-level acquaintances, and the "methods of the perpetrator tend to have a negative orientation designed to disconcert, unnerve, and thus take power away from the victim" (p. 76). The stalker progressively seeks to take power away from all aspects of the victim's life. While these authors claim that "the offender's gratification is rooted in the desire to extract evidence of the victim's powerlessness with inverse implications for his power" (p. 76), which implies sadism, it should be noted that this alone does not comport to the core of sadistic behavior. Power over a person is not enough to meet the criteria for sadistic behavior, which must specifically be linked to sexual arousal or gratification from physical or psychological pain (American Psychiatric Association, 2013).

In 2006 Mohandie, Meloy, McGowan, and Williams proposed the RECON typology of stalking, based on the relationship type between the victim and offender, and on the context of the stalking. Two of the authors reviewed over 2300 case files over a 17-month period involving stalking, criminal harassment, menacing, terrorist threats, or domestic violence. The study found four groups, some with subtypes: Intimate (IA, 50% of the sample), Acquaintance (IB, 13% of the sample), Public Figure (IIA, 27% of the sample), and Private Stranger (IIB, 10% of the sample).

Unless otherwise stated, all of the following information comes from Mohandie et al. (2006).

The Intimate Stalker is the most malignant and has a violent criminal history, abuses drugs and alcohol, but is not likely to be psychotic. Over one-half will physically assault their victims and virtually all will reoffend, and do so in a much shorter time frame than the other types. The authors identify that the risk of physical violence for this type is supported by other research indicating that a prior intimate relationship increases the possibility of violence. This type is likely to have an insecure attachment style and personality disorder.

Acquaintance Stalkers are mostly males, with about one in five being female. About one-third will assault the victim or engage in property damage. When there are threats, they will be made regularly, and pursuit while sporadic will endure for two years on average. With the Intimate Type, a less intimate bond with the target will likely reduce the possibility of violence though their desire to establish a relationship is described as "ravenous" (p. 153).

For the Public Figure type, targets are usually celebrity figures, or those otherwise in the public eye. Twenty-seven percent of this group are female and about one in three are male victims. The public figure pursuer is likely to be older and also more likely to be psychotic. They are less likely to threaten the target (14%) and are more likely to express their love or desire for help. These authors note that with regard to violence, this may be reduced owing to the increased security often found surrounding public figures. It is also noted that they may have a preference for nonproximity-based contact.

Representing the smallest number, the Private Stranger Stalker would be somewhere between the Public Figure and Intimate Stalker. Many are male, mentally ill, and about one in ten evidence suicidality. They are direct in their communications and are more likely to want to communicate with their victim. Half of this type threaten, and nearly one-third are violent to person or property. One in seven assaults their target, and about 25% repeat offend.

One of the strengths of the typology is that the authors go to great lengths to discuss and describe the associated research that supports their findings, demonstrating their reliability.

While not a typology on stalking, Petherick and Sinnamon (2014) discuss a general motivational typology that is useful for describing the motivation in stalking. This typology is different in that it describes the motivational milieu for both offenders and victims, which tells you not only why the stalker is pursuing a victim or victims but also why the victim behaved in the way that they did that led to the stalking in the first place. Moreover, when applied to victims, this typology leads to a better understanding of why some may be repeatedly victimized through stalking or any other crime. As such, it can help prevent further crimes from being perpetrated.

This typology is based on the pathways model, where motivation is tempered through the complex development and interplay of emotions, self-esteem, and personality development. It is based on the early seminal work of Groth (1979) and Groth, Burgess, and Holmstrom (1979), on the later work of Hazelwood (2009), and finally the first general adaptation of this in Turvey (1999 and subsequent editions). The Petherick and Sinnamon adaptation also incorporates other types not present in the previous works, including a type from the MTC-R3 (Massachusetts Treatment Center – Revision 3). Research is currently being undertaken to validate this typology, with promising early results. These typologies are presented in brief in the following discussion.

Reassurance-oriented individuals have low self-esteem and low self-worth, and their behavior represents an attempt to restore this. Their self-efficacy is also low, and this may be reflected in poor social skills. For offenders, they believe their intrusions upon the victim will eventually win them over predicated on the belief that repetition will eventually prove their worth and that the attention will ultimately be reciprocated. For victims, the attention may be viewed as flattering, and antisocial or criminal behavior may be tolerated because the attention they are receiving fills a void. They may also tolerate it because they believe that being in a relationship is better than being alone. Reassurance-oriented behavior is strongly represented by a negative inner narrative such as "this is what I deserve" or "abuse is part of being in a relationship."

In assertive-oriented behavior, the individual also has low self-esteem and low self-worth, but this is expressed through power and control over another individual. This can be manifested by making themselves feel better by making another feel bad. This can be through general behavior and demeanor, or verbally by putting others down, telling embarrassing or demeaning stories about them, spreading rumors and falsities, or any other similar behavior. They continually push their own agenda and will onto others, and they may cultivate a reputation for being unpleasant to be around for extended periods of time.

Operating from a general base of anger, retaliatory victims or offenders are fighting back against a real or perceived wrong. Victims may be specifically targeted over something they have actually done, or they may be representative of some group, agency, or institution. Retaliatory behavior may be easy to identify because the angry individual will usually identify what they believe you have done to them. This behavior will typically surface as a result of some trigger, and this may have nothing to do with anything the victim has actually done. In victims, they may be angry at what a partner has or has not done and act out accordingly. For example, one person stated that she thanked her husband's boss for allowing her husband to bring home stationery from work. He stated that he had not allowed him at all, and that this constituted theft. She was well aware of this fact, and claimed that she did it as payback for the long hours her husband put into his job. He was sanctioned as a result.

While not in any of the previous permutations, the pervasively angry type is in the MTC-R3, and represents a person who is not angry about a real or imagined wrong but is instead generally bitter about most or all aspects of their life. The pervasively angry offender isn't angry at the victim; they are usually just at the wrong place at the wrong time when the anger is expressed. It should go without saying that for victims, either of the anger types may be prone to further or escalated victimization when they express their anger at the wrong person.

Excitation-oriented offenders are sadistic. This means they get sexual satisfaction from the pain and suffering of others. While the term has taken on a casual meaning to describe anyone who inflicts suffering on another, the sexual satisfaction is a requirement for actual sadism to be identified. This type is rare and is the most difficult to adapt to victim behavior.

The materially oriented seek money or goods. This type was identified in the early versions of the typology as profit, but was changed to materialism because offenders and victim may not seek only money, nor may they actually profit in the literal sense of the word. For example, drug addicts who steal to support a habit may not be profiting at all but rather just taking enough to get by. Victims may stay with an abusive partner because they can't afford to live on their own, and their finances may be such that they are easy prey for scams and cons. Their position may be the result of low or poor employment, bad financial decisions, an overbearing partner who deprives them of money, or when they have costly habits (such as gambling or drugs).

The final type is preservation oriented. These individuals engage in behavior that, most usually, revolves around personal safety, or the safety of others for whom you feel responsible such as children. In offenders, this may result in a first-strike mentality where they feel like "it's me or them." Victims may feel compelled to stay in a bad relationship because they fear for their or their children's safety should they leave.

While not the newest typology, that developed by Mullen et al. (2009) is certainly one of the more widely discussed. It is also the only typology that is directly linked to an empirically derived risk assessment instrument specific to the crime of stalking, called the Stalking Risk Profile[2].

The typology on which the SRP is based was first presented in Mullen et al. (1999) and was later presented in *Stalkers and Their Victims* (Mullen et al., 2009). This typology is multiaxial in that it covers a number of different behaviors and outcomes, and does not focus on a single axis, such as motivation. As discussed in Mullen et al. (2009, p. 66):

> *This typology attempts to capture the function of the behavior for the stalker. What are the stalker's purposes in pursuing this particular course of action, and what needs and desires are being satisfied? The stalking behaviors have a meaning for the stalker which relates in some way to their goals.*

There are five types, being the rejected, the intimacy seeker, the incompetent (suitor), the resentful, and the predatory. As presented in Mullen et al. (1999), these are also presented in the order of their prevalence in the data set. Of the 145 stalkers initially studied, there were 52 Rejected, 40 Intimacy Seekers, 22 Incompetent, 16 Resentful, and 6 Predatory types (these ranking of the types is also the same in a later study as presented in Mullen et al. (2009)).

Each type will be discussed in more detail following (unless otherwise stated the following information is from Mullen et al., 1999 or 2009).

The rejected stalker is the most common type and the pursuit begins after the breakdown of an intimate relationship, or when their partner indicates that they want to end the relationship, where the aim of the stalking is to either reconcile the relationship or to exact revenge. The stalker may perceive that the rejection is humiliating or that the relationship is somehow special or that it will never be replaced. Because of the underlying emotional attachment, this type can be the most persistent and the most difficult to dislodge from the pursuit.

Loss could be combined with "frustration, anger, jealousy, vindictiveness, and sadness, in ever-changing proportions" (Mullen et al., 1999, p. 1246). These stalkers often had personality disorders, most prominent being narcissistic and antisocial, though nine of the original 52 had delusional disorders. While associating with masculine roles, they often have strong dependency traits and externalize blame.

Intimacy seekers and incompetent suitors make up the largest group of stranger stalkers, and both types are attempting to establish a relationship with the object of their affections. In their original study it was noted that this significant other was

---

[2] The author has done the SRP training and would recommend it to anyone should the opportunity arise.

identified as their "true love" (Mullen et al., 1999). In this group psychopathology was high, with the sample identified as having erotomania, schizophrenia, mania, and morbid infatuations or personality disorders. In this group, the romanticized or idealized relationship with the victim may become a substitute for a real relationship, and the feeling of being in love may reinforce the pursuit behaviors.

For the incompetent suitor type, they are typically unified in their lack of social skills, particularly as they relate to intimate partner skills. For some their attitude may be "willful ignorance" or "cavalier indifference" rather than actual social deficit (Mullen et al., 2009, p. 86). Incompetent suitors can range from those who are completely bereft of social functioning to those who are assertive, overbearing, or "insensitive egoists" (p. 86) who expect women to instantly fold to their display or machismo. Though predominantly male, females can also be incompetent suitors, and men as well as women can be targeted. Harassment from this type is usually brief, lasting for the shortest time in this typology, but they are also most prone to recidivate. This may be because they are unlikely to appreciate the gravity or impact of their behavior.

The resentful type originates in feelings of injustice, where the stalker takes on the role of the aggrieved party, and the stalking is a vehicle through which retribution is exacted. While the stalking may be brief, represented by feelings that a wrong has been righted, the duration may also be extended, where the feelings of power and control over the victim fuel continued harassment. The victim may also start out as, or become representative of, people who have responsible for indignations over the stalker's life. When being interviewed, this type will likely present as the victim.

In the predatory type, the stalking is usually preparatory to some other attack, whether physical or sexual. This type enjoys surveillance and observation of the victim, who may not even be aware of their attention focused upon them, until such a time as an approach or attack is effected. As with other types and studies, this group is small and quite specialized. In some situations, "these behaviors may in themselves by sexually arousing, providing erotic gratification from the sense of power over the victim and, in some instances, their capacity to humiliate them by unwanted intrusion and the arousal of fear" (Mullen et al., 2009, p. 110). So while the stalker's behavior may result in sexual arousal, in cases where the victim is not privy to the pursuit this would not be sufficient to meet the threshold for sadistic behavior. This would require both (1) that the stalker experiences sexual arousal or gratification, and (2) that the victim experiences physical or psychological pain or suffering.

As stated, this typology forms the basis of the new standard of stalking risk assessment instruments, the SRP. This tool is based on the results of research into stalking types, including those factors that are associated with an elevated risk for violence. Beyond being merely a tool for assessing risk, this instrument classifies risk across four domains: the risk of violence, the risk of persistence, the risk of recurrence, and the risk of psychosocial damage to the stalker. The SRP belongs to a general set of instruments collectively called structured professional judgements, where the evaluation is made based on the presence or absence of various features within a case. Coupled with the general risk factors for violence are a number of low-frequency but high-risk factors, such as threat/control override disorders (also known as delusional misidentification disorders) including the Capgras and Fregoli delusions. These "red flag risk factors" (Mackenzie et al., 2009) also include suicidal ideation, homicidal ideation, last-resort thinking, and psychopathy. The presence of any of these factors is typically viewed as automatically elevating the risk status to high.

While the training on the SRP takes a number of days, where minutiae of the instrument and scoring are taught, the use is relatively simple. It is this distilled presentation that will be employed in this chapter for the sake of brevity.

First, the evaluator uses a flowchart provided in the training manual to determine the type of stalker they are dealing with, based on the previous Mullen et al.s' typology. This is done by answering a series of IF-THEN or YES/NO type propositions. For example, "is the target the primary victim?" – YES – then "is the stalker known to the primary victim?" – YES. Following this are a series of flowchart questions based on the relationship, apparent initial motivation, and psychopathology, followed by the stalker type. So if the answer to the relationship question is "former sexual partner," and the apparent initial motivation is to reestablish the relationship, then the classification would be the rejected type.

Once the stalker type has been established, the evaluator consults the appropriate evaluation management sheet (EMS) and works progressively through each of the above sections. Once the form has been completed, the evaluator then makes a judgment, based on the presence or absence of the factors. As stated these relate to violence risk, the risk of persistence (whether the stalking will continue), the risk of recurrence (either with the same victim or a new one should the stalking stop), and finally the risk of psychosocial damage to the stalker.

Each EMS is subtly different from the others, representing different factors identified in the research on the stalking types relating to various risks. Once the process is finished, the evaluator then communicates their findings to the client or victim.

Should the reader want a further but still brief understanding of this tool, they should consult McEwan, Pathé, and Ogloff (2011).

PHYSICAL AND PSYCHOLOGICAL EFFECTS OF STALKING

With only limited information being available on the effects of stalking on victims (Meloy, 1996; Pathé & Mullen, 1997), there is a general lack of understanding about the nature and severity of its impact. Typically studies have focused on the classifications and diagnosis of stalkers. While this body of literature has been growing, historically "very few studies have considered the economic and social effect on victims of being stalked and even less attention has been paid to the psychological or psychiatric consequences of stalking" (Blaauw, Winkel, Sheridan, Malsch, & Arensman, 2002, p. 23). While it is reasonable to conclude that the latter may be a logical extension of the former, surprisingly few studies have addressed this (see Abrams & Robinson, 2002; Pathé & Mullen, 1997). Blaauw, Winkel, and Arensman (2000, p. 3) agree, "despite the growing awareness that stalking is a considerable public health issue, there is hardly any information available about the toll that stalking inflicts on victims."

When dealing with stalking victims, there can be little doubt about the injurious nature of the behavior. Hall (1998, p. 136) notes that "living in fear, especially over a prolonged duration of time, takes a toll on the quality of human life." The impact of stalking on a given victim can be manifested as either physical or psychological, or a combination of both, and may range from mild (restlessness or concern) to severe (akin to posttraumatic stress disorder, PTSD). Another interesting facet for study would be how immediate disruptions to the victims' functioning (general increases in anxiety and illness and an increase in time away from work) affect broader social concerns such as negative impacts on industry. Also, there is little exploration into the weighting of various stalking behaviors on victim psychopathology, for instance, whether physical pursuit is more injurious than repetitive telephoning.

In many cases, one of the difficulties in quantifying the effects of stalking is separating the physical (assault including sexual assault, damage to property, etc.) from the psychological (loss of sleep, absence from work, and social withdrawal) (Petherick, 2008). Indeed, the latter class of harm may not be identified by the victim as related to the stalking, even in cases where a physical ailment is the result of a mental one (Petherick, 2008). Furthermore, many legal proscriptions for stalking do not recognize psychological distress as a form of harm.

In one Australian study (Pathé & Mullen, 1997), 37% of the victims surveyed met the full diagnostic criteria for PTSD (see American Psychiatric Association, 1994), while another 18% met all of the criteria except a single episode of stress involving actual or threatened physical harm. Of the other features noted in this study, 82% of victims modified their typical activities, 73% engaged additional security measures, 70% curtailed social outings, and "a preponderance of victims described a deterioration in their physical and/or mental health since the onset of the harassment" (p. 14).

Overall, many victims become hypervigilant and socially withdrawn, exercising caution and suspicion in social relationships. Brewster (1997) showed that 44% of victims had become distrustful or suspicious, 42% fearful, 31% nervous, 27% angry, 36% paranoid, and 21% depressed.

One survey of the effects of stalking on victims in South-East Queensland (Monico, 1998) found that 89% of the participants made changes to their usual activities (which generally involved a downturn of activity). Eighty-four percent of those surveyed changed their habits relating to social outings with many noting they rarely go out alone. In addition, 43% changed their place of work, 14% decreased their work attendance, and 22% stopped work altogether. Most of the participants (68%) had moved residence to escape the harassment, and a majority (84%) altered security arrangements in some way. In another study primarily examining relationship and motivation (Ulvestad, 2002), the victims' reaction to stalking was worry or concern (84%), fear or fright (84%), irritation and annoyance (82%), flattering (11%), and indifference (16%).

Collins and Wilkas (2000, p. 317) detail stalking trauma syndrome (STS), "a condition that can occur when a victim is subjected to repeated and persistent stalking behavior." STS is characterized by three elements: (1) a cycle of crisis; (2) significant psychological effects that include helplessness, hopelessness, anxiety, depression, desperation, loss of control, and behavior change; (3) recovery-based coping tools for victims and their families. STS is diagnostically related to PTSD though it is felt that "PTSD does not, in effect, recognize the consequences which spawn from the repeated and persistent victimization stalking presents" (Collins & Wilkas, 2000, p. 319).

STALKING AMONG SUBPOPULATIONS

Stalking is among one of the most prevalent crimes, with many studies showing that between one in four to about one in six people will be stalked at some point in their life (see McLennan, 1996; Purcell et al., 2000; Tjaden, 1997, and others). While this reflects a fairly high incidence of the crime in the general population, there are some sectors of the general community that may be more prone to stalking victimization or to specific forms of victimization. For example, it is generally acknowledged that celebrities are more likely be victimized by those suffering from mental disorders.

Mental health professionals regularly deal with clients who may be experiencing mental or emotional difficulties. This may make them more susceptible to the wrong type of attention, either as a result of revenge or payback, or where care and attention is interpreted as more than the result of a professional and clinical relationship. Those with attachment difficulties, at the extreme end of the spectrum like those with borderline personality disorder, may be more prone to overinterpret the care and regard of the therapeutic alliance. In the case of forensic psychologists, they may be likely to be targeted when a report or evaluation represents less than the most favorable outcome for the client.

These and other scenarios mean that mental health workers may experience victimization at higher rates. Before looking into a number of the studies that have addressed this issue, it is also important to note that this group of professionals may also have protections not afforded members of the public. This would include using evidence of the stalking as part of any assessment, thus indicating an inability to moderate their own behavior or conform to conventions of prosocial behavior. This may not auger were for pre- and postsentencing reports, probation reports, and a host of other assessments where any stalking would result in, or increase the probability of, a negative outcome.

Gentile, Asamen, Harmell, and Weathers (2001) conducted a survey on stalking of psychologists by their clients in the United States. They limited their sample to those who offer mental health services, with 294 responding to the survey from an initial mailing out of 750. The respondents were split evenly between men and women. Most (n = 240) were married, were predominantly Caucasian (n = 278), and most had a PhD qualification (n = 252). Approximately 10% of the sample had been stalked at some time, and four of the respondents had been stalked twice. Contrary to findings from community surveys, more males were stalked (12.1%) than females (8.4%). Of the 34 total incidents of stalking, 67.6% were committed by females, with about half (32.4%) being committed by males. This is again noted as being inconsistent with the community surveys on stalking, where it is found that most (87%) stalking is perpetrated by males.

With regard to the characteristics of the clients, only 5.9% were married. Most had at least completed high school. Diagnostically, the findings were largely as expected, with 21 of the 34 clients who stalked having a mood disorder, five had no Axis I diagnosis, while 26 had an Axis II personality disorder (please note that the newer DSM 5 has no Axis classification, and that this study employed the Axis/Cluster system of an older DSM version). Two of these were diagnosed as having more than one personality disorder, borderline being the most common personality disorder, present in about two-thirds of the sample. As noted, this would be expected given that this disorder is characterized by a fear of rejection or abandonment. The stalkers had experienced a recent loss or stress (73.5%), with 41.2% experiencing a divorce or dissolution of intimate relationships. Many had a history of negative caregiver experiences during childhood (79.4%). This indicates, and supports the hypothesis, that stalking is predominantly a problem of attachment (see Kienlen, 1998).

Kivisto, Berman, Watson, Grubewr, and Paul (2015) also examined stalking among North American psychologists. Their sample was 157 psychologists, with the sample relatively evenly split among males and females. Slightly more than half (53.5%) claimed that they spent at least half of their time engaging in forensic activities. Results show that 71% of these respondents had, at a minimum, been harassed by clients at some point in their life, while one in seven had been stalked. Unlike the previous study, there were no sex differences in the stalking behavior, though there were differences in harassment, with men being more likely to be threatened and attacked than women. Those psychologists having a forensic focus were nearly twice as likely to be stalked than those who did not engage in forensic work (17.9% vs. 9%). This is, again, in line with expectation. Despite being more prone to harassment than those in nonforensic work, those doing forensic work were not more likely to be physically assaulted.

Most psychologists felt they could ascribe a motivation for the intrusion. Resentment was identified as the most common reason for the harassment (29.3%) or stalking (45.5%). For infatuation, stalking was more likely (22.7%) than harassment (10.2%), with infatuation resulting in a longer duration of intrusion. While threats were relatively common in this group, they were only moderately associated with actual attacks. While not all who were threatened were attacked, all who were attacked were threatened.

University students are another subpopulation that has been studied by numerous researchers. This group may be particularly prone to stalking harassment and intrusions for a number of reasons. For many this may be their first time away from home, meaning normal familial and peer support networks are not as accessible. For many, this may also be the first time they experience their first "adult" relationship. This may also mark the first period of drug and alcohol experimentation for many people

(Petherick, 2014). Either alone or together, these factors may put university students at greater risk.

Finn (2004), while not dealing with stalking directly, studied online harassment at the University of New Hampshire in the United States. The impetus for the study was the ubiquitousness of online communication on university campuses, and because "cyberstalking is part of the larger stalking problem on college campuses" (p. 469). The sample was 359 students from the undergraduate population, the majority (64%) of whom live on campus. Ten to 15% of the respondents experienced online harassment, either from strangers, acquaintances, or another. Strangers engaged in the highest proportion of email harassment (16.2%) and instant messaging (IM) (19.3%). Of those students who received email, 14.1% report still receiving the emails, even after asking the sender to stop. Similarly, this occurred in 13.1% of cases involving IM communications.

Most students (marginally, however, at 58.7%) received pornography, which could be part of stalking legislation (in the author's home state of Queensland, for example, giving offensive material to a person, directly or indirectly, is considered a stalking behavior). Finn notes that this may have been part of a larger "mail out" and not necessarily sent to individual students, however. Students who identified as LGBT reported harassment at greater levels then non-LGBT students.

Björklund, Häkkänen-Nyholm, Sheridan, and Roberts (2010) examined the prevalence of stalking among Finnish university students. Psychology students at five Finnish universities were recruited along with students from the Faculty of Arts at the University of Helsinki. A total of 615 students responded to the survey, 43.1% of whom were studying psychology. Slightly more females responded (86.6%) than their representation in the student composition (76.5%), perhaps indicating that female students are at higher risk. Stalking behaviors included sending unwanted letters, notes, or emails (56.4%), multiple unwanted telephone calls (52.7%), verbal abuse (50.7%), hurting emotionally (45.6%), engaging in inappropriate personal discussion (42.3%), repeatedly asking for a date (41.6%), manipulating or forcing the victim into a date (39.9%), seeking out information about the victim (32.9%), and asking out as "just friends" (31.5%).

Just under half of the respondents had been stalked in their life, with 22.3% being exposed to one episode (note, in many jurisdictions one episode of intrusion would not meet a legal threshold for stalking), while 26.2% were exposed to more than one incident. On average, victims report 10 episodes, and stalking was more common among women than men. About one in five were stalked by strangers, about one-quarter were ex-intimates, and just over half were some other type of acquaintance. The mean duration of stalking was 301 days, with the duration linked to the relationship between the stalker and victim, with stranger stalking occurring for less duration. Female stalkers stalked for longer on average.

Almost half 46%, experienced violence or threats, with violent behaviors also linked to relationship type. Stalking by ex-intimates involved a higher frequency of violent behaviors than that by acquaintances and strangers. This study may present a somewhat skewed presentation of stalking among this population, however, given the high proportion of female respondents, which will also change the nature and type of relationship between stalker and victim, and may also alter other sex and gender differences, and perhaps also influence the nature of threats and actual harm.

Last but not least are those stalking victims who comprise the group generally known as "celebrities." This could include film and television stars, members of the royal and other popular or high-profile families, politicians, and any other individual or group enjoying a high profile. This disparate group generally represent a prime target for stalking victimization as their lives are already well exposed to those who may harass them. In certain situations, such as those involving erotomania or other delusional disorders, the degree of familiarity or relationship may be grossly exaggerated or misinterpreted. Dietz, Matthews, van Duyne, et al. (1991, p. 195) note that "public figures are besieged by a constant onslaught of unwanted attention from mentally disordered persons in search of identity, love, power, relief, and—most of all—contact." While not identified as stalking per se, Dietz, Matthews, van Duyne, et al. (1991) and Dietz, Matthews, Martell, et al. (1991), examined threatening and inappropriate letters to both Hollywood celebrities and members of the US Congress, respectively, and the interested reader should consult these works independently.

As stated, the stalking of members of the public is likely to happen with far greater frequency, though representation of celebrities in media accounts of the phenomenon are more likely given their often sensational features and the fact that the target of the behavior is already well known. Indeed, it was the stalking of these celebrities that gave life to the widespread study and acknowledgment of stalking in the 1980s (Mullen et al., 2009).

James et al. (2009) and (2011) examined stalkers and harassers of the British royal family. The first study comprised 222 cases, with 193 cases (86.9% of the sample) having evidence of mental illness, with delusional beliefs in 151 cases, grandiose ideas in 135 cases, rambling or other incoherent utterances in 76 cases, and "persecutory preoccupations" in seven cases. Suicidal intention was present in seven cases and homicidal ideation in eight cases. The researchers further classified the cases according to the apparent motivation, finding 61 cases with delusions of royal identity (that the sufferer was either the real sovereign or a member of the royal family), 37 were amity seekers (looking for advice or friendship), 23 were infatuated with about one-half of this sample being erotomanic. Those seeking sanctuary and help comprised 15 cases, six claimed they were the focus of royal persecution, 14 saw themselves as counselors to the royals, while 13 were querulents, and the final 28 were described as "chaotic" where there was no clear motivation.

The second study (James et al., 2011), largely mirrored the results of the first, possibly because the data for both were drawn from the same pool of cases held by the Metropolitan Police Service's Royalty Protection Unit.

In Australia, Lowry et al. (2015) examined harassments and other problem behaviors experienced by staff working for members of parliament or the electoral office in the state of Queensland. Of the 199 respondents, 134 of these reported at least one episode of harassment or concerning behavior by a member of the public. The most frequent type of behavior encountered was inappropriate telephone calls (42%), threats of legal action (32%), threats of harm (28%), loitering outside the workplace (21%), and unwanted approaches (20%). Less frequent behaviors included inappropriate letters, faxes, or emails (17%), inappropriate social media contact (10%), distributing malicious material (7%), and actual or attempted physical attack, following, and property damage or interference (3% each). Males were more likely than females to experience intrusive behaviors in the workplace, and were more likely to be threatened with legal action, though females were more likely to experience telephone contact. Most of the respondents indicated that they had been on the receiving end of contact from more than one person (72%). Based on the responses, the types of contact were classified according to two main groups: those seeking help or making a personal grievance–based account (94%) or those who assumed a greater level of familiarity or intimacy than existed in reality (6%). About one-half of the respondents indicated that the harasser was mentally ill on the basis of their behavior. While the office of employment was the most likely place for harassment (90% of cases), this occasionally also spilled over into the start member's home and other public locations, such as shopping centers and schools.

SERIAL STALKING AND RECIDIVISM

It seems misplaced to talk about "serial" stalking, as stalking is a crime that must, by definition, repeat. This is typically referred to as a course or pattern of conduct and is a feature of many if not most laws on the behavior. Lloyd-Goldstein (2000) suggests that the term *serial stalking* should be defined as the sequential stalking by the same person. This could either be through victimizing multiple victims at once, or it could be moving from one different victim to the next. When considering the behavior of stalkers who move from victim to victim, we are essentially talking about recidivist offenders.

For those stalkers who legitimately believe that if the victim just got to know them they would like them, pursuing multiple "prospective partners" will increase their chance of success (a perceived success, not necessarily a logical or realistic one). From an evolutionary perspective, this will increase the likelihood that their genes will be passed along, ensuring continuity of familial lines. For the stalker who harasses out of anger, they are likely to acquire new, or more, victims when their anger reaches a threshold level. Predatory stalkers will seek out victims whenever the underlying reason for their predatory behavior surfaces.

Despite the fact that we are well into the third decade of stalking laws and research, surprisingly little work has been done thus far on serial stalking. Beyond a few book chapters and journal articles, there is no large body of literature from which to present a well-rounded picture of stalkers who harass more than one victim. Of those few works done, a fairly grim picture is painted of long-term outcomes, with most stalkers committing another offense following their initial conviction.

Malsch, de Keijser, and Debets (2011) carried out a study of stalkers using a database held by the Dutch Ministry of Justice. The sample had all offenders convicted for stalking between July 2000 and December 2003. Of the 709 offenders convicted for stalking, 53% recidivated during the period of the study, with those committing another stalking offense (11% of the overall sample) having repeated their offending within 7 months. These stalkers were convicted for a total of 1955 new crimes, with 58% committing a crime other than stalking, with 24% being related to stalking in some way. Violent crimes were committed by 17% of the convicted stalkers, and this occurred within 19 months. As may be expected, those with more historical stalking offenses were most at risk for reoffending. Frequent offenders had seven to nine previous convictions, and persistent offenders had 10 or more previous convictions, and for both groups the recidivism rate was 81%. For the first offenders, only about one-quarter reoffended, while those with a small number of offenses (between one and three), about half reoffended.

McEwan and Strand (2013) present findings from a study of psychopathology among stalkers, with one variable measured being recurrence. Two hundred and eleven stalkers in total were studied following referral to a specialist service in Melbourne, Australia. Of these 44 (32%) had at least one stalking episode prior to that which led to referral. Nine of these (20%) had previously targeted the same victim as that leading to referral, and the only difference between the single and serial stalkers was that the serial cohort tended to be unemployed to a higher degree. Those who had stalked previously were more likely to have a history of violence and also threatening behavior. Not surprisingly, the serial stalkers were more likely to have a personality disorder or "marked problematic personality traits" (p. 551).

Eke, Hilton, Meloy, Mohandie, and Williams (2011) examined the predictors of recidivism among stalkers. The sample of 78 offenders was drawn from a multisite study of 312 police cases. Of these 78 offenders, 60 (77%) committed at least one new offense, with four committing another offense while in prison by calling or writing to their victims. A mean time for recidivism was 9.8 months for the first new offense, though 50% of the new offenses were within two months. Nine percent occurred within less than one day. New stalking offenses were committed for slightly more than half of the subsample (56%) with a mean at-risk time of 11 months, though 47% repeat offended within three months, and about one-quarter within 24 days. Violent recidivism was found in 26 offenders, with an at-risk time of 17.5 months, though just short of half reoffended within eight months and about one-quarter within approximately two months.

It will be difficult to know how many serial stalkers there are, or whether the type that stalks multiple people at one time or stalks victims sequentially. To be able to get an accurate picture this would rely on the cases being reported, the reports being taken accurately, the cases being accurately linked (Petherick, 2014), and the perpetrator being arrested and prosecuted. Until then the herein studies are a useful barometer of the general state of affairs: upwards of half of all stalkers will offend again.

CONCLUSIONS

Stalking involves repeated intrusion and harassment of one person by another that occurs over time and is unwanted and brings about fear. The definition of stalking used in this chapter also identifies that these behaviors may, when taken in isolation, appear innocuous or innocent, but when viewed collectively and in context are maladaptive and potentially illegal.

The legal definition of stalking is relatively easy to find and can be found in any number of statutes around the world. Therefore, stalking will be legally proscribed by the criminal law in a given jurisdiction. As a deviance, the concept of stalking is a lot more difficult to define, and will typically rely on the thresholds any given victim employs to determine when the behavior moves through the continuum from courting, to deviant persistence, to criminal intrusion.

This chapter has demonstrated the wide variety of behaviors evident in stalking from telephoning to letter writing to surveillance. It has also demonstrated the vast array of victim responses to stalking, which are as many and varied as the multiple manifestations of stalking itself.

SUMMARY

- Stalking is a common crime impacting between one in four and one in six individuals.
- Stalking legislation is now over 30 years old and was first introduced in California in 1990, with Queensland being the first Australian state to introduce it in 1993. The United Kingdom didn't have specific antistalking legislation until 2012.
- Stalking laws differ by jurisdiction but generally include a pattern or course of conduct intentionally directed at another that causes fear or apprehension.
- Stalking was so named because of the hunter's use of a horse to get close to game. This horse was called the stalking horse.
- Stalking behaviors can range from the mild to the severe or life threatening. One of the problems faced by legislators has been in identifying which behaviors to proscribe as many of them are normal "courting" behaviors such as telephoning, sending gifts, and writing letters. These behaviors are typically identified as stalking when the victim reports experiencing fear or apprehension.
- The variety of stalking behaviors are as extensive as the characteristics of victims and stalkers. This can range from common romantic pursuit items such as flowers and chocolates, through to threatening or disturbing gifts such as weapons, dead animals, or other disturbing items. These gifts can tell you a great deal about the stalker and their intentions, which can subsequently help with intervention and resolution.
- While the introduction of stalking laws in California has been attributed to the stalking of Hollywood celebrities, most notably the murder of Rebecca

Schaeffer, the actual laws were introduced following a number of noncelebrity domestic homicides. These laws were first discussed and later introduced by Judge John Watson and Senator Ed Royce.

- When viewed in isolation, many stalking behaviors may appear to be relatively innocuous. However, when viewed as a collective whole representing an overall pattern of intrusion and harassment, these behaviors reveal a far more insidious pattern.
- While stalking is relatively prevalent in the general community, studies have found that certain populations may be at higher or particular risk. These include university students, mental health workers, and celebrities (not just actors but also politicians, the British royal family, or anyone else with a significant public profile).
- There have been a number of attempts made to develop risk assessment tools to determine the risk of violence posed by stalkers toward their victims. The current "gold standard" is the Stalking Risk Profile (SRP), which seeks not only to determine the risk of violence posed, but also the stalker's chance of continuing the harassment, starting again should they stop, and the risk of psychosocial harm. This risk instrument is based on the typology of stalkers developed by Mullen et al.
- Stalking is a crime that is prone to repeat by its very nature and definition. As such, it is a truly serial crime. However, there is little research that has been conducted on stalkers as a recidivist group. Of the small number done, it has been found that, depending on the study, about one-half of stalkers repeat offend, either with stalking or with another crime. Some findings indicate that stalkers more likely to repeat offend have problematic personality traits.

QUESTIONS

1. Lawmakers have had some trouble with the wording of stalking laws because they can involve the criminalization of courting behaviors. True or false?
2. The "gold standard" for stalking risk assessment is the:
   a. Violence Risk Appraisal Guide
   b. Stalking Risk Appraisal Guide
   c. Stalker Risk Assessment Inventory
   d. Stalking Risk Profile
   e. None of the above
3. Californian stalking laws were introduced largely because of the murder of actress _____ _____.
4. Most stalking laws require stalking intrusions to occur on:
   a. One or more occasions
   b. Two or more occasions
   c. Three or more occasions
   d. Four or more occasions
   e. There are no numerical requirements

5. What are some of the "special populations" that have been studied in stalking? Why might they be stalked at a greater rate than the general public?
6. There have been a large number of studies done on serial stalking. True or false?
7. List some of the effects of stalking on victims.
8. List some of the behaviors involved in stalking.

REFERENCES

Abrams, K. M., & Robinson, G. E. (2002). Occupational effects of stalking. *Canadian Journal of Psychiatry, 47*(5), 468–472.

American Psychiatric Association. (1994). *Diagnostic and statistical manual of mental disorders* (4th ed.). Washington: American Psychiatric Association.

American Psychiatric Association. (2013). *Diagnostic and statistical manual of mental disorders* (5th ed.). Washington: American Psychiatric Association.

Barlow, H. D., & Kauzlarich, D. (2002). *Introduction to criminology* (8th ed.). New Jersey: Prentice Hall.

Basile, K. C., Swahn, M. H., Chen, J., & Saltzman, L. E. (2006). Stalking in the United States: recent national prevalence estimates. *American Journal of Preventative Medicine, 31*(2), 172–175.

Björklund, K., Häkkänen-Nyland, H., Sheridan, L., & Roberts, K. (2010). The prevalence of stalking among Finnish university students. *Journal of Interpersonal Violence, 25*(4), 684–698. http://dx.doi.org/10.1177/0886260509334405.

Blaauw, E., Winkel, F. W., & Arensman, E. (2000). The toll of stalking: the relationship between features of stalking and psychopathology of victims. In *Paper presented at the Stalking: Criminal Justice Responses Conference, 7–8 December*. Sydney: Australian Institute of Criminology.

Blaauw, E., Winkel, F. W., Sheridan, L., Malsch, M., & Arensman, E. (2002). The psychological consequences of stalking victimization. In J. Boon, & L. Sheridan (Eds.), *Stalking and psychosexual obsession: Psychological perspectives for prevention, policing and harassment*. Chichester: Wiley and Sons.

Blackburn, R. (1993). *The psychology of criminal conduct: Theory, research and practice*. Chichester: John Wiley & Sons.

Brewster, M. P. (1997). *An exploration of the experiences and needs of former intimate stalking victims*. West Chester University. proposal no. 5-8432-PA-IJ.

Budd, T., Mattinson, J., & Myhill, A. (2000). *The extent and nature of stalking: Findings from the 1998 British Crime Survey*. Home Office Research, Development and Statistics Directorate. Research Study 110, October.

Coleman, F. L. (1997). Stalking behavior and the cycle of domestic violence. *Journal of Interpersonal Violence, 12*, 420–432.

Collins, M. J., & Wilkas, M. B. (2000). Stalking trauma syndrome and the traumatized victim. In J. A. Davis (Ed.), *Stalking crimes and victim protection: Prevention, intervention, threat assessment and case management*. Boca Raton: CRC Press.

Cupach, W. R., & Spitzberg, B. H. (1998). Obsessive relational intrusion and stalking. In B. H. Spitzberg, & W. R. Cupach (Eds.), *The dark side of close relationships*. New Jersey: Lawrence Erlbaum.

D'arcy, M. (2000). Stalking, sexual assault, domestic violence: what's in a name? In *Paper presented at the Stalking: Criminal Justice Responses Conference, 7–8 December*. Sydney: Australian Institute of Criminology.

Dennison, S., & Thompson, D. (2000). Community perceptions of stalking: what are the fundamental concerns? *Psychiatry, Psychology and Law, 7*(2), 159–169.

Dietz, P. E., Matthews, D. B., van Duyne, C., Martell, D. A., Parry, D. H., Stewart, T. M., et al. (1991). Threatening and otherwise inappropriate letters to Hollywood celebrities. *Journal of Forensic Sciences, 36*(1), 185–209.

Dietz, P. E., Matthews, D. B., Martell, D. A., Stewart, T. M., Hrouda, D. R., & Warren, J. (1991). Threatening and otherwise inappropriate letters to Members of the United States Congress. *Journal of Forensic Sciences, 36*(5), 1445–1468.

Eke, A. W., Hilton, Z., Meloy, J. R., Mohandie, K., & Williams, J. (2011). Predictors of recidivism by stalkers: a nine-year follow up of police contacts. *Behavioral Sciences & the Law, 29*, 271–283.

Finch, E. (2001). *The criminalization of stalking: Constructing the problem and evaluating the solution*. London: Cavendish Publishing.

Finn, J. (2004). A survey of online harassment at a university campus. *Journal of Interpersonal Violence, 19*(4), 468–483. http://dx.doi.org/10.1177/0886260503262083.

Fisher, B. S., Cullen, F. T., & Turner, M. G. (2002). *Being pursued: Stalking victimization in a national study of college women*. Criminology and Public Policy.

Fremouw, W. J., Westrup, D., & Pennypacker, J. (1997). Stalking on campus: the prevalence of strategies for coping with stalking. *Journal of Forensic Sciences, 42*(4), 666.

Geberth, V. J. (1992). Stalkers. *Law and Order, 10*, 1–6.

Gentile, S. R., Asamen, J. K., Harmell, P. H., & Weathers, R. (2001). The stalking of psychologists by their clients. *Professional Psychology, Research and Practice, 33*(5), 490–494.

Goode, M. (1995). Stalking: crime of the nineties? *Criminal Law Journal, 19*(1), 21–31.

Groth, N. (1979). *Men who rape. The psychology of the offender*. New York: Plenum Press.

Groth, N., Burgess, A. W., & Holmstrom, L. L. (1979). Rape: power, anger, and sexuality. *American Journal of Psychiatry, 134*(11), 1239–1243.

Häkkänen, H., Hagelstam, C., & Santilla, P. (2003). Stalking actions, prior offender-victim relationships and issuing of retraining orders in a Finnish sample of stalkers. *Legal and Criminological Psychology, 8*, 189–206.

Hagan, J. (1984). *Modern Criminology: Crime, Criminal Behaviour and its Control*. Reno: Sierra Nevada Press.

Hall, D. (1998). The victims of stalking. In J. R. Meloy (Ed.), *The psychology of stalking: Clinical and forensic perspectives*. London: Academic Press.

Hazelwood, R. R. (2009). Analysing the rape and profiling the offender. In R. R. Hazelwood, & A. W. Burgess (Eds.), *Practical aspects of rape investigation: A multidisciplinary approach* (4th ed.). Boca Raton: CRC Press.

Holmes, R. R. (2001). Criminal stalking: an analysis of the various typologies of stalkers. In J. A. Davis (Ed.), *Stalking crime and victim protection: Prevention, intervention, threat assessment, and case management*. Boca Raton: CRC Press.

James, D. V., Mullen, P. E., Meloy, J. R., Pathé, M. T., Preston, L., Darnley, B., et al. (2011). Stalkers and harassers of British royalty: an exploration of proxy behaviors for violence. *Behavioral Sciences & the Law, 29*, 64–80. http://dx.doi.org/10.1002/bsl.922.

James, D. V., Mullen, P. E., Pathé, M. T., Meloy, J. R., Preston, L. F., Darnley, B., et al. (2009). Stalkers and harassers of royalty: the role of mental illness and motivation. *Psychological Medicine, 39*, 1479–1490. http://dx.doi.org/10.1017/S0033291709005443.

Jordan, H. W., Lockert, E. W., Johnson-Warren, M., Cabell, C., Cooke, T., Greer, W., et al. (2006). Erotomania revisited: Thirty-four years later. *Journal of the National Medical Association*, 98(5), 787–793.

Keenahan, D., & Barlow, A. (1997). Stalking: A Paradoxical Crime of the Nineties. *International Journal of Risk, Security and Crime Prevention*, 2(4), 291–300.

Kienlen, K. K. (1998). Development and social antecedents of stalking. In J. R. Meloy (Ed.), *The Psychology of Stalking: Clinical and forensic perspectives*. London: Academic Press.

Kivisto, A. J., Berman, A., Watson, M., Grubewr, D., & Paul, H. (2015). North american psychologists' experience of stalking, threatening, and harassing behavior: a survey of ABPP displomates. *Professional Psychology, Research And Practice*, 46(4), 277–286. http://dx.doi.org/10.1037/pro0000025.

Lemon, N. K. D. (1994). *Domestic violence and stalking: A comment on the model anti-stalking code proposed by the National Institute of Justice*. Available from http://www.mincava.umn.edu/documents/bwjp/stalking/stalking.html.

Lloyd-Goldstein, R. (2000). Serial stalking: recent clinical findings. In L. Schlesinger (Ed.), *Serial offenders: Current throughts, recent findings*. San Diego: Academic Press.

Lowry, T. J., Pathé, M. T., Phillips, J. H., Haworth, D. J., Mulder, M. J., & Briggs, C. J. (2015). Harassment and other problematic behaviors experienced by the staff of public office holders. *Journal of Threat Assessment and Management*, 2(1), 1–10. http://dx.doi.org/10.1037/tam0000039.

Mackenzie, R., McEwan, T. E., Pathé, M., James, D. V., Ogloff, J. R. P., & Mullen, P. E. (2009). *Stalking risk profile: Guidelines for the assessment and management of stalkers*. StalkInc: Elwood.

Malsch, M., de Keijser, J. W., & Debets, S. E. C. (2011). Are stalkers recidivists? Repeated offending by convicted stalkers. *Violence and Victims*, 26(1), 3–15.

McEwan, T., Pathé, M., & Ogloff, J. R. P. (2011). Advances in stalking risk assessment. *Behavioral Sciences & the Law*, 29, 180–201. http://dx.doi.org/10.1002/bsl.973.

McEwan, T. E., & Strand, S. (2013). The role of psychopathology in stalking by adult strangers and acquaintances. *Australian and New Zealand Journal of Psychiatry*, 47(6), 546–555.

McFarlane, J. M., Campbell, J. C., Wilt, S., Sachs, C. J., Ulrich, Y., & Xu, X. (1999). Stalking and intimate partner femicide. *Homicide Studies*, 3(4), 300–316.

McLennan, W. (1996). *Women's safety Australia*. Canberra: Australian Bureau of Statistics. ABS Catalogue No. 4128.0.

Meloy, J. R. (1996). Stalking (obsessional following): a review of some preliminary studies. *Aggression and violent behavior*, 1, 147–162.

Meloy, J. R. (1998). The psychology of stalking. In J. R. Meloy (Ed.), *The psychology of stalking: Clinical and forensic perspectives*. London: Academic Press.

Meloy, J. R. (1999). Stalking: an old behavior, a new crime. *Forensic Psychiatry*, 22(1), 85–99.

Meloy, J. R., & Gothard, S. (1995). Demographic and clinical comparison of obsessional followers and offenders with mental disorders. *American Journal of Psychiatry*, 152, 258–263.

Miller, M. C. (March 2001). Stalking. *The Harvard Mental Health Letter*, 17.

Mohandie, K., Meloy, J. R., McGowan, M. G., & Williams, J. (2006). The RECON typology o stalking: reliability and validity based upon a large sample of north American stalkers. *Journal of Forensic Science*, 51(1), 147–155.

Monico, J. A. (1998). *The effects of stalking victimization and victim's responses to the crime* (Unpublished thesis). Gold Coast, Australia: Bond University.

Morowitz, S. J. (2003). *Stalking and violence: New patterns of trauma and obsession*. New York: Kluwer Academic/Plenum Press.

Mullen, P. E. (1997). Erotomanias (Pathologies of Love) and stalking. *Directions in Mental Health Counselling*, *7*(3), 3–16.

Mullen, P. E., Pathé, M., & Purcell, R. (2000). Stalking. *The Psychologist*, *13*(9), 454–459.

Mullen, P. E., Pathé, M., & Purcell, R. (2009). *Stalker and their victims* (2nd ed.). Cambridge: Cambridge University Press.

Mullen, P. E., Pathé, M., Purcell, R., & Stuart, G. (1999). Study of stalkers. *The American Journal of Psychiatry*, *156*(8), 1244–1249.

Pathé, M. (2002). *Victims of stalking*. Oxford: Oxford University Press.

Pathé, M., & Mullen, P. E. (1997). The impact of stalkers on their victims. *British Journal of Psychiatry*, *170*, 12–17.

Penney, T. L. (2014). Dark figure of crime (problems of estimation). *The Encyclopaedia of Criminology and Criminal Justice*, 1–6.

Perez, C. (1993). Stalking: when does obsession become a crime? *American Journal of. Criminal Law*, *20*(2), 263–280.

Petherick, W. A. (2008). Stalking. In B. E. Turvey (Ed.), *Criminal profiling: An introduction to behavior evidence analysis* (3rd ed.). London: Academic Press (2008).

Petherick, W. A. (2014). Serial stalking: looking for love in all the wrong places? In W. A. Petherick (Ed.), *Profiling and serial crime: Theoretical and practical issues*. Boston: Anderson Publishing.

Petherick, W. A., & Sinnamon, G. (2014). Motivations: victim and offender perspectives. In W. A. Petherick (Ed.), *Profiling and serial crime: Theoretical and practical issues*. Boston: Anderson Publishing.

Pinals, D. A. (2007). Stalking: classification and typology. In D. A. Pinals (Ed.), *Stalking: Psychiatric perspectives and practical approaches*. Oxford: Oxford University Press.

Purcell, R., Pathé, M., & Mullen, P. E. (2000). The incidence and nature of stalking victimization. In *Presented at the Australian Institute of Criminology Stalking: Criminal Justice System Responses Conference, December 7–8*.

Racine, C., & Billick, S. (2014). Classification systems for stalking behavior. *Psychiatry and Behavioral Sciences*, *59*(1), 250–254.

Sheridan, L. (2001). Stalking. *Journal of Interpersonal Violence*, *16*(2), 151–158.

Sheridan, L., & Boon, J. (2002). Stalking typologies: implications for law enforcement. In J. Boon, & L. Sheridan (Eds.), *Stalking and psychosexual obsession: Psychological perspectives for prevention, policing and treatment*. West Sussex: John Wiley and Sons.

Sheridan, L., & Davies, G. M. (2001). What is stalking? the match between legislation and public perception. *Legal and criminological psychology*, *6*(3), 3–17.

Sheridan, L., Davies, G. M., & Boon, J. (2001a). The course and nature of stalking: a victim perspective. *The Howard Journal*, *40*(3), 215–234.

Sheridan, L., Davies, G. M., & Boon, J. (2001b). Stalking: perceptions and prevalence. *Journal of Interpersonal Violence*, *16*(2), 151–167.

Sheridan, L. P., Blaauw, E., & Davies, G. M. (2003). Stalking: knowns and unknowns. *Trauma, Violence & Abuse*, *4*(2), 148–162.

Smoyak, S. A. (2000). Stalking: ambiguous language can mask a crime. *Journal of Psychosocial Nursing and Mental Health Services*, *38*(4), 6–7.

Stocker, M., & Nielssen, O. (2000). Apprehended violence orders and stalking. In *Presented at the Australian Institute of Criminology Stalking: Criminal Justice System Responses Conference, December 7–8*.

Swanwick, R. A. (1996). Stalkees strike back - the stalkers stalked: a review of the first two years of stalking legislation in Queensland. *University of Queensland Law Review*, *19*(1), 26–44.

Tjaden, P. (1997). *The crime of stalking: How big is the problem?* National Institute of Justice Research Preview.

Tjaden, P., & Thoennes, N. (April 1998). *Stalking in America: Findings from the national violence against women survey.* National Institute of Justice and the Centres for Disease Control and Prevention: Research in Brief.

Ulvestad, C. S. (2002). *Stalking: An investigation of relationships between victim and stalker, stalking behavior and motivation* (Unpublished thesis). Gold Coast, Australia: Bond University.

Watson, J. (1998). *First anti-stalking law in country.* Letter to the League of Women Voters. May 13. Available at: http://www.smartvoter.org/1998jun/ca/or/vote/watson_j/paper1.html.

Weiner, D. (January 1995). Stalking: criminal responsibility and the infliction of harm. *Law Institute Journal*, 30–33.

Wolff, R. (2008). *Stalking on facebook.* The Daily Gazette. May 12. Available from http://daily.swarthmore.edu/2008/5/12/stalking/print/.

Zona, M. A., Palarea, R. E., & Lane, J. C. (1998). Psychiatric diagnosis and the offender-victim typology of stalking. In J. R. Meloy (Ed.), *The psychology of stalking: Clinical and forensic perspectives.* San Diego: Elsevier.

Stalking Public Figures: The Fixated Loner

Michele Pathé

Queensland Forensic Mental Health Service, Brisbane, QLD, Australia; Queensland Fixated Threat Assessment Centre, Brisbane, QLD, Australia; Griffith University, Brisbane, QLD, Australia

CHAPTER OUTLINE

INTRODUCTION

In Western civilizations, people who pursue the famous pose a greater risk of death or serious injury to their targets than do terrorist groups or criminals (James et al., 2007; Meloy et al., 2004). Unfortunately, there is an abundance of individuals harboring intense preoccupations with a public figure or some related cause, and while only a minority progress to violent acts, this is a small proportion of a sizable group. The 1996 shooting massacre at Dunblane primary school in Scotland is a catastrophic example of violence perpetrated by a mentally disordered man with a long-standing grievance (Dunblane school massacre, 2015). Another is the 2011 shooting of U.S. politician Gabrielle Giffords by an obsessed, psychotic man. This attack resulted in multiple casualties, including the deaths of six bystanders and serious injuries to his intended target (Tucson Shooting, 2015). Extreme violence is an uncommon outcome for this group, whom we term "fixated" or "fixated loners," but other detrimental impacts are not, including psychological distress, embarrassment, disruption, adverse media attention, and dissipation of resources. Physical protection measures alone have not proved to be a sufficient defense against the fixated (Mullen, James, et al., 2009).

Ordinary citizens may be equally, if not more, at risk from fixated persons than the celebrities and politicians they target (James et al., 2007). The threat posed by fixated loners is as much a threat to public safety as it is to public figures. The systematic study of this concerning group has enabled the identification of risk factors, in particular mental illness, unearthing opportunities for intervention and risk mitigation at a much earlier stage. These findings have led to the establishment of effective threat assessment and management services to specifically address public figure stalking. This chapter will also consider wider applications for early intervention models of this type.

THE STALKING OF PRIVATE CITIZENS AND PUBLIC FIGURES

In the late 1980s, stalking behaviors had captured the interest of mental health researchers but public figure threats and stalking remained a law enforcement concern (Fein & Vossekuil, 1999). Some of the earliest descriptions of stalking behaviors did, however, involve public figure targets. For example, Esquirol (1965) reported a case of a man who lifted the skirt of an actress he was stalking and assaulted her husband, who he believed stood between him and his beloved. In 1881, the 20th American president, James Garfield, was fatally shot by Charles Guiteau, who had longstanding delusions of grandeur, including the belief that he had written Garfield's winning presidential speech. Guiteau stalked Garfield through repeated letters and approaches, demanding a diplomatic post for his vital contribution. The assassination at a train station in Washington, D.C., as Garfield was leaving for a much publicized summer holiday was primarily motivated by resentment fueled by narcissistic injury (Millard, 2011).

The word "stalking" was originally coined by the media in relation to "star stalkers," passionate fans who pursued celebrities (Lowney & Best, 1995). One such high profile stalking case was a catalyst for the passage of the world's first stalking legislation in California in 1990 (Mair, 1995; Rebecca Schaeffer, 2015);

Rebecca Schaeffer was a 21-year-old actress, best known for her role in the TV series "My Sister Sam." She was stalked for three years by an obsessive fan,

Robert Bardo, who sent her many letters, once receiving a reply from her fan service. In 1987 he travelled from Arizona to Los Angeles to speak to her on the set of "My Sister Sam" but was turned away by security guards. He returned a month later with a knife, but was again prevented from seeing the actress.

He subsequently fixated on other celebrity figures, including a couple of female singers. There are reports that he was also obsessed with child peace activist Samantha Smith, but after her death in a plane crash in 1985 he focused his attentions on Rebecca Schaeffer. Bardo's interest in Ms Schaeffer was rekindled after she starred in a black comedy involving a sex scene. Nineteen-year-old Bardo was incensed, paying a detective agency $250 to locate her home address through Department of Motor Vehicle (DMV) records. (He had read that in 1982 Arthur Jackson used a private detective and DMV records to track down Hollywood actress Theresa Saldana, who subsequently survived Jackson's vicious stabbing attack.) Bardo attended Ms Schaeffer's West Hollywood apartment and rang the doorbell. The actress answered, and after a brief conversation told him to leave. Bardo ate breakfast at a local diner and returned. When the actress answered the doorbell on this occasion, he fatally shot her in the chest at point-blank range with a recently acquired Ruger .357-caliber handgun.

Bardo was apprehended the next day, after running through traffic on an interstate highway. He was sentenced to life in prison without parole.

Stalking is a behavioral concept describing persistent and repeated harassment, in which one person imposes on another unwanted communications and/or contacts (Pathé & Mullen, 1997). It is targeted to a specific victim and includes both implicitly and explicitly threatening behavior that can persist for a protracted period (Kropp, Hart, & Lyon, 2002). Capturing this diverse constellation of behaviors under the rubric of stalking has inspired an ever-expanding discourse in the legal, social, and behavioral sciences.

In 1985, in response to the stalking of actress Jodie Foster and other public figures by university dropout John Hinckley Jr., culminating in Hinckley's attempted assassination in 1981 of President Ronald Reagan, Dietz, Matthews, Van Duyne, et al. (1991), and Dietz, Matthews, Martell, et al. (1991) undertook a series of studies of threatening and inappropriate communications and approaches to Hollywood celebrities and politicians. This body of work provided new insights into factors associated with a greater likelihood of progressing from communication with the target to approach behaviors. In particular, it contradicted existing assumptions about direct threats as a risk factor for subsequent approach activities. This finding was at odds with a growing literature on risk factors for general violence and the ensuing research on stalkers of private citizens, where prior threats were associated with an increased risk of progressing to approach and attack behaviors.

Meanwhile, Rebecca Schaeffer's murder prompted the Los Angeles Police Department (LAPD) to adopt a more proactive approach in threat and harassment cases, and the LAPD Threat Management Unit (TMU) was founded in 1990 to specifically investigate individuals who had engaged in abnormal, long-term patterns of threats or harassment (Zona, Palarea, & Lane, 1998). This was the first organizational structure established to specifically manage stalkers. Zona, Sharma, and Lane (1993) then undertook a systematic study of stalkers, analyzing 74 cases from the TMU database. Their pioneering typology of stalkers, conceptualized as "obsessional following," was drawn from this sample, and a further 126 case files were subsequently processed by the TMU (Zona et al., 1998). This study also emphasized that stalking impacted not only prominent figures but also ordinary citizens, and attention shifted from star stalkers to men who stalked their ex-partners.

Erotomania is "a conviction that one is loved, despite the supposed lover having done nothing to encourage or sustain that belief, but on the contrary having either made clear their lack of interest or remaining unaware of the claimed relationship" (Mullen, Pathé, & Purcell, 2009, p. 97). Erotomanic delusions are not uncommon among those who stalk the famous, particularly celebrity rather than political figures. The forensic implications of erotomania were first clearly articulated by Alexander Morrison (1848; cited in Enoch & Trethowan, 1979), who wrote that "erotomania sometimes prompts those laboring under it to destroy themselves or others, for although in general tranquil and respectful, the patient sometimes becomes irritable, passionate and jealous." More than a century later, Mullen and Pathé (1994a, 1994b) described an Australian clinical forensic cohort of male patients with erotomania. All of these patients had stalked the object of their affection, a mix of celebrities and private citizens. Most cases (79%) involved violent behaviors (overt threats to harm, property damage, physical and/or sexual assault). This study highlighted the disruptive, distressing, and occasionally fatal impact of erotomanic beliefs and underscored the damaging impact of stranger/acquaintance stalking, regardless of the victim's public profile.

Stalkers are a heterogeneous group, with differing psychopathology, motivations, risk profiles, and management approaches. While to date there is no truly comprehensive multifactor theory to account for stalking behaviors, various taxonomies of stalking have evolved in a bid to reduce diverse behaviors into manageable categories that can assist risk and management decisions (de Becker, 1997; McEwan & Pathé, 2013). One of the most commonly used typologies, endorsed by the Group for Advancement of Psychiatry Committee on Psychiatry and the Law (Pinals, 2007), is the functional classification developed by Mullen, Pathé, Purcell, and Stuart (1999) from an original sample of 145 Australian stalkers. As described later, this typology is based primarily on the motivation for the stalking behavior.

STRUCTURED RISK ASSESSMENT IN STALKING

The 1990s heralded the development of the first structured professional guidelines for violence risk assessment, including general measures such as the Historical Clinical Risk-20 (HCR-20; Webster, Douglas, Eaves, & Hart, 1997) and special-purpose risk assessment measures for specific forms of violence, including the Spousal

Assault Risk Assessment Guide (SARA; Kropp, Hart, Webster, & Eaves, 1999) and the Risk for Sexual Violence Protocol (RSVP; Hart, Kropp, & Laws, 2003). These instruments have been validated and incorporated into clinical forensic practice in most Western nations. White and Meloy (2007) have since advanced the Workplace Assessment of Violence Risk (WAVR-21), a structured tool for assessing targeted violence in the workplace.

Researchers in the stalking field recognized that existing tools were unsuitable or inadequate for measuring risk in stalking situations, and there was a paucity of robust, retrospective, and prospective studies in this area. The empirical literature on stalking risks (Farnham, James, & Cantrell, 2000; McEwan, Mullen, & Purcell, 2007; McEwan, Pathé, & Ogloff, 2011; Meloy, 2001; Rosenfeld, 2004; Spitzberg & Cupach, 2007), combined with more extensive data from general violence risk studies, led to the development in Canada of the first structured professional judgment tool for assessing risk in stalking, *Guidelines for Stalking Assessment and Management* (SAM: Kropp, Hart, & Lyon, 2008). The SAM considers the nature of the stalking, perpetrator risk factors, and victim vulnerability factors and has utility in forensic and correctional settings, law enforcement, and victim safety planning.

In 2009, MacKenzie and colleagues published the *Stalking Risk Profile: Guidelines for Assessment and Management of Stalkers* (SRP). The key principle underpinning the SRP is that different types of stalkers have different motivations, and risk therefore varies according to stalker type. The SRP, as for all structured professional judgment tools, is based on empirical research and clinical experience, and risk is assessed according to the Mullen, Pathé, et al. (2009) motivational typology (Table 9.1). The SRP appraises risk in several domains (the risk of violence, persistence, recurrence, and psychosocial damage) and assesses the presence and severity of these risk factors. It also aids in the identification of targets for clinical intervention and the evaluation of change in risk over time. Both the SAM and the SRP have undergone initial validation trials with promising results (Kropp, Hart, Lyon, & Storey, 2011; McEwan & Strand, 2015).

THE CONVERGENCE OF STALKING AND PUBLIC FIGURE THREAT ASSESSMENT

In 2003, in response to a study commissioned by the British Home Office, mental health researchers from the United Kingdom, the United States, and Australia with a shared interest and expertise in the stalking and threat assessment fields formed the Fixated Research Group (FRG). The project explored the characteristics of and risk posed by lone individuals who fixated on public figures, particularly the British Royal Family. Pathological "fixation" (from the Latin *figo*, to be "bound fast") is a psychological concept defined as "obsessive preoccupations pursued to an abnormally intense degree" (Mullen, James, et al., 2009, p. 202). These individuals can be fixated on a *person* (usually a celebrity figure such as an actor, newsreader, musician, or sports star) or some idiosyncratic *cause* (an intensely personal grievance or quest

Table 9.1 Stalker Typology (MacKenzie et al., 2009; Mullen, Pathé, et al., 2009)

	Rejected	Intimacy Seeker	Incompetent Suitor	Resentful	Predatory	Help Seeker	Attention Seeker	Chaotic
				Stalker Type				
Relevant to private citizens or public figures	Private citizens	Both	Both	Both	Both	Public figures	Public figures	Public figures
Context	Breakdown of intimate relationship	Lack of intimacy	Loneliness	Perceived injustice	Sexually deviant interests	Unresolved problems	Need to draw attention to themselves	Motives so confused, or so little information, that motivation unable to be discerned
Prior relationship	Usually sexually intimate	Acquaintance or stranger, including public figure	Acquaintance or stranger	Victim is perceived agent of injustice	Acquaintance or stranger	Public figure	Public figure or site	
Initial motivation	Reconciliation &/or revenge	Establish an intimate relationship	Seeking friendship or date	To avenge injustice	Preparing for attack, usually sexual	Seeking help from public figure because of public figure's position	Bolster self-worth	
Sustaining motivation	Stalking compensates for lost intimacy	Substitutes for real relationship	Usually not sustained	Power and control	Sexual gratification			
Diagnosis	Mostly personality disorders (usually narcissistic, antisocial, borderline, dependent)	Morbid infatuation, erotomanias	Intellectually or socially disabled	Paranoid disorders	Sexual deviation (paraphilias)	Dependent, poor coping skills	Personality disorders, bipolar disorder, adolescent anomie	Disturbed, chaotic group
Public figure sub-types		1. Entitlement to friendship 2. Delusions of kinship[a]					1. Acting independently on behalf of a political protest 2. Wanting to make grand public statement	

[a]Delusional belief that they themselves are the public figure, or that they are a close relative of the public figure. More common in stalkers of royalty.

for justice). Fixated individuals commonly engage in stalking behaviors as a consequence of their all-consuming beliefs.

The FRG undertook a retrospective analysis of 5000 case files held by the Royalty Protection Police, in relation to individuals who had engaged in inappropriate communications, approaches, and attacks on members of the British Royal Family (Fixated Research Group 2006). The group also conducted an historical study of attacks on members of the British Royal Family (James et al., 2009) and a study of attacks on Western European politicians (James et al., 2007). The discovery of substantial rates of mental illness among those who harassed and threatened public figures supported previous findings (Dietz, Matthews, Martell, et al., 1991; Scalora et al., 2002, 2003), but the Fixated Research Project dispelled the prevailing misconception that mental illness precluded the planning and execution of targeted acts of violence. The FRG observed that more organized and outwardly rational fixated persons were capable of undertaking such attacks, and their unwavering psychotic convictions strengthened their resolve. These findings had important implications for public figure protection, inviting proactive interventions (treatment of mental illness) rather than the more reactive strategies that were then available to police. The significance of mental illness in public figure stalking will be elaborated on later.

The Fixated Research Project built on the earlier work of Scalora et al. (2002, 2003), which underscored the important role of warning behaviors as antecedents to attacks on public figures. Indeed, half the cases who attacked elected politicians in Western Europe between 1990 and 2004 (James et al., 2007) had earlier engaged in warning behaviors. Thus, while not constituting direct threats to the target, such behaviors are a dynamic manifestation of the subject's fixation, which provide opportunities for appropriate intervention. These behaviors will be discussed in further detail later.

Several typologies have evolved in relation to public figure stalkers. Phillips' (2006, 2008) typology was derived from a U.S. sample of threateners and approachers to Secret Service protectees, while James et al. (2009) eight motivational types were derived from problematic approachers to members of the British Royal Family. The typology that forms the basis for assessment of risk in public figure stalkers (MacKenzie et al., 2009) is adapted from the motivational typology of stalkers of the general public (Mullen et al., 1999; Mullen, Pathé, et al., 2009; Mullen, James, et al., 2009) (Table 9.1). An important distinction between public figure stalkers and those who pursue private citizens is that although ex-partners are overrepresented among stalkers in general population samples, ex-intimate stalking is not relevant to the prominent person's public office. The public figure stalker typology overlaps with the general stalker typology, once the ex-intimate (rejected) stalkers are removed. It should be noted that incompetent suitors (those ineptly pursuing a friendship or date) and predatory (sexually motivated) stalkers are less commonly encountered by well-protected public figures. Two additional public figure stalker categories emerged from the FRG studies: attention seekers and help seekers (Table 9.1).

A direct comparison was made between an Australian clinic sample of stalkers of the general population and a sample of public figure stalkers from the Royalty Protection archives. Similarities were identified between the risk factors for the two groups of stalkers (James, Kerrigan, Forfar, Farnham, & Preston, 2010). Thus, despite the separate evolution of the stalking and public figure threat assessment fields, the data suggest we are essentially referring to the same phenomenon, if the stalkers of former sexual intimates are excluded. This has led to a sharing of empirical knowledge and the advancement of risk assessment and management approaches in these two disciplines.

Convergence in the stalking and public figure protection fields has enabled the utilization of the SRP in public figure stalking risk assessments. The SRP has a public figure section, in which the public figure motivational typology forms the basis for risk judgments in the standard domains of violence, persistence, recurrence, and psychosocial damage, as well as the additional public figure stalker risk domains of escalation (the risk that the behavior will become more intrusive) and disruption (the impairment that the stalking causes to the prominent person's public function and the associated demands on public resources) (MacKenzie et al., 2009).

KEY CONCEPTS FROM THE FIXATED RESEARCH
MENTAL ILLNESS

An influential study by the U.S. Secret Service, known as the Exceptional Case Study Project (Fein & Vossekuil, 1999), which investigated attacks and near-lethal attacks, predominantly on Secret Service protectees, deemphasized the contribution of mental illness. Indicators of severe mental illness were certainly present in this study but were not accorded operational significance (see Dietz & Martell, 2010; Mullen, Pathé, et al., 2009; Mullen, James, et al., 2009). However, there is now compelling evidence for high rates of serious mental illness in fixated individuals who pursue public figures (Every-Palmer, Barry-Walsh, & Pathé, 2015; FRG, 2006; Hoffmann, Meloy, Guldimann, & Ermer, 2011; James et al., 2007; 2009; Meloy, Mohandie, & McGowan, 2008; Mullen et al., 2008; Mullen, Pathé, et al., 2009; Mullen, James, et al., 2009; Pathé, Lowry, et al., 2015, Pathé, Haworth, et al., 2015).

This has been a key finding in the public figure threat assessment literature. As previously emphasized, the vast majority of fixated persons with mental illness will never progress to violent outcomes, but a small proportion do, and the presence of mental illness provides an avenue for risk mitigation.

Mental health data from cases referred to Fixated Threat Assessment Centers operating in the United Kingdom and Australia (described later), which assess and manage fixated loners, have consistently contained substantial rates of major mental illness, with only a minority of these cases receiving mental health care at the time of referral. For referred cases currently under the care of a mental health service, the treating clinician was often unaware of their patient's behaviors and associated risks. Others had disengaged from treatment leading to symptom relapse, while a significant minority were not known to the mental health system. In these instances, warning behaviors such as disordered correspondence to public office holders, heralded an illness which had deteriorated, often unnoticed, over several years. The following is an example from the files of the Queensland Fixated Threat Assessment Center. Nonessential details have been altered.

A 70-year-old single man had written frequently to public office holders over a 5-year period. These contained his various suspicions about the activities of neighbors and redevelopers in the area, but in recent months the letters had escalated in frequency and adopted a more desperate tone. He made references to "intruders" and "terrorists" on his roof at night and he begged for help.

The man was not known to any mental health agency and there were no police records other than his letter writing. A police officer and mental health clinician conducted a visit to his isolated property, which was surrounded by makeshift barricades. Inside, the elderly man was living in squalid conditions in a state of fear, with towels covering his windows and axes propped up against the doors.

An involuntary assessment order was prepared and the local mental health service arranged for his admission to hospital. Further history from estranged family members and neighbors suggested that he had been unwell over many years. His persecutory delusions responded to medication, and he was eventually discharged to supported accommodation. His disordered correspondence had effectively exposed his illness, improved his quality of life, and greatly reduced his assessed risk. He has abandoned his letter writing, preferring to watch television for the first time in 15 years.

WARNING BEHAVIORS

Threats are not uncommon among the stalkers of private citizens. They are frequently associated with ex-intimate (rejected) and resentful stalking patterns (Table 9.1). Resentful stalkers are typically gratified by the distress they evoke in their victims and few enact their threats. Ex-intimate stalkers are far more likely to progress to harmful outcomes, and threats in this group should be regarded as promises (McEwan et al., 2007, 2011; Mullen et al., 1999).

Studies of threats by public figure stalkers have generally demonstrated an inverse relationship between issuing a threat and subsequent approaches. As noted earlier, Dietz, Matthews, Van Duyne, et al. (1991) and Dietz, Matthews, Martell, et al. (1991) found that direct threats did not predict approach behaviors in subjects who engaged in threatening and inappropriate communications to Hollywood celebrities and politicians. However, it would be unwise to dismiss the predictive value of direct threats in those who harass the famous, as a substantial minority of threateners *do* proceed to approach and/or attack. Dietz, Matthews, Van Duyne, et al. (1991) and Dietz, Matthews, Martell, et al. (1991) found that 23% of correspondents who made threats to Hollywood celebrities and 33% of those sending threatening letters to members of the U.S. Congress did subsequently approach. Meloy et al. (2008) found that 35% of their celebrity stalkers who made prior threats went on to approach, and Scalora et al. (2003) found that 41% of threatening writers to U.S. congress members subsequently engaged in approach behaviors.

Although direct threats are not a reliable way to alert public figures and the authorities to fixated approaches and attacks, many fixated persons do engage in antecedent warning behaviors. As noted earlier, warning behaviors are effectively a manifestation of the subject's fixation and frequently also signal a mental disorder. Warning behaviors may be evident in the person's utterances or activities, and can be present for days, months, or even years. Examples include disordered, aggressive, or otherwise threatening correspondence or approaches to public office holders or other authorities; lone protests; hunger strikes; lawsuits against the public figure or government; posters; leaflets; media advertisements; and informing others of their intentions ("leakage"), typically through social media. To this can be added last resort thinking (see "Last Resort Language"), which is a "red flag" risk factor in stalking, signaling the potential for more serious or imminent violence.

LAST RESORT LANGUAGE

Examples: *This is my last chance; You give me no choice; I'm at the end of my tether; If I can't have her, nobody will; You are my only hope; I'm at my wit's end.*

The individual indicates that they have reached a point where they no longer feel constrained by legal or moral imperatives. They have relinquished hope of achieving the goals of their stalking by socially acceptable means. Their efforts have proved futile, they are exasperated and they believe they must now provoke a definitive outcome.

Last resort thinking may be triggered by recent losses or destabilisers, such as job retrenchment or a failed court case.

From Stalking Risk Profile (MacKenzie et al., 2009, p. 22).

The following composite case from the author's files illustrates warning behaviors that were not appreciated or acted on prior to a violent attack. Further examples can be found in James et al. (2007) study of attacks on Western European politicians.

A 60-year-old man who lived on the outskirts of a regional town had a longstanding grievance against the government. He believed that he won $100 million in the lottery 4 years earlier but his local Member of Parliament had conspired with police to steal his winning ticket. He was unswayed by evidence that there had never been a $100 million draw. He repeatedly petitioned his state and federal parliamentarians, sending numerous letters and emails over a 4-year period to his local MP, the federal member and the prime minister. He received a generic acknowledgement from the federal MP's office, and some social services pamphlets from his local electoral office.

In the meantime, by way of protest he ceased paying his bills, including his rent, and he was threatened with eviction. He refused to accept social welfare payments because he believed he was a multimillionaire, once he claimed what was rightfully his.

Over time, his correspondence increased in volume and frequency, with an angrier tone. His emails contained implied threats, and statements to the effect that they had left him no choice. No concerns were raised and no action was taken, and 2 days after his last missive he drove his truck through the home of his local MP.

This caused considerable damage to the MP's property and his teenaged son narrowly avoided injury.

The man's neighbors subsequently reported that he had been behaving oddly for at least 6 months. He had been seen walking along the highway at midnight, collecting rubbish, and he erected large placards around the periphery of his property, accusing the government of avarice and treachery.

The man was a divorcee who had worked in the mines and he still held a shot firer's license. When police subsequently searched his property, they discovered explosives in his shed, and a list of names of politicians with maps detailing their addresses.

The man was unknown to mental health services, and police holdings were confined to the 4-year history of unrewarding contact with politicians. He was charged with numerous offences. While remanded in custody he was diagnosed by prison mental health services with a delusional disorder and transferred to a psychiatric facility. He was subsequently found to be of unsound mind at the time of the offence, and was treated in hospital for an extended period.

This man engaged in a number of warning behaviors over several years which were not properly recognized or addressed, including inappropriate correspondence and threats to public office holders, posters, and last resort statements. These were missed opportunities to prevent the progression to destructive consequences, for the politician and his family, to their neighbor (whose home was also damaged), and to the man himself, who spent the next few years in prisons and secure hospitals. There was a clear potential for a more serious outcome, given the man had researched other public office holders and he could access and operate dangerous weapons. It unfortunately required a dramatic incident to bring about treatment for his erstwhile unrecognized psychotic illness. Thus, although the fixated less commonly issue direct threats, their attacks are potentially preventable, if there is a system in place to identify and assess warning behaviors (Meloy, Hoffmann, Guldimann, & James, 2012).

THREAT ASSESSMENT AND MANAGEMENT SERVICES FOR FIXATED PERSONS

Both law enforcement and mental health services encounter concerning, fixated individuals but until recently neither possessed sufficient information to properly assess or manage the risk. The FRG concluded that what was needed was a threat assessment agency to specifically address the threat posed by lone, fixated persons. The FRG also believed that such an agency would require the combined skills and resources of both police and mental health personnel. They envisaged that an integrated service of this type would need several key components: a referral process that screened out low concern cases (the "background noise"), an intelligence database, an investigative capacity, information governance processes, an evidence-based risk assessment tool for identifying cases requiring further intervention, a range of intervention options including mental health diversion, a case management system for high concern cases, and a process of regular case review. It was also evident that mental health professionals would need to be actively involved, both in the assessment of these individuals and in the facilitation of mental health care through liaison with colleagues in psychiatric services (James et al., 2010).

THE FIXATED THREAT ASSESSMENT CENTER – UNITED KINGDOM

These aims were realized in 2006, when the British Home Office established the Fixated Threat Assessment Center (FTAC) in London (Boyce, 2011; James et al., 2010, 2014). FTAC is the first integrated police–mental health intelligence agency of its kind in the world. Staffed and funded by the Metropolitan Police Service and National Health Service, the unit's core function is to assess and manage the risks posed by fixated persons to public figures, their workplaces, and prominent sites and events. Its referrers include members of the British Royal Family and politicians across the United Kingdom. Standardized risk assessments informed by mental health and police data are undertaken jointly by police and mental health staff. In cases determined to be of at least moderate concern (in terms of potential for harm), interventions are formulated. Given the high rates of mental illness in the fixated, many of whom have fallen through the care net, such interventions frequently entail linking the individual with mental health services. Outcomes are summarized later.

The success of FTAC's collaborative, early intervention model in reducing risk through the facilitation of care for mentally ill, fixated people has attracted the interest of forensic mental health and law enforcement agencies in other nations. Several countries including the Netherlands have taken steps to establish similar agencies (Voerman, 2014). However, differences in mental health legislation, information sharing, and resources have restricted the extent to which this model can be replicated in other European centers.

Serious assaults on public figures are rare in Australia, with just two recorded assassination attempts by mentally ill, fixated individuals: the near-fatal shooting in 1868 of Prince Alfred, son of Queen Victoria, by a man who had been recently released from a mental institution, and the attempted shooting of Australian political party leader Arthur Calwell in 1966 by a mentally ill teenager (Calwell, 2014). There have been many more reports of serious threats to harm or kill Australian politicians (for example, Paull, 2011). Moreover, a survey of Canadian politicians suggested that public figure harassment was relatively common and frequently perpetrated by mentally disordered individuals (Adams, Hazelwood, Pitre, Bedard, & Landry, 2009).

QUEENSLAND FIXATED THREAT ASSESSMENT CENTER – QUEENSLAND, AUSTRALIA

In 2011, forensic mental health researchers in the Australian state of Queensland conducted a survey of Queensland state parliamentarians, aimed at establishing the frequency of harassing behaviors experienced by these politicians, the nature and impact of the intrusions, and the likely contribution of mental illness. An anonymous questionnaire was distributed to all 89 members of Parliament. Almost half the MPs responded, and 93% of these reported at least one form of harassment, the most common being alarming behavior at the electoral office and receipt of inappropriate correspondence or telephone calls. Threats to harm were reported by 60% of respondents, with 14% reporting at least one attempted or actual physical assault. The duration of harassment ranged from less than 1 h to 8 years (median 2 months), and over 80% of those targeted reported some level of fear. Half of these parliamentarians considered their harasser to be mentally ill (Pathé, Phillips, Perdacher, & Heffernan, 2014).

This survey was originally administered to the Westminster parliament members in England and subsequently to parliamentarians in New Zealand (Every-Palmer et al., 2015; James et al., 2016). Despite differing parliamentary structures, sample sizes and response rates (United Kingdom 38%, Queensland 49%, New Zealand 84%), the results of these studies were remarkably consistent in many respects. As for the Queensland harassment survey, intrusive/aggressive behaviors featured prominently, being reported by 81% of the Westminster responders and 87% of New Zealand MPs. They also reported similarly disturbing levels of actual or attempted physical assault (18% for Westminster and 15% for New Zealand parliaments.) In the United Kingdom, 39% of MPs considered the perpetrator to be mentally ill. Half the New Zealand parliamentary sample formed this opinion, and a further 29% were unsure.

Queensland shares a similar legal framework and mental health laws to the United Kingdom. The Queensland Police Service (QPS) recognized that existing law enforcement processes for evaluating threats to public office holders were compromised by the lack of evidence-based tools and the inability to address the main problem underlying fixation: mental illness. With limited access to police information, mental healthcare providers were often unaware of the concerning behaviors of their patients and, thus, the risk they potentially posed. In some cases, the mentally ill fixated person had not even come to the attention of mental health services. Queensland had an established history of joint police–mental health initiatives and a preexisting memorandum of understanding that specified the parameters of information sharing between the police and health services. The Queensland MP harassment survey (Pathé et al., 2014) highlighted a significant threat to the democratic process and the need for an FTAC-style service in Australia.

The Queensland Fixated Threat Assessment Center (QFTAC) was established in 2013. It is a jointly funded service situated within the Security Operations Unit at the QPS Headquarters. Senior mental health clinicians are embedded in the unit.

While the UK FTAC has a national remit and its stakeholders include the British Royal Family and royal households, QFTAC's stakeholders are predominantly state MPs, federal politicians whose electorate lies in Queensland, ministerial and electoral offices, and members of the judiciary. As outlined in the following section, both FTAC and its more recent Australian incarnation have demonstrated their effectiveness in protecting public figures, improving public health, and, importantly, promoting public safety. Both centers are subject to ongoing evaluation and place an emphasis on training and research activities aimed at enhancing existing practices in this field. A comprehensive account of the functions and activities of FTAC and QFTAC can be found in James et al. (2014) and Pathé, Lowry, et al. (2015).

THE EFFECTIVENESS OF FIXATED THREAT ASSESSMENT AGENCIES

Integrated approaches to managing the fixated threat have demonstrated their efficacy in facilitating care and treatment for fixated persons and reducing the associated risks. FTAC's analysis of the first 100 consecutive cases assessed as a moderate or high concern found that 86% suffered from a psychotic illness, 57% were admitted to hospital, and 26% were accepted by community mental health teams. By catalyzing suitable health outcomes, 80% of cases were reduced to a low level of concern (James et al., 2010, 2014).

In a similar vein, in its first year of operations QFTAC found that more than half the individuals who had displayed problematic behaviors toward public office holders were seriously mentally ill, and almost three-quarters of these had either disengaged from care or were unknown to mental health services. A substantial proportion of cases had previously attracted the attention of police. At initial referral, two-thirds of cases were assessed as a moderate or high level of concern. There was a substantial reduction in concern levels at the conclusion of the 12-month reporting period (96% low, 4% moderate, 0% high). QFTAC's outcomes in the following year showed a similar trend, with over 60% of referrals having psychiatric issues, a third of whom were diagnosed with a serious mental illness such as schizophrenia, delusional disorder, or major mood disorder. Only a quarter of those with psychiatric issues were receiving mental health treatment at the time of referral. In addition to addressing other identified risk factors (such as removal of weapons), over 40% of these cases were referred by QFTAC to a public mental health service. Initially, 21% of QFTAC cases were assessed as being of high concern and 39% as a moderate concern. At the end of the annual reporting period following intervention, 96% of cases had fallen to a low level of concern.

The higher proportion of mentally ill fixated people reported by UK FTAC is likely to be a reflection of differences in the public figure populations serviced by FTAC and its Australian counterpart. Those who fixate on royalty—a large proportion of FTAC referrals—have a high prevalence of mental illness or at least the more overt forms of mental illness (James et al., 2009; van der Meer, Bootsma, & Meloy, 2012).

FIXATED PERSONS AT MAJOR EVENTS

Major public figure gatherings can be a drawcard for the fixated. Those who have an imagined relationship with a dignitary may seek access to that person at a major event. Those fixated on a cause rather than a specific delegate may view the event as a platform to publicly avenge a perceived injustice or an opportunity to draw attention to their cause on a global scale.

Mentally disordered individuals without fixated motives may also intrude at such events. They usually fall into one of the following groups.

THE DISORGANIZED

An acutely psychotic or intoxicated group, these individuals are typically disorganized in their presentation. They have often incorporated delegates and police into their delusional perceptions, but they have no history or current indicators of fixation. For example, a man with florid persecutory delusions who believes the pronounced police presence at a G20 meeting is specifically intended for him shouts at a police helicopter hovering overhead, convinced it is filming him.

THE CURIOUS

These are usually rather hapless and innocuous individuals, most of whom are mentally or intellectually disabled. Their intrusions at events stem from poor social skills and self-awareness, and they are often oblivious to the significance of the occasion or the security concerns. One man with chronic schizophrenia who was waiting on a park bench to meet a friend became intrigued by the dignitaries exiting a nearby hotel. He approached the hotel entrance and politely requested that a police officer photograph him with a world leader.

THE SUICIDAL

People who are seeking a dramatic exit may gravitate to major events because they are armed settings conducive to secondary suicide, or "suicide by cop." One man who wanted to exact revenge on his former employer threatened to disrupt a political party meeting so he could "go down in a hail of bullets." On advice from a family member, the man was apprehended by police, loitering on the outskirts of the venue.

THE PEST

This group is seeking attention for their own gratification, and they are not committed to any particular cause. Serious mental illness is uncommon in this group, and personality disorders predominate. These individuals are often known to police, having attracted publicity through their antics at previous events. One such individual, who had a severe borderline personality disorder, told his mental health case manager that he planned to attend the G20 wearing women's lingerie. He was admitted to hospital the next day following a suicidal gesture, surrendering his opportunity to attend the event.

In 2014, the G20 Finance Ministers' meeting and World Leaders' Summit were held in the Queensland cities of Cairns and Brisbane, respectively. This was the largest peacetime security and policing operation in Australia's history, and the risk posed by fixated persons at these events was duly recognized. Historically, the fixated consumed valuable policing and security resources at major events. Furthermore, major events, being secure and armed environments, constituted a risk to intrusive, mentally ill persons.

QFTAC developed a model for managing fixated persons at these events, comprising preoperational, operational, and postoperational phases (Pathé, Haworth, et al., 2015). There was a strong emphasis on preoperational planning, during which QFTAC liaised with partner agencies globally to obtain relevant information on persons who had demonstrated a fixation on a delegate or a cause and who were deemed to have the capacity to attend the event. QFTAC conducted risk assessments and risk management interventions in concerning cases. Some of these individuals were acutely unwell, necessitating psychiatric admission or more intensive community treatment. Preoperational training was also provided to mental health and law enforcement agencies, to enhance awareness of the fixated and the threat they posed to themselves and others at major events.

While QFTAC deployed joint police–mental health field teams during these events, the preoperational emphasis attenuated the fixated threat before the commencement of these meetings. This major event experience reinforced the benefits of the FTAC model, as prevention through mental health intervention again proved to be the most effective and appropriate way to circumvent fixated incidents.

THE FIXATED MODEL IN OTHER AREAS OF TARGETED VIOLENCE

Fixated threat assessment agencies owe their effectiveness to a collaborative, proactive strategy. They focus on *preventing* harmful consequences rather than attempting the impossible task of predicting which individual will progress to such outcomes. Earlier recognition and management of mental illness is relevant to other areas of targeted violence, suggesting a role for similar, suitably adapted proactive models.

HIGH-RISK STALKERS

The incidence of mental illness among stalkers of ordinary citizens, though somewhat lower than the rates for public figure stalkers, far exceed that of the general population. Up to 40% of a sample of 211 stalkers referred to a forensic problem behavior clinic had a major mental illness (McEwan & Strand, 2013; Warren, MacKenzie, Mullen, & Ogloff, 2005). Serious disorders are more commonly associated with intimacy seeking and resentful patterns of stalking (Table 9.1). Rates of violence and threats are highest for stalkers of ex-intimates, the rejected stalkers. Although this is typically a personality disordered group, it is not only possible but necessary to provide mental health intervention to rejected stalkers in order to reduce risk to the victim and third parties, and prevent a recurrence of stalking in future relationships. This entails skills-based training, targeting the skills deficits common to stalkers, particularly verbal and social skills, problem-solving/conflict resolution, and emotional regulation (MacKenzie & James, 2011).

There is a tendency to equate rejected stalking with domestic violence. Certainly, some of the behaviors that occur in domestic violence settings, such as following, surveillance, and checking, are redolent of stalking. However, the aim of stalking is to make one's presence felt where it would not otherwise exist. Where a relationship persists, however abusive, both partners still have a legitimate presence. Stalking behaviors can only begin when the relationship has unequivocally ended, and it is unrealistic to manage stalking situations while stalker and victim continue to cohabitate (McEwan & Pathé, 2013).

Of course, many domestic violence victims would choose to extricate themselves from the relationship if they felt safe to do so. There are numerous examples where women particularly have sought help to escape abusive relationships but the authorities have failed to appreciate the risks or lacked adequate resources to effectively intervene (e.g., Benny-Morrison, 2012). An early intervention model for high-risk stalkers, incorporating an evidence-based screening checklist for frontline police, would enable more informed prioritization of cases and the diversion of high-risk stalkers to treatment programs or the appropriate combination of legal sanctions and treatment (MacKenzie & James, 2011; McEwan & Strand, 2015). The approach should not be confined to ex-intimates, since stalking by strangers and acquaintances is more frequently associated with psychopathology, persistence, and stalking recidivism (McEwan & Strand, 2013).

THE "LONE ACTOR"

The "lone actor" or "lone wolf" terrorist has been variously defined. Spaaij (2010, p. 856) refers to "a person who operates individually, does not belong to an organised terrorist group or network and whose modus operandi are conceived and directed without any outside command or hierarchy." However, it is increasingly apparent that few terrorist acts are conceived by an individual extremist, given the influence of extremist groups on the Internet. A broader definition is "any individual who engages in hostile acts against others in pursuit of aims that have a particular meaning for them" (Lone actors, fixation and mental illness, 2015). Traditional counterintelligence methods employed against terrorist organizations and networks may be less applicable to lone actors. Recent research that has specifically focused on lone actor rather than group actor terrorists (Corner & Gill, 2014; Gill, 2015; Gill, Horgan, & Deckert, 2014) suggests that lone actor terrorists have more in common with fixated loners than group terrorists.

Fixated loners and terrorists differ in terms of their prevalence (the fixated are far more common) and risk of violence (substantially higher for terrorists, though the fixated can occasionally be extremely violent). Terrorists frame their actions as part of a wider group or movement, with a shared ideology, while fixated loners do not strongly affiliate with ideological groups and their cause is highly idiosyncratic. Current research also indicates that lone actor terrorists, whose average age is in the mid-30s, are older than their group counterparts (Gill, 2015) but younger than the fixated (average age mid-50s) (Pathé, Lowry, et al., 2015).

There are, however, important commonalities between lone actor terrorists and fixated loners. Both groups typically harbor a personal grievance or vendetta, triggered by perceived injustice or loss. They also share elevated rates of mental illness. While earlier studies on group terrorists dismissed the role of mental illness, the extant literature on lone actors has found considerably higher rates of mental illness relative to group actors. A study comparing mental illness in lone-actors and far-right terrorist groups found rates of 40.4% and 7.6%, respectively (Gruenewald, Chermak, & Freilich, 2013), while Corner and Gill (2014) found that 32% of their data set of 119 lone actors had been diagnosed with mental illness, a rate nearly 14 times that of a comparison sample of group-based terrorists. In short, lone actor terrorists and fixated loners have similar triggers and similar rates of mental illness.

As previously defined, lone actors engage in hostile acts against others, in pursuit of aims that have a certain meaning for them. If they are pursuing some highly personal or idiosyncratic cause, they are viewed as having fixated motives. Alternatively, if their quest is framed in some religious or political ideology, then they are generally considered to have terrorist motives (Lone actors, fixation and mental illness, 2015). However, early in the lone actor's destructive trajectory, it is not always possible to differentiate individuals with fixated and terrorist motives. When assessing the lone actor, instead of asking, "Is this a terrorist or a fixated person?" a more preemptive question would be, "Is this part of a pattern of behavior that could lead to an attack?" Regardless of motive, fixated or terrorist, there is a common need to identify vulnerable cases and intervene to address risk factors at the earliest opportunity. In the case of lone actor terrorists, mental illness may well be one of these risk factors and a potentially crucial component in terms of risk mitigation.

The FTAC model has demonstrated the capacity to apply evidence-based tools, informed by psychological understanding, to the assessment and risk management of fixated loners. A similar model could be adapted for the individual would-be terrorist with suspected mental illness or a known history of mental illness. Rather than identifying this group through their disordered correspondence to public office holders, sources of referral for lone actor extremists will need to draw on the antecedent events and behaviors, such as social media activity, monitored by security and policing agencies. Any integrated model of this type will be contingent on cooperation between agencies and the appropriate exchange of key information in the interests of public safety.

CONCLUSIONS

Fixation, mental illness, and warning behaviors play important roles in the identification, assessment, and management of those who threaten and stalk public figures. This is encapsulated in the words of Dietz and Martell (2010, p. 344): "Every instance of an attack on a public figure in the United States for which adequate information has been made publicly available has been the work of a mentally disordered person who issued one or more pre-attack signals in the form of letter, visits or statements." The recognition and effective management of fixated behaviors have wider implications, as fixated loners frequently pose a greater risk to themselves and those around them. The introduction of preventive services to specifically address the threat posed by these individuals has important implications for public health and safety. Research on stalkers of private citizens has advanced our knowledge in the public figure arena, enhancing our capacity to distinguish the masses of discontented, aggrieved, self-important, and ineffectual people from those with the potential to progress to seriously adverse outcomes.

SUMMARY

- In Western civilizations, people who pursue the famous pose a greater risk of death or serious injury to their targets than terrorist groups or criminals. Unfortunately, there is an abundance of individuals harboring intense preoccupations with a public figure or some related cause, and while only a minority progress to violent acts, this is a small proportion of a sizable group.
- Extreme violence is an uncommon outcome for this group, whom we term "fixated" or "fixated loners," but other detrimental impacts are not, including psychological distress, embarrassment, disruption, adverse media attention, and dissipation of resources. Physical protection measures alone have not proved to be a sufficient defense against the fixated.
- The word "stalking" was originally coined by the media in relation to "star stalkers," passionate fans who pursued celebrities. One such high-profile stalking case (that of actress Rebecca Schaeffer) was a catalyst for the passage of the world's first stalking legislation in California in 1990.
- Stalking is a behavioral concept describing persistent and repeated harassment, in which one person imposes on another unwanted communications and/ or contacts. It is targeted to a specific victim and includes both implicitly and explicitly threatening behavior that can persist for a protracted period. Capturing this diverse constellation of behaviors under the rubric of stalking has inspired an ever-expanding discourse in the legal, social and behavioral sciences.
- Erotomania is "a conviction that one is loved, despite the supposed lover having done nothing to encourage or sustain that belief, but on the contrary having either made clear their lack of interest or remaining unaware of the claimed

relationship." Erotomanic delusions are not uncommon among those who stalk the famous, particularly celebrity rather than political figures. The forensic implications of erotomania were first clearly articulated by Alexander Morrison in 1848, when he wrote that: "Erotomania sometimes prompts those laboring under it to destroy themselves or others, for although in general tranquil and respectful, the patient sometimes becomes irritable, passionate and jealous".

- The 1990s heralded the development of the first structured professional guidelines for violence risk assessment, including general measures such as the Historical Clinical Risk-20 (HCR-20; Webster et al., 1997) and special-purpose risk assessment measures for specific forms of violence, including the Spousal Assault Risk Assessment Guide (SARA; Kropp et al., 1999) and the Risk for Sexual Violence Protocol (RSVP; Hart et al., 2003). These instruments have been validated and incorporated into clinical forensic practice in most Western nations. White and Meloy (2007) have since advanced the Workplace Assessment of Violence Risk (WAVR-21), a structured tool for assessing targeted violence in the workplace.

- In 2009, MacKenzie and colleagues published *Stalking Risk Profile: Guidelines for Assessment and Management of Stalkers (SRP)*. The key principle underpinning the SRP is that different types of stalkers have different motivations, and risk therefore varies according to stalker type.

- Pathological "fixation" (from the Latin *figo*, to be "bound fast") is a psychological concept defined as obsessive preoccupations pursued to an abnormally intense degree. These individuals can be fixated on a person (usually a celebrity figure such as an actor, newsreader, musician or sports star) or some idiosyncratic cause (an intensely personal grievance or quest for justice). Fixated individuals commonly engage in stalking behaviors as a consequence of their all-consuming beliefs.

- An influential study by the U.S. Secret Service, known as the *Exceptional Case Study Project*, deemphasized the contribution of mental illness after investigating attacks and near-lethal attacks, predominantly on Secret Service protectees. While there were indicators of severe mental illness throughout the study, they were not considered to be operationally significant. However, this has largely been refuted, and there is now compelling evidence for high rates of serious mental illness in fixated individuals who pursue public figures. This has been a key finding in the public figure threat assessment literature. The vast majority of fixated persons with mental illness will never progress to violent outcomes; however, a small proportion do, and the presence of mental illness provides an avenue for risk mitigation.

- Threats are not uncommon among the stalkers of private citizens. They are frequently associated with ex-intimate (rejected) and resentful stalking patterns (Table 9.1). Resentful stalkers are typically gratified by the distress they evoke in their victims and few enact their threats. Ex-intimate stalkers are far more likely to progress to harmful outcomes, and threats in this group should be regarded as "promises." Integrated approaches to managing the fixated threat have demonstrated their efficacy in facilitating care and treatment for fixated persons and reducing the associated risks.

- Major public figure gatherings can be a drawcard for the fixated. Those who have an imagined relationship with a dignitary may seek access to that person at a major event. Those fixated on a cause rather than a specific delegate may view the event as a platform to publicly avenge a perceived injustice, or an opportunity to draw attention to their cause on a global scale.
- Mentally disordered individuals without fixated motives may also intrude at such events. They usually fall into one of the following groups: disorganized, curious, suicidal, and pest.
- **The Disorganized:** An acutely psychotic or intoxicated group. These individuals are typically disorganized in their presentation. They have often incorporated delegates and police into their delusional perceptions but they have no history or current indicators of fixation.
- **The Curious:** These are usually rather hapless and innocuous individuals, most of whom are mentally or intellectually disabled. Their intrusions at events stem from poor social skills and self-awareness, and they are often oblivious to the significance of the occasion or the security concerns.
- **The Suicidal:** People who are seeking a dramatic exit may gravitate to major events because they are armed settings conducive to secondary suicide, or "suicide by cop."
- **The Pest:** This group is seeking attention for their own gratification, and are not committed to any particular cause. Serious mental illness is uncommon in this group, and personality disorders predominate. These individuals are often known to police, having attracted publicity through their antics at previous events.
- Fixated threat assessment agencies owe their effectiveness to a collaborative, proactive strategy. They focus on preventing harmful consequences rather than attempting the impossible task of predicting which individual will progress to such outcomes. Earlier recognition and management of mental illness is relevant to other areas of targeted violence, suggesting a role for similar, suitably adapted proactive models.

QUESTIONS

1. Define "stalking," and explain the unique characteristics of public figure stalking.
2. What association is there between stalking and public figure threat assessment?
3. Describe the key elements of Mullen et al.'s Stalking Risk Profile Motivational Typology (see Table 9.1).
4. Provide a description of three structured risk assessment tools.
5. In threat assessment, discuss the issue of mental health as a risk factor.

6. In threat assessment, discuss the importance of awareness of warning behaviors. Describe the key warning behaviors identified by the research.
7. Provide an explanation of risk assessment and management practices and, in doing so, provide a summary of the effectiveness of these practices.
8. Detail the characteristics of the four primary motivational types of the fixated person most likely to engage with a target during public events, and provide examples of a characteristic engagement scenario.
9. Describe the relevance of the fixated person model in the context of high-risk stalking.
10. Describe the relevance of the fixated stalker model in the context of the "lone actor."

REFERENCES

Adams, S. J., Hazelwood, T. E., Pitre, N. L., Bedard, T. E., & Landry, S. D. (2009). Harassment of Members of Parliament and the Legislative Assemblies in Canada by individuals believed to be mentally disordered. *The Journal of Forensic Psychiatry & Psychology, 20*(6), 801–814.

de Becker, G. (1997). *The Gift of Fear: Survival signals that protect us from violence.* London: Bloomsbury.

Benny-Morrison, A. (June 18, 2012). *Man stalked ex before murders: Inquiry.* Retrieved November 21, 2015, from: http://www.news-mail.com.au/news/man-stalked-ex-murders-inquiry/1421575/.

Boyce, N. (2011). The UK's fix for fixated threats. *Lancet, 377*(9763), 367–368.

Calwell, A. (August 30, 2014). *Wikipedia, the free encyclopedia.* Retrieved August 30, 2014, from http://en.wikipedia.org/wiki/Arther_Calwell.

Corner, E., & Gill, P. (2014). A false dichotomy? Lone actor terrorism and mental illness. *Law and Human Behavior, 39*, 23–34.

Dietz, P. E., & Martell, D. A. (2010). Commentary: approaching and stalking public figures – a prerequisite to attack. *Journal of the American Academy of Psychiatry and the Law, 38*(3), 341–348.

Dietz, P. E., Matthews, D. B., Van Duyne, C., et al. (1991). Threatening and otherwise inappropriate letters to Hollywood celebrities. *Journal of Forensic Sciences, 36*, 185–209.

Dietz, P. E., Matthews, D. B., Martell, D. A., et al. (1991). Threatening and otherwise inappropriate letters to members of the United States Congress. *Journal of Forensic Sciences, 36*, 1445–1468.

Dunblane school massacre. (November 6, 2015). *Wikipedia, the free encyclopedia.* Retrieved November 6, 2015, from: https://en.wikipedia.org/wiki/Dunblane_school_massacre.

Enoch, M. D., & Trethowan, W. H. (1979). *Uncommon psychiatric syndromes.* Bristol: John Wright & Sons.

Esquirol, J. E. D. (1965). *Mental maladies: A treatise on insanity* (translated by R. de Saussure). New York, NY: Hafner. Original work published 1845.

Every-Palmer, S., Barry-Walsh, J., & Pathé, M. T. (2015). Harassment, stalking, threats and attacks targeting New Zealand politicians: a mental health issue. *Australian & New Zealand Journal of Psychiatry, 49*(7), 634–641.

Farnham, F. R., James, D. V., & Cantrell, P. (2000). Association between violence, psychosis, and relationship to victim in stalkers. *Lancet, 355*, 199.

Fein, R. A., & Vossekuil, B. (1999). Assassination in the United States: an operational study of recent assassins, attackers, and near-lethal approachers. *Journal of Forensic Sciences, 44*(2), 321–333.

Fixated Research Group. (2006). *Inappropriate communications, approaches and attacks on the British royal family, with additional consideration of attacks on politicians* (Research Report). London: Home Office.

Gill, P. (2015). *Lone-actor terrorists: A behavioural analysis.* London: Routledge.

Gill, P., Horgan, J., & Deckert, P. (2014). Bombing alone: tracing the motivations and antecedent behaviors of lone-actor terrorists. *Journal of Forensic Sciences, 59*(2), 425–435.

Gruenewald, J., Chermak, S., & Freilich, J. D. (2013). Distinguishing 'loner' attacks from other domestic extremist violence: a comparison of far-right homicide. Incident and offender characteristics. *Criminology & Public Policy, 12*(1), 65–91.

Hart, S. D., Kropp, P., & Laws, D. (2003). *The risk for sexual violence protocol (RSVP).* Vancouver: Mental Health, Law and Policy Institute, Simon Fraser University.

Hoffmann, J., Meloy, J. R., Guldimann, A., & Ermer, A. (2011). Attacks on German public figures 1968–2004: warning behaviors, potentially lethal and non-lethal acts, psychiatric status and motivations. *Behavioral Sciences & the Law, 29*(2), 155–179.

James, D. V., et al. (2016). Harassment and stalking of Westminster MPs: (2) associations and consequences. *Journal of Forensic Psychiatry & Psychology*, http://dx.doi.org/10.1080/14789949.2015.1124909.

James, D. V., Farnham, F. R., & Wilson, S. P. (2014). The fixated threat assessment centre: implementing a joint policing and psychiatric approach to risk assessment and management in public figure threat cases. In J. R. Meloy, & J. Hoffmann (Eds.), *International handbook of threat assessment* (pp. 299–320). New York, NY: Oxford University Press.

James, D. V., Kerrigan, T., Forfar, R., Farnham, F. R., & Preston, L. (2010). The Fixated Threat Assessment Centre: preventing harm and facilitating care. *The Journal of Forensic Psychiatry & Psychology, 21*(4), 521–536.

James, D. V., Mullen, P. E., Meloy, J. R., Pathé, M. T., Farnham, F. R., Preston, L., et al. (2007). The role of mental disorder in attacks on European politicians 1990–2004. *Acta Psychiatrica Scandinavica, 116*(5), 334–344.

James, D. V., Mullen, P. E., Pathé, M. T., Meloy, J. R., Preston, L., Darnley, B., et al. (2009). Stalkers and harassers of royalty: the role of mental illness and motivation. *Psychological Medicine, 39*, 1479–1490.

Kropp, P. R., Hart, S. D., & Lyon, D. R. (2002). Risk assessment of stalkers: some problems and possible solutions. *Criminal Justice and Behavior, 29*, 590–616.

Kropp, P. R., Hart, S. D., & Lyon, D. R. (2008). Risk assessment of public figure stalkers. In J. R. Meloy, L. Sheridan, & J. Hoffmann (Eds.), *Stalking, threatening and attacking public figures: A psychological and behavioral analysis.* New York: Oxford University Press.

Kropp, P. R., Hart, S. D., Lyon, D. R., & Storey, J. E. (2011). The development and validation of the guidelines for stalking assessment and management. *Behavioral Sciences & the Law, 29*(2), 3012–3016.

Kropp, P. R., Hart, S. D., Webster, C. D., & Eaves, D. (1999). *Manual for the spousal assault risk assessment guide.* Toronto: Multi-Health Systems.

Lone actors. (2015). *Fixation and mental illness.* Retrieved November 21, 2015, from: http://www.theseus11p.com/briefing-and-media/news-and-events/10/Lone-actors-fixation-and-mental-illness.

Lowney, K. S., & Best, J. (1995). Stalking strangers and lovers: changing media typifications of a new crime problem. In L. Best (Ed.), *Images of issues: Typifying contemporary social problems* (2nd ed.) (pp. 33–57). New York: Aldine de Gruyter.

MacKenzie, R. D., & James, D. V. (2011). Management and treatment of stalkers: problems, options and solutions. *Behavioral Sciences & the Law, 29*(2), 220–239.

MacKenzie, R. D., McEwan, T. E., Pathé, M. T., James, D. V., Ogloff, J. R. P., & Mullen, P. E. (2009). *The stalking risk profile: Guidelines for the assessment and management of stalkers.* Melbourne, Australia: Monash University & StalkInc.

Mair, G. (1995). *Star stalkers.* New York: Pinnacle Books, 21–38.

McEwan, T. E., & Pathé, M. (2013). Stalking. In G. Bruinsma, & D. Weisburd (Eds.), *Encyclopedia of criminology and criminal justice* (pp. 5026–5038). New York: Springer.

McEwan, T. E., & Strand, S. (2013). The role of psychopathology in stalking by adult strangers and acquaintances. *Australian & New Zealand Journal of Psychiatry, 47,* 546–555.

McEwan, T. E., & Strand, S. (November 2015). Improving assessment in stalking cases: the SAS-R and the SRP. In *Paper presented at the Asia Pacific association of threat assessment professionals. Bangkok, Thailand* (pp. 2–5) (November).

McEwan, T. E., Mullen, P. E., & Purcell, R. (2007). Identifying risk factors in stalking: a review of current research. *International Journal of Law & Psychiatry, 30,* 1–9.

McEwan, T. E., Pathé, M., & Ogloff, J. R. P. (2011). Advances in stalking risk assessment. *Behavioral Sciences & the Law, 29,* 180–201.

van der Meer, B. B., Bootsma, L., & Meloy, J. R. (2012). Disturbing communications and problematic approaches to the Dutch royal family. *The Journal of Forensic Psychiatry & Psychology, 23*(5–6), 571–589.

Meloy, J. R. (2001). Communicated threats and violence toward public and private targets: discerning differences among those who stalk and attack. *Journal of Forensic Sciences, 46*(5), 1211–1213.

Meloy, J. R., Hoffmann, J., Guldimann, A., & James, D. (2012). The role of warning behaviors in threat assessment: an exploration and suggested typology. *Behavioral Sciences & the Law, 30*(3), 256–279.

Meloy, J. R., James, D. V., Farnham, F. R., Mullen, P. E., Pathé, M., Darnley, B., et al. (2004). A research review of public figure threats, approaches, attacks, and assassinations in the United States. *Journal of Forensic Sciences, 49*(5), 1–8.

Meloy, J. R., Mohandie, K., & McGowan, M. G. (2008). A forensic investigation of those who stalk celebrities. In J. R. Meloy, L. Sheridan, & J. Hoffmann (Eds.), *Stalking, threatening, and attacking public figures: A psychological and behavioral analysis* (pp. 37–54). Oxford: Oxford University Press.

Millard, C. (2011). *Destiny of the republic: A tale of madness, medicine and the murder of a president.* New York: Doubleday.

Mullen, P. E., James, D. V., Meloy, J. R., Pathé, M. T., Farnham, F. R., Preston, L., et al. (2008). The role of psychotic illnesses in attacks on public figures. In J. R. Meloy, L. Sheridan, & J. Hoffmann (Eds.), *Stalking, threatening, and attacking public figures. A psychological and behavioral analysis* (pp. 55–82). Oxford: Oxford University Press.

Mullen, P. E., & Pathé, M. (1994a). Stalking and the pathologies of love. *Australian & New Zealand Journal of Psychiatry, 28,* 469–477.

Mullen, P. E., & Pathé, M. (1994b). The pathological extensions of love. *British Journal of Psychiatry, 165,* 35–43.

Mullen, P. E., Pathé, M., & Purcell, R. (2009), *Stalkers and their victims* (2nd ed.). Cambridge, UK: Cambridge University Press.

Mullen, P. E., James, D. V., Meloy, J. R., Pathé, M. T., Farnham, F. R., Preston, L., et al. (2009), The fixated and the pursuit of public figures. *Journal of Forensic Psychiatry & Psychology, 20,* 33–47.

Mullen, P. E., Pathé, M., Purcell, R., & Stuart, G. W. (1999). A study of stalkers. *American Journal of Psychiatry, 156,* 1244–1249.

Pathé, M., & Mullen, P. E. (1997). The impact of stalkers on their victims. *British Journal of Psychiatry, 170,* 12–17.

Pathé, M. T., Haworth, D. J., Lowry, T. J., Webster, D. M., Winterbourne, P., Mulder, M. J., et al. (2015), A model for managing the mentally ill fixated person at major events. *Australian & New Zealand Journal of Psychiatry.* 10.1177/00048677415581022.

Pathé, M. T., Lowry, T. J., Haworth, D. J., Webster, D., Winterbourne, P., Mulder, M. J., et al. (2015), Assessing and managing the threat posed by fixated persons in Australia. *Journal of Forensic Psychiatry & Psychology.* 10.1080/14789949.2015.1037332.

Pathé, M. T., & Meloy, J. R. (2013). Commentary: stalking by patients: psychiatrists' tales of anger, lust and ignorance. *Journal of the American Academy of Psychiatry and Law, 41,* 200–205.

Pathé, M., Phillips, J., Perdacher, E., & Heffernan, E. (2014). The harassment of Queensland Members of Parliament: a mental health concern. *Psychiatry, Psychology and Law, 21,* 577–584.

Paull, N. (June 10, 2011). *PM kill threat.* Retrieved October 2011 from: http://www.townsvillebulletin.com.au/article/2011/06/10/238375_news.html.

Phillips, R. T. M. (2006). Assessing presidential stalkers and assassins. *Journal of the American Academy of Psychiatry and the Law, 34,* 154–164.

Phillips, R. T. M. (2008). Preventing assassination: psychiatric consultation to the United States secret service. In J. R. Meloy, L. Sheridan, & J. Hoffmann (Eds.), *Stalking, threatening and attacking public figures: A psychological and behavioral analysis* (pp. 363–386). New York: Oxford University Press.

Pinals, D. A. (2007). Stalking: classification and typology. In D. A. Pinals (Ed.), *Stalking: Psychiatric perspectives and practical approaches* (pp. 27–60). New York: Oxford University Press.

Rosenfeld, B. (2004). Violence risk factors in stalking and obsessional harassment: a review and preliminary meta-analysis. *Criminal Justice & Behavior, 31,* 9–36.

Scalora, M. J., Baumgartner, J. V., Callaway, D., Zimmerman, W., Hatch-Maillette, M. A., Covell, C. N., et al. (2002). An epidemiological assessment of problematic contacts to members of Congress. *Journal of Forensic Sciences, 47,* 1360–1364.

Scalora, M. J., Baumgartner, J. V., Hatch-Maillette, M. A., Covell, C. N., Palarea, R. E., Krebs, J. A., et al. (2003). Risk factors for approach behavior toward the U.S. Congress. *Journal of Threat Assessment, 2*(2), 35–55.

Schaeffer, R. (November 6, 2015). *Wikipedia, the free encyclopedia.* Retrieved 6 November, 2015 from: https://en.wikipedia.org/wiki/Rebecca_Schaeffer.

Spaaij, R. (2010). The enigma of lone wolf terrorism: an assessment. *Studies in Conflict & Terrorism, 33*(9), 854–870.

Spitzberg, B. H., & Cupach, W. R. (2007). The state of the art of stalking: taking stock of the emerging literature. *Aggression & Violent Behavior, 12,* 64–86.

Tucson Shooting. (November 21, 2015). *Wikipedia, the free encyclopedia.* Retrieved November 21, 2015 from: https://en.wikipedia.org/wiki/2011_Tucson_shooting.

Voerman, B. (June 2014). Case study: ethical and other dilemmas in threat management. In *Paper presented at annual conference of the European network of public figure threat assessment agencies. Vilnius, Lithuania* (pp. 2–4) (June).

Warren, L. J., MacKenzie, R., Mullen, P. E., & Ogloff, J. R. P. (2005). The problem behavior model: the development of a stalkers clinic and a threateners clinic. *Behavioral Sciences & the Law*, *23*, 387–397.

Webster, C. D., Douglas, K. S., Eaves, D., & Hart, S. D. (1997). *HCR-20: Assessing risk of violence (Version 2)*. Burnaby, Canada: Mental Health, Law & Policy Institute, Simon Fraser University.

White, S., & Meloy, J. R. (2007). *The WAVR-21: A structured professional guide for the workplace assessment of violence risk*. San Diego, CA: Specialized Training Services.

Zona, M. A., Palarea, R. E., & Lane, J. (1998). Psychiatric diagnosis and the offender-victim typology of stalking. In J. R. Meloy (Ed.), *The Psychology of stalking: Clinical and forensic perspectives* (pp. 70–84). San Diego, CA: Academic Press.

Zona, M. A., Sharma, K. K., & Lane, J. (1993). A comparative study of erotomanic and obsessional subjects in a forensic sample. *Journal of Forensic Sciences*, *38*, 894–903.

Circumscribing Cyberbullying: Toward a Mutual Definition and Characterizations of Aggression, Assault, and Recklessness via Telecommunications Technology

10

Yolande Robinson[1], Wayne Petherick[2]

[1]Griffith University, Gold Coast, QLD, Australia; [2]Bond University, Gold Coast, QLD, Australia

CHAPTER OUTLINE

The Psychology of Criminal and Antisocial Behavior. http://dx.doi.org/10.1016/B978-0-12-809287-3.00010-9

INTRODUCTION

Until the seminal research conducted in the early 1990s by Dan Olweus (1993a, 1993b), little was known about the perpetration and experience of bullying. In fact, rather than conceptualizing bullying behaviors as deliberate, harmful, and worthy of intervention, bullying was widely perceived as a rite of passage, a normal child-to-adolescent-to-adult developmental milestone, a behavior that one would "grow out of" or be erased from memory with the passage of time without consequence (Bradshaw, O'Brennan, & Sawyer, 2008; Campbell, 2000; Carr-Gregg & Manocha, 2011). However, in the last 5 or so years, the vast amount of research into the prevalence and outcomes of bullying behaviors have dismissed these views, presenting compelling evidence of profound negative and potentially life-long effects of bullying that persist far beyond the time and space of the schoolyard.

The propensity for online aggression first came to the attention of researchers following a study of 1501 American students (Jones, Mitchell, & Finkelhor, 2012), and was the first to identify Internet chat rooms and email as modalities for bullying (Monks & Coyne, 2011). Since that time *cyberbullying* is considered by media, the public, and scholars as an emergent and significant problem with many unique characteristics such as round-the-clock access to the victim, the potential for offender anonymity, and access to a wide audience (Lazuras, Barkoukis, Ourda, & Tsorbatzoudis, 2013). Until relatively recent times, peer-to-peer victimization was, indeed, confined to the school yard or within other proximal contexts. The burgeoning Internet and the speed with which this has become a vehicle for aggression in the behavioral landscape may well explain the variability and inconsistency by which the phenomenon is defined and characterized (Calvete, Izaskun, Estévez, Villardón, & Padilla, 2010; Campbell, 2010; Låftman, Brolin, & Bitte Östberg, 2013; von Marées & Petermann, 2012; Sabella, Patchin, & Hinduja, 2013).

BACKGROUND

Thus far, academia has failed to agree on a universal definition for *online aggression/ cyberbullying* (Langos, 2012; Menesini et al., 2012). Sabella et al. (2013, p. 2704) listed the realities and myths of cyberbullying, the first of which was "that everybody knows what cyberbullying is." The most widely accepted definition of traditional, face-to-face bullying was forwarded by Olweus (1993a, p. 5): "aggressive, intentional act or behaviour that is carried out by a group or individual repeatedly over time against a victim who cannot easily defend him or herself." Smith et al. (2008) appended this definition by adding "using electronic forms of contact" to account for their construct of cyberbullying. Hinduja and Patchin (2009, p. 34) further added "intentional nature and repeated harms involved." This criterion of repetition is questioned by some who consider that one act of cyberbullying such as posting a denigrating picture, has the ability to remain in cyberspace indefinitely, meaning that one act can result in many violations or offenses (Langos, 2012). Some have added other elements such as there must be a suitable and vulnerable target (Whitney & Smith, 1993; Ybarra & Mitchell, 2004a), where others qualify the definition by including factors such as overt aggression or direct confrontation (Wade & Beran, 2011; Ybarra & Mitchell, 2004b).

Many definitions of online aggression proffered by the literature refer directly back to the traditional bullying construct and consider online aggression as an extension of traditional bullying (Naruskov, Luik, Nocentini, & Menesini, 2012) and just "old wine in a new bottle" (Li, 2007, p. 1777). As research into this area is growing, however, some contributors are doubtful that amendments to the traditional bullying definition are relevant, appropriate, or sufficient to describe online aggression (Hinduja & Patchin, 2009; Menesini & Nocentini, 2009; Naruskov et al., 2012; Slonje & Smith, 2008) arguing that cyberbullying is distinct and unique enough to be researched and measured as a different problem entirely. Therefore, a major issue for the area of cyberbullying, is the lack of a coherent and widely accepted definition of the phenomenon (Langos, 2012; Navarro & Jasinski, 2012).

The absence of a clear definition is further confounded by the inability of the literature to find agreement on to what to call the phenomenon (Law, Shapka, Hymel, Olson, & Waterhouse, 2012). *Cyberbullying* and *online aggression* are most frequently used; however, others include *online bullying, Internet harassment, online harassment,* and *electronic bullying.* Scholars cite numerous operational problems with each term. For instance, Law et al's exemplary study (2012) examining proactive and reactive online aggression argue that there are critical differences between *bullying* and *aggression.* Where the literature largely agrees that bullying involves three necessary conditions—intention to harm, repetition, and a power imbalance, only the intention to harm others is agreed as a necessary condition for *aggression* and that there are inherent problems with suggesting the elements of repetition and power imbalance with the use of the term *aggression.* In regard to repetition, two forms of cyberbullying identified by Willard (2007), whose typology of cyberbullying is extensively used, include masquerading and trickery where neither of these definitions require a repetition of acts. The latter condition of power imbalance is problematic as traditionally, the more popular, older, or stronger offenders tend to hold the balance of power, which is not necessarily the case in online aggression. For instance, Feinberg and Robey (2009) identified the *vengeful angel* as one of four in their typology of online aggressors. This category of offender may be smaller or younger than the target but takes on the role of the vigilante acting, often anonymously, to defend or retaliate on behalf of a friend who has been victimized in one setting or another (Huntingdon & Petherick, 2013).

A similar problem for researchers exists with the types of behaviors that ought to be included within the broader context of online aggression (Campbell, 2010). For instance, dependent variables for measuring cyberbullying behaviors in Navarro and Jasinski's study (2012, p. 88) were limited to rumor-mongering, "embarrassing pictures," threats, and reposting private conversations publicly. In contrast, Pettalia, Levin, and Dickenson (2013), adopted Willard's (2007) typologies of impersonation, denigration, outing/trickery, exclusion, harassment, and stalking; a similar model used by Huntingdon and Petherick (2013) who added "flaming" and omitted "denigration" (these terms will be explained later in this chapter). One 2011 examination categorized and measured cyberbullying perpetration as sending "unwanted emails," exclusion, uploading embarrassing emails without consent, impersonating, and changing victims' passwords (Walrave & Heirman, 2011).

Similarly, a recent study of Estonian students highlights a tendency for participants and researchers alike to confuse modality with forms of aggressive behaviors. In this study 20 secondary students identified *types* of online aggression behaviors as written-verbal, visual, exclusion, and impersonation, where the first two are clearly the modality, and the last two, forms of bullying (Naruskov et al., 2012). Moreover, some studies do not characterize cyberbullying at all, presenting participants with a definition of cyberbullying without explanation as to the behaviors this term represents, thus leaving the interpretation of the term to the respondents (Sabella et al., 2013).

The overall intention of the current chapter is to contribute to the burgeoning amount of literature on this important area, to discuss the importance of a consensus about the definition and conceptualization of online aggression, and to offer a workable and theoretically sound term to represent cyberbullying behaviors.

REACHING CONSENSUS: THE IMPORTANCE OF FIRST THINGS FIRST

Table 10.1 highlights the lack of empirical consensus in both defining and identifying the various forms that online aggression may take.

RELEVANCE TO RESEARCHERS

Researchers have discussed the importance of reaching consensus in regard to definitions and constructs of online bullying as, in order to adequately address the phenomenon, it is imperative to know what it is and how it presents (Langos, 2012). Menesini et al. (2012) posit that empirical agreement with the foundational elements of online aggression is essential as "different operationalization and conceptualization can affect the estimates of involvement in the phenomenon and consequently can affect the rationale for intervention" (Menesini et al., 2012, p. 455). Sabella et al. (2013) consider that the tendency for broad definitions, focusing on an array of specific examples of harm such as name-calling or social exclusion, or inconsistencies in the types of media through which cyberbullying occur can create confusion, incomplete pictures, and misinformation (Craig, Henderson & Murphy, 2000; Sabella et al., 2013; Smorti, Menesini, & Smith, 2003). Also addressing methodological concerns, Navarro and Jasinski (2012) underscore the importance of surveys being specific and clear and that "future studies work toward consistency in conceptualising cyberbullying by referencing previous studies" (Navarro & Jasinski, 2013, p. 301).

Table 10.1 Empirical Definitions of Online Aggression/Harassment/Cyberbullying

Nag and Goh (2010, p. 388)	The willful use of the Internet as a technological medium through which harm or discomfort is intentionally and repeatedly inflicted, targeting a specific person or group of persons.
Feinberg and Robey (2009, p. 26)	Sending or posting harmful or cruel text or images using the Internet (e.g., instant messaging, emails, chat rooms, and social networking sites) or other digital communication devices, such as cellphones.
Hindu and Patching (2009, p. 48). In Brown and Demery (2009, p. 19).	When someone repeatedly makes fun of another person online or repeatedly picks on another person through email or text messages or when someone posts something online about another person that they do not like.
Wolak, Mitchell, and Finkelhor (2007, p. 118)	Threats or other offensive behavior sent online to youth or posted online about youth for others to see.
Olweus (1999, p. 10)	[Exposure], repeatedly and over time, to negative actions on the part of one or more other students.
Smith et al. (2008, p. 376)	An aggressive, intentional act carried out by a group or individual, using electronic forms of contact, repeatedly, and over time against a victim who cannot easily defend him or herself."
Wade and Beran (2011, p. 41)	… intentional acts of aggression—or intentional acts causing harm toward someone else—that are perpetrated via an electronic medium.
Walther (2012, p. 533)	Cruelty to others by sending or posting harmful material or engaging in other forms of social aggression using the Internet or other digital technologies.

RELEVANCE TO RESEARCH PARTICIPANTS

The topic of relevance to participants was addressed by von Marées and Petermann (2012), arguing that, although numerous definitions for online aggression have been proposed, none have to date substantiated their relevance to particular target populations such as adolescents. Moreover, they add, successful intervention at the school level necessarily requires that educators are specifically aware of the various forms of online aggression. A number of scholars have also pointed to the importance of a robust, fitting, and universal definition, conceptualization, and operationalization of online aggression in regard to children and adolescents with learning or behavioral difficulties. Eden, Heiman, and Olenik-Shemesh (2013) suggest that children with learning or behavioral problems are the ones at particular risk of perpetrating, as well as being a victim of online aggression, an important contention in light of the findings that these populations, and young people in general have very little understanding of online aggression and too often lack awareness of its basic elements (Campbell, 2005; Cowie & Colliety, 2010; Li, 2007). This situation is particularly problematic where such participants are asked to report on frequencies, modalities, or effects of a behavior that has been inadequately defined, or a range of behaviors that lack homogeneity, uniformity, and clarity.

IMPORTANT FOR DETECTION, INTERVENTION, AND TREATMENT

Another problem with inconsistent or inaccurate definitions can be found at the ground zero of the behavior itself. Whether a child, adolescent, or adult is experiencing or perpetrating bullying or cyberbullying depends on the definition of the term and the characterizations and constructs used for identifying it. For educators, parents, victims, and offenders alike, it is important to recognize that not all instances of conflict indicate an act of bullying, but again, this depends on the characterizations within the definition itself and the elements included. From the stand point of logic and reasoning, defining the phenomenon under investigation is necessary for establishing relevant thresholds. That is, we must define the terms we use so we know when they have and have not occurred. This means knowing when one is a bully and knowing when one has been bullied.

Sabella et al. (2013) reiterate that bullying and cyberbullying require the elements of intent, repetition, harm, and power imbalance. For this reason, they contend, the terms *bullying* and *cyberbullying* are being overused, misrepresented, and misunderstood and, as such, bullying victimization is being claimed for such things as not being invited to a party, being ignored, or being shoved *on one instance*. For this reason, they contend, the element of repetition must be present to delineate these acts as peer conflict rather than bullying.

The importance of timely and adequate identification, intervention, and treatment for bullying victimization and perpetration is well discussed and documented throughout the literature. For victims, links have been found between being bullied/victimized and obesity, low body satisfaction and self-esteem (Fox & Farrow, 2009), poor grades (Adams & Lawrence, 2011), suicide, suicidal ideation and self-destructive behaviors (Bonanno & Hymel, 2010; Fisher et al., 2011), and various long-term mental health morbidities. High incidence of internalizing difficulties and psychopathology has also been associated with victimity including adult antisocial behavior, clinical depression, and anxiety disorders (McEachern & Snyder, 2012; Williford et al., 2012). For male perpetrators, strong associations have been found between bullying and adult antisocial and psychopathological behaviors and violent crime (Kim, Leventhal, Koh, Hubbard, & Boyce, 2006; Orpinas, Horne, & Staniszewski, 2003; Sourander & Klomek, 2011). In general, child bullies were found to be more likely to drop out of school, work in low-skill employment, be involved in domestic violence, and use harsh, coercive, and corporal punishment on their children. There is a strong multigenerational component to bullying, with children of authoritarian parents who were abusers in school more likely to become bullies themselves (Knafo, 2003).

Effective and accurate identification of bullying victimization and offending, and in particular the definition and constructs that describe this behavior, therefore, cannot be overstated as research suggests that the investment of time, money and resources into evidence-based antibullying programs yield significant benefits for victims, offenders, school and workplace environments, as well as social and economic benefits for society as a whole (Huntingdon & Petherick, 2013; Smith, Cousins, & Stewart, 2005). For this to occur, it is essential that the constructs and parameters are clearly defined.

CYBERBULLYING? ONLINE AGGRESSION? INTERNET HARASSMENT? IT'S ALL IN THE NAME

The author acknowledges that there are many terms that are conceptualized differently across disciplines and that this situation is widely accepted. As one example, the term *altruism* differs in concept across the disciplines of psychology, philosophy, biology, evolutionary anthropology, and experimental economics (Clavien & Chapuisat, 2013). However, there are calls for greater collaboration across disciplines in regard to research design and data collection and analysis (Clayton, 2011; Goodwin, 2008; Riccio, 1997; Weinstein et al., 2001) due to the positive impacts found in regard to expertise development, team effectiveness (Goodwin, 2008), deepened awareness of perspectives and concepts, practical development, enhanced awareness of one's own competences, flexible professionalism, and improved insights into research and development processes (Karlsson, Anderberg, Booth, Odenrick, & Christmansson, 2008). It is conceivable that empirical inquiry into cyberbullying may indeed benefit from an interdisciplinary approach as information specialists in the areas of Internet technology, software and device design, psychology, criminology, and perhaps others investigate a multipronged approach to this complex phenomenon. If this is to eventuate, it is important that consensus is reached in regard to terminology and conceptualization.

In order to construct a workable and theoretically sound label, the authors propose it is first necessary to deconstruct the existing terms that have thus far most satisfied and represented researchers' definitions and constructs of the behavior. These being various iterations of the terms *cyber, online,* and *Internet* connected to those of *bullying, aggression,* and *harassment.* Langos' (2012) methodology, whereby a literal approach to interpreting lingual meaning, combined with a semantic investigation of the unique and varying characterizations and conceptualizations of each term, is perhaps an appropriate method of deconstruction.

CYBER, ONLINE, OR INTERNET?

Academics involved in criminological and psychological inquiry (particularly in regard to bullying) largely define the term *cyber* as to broadly denote *generated by technology* (Langos, 2012) and includes SMS messages sent between cellphones (texting) in both definition and measurement. Specialists in areas such as international law, cyber security, economics, engineering, and Internet technology (Mainelli, 2013; O'Connell, 2012; Stastny, 2010) are more specific, however, limiting the application of the term to Internet technology only and do not allow for the term to represent communications via cellphones or any other type of technology (unless the Internet is accessed via these means).

Identifying modality as cyber, online, or Internet is therefore problematic as noncyber, online, and Internet modalities such as text messages via cellphones are a significant problem and as significant a problem as offending and victimization via the range of Internet technology (Buelga, Cava, & Musitu, 2010). To this end, the authors suggest that the term *telecommunications* (TC) supplant these terms as it represents all non–face-to-face communications over distance by technological means that are available now, as well as covering future technological communication possibilities that include but are not limited to:

- Fixed-line telephone/facsimile
- Satellite, such as cellphones
- Networked computers allowing for text via emails or video with webcams
- Internet chat rooms and social media networks such as Facebook, Twitter, voice-over Internet protocols, and gaming sites
- The broadcast system: radio and television networks
- Telematics: services and infrastructures that link computer and digital media equipment over telecommunication links (Kotval, 1999)

Second, in regard to the term *online*, TC is more accurate and appropriate as *online* and *offline* are Internet exclusive, *electronic* can denote any electrical appliance, *nontraditional* is a term fraught with conflicting interpretations, and *ICT* is Internet communication technology.

BULLYING: AGGRESSION OR HARASSMENT?

In regard to *bullying*, most definitions and operationalizations to date agree with Farrington's (1993) model—bullying can be physical, verbal, or psychological (Guerin & Hennessy, 2002). Some scholars also propose a suite of elements modeled on the Olweus-based definition of bullying and translate them into the TC context (Ybarra, Boyd, Korchmaros, & Oppenheim, 2012). These elements are intention to harm (Besag, 1989; Olweus, 1993a; Tattum, 1989), repetition (Olweus, 1999), provocation (absence of) (Farrington, 1993; Olweus, 1997; Swain, 1998), and imbalance of power (Olweus, 1997). However, not all researchers concur with these criteria, in tandem or individually. For instance, Ybarra et al. (2012) included just two of them, repetition and imbalance of power, plus one other—that the offense happened over a period of time. In contrast, Smith et al. (2008) included intent to harm, repetition, and Ybarra's (2012) addition of the construct of time. Individually, research is widely divided as to whether any of these elements do, in effect, translate into the bullying experience. Following is an examination of the four elements of bullying, as stated earlier: intent, repetition, absence of provocation, and imbalance of power. The terms *aggression* and *harassment* will also be examined for their contribution to the MT bullying construct.

INTENT TO HARM

Intent is considered a key aspect of any aggressive offense including bullying (Graham et al., 2006) and a primary measure by which the court may forgive or mitigate damage. Almost all the definitions of traditional and TC bullying include this attribute (Menesini et al., 2012), and several studies have found that the perpetrator must have the intention to harm in order for it to be defined as a bullying behavior; "otherwise the behavior is perceived as a joke" (Menesini et al., 2012, p. 457). The problem with establishing intent, however, is that it is an internal event and difficult to establish due to a number of neurological, legal, and philosophical considerations.

First, the frontocortical areas of the brain are largely accountable for regulating impulsive behavior, including angry and aggressive responses. This area is also responsible for overseeing higher executive functions such as motivation, planning, and empathy (Potegal, 2012; Sinnamon, 2015). The prefrontal cortex, the primary mediator of these higher executive functions, is subject to developmental limitations and is among the last neural structures to reach maturity (Luna, Paulsen, Padmanabhan, & Geier, 2013; Sinnamon, 2015). Changes in neurological maturity across childhood and adolescence result in substantially improved higher faculties, part of which includes (all things being equal) a move from a hedonism-driven morality to one that is guided by a more socially informed moral compass. This neurodevelopmentally mediated improvement to our sense of right and wrong and the accompanying awareness of the consequences of our actions as we move from childhood to adolescence may be the reasons that bullying tends to become less common in older cohorts. For example, the Australian Covert Bullying Prevalence Study (Child Health Promotion Research Centre, 2009) found that as children and teens progressed through school years, the incidence of bullying declined.

Distinct from developmental hindrances to establishing intent, Young et al. refer to the literature, including results of their own inquiry, and determine that "damage to ventromedial pre-frontal cortex (VMPC) impairs judgment of harmful intent" and that "[the] results highlight the critical role of the VMPC in processing harmful intent for moral judgment" (Young et al., 2010, p. 665). Establishing intent in children, adolescents, and adults, therefore, is a murky affair at best due to these neurological developmental and structural inhibiting factors.

Second, although the element of intent may have utility in regard to quantifying the severity of and motive for an aggressive behavior (Ames & Fiske, 2013; Graham et al., 2006), as well as providing the court a measure by which an act might be mitigated or aggravated, intent cannot speak to the severity of the actual harm (or absence of harm) caused to the victim. According to the harm principle, a conduct should be criminalized if, and only if, the result of it is a direct harm (Feinberg, 1984), but many scholars disagree, suggesting that the existence of harm is neither a necessary nor a sufficient reason for criminalizing it (Stewart, 2010). Moreover, criminal law is largely guided by two principles: the harm principle, which seeks to regulate harm incurred, and the offense principle, regulating certain kinds of offensive conduct that can reliably predict risk of harm to others (Dworkin, 2012). By this standard, then, it would not be necessary for a TC "bullying" offense, by definition, to have caused harm but to be of a nature to reliably predict that a victim of it may suffer damage or injury. We propose that the legal *reasonable person* threshold test would be sufficient for this task.

In support of this position, Guerin and Hennessy (2002) found that the majority of student participants did not perceive intent to harm as necessary for a TC or traditional bullying offense to occur, but that the effect of bullying was more important.

Sabella et al. (2013) concede that there may be a measure of truth to the notion that bullies are inspired by an antisocial or perverse sense of satisfaction from knowing that they have harmed another, but that they are more likely to be driven by "a need for control and domination [believing that] his or her actions will lead to greater peer acceptance and recognition" (Sabella et al., 2013, p. 2705). This suggestion has found accord with research where many traditional and TC bullies affront others for revenge, for fun, or as an outlet for their own anger or frustration.

Returning to Menesini et al's contention that if intent cannot be established the offense can only be considered a joke, the question must be asked—perceived as a joke by whom? Although the perpetrators may hold this view and, by definition researchers may be required to hold this view, it may not be considered so by a victim of TC bullying events whether or not the intent was to cause harm.

REPETITION

While some researchers agree that the element of repetition is a firmly established and key criterion for a TC bullying offense (Langos, 2012), others amend the definition of the term as applied to traditional bullying when applied to its TC counterpart. For instance, delineations have been made between TC bullying by one bully to one victim, one victim with multiple bullies, and the "serial" form of TC bullying, one bully with multiple victims (Huntingdon & Petherick, 2013). Here it is clear that repetition refers to victim and offender numbers. Some researchers limit the term *repetition* to numbers of messages sent (Gradinger, Strohmeier, & Spiel, 2009) to the victim or transmitted to others. Dracic (2009) suggests that in order for behavior to be considered repetitious, it must be the *same* behavior that is repeated, thus adding an additional typological layer to this construct.

Langos (2012) posits that, because of the nature of cyberspace, the element of repetition is best framed within two dichotomous forms of bullying that have been applied to traditional bullying: direct and indirect (cyber)bullying. Here the authors refer to Brenner and Rehberg's (2009) definitions where direct TC bullying occurs privately, involving communications limited to and only accessed by the perpetrator and victim. Indirect bullying, on the other hand, occurs in the "public cyber arena" in places where the information is unrestricted or publically accessible such as on "public blogs, Facebook, or via a video sharing Website" (Langos, 2012, p. 286). This is, of course, a reasonable account of these forms of TC bullying but may elicit further confusion to an already ambiguous construct as these explanations are very different from their traditional bullying counterparts. Specifically, when related to traditional bullying, the terms *indirect* and *direct* usually refer to covert/relational bullying (social exclusion, ignoring, malicious rumor-mongering, and backbiting) and overt bullying—physical and verbal (such as hitting, punching, pushing, threatening, name-calling) (Ang & Goh, 2010; Baldry, 2004; Law et al., 2012; Smith, Polenik, Nakasita, & Jones, 2012; de Wit, Hirasing, & van de Wal, 2003) rather than the terms relating to the accessibility or intended targets of the information.

Herein lies the problem in regard to establishing whether a TC offense is, indeed, repetitious. On the one hand, one, or a number of offenders can target one single victim with a number of harmful messages or posts. On the other hand, one offender may send one damaging message or posts to multiple parties or onto a site that can be accessed by a large local or global audience. Where it is reasonable to define two or more received messages as repetitious, it is less than clear that the same term can be applied to one post that is shared,or one post that is accessed (whether by accident or intention) by a larger audience. Moreover, in these cases, the victim may not directly receive any correspondence, but the harm may result from either knowing that they exist or from responses from the recipients. For instance, a seminaked photograph is taken with full knowledge and consent of the victim; it is then shared with one other who shares with one other, and so on. The recipient then bears the brunt of face-to-face denigration at school. As it may be reasonably argued that the face-to-face taunts resulted from one single TC offense, it is difficult to justify the element of repetition as a key and necessary element of TC bullying in every case (Menesini et al., 2012; Smith, 2011). Just as important to note is that one incident, if sufficiently embarrassing or provocative, may see a victim harassed incessantly. The behavior that initiated the bullying occurred on only one occasion, but the flow on effects of this are enduring and carried out by multiple people toward one target.

PROVOCATION

Research has supported the traditional bully stereotype as highly aggressive, self-sufficient, and impulsive and not as well integrated as their nonbully peers but more integrated than their victims (Carrera, DePalma, & Lameiras, 2011; Huntingdon & Petherick, 2013; Olweus, 1997). As a subtype of a violent antisocial, rule-breaking pattern of behavior, it may be provoked as a retaliatory, aggressive response to an external stimulus (Fite, Colder, Lochman, & Wells, 2007), or it can be unprovoked, perhaps a means by which a person gains acceptance within a particular peer-group or acts to gain from another's denigration or demise. Researchers have delineated these two models of behavior as proactive aggression (a premeditated and goal-orientated aggression) and reactive aggression (a retaliatory and impulsive form of aggression, a response to an immediate threat or frustration) (Fite et al., 2007). Within the construct of TC bullying, both forms of aggression may be apparent.

That the element of provocation is neither necessary nor sufficient to define or recognize a TC bullying offense is further illustrated by Feinberg and Robey's (2009) typologies of TC offenders, which speak to their varied motives for perpetrating a TC bullying event.

- *Vengeful angel*: takes on the role of the vigilante who protects, defends, or retaliates on behalf of a friend who has been bullied or cyberbullied. This offender does not see himself or herself as a bully, but thinks his or her actions are justified retaliation.
- *Power hungry*: (also known as "revenge of the nerds") offenders exert their authority and strike fear in the heart of the victim. These offenders are often

victims of face-to-face bullies who, for a variety of reasons (e.g., physical stature) avoid face-to-face bullying, feeling less fearful or more confident in cyberspace.

- *Mean girls*: usually bully out of boredom or for entertainment and torment their victim in social groups.
- *Inadvertent*: do not think about the consequences of their actions and harm or distress is unintentional.

IMBALANCE OF POWER

That a victim of an aggressive act cannot easily defend himself or herself is indicative of a power imbalance (Grigg, 2010; Olweus, 1997) and another element widely considered by literature as necessarily included within a TC bullying definition. Vandebosch and Van Cleemput (2008) argue that where bullying occurs in the traditional setting disparities of power will most likely refer to factors such as seniority, physical strength, or position within a social group, within cyberspace power may be measured by computer expertise, numbers of "friends" connected to a person's social networking site, or advantage may be found with access to particular types of gaming areas or chat rooms.

In either case, whether bullying occurs in the physical or TC space, victimization results from the inability of the target to adequately respond. The term *power*, however, when called upon to define a TC bullying act, can be somewhat misleading due to its historical associations with offenses, violent or otherwise, that have involved emotional, psychological, or physical superiority or advantage. Within a telecommunications environment, victimization or vulnerability is more associated with the concept of *advantage*, whereby an offender can subject a target to aggressive and harmful behaviors with the same potential to frighten and damage but can be done at a time convenient to the bully, in real-time, at any time, and anonymously. Indeed, under the cover of anonymity, bullies can act more aggressively than they would in face-to-face confrontations as well as avoid the risk of physical injury (Hinduja & Patchin, 2009; Sontage et al., 2011). Additionally, where traditional bullying can be witnessed and moderated by parents, teachers, or peers, TC bullying can be performed in private, without regulation or consequence (McDonald, 2004). These benefits for the TC bully are more benefits of convenience, security, and safety rather than benefits of power per se and may be more appropriately referred to as *advantage* within the defining construct of TC bullying.

We also take issue with the concept of a power imbalance within bullying relationships. Indeed, much bullying that occurs within any group is the result of all parties having equal social standing and social capital, and the bullying results from trying to increase one's own social standing, while simultaneously decreasing the social capital of others. This is done in order to garner or foster favor, increase social standing, establish or bolster relationships, or for any other possible gain or advantage. We concede that in this instance bullying is still about an imbalance of power;

our contention is that this imbalance does not have to exist before or during the bullying event/s, and that it can actually arise at the inception of the bullying, either in the planning or the execution phases of it.

AGGRESSION

Aggression is widely defined as any behavior directed toward another person/s that is carried out with intent to cause harm and with the understanding that the behavior will cause harm to the victim/s (Baron & Richardson, 1994; Berkowitz, 1993; Bushman & Anderson, 2001; Geen, 2001). Likewise, accidental harm is not considered as aggression because of the absence of intent. An example is the pain when being injected with a substance intended to cure an illness, such as receiving subcutaneous insulin injections; the pain is not the intention, the intention is the higher purpose—improved health for the recipient. This element of intent to cause harm and the difficulties associated with establishing intent to cause harm in all occurrences of TC bullying have been addressed here earlier. *Aggression* defined, therefore, as requiring the element of intent cannot, therefore, be a fundamental and necessary component or descriptive of an TC offense.

HARASSMENT

The terms *bullying, aggression,* and *harassment* are often used interchangeably, but they are distinguishable by both law and definition (Mason, 2002). Although widely accepted as a term to denote any aggressive or repetitive nuisance or harmful behavior, harassment refers to offensive and discriminatory treatment of one person by another based on a victim's personal characteristics such as age, race, religion, sexual orientation, disability, or gender and is sanctioned under laws regarding antidiscrimination and equal opportunity (Earle & Madek, 1993). Harassment, therefore, is more appropriately placed, for the purposes of identifying a TC event as a subset of this behavior more appropriately placed within discussions of typologies rather than a principal feature of the overarching definition.

As previously stated, proposing a term for the phenomenon widely labeled as *cyberbullying, online aggression,* or *Internet harassment* is a challenge due to the mercurial and volatile nature of TC technology and the variability and inconsistency by which the phenomenon presents (Calvete et al., 2010; Låftman et al., 2013; Sabellaa et al., 2013). Furthermore, the authors argue that there are two prevailing needs that require a concise and pragmatic term; the first is to enable parents, carers, educators, clinicians, victims, and offenders to recognize patterns of TC behavior in order to intervene, arrest, and treat. The second aim is to satisfy the requirements of the criminal justice system (CJS), which must address the element of intent to harm, which is not a necessary element in all TC offenses. In regard to the modality for nontraditional bullying/aggression/harassment, the authors suggest that the term TC satisfies all distance communication types. However, deciding on a term that represents the nature of the offense, as has been illustrated, poses a more profound and complex challenge.

To this end, the authors recommend the term *aggression, assault,* or *recklessness* be adopted as this term perhaps provides the most inclusive and indicative representation of the offense and satisfies the interests of those wishing to identify and ameliorate the behavior, as well as those required to arraign and prosecute. The term *aggression* provides for the elements of harm and intent to harm the target of the behavior, whereas the term *assault* allows for harms incurred and threats of harm made of both physical and psychological natures, which are able to be dealt with in either criminal or civil proceedings (Brewer, 1994). Importantly, in circumstances where intent is difficult to establish, the offender/s may be proved liable on the basis of *recklessness* wherein, although there may have been some thought to the consequences of the act, the offender decided to act anyway. The offender need not, therefore, had acted intentionally to harm the victim (Krone, 2004).

The authors propose, in the light of these discussions that the phrase and acronym *TC aggression, assault, or recklessness* (TAAR) supplant the terms *cyberbullying, online aggression,* and *Internet harassment.*

CONCLUSION

Bullying via traditional and telecommunications pathways, places, and systems has been described as the most significant and pervasive problems affecting schools, social environments, and workplaces. A lack of consensus in regard to an expanded definition of these phenomena has created considerable discrepancy and lack of corrective, empirical, and proscriptive direction in regard to the many aspects of this behavior or set of behaviors for the many key stakeholders that are attempting to mitigate the harm and significant cost for which TAAR has been responsible.

It is hoped that the definition proposed will go some way to contributing to the literature in regard to a defining conceptualization of aggression, abuse, and recklessness via telecommunications mediums. However, a number of foundational and fundamental aspects of TAAR require attention and inquiry, including efforts to establish a universally accepted typology of TAAR behaviors. Additionally, although the term *telecommunications* has been proposed in the current report, it would be helpful to formalize the associated modalities in order to provide a model for measurement and assessment.

SUMMARY

- Bullying via traditional and telecommunications pathways, places, and systems has been described as the most significant and pervasive problems affecting schools, social environments and workplaces. A lack of consensus in regard to an expanded definition of these phenomena has created considerable discrepancy and lack of corrective, empirical and proscriptive direction for prevention, mitigation, and intervention strategies. TAAR has been suggested as a coverall terminology to supplant the interchangeable terms otherwise used to describe the phenomenon including *cyberbullying, online aggression*, and *Internet harassment.*

- Cyberbullying is considered by media, the public, and academicians as an emergent and significant problem with many unique characteristics such as round-the-clock access to the victim, the potential for offender anonymity, and access to a wide audience. The burgeoning Internet and the speed with which this has become a vehicle for aggression in the behavioral landscape may well explain the variability and inconsistency by which the phenomenon is defined and characterized.
- Many definitions of online aggression proffered by the literature refer directly back to the traditional bullying construct and consider online aggression as an extension of traditional bullying. Some contributors are doubtful that amendments to the traditional bullying definition are relevant, appropriate, or sufficient to describe online aggression, arguing that *cyberbullying* is distinct and unique enough to be researched and measured as a different problem entirely. Therefore, a major issue for the area of cyberbullying is the lack of a coherent and widely accepted definition of the phenomenon. The absence of a clear definition is further confounded by the inability of the literature to find agreement upon to what to call the phenomenon.
- The literature largely agrees that bullying involves three necessary conditions: intention to harm, repetition, and power imbalance.
  Whether a child, adolescent, or adult is experiencing or perpetrating bullying or cyberbullying depends on the definition of the term and the characterizations and constructs used for identifying it. For educators, parents, victims, and offenders alike, it is important to recognize that not all instances of conflict indicate an act of bullying, but again, this depends on the characterizations within the definition itself and the elements included.
- For victims, links have been found between being bullied/victimized and obesity, low body satisfaction, self-esteem, poor grades, suicide, suicidal ideation, self-destructive behaviors, and various long-term mental health morbidities. High incidence of internalizing difficulties and psychopathology has also been associated with victimization, including adult antisocial behavior, clinical depression, and anxiety disorders.
- In male perpetrators, strong associations have been found between bullying and adult antisocial and psychopathological behaviors and violent crime.
- In general, child bullies were found to be more likely to drop out of school, work in low-skill employment, be involved in domestic violence, and use harsh, coercive, and corporal punishment on their children.
- There is a strong multigenerational component to bullying, with children of authoritarian parents who were abusers in school more likely to become bullies themselves.
- Academics involved in criminological and psychological inquiry, in the area of bullying, largely define the term *cyber* as broadly denoting the idea of

something that is generated by technology, including SMS messages sent between cellphones (texting) in both definition and measurement. Specialists in areas such as international law, cyber security, economics, engineering, and Internet technology are more specific, limit the term to mean Internet technology only, and do not allow for the term to represent communications via cellphones or any other type of technology (unless the Internet is accessed via these means). Identifying modality as cyber, online, or Internet is therefore problematic as noncyber, online, and Internet modalities such as text messages via cellphones are a significant media used in bullying.

- Intent to harm is considered a key aspect of any aggressive offense including bullying and is a primary measure by which the court may forgive or mitigate damage. Almost all the definitions of bullying include this attribute, and a widely held position is that there must be an intention to harm in order for a behavior to be defined as bullying. The problem with establishing intent, however, is that it is an internal event and difficult to establish due to a number of neurological, legal, and philosophical considerations.

- Repetition in telecommunications bullying may refer to one bully to one victim over several repetitions, one victim with multiple bullies, and one bully with multiple victims. Here it is clear that repetition refers to victim and offender numbers. Ultimately, in order for behavior to be considered repetitious, it must be the same behavior that is repeated. The variations to "repeated" adds an additional typological layer to this construct.

- Provoked and unprovoked bullying has been identified in the telecommunications space. As a subtype of a violent antisocial, rule-breaking pattern of behavior, bullying may be provoked as a retaliatory, aggressive response to an external stimulus, or it can be unprovoked, perhaps as a means by which a bully attempts to (a) gain acceptance within a particular peer-group, (b) gain control over circumstances, or (c) gain other favor from another's denigration or demise. Researchers have delineated these two models of behavior as proactive aggression (a premeditated and goal-orientated aggression) and reactive aggression (a retaliatory and impulsive form of aggression, a response to an immediate threat or frustration). Within the construct of TC bullying, both forms of aggression may be apparent.

- Research has supported the traditional bully stereotype as highly aggressive, self-sufficient, and impulsive. They have been characterized as being not as well integrated as their nonbully peers, but more integrated than their victims.

- When a victim of an aggressive act cannot easily defend him or herself, there is a clear indication of a power imbalance. Where bullying occurs in the traditional setting, disparities of power will most likely refer to factors such as seniority, physical strength, or position within a social group. However, within cyberspace, power may be measured by computer expertise, numbers of "friends" connected to a person's social networking site, or advantage may be found with access to particular types of gaming areas or chat rooms.

- Aggression is widely defined as any behavior directed toward another person/s that is carried out with intent to cause harm and with the understanding that the behavior will cause harm to the victim/s. Accidental harm is not considered as aggression because of the absence of intent. This element of intent to cause harm, and the difficulties associated with establishing intent to cause harm in most occurrences of TC bullying, means that aggression (when defined as requiring the element of intent) cannot be a fundamental and necessary component of bullying in the cyberspace.

- The terms *bullying, aggression*, and *harassment* are often used interchangeably but they are distinguishable by both law and definition. Although widely accepted as a term to denote any aggressive or repetitive nuisance or harmful behavior, harassment refers to offensive and discriminatory treatment of one person by another based on a victim's personal characteristics such as age, race, religion, sexual orientation, disability, or gende and is sanctioned under laws regarding antidiscrimination and equal opportunity. Harassment is a core feature of bullying in the cyberspace.

QUESTIONS

1. Define *bullying* in its traditional form.
2. Define *bullying* in the telecommunications space (i.e., TAAR), and explain the three conditions necessary for behavior to be considered as bullying.
3. What are the identified characteristics of a victim of TAAR, and what are the negative correlates?
4. What are the negative correlates associated with being a victim of TAAR?
5. What are the identified characteristics of a perpetrator of TAAR?
6. What are the negative correlates associated with being a perpetrator of TAAR?
7. Define and explain "intent to harm."
8. Define and explain "repetition."
9. Define and explain "provocation."
10. Define and explain "power imbalance."

REFERENCES

Adams, F. D., & Lawrence, G. J. (2011). Bullying victims: the effects last into college. *American Secondary Education, 40*(1), 4–13.

Ames, D., & Fiske, S. (2013). Association for psychological science; intent to harm: Wilful acts seem more damaging. *Medicine & Law Weekly, 140.*

Ang, R. P., & Goh, D. H. (2010). Cyberbullying among adolescents: the role of affective and cognitive empathy, and gender. *Child Psychiatry and Human Development, 41*(4), 387–397.

Baldry, A. (2004). The impact of direct and indirect bullying on the mental and physical health of Italian youngsters. *Aggressive Behaviour, 30*(5), 343–355.

Baron, R. A., & Richardson, D. R. (1994). *Human aggression.* New York: Plenum.

Berkowitz, L. (1993). Pain and aggression: some findings and implications. *Motivation and Emotion, 17,* 277–293.

Besag, V. (1989). *Bullies and victims in schools*. Milton Keynes: Open University Press.

Bonanno, R. A., & Hymel, S. (2010). Beyond hurt feelings: investigating why some victims of bullying are at greater risk for suicidal ideation. *Merrill-Palmer Quarterly*, *56*(3), 420.

Bradshaw, C. P., O'Brennan, L. M., & Sawyer, A. L. (2008). Examining variation in attitudes toward aggressive retaliation and perceptions of safety among bullies, victims, and bully/victims. *Professional School Counseling*, *12*(1), 10–21.

Brenner, S. W., & Rehberg, M. (2009). "Kiddie Crime"? the utility of criminal law. *First Amendment Law Review*, *8*, 1–85.

Brewer, J. D. (1994). *The danger from strangers: Confronting the threat of assault*. Norwell, Mass: Kluwer Academic.

Brown, C. F., & Demaray, M. K. (2009). Cyberbullying research. *National Association of School Psychologists. Communique*, *38*(4), 19.

Buelga, S., Cava, M., & Musitu, G. (2010). Cyberbullying: adolescent victimization through mobile phone and Internet. *Psicothema*, *22*(4), 784.

Bushman, B. J., & Anderson, C. A. (2001). Is it time to pull the plug on the hostile versus instrumental aggression dichotomy? *Psychological Review*, *108*, 273–279.

Calvete, E., Izaskun, O., Estévez, A., Villardón, L., & Padilla, P. (2010). Cyberbullying in adolescents: modalities and aggressors' profile. *Computers in Human Behavior*, *26*(5), 1128–1135.

Campbell, M. (2005). Cyber-bullying—an old problem in a new guise. *Australian Journal of Guidance and Counselling*, *15*(1), 68–76.

Campbell, M. (2010). Research on cyberbullying [online]. *Australian Journal of Guidance and Counselling*, *20*(2), 3–4.

Campbell, W. (2000). Techniques for dealing with student harassment at high school level. *American Secondary Education*, *29*(1), 34.

Carr-Gregg, M., & Manocha, R. (March 2011). Bullying: effects, prevalence and strategies for detection [online]. *Australian Family Physician*, *40*(3), 98–102.

Carrera, M. V., DePalma, R., & Lameiras, M. (2011). Toward a more comprehensive understanding of bullying in school settings. *Educational Psychology Review*, *23*(4), 479–499. http://dx.doi.org/10.1007/s10648-011-9171-x.

Child Health Promotion Research Centre. (2009). *Australian covert bullying prevalence study. Australian Government Department of Education, Employment and Workplace Relations*.

Clavien, C., & Chapuisat, M. (2013). Altruism across disciplines: one word, multiple meanings. *Biology & Philosophy*, *28*(1), 125–140.

Clayton, J. (2011). Collaboration across the disciplines: an experiment in interdisciplinary pedagogy. *Literature and Medicine*, *29*(1), 127–131.

Cowie, H., & Colliety, P. (2010). Cyberbullying: sanctions or sensitivity? *Pastoral Care in Education: An International Journal of Personal, Social and Emotional Development*, *28*(4), 261–268.

Craig, W., Henderson, K., Murphy, J. (2000). Prospective teachers' attitudes toward bullying and victimization. *School Psychology International*, *21*(1), 5–21

Dracic, S. (2009). Bullying and peer victimization. *Materia Socio-Medica*, *21*(4), 216.

Dworkin, G. (2012). Harm and the volente principle. *Social Philosophy & Policy*, *29*(1), 309–321.

Earle, B., & Madek, G. (1993). An international perspective on sexual harassment law. *Law & Inequality: A Journal of Theory and Practice*, *12*(1), 43.

Eden, S., Heiman, T., & Olenik-Shemesh, D. (2013). Teachers' perceptions, beliefs and concerns about cyberbullying. *British Journal of Educational Training, 44*(6), 1036–1052.

Farrington, D. P. (1993). Understanding and preventing bullying. In M. Tonry, & N. Morris (Eds.), *Crime and justice: An annual review of research* (17) (pp. 381–458). Chicago: University of Chicago Press.

Feinberg, J. (1984). *Harm to others*. New York: Oxford University Press.

Feinberg, T., & Robey, N. (2009). Cyberbullying: intervention and prevention strategies. *National Association of School Psychologists, 38*(4), 29.

Fisher, J., de Mello, M. C., Izutsu, T., Vijayakumar, L., Belfer, M., & Omigbodun, O. (2011). Adolescence: developmental stage and mental health morbidity. *International Journal of Social Psychiatry, 57*(1), 13–19.

Fite, P., Colder, C., Lochman, J., & Wells, K. (2007). Pathways from proactive aggression to substance use. *Psychology of Addictive Behaviours, 21*(3), 355–364.

Fox, C., & Farrow, C. (2009). Global and physical self-esteem and body dissatisfaction as mediators of the relationship between weight status and being a victim of bullying. *Journal of Adolescence, 32*(5), 1287–1301.

Geen, R. (2001). *Human aggression*. Buckingham: Open University Press.

Goodwin, G. (2008). Psychology in sports and the military: building understanding and collaboration across disciplines. *Military Psychology, 20*, 147–153.

Gradinger, P., Strohmeier, D., & Spiel, C. (2009). Traditional bullying and cyberbullying: identification of risk groups for adjustment problems. *Journal of Psychology, 217*(4), 205–213.

Graham, K., Tremblay, P., Wells, S., Pernanen, K., Purcell, J., & Jelley, J. (2006). Harm, intent, and the nature of aggressive behavior: measuring naturally occurring aggression in barroom settings. *Assessment, 13*, 280–297.

Grigg, D. (2010). Cyber-aggression: definition and concept of cyberbullying. *Australian Journal of Guidance and Counselling, 20*(2), 143–156.

Guerin, S., & Hennessy, E. (2002). Pupils' definitions of bullying. *European Journal of Psychology of Education, 17*(3), 249–261.

Hinduja, S., & Patchin, J. (2009). *Bullying beyond the schoolyard: Preventing and responding to cyberbullying*. Thousand Oaks, CA: Sage Publications (Corwin Press).

Huntingdon, Y., & Petherick, W. (2013). Serial bullying and harassment. In W. Petherick (Ed.), *Profiling and serial crime: Theoretical and practical issues* (pp. 263–293). Oxford: Elsevier Inc.

Jones, L. M., Mitchell, K. J., & Finkelhor, D. (2012). Trends in youth Internet victimization: findings from three youth Internet safety surveys 2000-2010. *The Journal of Adolescent Health, 50*(2), 179–186. http://dx.doi.org/10.1016/j.jadohealth.2011.09.015.

Karlsson, J., Anderberg, E., Booth, S., Odenrick, P., & Christmansson, M. (2008). Reaching beyond disciplines through collaboration. *Journal of Workplace Learning, 20*(2), 98–113.

Kim, Y. S., Leventhal, B. L., Koh, Y. J., Hubbard, A., & Boyce, A. T. (2006). School bullying and youth violence: causes or consequences of psychopathologic behavior? *Archives of General Psychiatry, 63*, 1035–1041.

Knafo, A. (2003). Authoritarians, the next generation: values and bullying among adolescent children of authoritarian fathers. *Analyses of Social Issues and Public Policy, 3*(1), 199–204.

Kotval, Z. (1999). Telecommunications: a realistic strategy for the revitalization of American cities. *Cities, 16*(1), 33–41.

Krone, T. (2004). *Hacking techniques. High tech crime brief no. 7.* Australian Institute of Criminology. Retrieved from http://www.aic.gov.au/publications/current%20series/htcb/1–20/htcb007.html.

Låftman, S., Brolin, M., Bitte, & Östberg, V. (2013). *Children and Youth Services Review, 35*(1), 112–119.

Langos, C. (2012). Cyberbullying: the challenge to define. *Cyberpsychology, Behavior and Social Networking, 15*(6), 285–289.

Law, D., Shapka, J., Hymel, S., Olson, B., & Waterhouse, T. (2012). The changing face of bullying: an empirical comparison between traditional and Internet bullying and victimization. *Computers in Human Behavior, 28*(1), 226–232.

Lazuras, L., Barkoukis, V., Ourda, D., & Tsorbatzoudis, H. (2013). A process model of cyberbullying in adolescence. *Computers in Human Behavior, 29*(3), 881–887.

Li, Q. (2007). New bottle but old wine: a research of cyberbullying in schools. *Computers in Human Behaviour, 23,* 1777–1791.

Luna, B., Paulsen, D., Padmanabhan, A., & Geier, C. (2013). The teenage brain: cognitive control and motivation. *Current Directions in Psychological Science, 22,* 94–100.

Mainelli, M. (2013). Learn from insurance: cyber bore. *Journal of Risk Finance, 14*(1), 100–102.

von Marées, N., & Petermann, F. (2012). Cyberbullying: an increasing challenge for schools. *School Psychology International, 33,* 467.

Mason, G. (2002). Harm, harassment and sexuality. *Melbourne University Law Review, 26,* 596–621.

McDonald, L., & Griffith University. School of Psychology. (2004). *Teachers' attitudes toward bullying: The effects of identification, years of experience, bully gender and type of bullying.*

McEachern, A. D., & Snyder, J. (2012). Gender differences in predicting antisocial behaviors: developmental consequences of physical and relational aggression. *Journal of Abnormal Child Psychology, 40*(4), 501.

Menesini, E., & Nocentini, A. (2009). Cyberbullying definition and measurement; some critical considerations. *Journal of Psychology, 217*(4), 230–232.

Menesini, E., Nocentini, A., Palladino, B., Frisén, A., Berne, S., Ortega-Ruiz, R., et al. (2012). Cyberbullying definition among adolescents: a comparison across six European countries. *Cyberpsychology, Behavior, and Social Networking, 15*(9), 455–463.

Monks, C., & Coyne, I. (2011). *Bullying in different contexts.* Cambridge: Cambridge University Press.

Naruskov, K., Luik, P., Nocentini, A., & Menesini, E. (2012). Estonian students' perception and definition of cyberbullying. *Trames, 16*(4), 323–343.

Navarro, J., & Jasinski, L. (2012). Going cyber: using routine activities theory to predict cyberbullying experiences. *Sociological Spectrum, 32*(1), 81–94.

Navarro, J., & Jasinski, L. (2013). Why girls? Using routine activities theory to predict cyberbullying experiences between girls and boys. *Women and Criminal Justice, 23*(4), 286–303.

Olweus, D. (1993a). *Bullying at school: What we know and what we can do.* Oxford: Blackwell Publishers.

Olweus, D. (1993b). *Bullying at school.* Oxford: Blackwell Publishers.

Olweus, D. (1997). Bully/victim problems in school. *Irish Journal of Psychology, 18*(2), 170–190.

Olweus, D. (1999). Sweden. In P. K. Smith, Y. Morit, J. Junger-Tas, D. Olweus, R. Catalano, & P. Slee (Eds.), *The nature of school bullying: A cross-national perspective* (pp. 7–27). London: Routledge.

Orpinas, P., Horne, A. M., & Staniszewski, D. (2003). School bullying: changing the problem by changing the school. *School Psychology Review, 32*, 431–444.

O'Connell, M. (2012). Cyber security without cyber war. *Journal of Conflict and Security Law, 17*(2), 187.

Pettalia, J., Levin, E., & Dickenson, J. (2013). Cyberbullying: Eliciting harm without consequence. *Computers in Human Behavior, 29*, 2758–2765.

Potegal, M. (2012). Temporal and frontal lobe initiation and regulation of the top-down escalation of anger and aggression. *Behavioural Brain Research, 231*(2), 386–395.

Riccio, C. (1997). A call for increased collaboration across disciplines. *Contemporary Psychology: A Journal of Reviews, 42*(11), 1018–1020.

Sabella, R., Patchin, J., & Hinduja, S. (2013). Cyberbullying myths and realities. *Computers in Human Behavior, 29*(6), 2703–2711.

Sinnamon, G. (2015). Psychopathology and criminal behaviour. In W. Petherick (Ed.), *Applied crime analysis: A social science approach to understanding crime, criminals, and victims.* Boston: Anderson Publishing.

Slonje, R., & Smith, P. (2008). Cyberbullying: another main type of bullying? *Scandinavian Journal of Psychology, 49*, 147–154.

Smith, H., Polenik, K., Nakasita, S., & Jones, A. P. (2012). Profiling social, emotional and behavioural difficulties of children involved in direct and indirect bullying behaviours. *Emotional & Behavioural Difficulties, 17*(3–4), 243–257.

Smith, J., Cousins, B., & Stewart, R. (2005). Antibullying interventions in schools: ingredients of effective programs. *Canadian Journal of Education, 28*(4), 739–762.

Smith, P. (2011). Cyberbullying and cyber aggression. In R. S. Jimerson, B. Nickerson, J. Mayer, & J. Furlong (Eds.), *Handbook of school violence and school safety: International research and practice.* New York: NY: Routledge.

Smith, P., Mahdavi, J., Carvalho, M., Fisher, S., Russell, S., & Tippett, N. (2008). Cyberbullying: its nature and impact in secondary school pupils. *Journal of Child Psychology and Psychiatry, 49*(4), 376–385.

Smorti, A., Menesini, E., & Smith, P. (2003). Parents' definitions of children's bullying in a five-country comparison. *Journal of Cross-Cultural Psychology, 34*(4), 417–432.

Sontag, L. M., Clemans, K. H., Graber, J. A., & Lyndon, S. T. (2011). Traditional and cyber aggressors and victims: a comparison of psychosocial characteristics. *Journal of Youth and Adolescence, 40*(4), 392–404. http://dx.doi.org/10.1007/s10964-010-9575-9.

Sourander, A., & Klomek, A. B. (2011). Bullying at age eight and criminality in adulthood: findings from the Finnish nationwide 1981 birth cohort study. *Social Psychiatry and Psychiatric Epidemiology, 46*(12), 1211–1219.

Stastny, R. P. (2010). Cyber battleground. *Oilweek, 61*(8), 36–40.

Stewart, H. (2010). The limits of the harm principle. *Criminal Law and Philosophy, 4*(1), 17–35.

Swain, J. (1998). What does bullying really mean? *Educational Research, 40*(3), 358–364.

Tattum, D. P. (1989). Violence and aggression in schools. In D. P. Tattum, & D. A. Lane (Eds.), *Bullying in school* (pp. 7–19). Stoke-on-Trent: Trentham Books.

Vandebosch, H., & Van Cleemput, K. (2008). Defining cyberbullying: a qualitative research into the perceptions of youngsters. *Cyber Psychology & Behaviour, 11*, 499–503.

Wade, A., & Beran, T. (2011). Cyberbullying: the new era of bullying. *Canadian Journal of School Psychology*, 26(1), 44–61.

Walrave, M., & Heirman, W. (2011). Cyberbullying: predicting victimisation and perpetration. *Children and Society*, 25, 59–72.

Walther, B. (2012). Cyberbullying: holding grownups liable for negligent entrustment. *Houston Law Review*, 49, 531–560.

Weinstein, M., Hermalin, A., Stoto, M., Evans, V., Ewbank, D., & Haaga, J. (2001). Greater collaboration across disciplines. *Annals of the New York Academy of Sciences*, 954(1), 311–321.

Whitney, I., & Smith, P. K. (1993). A survey of the nature and extent of bullying in junior/middle and secondary schools. *Educational Research*, 35, 3–25.

Willard, N. (2007). *Cyberbullying and cyberthreats: Responding to the challenge of online social aggression, threats and distress.* Champaigne, Illinois: Research Press.

Williford, A., Boulton, A., Noland, B., Little, T. D., Kärnä, A., & Salmivalli, C. (2012). Effects of the KiVa anti-bullying program on adolescents' depression, anxiety, and perception of peers. *Journal of Abnormal Child Psychology*, 40(2), 289–300.

de Wit, C., Hirasing, R., & van de Wal, M. (2003). Psychological health among young victims and offenders of direct and indirect bullying. *Pediatrics*, 111(6), 1312.

Wolak, J., Mitchell, K., & Finkelhor, D. (2007). Unwanted and wanted exposure to online pornography in a national sample of youth Internet users. *Pediatrics*, 119(2), 247–257. http://dx.doi.org/10.1542/peds.2006-1891.

Ybarra, M., Boyd, D., Korchmaros, J., & Oppenheim, J. (2012). Defining and measuring cyberbullying within the larger context of bullying victimization. *Journal of Adolescent Health*, 51(1), 53–58.

Ybarra, M. L., & Mitchell, K. J. (2004a). Online aggressor/targets, aggressors, and targets: a comparison of associated youth characteristics. *Journal of Child Psychology and Psychiatry*, 45, 1308–1316.

Ybarra, M. L., & Mitchell, K. J. (2004b). Youth engaging in online harassment: associations with caregiver-child relationships, Internet use, and personal characteristics. *Journal of Adolescence*, 27, 319–336.

Young, L., Bechara, A., Tranel, D., Damasio, H., Hauser, M., & Damasio, A. (2010). *Neuron*, 65(6), 845–851.

Domestic Violence: Psychological Issues Related to the Victim and Offender

11

Mauro Paulino

Mind/Institute of Clinical and Forensic Psychology, Lisbon, Portugal

CHAPTER OUTLINE

INTRODUCTORY ASPECTS: FRAMEWORK OF A SOCIAL SCOURGE NAMED DOMESTIC VIOLENCE

Meloy (2003) considers that one of the great paradoxes of human existence is the fact that the majority of interpersonal violence occurs between people who are related to each other. Within the family, many homes are marked by violence, making the home "one of the most dangerous places in modern societies. In statistical terms, regardless of sex and age, a person will become more susceptible to violence at home than in a street at night" (Giddens, 2001, p. 196). This underscores the seriousness of family violence.

In order to understand domestic violence, it is essential to appreciate that the violence occurs within the confines of a bidirectional interaction between the aggressor and the victim, that takes place within a particular context, and that these contextual characteristics must, in themselves, be recognized and explored as unique independent variables in the equation.

Violence is a complex and serious social problem that is intimately and inextricably linked to the human condition and spans the divide between culture, geography, and historical epochs (Machado, Gonçalves, & Matos, 2008). It constitutes a public health problem (Brandão, 2006; Corsi, 2003; Datner, Asher, & Rubin, 2003; Garcia, Ribeiro, Jorge, Pereira & Resende, 2008; Matias & Paul, 2014; Mota, Vasconcelos, & Assis, 2007; Oliveira & Souza, 2006). It is so widespread and burdensome that it has obtained a prominent place in scientific, political, and legal discourses as well as in literary circles and the media (Matos, 2006). In addition to a serious social problem, it is a serious medical and legal problem (Arroyo, 2004), and it is recognized worldwide with a number of socioeconomic repercussions not only for the victim but also for their family and wider society (Magalhães, 2010).

According to the World Health Organization, violence can take two forms: unintended violence and intentional violence. Unintentional violence refers to the variety of accidental events (e.g., accidents, road accidents, domestic accidents), while intentional acts are those violent behaviors that are enacted with purpose (e.g., physical assault, sexual assault, psychological abuse, domestic violence, homicides, and others) (Magalhães, 2010).

Intentional violence is a dynamic concept, which refers broadly to "a transgression of social norms and values established in each moment" (Lisboa, Barroso, Leandro, & Patrício, 2009, p. 23). According to Magalhães (2010), the intentionally violent behavior occurs in situations in which relational power imbalance between two or more parties is characterized by the use of force and coercion that causes damage to the victim's physical and psychological integrity.

Assuming various forms of manifestation, violence is often grouped into three categories—physical violence, psychological/emotional violence, and sexual violence (Almeida, 2009; Coker, Smith, McKeown, & King, 2000; Magalhães, 2010)—which all manifest in different contexts (e.g., domestic violence, collective violence, youth violence).

Physical violence consists of the use of physical force and the intentional infliction of harm to an individual's person; psychological/emotional violence involves threat, intimidation, humiliation, criticism, and other acts designed to degrade self-esteem, beliefs of self efficacy, financial independence, and erode access (whether real or perceived) to external social supports; and, finally, sexual abuse involves the forced engagement in sexual acts against the will of the victim. Although not formally recognized until relatively recently, sexual violence can occur within the confines of an intimate partner relationship. According to Article 36 of the Council of Europe Convention on preventing and combating violence against women and domestic violence (Istanbul Convention), in effect since the first of August 2014, sexual violence, including rape, is equally applied to acts committed against spouses or partners or against ex-spouses or ex-partners in accordance with respective national laws. Portugal was the first state of the European Union to ratify this international instrument. Similar laws exist across most of the developed world in some form; however, numerous countries around the world continue to uphold laws in which there is no provision for rape or other sexual assault by a husband on his wife.

According to the Portuguese Association for the Support of Victims (APAV), domestic violence is defined as "any conduct or omission of a criminal nature, repeated and/or intense or not, that inflicts physical, sexual, psychological or economic suffering directly or indirectly to any person who lives as a resident in the same domestic space or even if not a resident, is a spouse or former spouse, partner or ex-partner, boyfriend or ex-boyfriend, or parent, or has been in a similar situation; or is an ascendant or descendant, by blood, adoption or marriage " (APAV Statistics, Annual Report 2014, p. 9).

Domestic violence is a cross-over crime that can affect anyone, regardless of gender, age, race, religion, sexual orientation, or socioeconomic status. Domestic violence was legitimized and silenced for centuries and, during this time, was considered an accepted element of an intimate partnership (e.g., *entre marido e mulher ninguém mete a colher*, a Portuguese expression stating nobody should intervene in a marriage; or *Patria Potestas in Romana*, the Roman statute in which the familial patriarch was afforded absolute sovereignty over others in the household, including wives, children, and slaves). However, it has become increasingly unaccepted during the course of the past 150 years. Today, domestic violence is no longer acceptable across much of the world, and the issues surrounding domestic violence are prominent in the legal, social, scientific, and moral conversation. While it was no longer permitted after this time, it was not made explicitly illegal and did not receive specific attention under domestic violence laws until 2007.

According to the annual monitoring report of domestic violence in Portugal, in 2013 police forces recorded 27,318 reports of domestic violence, which corresponds to an increase of 2.4% over the previous year. The first half of 2014 included 13,071 reports of domestic violence in Portugal. The number of domestic violence reports for this period was equivalent to 78.4% of all other crimes reported for the same period (all other crimes = 17,786 cases for the same period; APAV statistics, annual report 2014). The acts of violence that may constitute domestic violence include physical abuse, psychic/emotional abuse, child maltreatment, threats/coercion, slander/libel, intimidation, nonconsensual sexual contact, social isolation, social control, and homicide (attempted or completed) (Madeira & Alves 2014). According to Morgado (2004; cited in Falcke, Oliveira, Rosa, & Bentancur, 2009), domestic violence is the sixth leading cause of death or disability in women aged 15–44 years.

In Brazil, the Brazil's Federal Law 11340/06, also called Maria da Penha Law (Lei Maria da Penha), was ratified on August 7, 2006, which contains mechanisms to restrain and prevent domestic and family violence against women in honor of the pharmaceutist, Maria da Penha Maia Fernandes, who in 1983 was shot by her husband while she was sleeping. According to the Central de Atendimento à Mulher – Ligue 180 (Central for assistance to women—dial 180), in the first half of 2013, 37,582 reports of violence were recorded (physical, psychological, moral, property, sexual, and human trafficking) (SPM, Políticas Pelos Direitos das Mulheres, 2013).

Sousa (2012) mentions that in the 13,800 cases of domestic violence registered by the Portuguese authorities, in 2009, more than half the cases indicated the presence of a child. It is recalled that future social order is influenced by the education of children today (Dreikurs, 2001). Seen as silent victims, when exposed to interparental violence, they have increasingly been the focus of research and intervention, creating a unanimous decision that the exposure of children to domestic violence is a social, emotional, and cognitive risk (Holt, Buckley & Whelan, 2008; Paulino, 2016).

THE OFFENDER, VICTIM, AND CONTEXT: RISK FACTORS IDENTIFICATION

Professionals working with domestic violence and with high-risk populations must be well versed in risk assessment. Risk assessment does not only include identifying the presence of environmental and/or event-related lineal causation factors. Risk assessment also involves the ability to recognize indicators of internal psychological risk factors and the factors associated with the complex dynamics of all of the individual features present that, when combined, result in an elevation of the risk of violence.

Generally speaking, no single risk factor in itself guarantees that violence is imminent or has indeed already taken place. In fact, abuse can occur spontaneously, even in the absence of the stereotypically evident risk factors, and conversely, violence may not eventuate even when there is an overwhelming presence of these risk factors. However, despite the importance of recognizing that exceptions to the rule can and do happen, Magalhães (2010, p. 71) reminds us that the evidence suggests that "the combination of several risk factors [typically] increases the likelihood of abuse."

OFFENDER RISK

As a general rule, the risk of perpetration of domestic violence increases with the increased presence of a range of identified personal characteristics. These include the following (APAV, 2010; Magalhães, 2010; Matias & Paulino, 2014):

1. Being young and male—the younger the age (once into adulthood), the higher is the risk of initiating violent behavior
2. Low levels of education, employment, and economic resources
3. History of family violence in household of origin: interparental violence, child mistreatment, etc.
4. An established history of prior domestic violence
5. The presence of an attitude that legitimizes violence, and supports traditional and stereotypical beliefs as to social, familial, and relational gender roles
6. The presence of addictive personality features and evidence of addictive behaviors (alcohol, substances, etc.)
7. Presence of certain mental illnesses such as depressive disorders with psychotic features and schizophrenia
8. Evidence of personality disorders and/or personality characteristics marked by historical patterns of instability in interpersonal relationships, self-image, affect regulation, and substantial behavioral impulsivity and/or by antisocial and/or narcissistic tendencies such as behaviors that show a distinct disregard for, and violation of, the rights of others

9. The absence of emotional resilience or emotional flexibility needed to cope with stressful life events (coping self-efficacy)—this may manifest in behaviors such as low impulse control, low frustration tolerance, low self-esteem (and the need for external validation to maintain and/or restore self-esteem), and a high level of vulnerability to stress
10. Unrealistic expectations regarding existing resources
11. Demonstrated lack of empathy
12. History of deviant and/or high-risk behavior
13. Lack of experience in providing care, particularly to minors and the elderly, and having, for example, an unrealistic expectation regarding what is age-appropriate behavior or developmental characteristics in children
14. Inability to anticipate the consequences of one's actions, and cannot generally evaluate the risk versus reward, in a behavior choice
15. Demonstration of moral dissociation (deficit in social, psychological and cognitive skills required for a moral assessment of a behavior, such as a violent act
16. Distorts and exaggerates the perception of stimulation that provokes the aggressive response, while cognitively minimizing its consequences
17. A general and pervasive pattern of behavioral and attitudinal aggression
18. Generally apparent deficits in social-cognitive function
19. Externalizes blame
20. Denies responsibility for one's own actions

Samson (2010), points out a number of indications that are considered relevant to identifying potential perpetrators and/or the potential danger these individuals present. Some of these include:

1. The way they speak poorly of previous partners
2. How easily they lose control
3. Cruelty to animals
4. Excessive planning
5. Lack of mutual sharing of biographical life content
6. Intention and/or attempts to isolate the (potential) victim
7. Imposing their own life perspectives/beliefs, and lifestyle choices, onto others
8. Abrupt mood swings, among others

However, it should be noted that perpetrators of spousal violence are not a homogeneous group nor do they have consistent, predictable profiles. To this end, there remains a substantial number of offenders who, from both a behavioral and a psychological perspective, appear well adjusted and functionally "normal" (Echeburúa & Corral, 2009; cited in Gonçalves, Cunha, & Dias, 2011).

According to Holtzworth-Munroe and Stuart (1994, cited in Gonçalves et al., 2011), the violent behavior of perpetrators of spousal abuse can be presented along three dimensions:

1. The severity and frequency of spousal violence

2. The character of the majority of the violence perpetrated (e.g., intrafamilial or extrafamilial)
3. The presence and character of any associated psychopathology or personality disorders

Becerra-Garcia (2015) found that both the perpetrators of domestic violence and the perpetrators of sexual assault show evidence of impaired executive function in areas of cognitive flexibility and executive control of task management such as task switching and set maintenance. This finding illustrates the importance of executive function in behavior and emotion management and in the mediation of aggression responses, self-esteem formation, and social-cognitive function. Executive function is an essential element of higher-order cognitive performance, part of which involves mediating lower-order aggression, emotion, sexual, and reactive behavior, and responses, and therefore plays a central role in mediating physical and sexual violence risk. Furthermore, these findings raise the level of importance that should be given to interventions that address neuropsychological function and attempt to enhance adaptive social responses and promote a change in the perspective of the aggressor. This policy approach can be a complementary part of the psychoeducational and cognitive-behavioral programs that are usually used to treat domestic abusers and sex offenders.

VICTIM RISK

As with offenders, the risk of becoming a victim of domestic violence increases with the increased presence of a range of identified personal characteristics. These include the following (APAV, 2010; Magalhães, 2010; Matias & Paulino, 2014):

1. Being female
2. Having age or experience-related vulnerabilities: children, young and naïve adults, older adults
3. Having personality and temperament characteristics that create co-dependence and other maladaptive interaction and relational connections with the perpetrator
4. Depending physically, emotionally, and/or financially on the perpetrator
5. Being characteristically submissive in nature
6. Tendency to internalize guilt
7. History of family violence in their family of origin: interparental violence, child maltreatment
8. Presence of addictive personality features, and evidence of addictive behaviors (alcohol, substances, etc.)
9. Presence of physical and/or mental illness
10. Low level of education
11. Social isolation
12. Low self-esteem
13. Limited economic resources
14. Living in poor conditions
15. Characteristic patterns of denial
16. Idealized view of own spousal relationship, and spousal relationships in general

17. In children only: premature birth and low birth weight

Interestingly, women who have experienced a history of psychological abuse show a greater preference for partners with characteristics associated with abusive personalities. Women characterized by a high level of anxiety report more experiences of emotional/psychological abuse (O'Hear & David, 1997 cited in Zayas & Shoda, 2007) and physical abuse (Henderson, Bartholomew & Dutton, 1997 cited in Zayas & Shoda, 2007) at the hands of their spouses. Conversely, men with a history of inflicting psychological abuse on their spouses showed a greater preference for partners with anxiety traits.

Baccino (2006) adds that the victims of domestic violence (women) lose a child during pregnancy twice as often (either accidental or induced miscarriage) and consume three times more psychotropic drugs. During pregnancy, female victims of domestic violence are less likely to receive sufficient levels of prenatal care, and are more likely to develop issues associated with weight control and other health concerns during their pregnancy and to develop postpartum disorders associated with depression, adjustment, and trauma. Moreover, the newborn children of victims have a higher risk of having low birth weight and other neonatal health challenges (Markowitz, Polsky, & Renker, 2006).

Domestic violence victimization has significant adverse consequences for the victim, their families, the victim's peers, and the broader community. The longer the abuse continues, the more severe are the consequences. In the short term, victimization is associated with:

1. Severe emotional reactions (fear, anger, isolation, and malaise) and associated cognitive disorganization
2. (Psycho)somatic complaints (insomnia, headaches, gastrointestinal problems, pelvic pain)
3. Physical sequelae directly related to the violence (broken bones, vaginal trauma, bruising, etc.)

As the period of abuse extends, additional consequences may manifest. These include:

1. Depression
2. Anxiety
3. Posttraumatic stress disorder
4. Eating disorders
5. Alcohol and substance abuse
6. Dissociative disorders
7. Sexual dysfunction
8. Paranoia and distrust of members of the opposite sex (or subgroup of the perpetrator)
9. Autonomic hyperarousal, hypervigilance to threat/control signals
10. Low self-esteem
11. These and a range of other physical conditions, behaviors, emotional states, and cognitive operations that can be characterized as either direct and indirect consequences of the physical, psychological, sexual, and/or financial abuse, or associated maladaptive coping strategies across a range of complex defense mechanisms aimed at maintaining physical and mental functionality (APAV, 2010)

HISTORICAL AND ENVIRONMENTAL RISK

There are certain family background characteristics that may trigger violent behavior. These include (APAV, 2010; Magalhães, 2010):

1. Single-parent family
2. Blended families (stepchildren, half-siblings, etc.)
3. Family financial, socioeconomic, and housing problems: social isolation, lack of family support, poverty, inappropriate housing for familial/personal needs
4. Large families with limited resources
5. Unstructured/chaotic family environment with dysfunctional relationships: violence, poor parenting skills, poor attachments, specific illnesses and physical conditions in children or parents with inappropriate resourcing to cope/manage
6. Significant levels of current and/or historical family stress: death, separation, unemployment, financial problems
7. Family circumstances in which there is an added externally driven burden of care placed on the family with limited resources (personal, emotional, competency, financial) to cope: care of a child, elder, other relative/s, community needs, etc.

In addition, there are several reasons why a victim may stay in a violent/abusive relationship. These may be internal or they may be external and include:

1. Absence of an alternative place to live
2. Economic dependency on the perpetrator
3. Religious or social beliefs ("married till death do us part," etc.)
4. Social desirability associated with relationship
5. The lack of successful outcomes from previous interventions, whether social or criminal
6. Learned helplessness
7. A fear of reprisals from the perpetrator and/or family, and community members
8. Social isolation and the consequent loss of identity

Internal factors may include:

1. Codependence
   a. Maladaptive coping strategy aimed at minimizing violence: passivity response
   b. Guilt
   c. Desire to maintain family life: Belief in importance of continued cohabitation with spouse for sake of children, even when the spouse (perpetrator) does not have a positive connection with the spouse
   d. (Misguided) sense of loyalty to spouse
   e. Continued belief in own "love" of perpetrator, and/or belief in perpetrator's "love" for victim
   f. Belief that the offender will change
   g. Emotion and physical "exhaustion" and skepticism

A person is especially vulnerable when he or she is directly dependent on the perpetrator (emotionally, economically), as this ultimately reduces the capacity to objectively see the situation and act in one's own (and the children's) best interests. Dependence impacts a victim's cognitive appraisals, reinforces prevailing dependent personality traits, and ultimately increases the victim's fear, however this may be manifest (fear of reprisal, fear of loss of social status, fear of being alone, and fear of economic vulnerability, among others). These factors then serve to compromise the victim's capacity to make the decision to leave (Plana, 1999). According to Damas (2010, p. 36): "The lack of courage delays, but fear prevents, any action." Turvey (2009), states that female victims of domestic violence do not always see themselves as victims, because, as in many of the social problems, denial serves as a psychological means of survival.

It is crucial to take into account the perspective of the victim in relation to the acts of the perpetrator. That is, one must take into account the meaning that the victim attributes to the behavior, and in some cases, whether these acts are, in fact, considered as abusive (Ali, 2003). Sometimes victims assimilate norms and cultural discourses that blame and legitimize the behavior of offenders (Machado, Matos, & Gonçalves, 2001). Victims often interpret events differently to those who have not experienced domestic violence and will generally legitimize or "normalize" aggressive behaviors. Victims of physical violence in particular have been found to be more tolerant than those who are not victims of violence. Psychologically, victims will often rationalize, minimize, or deny violent/abusive behaviors against them (or against their children) as an attempt to make sense of it, to maintain their own cognitive legitimacy of their spousal status, and as a (maladaptive) coping mechanism to help them survive the ordeal (Machado et al. 2001). Ferraro and Johnson (1983), have identified six rationalizations made by victims to legitimize their decision to stay in an abusive relationship:

1. Appeal to ethical salvation: they may convince themselves that they can stay and the perpetrator from those circumstances is blamed for the behavior
2. Denial of the event: perhaps even the perpetrator's
3. Denial of damage: the denial of the damage means they do not recognize the physical or sexual abuse that the victim is endures, and self-defines the acts/experiences as tolerable, normal and *non delitivo*
4. Denial of victimization: denial of victimization is characterized by taking the blame and responsibility for the abuse, and thereby negating any responsibility on the part of the offender
5. Denial of the availability of alternative options: the victim believes that help is ultimately unavailable or futile, and the possibility of an alternative life is limited or nonexistent
6. Appeal/deference to the power and/or will of higher entities: the victim maintains the relationship based on traditional or religious principles to which the victim holds, and rationalizes that it is "God's will."

The cooperative attitude, or lack thereof, is another factor to consider when investigating a suspected case of domestic violence. Some victims will readily identify the abuse and name the perpetrator; some will identify the situation but refuse to name the perpetrator; and still others will deny any abuse has occurred.

In cases where the victim does not want to report the situation, experts must, during the investigation, pay special attention to certain factor and behaviors, such as (Matias & Paulino, 2014):

1. Minimizing the extent of injuries or attempts to conceal them
2. Frequent injuries in certain parts the body
3. Tense and frightened posture
4. Depression and anxiety symptoms
5. History of psychiatric illness and substance dependence
6. The constant presence of an aggressive and dominant companion, who is responsible for the victim or partner's silent negligence
7. Submissive attitude of the woman against the partner
8. Unexplained delays in seeking treatment
9. Injuries that are incompatible with the given explanation
10. Successive inconsistent or incoherent versions of the same accident
11. Vague and confused explanations for what happened
12. Frequent and recurring use of health services
13. Suicidal ideation

It is important to take into account that a significant portion of people assisted in a hospital or health center will not want to reveal the cause of the trauma and will therefore provide an alternative cause of the presentation (injuries) that may sound unlikely given the nature of the injuries and the medical knowledge of the attending physicians. The common stories are that they fell down the stairs, bumped into a door, or slipped in the bath/shower.

Some of the most important questions and indicators to identify/synthesize a possible case of domestic violence are:

1. The regular presentation to health professionals with a variety of physical markings and bruises accompanied by vague explanations and symptom descriptions
2. A lack of regular consultation with health care professionals, or frequent delays, reappointing, or "no shows" to scheduled consultations
3. Injuries that are incompatible with the descriptions provided by the victim
4. Common injuries in the hands, face, head, neck, chin, chest, and abdomen
5. Evidence of multiple injuries in different stages of healing
6. Attempts to minimize the severity of injuries and/or try to hide them with clothes
7. The (suspected) victim seems timid, frightened, overly anxious, or depressed
8. The victim is constantly monitored in consultations by partners or other family members, who may dominate and answer questions or offer explanations on behalf of the (suspected) victim
9. The (suspected) victim seems too passive or appears afraid of, or to defer substantially to, their partner or other family member

10. The partner seems aggressive or controlling and is reluctant to let the woman speak or be alone with health experts
11. Refers to spousal problems without particularizing situations of violence
12. History of miscarriages or premature births

The screening of domestic violence while conducting a medical history can be done by considering three questions during the consultation:

1. Has the patient suffered some kind of physical injury, or been harmed by someone, in the previous year, or in the case of pregnancy or recent childbirth, since falling pregnant or since childbirth? Remember that pregnancy and childbirth are two significant triggers of domestic violence against expectant/recent mothers.
2. Does the patient maintain a relationship with any person who has previously caused them harm or threatened to do so?
3. Has the patient been coerced, or forced to engage in sexual activity or to perform sex acts with which he or she was uncomfortable with, objected to, or was against his or her will?

If domestic violence has been established, then it is critical to conduct a thorough risk assessment and prepare a victim security plan, based on the calculated risk. It will be up to the expert to assess the level of recurrence of assaults, the probability of a sharp escalation of aggression occurring, the risk of serious harm or homicide, and any potential suicide risk (Matias & Paulino, 2014). The research shows a distinction between the risk of spousal violence and the risk of spousal homicide. Nonetheless, there is a clear relationship between domestic violence and intimate partner homicide and filicide. Therefore, risk assessment and appropriate action are essential. These should account for the key indicators of risk, including (Gonçalves et al., 2011; Matias & Paulino, 2014):

For spousal violence risk:

1. Alcohol abuse
2. Low frustration tolerance
3. Deficits of assertiveness (behavioral/vocal)
4. Disturbance of antisocial personality
5. Different religious orientations in the couple
6. Incidental factors (early marriage, unemployment, separation)
7. Academic/professional superiority of the (potential) victim
8. Violence or other aggressive position taken toward the children
9. Violence in the family of origin of either party

For spousal homicide risk:

1. Alcohol and drug abuse
2. Possession of, or access to, firearms and other weapons
3. Previous armed threats
4. Previous death threats

5. Threats of suicide
6. Attitudes of extreme power and dominance
7. Obsessive attitudes/behaviors
8. Rumination and excessive jealousy
9. Pervasive violent behavior and/or attitudes
10. Serious injuries in previous incidents
11. Psychiatric morbidity/psychopathology
12. Previous forced sexual behaviors with victim or others
13. Use of weapons in prior incidents

CONCLUSION

Reported cases of domestic violence are on the increase; however, there is evidence that the number of cases reported is a small percentage of actual incidents. Many of the existing cases are not reported and therefore are not identified in the official statistics. This is despite a marked change in community attitudes toward domestic and intimate partner violence. Even though this change is tangible and has helped reduce the stigma and victim-blaming long associated with acts of domestic violence, a significant number of cases remain "behind closed doors." This fact underscores the importance of continued public awareness, legal reform to protect victims and punish perpetrators, and professional support and advocacy for victims and others who are impacted by violence in the family. This includes further scientific and professional endeavors to better understand the nature of this crime and the characteristics of both perpetrators and victims alike. As has been demonstrated throughout this chapter, due to its inherent complexity, recognizing domestic violence is not always easy, and successfully intervening may be harder still. However, public education and the provision of appropriate training and support to frontline professionals in this field (psychologists, social workers, doctors, lawyers, police officers, child safety workers, etc.) and to secondary professionals whose work often intersects with domestic violence and its consequences (e.g., teachers, childcare staff, sports coaches, etc.) can help to bring domestic violence further into the light and help provide meaningful and timely assistance to those affected.

Health experts have a privileged place in the observation and identification of domestic violence. Identifying and recognizing signs are the first step of intervention in health care. Often these professionals are faced with the feeling "that something is not right" but do not know what to do or how to act. Throughout this process, the victim should feel that professionals, apart from being able to provide proper care, are available to listen and help without judging.

In summary, family violence is a problem of epidemic proportions and one of the most serious of public health problems, requiring society as a whole to engage collectively with a process of change. To paraphrase Magalhães (2010, p. 138), it is important to promote "(…) a multidisciplinary and necessarily articulated intervention, (…) [for] isolated interventions, even well intentioned, may cause more harm than good. [However] (…) it is always better to intervene than to be waiting for a natural resolution of the case."

SUMMARY

- One of the great paradoxes of human existence is the fact that the majority of interpersonal violence occurs between people who are related to each other. Within the family, many homes are marked by violence, making home as "(…) one of the most dangerous places in modern societies. In statistical terms, regardless of sex and age, a person will become more susceptible to violence at home than in a street at night" (Giddens, 2001, p. 196). This underscores the seriousness of family violence.

- In order to understand domestic violence, it is essential to appreciate that the violence occurs within the confines of a bidirectional interaction between the aggressor and the victim, that takes place within a particular context, and that these contextual characteristics must, in themselves, be recognized and explored as unique independent variables in the equation.

- According to the World Health Organization, the word "violence" can take two forms: unintended violence and intentional violence. Unintentional violence refers to the variety of accidental events (e.g. accidents, road accidents, domestic accidents), while intentional acts are those violent behaviors that are enacted with purpose (e.g. physical assault, sexual assault, psychological abuse, domestic violence, homicides, and others).

- Professionals working with domestic violence and with high-risk populations, must be well versed in risk assessment. Risk assessment does not only include identifying the presence of environmental and/or event-related lineal causation factors. Risk assessment also involves the ability to recognize indicators of internal psychological risk factors, and the factors associated with the complex dynamics of all of the individual features present, that, when combined, result in an elevation of the risk of violence.

- Generally speaking, no single risk factor in itself guarantees that violence is imminent, or has indeed taken place already. In fact, abuse can occur spontaneously, even in the absence of the stereotypically evident risk factors, and conversely, violence may not eventuate even when there is an overwhelming presence of these risk factors. However, despite the importance of recognizing that exceptions to the rule can, and do happen, Magalhães (2010, p. 71) reminds us that the evidence suggests that "(…) the combination of several risk factors [typically] increases the likelihood of abuse."

- As a general rule, the risk of perpetration of domestic violence increases with the increased presence of a range of identified personal characteristics. However, it should be noted that perpetrators of spousal violence are not a homogeneous group nor do they have consistent, predictable profiles. To this end, there remains a substantial number of offenders who, from both a behavioral and psychological perspective, appear well adjusted and functionally "normal."

- Becerra-Garcia (2015) found that both the perpetrators of domestic violence, and of sexual assault, show evidence of impaired executive function in areas of cognitive flexibility, and executive control of task management such as task switching and set maintenance. This finding illustrates the importance of executive function in behavior and emotion management, and in the mediation of aggression responses, self-esteem formation, and social-cognitive function

- As with offenders, the risk of becoming a victim of domestic violence increases with the increased presence of a range of identified personal characteristics. Interestingly, women who have experienced a history of psychological abuse, show a greater preference for partners with characteristics associated with abusive personalities. Women characterized by a high level of anxiety report more experiences of emotional/psychological abuse and physical abuse at the hands of their spousal partners. Conversely, men with a history of inflicting psychological abuse on their spouses showed a greater preference for partners with anxiety traits.
- A person is especially vulnerable when they are directly dependent upon the perpetrator (emotionally, economically), as this ultimately reduces their capacity to objectively see the situation and act in their own (and their children's) best interests. Dependence impacts a victim's cognitive appraisals, reinforces prevailing dependent personality traits, and ultimately increases the victim's fear; however, this may be manifest (fear of reprisal, fear of loss of social status, fear of being alone, fear of economic vulnerability, etc.). These factors then serve to compromise the victim's capacity to make the decision to leave.
- Female victims of domestic violence do not always see themselves as victims, because, as in many of the social problems, denial serves as a psychological means of survival. It is crucial to take into account the perspective of the victim in relation to the acts of the perpetrator. That is, one must take into account the meaning that the victim attributes to the behavior and in some cases, whether these acts are, in fact, considered as abusive. Sometimes victims assimilate norms and cultural discourses that blame and legitimize the behavior of offenders. Victims often interpret events differently to those who have not experienced domestic violence and will generally legitimize or "normalize" aggressive behaviors.
- It is important to take into account that a significant portion of people assisted in a hospital or health center will not want to reveal the cause of trauma and will therefore provide an alternative cause of the presentation (injuries), that may sound unlikely given the nature of the injuries and the medical knowledge of the attending physicians. The common stories are that they, fell down the stairs, bumped into a door, or slipped in the bath/shower.
- If domestic violence has been established then it is critical to conduct a thorough risk assessment and prepare a victim security plan, based on the calculated risk. It will be up to the expert to assess the level of recurrence of assaults, the probability of occurring a sharp escalation of aggression, the risk of serious harm or homicide, and any potential suicide risk. The research shows a distinction between the risk of spousal violence and the risk of spousal homicide; nonetheless, there is a clear relationship between domestic violence and intimate partner homicide and filicide. Therefore, risk assessment and appropriate action are essential.

QUESTIONS

1. According to the World Health Organization, violence can take two forms. What are these two forms, and what are their characteristics?
2. What are the general personal characteristics (20) that have been identified as risk factors associated becoming a perpetrator of domestic violence?
3. Samson (2010) points out a number of indications that are considered relevant to identifying potential perpetrators and/or the potential danger these individuals present. What are these indicators?
4. What are the three dimensions along which the violent behavior of perpetrators of spousal abuse can be presented?
5. As with offenders, the risk of becoming a victim of domestic violence increases with the increased presence of a range of identified personal characteristics
6. Domestic violence victimization has significant short- and long-term adverse consequences for the victim. Describe these consequences.
7. What are the family background characteristics that are associated with domestic violence risk?
8. Why might a victim choose to stay in a violent relationship? Discuss both internal and external factors.
9. Ferraro and Johnson (1983) have identified six rationalizations made by victims to legitimize their decision to stay in an abusive relationship. Name and describe them.
10. In cases where the victim is reluctant/does not want to report domestic violence, what are the factors and behaviors that investigators must be aware of?
11. If healthcare experts only focus their attention on the treatment of injuries, without asking their causes, they will do little to help the victim. What are some of the most important questions and indicators to identify/synthesize a possible case of domestic violence?
12. The screening of domestic violence while conducting a medical history can be done by considering three questions during the consultation. What are they?
13. The research shows a distinction between the risk of spousal violence, and the risk of spousal homicide. What are the key indicators of spousal violence?
14. What are the key indicators of spousal homicide?

REFERENCES

Ali, S. M. (2003). Domestic violence against women: perspective from Pakistan. *Pakistan Journal of Medical Sciences, 19*(1), 23–28.
Almeida, M. (2009). *Violência conjugal e álcool: (in) existência de uma relação causal?* Dissertação de Mestrado. Coimbra, Portugal: Faculdade de Medicina, Universidade de Coimbra.
APAV Statistics, Annual Report 2014, Retrieved from http://apav.pt/apav_v2/images/pdf/Estatisticas_APAV_Relatorio_Anual_2014.pdf.

APAV. (2010). *Manual Alcipe – Para o atendimento de mulheres vítimas de violência* (2nd Ed).

Arroyo, M. (2004). Violencia familiar. In E. Cañadas (Ed.), *Gisbert Calabuig: Medicina legal y toxicologia* (6th Ed) (pp. 486–504). Barcelona: Masson.

Baccino, É. (2006). Violence conjugales. In É. Baccino (Ed.), *Médecine de la violence: Prise en charge des victims et des agresseurs* (pp. 119–129). Paris: Masson.

Becerra-García, J. (2015). Neuropsychology of domestic violence: a comparative preliminary study of executive functioning. *Medicine, Science and the Law*, 55(1), 35–39.

Brandão, E. R. (2006). Renunciantes de direitos? A problemática do enfrentamento público da violência contra a mulher: o caso da delegacia da mulher. *PHYSIS: Revista Saúde Coletiva*, 16, 207–231.

Coker, S. L., Smith, P. H., McKeown, R. E., & King, M. J. (2000). Frequency and correlates of intimate partner violence by type: physical, sexual, and psychological battering. *American Journal of Public Health*, 90(4), 553–559.

Corsi, J. (2003). La violencia en el contexto familiar como problema social. In J. Corsi (Ed.), *Maltrato y abuso en el âmbito doméstico* (pp. 15–40). Buenos Aires: Paidós.

Damas, M. (2010). *Os Portugueses São Analfabetos Sexuais...E Emocionais.* Alfragide: Livros d'Hoje.

Datner, E., Asher, J., & Rubin, B. (2003). Domestic violence and partner rape. In A. Giardino, E. Datner, & J. Asher (Eds.), *Sexual assault victimization across the life span* (Vol. 1) (pp. 347–362). Universidade de Michigan: G.W. Medical Pub.

Dreikurs, R. (2001). *Educação: Um desafio aos pais.* Amadora: McGraw-Hill.

Echeburúa, E., & Corral, P. (2009). *Manual de violencia familiar.* Madrid: Siglo.

Falcke, D., Oliveira, D. Z., Rosa, L. M., & Bentancur, M. (2009). Violência conjugal: um fenômeno internacional. *Contextos Clínicos*, 2(2), 81–90.

Ferraro, K. J., & Johnson, J. M. (1983). How women experience battering: the process of victimization. *Social Problems*, 325–339.

Garcia, M. V., Ribeiro, L. A., Jorge, M. T., Pereira, G. R., & Resende, A. P. (2008). Caracterização dos casos de violência contra a mulher atendidos em três serviços na cidade de Uberlândia, Minas Gerias, Brasil. *Cadernos de Saúde Pública*, 24, 2551–2563.

Giddens, A. (2001). *Sociologia.* Lisboa: Fundação Calouste Gulbenkian.

Gonçalves, R., Cunha, O., & Dias, A. (2011). Avaliação Psicológica de Agressores Conjugais. In M. Matos, R. Gonçalves, & C. Machado (Eds.), *Manual de Psicologia Forense: Contextos e Desafios* (pp. 223–245). Braga: Psiquilíbrios Edições.

Holt, S., Buckley, H., & Whelan, S. (2008). The impact of exposure to domestic violence on children and young people: a review of the literature. *Child Abuse & Neglect*, 32, 797–810.

HYPERLINK "http://www.itajuba.mg.gov.br/semug/legislacao_cppmi/lei_maria_penha.pdf" \o "http://www.itajuba.mg.gov.br/semug/legislacao_cppmi/lei_maria_penha.pdf"http://www.itajuba.mg.gov.br/semug/legislacao_cppmi/lei_maria_penha.pdf.

Lei Maria da Penha, Lei n. 11.340. Biblioteca Digital, Câmara dos Deputados.

Lei n.11.340, de 7 de Agosto de. (2006). *Presidência da Republica, Casa Civil.* Consultado em http://www.planalto.gov.br/ccivil_03/_Ato2004-2006/2006/Lei/L11340.htm. a 24 de Março 2015.

Lisboa, M., Barroso, Z., Leandro, A., & Patrício, J. (2009). *Violência e Género: Inquérito Nacional sobre a Violência Exercida contra Mulheres e Homens.* Lisboa: Comissão para a Cidadania e Igualdade de Género.

Machado, C., Gonçalves, M., & Matos, M. (2008). *Manual da Escala de Crenças Sobre Violência Conjugal (E.C.V.C.) e do Inventário de Violência Conjugal (I.V.C.)* (2nd Ed.). Braga: Psiquilíbrios Edições.

Machado, C., Matos, M., & Gonçalves, M. (2001). Cultural beliefs and attitudes about violence against women and children. In R. Gonçalves (Ed.), *Victims and offender: Chapter on psychology and law* (pp. 137–154). Bruxelas: Politeia.

Madeira, C., & Alves, S. (2014). Violência Doméstica: Princípios orientadores de atuação no serviço de urgência. In A. Gomes (Ed.), *Enfermagem forense* (Vol. 2) (pp. 586–605). Lisboa: Lidel.

Magalhães, T. (2010). *Violência e abuso*. Coimbra: Estado da Arte.

Markowitz, J., Polsky, S., & Renker, P. (2006). Aproximación clínica a la violencia doméstica. In S. Polsky, & J. Markowitz (Eds.), *Atlas en color de violencia doméstica* (pp. 1–19). Barcelona: Masson.

Matias, M., & Paulino, M. (2014). *O Inimigo em Casa. Dar voz ao silêncio da violência doméstica.* (2nd Ed.). Lisboa: Prime Books.

Matos, M. (2006). *Violência nas relações de intimidade: Estudo sobre a mudança psicoterapêutica na mulher.* Tese de Doutoramento não publicada. Universidade do Minho: Instituto de Educação e Psicologia.

Meloy, J. (2003). Pathologies of attachment, violence, and criminality. In A. Goldstein (Ed.), *Handbook of psychology – Vol XI forensic psychology.* (pp. 509–526). New Jersey: John Wiley & Sons.

Mota, J., Vasconcelos, A., & Assis, S. (2007). Análise de correspondência como estratégia para a descrição do perfil da mulher vítima do parceiro atendida em serviço especializado. *Ciência & Saúde Colectiva, 12*(3), 799–880.

Oliveira, D. C., & Souza, L. (2006). Gênero e violência conjugal concepções de psicólogos. *Estudos e Pesquisas em Psicologia, 6*, 34–50.

Paulino, M. (2016). Spousal violence: Psychodynamics, forensic mental health issues and research. San Diego: Elsevier Academic Press.

Plana, J. (1999). *Manual de actuación sanitaria, policial, legal y social frente a la violencia doméstica.* Guión de actuación y formulários. Barcelona: Masson.

Samson, A. (2010). *A Violência Doméstica: Aprenda a Identificar Situações de Abuso e a Ser Feliz.* Lisboa: Livros de Seda.

Sousa, A. B. (2012). *Problemas da família e da criança.* Coimbra: Edições Almedina.

SPM, Politicas Pelos Direitos das Mulheres. (2013). *Secretaria de Politicas Pelos Direitos das Mulheres, Presidência da República.*

Turvey, B. (2009). Intimate partner violence. In B. Turvey, & W. Petherick (Eds.), *Forensic victimology: Examining violent crime victims in investigative and legal contexts* (pp. 299–327). San Diego: Elsevier.

Zayas, V., & Shoda, Y. (2007). Predicting preferences for dating partners from past experiences of psychological abuse: identifying the psychological ingredients of situations. *Personality & Social Psychology Bulletin, 33*(1), 123–138.

Honor Killings and Domestic Violence: The Same or Different?

12

Carletta Xavier[1], Wayne Petherick[1], Grant Sinnamon[1,2]

[1]Bond University, Gold Coast, QLD, Australia; [2]Bela Menso Brain and Behaviour Centre, Varsity Lakes, QLD, Australia

CHAPTER OUTLINE

INTRODUCTION

In Australia, 75% of the women killed between 2011 and 2012 were killed by their male partner (Australian Institute of Criminology, 2015). Comparatively for the same period, 25% of male homicides were perpetrated by the victim's female intimate partner (Australian Institute of Criminology, 2015). It should be noted that these figures do not include victims of violence who have survived or who have suffered minor injuries. These figures and other similar statistics from around the world highlight the substantial link between the risk of interpersonal violence and intimate relationships (Reddy, 2008). Attention to this relationship has increased in recent years through an extensive range of campaigns such as those promoted by White Ribbon, Amnesty International, and #ShineALight. In addition, recent high profile cases of domestic violence (DV)-related homicide have generated widespread media coverage of intimate-partner violence, and particularly intimate-partner crimes against women (Reddy, 2008). Many behaviors against women that are criminal in the majority of "Westernized" societies are often considered acceptable in other cultures (e.g., honor killings). These acts of violence have captured the attention of the public and become an increasingly popular social and political issue (Siddiqui, 2005). Of particular note is the increasing "vox populi" questioning how violence against women can be labeled as "honorable," rather than as criminal DV, assault, and homicide.

The aim of this chapter is to compare the commonalities and differences between honor killings and DV and in no way purports to rationalize, condone, or excuse violence against women, no matter where it is perpetrated, or by whom. Specifically, this chapter aims to explore and characterize the victims, perpetrators, and environments in which DV and honor killings take place, along with the individual and cultural motivations behind these acts. Moreover, this chapter aims to demonstrate whether honor killings are similar to DV, in relation to modus operandi and other underlying factors, in order to determine whether honor killings can be classified as a type of DV or whether they are best viewed as unique to one another.

DOMESTIC VIOLENCE

Historically, the stereotypical domestic role of the male and female have prevailed. Many of the stereotypical domestic gender roles are universally identified across numerous cultures and historical epochs (Cohan, 2010). Often, the roles of the breadwinner and homemaker, and controller and controlled, stem from underlying prejudicial beliefs relating to women's inferiority and a common position akin to the Ancient Roman Statute of Patria Potestas Romana (The Power of the Father), in which children and wives were legally and morally identified as the property of the Patriarch and subject to his rule, including decisions regarding life and death (Brotto, Sinnamon, & Petherick, 2016; Cohan, 2010). Arguably, whether stemming from a cultural or religious genesis, violence against women within any given culture or context has significant foundation in these historical patriarchal positions.

DV is a widespread problem across Australia (Healey, 2014) and other parts of the world. Definitions of DV are socially constructed and reflect the underlying understandings, perceptions, and interests of the culture in question (Muehlenhard & Kimes, 1999). While there are many definitions for DV, consistent across most is the notion that DV is multifaceted, that it does not necessarily involve actual physical violence, and that it involves excessive control. According to Healy (2014, p. X):

> Domestic violence refers to an abuse of power within an intimate relationship … when one partner attempts to physically or psychologically dominate, control, or harm the other partner. Common forms include physical and sexual violence, threats, intimidation, and any acts associated with deprivation, or neglect.

Almedia and Durkin (1999, p. 313) define DV as "the patterned and repeated use of coercive and controlling behavior to limit, direct, and shape a partner's thoughts, feelings, and actions. Power and control tactics are often utilized to establish dominance." Three of the primary rationales or motivations for DV offenders have been identified: sexual jealously, cause (fail to meet expectations), and will (expression of power) (Baker, Gregware, & Cassidy, 1999; Levinson, 1988).

TYPES OF DV

The stereotypical DV situation involves direct acts of physical violence within an intimate partner relationship toward the offender's intimate partner or children in their care. However, the National Plan to Reduce Violence against Women and Children (2011, p. 2) identified that "a central element of DV is that of an ongoing pattern of behavior aimed to control, dominate, and exercise power over the other, in both criminal and noncriminal manners." As such, DV has been recognized as flexible and is composed of many additional facets not directly involving physical violence and may therefore involve other acts such as coercion, threat, intimidation, financial control, and social isolation. In this way, physical abuse, sexual abuse, psychological abuse, verbal abuse, emotional abuse, social abuse, spiritual abuse, and economic abuse have all been established as acts of DV (Mitchell, 2011).

Physical abuse refers to direct assault, injury, and harm to the body (Domestic Violence Centre, 2016; Mitchell, 2011; New York State Office for the Prevention of Domestic Violence, 2014; White Ribbon, 2016). This includes the use of weapons, driving dangerously, the destruction of property, assault of children, sleep deprivation, punching, choking, hitting, pushing, and shoving (Mitchell, 2011; Ouzos & Makkai, 2004). Sexual assault is also another form of physical abuse. This refers to pressured or unwanted sex or degradation, coercive sex, degrading and criticizing sexual acts, and any additional related acts that cause the victim any type of harm (Domestic Violence Prevention Centre, 2016; Mitchell, 2011; Mouzos & Makkai, 2004; New York State Office for the Prevention of Domestic Violence, 2014; White Ribbon, 2016).

Nonviolent types of abuse such as psychological abuse, emotional abuse, and verbal abuse are commonly recognized as the most prevalent types of DV. Psychological abuse refers to impacts on the victim's psychological state, which causes the victim distress and harm (Domestic Violence Prevention Centre, 2016; Mitchell, 2011; New York State Office for the Prevention of Domestic Violence, 2014; White Ribbon, 2016). Acts of this nature include, but are not limited to, threatening custody of children, implanting false beliefs, humiliation, threats, insults, swearing, and harassment (Mitchell, 2011; Mouzos & Makkai, 2004). Emotional abuse refers to the offender blaming the victim for their marital or relationship problems. By doing this, the offender seeks to undermine the self-esteem and self-worth of the victim for easier control over their behavior (Domestic Violence Prevention Centre, 2016; Mitchell, 2011; New York State Office for the Prevention of Domestic Violence, 2014; White Ribbon, 2016). Additionally, the offender will withdraw interest and engagement with the victim (e.g., long periods of silence) (Mitchell, 2011). Verbal abuse includes humiliation and degradation centered round factors relating to intelligence, sexuality, body image, or capacity as a parent and/or spouse (Domestic Violence Prevention Centre, 2016; Mitchell, 2011; New York State Office for the Prevention of Domestic Violence, 2014; White Ribbon, 2016).

The last cluster of abuse characteristics are socially based and include social abuse, spiritual abuse, and economic abuse. Social abuse includes the victim being isolated from their family and/or friends, the offender controlling residency, denying their partner access to the telephone, and restricting the locations their partner can go (Domestic Violence Prevention Centre, 2016; Mitchell, 2011; Mouzos & Makkai, 2004; New York State Office for the Prevention of Domestic Violence, 2014; White Ribbon, 2016). Moreover, the couple will likely be residing in an area where the victim has no social circle readily available to them and no opportunities for employment, thus hindering the victim's ability to meet new people (Mitchell, 2011). Spiritual abuse is understood to comprise the misuse of religious beliefs and/or practices to force victims to be the subordinate, which "justifies" their abuse and violence toward the victim (Mitchell, 2011; Mouzos & Makkai, 2004). Economic abuse refers to the control over all finances, forbidding victims from accessing "personal" funds, giving the victim an "allowance," hindering employment opportunities for the victim, and having control over any wages (Domestic Violence Prevention Centre, 2016; Mitchell, 2011; Mouzos & Makkai, 2004; New York State Office for the Prevention of Domestic Violence, 2014; White Ribbon, 2016).

VICTIMS OF DV

Violence against women is considered to be a significant social problem across the globe (Lombard & McMillan, 2012), and while DV is not a gender-specific problem, it does impact females at considerably higher rates than males and can therefore be identified as a female-biased form of violence and an abuse of power, within an intimate relationship. This includes de facto and separated couples, couples who are not cohabiting, and homosexual relationships (Flood & Fergus, 2008). Although this chapter is predominantly about DV and honor killings directed at female victims and females have significantly higher rates of victimization compared to men (Department of Social Services, 2013); the literature suggests that this form of violence against men is underreported (often due to stereotypical factors surrounding idealized notions of masculinity; Evans, 2012), and therefore, true comparative rates of prevalence are unknown.

There are several factors that have been identified as being associated with an increased risk of DV. These vulnerabilities include being younger, indigenous, a woman living in a remote location, physical and mental disability, immigration from a culturally divergent country-of-origin, low education, and being unemployed (Mitchell, 2011). However, it is important to note that while these factors increase a woman's vulnerability, DV is found in almost all cultural and subcultural social demographics.

DV OFFENDERS

There is a common misconception that males exclusively commit DV (Flood & Fergus, 2008; McKeown, 2014; Morgan & Chadwick, 2009). Research into DV perpetrators indicates that violence is used as a maladaptive coping mechanism, and perpetrators exhibit a variety of associated maladaptive behaviors and personality characteristics, including low self-esteem, fear of abandonment, low assertiveness and high aggression, poor social skills, poor self-control, and poor emotional skills (Rode, 2010). As these characteristics are classically associated with a need for control and a perpetual sense of being "out of control" (Sinnamon, 2015); perpetrators use acts of violence and other behaviors associated with DV (threat, intimidations, etc.) as a means to obtain control over the spatial and temporal threats to their self-esteem and ego-driven personal needs (Rode, 2010; Sinnamon, 2015).

There are several factors in males that result in an increased risk of becoming a DV offender. These include being a victim of childhood trauma and abuse (Murrell, Christoff, & Henning, 2007), alcohol and drug abuse, financial stress, personal psychological stress, and lack of social support (Mitchell, 2011). Alcohol abuse is the strongest predictor for DV, with 49% of female DV victims experiencing episodic violence at the hands of an intoxicated male perpetrator (Australian Bureau of Statistics, 2005). In Australia, between 2000 and 2006, 44% of intimate-partner homicides involved an intoxicated perpetrator (Dearden & Payne, 2009). However, according to Dearden and Payne (2009), those involving a female perpetrator and male victim involve a greater number of intoxicated offenders (73%), compared to those involving a male offender and female victim (36%). In First Australian Populations, almost 9 of 10 (87%), intimate-partner homicides involve an intoxicated perpetrator (Dearden & Payne, 2009). These figures illustrate the significant role played by alcohol in DV deaths; however, other factors also play a role. When examining the factors associated with an intimate-partner homicide, such as alcohol, other substances, environmental considerations, and background of both the victim and perpetrator, it is important to examine the interrelationships between all factors involved and the extent to which the various elements play a direct and/or indirect role in the spatial, temporal, and personal circumstances leading up to and surrounding the event.

Male perpetrators of DV have been commonly identified with antisocial, borderline, dependent, and narcissistic personality characteristics and are often diagnosed with depressive disorders such as major depression and hypomania (Murrel et al., 2007; Sinnamon, 2015). These characteristics are more common in violent men compared to nonviolent men, and the level of associated impairment is directly correlated to the perpetrator's personal level of exposure to childhood abuse and trauma (Murrell et al., 2007). Moreover, 40% of male perpetrators had a criminal record prior to their arrest for DV (Murrell et al., 2007).

While females also commit acts of DV, the true extent to which women engage in acts of violence against their intimate partners is unknown. This is largely due to the previously mentioned factors around masculinity and stigma that serve to impede male victims' reporting of domestic victimization (Lombard & McMillan, 2012). A small proportion of female perpetrators of DV have been discussed in the literature. From what is known about the female perpetrator of DV, it has been suggested that women are less likely than males to use coercive or controlling tactics, systematic threats, or overt physical violence (Hester, 2012). Instead, the research indicates that women are more likely to use tactics that do not require physical strength such as psychological abuse, emotional manipulation, and indirect or nonphysical acts of aggression (Drijber, Reijnders, & Ceelen, 2012; McKeown, 2014; Straus, 1980). While the behavior may differ somewhat to that of male perpetrators, much of the inherent motivation remains the same, namely the need to control the environment and the people in it as a means of protecting or restoring self-esteem.

One common argument as to why women behave violently toward a partner is that they are often engaging in acts of "violent resistance." This concept is understood to include both self-defense and retaliation against intimate partners (usually males) who are violent, threatening, or coercive (Downs, Rindels, & Atkinson, 2007; Hester, 2012). Though less likely to commit violent acts than males, when they do commit them, women are statistically more likely to murder their intimate partner or child (McKeown, 2014; Polk, 1993).

HONOR KILLINGS

Honor killing, otherwise known as a customary killing, is a specific form of honor-based violence defined as the murder of a family member, primarily a female, whose murder is undertaken by another family member or members as an act of restoring honor to the family (Byreshwar, 2014; Gill, 2009). At a broader level, the community believes the female has dishonored their family by engaging in acts that are deemed inappropriate or wrong (Baker et al., 1999; Byreshwar, 2014). Honor-related crimes are dynamic in nature and change depending on time, place, cultural norms, and practices (Byreshwar, 2014). Thus, honor killings can be identified as a cultural tradition (Byreshwar, 2014). Historically, and across a number of contemporary cultures, societies have condoned violence against women in the context that men have the "right" to discipline women who bring shame upon their family (United Nations Population Fund, 2000). When this "discipline" extends to homicide, the term "honor killing" is often used. It is poorly understood in the Western social sphere and is an underscrutinized practice that is considered, at the same time, an accepted cultural practice, a deviant behavioral phenomenon, and a horrendous criminal act (Grewal, 2013). The question that arises is: In the Western legal vernacular, are honor killings and DV homicides synonymous?

There are approximately 5000 reported cases of honor killings around the world each year (Kljun, 2014; United Nations Population Fund, 2000). However, the true prevalence of honor-related crimes is unknown as many honor-related deaths and violent attacks are concealed or perceived to be accidental or suicidal in nature

(Kulczycki & Windle, 2011). It is also important to note that the fundamental rationality for honor killings is because they are an integral part of some cultures, where the reputation, or "honor," of the patriarchal lineage is considered to be of greater importance than the welfare of women (Baker et al., 1999).

Honor killings are reported in numerous countries around the world, underscoring the heterogeneity of ethnicity, culture, class, and religious affiliations that are associated with this form of patriarchal-dominant behavior (Elakkary, Franke, Shokri, Hartwig, Tsokos, Puschel, 2013; Kljun, 2014; Tripathi & Yadav, 2004). Countries with the highest reported incidents of honor killing include India, Pakistan, Egypt, Jordan, Lebanon, Morocco, Pakistan, the Syrian Arab Republic, Turkey, Yemen, and other Mediterranean and Persian Gulf countries (Honour Based Violence Awareness Network, 2015). Additionally, Western countries such as France, Germany, and the United Kingdom that have large migrant communities also have reports of honor killings. Other Western nations have high rates of intimate partner homicide and fratricide that may be more akin to the classic notions of honor killings but are not formally recognized as such.

The concept of honor is used to rationalize killing and extreme violence on the notion that the family's or man's honor is primarily dependent on the behavior of the woman (Baker et al., 1999). The perceived loss of honor has been associated with both internal and external characteristics (Cohan, 2010). Internal loss of honor refers to individual loss where the individual may feel shame, guilt, or similar feelings after challenging or violating the cultural norms of behavior or after another has violated those norms in a manner that is perceived by the aggrieved to reflect poorly on their own identity (Cohan, 2010). Conversely, external loss of honor refers to community loss, in that the community will form an opinion on the individual who allegedly, or did, violate the norms, thus, believing the individual should be shamed (Cohan, 2010). In this way, the behavioral control of women is seen as a protective factor for the woman, their family, and their wider community (Baker et al., 1999). Moreover, if the patriarchal authority is perceived to be threatened by a woman's behavior, then the entire family, in this cultural context, will often experience feelings of shame, humiliation, and a loss of face (Cohan, 2010).

Subsequently, honor requires females to behave and conform to cultural norms of female etiquette, which typically revolve around notions of feminine humility, docility, and submission to male authority. These are often expressed in expectations of behavior such as "do not go out in public unaccompanied by a male relative," "do not talk to men outside of the family unit without permission and without a chaperone present," "do not talk back to your husband," "do not criticize laws or proffer an opinion on politics or other matters of male dominion," and "do not stray from feminine expectations" (Baker et al., 1999). These behaviors extend to factors such as sexual and interpersonal relational behaviors (premarital sex, female extramarital relations, eloping with a nonapproved man, romantic involvement with someone not approved by the family, unapproved nonsexual friendship with males outside of the family, suspected pregnancy outside marriage, being a victim of rape, flirting, seeking a divorce, and having various arbitrarily defined unsuitable individual mannerisms) (Byreshwar, 2014; Cohan, 2010; Eisner & Ghuneim, 2013; Elakkary et al., 2013; Kljun, 2014; Tripathi & Yadav, 2004). Once these acts and/or norms are broken or challenged the punishment, including honor killings, are justified on the premise that the male/s of the family are obligated to restore honor to the household, and that the female has brought the punishment on herself through her choice to behave "dishonorably" (Dogan, 2013; Elakkary et al., 2013). In this way, family honor and reputation are only restored once a punishment is carried out against the "offender" (Baker et al., 1999; Cohan, 2010; Eisner & Ghuneim, 2013).

As such, the role of the [women's] family is to reestablish, or restore, honor by engaging in the aforementioned acts (Kljun, 2014). The necessity to punish dishonor is rooted in cultural norms and societies, where family honor is a justification for murder because of the perception of the female as a vessel for family reputation (Kulczycki & Windle, 2011). Communities and/or families who fail to implement punishment for wrongful behavior can further increase the dishonor already perceived to have been brought upon the family (Baker et al., 1999). Thus, families or men who are able to maintain such control over their women benefit from respectable reputations within their community and are not subjected to the consequences surrounding loss of honor (Baker et al., 1999).

Traditionally, all punishments and honor killings relating to the restoration of family honor are associated with extreme acts of violence (Elakkary et al., 2013). Common methods undertaken to restore family honor include, but are not limited to, stoning, stabbing, beating, shooting, acid attacks, disfigurement of organs, rape, and ultimately acts culminating in the murder of the female "offender" (Cohan, 2010; Eisner & Ghuneim, 2013). However, it should be noted that "different violations of the honor code are associated with different punishments, thus enforcing that honor violence manifests in a multifaceted way" (Gill & Brah, 2014, p. 73). These acts receive considerable social support in their respective cultural contexts, thus enabling lenient treatment within that criminal justice system (Eisner & Ghuneim, 2013; Sen, 2005; Wikan, 2008). It is said that honor is an essential capital that makes the killing socially acceptable and somewhat of a necessity (Eisner & Ghuneim, 2013).

VICTIMS OF HONOR KILLINGS

In societies in which honor killings are commonly practiced, women are, to varying degrees, legally, culturally, and often religiously considered to be under the dominion of the patriarchal male of their household. This is not a "Third World" or religion-based position, but rather has heterogeneous roots from across the world. The most direct origin for this patriarchal norm has come from pre-Christian Greco-Roman society in which, according to Brotto et al. (2016, this volume):

> … a wife was subject to patria potestas in Romana. This was a legal state under
> which the patriarch of the family had absolute sovereignty (including the power

of life and death) over the other family members including, wife, children, and grandchildren. Female children were only subjected to this authority until they were married, at which time they became a part of the family into which they were married and therefore became subject to the patriarch of her new familial group. In Roman Society, women were considered intellectually and physically inferior and in need of protection, therefore the law was applied to women with the intention of proffering protection rather than dominion over wives. This provision became blurred over the last two millennia and women were ultimately folded into the general structure of patria potestas throughout the era of the Holy Roman Empire and the Western Social 'spin-off' social systems. Various legal and social systems have slowly changed some of tenets of patria potestas. For example, the permission to control life and death was revoked in many countries by the 18th or 19th century. However, other provisions remained such as 'The Rule of Thumb' in which a man could beat his wife and children provided the stick used was no bigger than the width of his thumb.

This position is characteristic of patriarchal societies and continues today in locations where the culture remains, whether by social or religious tenet, male dominated (Brotto et al., 2016; Elakkary et al., 2013; Hamad, 2015). The nature of patriarchy means that females are the primary victims of honor killings, and other honor-related violence. Given that rumor and innuendo are often enough to damage reputation, women are often subjected to honor violence, including homicide, on little more than suspicion. In many instances, particularly where the patriarchal notions of "honor" are intimately intertwined with theocratic rule of law, women are seldom provided a fair opportunity to defend any accusations made against them (Tripathi & Yadav, 2004).

Females are considered the honor of their family and, as such, play an important role in the maintenance of the whole family's honor (Gill & Brah, 2014). Women are expected to avoid shameful behavior, police the behavior of other women, and maintain their purity and chastity (Gill & Brah, 2014). Considerable emphasis is placed on a woman's behavior within these cultural contexts, as "a man's honor lies between the legs of a woman" (Cohan, 2010, p. 10). A female, in the given context, is denied of individual entity, and as such, their individual actions and behaviors significantly impacts collective family honor (Baker et al., 1999; Cohan, 2010; Dogan, 2013). Simply, this is because honor is believed to be of sacred importance, viewed as more important than the life of the family (Baker et al., 1999; Cohan, 2010; Dogan, 2013).

Consistent among literature is the notion that honor killings are specific acts of violence against female family members perceived to have brought shame or humiliation to their family by engaging in a dishonorable act (Eisner & Ghuneim, 2013). This means that the greatest risk factor for being a victim of honor-based violence is being a female. Male victims of honor crime are almost nonexistent; however, a Pakistani study did identify a small number of male victims (Devers & Bacon, 2010). Men who are believed to have engaged in relationships with females outside marriage have been acknowledged as victims of honor killings (Eisner & Ghuneim, 2013; Reddy, 2008). For example, if the male allegedly ruined a reputation by withdrawing a promise of marriage, or a relationship is assumed, or suspected, the male will be subjected to honor violence and/or killing (Reddy, 2008). However, male victims are occasionally able to escape sanctions caused by the violation of honor, which is not an option to female victims (Reddy, 2008). Men may be given the opportunity to negotiate pardons with family members, and additionally, acts men engage in are perceived differently within society (Mallicoat & Ireland, 2014). As such, males engaging in sexual taboos is treated on an individual basis and are only considered taboo inside the nuptial home, resulting in a lesser punishment (Devers & Bacon, 2010).

OFFENDERS IN HONOR KILLINGS

It is common for honor killings and honor-related violence to be committed by the "offender's" male relatives, who finds the violence a necessary means to preserve or restore the entire family's honor (Elakkary et al., 2013; Kljun, 2014; Reddy, 2008). Typically, the male is recognized as the head of the family and has the responsibility of defending and upholding the family or social group's honor and the honor of their own conduct (Elakkary et al., 2013; Gill & Brah, 2014). It is common for honor killings to involve multiple offenders (those who conduct the discipline or homicide), which is one main difference from typical DV situations. Punishment can be undertaken by fathers, grandfathers, uncles, brothers, and cousins, who were directly or indirectly involved in the dishonor and, thus, need to partake in restoring honor (Eisner & Ghuneim, 2013; Elakkary et al., 2013; Kulczycki & Windle, 2011; Tripathi & Yadav, 2004). Moreover, it is demonstrated that men of a lower socioeconomic status may be more inclined to engage in acts of honor killings and/or violence, because "all they have is their honor" (Kulczycki & Windle, 2011). In many cultures, women of low socioeconomic standing are financial assets to the family. When married, the family may receive a payment for the female from the family of her male spouse. If a woman is deemed to be "tainted" in some way and her family of less standing, then she is worth less in any marriage transaction and will potentially remain at home with no prospect of marriage or of bearing legitimate children for the "honor" of her family. Thereby, the female becomes a financial burden on her family rather than an asset to secure financial benefit or social connection through marriage. In this instance, honor killings serve to protect the honor of the family and the economic value of any remaining females.

Additionally, literature has identified instances wherein females have participated in honor killings and violence. It has been recognized that mothers, aunts, sisters, and mothers-in-law have been directly or indirectly involved in the perpetration of honor killings (Eisner & Ghuneim, 2013; Elakkary et al., 2013; Kulczycki & Windle, 2011; Tripathi & Yadav, 2004). This is another major difference between DV and honor killings. However, unlike male offenders, women more often than not participate indirectly as instigators of gossip or pressure the male family members to restore or preserve the honor of the family (Kulczycki & Windle, 2011). As mentioned, offenders tend to be from the family of the involved female; however, in cases of affairs, perpetrators are recognized to include the male's family (Kulczycki & Windle, 2011).

Perpetrators of honor killings consistently go unpunished or receive lighter sentences for their crimes (Kulczycki & Windle, 2011). Perpetrators are very rarely sentenced to full convictions by courts in their culture (SURGIR, 2012). Explanations for this include blameworthy indulgence, inadequate laws, the complicity of judges and public authorities, and the lack of witnesses (SURGIR, 2012). One example of how the criminal justice system prosecutes crimes of honor is the Jordanian Penal Code (1960), which states that "he who catches his wife or one of his female close relatives committing adultery with another, and he kills, wounds or injures one of both of them, is exempt from any penalty" (Eisner & Ghuneim, 2013, p. 2). Thus, customary tradition remains, and the crime goes unpunished.

CHARACTERISTICS OF HONOR KILLING AND DV

As noted previously, there is a legitimate question as to whether DV and honor-based violence are synonymous.

Honor Killings

Factors identified specifically in honor killings were extreme acts of violence; identified by stoning, stabbing, beating, shooting, acid attacks, disfigurement of organs, rape, and murder. Moreover, there are often multiple offenders, and the victims of crimes are often female family members. Additionally, attacks were found to be planned, and used as a means of control for the female's behavior. The behavior of the offender is justified as normative to the given culture, because they were the "victim" of shame and dishonor. As such, the perpetrators were not found to exhibit remorse. The common perpetrator of honor killings was identified as male and the common victim a female, although there are some instances of female perpetrators and male victims.

Domestic Violence

A factor identified specifically in DV was its acknowledgment as a criminal act, punishable by the criminal justice system. Additionally, DV was found to be an unplanned and spontaneous crime that involves one offender. The common victim in DV cases was recognized to be an intimate partner/spouse or child, where sometimes the perpetrator exhibits remorse for their criminal acts. Ultimately, the acts of violence are extreme and include beating, stabbing, shooting, sexualized violence, and violence aimed to humiliate and/or control the victim. The common perpetrator of DV was identified as male and the common victim a female, although there are some instances of female perpetrators and male victims (Table 12.1).

Table 12.1 A Comparison of the Characteristics of DV and Honor Killing

Honor Killings	Domestic Violence
Committed mainly by male relatives against female family members	Committed by an adult male against female spouse or intimate partner
Carefully planned	Unplanned and spontaneous
Used as a threat for control of women	Used for a sense of power and control in perpetrator's life
Can involve multiple family members: mother, father, sister, brother, extended family	Does not involve multiple offenders
Involvement of the community	Community detests DV
Motive because individual brought dishonor to family	Motivations range from a poorly cooked meal to suspected infidelity
Tactics are very gruesome [rape, beating, burning, stoning, decapitation]	Tactics include shooting, stabbing, beating, sexual assault, aggressive humiliation, and control
Normative behavior for culture	Criminal act
No remorse by offender, they are seen as victims because of the shame	Remorse of regret is sometimes exhibited
Men against women	Men against women primarily
Physical violence	Not always physical violence
No literature suggestive of any disorders, or conditions specific to risk factors	Personality and/or mood disorders, mental illness, low self-esteem sometimes evident

DISCUSSION

When comparing and contrasting DV and honor killings, the majority of research argues that honor killings are merely an extension of DV and should not be treated differently simply due to some notion of "cultural tradition" (Meetoo & Mirza, 2007). However, by examining the characteristics of both crimes, it is evident that both cases are complex and multifaceted, and this impacts on the ability to simply classify honor killings as an extension of DV.

SIMILARITIES IN THE CHARACTERIZATION OF DV AND HONOR KILLINGS

Three main similarities were recognized between DV and honor-related violence:

1. Males as the primary perpetrator
2. Females as the primary victim
3. The use of physical violence

In cultures where individual (male) and family honor is held in high esteem, a man's position is upheld by a combination of personal moral integrity (whatever this means within the unique cultural/subcultural context in which they live), as well as the reputation attributed to him by his relatives' proxy (Caffaro, Ferraris, & Schmidt, 2014). Thus, as the male is the leader or head of the family, he is responsible for the preservation and, when necessary, restoration, of the honor of himself as well as the whole family (Caffaro et al., 2014; Elakkary et al., 2013). As such, the head of the family, and other males (extended family) shamed by a family member's misbehavior, are obliged to engage in direct acts of intercession to remediate the situation (Eisner & Ghuneim, 2013; Elakkary et al., 2013; Kulczycki & Windle, 2011; Tripathi & Yadav, 2004).

Similarly, it is most commonly dominant males who are the perpetrators of DV (Flood & Fergus, 2008; McKeown, 2014; Morgan & Chadwick, 2009). These males are characteristically suffering from low self-esteem, poorly developed social skills, a variety of personality and emotional disorders, and a lack of self-control. All of these contribute to a significant increase in the risk of impulsive violent behaviors (Rode, 2010; Sinnamon, 2015). Additionally, when females were recognized as perpetrators, in both cases, a more indirect approach was identified. Research suggests female perpetrators of DV engaged in less physical methods of violence and tended to engage in psychological tactics (Drijber et al., 2012). Similarly, female's involvement in honor killings tended to be indirect, in that they engaged in encouraging and manipulating the instigation of the punishment of other females' alleged misbehavior (Kulczycki & Windle, 2011).

Physical (often extreme) violence is a shared characteristic of DV and honor-related violence. As has been identified in the extant literature, the restoration of honor is commonly associated with extreme acts of violence (Ekkary et al., 2014), and while DV is flexible and encompasses many forms of abuse, physical violence is considered the most common (Mitchell, 2011). However, while perpetrators of both DV and honor-related violence engage in physical aggression, the nature of the violence digresses. While both forms of violence are deemed malicious, they are considered to occur along different parts of the spectrum. DV appears to occur along an impulsive harm line whereby weapons and other means used against the victim are often opportunistic, and selected based on objects or methods "to hand." These include beating with hands or readily accessible objects, stabbing, shooting, dangerous driving, destruction of property, abuse of children and/or pets, forced sleep deprivation, or other improvised acts of humiliation and submission (Mitchell, 2011; Mouzos & Makkai, 2004). Comparatively, physical acts of honor violence are considered to be more premeditated and designed to make a public statement, as well as provide vengeful "satisfaction" to the perpetrators who identify themselves as the aggrieved party. These include behaviors such as physical beating with specifically selected objects, stoning, stabbing (often ritualistic), shooting, disfiguration with acid, organ and/or appendage disfiguration/amputation, and "punitive" or "restitutional" rape. All of these are also used as a means of deliberately killing the accused in a manner that makes a clear statement to other family members and the community (Cohan, 2010; Eisner & Ghuneim, 2013). Ultimately, while all acts inflict serious harm on the victim and these acts should never be ascribed any form of hierarchical value, it is evident that the more "creative" methods used in honor violence are comparatively rarer (though not absent) in DV. Indeed, honor violence and honor killings characteristically involve the use of deliberate and premeditated torture more frequently than does DV.

DIFFERENCES IN CHARACTERISTICS OF DV AND HONOR KILLINGS

Four primary characteristics have been identified as the common differences between DV and honor-related violence (Sen, 2003; Welchman & Hossain, 2005). These are:

1. Honor-based violence occurs within a collective family structure, community, and society, while DV occurs within a nuclear family framework.
2. Honor-based violence involves premediated and carefully planned acts aimed at restoring honor and shaming the victim, due to a cultural tradition, while acts of DV often occur spontaneously and without planning and are not considered culturally normative.
3. Honor-based violence is centered on the patriarchal right to control women—sexually and socially, with women being considered as either property or under the dominion of male authority, while DV is centered on the perpetrators' individual feelings and/or struggles specific to their own life.
4. Methods of honor-based violence are considered more extreme than those of DV.

When comparing DV and honor-related violence and/or killing, one consistent difference is the underlying fact that honor-related violence is a condoned and collective family matter, while DV is seldom condoned by the wider family (although it is often known to other family members) and is generally an act between members within a nuclear familial component. Honor-based violence and/or killings tend to involve multiple family members and, either directly or indirectly, the community as a whole, in the carrying out of punitive and restitutional sentences against someone accused of dishonorable conduct (Chesler, 2009; Eisner & Ghuneim, 2013; Elakkary et al., 2013; Kulczycki & Windle, 2011; Tripathi & Yadav, 2004). This includes the participation by extended family such as cousins, uncles, and grandparents. Comparatively, DV is understood as an individual crime, committed by violent men, particularly intimate or ex-intimate partners and/or spouses (Akpinar, 2003; Hamad, 2015). In typical DV, it is uncommon for brothers to kill sisters and males to kill their female cousins (Chesler, 2009). Rather, DV most commonly involves a male inflicting violence on an intimate partner, or children, in order to assert control and restore or protect self-esteem (Baker et al., 1999).

DV also differs from honor-related violence in the character of the premeditation of the behavior. DV has been identified as generally spontaneous in nature. The specific act is usually unplanned and reactive. In comparison, acts of honor-related violence is often premeditated and carefully planned (Hanlon, Brook, Demrey & Cunningham, 2016; Rode, 2010). Honor is commonly associated with moral integrity and self-esteem related to virtue or talent (Sev'er & Yurdakul, 2001). However, this common understanding is culturally dependent and as such is subject to definitional diversity across cultural contexts (Abu-Lughod, 1986; Sev'er & Yurdakul, 2001). In cultures where honor-related violence against women is, to some extent, condoned, honor is generally perceived as an integral part of a males' identity and as a foundational component of the social status of the family unit. In this way, honor is a seen as being a high-value tangible currency (Sev'er & Yurdakul, 2001). Therefore, in this cultural context, honor, or the perceived lack of it, has a direct and observable impact on the social wealth of an individual, their family, and others associated with them.

Honor, by definition, acts as the primary, if not exclusive, motivation for honor-related violence (Elakkary et al., 2013; Kljun, 2014; Reddy, 2008). This is not typically the case in DV, which is instead usually provoked by a variety of internal personality and psychological characteristics that drive the perpetrator to seek to use violence as a means to exert control and restore self-esteem (Brotto et al., 2016; Kljun, 2014; Rode, 2010). This marks a fundamental difference between the two forms of violence. The motivation for honor-based violence is the restoration of a definition of honor that has its roots firmly entrenched in the collective social, legal, and religious norms, traditions, practices, and beliefs of the cultural context in which it occurs. In contrast, the motivation for DV is the internally-derived need for control due to poor or fragile self-esteem, and maladaptive coping. Perpetrators of DV are more likely than not to suffer from personality and/or mood disorders or other mental illness (Brotto et al., 2016; Hanlon et al., 2016; Murrell et al., 2007). Again, this differs from honor-based violence, where violence is used to punish (usually female) family members who digress from the accepted (and expected) behavioral norms, and to restore personal and familial "face" in the wake of this digression (Kljun, 2014).

In their typical cultural contexts, acts of DV are generally detested among large parts of the community, with few voices providing justification or excuses for perpetrators (Chesler, 2009). Moreover, victims of DV are commonly assisted with support, medical assistance, counseling, and advocacy. These supports and services can help to empower victims to leave their abusers and find a safe environment (Geffner & Rosenbaum, 2001). This differs from victims of honor-based violence, where often the whole, or a large proportion, of their community condones and may be involved in the metering out of "punishment." Therefore, victims of honor-related violence are seldom afforded the same rights and assistance as their DV counterparts, as their cultural context dictates that the right of restoring honor outweighs the basic human right of the individual.

The types of behavior that associated with DV and honor -related violence are also different. DV is a multifaceted crime that encompasses several types of abusive behaviors and not just physical violence. These can include sexual, psychological, verbal, emotional, social, spiritual, and economic abuse (Mitchell, 2011). Each type of abuse is associated with threatening, intimidating, controlling, and fearful behavior from the perpetrator to the victim as a means of asserting control (Australian Government Department of Human Services, 2016). In comparison, honor-based violence and killings are solely associated with physical acts of violence against the victim, as it is the physical harm caused to the individual that constitutes the oath to restoring honor and/or exacting restitution (Cohan, 2010; Baker et al., 1999; Eisner & Ghuneim, 2013). As such, those who engage in committing honor violence rarely feel guilt or remorse because they are considered the victim of shame and dishonor and are therefore justified and deserving (Chesler, 2009). By comparison in DV, perpetrators may commonly exhibit remorse and guilt for their actions, as their violence is recognized to be more sporadic, unplanned, and spontaneous (Hanlon et al., 2016).

A final and socially important difference between these two forms of violence is that in the respective cultural contexts in which DV and honor-related violence commonly occur, DV is generally a criminal act and this position has popular support, and perpetrators are increasingly treated as serious criminals (Brotto et al., 2016; Elakkary et al., 2013; Kljun, 2014; Reddy, 2008). However, honor-related violence and killings are often considered a social, legal, and/or religious right for an aggrieved male or family. This often means that, even where the practice has begun to lose legal protection, perpetrators receive significant leniency, clemency, and, in a number of jurisdictions, protection from prosecution. Indeed, some contexts continue to treat perpetrators of honor-related violence as moral crusaders (Caenegem, 1999; Sev'er & Yurdakul, 2001).

CONCLUSION

This chapter has explored the nature of DV and honor-related violence and highlighted the areas in which they share characteristics and areas in which they are divergent. Ultimately, while both forms of violence share several characteristics, they are clearly motivated by different intentions and underlying phenomena. As such, they should be viewed as separate constructs, albeit with some covariate dimensions. Honor killings are essentially the product of a social context in which personal, social, familial, religious beliefs, traditions, and behavioral norms dictate that women are subservient to men, and that patriarchal honor is a tangible currency that trumps other individual human rights. By contrast, DV is a product of maladaptive coping mechanisms of internally mediated personality and psychological characteristics that drive an individual's need to exert overt control over one's immediate intimate environment, in order to maintain control and to protect and/or restore self-esteem.

SUMMARY

- Statistics from around the world, highlight the substantial link between the risk of interpersonal violence and intimate relationships.
- Many behaviors against women that are criminal in the majority of "Westernized" societies, are often considered acceptable in other cultures (e.g., honor killings). These acts of violence have captured the attention of the public and become an increasingly popular social and political issue.

- Many of the stereotypical domestic gender roles are universally identi-fied across numerous cultures and historical epochs. Often, the roles of the breadwinner and homemaker, and controller and controlled, stem from underlying prejudicial beliefs relating to women's inferiority, and a common position akin to the Ancient Roman Statute of Patria Potestas Romana (The Power of the Father), in which children and wives were legally and morally identified as the property of the Patriarch and subject to his rule, includ-ing decisions regarding life and death. Arguably, whether stemming from a cultural or religious genesis, violence against women within any given culture or context, has significant foundation in these historical patriarchal positions.
- Definitions of DV are socially constructed, and reflect the underlying under-standings, perceptions, and interests of the culture in question. While there are many definitions for DV, consistent across most is the notion that DV is multi-faceted, that it does not necessarily involve actual physical violence, and that it involves excessive control.
- DV can be defined as: "an abuse of power within an intimate relationship… when one partner attempts to physically or psychologically dominate, control, or harm the other partner. Common forms include physical and sexual violence, threats, intimidation, and any acts associated with deprivation, or neglect." Another way of defining DV is: "The patterned and repeated use of coer-cive and controlling behavior to limit, direct, and shape a partner's thoughts, feelings, and actions. Power and control tactics are often utilized to establish dominance."
- Three of the primary rationales or motivations for DV offenders have been iden-tified as sexual jealously, cause (fail to meet expectations), and will (expression of power).
- The stereotypical DV situation involves direct acts of physical violence within an intimate partner relationship toward the offender's intimate partner or chil-dren in their care.
- "a central element of DV is that of an ongoing pattern of behavior aimed to control, dominate, and exercise power over the other, in both criminal and non-criminal manners."
- DV has been recognized as flexible, and is comprised of many additional facets not directly involving physical violence, and may therefore involve other acts such as coercion, threat, intimidation, financial control, and social isolation. In this way physical abuse, sexual abuse, psychological abuse, verbal abuse, emotional abuse, social abuse, spiritual abuse, and economic abuse have all been established as acts of DV.
- Violence against women is considered to be a significant social problem across the globe, and while DV is not a gender-specific problem, it does impact females at considerably higher rates than males, and can therefore be identified as a female-biased form of violence and an abuse of power, within an intimate relationship.

- There are several factors that have been identified as being associated with an increased risk of DV. These vulnerabilities include being younger, indigenous, a woman living in a remote location, physical and mental disability, immigration from a culturally divergent country-of-origin, low education, and being unemployed. However, it is important to note that, while these factors increase a woman's vulnerability, DV is found in almost all cultural and sub-cultural social demographics.
- Research into DV perpetrators indicates that violence is employed as a maladaptive coping mechanism, and perpetrators exhibit a variety of associated maladaptive behaviors and personality characteristics, including low self-esteem, fear of abandonment, low assertiveness and high aggression, poor social skills, poor self-control, and poor emotional skills.
- There are several factors in males that result in an increased risk of becoming a DV offender. These include, being a victim of childhood trauma and abuse, alcohol and drug abuse, financial stress, personal psychological stress, and lack of social support. Alcohol abuse is the strongest predictor for DV.
- When examining the factors associated with an intimate-partner homicide, such as alcohol, other substances, environmental considerations, and background of both the victim and perpetrator, it is important to examine the interrelationships between all factors involved and the extent to which the various elements play a direct and/or indirect role in the spatial, temporal, and personal circumstances leading up to and surrounding the event.
- While females also commit acts of DV, the true extent to which women engage in acts of violence against their intimate partners is unknown. This is largely due to the previously mentioned factors around masculinity and stigma that serve to impede male victims' reporting of domestic victimization.
- Honor killing, otherwise known as a customary killing, is a specific form of honor-based violence defined as the murder of a family member, primarily a female, whose murder is undertaken by another family member or members as an act of restoring honor to the family. Honor related crimes are dynamic in nature, and change depending on time, place, cultural norms, and practices. Thus, honor killings can be identified as a cultural tradition. Honor killings are reported in numerous countries around the world, underscoring the heterogeneity of ethnicity, culture, class, and religious affiliations that are associated with this form of patriarchal-dominant behavior.
- Internal loss of honor refers to individual loss where the individual may feel shame, guilt, or similar feelings after challenging or violating the cultural norms of behavior, or after another has violated those norms in a manner that is perceived by the aggrieved to reflect poorly on their own identity. External loss of honor refers to community loss, in that the community will form an opinion on the individual who allegedly, or did, violate the norms, thus, believing the individual should be shamed.
- Traditionally, all punishments and honor killings relating to the restoration of family honor are associated with extreme acts of violence. Common methods

undertaken to restore family honor include, but are not limited to, stoning, stabbing, beating, shooting, acid attacks, disfigurement of organs, rape, and ultimately acts culminating in the murder of the female "offender".

- The nature of patriarchy means that females are the primary victims of honor killings, and other honour-related violence. Given that rumor and innuendo are often enough to damage reputation, women are often subjected to honor violence, including homicide, on little more than suspicion. In many instances, particularly where the patriarchal notions of "honor" are intimately intertwined with theocratic rule of law, women are seldom provided a fair opportunity to defend any accusations made against them.

- Perpetrators of honor killings consistently go unpunished or receive lighter sentences for their crimes. Explanations for this include blameworthy indulgence, inadequate laws, the complicity of judges and public authorities, and the lack of witnesses. One example of how the criminal justice system prosecutes crimes of honor is the Jordanian Penal Code (1960) which states that "he who catches his wife or one of his female close relatives committing adultery with another, and he kills, wounds or injures one of both of them, is exempt from any penalty."

- Three main similarities were recognized between DV and honor related violence: a) Males as the primary perpetrator; b) Females as the primary victim, and c) The use of physical violence.

- Four primary characteristics have been identified as the common differences between DV and honor-related violence: a) Honor-based violence occurs within a collective family structure, community and society, while DV occurs within a nuclear family framework; b) Honor-based violence involves pre-mediated and carefully planned acts aimed at restoring honor and shaming the victim, due to a cultural tradition, while acts of DV often occur spontaneously and without planning, and are not considered culturally normative; c) Honor-based violence is centered on patriarchal right to control women: sexually and socially, with women being considered as either property or under the dominion of male authority, while DV is centered on the perpetrators individual feelings and/or struggles specific to their own life; d) Methods of honor-based violence are considered more extreme than DV.

- Ultimately while both forms of violence share several characteristics, they are clearly motivated by different intentions and underlying phenomena. As such, they should be viewed as separate constructs, albeit with some covariate dimensions.

QUESTIONS

1. Define domestic violence
2. Define intimate-partner violence and intimate-partner homicide
3. Define honor-related violence and honor killing

4. What are the main similarities between domestic violence and honor-related violence? Describe these similarities.
5. What are the primary differences between domestic violence and honor-related violence? Describe these differences.
6. Describe Patria Potestas Romana and how this historical legal statute could have contributed to both the condoning of honor-related violence/killings.
7. Describe the types of behavior that can be associated with domestic violence.
8. Describe the typical victims and perpetrators of domestic violence.
9. Describe the types of acts that are commonly associated with honor-related violence/killings.
10. Describe the typical victims and perpetrators of honor-related violence/killings.

REFERENCES

Abu-Lughod, L. (1986). *Veiled sentiments: Honour and poetry in a Bedouin society*. Berkeley, CA: University of California Press.

Akpinar, A. (2003). The honour/shame complex revisited: violence against women in the migration context. *Women's Studies International Forum*, 26(5), 425–442. http://dx.doi.org/10.1016/j.wsif.2003.08.001.

Almeida, R. V., & Durkin, T. (1999). The cultural context model: therapy for couples with domestic violence. *Journal of Marital and Family Therapy*, 25(3), 313–324. http://dx.doi.org/10.1111/j.1752-0606.1999.tb00250.x.

Australian Bureau of Statistics. (2005). *Personal safety survey*. Retrieved from http://www.ausstats.abs.gov.au/ausstats/subscriber.nsf/0/056A404DAA576AE6CA2571D00080E985/$File/49060_2005%20(reissue).pdf.

Australian Government Department of Human Services. (2016). *Family and domestic violence strategy 2016–2019*.

Australian Institute of Criminology. (2015). *Australian crime: Facts and figures*. Retrieved from http://aic.gov.au/publications/current%20series/facts/1-20/2013.html.

Baker, N. V., Gregware, P. R., & Cassidy, M. A. (1999). Family killing fields: honour rationales in the murder of women. *Violence Against Women*, 5(2), 164–184. http://dx.doi.org/10.1177/107780129952005.

Brotto, G. L. M., Sinnamon, G. C. B., & Petherick, W. (2016). Victimology and predicting victims of personal violence. Of crime. In W. Petherick, & G. C. B. Sinnamon (Eds.), *The psychology of antisocial and criminal behaviour*. Boston, MA: Anderson Publishing.

Byreshwar, P. (2014). "Honour killing" the menace. *Indian Journal of Applied Research*, 4(1), 259–261. Retrieved from http://www.worldwidejournals.com/ijar/file.php?val=January_2014_1388584173_ee78c_75.pdf.

Caenegem, W. V. (1999). Advantages and disadvantages of the adversarial systems in criminal proceedings. *Law Faculty Publications*, 1(1), 69–102. Retrieved from http://epublications.bond.edu.au/law_pubs/224.

Caffaro, F., Ferraris, F., & Schmidt, S. (2014). Gender differences in the perception of honour killing in individualist versus collectivistic cultures: comparison between Italy and Turkey. *Sex Roles*, 71(9–10), 296–318. http://dx.doi.org/10.1007/s11199-014-0413-5.

Chesler, P. (2009). Are honour killings simply domestic violence? *The Middle East Quarterly*, 16(2), 61–69. Retrieved from http://www.meforum.org/2067/are-honour-killings-simply-domestic-violence.

Cohan, J. A. (2010). Honour killings and the cultural defense. *California Western International Law Journal, 40*(2), 177–252. Retrieved from http://scholarlycommons.law.cwsl.edu/cgi/viewcontent.cgi?article=1086&context=cwilj.

Council of Australian Governments (2011). The National Plan to Reduce Violence Against Women and Children. Available from a central element of DV is that of an ongoing pattern of behavior aimed to control, dominate, and exercise power over the other, in both criminal and noncriminal manners.

Dearden, J., & Payne, J. (2009). *Alcohol and homicide in Australia: Trends & issues in crime and criminal justice (372)*. Retrieved from Australian Institute of Criminology website: http://www.aic.gov.au/publications/current series/tandi/361–380/tandi372.aspx.

Department of Social Services. (2013). *Literature review on domestic violence perpetrators*. Retrieved from https://www.dss.gov.au/sites/default/files/documents/09_2013/literature_review_on_domestic_violence_perpetrators.pdf.

Devers, L. N., & Bacon, S. (2010). Interpreting honour crimes: the institutional disregard towards female victims of family violence in the Middle East. *International Journal of Criminology and Sociological Theory, 3*(1), 359–371. Retrieved from http://ijcst.journals.yorku.ca/index.php/ijcst/article/viewFile/25925/24007.

Dogan, R. (2013). Did the coroners and justice act 2009 get it right? Are all honour killings revenge killings? *Punishment & Society, 15*(5), 488–514. http://dx.doi.org/10.1177/1462474513504797.

Domestic Violence Prevention Centre. (2016). *Forms of abuse*. Retrieved from http://www.domesticviolence.com.au/pages/forms-of-abuse.php.

Downs, W. R., Rindels, B., & Atkinson, C. (2007). Women's use of physical and nonphysical self-defense strategies during incidents of partner violence. *Violence Against Women, 13*(1), 28–45. http://dx.doi.org/10.1177/1077801206294807.

Drijber, B. C., Reijnders, U. J., & Ceelen, M. (2012). Male victims of domestic violence. *Journal of Family Violence, 28*(2), 173–178. http://dx.doi.org/10.1007/s10896-012-9482-9.

Eisner, M., & Ghuneim, L. (2013). Honour killing attitudes among adolescents in Amman, Jordan. *Aggressive Behavior, 39*(5), 405–417. http://dx.doi.org/10.1002/ab.21485.

Elakkary, S., Franke, B., Shokri, D., Hartwig, S., Tsokos, M., & Püschel, K. (2013). Honour crimes: review and proposed definition. *Forensic Science, Medicine, and Pathology, 10*(1), 76–82. http://dx.doi.org/10.1007/s12024-013-9455-1.

Evans, K. (2012). *Media representations of male and female "co-offending": How female offenders are portrayed in comparison to their male counterparts* (Master's thesis, University of Chester, Chester, England). Retrieved from http://www.internetjournalofcriminology.com/Evans_Media_Representations_of_Male_and_Female_Co-Offending_IJC_Dec_2012.pdf.

Flood, M., & Fergus, L. (2008). *An assault on our future: The impact of violence on young people and their relationships*. Retrieved from White Ribbon Foundation website: http://www.whiteribbon.org.au/uploads/media/Research_series/An_assault_on_our_future_FULL_Flood__Fergus_2010.pdf.

Geffner, R. A., & Rosenbaum, A. (2001). Domestic violence offenders: treatment and intervention standards. In *Domestic violence offenders: Current interventions, research, and implications for policies and standards* (pp. 1–9). Binghamton, NY: The Haworth Press.

Gill, A. (2009). Honour killings and the quest for justice in black and minority ethnic communities in the United Kingdom. *Criminal Justice Policy Review, 20*(4), 475–494. http://dx.doi.org/10.1177/0887403408329604.

Gill, A. K., & Brah, A. (2014). Interrogating cultural narratives about "honour"- based violence. *European Journal of Women's Studies*, *21*(1), 72–86. http://dx.doi.org/10.1177/1350506813510424.

Grewal, L. (2013). Outsourcing patriarchy. *International Feminist Journal of Politics*, *14*(1), 1–19. http://dx.doi.org/10.1080/14616742.2012.755352.

Hamad, R. (June 9, 2015). *Is there any difference between domestic violence and honour killings?*. Retrieved from http://www.dailylife.com.au/news-and-views/dl-opinion/is-there-any-difference-between-domestic-violence-and-honour-killings-20150608-ghixcv.html.

Hanlon, R E., Brook, M., Demery, J A., & Cunningham, M. D. (2016). Domestic homicide: neuropsychological profiles of murderers who kill family members and intimate partners. *Journal of Forensic Science*, *61*(1), S163–S170. http://dx.doi.org/10.1111/1556-4029.12908.

Healey, J. (Ed.). (2014). *Domestic and family violence*. Sydney: The Spinney Press.

Hester, M. (2012). Portrayal of women as intimate partner domestic violence perpetrators. *Violence Against Women*, *18*(9), 1067–1082. http://dx.doi.org/10.1177/1077801212461428.

Honour Based Violence Awareness Network. (2015). *Today*. Retrieved from http://hbv-awareness.com/today/.

Kljun, S. (2014). In the name of honour. *Bulletin (Law Society of South Australia)*, *36*(7), 18–19. Retrieved from http://search.informit.com.au/fullText;dn=574408421582397;res=IELAPA.

Kulczycki, A., & Windle, S. (2011). Honour killings in the Middle East and North Africa: a systematic review of the literature. *Violence Against Women*, *17*(11), 1442–1464. http://dx.doi.org/10.1177/1077801211434127.

Levinson, D. (1988). *Family violence in cross-cultural perspective*. *Handbook of family violence*, 435–455. http://dx.doi.org/10.1007/978-1-4757-5360-8_18.

Lombard, N., & McMillan, L. (2012). Taking stock: theory and practice in violence against women. In *Violence against women: Current theory and practice in domestic abuse, sexual violence and exploitation* (pp. 233–242). London, United Kingdom: Jessica Kingsley Publishers.

Mallicoat, S. L., & Ireland, C. (2014). International issues in the victimization of women. In *Women and crime: The essentials* (pp. 137–142). California, CA: Sage Publications.

McKeown, A. (2014). Female offenders who commit domestic violence: aggression characteristics and potential treatment pathways. *The Journal of Forensic Practice*, *16*(2), 127–138. http://dx.doi.org/10.1108/jfp-01-2013-0007.

Meetoo, V., & Mirza, H. S. (2007). There is nothing "honourable" about honour killings: gender, violence and the limits of multiculturalism. *Women's Studies International Forum*, *30*, 187–200. http://dx.doi.org/10.1016/j.wsif.2007.03.001.

Mitchell, L. (2011). *Domestic violence in Australia—an overview of the issues*. Retrieved from Department of Parliamentary Services website: http://parlinfo.aph.gov.au/parlInfo/download/library/prspub/1246402/upload_binary/1246402.pdf;fileType=application/pdf#search=%22background%20note%20(parliamentary%20library,%20australia)%22.

Morgan, A., & Chadwick, H. (2009). *Key issues in domestic violence* (7). Retrieved from Australian Institute of Criminology website: http://www.aic.gov.au/media_library/publications/rip/rip07/rip07.pdf.

Mouzos, J., & Makkai, T. (2004). *Women's experiences of male violence: Findings from the Australian component of the international violence against women survey (IVAWS)*

(56). Retrieved from Australian Institute of Criminology website: http://www.aic.gov.au/media_library/publications/rpp/56/rpp056.pdf.

Muehlenhard, C. L., & Kimes, L. A. (1999). The social construction of violence: the case of sexual and domestic violence. *Personality and Social Psychology Review*, *3*(3), 234–245. http://dx.doi.org/10.1207/s15327957pspr0303_6.

Murrell, A. R., Christoff, K. A., & Henning, K. R. (2007). Characteristics of domestic violence offenders: associations with childhood exposure to violence. *Journal of Family Violence*, *22*(7), 523–532. http://dx.doi.org/10.1007/s10896-007-9100-4.

New York State Office for Prevention of Domestic Violence. (2014). *Domestic violence: Finding safety and support*. Retrieved from http://www.opdv.ny.gov/help/fss/fss.pdf.

Polk, K. (1993). *Homicide: Women as offenders* (Retrieved from Australian Institute of Criminology website).

Reddy, R. (2008). Gender, culture and the law: approaches to "honour crimes" in the UK. *Feminist Legal Studies*, *16*(3), 305–321. http://dx.doi.org/10.1007/s10691-008-9098-x.

Rode, D. (2010). Typology of perpetrators of domestic violence. *Polish Psychological Bulletin*, *41*(1). http://dx.doi.org/10.2478/s10059-010-0005-3.

Sen, P. (2003). Successes and challenges: understanding the global movement to end violence against women. In M. Kaldor, H. K. Anheier, & M. Glasius (Eds.), *Global civil society* (pp. 119–150). London: Oxford University Press.

Sen, P. (2005). Crimes of honour: value and meaning. In L. Welchman, & S. Hossain (Eds.), *"Honour": Crimes, paradigms, and violence against women* (pp. 42–63). London, United Kingdom: Zed Books.

Sev'er, A., & Yurdakul, G. (2001). Culture of honour, culture of change: a feminist analysis of honour killings in rural Turkey. *Violence Against Women*, *7*(9), 964–998. http://dx.doi.org/10.1177/10778010122182866.

Siddiqui, H. (2005). "There is no "honour" in domestic violence, only shame!" Women's struggles against "honour" crimes in the UK. In L. Welchman, & S. Hossain (Eds.), *"Honour": Crimes, paradigms, and violence against women* (pp. 263–281). London, United Kingdom: Zed Books.

Sinnamon, G. (2015). Psychopathology and criminal behaviour. In W. Petherick (Ed.), *Applied crime analysis: A social science approach to understanding crime, criminals, and victims*. Boston: Anderson Publishing.

Straus, M. (1980). Victims and aggressors in marital violence. *American Behavioral Scientist*, *23*(5), 681–704. http://dx.doi.org/10.1177/000276428002300505.

SURGIR. (2012). *Combating honour crimes in Europe*. Retrieved from http://www.surgir.ch/userfiles/file/surgir-brochure-honour-crimes-en.pdf.

Tripathi, A., & Yadav, S. (2004). For the sake of honour: but whose honour? "Honour Crimes" against women. *Asia-Pacific Journal on Human Rights and the Law*, *5*(2), 63–78. http://dx.doi.org/10.1163/157181504774852050.

United Nations Population Fund. (2000). Lives together, worlds apart: men and women in a time of change. *The State of World Population*. 25–30, Retrieved from http://www.unfpa.org/sites/default/files/pub-pdf/swp2000_eng.pdf.

Welchman, L., & Hossain, S. (2005). In *"Honour": Crimes, paradigms, and violence against women*. London: Zed Press.

White Ribbon. (2016). *Family and domestic violence*. Retrieved from http://www.whiteribbon.org.au/uploads/media/updated_factsheets_Nov_13/Factshee_6_Family_and_domestic_violence.pdf.

Wikan, U. (2008). *In honour of fadime: Murder and shame*. Chicago, IL: University of Chicago.

Homicide in Australia

13

Amber McKinley

Charles Sturt University, Canberra, ACT, Australia

CHAPTER OUTLINE

INTRODUCTION

The stereotypical homicidal maniac in popular myth and theory is portrayed a madman who preys on innocent and unsuspecting victims down dark alleys. The truth is far more mundane; men are overwhelmingly the offenders and victims in Australian homicides, and more often than not, they are known to each other. Their madness, if it exists at all, is of a kind all too familiar in human relationships. The image of the killer and their victim has been constructed over time out of infrequent yet sensational cases and should, in fact, be replaced with a more realistic picture.

Homicide is a relatively rare event in Australia, with current data showing 264 victims in 2012 (Bryant & Cussen, 2015). Homicide is not usually a crime committed by a deviant individual operating in a social vacuum, in most cases, detailed throughout this chapter, it is the outcome of a violent interpersonal relationship. As a result, murder enjoys the highest public profile of any crime. The public, it seems, has an almost insatiable appetite for, and macabre fascination with, the details of individual murder cases, as both newspaper editors and writers of fiction will testify.

Media headlines are typically sensationalized often including homicides that are based on unprovoked attacks by strangers or cases with unique or bizarre aspects. Authors and movie producers also play their part in perpetuating this view of homicide by creating fictionalized stereotypes of the murderer as cold and calculating, acting out of motives of greed, lust, or revenge. Mundane motives such as powerlessness, the desire for freedom, or even resentment at having to do the dishes are rarely attributed to the murderers in Agatha Christie's or Cornwell's mysteries. The resultant view of murder is that it is usually premeditated and concealed by the offender; however, the reality of homicide in Australia is very different.

This chapter will review the most current Australian data available from the National Homicide Monitoring Program (NHMP) (2010–12 financial year) and compare it to the past 24 years, to illustrate trends, patterns, and specific psychological aspects relevant to these events. Topics covered will include what homicide currently looks like in Australia, who are the victims, the contextual and situational factors surrounding the events, and the behavioral aspects involved.

In 2013, global mortality data conservatively estimated that just under half a million people died in homicide-related incidences (UNODC, 2014). Of this number, more than one-third of the violent deaths occurred in impoverished developing countries. These violent deaths occur for many reasons, in general terms, homicide is perpetrated as a result of greed, passion, the effects of alcohol/illicit drug consumption, gender, ethnic and racial differences, religion, sexual property, social status, mental illness, and a need for power and control. Globally, there appears to be a shift in the type of homicide occurring within different countries, from intimate family-related homicides to stranger-, gang-, and organized crime–related deaths (UNODC, 2014).

According to Bryant and Cussen (2015), the rate of homicide in Australia is relatively low by global standards and has decreased over the past two decades. Acts of homicide have far-reaching social consequences; they create fear in communities as well as affect those responsible for investigating them. It is imperative that researchers and investigators examine, understand and work toward the development of strategies to better comprehend the demographic variables and behavioral aspects associated with the victims, perpetrators, and incidents of homicide in Australia.

Despite a slight increase in the number of homicide victims over the last 2 financial years, where data are available, 2010–12, the overall national rate of victimization has been on a downward trend since 2001–02. The rate of homicide per 100,000 of the population in Australia (2010–12) remained stable at 1.2 incidents, unchanged from the previous year of collection. It is one of the lowest recorded since the establishment of the NHMP in 1989. In the past 24 years, the number of homicides across Australia has decreased overall (see Fig. 13.1), a trend that is mirrored internationally (UNODC, 2014).

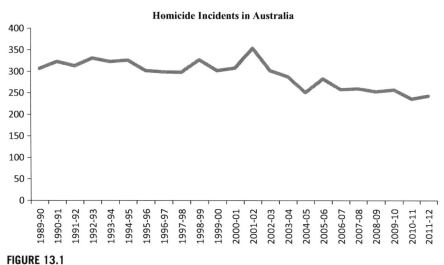

FIGURE 13.1

Homicide incidents in Australia, 1989–90 to 2011–12 (number).

National Homicide Monitoring Program 1989–90 to 2010–12 Annual Report (2015).

The statistics for this chapter were sourced from the NHMP and their framework categorizes homicide victim and offender-related data according to age, gender, marital status, racial appearance, prior criminal history, employment, alcohol/illicit drug use, and cause of death. This framework is used so that it is possible to determine the social factors likely to coexist in particular types of homicides, thus assisting different disciplines within this space to identify vulnerable groups of people.

IMPACT OF HOMICIDE IN AUSTRALIA

Even though levels of homicide in Australia are comparatively low in the global context, costs to the government, citizens, and the nation overall are estimated to exceed $930 million per annum (Mayhew, 2003). This cost can be broken down into categories, such as medical costs, legal expenses, and lost earnings. Medical costs associated with homicide are estimated at $7600 per victim, or a total of $4.5 million per annum, with lost earnings accounting for the greatest proportion of the total cost. For example, it has been estimated that a victim 15–24 years of age would, due to a lack of productivity, cost the nation approximately $1.6 million (Mayhew, 2003).

The Homicide Victims' Support Group (Australia) Inc. (2013) suggests that another major factor for consideration is the intangible losses that cannot automatically be equated with a monetary value. Examples of these losses include quality of life for secondary victims posthomicide, emotional trauma, and posttraumatic stress. Each of these traumas carries a concomitant cost with respect to counseling, loss of income due to absence from work, and other costs associated with reconstructing their lives. The total cost of intangible losses is estimated at approximately $225 million overall per annum (Mayhew, 2003).

WHY PEOPLE KILL

Homicides should be seen within a social context; they are complex interactions between the perpetrator and victim, involving a physical altercation. The actual act includes the dynamic risk of all parties, the context leading up to the event, which goes to inform context that the homicide occurs in (McKinley, 2016). Situational contexts have changed little from the 1900s to the 2000s, with the typical characteristics of a homicide event starting with an assault or sharp force trauma, committed by a single adult male known to the victim, having an in intraracial, intraage argument (McKinley, 2016).

Since 2000, there has been a steady increase in homicide incidents where multiple offenders are recorded with an instrumental motive, which has in turn increased acquaintance and stranger homicides (Bryant & Cussen, 2015). A homicide is *instrumental* if the immediate and primary goal is to obtain money or property and *expressive* if the offender's immediate and primary motive is to hurt the other person (Adjorlolo & Chan, 2015).

Expressive homicides are more prevalent than those categorized as instrumental. Expressive homicides typically commence with trivial altercations, victim precipitation, and the presence of alcohol (Adjorlolo & Chan, 2015). Contrary to popular belief, confrontational homicides now indicate that both male and female offenders (not in only minority groups) in both public and private spaces are involved. In relation to these types of homicides, both stability and change are found in the data since NHMP started recording in 1989.

People kill each other for a number of reasons; however, there does not appear to be any universally agreed method for classification of homicides (Harries, 1997). Many of the previous classifications focused on qualitative variables, such as prior victim–offender relationship or precipitative events, as opposed to those based on specific quantitative measures, such as the total number of victims (Wellford & Cronin, 1999). Although there are a range of reasons why people kill each other, most events can be classified into one of three categories. These categories are organized according to the principal relationship shared between the victim and the perpetrator. The categories are:

- Domestic/intimate homicides: The definition of "domestic relationship" was taken from the Crimes (Domestic and Personal Violence) Act (2007). The perpetrator usually knows the victim and in most cases there is a clear motive. The essence of the definition of domestic is a blood relation, as opposed to intimate where there is normally a sexual aspect to the relationship. Research states that the motive in this homicide typology is frequently based on factors such as anger, hate, jealously, rage, or revenge (Mouzos & Rushforth, 2003a,b; Shackelford & Mouzos, 2005; Stöckl et al., 2013). The psychological dynamics involved in such violent interpersonal disputes often involve violence and offender attitudes of "…if I can't have you, then nobody will have you." In many instances, the event is initiated when the victim attempts to end the relationship, reports to authorities in order to get help for themself and their child(ren), or petitions the court for an Apprehended Violence Order (AVO) in order to stop their offenders' abusive behavior. The court order will direct the offender to stay away from the victim and refrain from any further contact. Once external parties are involved in what was once a private relationship, the offender becomes infuriated with their perceived lack of control and the attempt by their partner to destroy their relationship and may engage in a number of acts of harassment, which may include assault, stalking, and threats (Mouzos & Rushforth, 2003a,b; Polk, 1994). Cases such as the murder of Rachelle Yeo by her ex-lover (*R v Mulvihill* [2014] NSWSC 443), the murder of Mabel Walsh and her two grandchildren by her husband and their grandfather (*R v Walsh* [2009] NSWSC 764), the murder of Christine Anthony (aka Christine Darcy) by her lover (*R v Harding* [2013] NSWSC 513), and the murder of Lisa Harnum by her lover (*R v Gittany* [2013] NSWSC 1503) are examples of this homicide typology.

- Acquaintance homicide: An incident involving a victim and offender who were known to each other but who were not related to each other or living in a domestic relationship (Chan & Payne, 2013). These types of homicides usually involve contributing factors, such as arguments stemming from a verbal confrontation, where victim and/or perpetrator are under the influence of alcohol or illicit drugs and have "lost face" in front of peers (Polk, 1994). The murder of Dorothy Davis and Kerry Whelan by an acquaintance of both women (*R v Burrell* [2006] NSWSC 581, 9 August 2006, *Burrell and the Queen* [2009] NSWCCA 163, 17 June 2009, *R v Burrell* [No 3] [2008] NSWSC 30; 8 February 2008, *R v Burrell* [2009] NSWCCA 193); the murders of 11 nursing home victims by their hired carer (*R v Dean* [2013] NSWSC 1027, NSW Supreme Court, Latham J, 1 August 2013); the murder of Ziad Razzak and Melissa Nemra in a drive-by shooting by rival gang members (*R v Darwiche & Others* [2006] NSWSC 1167; 10 November 2006, *R v Darwiche & Others* [2006] NSWSC 924; NSWSC 926; NSWSC 927; 19 April 2006; *R v Darwiche & Others* [2011] NSWCCA 62, 8 April 2011) are examples of this homicide typology.
- Stranger homicides: Unlike acquaintance homicides, which generally start with personal conflict between the offender and victim, stranger homicides often have no discernible relationship, reflected in the title of typology. Stranger homicides sometimes involve a co-committed crime that required extensive planning, such as a robbery/homicide. These types of crime are usually premeditated, with forensic awareness in some cases, so that the likelihood that physical evidence will be left behind for investigators to discover is decreased, reducing the potential of identifying an offender. In a stranger homicide, the

offender usually commits the crime in secrecy, without witnesses, thereby thwarting investigative effort in obtaining evidence. Many of the stranger homicides have no obvious motive recorded, unknown crime scenes (where the victim's body is dumped and the initial place of the violent attack is not known) and no obvious nexus between the victim and the offender. Police have to rely heavily on information gleaned from the public and when little or no information is forthcoming, the homicide can often remain unsolved. Cases such as the murder of Shahab Kargarian and Shabnam Faiz (*R v Collisson* [2002] NSWSC 229, 26 March 2002; *R v Bradley* [2002] NSWSC 1018, 1 November 2002 and *R v Collisson* [2003] NSWCCA 212, 29 July 2003), the murder of Peter Falconio and kidnapping of Joanne Lees (*R v Murdoch* [2005] NTSC 75, NTSC 76, NTSC 80), the manslaughter by unlawful and dangerous act of Thomas Kelly (*R v Loveridge* [2013] NSWSC 1638, 8 November 2013, *R v Loveridge* [2014] NSWCCA 120, 4 July 2014) are examples of this homicide typology.

CHANGES IN HOMICIDE TRENDS

Even though the total number of homicides has decreased in Australia over the last 25 years, the number of stranger homicides have increased during the same period, altering the ratio of domestic to stranger homicides (Bryant & Cussen, 2015). This phenomenon can be seen in the United States and United Kingdom (Fox & Zawitz, 2011; McClellan, 2007; Regoeczi & Miethe, 2003; Wellford & Cronin, 2000). Additionally, many of the stranger homicides are drug related and include unwilling witnesses due to the fear of intimidation, a lack of positive community relationships with law enforcement and a general and pervasive distrust of police (Regoeczi & Miethe, 2003; Richardson & Kosa, 2001; Wellford & Cronin, 2000). Research states that stranger related homicides occur because of organized gangs and drug use and access; trafficking of humans, drugs; munitions; increased migration; and the ease in which people can access and trawl the Internet for victims and ideas (Comber, 2009; Kaplan & Dubro, 2012; Paoli, 2003).

Wolfgang's seminal work (1958) argued that the construction of communities was based on dichotomous categorizations, in both socioeconomic and cultural terms, which could give rise to conflict. Smith and Zahn (1999) argued that the motives for, and the commission of, homicide have not altered substantially for centuries except that over the previous 20 years, there has been an increase in stranger homicides in some Western countries. More recently, Pinker (2011) has proposed five reasons for the reduction in rates of homicide, which he argues have declined steadily over the centuries of human existence. He suggests that the coercive power of a benevolent state imposing law and order provides a framework for life to shift from purely survival to an environment that allows scope for society to develop. Commerce can then occur, which promotes interdependency, discouraging aggressive violence between neighbors. The status and treatment of women improve, which leads to feminization of society that honors the gentler values and diverts away from hypermasculine social values (Pinker, 2011, p. 684). He argues that these societal values then have a pacifying force where the power of reason slowly expands to overcome prejudice, hatred, and the right of might, producing a better society where people apply the principles of reason in their interpersonal dealings, which he terms the "escalator of reason" (Pinker, 2011, p. 686).

AUSTRALIAN DATA

According to Bryant and Cussen (2015), the populations with the greatest risk of homicide victimization are middle-aged males from minority groups. Victims were most commonly male ($n=328$, 64%) for the period of 2010–12, followed by 30% ($n=99$) who were between the ages of 35 and 45, and 17% who were identified as Indigenous ($n=50$). These data support the work of Australian researchers such as McKinley (2016), Mouzos (1999), and Polk (1994), who all argue that it is male *bravado*, aggression, loss of face, intoxication, and confrontational behaviors that ultimately victimize this population.

AGE AND SEX

With the total number of Australian homicides in decline, it comes as a surprise that the number of homicide events involving children, those under the age of 18, remains relatively stable (Bryant & Cussen, 2015). In most countries, homicide rates tend to be lowest in the youngest ages, to peak among adults aged 35 years and then decline. During the period of 1989–2012, the total number of homicides dropped from 307 in 1989–90 (1.9 per 100,000 population) to 243 in 2011–12 (1.1 per 100,000 population), with the highest number ($n=354$) occurring in 2001–02 (1.8 per 100,000 population; Bryant & Cussen, 2015).

In this same time period, the number of child homicides fluctuated from 42 in 1989–90 to 53 in 2001–02, and to 19 in 2008–09, and then increased once again to 30 in 2011–12 (see Fig. 13.1; Bryant & Cussen, 2015). In 2011–12, the Australian child homicide rate compared to other Western countries' rates in the following manner: New Zealand, 1 per 100,000 population; United States, 4 per 100,000 population; Canada, 2 per 100,000 population, and the United Kingdom, 0.4 per 100,000 population (UNICEF, 2014) (Fig. 13.2).

Previous research states that many child homicide events occur when the young victim's normal, repetitive requirements for attention, clothing, or food cause their carer to violently react (Nielssen, Large, Westmore, & Lackersteen, 2009). The majority of children fatally assaulted were aged less than 8 and approximately half of all children who died as a result of 'assaultive force'[1] were under 1 year of age. This number is statistically significant and links directly to the perpetrators of these crimes; it demonstrates that the majority of deaths were brought on by the victim's

---

[1] Defined as assault where the perpetrator uses their hands and/or feet.

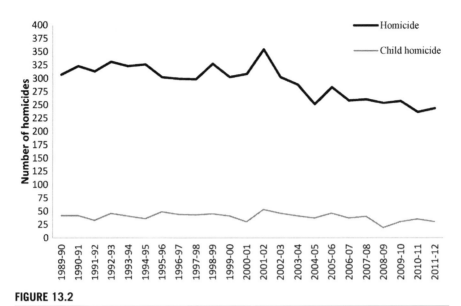

FIGURE 13.2

Homicide incidents in Australia, 1989–90 to 2011–12 (number).

National Homicide Monitoring Program Annual Report; Bryant, W., & Cussen, T. (2015). Homicide in Australia: 2010–12 national homicide monitoring program annual report, monitoring report no. 23. *Canberra: Australian Institute of Criminology. p. 29.*

carer, whether their natural mother or significant male guardian (natural father or de facto). Since the inception of the NHMP, nonbiological fathers were overrepresented as offenders (Bryant & Cussen, 2015).

A theory that was raised in relation to this phenomenon has been labeled the "Cinderella effect." Although it has received some criticism, there appears to be logic to the concept. It has been noted by various researchers that child abuse is a complex issue and is affected by a multitude of factors. The Cinderella effect was first posited by Daly and Wilson (2001). Their study, using evolutionary psychology, argued that there was a higher incidence of child abuse and maltreatment by stepparents than by biological parents. Their theory was based on "adaptive reproductive strategy" between primates, where males commonly kill the offspring of other males in an attempt to start the estrus surge within the mother, giving the mate the best chance to impregnate her himself (Hrdy, 1977).

For over 30 years, research demonstrated that stepchildren in Canada, the United Kingdom, and the United States were at a greater risk of child abuse and maltreatment, especially fatal beatings, when nonbiological stepparents were involved (Daly & Wilson, 2001; Harris, Hilton, Rice, & Eke, 2007; Weekes-Shackelford & Shackelford, 2004). Roach's (2011) study recorded that children were up to a 100 times more likely to die at the hand of a nonbiological than a biological parent. Strong evidence suggests that in families made up of both stepchildren and genetically related children, abusive parents will more often target the stepchildren and forgive their own offspring.

Crawford and Kreb's (2008) findings demonstrate that stepchildren were specifically targeted 9 of 10 times in one of their studies and in 19 of 22 in another (p. 387). Quantitative research that found a child residing with a stepparent is the single best predicator of child abuse and neglect, even after controlling for socioeconomic effects (Weekes-Shackelford & Shackelford, 2004, p. 76). Lamont (2011, p. 5) cites Yampolskaya, Greenbaum, and Berson (2009), who examined the profiles of 126 filicide perpetrators in United States and found that nonbiological fathers were 17 times more likely to fatally assault a child than were biological parents.

Tooley, Karakis, Stokes, and Ozannesmith (2006) found similar results in Australia. Case study one illustrates the death of a minor at the hands of his stepfather.

CASE STUDY ONE

Over a period of 2 years, the Department of Community Services (DoCs) received and recorded notifications of suspected physical abuse, neglect, and supervision issues regarding a 3-year-old boy. He was later found dead in his home, and according to his mother and her de facto, had suffered from a seizure and consequently died. The postmortem examination recorded cause of death as "severe head injury, with marked brain swelling." Multiple bruises and recent and historic fractures were discovered on the victim's body. The forensic pathologist concluded that the victim had suffered from long-term abuse and neglect. At the time of the victim's death, his biological father was in prison, the mother's parents lived interstate, and there was a female infant (the offspring of the victim's mother and the offender) who survived the victim living at their residence.

During the first week of the investigation, the police narrowed their focus to the de facto male living with the victim's mother. He had a prior criminal history in minor, but violent, assaults and had often stated to his friends and family that he did not like the boy and wished that he were not around so that he and the child's mother could be free of the responsibility. When faced with all of the forensic evidence, the medical examiner's report, and witness statements, the offender pleaded guilty and received an 8-year sentence. The child's mother was charged with failing to report the abuse and complicity in the act, but due to a plea and giving evidence against the offender, all charges were withdrawn.

Strang (1996, p. 1) found that 1 in 12 homicides in Australia involved a child under 15, and that for children under the age of 1, the number of deaths caused by filicide equals or exceeds the number of deaths caused by motor vehicle accidents, accidental poisonings, falls, or drowning. This is significant as children are more vulnerable to fatal mistreatment or abuse however often, "children are more likely to be killed in their own home by members of their own family than by anywhere else or by anyone else in society" (Browne & Lynch, 1995, p. 309).

Extensive research in this field illustrates that the circumstances surrounding a child's death can be considerably different, such as recurring violent assaults over a prolonged period of time; an isolated event in which the perpetrator suddenly experiences an overwhelming set of emotions (in combination with specific situational factors) and loses self-control; or chronic neglect and mistreatment or psychotic delusions about the victim (Nielssen et al., 2009). Other researchers name the following issues as the reasons that people kill their children: the individual child's traits, such as disability and age, the offender's previous convictions or drug abuse problems, a perceived or real custody battle loss, and mental health problems (Burgess & Drais, 1999; Temrin, Buchmayer, & Enquist, 2000).

Still other reasons for parents taking their children's lives include "altruistic" reasoning, meaning that the parent believes that the children are better off with them "in the afterlife," leading to a murder-suicide event. Another reason is to dispose of an unwanted baby, such as if the child is born outside of a marriage. The final reason offered is spousal revenge, which can occur when a parent kills their child(ren) to hurt their partner. Typically, this type of homicide motive is seen in cases of infidelity (Coorg & Tournay, 2013). Older children (teenagers) more often died as the result of knife wounds or firearm injuries (Bryant & Cussen, 2015; Dearden & Jones, 2008).

The age group with the highest percentage of victims in the NHMP data was 35–49 years for most forms of homicide, constituting 30% of the total number of homicides for the period of 2010–12. Of note is that this variable has remained constant over 24 years of data collection period by the NHMP (Bryant & Cussen, 2015). Authorities and policy makers in Australia already specifically target the age group 18–35 years to focus on the main catalysts for aggression, so the results for these groups suggest some success in the implementation of these initiatives. However, the continued high rate of homicide in the category 35–49 years suggests a need to focus on this group. The reasons that this specific group appear to be victimized are numerous and detailed later, but the author acknowledges that although there are certain dangerous moral assumptions underlying some elements of victimology, the notion of victim precipitation can add value in relation to understanding the victimization rate in this type of homicide.

Victims, specifically, men aged 35–49 years, appear to be involved in homicide cases where self-defense or provocation was evident, as well as cases where a spur-of-the-moment attack, between males of the same age group, in fights during social occasions where alcohol or drugs are present. The majority of cases demonstrate behaviors either driven by biological imperatives (testosterone), sociological issues (differential opportunities, gender roles, social learning, and value conflict), or evolutionary psychology (changing economic opportunity, male competition, or changes in the socialization process).

Gender is defined as "not a natural fact but a complex social, historical, and cultural product; it is related to, but simply derived from, biological sex differences" (Lilly, Cullen, & Ball, 2014, p. 246). Research acknowledges that "the gender differences in filicide motivation indicate that an understanding of the social construction of masculinity and femininity may be crucial to an adequate understanding of filicide" (Wilczynski, 1995, p. 369).

For several decades, the research between gender and homicide has shown that males commit between 85% and 90% of homicides (Harne, 2011). However, in the case of filicide, women are as likely to be the perpetrators (Alder & Polk, 1996, p. 2). Kajese et al. (2011, p. 147) found that the most common perpetrator was the victim's biological father (44%), the victim's biological mother (27%), and the male partner of the victim's mother (20%). McKee and Egan (2013, p. 759), who found that maternal filicides were committed by mothers whom, among other things, "found their maternal role threatened."

In relation to gender, 85% of offenders identified as male ($n=453$), and 15% were female ($n=79$). The female population of offenders remained comparatively stable in relation to previous years of recording. In contrast, the rate of offending for males continues to decline; for example, in 1992–93, the figure was 3.8 per 100,000, and in 2010–12, it was 2.0 per 100,000, demonstrating a difference of 47%.

NHMP data illustrate, since 1989, that males comprise in excess of 80% of all known homicide offenders. The reasons that this particular group are more frequently represented appears to be due to a number of factors which include a propensity for males to exhibit more aggression particularly toward other males and especially in public places when alcohol or drugs may act to lower inhibitions; a need for some males to prove that their levels of strength and power have not diminished as they age; and the desire to demonstrate to potential sexual partners that they can "protect them" through displays of aggression toward other would-be suitors (McKinley, 2016; Mouzos, 2003; Polk, 1994).

Most studies examine gender differences with respect to particular variables, such as victim–offender relationships, motive or age, rather than in the totality of combinations of offender, victim, and offense elements that define the basic structure of homicide situations (Harris, 2003; Moffit, 2001). Theories of gender-based offender motivations tend to be nomothetic explanations for difference in prevalence across groups and context. When women are the offenders in a homicide, it is usually an act of infanticide or against an intimate partner, with their motive being self-protection or as a precipitating motive argumentative abuse.

Data illustrate that the victimization rate for males has always been higher than that for females. The years 2009 and 2010 do not show any change from the previous year of data collection (2008–09) in that the rate of victimization for males: males were 1.5 per 100,000 and females were 1.0 per 100,000 (Bryant & Cussen, 2015), and these ratios are consistent in the United States (Zahn & McCall, 1999), United Kingdom (Francis et al., 2004), Canada (Canadian Center for Justice Statistics, 2010), and New Zealand (Simpson, Mckenna, Moskowitz, Skipworth, & Barry-Walsh, 2004). Extant research states that the relationship between gender and risk of victimization is complex (Johnson & Hotton, 2003). Violence and the consequent victimization of women are pervasive in Australian society, afflicting women from all ages, cultures, classes, and backgrounds (Lloyd, 1997). Empirical evidence demonstrates that women are at greater risk of violence at the hands of someone they know and in the context of a home than by a stranger or in public, particularly when they are trying to leave a relationship (Mouzos, 2003). Research has shown that females are more likely than males to kill and be killed by acquaintances (Browne & Williams, 1993; Browne, Williams, & Dutton, 1999).

Data indicate that 30% ($n=161$) of the offenders identified in the collection period had a previous criminal history, involving at least one conviction (Bryant & Cussen, 2015). Generally, female offenders (14%, $n=11$) are less likely than male offenders (33%, $n=150$) to possess prior criminal convictions. Fourteen percent of offenders ($n=76$) did not have a prior criminal conviction recorded. Previous criminal records, for both male and female offenders (15% for males and 8% for females), can be categorized by the single most commonly recorded offense, "assault" (14%, $n=75$), followed by property offenses (4%, $n=23$), drug offenses (3%, $n=15$), and robbery (2%, $n=11$) (Bryant & Cussen, 2015).

The rate of male offending is 2.3 per 100,000 compared to the rate of females, which is 0.5, slightly less than the previous year's numbers (0.8). Of the 532 known offenders, 3% ($n=16$) were under 18 years and only one of this group was female (Bryant & Cussen, 2015). The youngest recorded offender was aged 14 years at the time of the incident they were charged. Research identified a uniform distribution of offenders across the age range from 18 to 49 years. Approximately 3.1% of known offenders ($n=17$) were over the age of 65 years, the oldest being 81 years at the time of the homicide event. The average age of offenders has remained relatively stable since the NHMP commenced; with a modest decrease in mean age from 1989 to 90 (36 years) to 2011–12 (33 years) (Bryant & Cussen, 2015)[2]. Case study two demonstrates the intersection of age, gender, victim–offender relationship, and motive.

CASE STUDY TWO

The victim of this incident was in her mid-30s and a single working mother of a toddler. Her ex-partner, the child's father, had since remarried and moved intrastate. She had been dating a number of men casually, who were not known to each other. At the time of her death, the victim worked as a sales representative, and during the police investigation after her death, they discovered that she was actively engaged in prostitution.

She was living alone with her child but had a domestic partner who spent some nights at her residence. A dispute between the victim and her de facto, the perpetrator, occurred while on a family outing when the victim told him that she was seeing someone else. Her new partner was younger and wealthier than the perpetrator and she wanted to break up with him to pursue this new relationship.

The perpetrator drove to a secluded area, intent on convincing her to stay. The victim would not consider it and they verbally fought for some period of time. The perpetrator then shot the victim in the back of her head while she sat in the passenger seat of the vehicle and dumped her body in bushland. The perpetrator was a middle-aged former government employee and corrupt former police officer. The perpetrator was arrested 4 months after the murder when he attempted to retrieve the victim's remains to dispose of them elsewhere. He was charged with murder and multiple firearms offenses.

He pleaded guilty to manslaughter, not murder, on the grounds of provocation.

CRIME SCENE LOCATION

The crime scene location of a homicide is principally shaped by the homicide typology. During the period of 2010–12, the majority of all homicide incidents occurred within a residence ($n=336$; 70%). Of this number the largest number of victims were in an intimate or domestic relationship with their killer ($n=158$; 84%). Given the intimate

---

[2] Information was not available for 25 offenders (Bryant & Cussen, 2015).

nature of a private location,[3] where individuals known to each other consistently interact, it is a logical conclusion and the recorded data support existing literature (Keppel & Weiss, 1992; Wellford & Cronin, 1999). There appears to be links between crime scene location, homicide typology, and case solvability (McKinley, 2016). As an example, several studies have found that homicides occurring in residential locations are more likely to be solved than those occurring in outside, secluded areas (Litwin & Xu, 2007), in general public (Litwin, 2004), or in all other locations (Addington, 2006; Regoeczi, Kennedy, & Silverman, 2000). They have also found that homicides occurring in public areas are more likely to be solved than those occurring in secluded areas (Litwin & Xu, 2007) and those occurring in bars/public houses (Litwin, 2004).

Acquaintance ($n=119$; 68%) and stranger ($n=21$; 41%) homicides are less likely to occur in private spaces. An illustration of an unsolved homicide occurring between an unknown offender and a young woman of no-fixed address is in Case Study Three.

CASE STUDY THREE

A white female in her late teens, known to police as a heroin addict and sex worker, was found at an inner city derelict premises. The victim was discovered where she died. She had a boyfriend and she was employed at the time of her death. The forensic pathologist recorded her cause of death as severe head injuries. A dozen separate wounds were discovered at her postmortem, consistent with being beaten with a length of timber. A baseball bat was discovered within the crime scene and was confirmed as one of the murder weapons. Several persons of interest were listed in this matter; however, to date no one has been charged.

Other than the homicides that occur within a residence, the next most prevalent locations for homicide incidents were on a street ($n=56$) or in open areas ($n=20$). Conversely, a larger number of acquaintance homicides occurred in a street or open area ($n=33$; 19%), as did 35% ($n=18$) of stranger homicides. Case study four details the unsolved death of man in a public park and is like another 11 homicides involving acquaintances or strangers (18%) that occurred at the vicinity of a recreational venue.

CASE STUDY FOUR

A single white man in his 40s was found beaten to death in a public park. His time of death was listed as between midnight and 7 a.m. He was long-term unemployed as he suffered from an intellectual handicap and schizophrenia. He did not use drugs or alcohol. Police discovered that the victim had been previously assaulted in the same park where he eventually died. Known at local homeless shelters, religious centers and railway attendants in the area considered him considered a quiet, unassuming man. He did not have a strong bond with his biological family due to his illness. His cause of death was listed as blunt force trauma to the head and chest. A person of interest was identified and was later requested by police to give a statement at a Coronial inquest. Upon receiving legal advice, he declined to answer any questions. This case remains unsolved.

---

[3] For the purposes of this chapter, a private location is considered a dwelling, whether it is a house or apartment, where a person has established a residence regardless of the amount of time they have lived there. A public location is defined as a public space accessible to anybody, such as a street, parkland, or public house.

IN THE COURSE OF ANOTHER CRIME

As with previous decades, the majority of homicide events that occurred in the 2010–12 period (73%, $n=351$) were not committed during the course of another crime. Extant research states that the most significant factor found to differentiate solved and unsolved homicides was whether the incident occurred during the commission of another offense (Mouzos & Muller, 2001; Salfati, 2000; Salfati & Haratsis, 2001). During 2010–12, comparative analysis indicates that unsolved homicides were significantly more likely than solved homicides to occur during the course of another crime (22.6% and 11.9%, respectively). Seventy-two events (15%) did occur concurrently with another crime; the most common precipitating offense was robbery ($n=17$; 4%), and then drug offenses ($n=14$; 3%) followed by breaking and entering ($n=11$; 2%). These actions are associated with more organized offenders who are cognizant of forensic techniques and demonstrate that homicides that involve the commission of property and/or sexual crimes are less likely to be solved.

INTOXICATION

The Australian Institute of Criminology (Morgan & McAnarney, 2009, p. 2) classifies a homicide as "alcohol related" if:

- Postmortem toxicological analysis found alcohol in the victim's bloodstream
- Police records reveal that the offender was intoxicated or had been drinking at the time of the incident

Graham, Wells, and West discovered when they presented their research in 1997 that there was a strong association between alcohol intoxication and the drinker's behavior. The personality of the drinker was impacted by the amount they drank and the context in which they drank. They also found that environmental factors present at the time of the incident, cultural attitudes, and social acceptability of alcohol-related violence directly affected the drinker's behavior. Cranach and Conroy (2001) reviewed Australian homicide events from 1989 to 2000 using the NHMP's database and discovered that 13% of homicide incidents were the direct result of an alcohol-related argument.

Makkai and Payne (2003) presented research that stated that one in three (34%) Australian prisoners, incarcerated for homicide offenses, self-reported addiction to alcohol, while just under half (44%) reported being intoxicated at the time of their most serious offense. The most recent study published in 2008 by Darke and Duflou examined 473 toxicological reports related to New South Wales homicide victims. Data revealed that victims had consumed alcohol prior to or during the incident that caused their death in 42% of cases and that those victims had a median blood alcohol content of 0.14 g/100 mL, which for context is nearly 3 times over the legal limit for driving in Australia (Darke & Duflou, 2008).

Results from the NHMP database for 2010–12 demonstrate that over one-third ($n=179$; 37%) of all homicide events involved excessive alcohol consumption. These numbers illustrate a decrease, from 2008–10 findings, which indicated that alcohol had been consumed in almost half of all incidents. By homicide type, alcohol consumption by the victim was more commonly recorded for acquaintance homicides (46%) than for stranger (18%) or domestic (26%) homicides. By contrast, alcohol consumption by a perpetrator was relatively evenly distributed between acquaintance (43%) and domestic (36%) homicides.

Consuming copious amounts of alcohol directly affects people's behavior (Dingwall, 2006; Graham & Homel, 2008). Some of the ways alcohol change people's behavior is by causing short sightedness or "myopia." Myopia occurs when people focus on proximal issues with little regard to the consequences of their actions. Alcohol consumed in excess can increase potential for violence and cause consumers to become confrontational due to the way alcohol affects their brain, particularly when the person drinking is predisposed to violent outbursts (Felson, Teasdale, & Burchfield, 2008). Alcohol reduces the consumer's ability to think, narrowing their focus of attention and producing tunnel vision. Alcohol has been shown to cause impulsive behavior, introspection, and emotional outbursts. It also reduces anxiety, which actually protects us by telling us to avoid certain situations. Continuous drinking affects the way a person processes information, such as a consumer may misinterpret another person's behavior and misread social cues. This may be why many drunken altercations begin with little more than a "dirty look."

In relation to acquaintance homicide events, the offender was identified as having consumed alcohol in 52% of cases ($n=75$), while the rate was 32% ($n=46$) for domestic homicides and stranger homicide (8%, $n=12$) (Bryant & Cussen, 2015). Offenders' alcohol consumption was found to be higher in acquaintance homicides ($n=53$; 46%) as opposed to domestic homicide ($n=44$; 38%).

CASE STUDY FIVE

After his first wife died, the offender met and befriended the deceased, who was a female from a non–English-speaking background staying in this country on a student visa. They went out socially several times and had sexual intercourse once before the deceased moved in with the offender to his house in the suburbs within 1 year of their first meeting. After a short period, she told him that her visa was due to expire and suggested they marry so that she could obtain permanent residency to become an Australian citizen. They were married 8 months after they met in the presence of the offender's sister and brother-in-law; his own children were not informed of the marriage because the offender believed they would not approve of his choice of wife, since at the time of their marriage, he was in his mid-60s and his new wife was in her mid-20s.

According to the person of interest, after the wedding everything changed, sexual intercourse ceased and they occupied separate bedrooms. She became very demanding as to her domestic requirements, forced him to drive her to and from her place of employment, and accused him of stealing her residency papers. He in turn accused her of stealing his mail and removing other items from his bedroom. She said she needed to be able to show that she had the resources to finance her proposed university studies, so the offender obtained a substantial loan from one of his children that he believed was to be deposited in a joint account. Instead, she placed it into her newly opened private account. Ongoing disputes over money and personal property ensued. The deceased allegedly obtained money from his bank by forging his signature and she pawned their wedding rings. The offender stated she was known to stay out many nights in a row and was argumentative and emotionally abusive. To avoid confrontation, he locked himself in his room and rarely came out.

Police were called to the premises on two separate occasions prior to the deceased's death for noise and abuse complaints. On both occasions, both parties chose to stay at their residence. On the day of her death, the deceased arrived home in the early hours of the morning and banged on the door to be let in. The offender got up, let her in, and returned to his bedroom, where he locked the door and attempted to go back to sleep. The deceased spoke, yelled, and kicked at his bedroom door for about 40 min. He then opened the door, shook her by the arms, and asked her to stop, whereupon she stepped into his bedroom and a scuffle ensued. They physically fought each other and both ended up on the bedroom floor, when the offender kneed her in the stomach and hit her on the head. At this stage, he says the deceased was screaming, and in order to quieten her, he put a cloth over her mouth and held it there. He took her shoe and repeatedly hit her over the head with the heel. Shortly after he stopped, he realized that she was dead.

He had a drink of water, a cigarette, and a shower. He then telephoned police and his daughter and waited at the house until they arrived. The photographs of the deceased taken at the scene and the postmortem examination revealed multiple and extensive injuries to her head and body. Cause of death was recorded as blunt force trauma to the head and trunk and asphyxia. An examination of the offender showed eight lacerations on his right forearm and fractured fingers on his right hand. He admitted his actions to investigating police and pleaded guilty.

Illicit drug use was recorded in 101 homicides (21%) during 2010–12 (Bryant & Cussen, 2015). Victim illicit drug use ($n=92$; 19%) was more commonly recorded than offender drug use ($n=54$; 12%). Although initial drug use may be voluntary, drugs have been shown to alter brain chemistry, which interferes with an individual's ability to make decisions and can lead to compulsive craving, seeking, and use. This leads to substance dependency. All drugs, such as nicotine, cocaine, marijuana, heroin, and others, directly affect part of the limbic system, which is the brain's "reward" circuit. Drugs hijack this "reward" system, causing unusually large amounts of dopamine to flood the system. It is this flood of dopamine that causes the euphoria associated with drug use. Subsequent and serious side effects of illicit drug use include addiction, aggressiveness, paranoia, hallucinations, impaired judgment, impulsiveness, and a loss of self-control. In 21% of homicides ($n=101$), illicit drugs precipitated the event and 12% ($n=54$) of offenders were recognized as being intoxicated at the time of the event.[4]

ETHNICITY

Historically, prior to colonial contact, most conflict resolution within the Indigenous communities was structured in tradition and occurred at sacred places. Fighting behavior was controlled by elders and was carried out according to social rules in response to specified offenses. Violence was thus a form of institutionalized conflict resolution. (Craig, 1979; Langton, 1988; Thomson, 1935; cited in Memmott, Stacy, Chambers, & Keys, 2001, p. 30). While it is essential to any analysis of Indigenous homicide that a full understanding of the cultural contexts in which violence occurs be understood and stated, it is also important that this does not obscure other aspects of violence, particularly the destruction of individuals, families, and communities that has reached epidemic proportions in some places (Mouzos, 1999). It is thus

---

[4] Noteworthy, offender intoxication is a subjective assessment made by investigating officers, whereas postmortem toxicological tests can confirm whether the victim ingested any intoxicating substances.

arguable that whereas some forms of violence may provide acceptable avenues for conflict resolution as they did in traditional times, these forms are discernible and definable by their limits and rules, a level of constraint, often supervised, and most probably in the absence of alcohol.

Research from the Australia Institute of Criminology (AIC) shows that Indigenous Australians account for a disproportionately high number of both victims and offenders of homicide (McLaughlin, 2001). Although Indigenous Australians represent approximately 2% of the total Australian population, they accounted for 15.1% of homicide victims and 15.7% of homicide offenders over the 11-year period between July 1989 and June 2000. The rate per 100,000 for homicide victimization of Indigenous persons fluctuated between 12.6 and 13.8 in the early 1990s. By contrast, the non-Indigenous homicide victimization rate has remained between 1.3 and 1.8 per 100 000 over the same 11-year period (Mouzos, 2001) (Fig. 13.3).

Of all the homicide victims throughout the 2010–11 and 2011–12 financial years, 60 were identified as Indigenous Australians—34 males and 26 females. The rate of Indigenous homicide victimization was 4 times higher than that for non-Indigenous Australians, although these results varied significantly by gender. Indigenous males for example were 3 times more likely (4.6 per 100,000) than non-Indigenous males

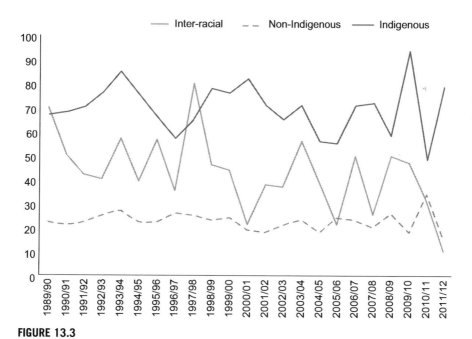

FIGURE 13.3

Rates of homicide victimization by race.

National Homicide Monitoring Program Annual Report 2010–2012; Bryant, W., & Cussen, T. (2015). Homicide in Australia: 2010–12 national homicide monitoring program annual report, monitoring report no. 23. Canberra: Australian Institute of Criminology. p. 29.

to be victims of homicide. Indigenous females were 5 times more likely (3.5 per 100,000) to be victims than non-Indigenous females. For all Indigenous homicide victims, 55% were killed in a domestic homicide, of which the most common subcategory was intimate partner homicide (42%, $n=25$). Use of knives/sharp instruments was particularly prevalent in domestic and acquaintance homicides. For homicide victims, 62 were aged 17 years or younger, while 16 children in the same age bracket were identified as homicide offenders.

Fig. 13.4 illustrates the trends in homicide victimization across Australian States and Territories. The sudden and substantial increase in the number of homicide victims in Tasmania in 1996 is attributed to the Port Arthur massacre. The anomalous peaks shown for the Northern Territory can be attributed to the large population of Indigenous persons residing in this area who have a disadvantaged background and therefore a higher concentration of factors that put them at greater risk of being a victim of homicide (Mouzos & Segrave, 2004).

There were no incidents recorded where an Indigenous victim was killed by a stranger; in fact, 47% of the victims were killed in a domestic homicide ($n=40$). Others were killed by an acquaintance ($n=26$). There were two victims where the victim–offender relationship was not recorded by police (Bryant & Cussen, 2015). Even though Indigenous people are overrepresented as victims of homicide there are similarities with non-Indigenous victimization. For example, females make up the majority of domestic homicide events (Cussen & Bryant, 2015).

MOTIVE

Determining the motive behind a homicide can assist in understanding certain situations or factors that may trigger a homicide event. However, assigning a motive to a homicide event is difficult because the reasons, or lack thereof, are as varied and complex as the

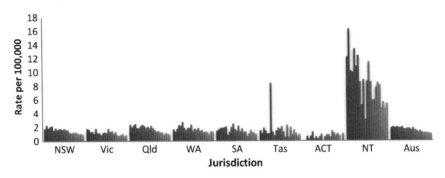

FIGURE 13.4

Homicide incidents by jurisdiction, 1989–90 to 2011–12 (rate per 100,000).[5]

---

[5] Note. Data sourced from NHMP annual reports (Bryant & Cussen, 2015; Chan & Payne, 2013; Dearden & Jones, 2008; Virueda & Payne, 2010).

persons involved in the crime. Motivation informs risk, both from the victim's perspective and that of the perpetrator. All motivated parties within a homicide, have a conscious imposition of risk even when there is a disjunction between the premise and the conclusion. NHMP data showed that motive was only recorded in 53% of homicide cases (511 victims, 1 July 2010–30 June 2012; Bryant & Cussen, 2015).

Female victims are more likely to have been killed as a result of a domestic argument, breakdown, or termination of their relationship, whereas male victims were more likely to have been victimized where motives were related to revenge, money, drugs, or alcohol-fueled arguments. In the majority of incidents, the motive either could not be determined (n=198; 39%) or was attributed to an unspecified altercation, either related to an "other" argument (n=118; 23%) or domestic circumstances (n=23; 4%). Only in a small number of incidents was the precipitating cause identified, for example, alcohol-fueled argument (n=19; 4%), money (n=48; 9%), or revenge (n=23; 4%).

Police are not required to have to prove motive in Australia so this may be why it is not frequently recorded. Other possible explanations include that the offender simply does not know why they reacted the way they did, the offender denies involvement so they will not discuss motive, that the motive is not obvious and the offender is deceased, or simply that the person charged with the homicide will not give a reason (McKinley, 2016).

Previous studies demonstrate that many researchers have attempted to categorize homicidal motive in order to give a reason for the offender's behavior. In 1988, Holmes and De Burger created numerous categories that could divide cases into as a way to describe the contributing factors, such as:

1. Visionary: these are homicides that were committed in response to voices or visions that demand that a person or group of persons be eliminated
2. Mission oriented: Conscious goal of eliminating a particular group or category of people
3. Hedonistic thrill seeking: Derives pleasure directly from the murder event
4. Comfort: Instrumental homicides in meeting the killer's goal of pleasure, creating comfort, the good life
5. Lust: Sexual arousal and gratification are integral to the homicidal act
6. Power-control oriented: Derives profound satisfaction from the process of having complete life-or-death control over his victim

Later, Douglas and Munn (1992) took Holmes and De Burger's work and broke down their categories and then added criminal enterprise, personal cause, sexual, and group cause, with each motivation divided into a number of smaller subcategories. Levin and Fox (1996) redeveloped the list again and specifically highlighted revenge (individual, category specific or nonspecific), love, profit, and terror. Ten years from when Holmes and DeBurger (1998) first published their study, Keppel and Walter (1999) published their findings renaming categories to:

1. Power–assertive: Increasing aggression with the victim ensures control and power
2. Power–reassurance: Acts out fantasy and seeks reassurance from the victim

3. Anger–retaliation: Seeks revenge for his anger toward another person by attacking a symbolic person
4. Anger–excitation: Engages in prolonged torture, exploitation, and/or mutilation, which energizes the killer's fantasy

In 2005, Tita and Griffiths reported that gangs, drugs, felony, argument, and familial/domestic were the main motives behind incidents of homicide in the United States. Soon after, Schmidt, Padosch, Rothschild, and Madea (2005) developed a more specific list of motives, which included concealment of a prior homicide, greed, domestic argument, revenge, family honor, jealousy, and sexual motives. Just a year later, Bijleveld and Smit (2006) added to previous research by asserting that criminal contract killing, disputes between inmates, and persons suffering psychotic breaks were also significant motives for homicide events.

Turvey (2011) reworked previous research on motive by re-categorizing motive based on his own involvement in numerous US cases. His categories include power reassurance or compensatory where the actual crime acts as a "restorative" to the offender, due to the doubts they hold about themselves, and power assertive, where the offender wants to appear to have no doubt about his own masculinity or capacity, using his crimes to express his virility. The anger retaliatory or displaced anger category becomes evident when the offender acts out based amassed real or imagined wrongs; the victim could be a person who wronged them or may symbolize that person to the offender. The sadistic or anger excitation category is recognized by brutality toward the victim. They will be tortured, humiliated, and more often bound due to the fact that the offender is motivated by causing intense pain as part of their own fantasies. These fantasies are solely for the offender's sexual pleasure. Turvey's final category is profit or material gain (2011).

Most recently, Australian researcher Parker (2016) while researching her PhD discovered that situational characteristics of homicide motive are most often related to gain, jealousy, revenge, love, concealment, hate/conviction, and thrill. She lists them as fundamental motives, rather than psychological or pure police recorded motives. The following case study illustrates the intersection between victim–offender relationship, motive, and violence.

CASE STUDY SIX

A young man in his early 20s was killed late at night at his place of work as a result of a gunshot wound to his head. Police intelligence sources suggested that prior to his death; he had been heavily involved in gang activity, drugs, and violent street crime and had a lengthy criminal history. Although he did not use alcohol or illicit or prescription drugs, it was generally known among his friends and family that he had a gambling habit. He was a member of a gang and had a history of being aggressive toward police. In fact, at the time of his death, he was being investigated in relation to the murder of a police member. The weapon was later proved to have been a 9-mm-caliber firearm. Robbery did not appear to be the motive in this case as ecstasy, cannabis, and over $1000 cash were located on the body of the deceased. However, witnesses stated that the victim had spoken of going to purchase 2 kg of cocaine and had been in the possession of $300,000 at the time he was last seen alive, which was not recovered.

Subsequent investigations identified a number of persons of interest; however, forensic evidence led to the offender who was charged with the offense. This man was found to be in his early 30s, married, and of the same ethnicity as the victim. He, too, had prior criminal convictions, including charges for drugs and armed robbery; he also worked in the same industry as the victim. There was no firearms license or registration listed against the offender. The firearm used in the homicide was never recovered. The offender was later convicted of armed robbery and was serving a 6-year sentence at the time that homicide detectives identified him as the offender in this case after lengthy investigations. He was subsequently tried and found guilty of murder, for which he is serving 20+ years.

VICTIM–PERPETRATOR RELATIONSHIP

Homicide is unique in terms of the nature of the crime, in particular the relationship between victim and offender. It is a crime that is most often committed against the offender's own circle of acquaintances. The homicide victim is typically an intimate of the offender, most commonly a family member or friend. Stranger killings, so often portrayed in the media, account for less than one in five killings in Australia.

Homicide, more than any other crime, frequently arises out of long and hostile interaction between victim and offender, rather than from a sudden unprovoked and premeditated action by an offender. It is perhaps this intimacy between victim and offender that explains why a proportion of homicide offenders commits suicide. In Australia, during 2010–12, there were 532 offenders recorded and 31 committed suicide (6%), either as part of the homicide event or just after.

Many people who commit murder have never offended previously and are not likely to again. Moreover, few could be classed as "dangerous" or criminally insane. In all but ultra-rare cases, they have killed the one person they are ever likely to kill and are no longer dangerous. Many of those convicted of murder have no prior criminal history, and previous convictions for violent offenses are uncommon (McKinley, 2016). Furthermore, homicide offenders enjoy the lowest recidivism rate of any other class of violent offender (Neuilly, Zgoba, Tita, & Lee, 2011).

In Australia, the majority of homicide victims are killed by someone they know. Of the 511 homicide victims recorded in 2010–12, 187 (36%) were classified as domestic homicides, 191 (37%) were classified as acquaintance homicide, and 66 (13%) as stranger homicide. The remaining 68 incidents (14%) could not be classified at the time of recording, as the relationship was unknown (Bryant & Cussen, 2015).

Of the 187 domestic homicide events, the bulk were classified as intimate partner incidents ($n = 109$, 58%). There were also 34 incidents classified as filicide (18%) where the offender was a parent and the victim was their child, 22 as parricides (12%) where the child has killed their parent, and six of siblicide (3%) where the victim and offender are brother/s or sister/s. This is a slight increase in domestic homicides between the 2008–10 and 2010–12 reporting periods (36% compared to 39%, respectively) (Bryant & Cussen, 2015; Chan & Payne, 2013).

Cultural guidelines shape the behavior of individuals who employ violent means to achieve their end goal, such as homicides that involve adult males cannot be divorced from their social or culturally defined roles as aggressors and providers. In the same way, analysis of intimate homicides cannot be separated from social norms governing the relationships. An overwhelming feature of many of the homicides involving wives or lovers as victims is the widespread use of violence by their partners in an effort to control their wives' activities. A variety of behaviors ranging from the threat of desertion to not having the house tidy upon the male's arrival home from their workplace legitimized the use of physical force.

The proportion of homicide by principal relationship has fluctuated since 1989–90, particularly with regard to domestic homicides. Virueda and Payne (2010) reported that during the period of 2007–08, more than half of Australia's homicides had a domestic nature (52%) but in more recent years this proportion has decreased to 39% of the total number of homicides for the period of 2010–12 (Bryant & Cussen, 2015). At 39%, the proportion of domestic homicides has reached an historic low; however, this finding may change somewhat when the victim–offender relationships in the currently unclassified cases (a higher proportion in 2010–12 than in previous years) become known.

Of the domestic homicides recorded in the NHMP, the majority was classified as intimate partner homicide. The frequency of intimate partner homicides has remained stable and while, overall, female victims are not as prevalent as males, they remain overrepresented in this category of homicide. For other homicide types, the results in 2010–11 and 2011–12 were relatively stable compared with previous years.

During the reporting period for jurisdictions reporting 10 or more homicides, stranger homicides were more prevalent in South Australia ($n=6$, 17%) and ranged in other jurisdictions from 4% ($n=1$) in the Northern Territory to 12% ($n=18$) in New South Wales. The three types of homicides that appear to be the most difficult to solve are those that are recorded as stranger homicides, gang/organized crime related (Finn & Healey, 1996; Koedam, 1993), and drug-related homicides. Mouzos and Muller (2001) also argue that homicides that occur during the committal of another crime are less likely to be solved. It can be argued that there are three distinct reasons for this phenomenon. First, offenders typically employ tactics such as witness intimidation and active obstruction, which impedes police investigations (Litwin, 2004; Puckett & Lundman, 2003; Regoeczi et al., 2000; Wellford & Cronin, 1999, 2000). Second, organized crime– or gang-related homicides are often well planned and executed at a time and place of the offender's choosing, to minimize forensic opportunities for investigators. Third, when multiple crimes occur at the same time, such as a rape homicide, then the crime scene may be more complex and include more forensic samples, and cross-contamination.

Kelchner and Kolnes (2008) argued that the probability of solving a homicide outside of the first 48 hours is severely diminished irrespective of other factors. This research suggests that there are two main reasons for this. First, when there is no obvious connection between the victim and offenders after detectives complete a victimology, there is very little chance of identifying an offender. Therefore, in stranger homicides, potential witnesses rarely exist due to the location and/or time the homicide was committed; for example, a homicide between unknown parties in a public place at 2 a.m. on a weekday – there is usually nothing but forensic evidence (if present) to assist police. In contrast, with numerous intimate homicides, the offender often contacts police, is found in situ at the crime scene, commits suicide, or evidence otherwise provides other clear links between offender and victim (Kelchner & Kolnes, 2008).

The second reason that detectives solve less "stranger" homicides is the increased difficulty of determining the offender's motive (Polk, 1994). The task for investigators in these homicides is to analyze the specific aspects of each individual case to draw out the relationship ties between victim and offender if any exist, which could arguably lead to establishing motivation. It can be argued the overall decrease in clearance rates longitudinally has been in some part due to the increase in stranger homicides. In comparison with intimate homicides, which are usually a product of a disagreement or conflict between the offender and victim and are often spur of the moment and not premeditated, stranger homicides often include a co-committed crime, such as robbery. These crimes are often well planned, synchronized, and committed "after hours" with "third party awareness" in mind, and if the offender(s) is forensically aware, there is little likelihood that physical evidence will be left behind.

One of the most provocative issues raised in relation to victim–offender relationships was raised by Wolfgang in 1958. He stated that in his analysis of homicide in Philadelphia, 25.5% of victims played a significant part in their own demise and coined the phrase *victim-precipitated homicide*.

> *...the term victim-precipitated is applied to those criminal homicides in which the victim is a direct, positive precipitator in the crime. The role of the victim is characterized by his having been the first in the homicide drama to use physical force directed against his subsequent slayer (Wolfgang, 1958, p. 252).*

Criticisms of Wolfgang's research span from victim-blaming to the information he collected and analyzed was only reliable and sufficient in 311 cases, and that in the remaining 83 cases the description was either too vague or nonexistent to make a judgment.

Irrespective of the issues raised here, the distinction between the victim and the offender can become blurred in some cases; for example, when a chronically abused wife kills her husband in self-defense. Victim-precipitated homicides are more likely to involve close friends, family members, and casual acquaintances who are intoxicated at the time of the homicide event (Voss & Hepburn, 1968; Wolfgang, 1958).

CAUSE OF DEATH

During 2010–11 and 2011–12, the largest category in relation to cause of death was stab wounds ($n=187$, 37%). This was followed by beatings ($n=125$, 24%) and gunshot wounds ($n=69$, 14%). A further 34 victims died from strangulation or suffocation (7%), and 24 died from smoke inhalation or burns (5%). Stab wounds were the

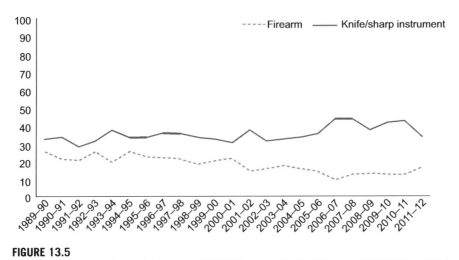

FIGURE 13.5

Weapon use in homicide incidents by year, 1989–90 to 2010–12.

most commonly recorded cause of death for both domestic and acquaintance homicides (42% and 39%, respectively).

In stranger-related homicide events, beatings ($n=19$, 37%) and stab wounds ($n=18$, 35%) were the most common causes of death. A greater proportion of acquaintance homicide victims ($n=25$, 14%) were killed as a result of gunshot wounds than domestic homicide victims ($n=13$, 7%). Knives were the most commonly used weapon in homicides where victims died from stab wounds ($n=165$, 88%). Another 11 victims (6%) died as a result of being stabbed with another sharp implement, such as broken glass or a screwdriver (Bryant & Cussen, 2015).

Since the inception of the NHMP in 1989–90, homicides resulting from firearm use have decreased. In 1989–90, 25% of homicides ($n=76$) involved the use of a firearm, while in 2011–12 firearms were used in 16% of homicide incidents ($n=38$) (see Fig. 13.5). Where a firearm was the weapon of choice, the bulk of these weapons were neither registered nor licensed (Mouzos & Rushforth, 2003a,b). By contrast, homicides involving the use of knives have remained relatively stable (32% in 1989–90; 33% in 2011–12).

CONCLUSION

Since the inception of the NHMP in 1989, the Australian Institute of Criminology has collected, analyzed, and reported on the facts and variables of homicide in Australia and the social context in which it is committed. Consequently, the NHMP has been able to advise government, law enforcement, and academia alike about the reality of homicide in this country. It has provided data for public debate on matters of the causes of homicide, factors associated with its etiology and prevention, as well as providing reports for legislative reform and offender programs. Although the data for homicide from the NHMP show that violent crime is declining, those that are still occurring have innumerable costs, not only to the individual victim and their families but also to the community and the nation.

Emerging from this chapter were several important points: first, that homicide is a product of complex interactions between individuals within the society they belong too. Homicide fluctuates across cultures and time. It is one of the most serious crimes in our society and is culturally, historically, and socially controlled as opposed to a random act of an unhinged or pathological individual.

Second, homicide comprises a variety of offenders and victims in different social settings. Homicide is committed by different people under different sets of pressures or circumstances. Differences in the characteristics of particular cases, in terms of both the participants and the precipitating events, leads to the development of a typology of homicide. Homicide typologies were developed according to the primary relationship between the victim and offender, and then the circumstances surrounding the crime. For example, the circumstances in which a teenager kills her abusive parent are vastly different from those where a neighbor kills a neighbor in the course of a spontaneous dispute. Both of these examples are different again from the circumstances in which a drug dealer kills their supplier for financial gain. These variations in homicide are not random: they are largely the product of specific social determinants.

In Australia, three of five homicides were interpersonal in nature, rather than motivated by ideology or greed. The majority of victims during the period of 2010–12 had a domestic (related by blood or marriage) or intimate (sexual aspect to the relationship) connection with the offender. Previous research suggests that a substantial amount of such homicides are an almost inevitable result of their high frequency and intense social interactions. A small minority of homicides were classified as instrumental, occurring in the course of another crime. Instrumental homicides were most likely to occur in conjunction with a theft or robbery and the victim and offender were usually strangers.

An advantage of analyzing acts of homicide as a feature of specific relationships and circumstances is that instead of focusing on the individual offender and act, research can examine specifics that determine what makes one type of relationship prone to violence more than any other. As an example, the development over time in relation to the unique roles and expectations surrounding the nature of the relationship between men and women becomes critical in understanding the interpersonal relationship between domestic/intimate homicide offenders and victims.

The NHMP data demonstrated that the majority of homicides recorded prior to 2012 were spontaneous rather than premeditated crimes. Naturally, some of the homicides presented in this chapter were premeditated, aside from the obvious gang homicides, a level of premeditation was evident in a number of the cases involving intimates and children, particularly those where a breakdown in the relationship and separation had occurred. Premeditation was apparent in a number of murder-suicides. Apart from these cases, the majority of homicides involved parties reacting to relatively unplanned circumstances. In just under half of the homicides, intoxication exacerbated the violence.

The aim of this chapter has been to provide the current social reality of homicide in Australia using the most current available Australian homicide data from the NHMP (2010–12 financial year). This chapter was divided into distinct areas so as to produce a clear and detailed review of what homicides look like in Australia. The main factors associated with homicide, such as the victims' age, gender, ethnicity, and cause of death, were analyzed making empirical connections between them, the offenders, their sociodemographic situation, the reasons behind the violence, and the circumstances in which the crime occurred. Finally, the chapter reviewed the contextual and situational factors surrounding different cases and provided information on motive and behavior.

SUMMARY

- Men are overwhelmingly the offenders and victims in Australian homicides and, more often than not, they are known to each other.
- Homicide is a relatively rare event in Australia, with current data showing 264 victims in 2012. In 2013, global mortality data conservatively estimated that just under half a million people died in homicide-related incidences. Of this number, more than one-third of the violent deaths occurred in impoverished, developing countries. Even though levels of homicide in Australia are comparatively low in the global context, costs to the government, citizens and the nation overall are estimated to be around $1 billion annually.
- Violent deaths occur for many reasons, in general terms, homicide is perpetrated as a result of greed, passion, the effects of alcohol/illicit drug consumption, gender, ethnic and racial differences, religion, sexual property, social status, mental illness, and a need for power and control. Globally, there appears to be a shift in the type of homicide occurring within different countries, from intimate family-related homicides to stranger-, gang-, and organized crime–related deaths.
- Homicide should be seen within a social context, they are complex interactions between the perpetrator and victim, involving a physical altercation. The actual act includes a dynamic risk to all parties, the context leading up to the event, which goes to inform the context in which the homicide occurs.
- Situational contexts have changed little from the 1900s to 2000s, with the typical characteristics of a homicide event starting with an assault or sharp force trauma, committed by a single adult male known to the victim, and occurring within the context of an intraracial, intraage argument.
- Since 2000 there has been a steady increase in homicide incidents where multiple offenders are recorded with an instrumental motive, which has in turn increased acquaintance and stranger homicides. A homicide is instrumental if the immediate and primary goal is to obtain money or property and expressive if the offender's immediate and primary motive is to hurt the other person.

Expressive homicides are more prevalent than those categorized as instrumental. Expressive homicides typically commence with trivial altercations, victim precipitation, and the presence of alcohol.

- Domestic/intimate homicides: The perpetrator usually knows the victim, and in most cases there is a clear motive. The essence of the definition of domestic is a blood relation, as opposed to intimate where there is normally a sexual aspect to the relationship. Research states that the motive in this homicide typology is frequently based on factors such as anger, hate, jealously, rage, or revenge.
- Acquaintance homicide: An incident involving a victim and offender who were known to each other but who were not related to each other, nor living in a domestic relationship. These types of homicides usually involve contributing factors, such as arguments stemming from a verbal confrontation, where victim and/or perpetrator are under the influence of alcohol or illicit drugs and have "lost face" in front of peers.
- Stranger homicides: Stranger homicides often involve a co-committed crime that required extensive planning, such as a robbery/homicide. These types of crime are usually premeditated, with forensic awareness in some cases, such that the likelihood that physical evidence will be left behind for investigators to discover is decreased, reducing the potential solvability of the homicide.
- Even though the total number of homicides has decreased in Australia over the last 25 years, the number of stranger homicides have increased during the same period, altering the ratio of domestic to stranger homicides There is a similar trend in both the United States and United Kingdom.
- The populations with the greatest risk of homicide victimization are middle-aged men from minority groups.
- For several decades, the research between gender and homicide has shown that males commit between 85% and 90%; however; in case of filicide, women are equally likely as to be the perpetrator.
- Most studies examine gender differences with respect to particular variables, such as victim–offender relationships, motive, or age, rather than in the totality of combinations of offender, victim, and offense elements that define the basic structure of homicide situations. Theories of gender-based offender motivations tend to be nomothetic explanations for differences in prevalence across groups and contexts. When women are the offenders in a homicide, it is usually an act of infanticide or against an intimate partner, with their motive being self-protection or as a precipitating motive argumentative abuse.
- The rate of victimization in English-speaking countries is around 1.5 per 100,000 for males and 1.0 per 100,000 for females. These ratios are consistent across Australia, the United States, United Kingdom, Canada, and New Zealand.
- One in three Australian prisoners (34%) incarcerated for homicide offenses self-report addiction to alcohol, and almost half (44%) report being intoxicated at the time of their most serious offense. Evidence indicates that 42% of victims had consumed alcohol in the period immediately preceding their death.

- Indigenous Australians account for a disproportionately high number of both victims and offenders of homicide. Although Indigenous Australians represent approximately 2% of the total Australian population, they accounted for around 15% of homicide victims and almost 16% of homicide offenders over the 11-year period between July 1989 and June 2000.
- Female victims are more likely to have been killed as a result of a domestic argument, breakdown, or termination of their relationship. Males were more likely to have been victimized where motives were related to revenge, money, drugs, or alcohol-fueled arguments. In the majority of incidents, the motive either cannot be determined (~40%) or was attributed to an unspecified altercation, either related to an "other" argument (23%) or domestic circumstances (4%). In only a small number of incidents, the precipitating cause was able to be identified (e.g., alcohol-fueled argument, 4%; money, 9%; and revenge, 4%).
- Homicide is unique in terms of the nature of the crime, in particular the relationship between victim and offender. It is a crime that is most often committed against the offender's own circle of acquaintances. The homicide victim is typically an intimate of the offender, most commonly a family member or friend. Stranger-killings, so often portrayed in the media, account for less than one in five killings in Australia. Homicide, more than any other crime, frequently arises out of long and hostile interaction between victim and offender, rather than from a sudden unprovoked and premeditated action by an offender. It is perhaps this intimacy between victim and offender that explains why a proportion of homicide offenders commits suicide. In Australia, during 2010–12, 6% of homicide offenders committed suicide either as part of the homicide event or soon after.
- Many people who commit murder have never offended previously and are not likely to again. Moreover, few could be classed as "dangerous" or criminally insane. In all but ultra-rare cases, they have killed the one person they are ever likely to kill and are no longer dangerous. Many of those convicted of murder have no prior criminal history and previous convictions for violent offenses are uncommon. Furthermore, homicide offenders enjoy the lowest recidivism rate of any other class of violent offender.
- The three types of homicides that appear to be the most difficult to solve are those that are recorded as stranger homicides, gang/organized crime–related, and drug-related homicides. Moreover, homicides that occur during the committal of another crime are less likely to be solved. It can be argued that there are three distinct reasons for this phenomenon. First, offenders typically employ tactics such as witness intimidation and active obstruction, which impedes police investigations; second, organized crime or gang related homicides are often well planned and executed at a time and place of the offender's choosing, to minimize forensic opportunities for investigators; and third, when multiple crimes occur at the same time, such as a rape-homicide, then the crime scene may be more complex and include more forensic samples and therefore cross-contamination.

- During 2010–11 and 2011–12, the largest cause of death in Australia was stab wounds (37%), followed by beatings (24%), gunshot wounds (14%), strangulation/suffocation (7%), and smoke inhalation or burns (5%). Stab wounds were the most commonly recorded cause of death for both domestic and acquaintance homicides (42% and 39%, respectively).

QUESTIONS

1. In recent years, there has been a shift in homicide typologies. What is the shift, and what are the main causes?
2. Homicide has consequences that reach beyond the victim that are both tangible and intangible. Explain and give examples.
3. Explain the three categories of homicides.
4. Pinker (2011) purposed five reasons for a reduction in homicide rates. What are they?
5. Explain the Cinderella effect, as posited by Daly and Wilson (2001).
6. In Australia homicides, men aged 35–49 years are over represented as victims; provide some reasons for this phenomenon.
7. Research has shown that homicides committed in the commission of other offenses are less likely to be solved than those that occur in isolation. Provide reasons for this.
8. Parker (2016) identified seven fundamental motives; name them.
9. Explain what is meant by "expressive" homicides.
10. How does alcohol influence a person's behavior?

REFERENCES

Addington, L. A. (2006). Using national incident-based reporting system murder data to evaluate clearance predictors a research note. *Homicide Studies, 10*(2), 140–152.

Adjorlolo, S., & Chan, H. C. (2015). The nature of instrumentality and expressiveness of homicide crime scene behaviors: a review. *Trauma, Violence, & Abuse*, 391–400.

Alder, C. M., & Polk, K. (1996). Masculinity and child homicide. *British Journal of Criminology, 36*(3), 396–411.

Bijleveld, C., & Smit, P. (2006). Homicide in the Netherlands on the structuring of homicide typologies. *Homicide Studies, 10*(3), 195–219.

Browne, A., & Williams, K. R. (1993). Gender, intimacy, and lethal violence: trends from 1976 through 1987. *Gender and Society, 7*, 78–98.

Browne, A., Williams, K. R., & Dutton, D. G. (1999). Homicide between intimate partners: 20-year review. In M. D. Smith, & M. A. Zahn (Eds.), *Homicide: A sourcebook of social research* (pp. 149–164). Thousand Oaks, CA: Sage Publications.

Browne, K. D., & Lynch, M. A. (1995). The nature and extent of child homicide and fatal abuse. *Child Abuse Review, 4*(5), 309–316.

Bryant, W., & Cussen, T. (2015). *Homicide in Australia: 2010–12 national homicide monitoring program annual report, monitoring report no. 23*. Canberra: Australian Institute of Criminology, p. 29.

Burgess, R. L., & Drais, A. A. (1999). Beyond the "Cinderella effect". *Human Nature, 10*(4), 373.

Carcach, C., & Conroy, R. (2001). Alcohol and homicide: a routine activities analysis. In *Alcohol, young persons and violence. Research and public policy series* (35) (pp. 183–202).

Canadian Centre for Justice Statistics (CCJS) Policing Services Program. (2010). *Uniform crime reporting incident-based survey manual*. Ottawa: Statistics Canada.

Chan, A., & Payne, J. (2013). *National homicide monitoring program annual report: Homicide in Australia 2008–09 to 2009–10*. Canberra: Australian Institute of Criminology.

Comber, L. (2009). *The triads: Chinese secret societies in 1950s Malaya and Singapore*. United Kingdom: Whittles Publishing.

Coorg, R., & Tournay, A. (2013). Filicide-suicide involving children with disabilities. *Journal of Child Neurology, 28*(6), 742–748.

Craig, D. (1979). *The effects of state policy and queensland's laws on an aboriginal reserve: a look at Yarrabah*. In: AIAS Newsletter No. 11, March, pp. 69–71.

Crawford, C., & Krebs, D. (2008). *Foundations of evolutionary psychology*. New York: Lawrence Erlbaum Associates.

Crimes (domestic and personal violence) act 2007 No 80.

Cussen, T., & Bryant, W. (2015). *Domestic/family homicide in Australia. Research in practice no. 38*. Canberra: Australian Institute of Criminology.

Daly, M., & Wilson, M. (2001). An assessment of some proposed exceptions to the phenomenon of nepotistic discrimination against stepchildren. *Annales Zoologici Fennici, 38*, 287–296.

Darke, S., & Duflou, J. (2008). Toxicology and circumstances of death of homicide victims in New South Wales 1996–2005. *Journal of Forensic Sciences, 53*(2), 447–451.

Dearden, J., & Jones, W. (2008). *Homicide in Australia: 2006-07 National Homicide monitoring program annual report (Vol. 2)*. Australian Institute of Criminology.

Dingwall, G. (2006). *Alcohol and crime*. Devon, UK: Willan Publishing.

Douglas, J. E., & Munn, C. (February 1992). Violent crime scene analysis: modus operandi, signature, and staging. *FBI Law Enforcement Bulletin*, 1–10.

Felson, B., Teasdale, B., & Burchfield, K. B. (2008). The influence of being under the influence: alcohol effects on adolescent violence. *Journal of Research in Crime and Delinquency, 45*(2), 119–141.

Finn, P., & Healey, K. M. (1996). *Preventing gang- and drug-related witness intimidation*. Darby, PA: DIANE Publishing.

Fox, J. A., & Zawitz, M. W. (2011). *Homicide trends in the U.S.* Retrieved from http://bjs.ojp.usdoj.gov/content/homicide/homtrnd.cfm.

Francis, B., Barry, J., Bowater, R., Miller, N., Soothill, K., & Ackerley, E. (2004). *Using homicide data to assist homicide investigations, no. 26/04*. London: Home Office. Retrieved from http://eprints.lancs.ac.uk/9492/1/francishomicide2004.pdf.

Graham, K., & Homel, R. (2008). *Raising the bar: Preventing aggression in and around bars, pubs and clubs*. Cullompton, UK: Willan Publishing.

Graham, K., Wells, S., & West, P. (1997). A framework for applying explanations of alcohol-related aggression to naturally occurring aggressive behaviour. *Contemporary Drug Problems, 24*, 625–666.

Harne, L. (2011). *Violent fathering and the risks to children: The need for change*. Policy Press.

Harries, K. D. (1997). *Serious violence: Patterns of homicide and assault in America.* Springfield, IL: Charles C Thomas.

Harris, C. R. (2003). A review of sex differences in sexual jealousy, including self-report data, psychophysiological responses, interpersonal violence, and morbid jealousy. *Personality and Social Psychology Review, 7*(2), 102–128.

Harris, G. T., Hilton, N. Z., Rice, M. E., & Eke, A. W. (2007). Children killed by genetic parents versus stepparents. *Evolution and Human Behavior, 28*(2), 85–95.

Holmes, R. M., & De Burger, J. (1988). *Serial murder.* Thousand Oaks, CA: Sage Publications.

Holmes, R. M., & DeBurger, J. E. (1998). *Profiles in terror: The serial murderer. Contemporary perspectives on serial murder,* 5–16.

Homicide Victims' Support Group (Aust) Inc. (2013). *Intangible costs of homicide.*

Hrdy, D. B. (1977). Infanticide as a primate reproductive strategy. *American Scientist, 65*(1), 40–49.

Johnson, H., & Hotton, T. (2003). Losing control homicide risk in estranged and intact intimate relationships. *Homicide Studies, 7*(1), 58–84.

Kajese, T. M., Nguyen, L. T., Pham, G. Q., Pham, V. K., Melhorn, K., & Kallail, K. J. (2011). Characteristics of child abuse homicides in the state of Kansas from 1994 to 2007. *Child Abuse & Neglect, 35*(2), 147–154.

Kaplan, D. E., & Dubro, A. (2012). *Yakuza: Japan's criminal underworld.* Berkeley, CA: University of California Press.

Kelchner, T., & Kolnes, A. (2008). The first 48: homicide solvability factors that lead to rapid clearance. In *Proceedings of the ASC annual meeting, St. Louis Adam's Mark, St. Louis, Missouri, Nov 12,* pp. 37–46.

Keppel, R. D., & Walter, R. (1999). Profiling killers: a revised classification model for understanding sexual murder. *International Journal of Offender Therapy and Comparative Criminology, 43*(4), 417–437.

Keppel, R. D., & Weiss, J. G. (1992). *Improving the investigation of violent crime: The homicide investigation and tracking system (HITS).*

Koedam, W. S. (1993). Clinical considerations in treating participants in the federal witness protection program. *American Journal of Family Therapy, 21*(4), 361–368.

Lamont, A. (2011). *Child abuse and neglect statistics.* Australian Institute of Family Studies.

Langton, M. (1988). Medicine Square. In K. Keen (Ed.), *Being Black (pp. 201–225).* Canberra: Aboriginal Studies Press.

Levin, J., & Fox, J. A. (1996). Psycho-social analysis of mass murder. In T. O'Reilly-Fleming (Ed.), *From serial and mass murder: Theory, research and policy* (pp. 55–76) See NCJ-169306.

Lilly, J. R., Cullen, F. T., & Ball, R. A. (2014). *Criminological theory: Context and consequences.* Sage Publications.

Litwin, K. J. (2004). A multilevel multivariate analysis of factors affecting homicide clearances. *Journal of Research in Crime and Delinquency, 41,* 327–351.

Litwin, K. J., & Xu, Y. (2007). The dynamic nature of homicide clearances a multilevel model comparison of three time periods. *Homicide Studies, 11*(2), 94–114.

Lloyd, S. (1997). The effects of domestic violence on women's employment. *Law & Policy, 19*(2), 139–167.

Makkai, T., & Payne, J. (2003). *Key findings from the drug use careers of offenders (DUCO) study.* Trends & issues in crime and criminal justice no.267 http://www.aic.gov.au/publications/tandi2/tandi267.html.

Mayhew, P. (2003). *Counting the cost of crime in Australia.* Trends and issues in criminal justice, no. 247. Canberra: Australian Institute of Criminology.

McClellan, J. (2007). Unsolved homicides: what we do and do not know. *Journal of Security Education, 2*(3), 53–69.

McKee, A., & Egan, V. (2013). A case series of twenty-one maternal filicides in the UK. *Child Abuse & Neglect, 37*(10), 753–761.

McKinley, A.C. *Homicide solvability and applied victimology in New South Wales, 1994–2013.* Queensland: Bond University. [Unpublished Ph.D. thesis].

McLaughlin, H. (2001). Are we headed in the right direction? In G. Johns (Ed.), *Waking up to dreamtime: The illusion of Aboriginal self-determination* (pp. 125–151). Singapore: Media Masters.

Memmott, P., Stacy, R., Chambers, C., & Keys, C. (2001). *Violence in Indigenous communities, report to crime prevention Branch of the Attorney-General's Department.* Australia: Attorney-General's Department, Canberra.

Moffitt, T. E. (2001). *Sex differences in antisocial behaviour: Conduct disorder, delinquency, and violence in the Dunedin Longitudinal Study.* Cambridge University Press.

Morgan, A., & McAtamney, A. (2009). *Key issues in alcohol-related violence.* Research in practice no. 4. Canberra: Australian Institute of Criminology.

Mouzos, J. (1999). New statistics highlight high homicide rates for Indigenous women. *Indigenous Women and Law, 4*(25), 16–17.

Mouzos, J. (2001). *Indigenous and non-Indigenous homicides in Australia: A comparative analysis.* Trends and issues in crime and criminal justice, no. 210. Canberra: Australian Institute of Criminology.

Mouzos, J. (2003). *Homicide in the course of other crime in Australia.* Trends and issues in crime and criminal justice, no. 252. Canberra: Australian Institute of Criminology.

Mouzos, J., & Muller, D. (2001). *Solvability factors of homicide in Australia: An exploratory analysis.* Trends and issues in crime and criminal justice, no. 216. Canberra: Australian Institute of Criminology.

Mouzos, J., & Rushforth, C. (2003a). *Family homicide in Australia.* Trends & issues in crime & criminal justice no. 255. Canberra: Australian Institute of Criminology.

Mouzos, J., & Rushforth, C. (November 2003b). *Firearm related deaths in Australia, 1991–2001.* Trends & issues in crime and criminal justice no. 269. Canberra: Australian Institute of Criminology.

Mouzos, J., & Segrave, M. (2004). *Homicide in Australia: 2002–2003. National Homicide Monitoring Program (NHMP) annual report.* Canberra: Australian Institute of Criminology.

Neuilly, M. A., Zgoba, K. M., Tita, G. E., & Lee, S. S. (2011). Predicting recidivism in homicide offenders using classification tree analysis. *Homicide Studies, 15*(2), 154–176.

Nielssen, N., Large, M., Westmore, B., & Lackersteen, S. (2009). Child homicide in New South Wales from 1991 to 2005. *The Medical Journal of Australia, 190*(1), 7–11.

Paoli, L. (2003). *Mafia brotherhoods: Organized crime, Italian style.* Oxford University Press.

Parker, B. *The seven deadly Sins: The development of a qualitative understanding of homicide offender motive.* [Unpublished thesis].

Pinker, S. (2011). *The better angels of our nature: Why violence has declined.* Viking Books.

Polk, K. (1994). *When men kill: Scenarios of masculine violence.* Melbourne: Cambridge University Press.

Puckett, J. L., & Lundman, R. J. (2003). Factors affecting homicide clearances: multivariate analysis of a more complete conceptual framework. *Journal of Research in Crime and Delinquency, 40,* 171–193.

R v Burrell [2006] NSWSC 581, 9 August 2006, *Burrell and the Queen* [2009] NSWCCA 163, 17 June 2009, *R v* Burrell [No 3] [2008] NSWSC 30; 8 February 2008, *R v Burrell* [2009] NSWCCA 193.

R v Collisson [2002] NSWSC 229, 26 March 2002; *R v Bradley* [2002] NSWSC 1018, 1 November 2002 and *R v Collisson* [2003] NSWCCA 212, 29 July 2003.

R v Darwiche & Others [2006] NSWSC 1167; 10 November 2006, *R v Darwiche & Others* [2006] NSWSC 924; NSWSC 926; NSWSC 927; 19 April 2006; *R v Darwiche & Others* [2011] NSWCCA 62, 8 April 2011.

R v Dean [2013] NSWSC 1027, NSW Supreme Court, Latham J, 1 August 2013.

R v Gittany [2013] NSWSC 1503.

R v Harding [2013] NSWSC 513.

R v Loveridge [2013] NSWSC 1638, 8 November 2013, *R v Loveridge* [2014] NSWCCA 120, 4 July 2014).

R v Mulvihill [2014] NSWSC 443).

R v Murdoch [2005] NTSC 75, NTSC 76, NTSC 80.

R v Walsh [2009] NSWSC 764.

Regoeczi, W. C., Kennedy, L. W., & Silverman, R. A. (2000). Uncleared homicide: a Canada/United States comparison. *Homicide Studies*, *4*(2), 135–161.

Regoeczi, W. C., & Miethe, T. D. (2003). Taking on the unknown: a qualitative comparative analysis of unknown relationship homicides. *Homicide Studies*, *7*(3), 211–234.

Richardson, D. A., & Kosa, R. (2001). *An examination of homicide clearance rates: Foundation for the development of a homicide clearance model*. Washington, DC: Police Executive Research Forum.

Roach, J. (2011). Evolution and the prevention of violent crime. *Psychology*, *02*(4), 393–404.

Salfati, C. G. (2000). The nature of expressiveness and instrumentality in homicides: implications for offender profiling. *Homicide Studies*, *4*(3), 265–293.

Salfati, C. G., & Haratsis, E. (2001). Greek homicide: a behavioural examination of offender crime-scene actions. *Homicide Studies*, *5*, 335–362.

Schmidt, P. H., Padosch, S. A., Rothschild, M. A., & Madea, B. (2005). Forensic case profiling aspects on multiple homicides from the Cologne–Bonn Metropolitan Area 1985–2000. *Forensic Science International*, *153*(2), 168–173.

Shackelford, T. K., & Mouzos, J. (2005). Partner killing by men in cohabiting and marital relationships: a comparative, cross-national analysis of data from Australia and the United States. *Journal of Interpersonal Violence*, *20*(10), 1310–1324.

Simpson, A. I., Mckenna, B., Moskowitz, A., Skipworth, J., & Barry-Walsh, J. (2004). Homicide and mental illness in New Zealand, 1970–2000. *The British Journal of Psychiatry*, *185*(5), 394–398.

Smith, M. D., & Zahn, M. A. (Eds.). (1999). *Homicide: A sourcebook of social research*. London: Sage Publications, pp. 3–8.

Stöckl, H., Devries, K., Rotstein, A., Abrahams, N., Campbell, J., Watts, C., et al. (2013). The global prevalence of intimate partner homicide: a systematic review. *Lancet*, *382*(9895), 859–865.

Strang, H. (1996). *Children as victims of homicide* (vol. 53). Australian Institute of Criminology.

Temrin, H., Buchmayer, S., & Enquist, M. (2000). Step-parents and infanticide: new data contradict evolutionary predictions. *Proceedings of the Royal Society B: Biological Sciences*, *267*(1446), 943.

Tita, G., & Griffiths, E. (2005). Traveling to violence: the case for a mobility-based spatial typology of homicide. *Journal of Research in Crime and Delinquency*, *42*(3), 275–308.

Tooley, G., Karakis, M., Stokes, M., & Ozannesmith, J. (2006). Generalising the Cinderella Effect to unintentional childhood fatalities. *Evolution and Human Behavior, 27,* 224–230.

Thomson, D. F. (1935). The joking relationship and organised obscenity in North Queensland. *American Anthropologist, 37.*

Turvey, B. E. (2011). *Criminal profiling: An introduction to behavioral evidence analysis.* Academic press.

UNICEF. (2014). *Hidden in plain sight: A statistical analysis of violence against children* New York, NY: Author.

United Nations Office on Drugs and Crime (UNODC). (2014). *World drug report.* https://www.unodc.org/documents/wdr2014/World_Drug_Report_2014_web.pdf.

Virueda, M., & Payne, J. (2010). *Homicide in Australia: 2007–08 national homicide monitoring program annual report, monitoring report no. 13.* Canberra: Australian Institute of Criminology.

Voss, H. L., & Hepburn, J. R. (1968). Patterns in criminal homicide in Chicago. *The Journal of Criminal Law, Criminology, and Police Science, 59*(4), 499–508.

Weekes-Shackelford, V. A., & Shackelford, T. K. (2004). Methods of filicide: stepparents and genetic parents kill differently. *Violence and Victims, 19*(1), 75–81.

Wellford, C., & Cronin, J. (1999). *An analysis of variables affecting the clearance of homicides: A multi-state study.* Washington, DC: Justice Research and Statistics Association.

Wellford, C., & Cronin, J. (2000). Clearing up homicide clearance rates. *National Institute of Justice Journal, 243,* 2–7.

Wilczynski, A. (1995). Child killing by parents: a motivational model. *Child Abuse Review, 4*(5), 365–370.

Wolfgang, M. (1958). *Patterns in criminal homicide.* Philadelphia: University of Pennsylvania Press.

Yampolskaya, S., Greenbaum, P. E., & Berson, I. R. (2009). Profiles of child maltreatment perpetrators and risk for fatal assault: a latent class analysis. *Journal of Family Violence, 24*(5), 337–348.

Zahn, M. A., & McCall, P. L. (1999). Trends and patterns of homicide in the 20th century. In M. D. Smith, & M. A. Zahn (Eds.), *Homicide: A sourcebook of social research.* London: Sage Publication.

Victims of Child Sexual Abuse: The Psychology of Victims

14

Larissa Christensen

Griffith University, Gold Coast, QLD, Australia

CHAPTER OUTLINE

INTRODUCTION

Child sexual abuse (CSA) encompasses a wide variety of sexual behaviors including penetration of the vagina or anus (by a penis, finger, or any object), oral sex, touching of the breasts or genitals, masturbation, exhibitionism (exposing oneself), voyeurism (spying/watching), exposing a child to or involving a child in pornography, and soliciting a child to engage in sexual activity. The current chapter begins by highlighting the difficulties in defining and conceptualizing CSA. This is followed by a review of the international literature on the prevalence of CSA, the characteristics often associated with victims of CSA, common misconceptions surrounding CSA, and the reasons why many children delay or do not disclose the abuse. The chapter will conclude with the short- and long-term outcomes for victims of CSA.

The Psychology of Criminal and Antisocial Behavior. http://dx.doi.org/10.1016/B978-0-12-809287-3.00014-6

DIFFICULTIES DEFINING AND CONCEPTUALIZING CHILD SEXUAL ABUSE

There are many definitions for child sexual abuse, varying by location. Goldman and Goldman (1988) defined CSA as a form of exploitation or sexual abuse performed by an offender who is at least 5 years older than the child (who is under the age of 18 years). In contrast, in New Zealand, CSA is defined as sexual behavior in which an adult, or a more powerful individual, involves a child in sexual acts or behaviors (Best Practice Advocacy Centre New Zealand, 2015). Different again, The Children's Bureau of the United States Department of Health and Human Services (2013) defined CSA as involving a child in sexual activity for the sexual or financial benefit of the perpetrator. Other definitions have taken a developmental perspective (see Kempe & Kempe, 1978).

In addition to the many definitions of CSA are the various age of consent laws. Essentially, age of consent dictates the age at which an individual is identified as able to give informed consent to engage in sexual activity (Australian Institute of Family Studies, 2014). It is irrelevant if the child perceives the sexual activity to be consensual, if a person engages in sexual activity with a child who is under the age of consent, a criminal offense (child sexual abuse) has been committed. Age of consent laws differ across countries. In Peru, the age of consent for sexual activity is 14 years, while in South Africa the age of consent for sexual activity is 16 years. Different again, in Ireland, the age of consent for sexual activity is 17 years. Notably, in Saudi Arabia, the couple must be married to engage in sexual activity, with homosexual intercourse being illegal and punishable by death.

The disparity in age of consent laws is also evident *within* countries. While most states and territories in Australia have the age of consent for sexual activity as 16 years, the age of consent in South Australia and Tasmania is 17 years. Further, Queensland is the only state in Australia that has different age of consent laws for various forms of sexual activity; the age of consent for anal intercourse is 18 years while the age of consent for other forms of sexual activity is 16 years. The disparity in age of consent laws is evident within the United States of America. Some states have a standard age of consent of 16 (e.g., New Jersey), 17 (e.g., New York), or 18 years (e.g., California) regardless of the gender involved. In other states, age of consent for homosexual activity is older. In both Nevada and New Hampshire, the age of consent for heterosexual activity is 16 years while the age of consent for homosexual activity is 18 years.

PREVALENCE OF CHILD SEXUAL ABUSE

Prevalence rates of child sexual abuse refers to the amount of individuals who were victimized during childhood. Prevalence rates are important to explore as they allow researchers and clinicians to understand how widespread CSA is over time. In one study, Pérez-Fuentes et al. (2013) used a large national sample in the United States that involved over 34,000 adults aged 18 years and older. They surveyed participants about any adverse sexual activity experienced in their first 17 years of life. Pérez-Fuentes et al. (2013) calculated a weighted prevalence of 10.14%; that is, the prevalence for CSA was 101 out of 1000 individuals. Pérez-Fuentes et al. (2013) concluded that the prevalence rate for child sexual abuse is high.

Stoltenborgh, van IJzendoorn, Euser, and Bakermans-Kranenburg (2011) conducted a meta-analysis on 217 publications involving 9,911,748 participants published between 1982 and 2008. The studies involved victims who were sexually abused before the age of 18 and covered samples from Australia, New Zealand, North America, South America, Asia, Europe, and Africa. Stoltenborgh et al. calculated a global prevalence of 11.8%; that is, 118 out of 1000 individuals were victims of CSA. They concluded that CSA is a problem of considerable magnitude across the globe.

COMMON CHARACTERISTICS OF CHILD SEXUAL ABUSE VICTIMS

While any child can potentially fall victim to child sexual abuse, a number of characteristics have been found to be commonly associated with victims of CSA. These characteristics include: victim gender, the victim's relationship to the perpetrator, and the type of abuse endured. For victim gender, research has found that females are more likely to be victims of CSA than males. Stoltenborgh et al. (2011) found a much higher prevalence rate among females than males for self-report studies: 180 out of 1000 females (18%) and 76 out of 1000 males (7.6%). These findings were consistent with Pereda, Guilera, Forns, and Gómez-Benito (2009) who conducted a meta-analysis on 65 articles covering 22 countries regarding CSA prior to the age of 18. Pereda et al. (2009) found that females were more likely to have suffered CSA (19.7%) than males (7.9%). These findings were consistent with other studies that have found females to be two to three times more likely to be victims of CSA than males (e.g., Barth, Bermetz, Heim, Trelle, & Tonia, 2012; Pérez-Fuentes et al., 2013).

The victim's relationship to the perpetrator also appears to be associated with CSA. The research indicates that a substantial amount of abuse is committed by someone known, often related, to the child. The Australian Personal Safety Survey found that the most common perpetrator of CSA was a male relative (other than the victim's father/stepfather; 30.2% of perpetrators), followed by a family friend (16.3%), an acquaintance or neighbor (15.6%), another known person (15.3%), the victim's father/stepfather (13.5%), and a stranger (11.1%; Australian Bureau of Statistics, 2005).[1] All remaining categories were below 1.0% (e.g., the victim's mother).

Similar findings are evident in developing countries. Mwangi et al. (2015) administered a survey on violence in Kenya with a sample comprising 2683 respondents aged 13–24 years. Of the younger respondents (13–17 years), over 78% of victims reported that they knew the perpetrator of sexual touching and over 90% knew the perpetrator of physically forced sex. Of the older respondents (18–24 years) who experienced CSA

---

[1] These figures do not add to 100%; this is because more than one perpetrator may have taken part in the abuse.

before the age of 18, over 91% reported that they knew the perpetrator of sexual touching and 95.3% of females knew the perpetrator of physically forced sex.[2]

Finally, some types of child sexual abuse are more prevalent than others. The literature suggests that CSA victims are more likely to endure nonpenetrative abuse than penetrative abuse. Published data over 4 years in New South Wales, Australia, from 1994 to 1995 and 1997 to 1998 indicated that the most prevalent type of abuse was nonpenetrative, specifically, touching (average=22.3%). This type of abuse was followed by vaginal penetration (16.2%), digital stimulation (fingers inserted into the vagina or anus; 8.8%), indecent assault (7.7%), anal penetration (5.8%), attempted abuse (any type; 5.8%), masturbation on victim (3.8%), fellatio on abuser (3.7%), masturbation on abuser (2.5%), fellatio on victim (2.0%), cunnilingus on victim (1.7%), and exposure to pornography (1.6%; see Table 3.14, Australian Bureau of Statistics, 2004). All remaining categories were below 1.0%. In a different study, Barth et al. (2012) found the highest prevalence estimates of CSA were for noncontact abuse (e.g., indecent exposure), followed by mixed sexual abuse (for example, various types of abuse or abuse not specified), contact abuse (e.g., fondling), and finally, forced intercourse (e.g., attempted, oral, vaginal, or anal intercourse). These findings were similar to Mohler-Kuo et al. (2014) who utilized an epidemiological survey on 6787 ninth-grade students in Switzerland. From the self-report questionnaires, Mohler-Kuo et al. (2014) found that most CSA victims endured noncontact offences, followed by contact without penetration, and finally, penetration.

MISCONCEPTIONS OF CHILD SEXUAL ABUSE

There are a number of common misconceptions held surrounding child sexual abuse. These include that children are unreliable witnesses, anatomically correct dolls are effective to use during interviews with children, and CSA is commonly diagnosable through genital examinations. In terms of the misconception that children are unreliable witnesses, historically, in Australia, common law considered children to be unreliable witnesses who could affect jurors' evaluations of the evidence (Australian Law Reform Commission, report 114, 2010). The widespread view of children was that they were incapable to decipher fantasy from reality. Judges were required to warn juries about the reliability of children's evidence (Australian Law Reform Commission, report 114, 2010). Similarly, in North America, judges would give cautionary instructions to juries to consider the child's testimony with care. However, research has since found that children are capable of providing forensically relevant accounts (Ceci & Bruck, 1993) that are accurate and detailed (Klemfuss & Ceci, 2012).

Rather, one of the main issues surrounding the reliability of children is their proneness to suggestibility when being questioned by their parents or even by professionals (e.g., police, child protection, medical professionals, defense attorneys).

[2] Mwangi et al. (2015) did not provide the percentage for male respondents who were victim of physically forced sex due to the small subsample.

Suggestibility is defined as "the degree to which children's encoding, storage, retrieval, and reporting of events can be influenced by a range of social and psychological factors" (Ceci & Bruck, 1993, p. 404). Suggestive questioning has the potential to taint the child's memory, particularly in younger children. Such questioning is problematic because the child may change their account either by acquiescing to the interviewer's questions (such as agreeing with an interviewer's suggestion out of a perceived pressure to conform) or integrate suggested information into their memories (such as accepting suggested information to fill in missing events; Ceci & Bruck, 1993). Suggestive questioning includes the use of: yes/no questions (e.g., "Did Uncle Johnny touch your doodle?"), selective reinforcement (that is, providing confirmatory feedback to certain responses), repetitious questioning (this may lead the child to believe that their previous response was incorrect), forced choice questioning ("Did Uncle Johnny touch your doodle *or* your bum?"), and misleading questioning (e.g., "Did Uncle Johnny make your sister take her clothes off too?").

Oddly, the attacks on the competency and reliability of children have, in fact, had positive effects. In particular, research has developed specialist interviewing protocols in order to prevent suggestibility and enhance the quality and amount of information elicited from the child during the interview (see Sternberg et al., 1997). This research has found—in contrast to the historical views once held in the judicial system—that children are able to encode and retrieve great amounts of information (Ceci & Bruck, 1993). In fact, children (including preschoolers) are able to accurately recall forensically relevant information in the absence of suggestive techniques (Bruck & Ceci, 1999). From this research, it appears that the reliability of children's reports rest more in the hands of the interviewer's skill than to any limitations in the child's memory (Bruck & Ceci, 1999).

A second common misconception is that anatomically correct dolls are effective to use during interviews with children. The use of anatomical dolls is one of the most contentious practices discussed in the literature for interviewing victims of CSA (Cronch, Viljoen, & Hansen, 2006). Anatomical dolls come in a variety of shapes, sizes, and colors; some dolls are Cabbage Patch dolls with sewn on genitals while others are specially made with vaginal, anal, and mouth openings (Boat & Everson, 1988). Anatomical dolls were widely used in the 1980s and 90s. For example, Boat and Everson (1988) found that of 295 professionals in North Carolina, 68% of child protection workers, 28% of mental health professionals, and 35% of law enforcement officers were using the dolls in CSA evaluations. They also found that 94% of child protection workers, 67% of mental health professionals, and 46% of law enforcement officers reported that they would be using the dolls within the next year. In a different study, Conte, Sorenson, Fogarty, and Rosa (1991) found that of 212 professionals, 92% responded that they utilized anatomical dolls in CSA evaluations.

There are a number of reasons why anatomical dolls were once believed to be effective when interviewing suspected victims of CSA. For example, Everson and Boat (1994) found the two most common uses of anatomical dolls in CSA evaluations were first as demonstration aids and secondly as anatomical models. In terms of demonstration aids, it was argued that the dolls served as props, allowing children to "show" as opposed to "tell" the abuse, especially when children were embarrassed, fearful, or did not have the verbal skills to provide a description (Everson & Boat, 1994). For anatomical models, it was suggested that the dolls were used to assess the names the child would allocate to different body parts, gauge the child's understanding of bodily functions, and identify the child's knowledge on the process of sexual intercourse (Everson & Boat, 1994). Essentially, such props were thought to assist children in bridging the gap between what the child knew (what had happened to them) and what they could articulate (or what they were willing to articulate; Poole & Bruck, 2012).

There are many reasons why anatomical dolls are ineffective when interviewing suspected victims of CSA. These reasons include the issue of symbolic representation and the quality of children's responses during interviews. First, some children have issues correctly reporting touches on dolls because of their poor symbolic representation. Symbolic representation is particularly an issue for very young children (i.e., under the age of four) as they cannot understand the self-representational nature of the dolls (DeLoache & Marzolf, 1995)—that the dolls are supposed to signify symbols of their own body (Dickinson, Poole, & Bruck, 2005). These young children fail to appreciate the symbol-referent relationship of the symbol to themselves (DeLoache & Marzolf, 1995). Even of the young children who are capable of dual representation, these children need to mentally sustain awareness on the symbolic purpose of such dolls and not go off topic (e.g., play with the doll; Dickinson et al., 2005).

For quality of responses, a number of studies have found that anatomical dolls decreased the quality of children's responses during interviews. For example, Bruck, Ceci, and Francoeur (2000) studied the influence of anatomical dolls on 3- and 4-year-olds' reports of a routine medical exam—there was no suspicion or knowledge that any child had ever been sexually abused. Children were randomly assigned to a nongenital examination or a genital examination. They were interviewed immediately after their examination and were asked to demonstrate certain events on an anatomical doll and on their own bodies. Bruck et al. (2000) found that for females, commission errors (i.e., false claims of touching) were more common when dolls were utilized; for example, some children incorrectly demonstrated insertions into the genital or anal cavity. Bruck et al. (2000) concluded that anatomical dolls should not be utilized in interviews with children younger than 5 years of age.

In a different study, Santtila, Korkman, and Sandnabba (2004) examined 27 transcribed forensic interviews with suspected victims of CSA in Finland. When compared to the children who did not have anatomical dolls present during their interviews, the children with anatomical dolls present gave shorter responses, provided fewer details, and the interviewer asked longer questions. Santtila et al. (2004) concluded that the dolls were unlikely to be an efficient tool. These findings were consistent with Lamb, Hershkowitz, Sternberg, Boat, and Everson (1996) who found that children interviewed with dolls provided responses that were shorter and less detailed than responses provided by children who were interviewed without dolls.

In a different study, Thierry, Lamb, Orbach, and Pipe (2005) examined the use of anatomical dolls on reports given by 3- to 12-year-olds who were suspected victims of CSA. While younger children (3- to 6-year-olds) were more likely to contradict details and play suggestively with the dolls than older children (7- to 12-year-olds), overall, regardless of the age group, children produced proportionally more fantasy details when the dolls were present. Thierry et al. (2005) concluded that other interview techniques that excluded anatomical dolls were just as effective and less risky.

In light of the growing concern of anatomical dolls, the use of anatomical drawings became popular as it was believed that drawings were less likely to elicit fantasy play and exploration. Willcock, Morgan, and Hayne (2006) assessed the abilities of 5- to 6-year-olds to use anatomical drawings to report where they were touched by a confederate. The authors found that the children's reports were inaccurate or incomplete when the anatomical drawings were used (in comparison with children's reports in the standard verbal interview). Willcock et al. (2006) concluded that anatomical drawings do not facilitate children's reports of touch and should not be used in interviews with children of such an age. Similarly, Bruck (2009) assessed whether the addition of anatomical drawings to interviews would increase errors or accuracy for 3- to 7-year-olds. While children had poor recall of the touches regardless of their group (anatomical drawing used versus no anatomical drawing used), children in the anatomical drawing group produced more errors than the nonanatomical drawing group. Bruck (2009) concluded that anatomical drawings do not assist children to provide accurate reports. Also, Poole and Dickinson (2011) found that such drawings increased the amount of false reports of touching. One reason for why children may have difficulty correctly reporting touches on drawings again stems back to their poor symbolic representation of the concept (particularly for younger children).

A third common misconception is that CSA is commonly diagnosable through genital examinations. Over the past decades, the reported rates of abuse-supportive genital findings have been declining. In the 1980s, the rate of abuse-supportive findings was high, spanning from 50% to 90% of children who were referred for examination due to suspected abuse (e.g., Cantwell, 1983). In the 1990s, this number dropped to 15–20% (e.g., Kellogg, Parra, & Menard, 1998). Since 2000, the rate of abuse-supportive findings has fallen to below 4% (e.g., Berenson et al., 2000). It has been suggested that genital findings, which were once believed to be diagnostic of penetration, have since been discovered to occur in nonabused children (Pillai, 2005). Therefore, other reasons for such genital findings cannot be ruled out (Berenson et al., 2000; Heger, Ticson, Velasquez, & Bernier, 2002).[3] For example, redness of the genital area may be due to dermatitis; tearing of the anus can be caused by constipation; genital warts in young children may be from caretaking activities or perinatal exposure (Adams, 2011).

In one study, Modelli, Galvão, and Pratesi (2012) used a retrospective analysis of 1762 children suspected to be victim of CSA that were examined in the pediatric

---

[3] However, a lack of physical evidence does not prove that CSA did not occur as abuse-supportive findings are rare.

population of the Federal District (Brazil) between 2008 and 2009. They found that around 90% of victims did not show evidence of physical damage. Of the females examined, about 2.1% showed abuse-supportive findings for suspected rape and 5.3% for libidinous acts (e.g., fondling and biting). Of the males examined for libidinous acts, abuse-supportive findings were found in 9.6% of cases.[4] Modelli et al. (2012) concluded that physical signs should not be the only indicator used when evaluating CSA as physical signs are difficult to recognize.

There are two main reasons for why physical signs of CSA are difficult to recognize. First, the perpetrator is generally someone the child knows whose interest is not to hurt the child (that is, to not violently penetrate the child), but rather, to have continued access to the child (avoiding the detection of abuse by others). Second, due to the delay in the child disclosing the abuse, superficial lesions are given time to heal (Modelli et al., 2012). For example, McCann, Miyamoto, Boyle, and Rogers (2007) studied the healing process of nonhymenal genital injuries in 239 prepubertal and pubertal girls (aged 4 months to 18 years). They found that most contusions and abrasions healed within just days. Deep lacerations required only up to 20 days to heal. McCann et al. (2007) concluded that such genital injuries leave little to any evidence. They recommended that children should be examined as soon as there is suspicion of CSA due to the rapid healing of such injuries.

WHY MANY CHILDREN DELAY OR DO NOT DISCLOSE SEXUAL ABUSE

The detection of CSA is often very difficult as CSA rarely leaves any physical signs and often has no witnesses due to the insidious behavior of the perpetrator (Hershkowitz, Lanes, & Lamb, 2007). In turn, the child's disclosure is often central to the abuse being discovered as well as for the commencement of legal and therapeutic intervention (Paine & Hansen, 2002). While society would like to think that children who are being sexually abused would disclose the abuse to someone the child trusted, this is not always the case. In fact, lengthy delays and nondisclosures are very common. For example, Kogan (2004) found that of a subsample of 263 adolescent females who took part in a survey, 19% delayed disclosure for longer than one year and 26% had not disclosed prior to the survey. In a different study, involving a sample of adult women sexually victimized as children, Smith et al. (2000) found that 47% of the women delayed disclosure for more than 5 years and 28% had not disclosed prior to the survey. Smith et al. (2000) concluded that long delays of disclosure are very common.

One major reason for the nondisclosure or long delay of disclosure for CSA is due to the grooming process, which plays a major role in the preparatory stage of sexual abuse. Grooming is a type of emotional seduction in which the perpetrator uses trust and affection to interact and manipulate the victim (Salter, 1995). Some perpetrators will also skillfully establish a friendship with the victim's parents—essentially

---

[4] Modelli et al. (2012) did not provide the percentage of males who had abuse-supportive findings for suspected rape.

grooming the victim's family—to gain easy access to the victim; that is, the victim's parents trust the perpetrator and allow for the perpetrator to have unsupervised access to the victim. Due to the established friendship with the victim's family, this makes it difficult for the victim to understand that the situation is abusive (Paine & Hansen, 2002). Institutional grooming may also occur; this is where the individual's job and status in society easily allows for deception (Mcalinden, 2006). In fact, perpetrators often have good social skills and advanced deception skills that allow them to play a double role in the community, thereby avoiding suspicion.

The perpetrator cultivates a "special" relationship with the victim, by offering the victim a number of inducements such as material items and privileges (such as toys) or even affection (the victim may have emotionally detached parents and instead receive most attention and affection from the perpetrator; Paine & Hansen, 2002). This enables the perpetrator to control the victim by not only giving inducements but also by threatening to take away such inducements. Threats may also include physical harm or punishment. For example, the perpetrator may threaten to hurt the victim or victim's parents if the victim was to disclose the abuse (Kaufman, Hilliker, & Daleiden, 1996). The perpetrator may also suggest that no one would believe the victim and that the victim would be called a liar if he or she were to tell anyone. Essentially, the perpetrator suggests that the only thing keeping the victim and his or her family safe is the victim keeping the abuse a secret (Summit, 1983).

There are a number of characteristics associated with the victim's disclosure, including the victim's gender, the victim's age, and the victim's relationship to the perpetrator. For victim gender, research has consistently found that male victims of CSA were less likely to disclose the abuse than female victims (Leclerc & Wortley, 2015; Priebe & Svedin, 2008; Tang, Freyd, & Wang, 2007; Ullman & Filipas, 2005). For example, Tang et al. (2007) reviewed disclosure rates of both retrospective and prospective studies and found that males were significantly less likely to disclose sexual abuse than females. In a different study, Priebe and Svedin (2008) found that of 1962 surveyed adolescents who reported CSA, nearly 20% of females and nearly 40% of males had not previously told anyone about the abuse. Romano and De Luca (2001) suggested that male victims disclose less than females due to the socialization that it is not masculine to seek help or the fear of being viewed as a homosexual if abused by a male perpetrator. Other reasons included a male's fear of losing his freedom if he disclosed the abuse (e.g., his parent's implementing firm supervision) or that he perceived that he desired the abuse through visible physiological responses (e.g., erection, ejaculation; Romano & De Luca, 2001).

For victim age, research has found victim disclosure to decrease with the age of the victim (Hershkowitz, Horowitz, & Lamb, 2005; Leclerc & Wortley, 2015; Pipe, Lamb, Orbach, & Cederborg, 2007). For example, Hershkowitz et al. (2005) found the age group with the greatest disclosure rate was 11–14-year-olds (82%) as opposed to 7–10-year-olds (72%) and 3–6-year-olds (48%). Similarly, Pipe et al. (2007) found the age group with the greatest disclosure rate was 9–13-year-olds (85%), followed by 6–8-year-olds (76%) and 4–5-year-olds (63%). One reason for why younger children were less likely to disclose was because they did not understand that the abuse was wrong (that such behavior constitutes abuse; Goodman-Brown, Edelstein, Goodman, Jones, & Gordon, 2003), whereas older children were better able to identify that the experience was abusive. A second reason for why younger children were less likely to disclose was because they were more vulnerable to the perpetrator's strategies for maintaining compliance and secrecy (Kogan, 2004).

In terms of the victim's relationship to the perpetrator, research has found that victims of intrafamilial abuse (that perpetrated by a family member) were less likely to disclose (or more likely to delay their disclosure) than victims of extrafamilial abuse (i.e., abuse perpetrated by a nonfamily member; e.g., family friend, neighbor, stranger; Goodman-Brown et al., 2003; Hershkowitz et al., 2007; Kogan, 2004; Smith et al., 2000). For example, Hershkowitz et al. (2007) found that most victims who were related to the perpetrator delayed their disclosure (78%) whereas only 17% of victims delayed their disclosure when the perpetrator was a stranger. Similarly, Smith et al. (2000) found that an intrafamilial relationship with the perpetrator was associated with lengthier delays, whereas no relationship to the perpetrator was associated with more rapid disclosure. One suggestion for why victims of intrafamilial abuse had lengthier delays of disclosure is because they experienced greater emotional conflict when deciding to disclose compared to victims of extrafamilial abuse. This is because these victims often feared the impact the disclosure would have on the family (for example, fear of breaking the family apart) or concerns of disloyalty toward one's own family member (Pipe et al., 2007).

SHORT- AND LONG-TERM OUTCOMES FOR CHILD SEXUAL ABUSE VICTIMS

Over the past two decades, there has been considerable research on the outcomes for victims of CSA (see Maniglio, 2009). The short- and long-term outcomes of CSA can vary from no obvious effects on the victim to very severe effects. The effects of CSA are not purely psychological but can also include physical, cognitive, social, and behavioral effects (Perry, Pollard, Blakley, Baker, & Vigilante, 1995). For example, in terms of physical effects, the stress endured in childhood from the abuse may disturb the neuroendocrine system as well as the sympathetic nervous system. Such disturbances can impact other systems in the body, potentially resulting in health problems such as cardiopulmonary and gynecological symptoms, obesity, and pain (Shonkoff, Boyce, & McEwen, 2009). However, most of the research has focused on the psychological effects of CSA.

CSA is a suggested risk factor to a wide array of mental health disorders in later life (Australian Psychological Society, 2013). Such disorders include somatoform conditions, depression, eating disorders, posttraumatic stress disorder (PTSD), anxiety, and sexual dysfunction (Bremner, 2003). Interestingly, a number of characteristics have been identified as being related to the short- and long-term outcomes of CSA. These characteristics include: victim gender, victim age, victim relationship to perpetrator, abuse severity, and maternal support. In terms of victim gender, research has found short-term outcomes to differ between male and female victims.

The research has found that female victims were more likely to display internalizing outcomes (such as depressive symptoms and submissive behaviors) whereas male victims were more likely to display externalizing outcomes (such as substance abuse, aggressive behaviors, and conduct problems; Gault-Sherman, Silver, & Sigfúsdóttir, 2009; Kendall-Tackett, Williams, & Finkelhor, 1993). The research has not found a relationship between victim gender and long-term outcomes (Fergusson, Boden, & Horwood, 2008; Fergusson, McLeod, & Horwood, 2013).

For victim age, research has found different outcomes for victims depending on the age of their first experience of CSA. In terms of short-term outcomes, victims who experienced abuse at a younger age were more likely to display symptoms of PTSD, whereas victims who experienced abuse at an older age were more likely to display depressive symptoms (Gries et al., 2000). Gries et al. (2000) suggested that younger children experienced PTSD because they were concerned about future victimization attempts whereas older children experienced depressive symptoms due to the abuse happening during a time (of pubescent and postpubescent sexuality) when they were gaining their sexual identity. In terms of long-term outcomes, the research has found that victims who were older at their first abusive experience tended to have more negative outcomes than victims who were younger at their first abusive experience. For example, Cutajar et al. (2010) studied forensic medical records of 2759 sexually abused children evaluated between 1964 and 1995 and linked these individuals to a public psychiatric database from 12 to 43 years later. Cutajar et al. (2010) found that victims who were older at the time of abuse had a greater risk for psychopathology. Cutajar et al. (2010) suggested that individuals who were abused during pubertal years whilst still undergoing sexual development held a greater understanding that such behavior constituted gross violations of sexual boundaries than victims who were younger at the time of abuse.

In terms of the victim's relationship to the perpetrator, research has found different outcomes depending on the victim's relationship; overall, a closer relationship between the victim and perpetrator is associated with more adverse outcomes (Putnam, 2003; Trickett, Noll, Reiffman, & Putnam, 2001; Tyler, 2002). For short-term outcomes, Trickett et al. (2001) found CSA perpetrated by a biological father showed the most extreme pattern of behavioral problems and maladjustment in comparison to those who had not been abused by a biological father (even of those victims who had multiple perpetrators). Trickett et al. (2001) suggested that this is because the role of the father is to protect the child and, in turn, sexual abuse is an extreme betrayal of such a role. In terms of long-term outcomes, Ullman (2007) examined the victim–perpetrator relationship and PTSD in adult survivors of CSA and found those abused by a relative reported more PTSD symptoms in comparison to those abused by a nonrelative. Ullman (2007) used Freyd (1996) betrayal trauma theory to suggest that it was more harmful to the victim's psychological symptomatology when the abuse was perpetrated by someone the child was dependent on (e.g., a relative) as it violated such trust as opposed to someone with whom the child was not close to.

Abuse severity has been found to be a characteristic associated with both short- and long-term victim outcomes; overall, more severe abuse is associated with more adverse outcomes. In terms of short-term outcomes, Gries et al. (2000) found that children victimized by the most severe forms of CSA (e.g., vaginal or anal penetration) were found to report significantly higher scores on depression than victims who experienced less severe forms of CSA (exposure to pornography and fondling among others). Gries et al. (2000) suggested that in cases of penetration, where the child's body was grossly violated, the child felt a greater sense of powerlessness and helplessness realizing that they cannot even control who comes into contact with them. For long-term outcomes, Fergusson, Lynskey, and Horwood (1996) followed a cohort of 1019 children over 18 years, where they compared four groups of individuals: no CSA, noncontact CSA, contact CSA without penetration, and contact CSA with penetration. Fergusson et al. (1996) found that even after controlling for childhood factors, individuals who experienced contact CSA with penetration had the highest rates of depressive symptoms, anxiety symptoms, conduct problems, certain substance use, and made more suicide attempts than any of the other three groups.

Finally, maternal support has been found to be associated with both short- and long-term victim outcomes; overall, less maternal belief and support is associated with more adverse victim outcomes. In terms of short-term outcomes, Zajac, Ralston, and Smith (2015) conducted a study on 118 mother–child dyads. They found that victims who gave lower ratings of maternal support postdisclosure had significantly higher levels of postadjustment outcomes (posttraumatic stress disorder, depression, and anger). Zajac et al. (2015) concluded that appropriate maternal support promotes the victims' psychological adjustment and can ameliorate against the harmful effects of CSA whereas less supportive mothers may put the victim at an increased risk for dysfunctional coping strategies (e.g., self-blame and avoidance). For long-term outcomes, Godbout, Briere, Sabourin, and Lussier (2013) examined the role of parental support in the relationship between CSA and later romantic attachment, couple adjustment, and psychiatric symptoms. The sample involved 348 adults engaged in stable romantic relationships of which 59 reported CSA. The participants who reported having nonsupportive parents post CSA disclosure reported higher levels of dyadic maladjustment, psychological symptoms, and levels of anxious attachment. In comparison, the participants who reported having supportive parents post disclosure of CSA had psychological and couple adjustment relative to that of the nonabused group. Godbout et al. (2013) concluded that perceived parental support is a protective factor for those who have been victims of CSA.

CONCLUSIONS

In conclusion, child sexual abuse is a difficult concept to define due to the varying definitions and ages of consent. This aside, it is evident that CSA is a global issue. While any child can potentially be a victim of CSA, this chapter highlighted a number of common victim characteristics, also exploring misconceptions of CSA in order to highlight some common myths. The reasons behind why many children delay or do not disclose the abuse were also canvassed; here, a particular focus was paid on the grooming process. Finally, the short- and long-term victim outcomes were explored in light of a number of characteristics. In sum, CSA is a worldwide issue that requires ongoing attention and research.

SUMMARY

- Child sexual abuse (CSA) encompasses a wide variety of sexual behaviors including penetration of the vagina or anus (by a penis, finger, or any object), oral sex, touching of the breasts or genitals, masturbation, exhibitionism (exposing oneself), voyeurism (spying/watching), exposing a child to or involving a child in pornography, and soliciting a child to engage in sexual activity.
- There are many definitions for CSA, which vary across jurisdictions. For example, Australian researchers have proposed that CSA is a form of exploitation or sexual abuse performed by an offender who is at least 5 years older than the child (who is under the age of 18 years); in New Zealand, CSA is defined as sexual behavior in which an adult, or a more powerful individual, involves a child in sexual acts or behaviors; and the United States defines CSA as involving a child in sexual activity for the sexual or financial benefit of the perpetrator. Yet other definitions take a developmental perspective.
- Age of consent dictates the age at which an individual is identified as able to give informed consent to engage in sexual activity. It is irrelevant if the child perceives the sexual activity to be consensual if a person engages in sexual activity with a child who is under the age of consent. Age of consent laws differ across countries and generally range from a low of around 14 years of age to a high of about 18 years. Some countries legally require a couple to be married before becoming sexually active; continue to render homosexuality as an illegal sexual act regardless of age or gender; and have different ages of consent for males and females, and for heterosexual and homosexual behaviors.
- The global prevalence rate of CSA is estimated to be around 11.8%.
- Characteristics found to be commonly associated with CSA victimization include: gender (females are at higher risk), relationship to the perpetrator (more common for perpetrator and victim to know each other), and the type of abuse endured.
- The Australian Personal Safety Survey found that the most common perpetrator of CSA was a nonguardian male relative (i.e., not the victim's father or stepfather); followed by a family friend; an acquaintance or neighbor; another person known to the victim; victim's father or stepfather; and finally, a stranger.
- CSA victims are more likely to endure nonpenetrative abuse than penetrative abuse. The most prevalent type of abuse is nonpenetrative touching; followed by vaginal penetration; digital stimulation (fingers inserted into the vagina or anus); indecent assault; anal penetration; attempted sexual assault; masturbation on victim; fellatio on abuser; masturbation on abuser; fellatio on victim; cunnilingus on victim; and exposure to pornography.

- Common CSA misconceptions include, that children are unreliable witnesses; that anatomically correct dolls are effective to use during interviews with children; and that CSA is commonly identifiable through genital examination.
- There are two main reasons why physical signs of CSA are difficult to recognize: (1) the perpetrator is generally someone the child knows whose interest is not to hurt the child (that is, to not violently penetrate the child), but rather, to have continued access to the child (avoiding the detection of abuse by others); and (2) the common delay in the child disclosing the abuse provides time for any superficial lesions to heal.
- Grooming is a type of emotional seduction in which the perpetrator uses trust and affection to interact and manipulate the victim, and often the victim's family and social circle (to gain unsupervised, "easy access" to the victim by developing the trust of the victim's usual protective supports). Institutional grooming may also occur in which the individual's job and social status allow for manipulation and deception to improve access to a victim(s). In fact, perpetrators often have good social skills and advanced deception skills that allow them to play a double role in the community, thereby avoiding suspicion, sometimes for quite extended periods of time.
- In CSA, the perpetrator generally groom's the victim by offering the victim a number of inducements such as material items and privileges (such as toys) or even affection (the victim may have emotionally detached parents and instead receive most attention and affection from the perpetrator). This enables the perpetrator to control the victim by not only giving inducements but also by guilt, and/or threatening to take away any proffered inducements. Threats may also include physical harm or punishment of the victim directly or of their family.
- Research has found that victims of intrafamilial abuse (that perpetrated by a family member) were less likely to disclose (or delay their disclosure) than victims of extrafamilial abuse (abuse perpetrated by a nonfamily member).
- The short- and long-term outcomes of CSA can be substantial. The effects of CSA are not purely psychological but can also include physical, cognitive, social, and behavioral effects.
- Outcomes differ depending on the victim–perpetrator relationship. Generally speaking, the closer the relationship between the victim and the accuser, the more adverse the outcome. Short-term outcomes are worst when the abuser is the victim's biological father, and are associated with extreme patterns of behavioral problems and maladjustment. In the long-term, children abused by a relative report greater symptoms of PTSD as adults.
- Maternal support for the victim in all cases (where the maternal guardian is not an active party to the abuse) has been shown to be directly related to better outcomes in both the short and long term.

QUESTIONS

1. How would you define child sexual abuse?
2. Why are there challenges in defining and conceptualizing child sexual abuse? What are some of the issues that make it challenging to do so?
3. Who is at greatest risk for child sexual abuse? Discuss the risk factors associated with child sexual abuse, the common characteristics of victims, and the prevalence of abuse based on these factors.
4. What are some other common misconceptions surrounding child sexual abuse? What role might the media play in some of these common misconceptions?
5. How would you explain the "grooming" process in layman's terms?
6. Are characteristics such as the victim's age and victim's gender related to the charging of the perpetrator and the prosecution of the case? Why/Why not?
7. How can professionals avoid suggestive questioning when interviewing children about sexual abuse? Create some guidelines professionals could adhere to.
8. Discuss how maternal belief and support, after the victim's disclosure of abuse, might differ when the victim's mother is in a relationship with the perpetrator in comparison with the perpetrator being a stranger.
9. Identify five "risk" factors that may contribute to poorer outcomes for children who have been victims of child sexual abuse. Explain the potential role of each of these risk factors in the child's recovery.

REFERENCES

Adams, J. (2011). Medical evaluation of suspected child sexual abuse: 2011 update. *Journal of Child Sexual Abuse, 20*, 588–605. http://dx.doi.org/10.1080/10538712.2011.606107.

Australian Bureau of Statistics. (2004). *Sexual assault in Australia: A statistical overview. (4523.0).* Retrieved from http://www.ausstats.abs.gov.au/ausstats/subscriber.nsf/0/C41F8B2864D42333CA256F070079CBD4/$File/45230_2004.pdf.

Australian Bureau of Statistics. (2005). *Personal safety survey Australia. (4906.0).* Retrieved from http://www.abs.gov.au/AUSSTATS/abs@.nsf/Lookup/4906.0Main+Features12012?OpenDocument.

Australian Institute of Family Studies. (2014). *Age of consent laws.* Retrieved from https://aifs.gov.au/cfca/publications/age-consent-laws.

Australian Law Reform Commission. (2010). *Family violence – a national legal response (114).* Retrieved from http://www.alrc.gov.au/sites/default/files/pdfs/publications/ALRC114_WholeReport.pdf.

Australian Psychological Society. (2013). *Child sexual abuse in the general community and clergy-perpetrated child sexual abuse.* Retrieved from https://www.psychology.org.au/Assets/Files/Child%20sexual%20abuse%20in%20the%20general%20community%20and%20clergy-perpetrated%20child%20sexual%20abuse.pdf.

Barth, J., Bermetz, L., Heim, E., Trelle, S., & Tonia, T. (2012). The current prevalence of child sexual abuse worldwide: a systematic review and meta-analysis. *International Journal of Public Health, 58*, 469–483. http://dx.doi.org/10.1007/s00038-012-0426-1.

Berenson, A., Chacko, M., Wiemann, C., Mishaw, C., Friedrich, W., & Grady, J. (2000). A case-control study of anatomic changes resulting from sexual abuse. *American Journal of Obstetrics and Gynecology, 182,* 820–834. http://dx.doi.org/10.1016/S0002-9378(00)70331-0.

Best Practice Advocacy Centre New Zealand. (2015). *Upfront: Detecting child abuse in general practice.* Retrieved from http://www.bpac.org.nz/BPJ/2011/september/upfront.aspx.

Boat, M., & Everson, M. (1988). Use of anatomical dolls among professionals in sexual abuse evaluations. *Child Abuse & Neglect, 12,* 171–179. http://dx.doi.org/10.1016/0145-2134(88)90025-7.

Bremner, J. D. (2003). Long-term effects of childhood sexual abuse on brain and neurobiology. *Child and Adolescent Psychiatric Clinics of North America, 12,* 271–292. http://dx.doi.org/10.1016/S1056-4993(02)00098-6.

Bruck, M. (2009). Human figure drawings and children's recall of touching. *Journal of Experimental Psychology: Applied, 15,* 361–374. http://dx.doi.org/10.1037/a0017120.

Bruck, M., & Ceci, S. J. (1999). The suggestibility of children's memory. *Annual Review of Psychology, 50,* 419–439. http://dx.doi.org/10.1146/annurev.psych.50.1.419.

Bruck, M., Ceci, S. J., & Francoeur, E. (2000). Children's use of anatomically detailed dolls to report genital touching in a medical examination: developmental and gender comparisons. *Journal of Experimental Psychology: Applied, 6,* 74–83. http://dx.doi.org/10.1037/1076-898X.6.1.74.

Cantwell, H. B. (1983). Vaginal inspection as it relates to child sexual abuse in girls under thirteen. *Child Abuse & Neglect, 7,* 171–176. http://dx.doi.org/10.1016/0145-2134(83)90069-8.

Ceci, S. J., & Bruck, M. (1993). Suggestibility of the child witness: a historical review and synthesis. *Psychological Bulletin, 113,* 403–439. http://dx.doi.org/10.1037/0033-2909.113.3.403.

Children's Bureau (Administration on Children, Youth and Families, Administration for Children and Families) of the United States Department of Health and Human Services. (2013). *Child maltreatment 2012.* Retrieved from http://www.acf.hhs.gov/sites/default/files/cb/cm2012.pdf.

Conte, J. R., Sorenson, E., Fogarty, L., & Rosa, J. D. (1991). Evaluating children's reports of sexual abuse: results from a survey of professionals. *American Journal of Orthopsychiatry, 61,* 428–437. http://dx.doi.org/10.1037/h0079264.

Cronch, L. E., Viljoen, J. L., & Hansen, D. J. (2006). Forensic interviewing in child sexual abuse cases: current techniques and future directions. *Aggression and Violent Behavior, 11,* 195–207. http://dx.doi.org/10.1016/j.avb.2005.07.009.

Cutajar, M. C., Mullen, P. E., Ogloff, J. R., Thomas, S. D., Wells, D. L., & Spataro, J. (2010). Psychopathology in a large cohort of sexually abused children followed up to 43 years. *Child Abuse & Neglect, 34,* 813–822. http://dx.doi.org/10.1016/j.chiabu.2010.04.004.

DeLoache, J. S., & Marzolf, D. P. (1995). The use of dolls to interview young children: issues of symbolic representation. *Journal of Experimental Child Psychology, 60,* 155–173. http://dx.doi.org/10.1006/jecp.1995.1036.

Dickinson, J. J., Poole, D. A., & Bruck, M. (2005). Back to the future: a comment on the use of anatomical dolls in forensic interviews. *Journal of Forensic Psychology Practice, 5,* 63–74. http://dx.doi.org/10.1300/J158v05n01_04.

Everson, M. D., & Boat, B. W. (1994). Putting the anatomical doll controversy in perspective: an examination of the major uses and criticisms of the dolls in child sexual abuse evaluations. *Child Abuse & Neglect, 18,* 113–129. http://dx.doi.org/10.1016/0145-2134(94)90114-7.

Fergusson, D. M., Boden, J. M., & Horwood, L. J. (2008). Exposure to childhood sexual and physical abuse and adjustment in early adulthood. *Child Abuse & Neglect*, *32*, 607–619. http://dx.doi.org/10.1016/j.chiabu.2006.12.018.

Fergusson, D. M., Lynskey, M. T., & Horwood, L. J. (1996). Childhood sexual abuse and psychiatric disorder in young adulthood: I. Prevalence of sexual abuse and factors associated with sexual abuse. *Journal of the American Academy of Child and Adolescent Psychiatry*, *35*, 1355–1364. http://dx.doi.org/10.1097/00004583-199610000-00023.

Fergusson, D. M., McLeod, G. F., & Horwood, L. J. (2013). Childhood sexual abuse and adult developmental outcomes: findings from a 30-year longitudinal study in New Zealand. *Child Abuse & Neglect*, *3*, 664–674. http://dx.doi.org/10.1016/j.chiabu.2013.03.013.

Freyd, J. J. (1996). *Betrayal trauma theory: The logic of forgetting abuse*. Cambridge, MA: Harvard University Press.

Gault-Sherman, M., Silver, E., & Sigfúsdóttir, I. D. (2009). Gender and the associated impairments of childhood sexual abuse: a national study of Icelandic youth. *Social Science & Medicine*, *69*, 1515–1522. http://dx.doi.org/10.1016/j.socscimed.2009.08.037.

Godbout, N., Briere, J., Sabourin, S., & Lussier, Y. (2013). Child sexual abuse and subsequent relational and personal functioning: the role of parental support. *Child Abuse & Neglect*, *38*, 317–325. http://dx.doi.org/10.1016/j.chiabu.2013.10.001.

Goldman, R. J., & Goldman, J. D. (1988). The prevalence and nature of child sexual abuse in Australia. *Australian Journal of Sex, Marriage and Family*, *9*, 94–106. http://dx.doi.org/10.1080/01591487.1988.11004405.

Goodman-Brown, T. B., Edelstein, R. S., Goodman, G. S., Jones, D. P., & Gordon, D. S. (2003). Why children tell: a model of children's disclosure of sexual abuse. *Child Abuse & Neglect*, *27*, 525–540. http://dx.doi.org/10.1016/S0145-2134(03)00037-1.

Gries, L. T., Goh, D. S., Andrews, M. B., Gilbert, J., Praver, F., & Stelzer, D. N. (2000). Positive reaction to disclosure and recovery from child sexual abuse. *Journal of Child Sexual Abuse*, *9*, 29–51. http://dx.doi.org/10.1300/J070v09n01_03.

Heger, A., Ticson, L., Velasquez, O., & Bernier, R. (2002). Children referred for possible sexual abuse: medical findings in 2384 children. *Child Abuse & Neglect*, *26*(6), 645–659.

Hershkowitz, I., Horowitz, D., & Lamb, M. E. (2005). Trends in children's disclosure of abuse in Israel: a national study. *Child Abuse & Neglect*, *29*, 1203–1214. http://dx.doi.org/10.1016/j.chiabu.2005.04.008.

Hershkowitz, I., Lanes, O., & Lamb, M. E. (2007). Exploring the disclosure of child sexual abuse with alleged victims and their parents. *Child Abuse & Neglect*, *31*, 111–123. http://dx.doi.org/10.1016/j.chiabu.2006.09.004.

Kaufman, K. L., Hilliker, D. R., & Daleiden, E. L. (1996). Subgroup differences in the modus operandi of adolescent sexual offenders. *Child Maltreatment*, *1*, 17–24. http://dx.doi.org/10.1177/1077559596001001003.

Kellogg, N. D., Parra, J. M., & Menard, S. (1998). Children with anogenital symptoms and signs referred for sexual abuse evaluations. *Archives of Pediatrics & Adolescent Medicine*, *152*, 634–641. http://dx.doi.org/10.1001/archpedi.152.7.634.

Kempe, R. S., & Kempe, C. H. (1978). *Child abuse*. Cambridge, MA: Harvard.

Kendall-Tackett, K. A., Williams, L. M., & Finkelhor, D. (1993). Impact of sexual abuse on children: a review and synthesis of recent empirical studies. *Psychological Bulletin*, *113*, 164. http://dx.doi.org/10.1037/0033-2909.113.1.164.

Klemfuss, J. Z., & Ceci, S. J. (2012). Legal and psychological perspectives on children's competence to testify in court. *Developmental Review*, *32*, 268–286. http://dx.doi.org/10.1016/j.dr.2012.06.005.

Kogan, S. M. (2004). Disclosing unwanted sexual experiences: results from a national sample of adolescent women. *Child Abuse & Neglect*, 28, 147–165. http://dx.doi.org/10.1016/j. chiabu.2003.09.014.

Lamb, M. E., Hershkowitz, I., Sternberg, K. J., Boat, B., & Everson, M. D. (1996). Investigative interviews of alleged sexual abuse victims with and without anatomical dolls. *Child Abuse & Neglect*, 20, 1251–1259. http://dx.doi.org/10.1016/S0145-2134(96)00121-4.

Leclerc, B., & Wortley, R. (2015). Predictors of victim disclosure in child sexual abuse: additional evidence from a sample of incarcerated adult sex offenders. *Child Abuse & Neglect*, 43, 104–111. http://dx.doi.org/10.1016/j.chiabu.2015.03.003.

Maniglio, R. (2009). The impact of child sexual abuse on health: a systematic review of reviews. *Clinical Psychology Review*, 29, 647–657. http://dx.doi.org/10.1016/j.cpr.2009.08.003.

Mcalinden, A. M. (2006). 'Setting'em up': personal, familial and institutional grooming in the sexual abuse of children. *Social & Legal Studies*, 15, 339–362. http://dx.doi. org/10.1177/0964663906066613.

McCann, J., Miyamoto, S., Boyle, C., & Rogers, K. (2007). Healing of nonhymenal genital injuries in prepubertal and adolescent girls: a descriptive study. *Pediatrics*, 120, 1000–1011. http://dx.doi.org/10.1542/peds.2006-0230.

Modelli, M. E., Galvão, M. F., & Pratesi, R. (2012). Child sexual abuse. *Forensic Science International*, 217, 1–4. http://dx.doi.org/10.1016/j.forsciint.2011.08.006.

Mohler-Kuo, M., Landolt, M. A., Maier, T., Meidert, U., Schönbucher, V., & Schnyder, U. (2014). Child sexual abuse revisited: a population-based cross-sectional study among swiss adolescentsw. *The Journal of Adolescent Health*, 54, 304–311. http://dx.doi.org/10.1016/j. jadohealth.2013.08.020.

Mwangi, M. W., Kellogg, T. A., Brookmeyer, K., Buluma, R., Chiang, L., Otieno-Nyunya, B., et al. (2015). Perpetrators and context of child sexual abuse in Kenya. *Child Abuse & Neglect*, 44, 46–55. http://dx.doi.org/10.1016/j.chiabu.2015.03.011.

Paine, M. L., & Hansen, D. J. (2002). Factors influencing children to self-disclose sexual abuse. *Clinical Psychology Review*, 22, 271–295. http://dx.doi.org/10.1016/ S0272-7358(01)00091-5.

Pereda, N., Guilera, G., Forns, M., & Gómez-Benito, J. (2009). The prevalence of child sexual abuse in community and student samples: a meta-analysis. *Clinical Psychology Review*, 29, 328–338. http://dx.doi.org/10.1016/j.cpr.2009.02.007.

Pérez-Fuentes, G., Olfson, M., Villegas, L., Morcillo, C., Wang, S., & Blanco, C. (2013). Prevalence and correlates of child sexual abuse: a national study. *Comprehensive Psychiatry*, 54, 16–27. http://dx.doi.org/10.1016/j.comppsych.2012.05.010.

Perry, B. D., Pollard, R. A., Blakley, T. L., Baker, W. L., & Vigilante, D. (1995). Childhood trauma, the neurobiology of adaptation, and "use-dependent" development of the brain: how "states" become "traits". *Infant Mental Health Journal*, 16, 271–291. http://dx.doi. org/10.1002/1097-0355(199524)16:4271::AID-IMHJ22801604043.0.CO;2-B.

Pillai, M. (2005). Forensic examination of suspected child victims of sexual abuse in the UK: a personal view. *Journal of Clinical Forensic Medicine*, 12, 57–63. http://dx.doi. org/10.1016/j.jcfm.2004.10.012.

Pipe, M.-E., Lamb, M. E., Orbach, Y., & Cederborg, A.-C. (2007). *Child sexual abuse: Disclosure, delay and denial*. New York: Routledge.

Poole, D. A., & Bruck, M. (2012). Divining testimony? The impact of interviewing props on children's reports of touching. *Developmental Review*, 32, 165–180. http://dx.doi. org/10.1016/j.dr.2012.06.007.

Poole, D. A., & Dickinson, J. J. (2011). Evidence supporting restrictions on uses of body diagrams in forensic interviews. *Child Abuse & Neglect, 35,* 659–669. http://dx.doi.org/10.1016/j.chiabu.2011.05.004.

Priebe, G., & Svedin, C. G. (2008). Child sexual abuse is largely hidden from the adult society: an epidemiological study of adolescents' disclosures. *Child Abuse & Neglect, 32,* 1095–1108. http://dx.doi.org/10.1016/j.chiabu.2008.04.001.

Putnam, F. W. (2003). Ten-year research update review: child sexual abuse. *Journal of the American Academy of Child and Adolescent Psychiatry, 42,* 269–278. http://dx.doi.org/10.1097/00004583-200303000-00006.

Romano, E., & De Luca, R. V. (2001). Male sexual abuse: a review of effects, abuse characteristics, and links with later psychological functioning. *Aggression and Violent Behavior, 6,* 55–78. http://dx.doi.org/10.1016/S1359-1789(99)00011-7.

Salter, A. C. (1995). *Transforming trauma: A guide to understanding and treating adult survivors of child sexual abuse.* Thousand Oaks, CA: SAGE Publications.

Santtila, P., Korkman, J., & Sandnabba, K. (2004). Effects of interview phase, repeated interviewing, presence of a support person, and anatomically detailed dolls on child sexual abuse interviews. *Psychology, Crime and Law, 10,* 21–35. http://dx.doi.org/10.1080/1068316021000044365.

Shonkoff, J. P., Boyce, W. T., & McEwen, B. S. (2009). Neuroscience, molecular biology, and the childhood roots of health disparities: building a new framework for health promotion and disease prevention. *The Journal of the American Medical Association, 301,* 2252–2259. http://dx.doi.org/10.1001/jama.2009.754.

Smith, D. W., Letourneau, E. J., Saunders, B. E., Kilpatrick, D. G., Resnick, H. S., & Best, C. L. (2000). Delay in disclosure of childhood rape: results from a national survey. *Child Abuse & Neglect, 24,* 273–287. http://dx.doi.org/10.1016/S0145-2134(99)00130-1.

Sternberg, K. J., Lamb, M. E., Hershkowitz, I., Yudilevitch, L., Orback, Y., Esplin, P. W., et al. (1997). Effects of introductory style on children's abilities to describe experiences of sexual abuse. *Child Abuse & Neglect, 21,* 1133–1146.

Stoltenborgh, M., van IJzendoorn, M. H., Euser, E. M., & Bakermans-Kranenburg, M. J. (2011). A global perspective on child sexual abuse: meta-analysis of prevalence around the world. *Child Maltreatment, 16,* 79–101. http://dx.doi.org/10.1177/1077559511403920.

Summit, R. C. (1983). The child sexual abuse accommodation syndrome. *Child Abuse & Neglect, 7,* 177–193. http://dx.doi.org/10.1016/0145-2134(83)90070-4.

Tang, S. S. S., Freyd, J. J., & Wang, M. (2007). What do we know about gender in the disclosure of child sexual abuse? *Journal of Psychological Trauma, 6,* 1–26. http://dx.doi.org/10.1080/19322880802096442.

Thierry, K. L., Lamb, M. E., Orbach, Y., & Pipe, M. E. (2005). Developmental differences in the function and use of anatomical dolls during interviews with alleged sexual abuse victims. *Journal of Consulting and Clinical Psychology, 73,* 1125. http://dx.doi.org/10.1037/0022-006X.73.6.1125.

Trickett, P. K., Noll, J. G., Reiffman, A., & Putnam, F. W. (2001). Variants of intrafamilial sexual abuse experience: implications for short-and long-term development. *Development and Psychopathology, 13,* 1001–1019. Retrieved from http://journals.cambridge.org.

Tyler, K. A. (2002). Social and emotional outcomes of childhood sexual abuse: a review of recent research. *Aggression and Violent Behavior, 7,* 567–589. http://dx.doi.org/10.1016/S1359-1789(01)00047-7.

Ullman, S. E. (2007). Relationship to perpetrator, disclosure, social reactions, and PTSD symptoms in child sexual abuse survivors. *Journal of Child Sexual Abuse, 16,* 19–36. http://dx.doi.org/10.1300/J070v16n01_02.

Ullman, S. E., & Filipas, H. H. (2005). Gender differences in social reactions to abuse disclosures, post-abuse coping, and PTSD of child sexual abuse survivors. *Child Abuse & Neglect, 29,* 767–782. http://dx.doi.org/10.1016/j.chiabu.2005.01.005.

Willcock, E., Morgan, K., & Hayne, H. (2006). Body maps do not facilitate children's reports of touch. *Applied Cognitive Psychology, 20,* 607–616. http://dx.doi.org/10.1002/acp.1212.

Zajac, K., Ralston, M. E., & Smith, D. W. (2015). Maternal support following childhood sexual abuse: associations with children's adjustment post-disclosure and at 9-month follow-up. *Child Abuse & Neglect, 44,* 66–75. http://dx.doi.org/10.1016/j.chiabu.2015.02.011.

Child Sexual Offenders: The Psychology of Offending

15

Larissa Christensen

Griffith University, Gold Coast, QLD, Australia

CHAPTER OUTLINE

INTRODUCTION

This chapter explores the psychology behind child sexual offending.

In order to design precise prevention and intervention programs, researchers, clinicians, and policy makers need to have insight into the psychology of child sexual offending. First, some of the common misconceptions held by society surrounding child sexual offenders will be addressed, followed by a discussion on female child sexual offenders, how and why individuals may become child sexual offenders, and crime scripts held by child sexual offenders. Finally, the ever-advancing issue of online child predators will be discussed.

The Psychology of Criminal and Antisocial Behavior. http://dx.doi.org/10.1016/B978-0-12-809287-3.00015-8

MISCONCEPTIONS OF CHILD SEXUAL OFFENDERS

There are a number of common misconceptions surrounding child sexual offenders. Some of these include that all child sexual offenders are pedophiles, child sexual offenders mostly target strangers, and all child sexual offenders were once victims of sexual abuse themselves (Richards, 2011). In terms of the first common misconception, the terms *child sexual offender* and *pedophile* cannot be used interchangeably (Feelgood & Hoyer, 2008). Not all pedophiles are child sexual offenders and, likewise, not all child sexual offenders are pedophiles.

A pedophile is an individual who is sexually attracted to, or has a sexual preference toward, prepubescent children. However, these individuals may not necessarily "act" on this attraction and instead solely experience sexually arousing fantasies or urges. Furthermore, pedophilia is considered a mental disorder (pedophilic disorder) listed within the class of paraphilic disorders in the Diagnostic and Statistical Manual of Mental Disorders (DSM5; American Psychiatric Association, 2013).

In contrast, a child sexual offender is an individual who *has* had some form of sexual contact or involvement with children. This may include contact offenses (e.g., penetration, fondling, masturbation) and noncontact offenses (e.g., exhibitionism, exposing the child to pornography, indecently recording the child). While some child sexual offenders may be attracted to children, other child sexual offenders may hold a sexual preference toward adults yet offend against children merely due to an *opportunity* for sexual gratification. Unlike pedophilia, there is no psychological diagnostic label for child sexual offending.

A second common misconception is that child sexual offenders mostly target strangers (Richards, 2011). Despite a persistent fear in society that strangers are the key sexual abusers of children, research demonstrates that a much higher number of child sexual offenders are, in fact, known to their victim. The Australian Bureau of Statistics (2005) estimated that of the 1,294,000 people living in Australia who had experienced sexual abuse before the age of 15, 90% of victims knew their offender and only 10% of victims were abused by a stranger. Similar findings are noted in other countries. In the United States, it has been found that strangers are the minority of child sexual offenders, with some studies finding as little as 7% of victims being targeted by strangers (for example, Finkelhor, Ormrod, Turner, & Hamby, 2005). This finding is also evident in less-developed countries. Aydin et al. (2015) studied 1002 cases of child sexual abuse (CSA) referred over a 7-year period to a forensic medicine department in Turkey. They found that about 88% of victims knew their offender and only 12% of victims were abused by a stranger.

A third common misconception is that all child sexual offenders were once victims of sexual abuse themselves (Richards, 2011). Foremost, it is difficult to accurately identify the percentage of offenders who experienced sexual abuse as a child, because some offenders, particularly males, are hesitant to disclose their victimization due to the personal shame of having been a victim of sexual abuse. At the other end of the spectrum, some offenders may embellish claims in order to "justify their offending or to elicit sympathy from therapists, courts, and parole board members"

(Simons, 2007, p. 61). It has, been suggested that the minority of sexual offenders were once victims of sexual abuse themselves (e.g., Salter et al., 2003).

Salter et al. (2003) conducted a longitudinal study of 224 adult males who were former victims of sexual abuse. They sought objective evidence from caution and conviction data as well as social services data. Salter et al. (2003) found that of the 224 former victims, only 26 had committed sexual offenses in later life. Further, it was found that particular experiences (for example, material neglect, lack of supervision appropriate to the child's age, rejection by parents) and patterns of childhood behavior (for example, cruelty to animals) were associated with an increased risk of victims becoming abusers in later life above and beyond previous CSA victimization.

FEMALE CHILD SEXUAL OFFENDERS

The research on female child sexual offenders has remained atheoretical for decades (Harris, 2010). Little is known about the characteristics of female child sexual offenders, including psychopathology, offense cycles, motivations, and deviant arousal. Two reasons stand out for why female child sexual offenders have been an underresearched and underrecognized area. One reason for the limited research may be due to the seemingly low prevalence rate of CSA perpetrated by females.

Cortoni and Hanson (2005) conducted a systematic review to highlight the prevalence of female sexual offending; samples included Canada, the United Kingdom, the United States, Australia, and New Zealand. They utilized two sources of information: official police/court records and victimization studies. Across both sources of information, Cortoni and Hanson (2005) found that prevalence rates of sexual offenses perpetrated by females were generally between 4% and 5% of all sexual offenses.

A second reason for the limited research on female child sexual offenders may be due to misguided perception of gender roles, making it difficult for both the victim and society to recognize the sexual behavior as abusive. At one end of the continuum, females can mask the offending as "normal activities" associated with their nurturing role (i.e., dressing, affection, and bathing; Lewis & Stanley, 2000) and at the other end of the continuum, females may be seductive and play the role of the "lover." Perceptions of such gender bias surrounding CSA has been found in a number of studies.

Geddes, Tyson, and McGreal (2013) provided a questionnaire to a random stratified sample that included one of two short hypothetical vignettes about a teacher (offender) and student (victim) in a sexual relationship. Other than the gender of the offender and victim, the two vignettes were identical. The 130 respondents reported significantly greater anger and the want for harsher consequences for the male teacher in a sexual relationship with a female student rather than the female teacher in a sexual relationship with a male student. Geddes et al. (2013) concluded that attributions made by both men and women pertaining to teacher–student sexual relationships were in line with traditional gender roles.

Typologies are used to understand the differences between types of offenders and consist of offender characteristics and victim-choice information (Robertiello & Terry, 2007). Matthews, Matthews, and Speltz (1989) constructed one of the most commonly referenced typologies for female sexual offenders: (1) male-coerced, (2) teacher/lover, and (3) predisposed molester. The *male-coerced* offender is forced or coerced by her partner (who is the initiator of the sexual abuse) to take part in the abuse generally on her own children. She is usually a passive female in a relationship with a dominant and abusive male (Grattagliano et al., 2012). She generally feels powerless, has low self-esteem, is of low intelligence, and takes part in the abuse out of fear of repercussion from her partner (Syed & Williams, 1996). While male coercion is often discussed synonymously with "female coperpetrators," not all co-offending females are coerced by their male partner (Nathan & Ward, 2002). In fact, some females who are coperpetrators may play a forceful and active role in the abuse and enjoy the experience (Nathan & Ward, 2002). Other reasons for why females may co-offend include rejection, jealousy, or the desire to establish a personal sense of control (Nathan & Ward, 2002). For instance, the female may feel rejected in her primary relationship with her partner, so instead she seeks attention from her partner through involving herself in the sexual abuse.

The *teacher/lover* offender is a female offender who almost entirely offends against male victims via a position of power (e.g., a high school teacher). She generally denies any abusive behavior as she perceives the victim (generally an adolescent) as being part of a consenting romantic relationship (Grattagliano et al., 2012). She turns to the adolescent male for sexual expression and acceptance as she has been unable to attain this in adult relationships (Grattagliano et al., 2012); this is likely a result of having been with a sexually abusive partner in the past (Syed & Williams, 1996).

In contrast, the *predisposed molester* is a female offender who is troubled by addictive behavior, emotional instability, and commonly comes from an abusive background (Grattagliano et al., 2012). She generally suffers from a serious psychological disorder and has difficulty in establishing functional sexual relationships with adults. She has a strong desire for attention and love, and victimizes any available child including her own children or children in her care. Common characteristics of the predisposed molester include extreme distrust, distorted thinking, feelings of persecution, and substance dependence (Grattagliano et al., 2012). As the majority of the child sexual offending research focuses on males as the perpetrators, the remainder of the chapter will primarily draw from the male child sexual offender literature.

HOW AND WHY INDIVIDUALS OFFEND

How is it possible for an adult to become sexually aroused by children? What causes an adult to sexually abuse a child? Why would a man in a stable marriage sexually abuse a child? These are questions commonly asked by many, and such questions are also of some importance to researchers, clinicians, and policy makers because understanding why CSA occurs can aid in the design of prevention and treatment interventions. Theories are central to the field of criminology because they provide explanations and interpretations of crimes, and a number of theories have been developed to explain and interpret why adults sexually offend against children. Some of these include: cognitive distortions, attachment theories, the precondition model (Finkelhor, 1984), and the pathways model (Ward & Siegert, 2002). Each of these will now be discussed.

COGNITIVE DISTORTIONS

Clinicians and researchers have found evidence that sexual offenders show distorted thinking patterns as well as offense-supportive thinking patterns (Beech, Bartels, & Dixon, 2013; Sinnamon, 2015). In fact, cognitive distortions have been found to be related to the onset and maintenance of sexual offending (Ó Ciardha & Ward, 2012). Since the mid-1980s, there has been a growing body of research related to the role of cognition in child sexual offending. Cognitive distortions are commonly referred to as maladaptive attitudes and beliefs as well as problematic thinking styles (Sinnamon, 2015; Ward, Hudson, Johnston, & Marshall, 1997).

Abel, Becker, and Cunningham-Rathner (1984) first introduced cognitive distortions to the sexual offending literature. They suggested that cognitive distortions result from the individual realizing that their sexual interests (toward children) are not in line with societal norms. The individual realizes the discrepancy between the two (his sexual interests and societal norms) and adjusts by producing an individualized set of cognitions; these cognitions support his beliefs that sexual involvement with children is appropriate in order to feel at ease with himself.

Abel et al. (1984) identified a number of key cognitive distortions that adults who are aroused by children may develop that support such sexual behavior with children. For example, "a child who does not physically resist my sexual advances really wants to have sex with me" (Abel et al., 1984, p. 98). Here, the individual assumes that children are capable of expressing themselves in an adult manner; that is, children will refuse sexual advances if they do not want to take part in sexual activity. In reality, children may respond with muteness due to fear or obedience of an adult figure and, in turn, the adult interprets this as the child accepting the behavior (Abel et al., 1984). Another example of a cognitive distortion is "having sex with a child is a good way for an adult to teach the child about sex" (Abel et al., 1984, p. 99). This indicates that some individuals rationalize their behavior as having positive effects on children. In reality, there are many negative short- and long-term effects suffered by victims of CSA (Daigneault, Hébert, & McDuff, 2009; Kwako, Noll, Putnam, & Trickett, 2010; Maniglio, 2010).

Ward and Keenan (1999) and Ward (2000) proposed the idea that child sexual offenders hold a set of beliefs referred to as *implicit theories* (ITs); the way an individual understands other people and the world can be understood as an implicit theory-like structure. As opposed to superficial postoffense rationalizations, in an attempt for the child sexual offender to justify his behavior, ITs suggest entrenched attitudes and beliefs held prior to, during, and after the offense regarding himself, the victim, and the social world.

Ward and Keenan (1999) suggested five implicit theories that are offense-endorsing cognitions held by child sexual offenders: *children as sexual objects* (children have the sexual motivations of adults and are capable of desiring sex); *nature of harm* (sexually abusing children is not always harmful and can sometimes be beneficial for children); *uncontrollability* (sexually abusing children is outside the offender's control); *entitlement* (the offender's needs surpass those of others); and *dangerous world* (the world is a hostile place where, if anyone, only children can be trusted). Put simply, ITs lead child sexual offenders to infer and understand the world around them in offense-congruent ways (Ward, 2000).

More recently, Ward, Gannon, and Keown (2006) developed the judgment model of cognitive distortions. They proposed that cognitive distortions can be explained by three types of judgments: belief-based judgments, value-based judgments, and action-based judgments. These judgments are sensitive to the individual's social and cultural conditions. Ward et al. (2006) suggested that careless reasoning over time can create false beliefs and associated values that can lead to offense-endorsing statements. In terms of belief-based judgments, irrational and misleading beliefs are most likely acquired from certain childhood experiences. Poor modeling and abusive family environments yield distorted interpersonal experiences for these individuals in which they develop misleading beliefs of themselves and other people (Ward et al., 2006).

Value-based judgments are those that the individual considers to either be of worth (beneficial) or of little value (harmful). Child sexual offenders may make a value-based judgment that they are better to have relationships with children than adults as they perceive children as more accepting, trustworthy, loving, and safe.

Finally, action-based judgments result from the offender's actions and are offense-supportive statements. They include minimizations, justifications, and denials. For example, an offender may deny that he sexually abused his niece but was merely checking her diaper to see if it was soiled. Over time, and if repeated enough, these statements may feed back to form offense-supportive beliefs. While cognitive distortions cannot completely explain the onset and maintenance of sexual offending (as they are single-factor theories), cognitive distortions are still a crucial piece in the etiological puzzle (Ó Ciardha & Ward, 2012).

ATTACHMENT THEORIES

Childhood attachments are centered on the child's bond to their caregiver and provide children with a template for their own future relationships (Bowlby, 1973). Ainsworth and Bowlby (1991) conceptualized three types of attachment styles: *secure attachment* (when the child's parent is responsive to the child's needs), *anxious-ambivalent attachment* (an insecure form of attachment when the parenting of the child is inconsistent), and *avoidant attachment* (an insecure form of attachment when the parenting of the child is unresponsive and detached). It has been suggested that attachment insecurity plays both a predisposing and precipitating role in CSA (McKillop, Smallbone, Wortley, & Andjic, 2012). These insecure early attachments are thought to negatively affect the working models individuals hold into adulthood. Working models are the individual's beliefs of the emotional availability of significant others as well as the value they place on significant others. Simons, Wurtele, and Durham (2008) argued that without the experience of secure attachments to caregivers in childhood, children can lack the positive working models to form healthy relationships with individuals; such working models can create a bridge between early insecure attachments and future problems with adult intimacy.

In support of attachment theory and sexual offending, Simons et al. (2008) conducted a retrospective study where they asked 269 offenders (132 child sexual offenders and 137 adult sexual offenders) to rate the attachment they had with their parents during childhood. They found that 94% of offenders described having insecure parental attachment bonds. In particular, 62% of child sexual offenders reported anxious-ambivalent attachment bonds, while 76% of adult sexual offenders reported avoidant attachment bonds. It is suggested that individuals with an insecure attachment style may have deficits in empathy, self-confidence, and interpersonal skills (Marshall, 1989; Ward, Hudson, Marshall, & Siegert, 1995). Further, these individuals grow up having severe anxiety about oneself and anxiety about experiencing intimacy with other adults (Marshall, 1993). In order to have intimate relationships that are nonintimidating, the individual finds safety in indulging in sexual behaviors with children because children are perceived to be less intimidating than adults (Stinson, Sales, & Becker, 2008).

THE PRECONDITION MODEL

Finkelhor (1984) developed the precondition model, which was the first multifactorial model created to account for CSA. He argued the importance of understanding the various needs of different offenders through a multifaceted lens including contextual and situational variables. He highlighted that generally four factors have been cited in the literature to explain the reasons behind why some individuals develop sexual interests in children. The four underlying factors are comprised of: (1) emotional congruence (the offender finds that sexual activity with children is emotionally satisfying); (2) sexual arousal (the offender finds that sexual activity with children is sexually arousing); (3) blockage (the offender engages in sexual activity with children because the offender is unable to meet their sexual needs in more socially appropriate ways, that is, with adults); and (4) disinhibition (the offender becomes disinhibited and behaves in ways that he would not normally behave). Finkelhor (1984) suggested that these four factors can be assembled into four preconditions: (1) motivation to sexually abuse a child; (2) overcoming of internal inhibitions; (3) overcoming of external inhibitions; and (4) dealing with a child's possible resistance to the abuse. It is suggested that each of these preconditions must be satisfied, in temporal sequence, before an individual can sexually abuse a child (Finkelhor, 1984).

Precondition 1 is where an individual needs to be motivated to sexually abuse a child. Three of the four factors (emotional congruence, sexual arousal, and blockage) belong to precondition 1 (that is, these factors constitute various motives for sexually abusing children). Emotional congruence may motivate the offender to engage in CSA because they may feel that children will respond best to the offender's need for safety and closeness. Sexual arousal toward children is suggested to be the result of the offender's childhood sexual experiences, inappropriate early conditioning experiences, or the modeling of sexual interests in children. For instance, the offender may have been exposed to child pornography at a young age. Finally, blockage is suggested to stem from the offender's marital problems, fear of adult females, or social skills deficits; these factors may work in combination or individually (Ward & Hudson, 2011).

Precondition 2 is where an individual needs to overcome internal inhibitors acting against the motivation. The fourth factor, disinhibition, belongs to precondition 2. For example, the offender may be under the influence of alcohol, which may disengage the offender's self-regulatory mechanisms and makes it easier for him to engage in sexually abusive behavior.

Precondition 3 is where an individual needs to overcome external inhibitors to commit the offense. This may include opportunistic behavior, such as targeting an unsupervised child or a child whose mother is distant.

Finally, **Precondition 4** refers to when an individual needs to deal with a child's possible resistance to the abuse. In contrast to the other preconditions, precondition 4 refers to the offense process rather than the causal factors (see Finkelhor, 1984). At this stage, the offender may also utilize a number of methods in order to gain and maintain the child's compliance, for example, the giving of material goods or using threats. While the precondition model does come with some criticisms (see Ward & Hudson, 2011 for a critique of the model), the model was the first comprehensive theory on the sexual offending of children and represents a significant achievement (Ward & Hudson, 2011).

THE PATHWAYS MODEL

The pathways model developed by Ward and Siegert (2002) suggests that there are many pathways that lead to the sexual offending of children with each pathway involving developmental influences, psychological mechanisms, and an opportunity to commit the offense. Similar to past theorists (e.g., Finkelhor, 1984; Hall & Hirschman, 1992), Ward and Siegert (2002) accepted that the reasons behind sexual offending are multifactorial, including factors such as family context, developmental adversity, biological variables, cultural values, situational variables, and belief systems. They suggested that the sexual offending is generated by four interacting types of psychological mechanisms: intimacy and social skill deficits, distorted sexual scripts, emotional dysregulation, and cognitive distortions. The pathways model identifies five etiological pathways that interact with the psychological deficits to create a vulnerability to sexual offending behavior:

- *Pathway 1:* Intimacy deficits
- *Pathway 2:* Deviant sexual scripts

- *Pathway 3:* Emotional dysregulation
- *Pathway 4:* Antisocial cognitions
- *Pathway 5:* Multiple dysfunctional mechanisms

NB: Factors, such as culture, biology, and development, mediate these mechanisms.

It is suggested that offenders who follow pathway 1 (intimacy deficits) possess somewhat normal sexual scripts and prefer sex with adults, however, will offend at specific times against children if a preferred partner is unavailable. The offender's loneliness and intimacy deficits lead to the need to engage in sexual activity with another person. These offenders regard the child as a "pseudo-adult" and perceive the function of the child merely as a surrogate partner. It is suggested that the type of intimacy deficits experienced by these offenders stem from insecure attachment styles (Ward & Siegert, 2002).

For pathway 2 (deviant sexual scripts), these individuals have distortions in their sexual scripts. Some examples of distorted sexual scripts may surround the type of preferred partner, the kinds of sexual activities to take part in, and the context for these activities. Such sexual scripts are suggested to have derived from adverse experiences such as early abuse (Ward & Siegert, 2002).

Pathway 3 (emotional dysregulation) involves individuals who have difficulties in some aspect of their emotional regulation system. This can include both the inhibition of behavior as well as the enhancement of behavior. While these individuals are likely to have sexual preferences for age-appropriate partners, it is suggested that these individuals sexually abuse children under certain circumstances. An offender experiencing a strong negative mood might result in a loss of control and, in turn, lead an individual to opportunistically use a child for sexual gratification (Ward & Siegert, 2002). Basically, these individuals have difficulty managing negative emotions and utilize sex as a soothing strategy.

Pathway 4 (antisocial cognitions) involves offenders who do not have distorted sexual scripts but, rather, possess procriminal beliefs and attitudes and disregard social norms. Such offenders may also hold a sense of their own superiority or patriarchal attitudes toward children. In turn, the cognitive distortions in conjunction with sexual needs and opportunity may result in sexual abuse.

Finally, pathway 5 (multiple dysfunctional mechanisms) involves individuals who have developed distorted sexual scripts (generally having stemmed from sexual abuse or exposure to sexual material as a child) in addition to flaws in other primary psychological mechanisms (e.g., poor emotional regulation, impaired intimacy deficits, and antisocial cognitions). These offenders are likely to be true pedophiles; they believe the ideal relationship is one between an adult and child and see that these interests are healthy and legitimate (Ward & Siegert, 2002).

CRIME SCRIPTS

While the literature highlights that child sexual offenders have deficiencies in various aspects of their lives, it is also important to look at child sexual offenders' areas of "competency" in their offending. A script arranges one's knowledge about how to perform in everyday life (Cornish, 1994) and assists offenders with the automatic processing of offense-related information and decision-making (Ward, 1999). Crime scripts include instructions about how to execute certain actions, the order of how the actions should be carried out, and the probable consequences of a particular action (Fortune, Bourke, & Ward, 2015). Specifically, Fortune et al. (2015) suggested that child sexual offender scripts may contain information surrounding how to: choose victims, groom victims, plan an offense, carry out an offense, attain victim compliance, deal with victim resistance, and avoid detection. There are also interconnected cognitive scripts on their past offenses and victims, which can facilitate future planning and execution (Fortune et al., 2015). Furthermore, when a script has been implemented successfully and repeatedly in the past, it is likely to be easily activated in the future (Tedeschi & Felson, 1994). Crime scripts provide researchers with a framework for the systematic investigation of a specific crime and allows for the exploration of all stages of the crime-commission process by breaking down the process into various stages (Cornish, 1994).

DECISION-MAKING AND CRIME COMMISSION

The internal and external constraints that shape crime scripts are referred to as *choice-structuring properties* and denote the choices and actions taken by the offender to commit a crime (Cornish & Clarke, 1987). Similar to other crimes, child sexual offenses are subject to specific choice-structuring properties. For instance, not only does the offense need to occur in an isolated place but the place needs to remain isolated for long enough so the offender can experience sexual gratification (Beauregard, Leclerc, & Lussier, 2012).

One of the first studies that investigated the decision-making of sexual offenders during crime commission implemented a "rational choice approach" (Proulx, Ouimet, & Lachaîne, 1995). The rational choice perspective suggests that offenders are active decision makers whose choices are directed by the costs and benefits of a desired outcome; that is, offenders want to minimize the costs and maximize the gains (Cornish & Clarke, 1987). In their study, Proulx et al. (1995) evaluated the decisions of 10 child sexual offenders and found that the offenders made a series of decisions and choices prior to sexually abusing children, which included: (1) where (the place) the offender is to encounter a potential victim; (2) the time of the attack; (3) the victim (such as gender, appearance/erotic value, vulnerability, and relationship of the victim to the offender); (4) the strategy to approach the victim; and (5) the strategy to involve the victim in sexual activity. Proulx et al. (1995) found that at each of the decisional steps, offenders took part in an assessment of the risk of negative consequences (for example, "What is the probability of getting caught?" "What is the probability of being incarcerated?").

Building on Proulx et al. (1995) study, Leclerc, Wortley, and Smallbone (2011) proposed an empirically based script model in child sexual offending. The eight steps that comprise the decision-making model are split over two phases: crime setup phase and crime achievement phase. Phase 1, crime setup phase, has five steps.

Entry to setting: prior to committing the crime the offender must encounter the victim (this step does not apply to offenders who offend against their own children).

Instrumental initiation: the offender must gain the victim's trust. Trust may be gained through providing the child attention and love while in other cases it may involve giving material goods (e.g., candy and toys).

Continuation: once trust is gained, some offenders will implement strategies to proceed to the location (e.g., inducements such as money or the use of threats and violence).

Location selection: in most cases, due to the established intimate relationship with the victim, the location where the crime takes place is generally the offender's home or sometimes the victim's home.

Instrumental actualization: the offender needs to create a set of circumstances in which they can be alone with the victim (e.g., inviting the victim over to the offender's home alone).

Phase 2, crime achievement phase, has three steps.

Completion: the offender attempts to gain the victim's cooperation in sexual activity through making it appear as normal interaction (e.g., in the form of a game).

Outcomes: this step refers to the amount of time the offender spends engaging in sexual activity with the victim and the type of sexual behaviors the victim is involved in.

Postoffense condition: the final step refers to preventing the victim from disclosing. The nature of offender–victim interaction during the offense will impact the extent to which the offender needs to adopt strategies consisting of preventing disclosure. While in some instances the offender may not have to implement such strategies (as the victim is too young to understand that sexual abuse occurred), in other situations the offender may give or threaten to withdraw enticements (e.g., money, attention) to prevent the child from disclosing.

Leclerc et al. (2011) highlighted that the process does not involve the offender to undergo every step of the process—some stages can be skipped. For example, if the victim is too young to understand that the behavior is abusive, the offender does not need to implement strategies at the final step (postoffense condition) to prevent the victim from disclosing. Leclerc et al. also pointed out that feedback loops may occur. A child's parent may decide to go along to the destination where the offender had planned to abuse the child. This would "force" the offender to create another set of circumstances in which he could isolate the child. Leclerc et al. (2011) concluded that child sexual offenders go through a manipulative process that requires decisions to be made at many steps along the way.

Beauregard et al. (2012) also utilized the rational choice approach to explore the decision-making process (surrounding offense planning, offense strategy, and aftermath of the offense) across various types of sexual offenders: child sexual offenders, adult sexual offenders, and victim-crossover sexual offenders (those who offend against both children and adults). They found that child sexual offenders utilized structured planning, making sure to select a cooperative victim and the right environment. In contrast, adult sexual offenders did not utilize planning as much but protected their identity through "forensic awareness" (e.g., took safety measures not to leave evidence). Beauregard et al. also found that child sexual offenders focused on gaining control of the situation (i.e., grooming) before sexually offending against a victim. In contrast, adult sexual offenders had less control over the situation but instead controlled the victim (for example, by using force). They found that for victim-crossover sexual offenders, their decision-making was adapted based on the "type" of victim. Beauregard et al. (2012) concluded that different types of sexual offenders use different types of decision-making, in particular, the important role of victim age and situational factors.

EXPERT OFFENDERS

Similar to other offenders, child sexual offenders have been suggested to vary in expertise from novice or "midway" offenders through to experienced and expert offenders. The way that child sexual offenders plan and skillfully commit their offenses suggests that some level of expertise is present (Fortune et al., 2015). Ward (1999) suggested that offenders can evade detection over numerous years through refining one's offense-related skills, for example, the selectivity in victim choice and offense location. Bourke, Ward, and Rose (2012) argued that sexual offenders can be placed on a continuum from novice to expert and that the difference between the two ends is the offender's level of knowledge, technique, and skill. Offenders who are considered expert have gained knowledge through a number of various means. These means include engaging in early sexualized fantasy, histories of CSA, and social learning, as well as reflecting on previous offenses and refining the methods (Bourke et al., 2012).

Bourke et al. (2012) tested whether the notion of an "expert" child sexual offender could be empirically supported through the identification of a group of child sexual offenders who demonstrated high levels of proficiency in their offending (for example, grooming techniques, target selection). They analyzed the interviews of 47 child sexual offenders and developed the expertise related competency (ERC) model. Bourke et al's. (2012) study supported Ward's (1999) theory that offense-related knowledge is structured off behavioral scripts. Bourke et al. (2012) found that the richer and more organized the child sexual offender's knowledge framework was, the greater success the offender had carrying out the offense. They suggested that information pertaining to prior victims, as well as present and future victims, is stored as interconnected offense scripts. These scripts allow the individual to readily access the script when selecting strategies for future offenses. In addition to well-planned strategies drawn from offense-related scripts, other important indicators of expertise include the offender's ability to alternate between offense strategies with ease and speed as well as the detection of opportunities (Fortune et al., 2015).

ONLINE CHILD PREDATORS

For more than a decade, the threat of online child predators has been prominent in media stories, research, and preventative efforts (Wolak & Finkelhor, 2013). As of 2015, there were 843,260 registered online sexual offenders in the United States

(National Center for Missing and Exploited Children, 2015). Seto, Wood, Babchishin, and Flynn (2012) suggested that there are a number of types of online offenders, including *contact-driven offenders* (groom online for the purpose of offline sexual contact), *fantasy-driven offenders* (solely to keep the relationship online), and *child pornographers* (download, collect, and disseminate child pornography). Other offenders also use the Internet to network with individuals who hold similar sexual interests in children (such as pedophile organizations).

Some differences exist between online child predators and in-person child sexual offenders. Seto et al. (2012) studied 38 individuals convicted of contact child sexual offenses, 38 individuals convicted of child pornography offenses, and 70 individuals convicted of online solicitation offenses. The authors found that child pornography and online solicitation offenders differed from contact offenders in terms of education levels; child pornography and online solicitation offenders were better educated than contact offenders. In another study, Burke, Sowerbutts, Blundell, and Sherry (2002) suggested child pornography users were generally better educated, had higher levels of intelligence, and had no prior criminal history, in comparison with contact child sexual offenders. While there appear to be some common characteristics amongst online child sexual offenders (e.g., education, intelligence, no prior criminal history), they represent a heterogeneous group in terms of their motivations. The offender who disseminates child pornography may be driven by monetary profits, whereas, the fantasy-driven offender may be motivated to discuss sexual activities online with children (Briggs, Simon, & Simonsen, 2011; Marcum, 2007).

The grooming processes between online and offline predatory relationships differ also. Online predators are faced with the initial lack of certainty regarding exactly "whom" they are interacting with (O'Connell, 2003); this is not an issue for contact offenders. O'Connell (2003) developed a five-stage model to explain the process of online grooming. The first stage, "friendship forming," is where the offender gets to know the child. This includes gathering information about the child's gender, age, and interests. Next, "relationship forming" takes place. This is where the offender forms a bond with the child by appearing compassionate and understanding and attempts to gain the child's trust. The offender then undergoes "risk assessment" in which he attempts to determine the likelihood of being caught, by inquiring about the child's location and the child's parents' schedules. Sexual topics may be introduced into the conversation here to test whether the child would engage in sexual activity. The "exclusivity" stage is when the offender encourages the child not to divulge their relationship to others. Finally, the "sexual stage" is where the offender perceives that the victim trusts them and thereby becomes explicit about their intentions toward the child. This may include asking the child about past sexual experiences, outlining sexual acts that he wants to perform on the child, or sending the child pornography. It is at this stage that the offender may suggest travel arrangements.

Black, Wollis, Woodworth, and Hancock (2015) empirically tested O'Connell's (2003) online grooming process in light of contact-driven offenders (those who engage with children online with the intention to offend against the child in person) and analyzed 44 transcripts of convicted online child sexual offenders. While Black et al. (2015) noted the presence of each of the five stages in the online interactions, the stages did not occur in the linear order proposed by O'Connell (2003). For instance, Black et al. (2015) noted that the risk assessment stage was most prevalent in the initial stage of the conversation. They argued that this may occur early on due to the individual attempting to determine whether it is worth investing time in the child as a potential victim. Also, they noted that many offenders questioned the child about their living situation and location at the outset of their conversation, deciphering how much of a logistical challenge it would be to gain physical contact with the victim. Results concluded that online offenders expedite the grooming process, in particular, the immediate assessment of risk and the early introduction of sexually explicit language and topics to the child (Black et al., 2015).

The popular view of contact-driven offenders is adults posing as children online in order to lure the child into meeting in person (i.e., the adult deceiving the child of their actual age); however, this is not the case. Wolak, Finkelhor, and Mitchell (2004) conducted telephone interviews with law enforcement agencies (local, state, and federal) concerning 129 cases of sexual offenses against children that were initiated with online encounters. While they found that 76% of offenders were older than 26 years of age, only 5% of offenders portrayed themselves online as being 17 years of age or younger. The authors also found that the deception of sexual motives was scarce; while the offenders made deceitful promises to the child pertaining to romance and love, most offenders were open about their interest in having sexual relations with the child. Interestingly, Wolak et al. (2004) found that 73% of victims met their offenders in person more than once, 39% of victims met their offender three or more times in person, and 20% of victims lived with the offender for some time. Half of the victims were described to have been in love with the offender (or held feelings of close friendship) and perceived the relationship as desirable. Wolak et al. (2004) highlighted the need for parents and the media, as well as health care professionals and educators, to be aware of the nature, existence, and dynamics of online relationships.

CONCLUSIONS

This chapter explored the psychology behind child sexual offending. In particular, a few of the common misconceptions surrounding child sexual offenders were raised. This was followed by a discussion on female child sexual offenders, how and why individuals become child sexual offenders, crime scripts, and online child predators. Overall, child sexual offenders are not a homogenous group of individuals. While one-factor theories can be used to explain why people become child sexual offenders, this chapter highlighted the importance of taking a multifactorial approach. The chapter also discussed the decision-making processes and choices that child sexual offenders undergo in the lead up to, and during, the offense; through refining one's offense-related skills, it is evident that offenders can evade detection over numerous years. Finally, the issue of online child predators was discussed, in particular, that the real-life dynamics of online child predators do not fit society's stereotype.

SUMMARY

- Conceptions surrounding child sexual offenders include: all child sexual offenders are pedophiles; child sexual offenders mostly target strangers; and all child sexual offenders were once victims of sexual abuse themselves. None of these are founded in evidence.
- The terms *child sexual offender* and *pedophile* cannot be used interchangeably (Feelgood & Hoyer, 2008). Not all pedophiles are child sexual offenders and, likewise, not all child sexual offenders are pedophiles.
- A pedophile is an individual who is sexually attracted to, or has a sexual preference toward, prepubescent children. However, these individuals may not necessarily act on this attraction and may instead solely experience sexually arousing fantasies or urges. Furthermore, pedophilia is considered a mental disorder (pedophilic disorder) listed within the class of paraphilic disorders in the *Diagnostic and Statistical Manual of Mental Disorders* (DSM5; American Psychiatric Association, 2013).
- A child sexual offender is an individual who has had some form of sexual contact or involvement with children. This may include contact offenses (e.g., penetration, fondling, masturbation) and noncontact offenses (e.g., exhibitionism, exposing the child to pornography, indecently recording the child). While some child sexual offenders may be attracted to children, other child sexual offenders may hold a sexual preference toward adults yet offend against children merely due to an opportunity for sexual gratification. Unlike pedophilia, there is no psychological diagnostic label for child sexual offending.
- About 90% of victims know their offender and only around 10% of victims are abused by a stranger.
- The research on female child sexual offenders has remained atheoretical for decades. Little is known about the characteristics of female child sexual offenders, including psychopathology, offense cycles, motivations, and deviant arousal. Typologies are used to understand the differences between types of offenders and consist of offender characteristics and victim-choice information. Matthews et al. (1989) constructed one of the most commonly referenced typologies for female sexual offenders: (1) male-coerced, (2) teacher/lover, and (3) predisposed molester.
- Theories are central to the field of criminology because they provide explanations and interpretations of crimes, and a number of theories have been developed to explain and interpret why adults sexually offend against children. Some of these include cognitive distortions, attachment theories, the precondition model (Finkelhor, 1984), and the pathways model (Ward & Siegert, 2002).

- While the literature highlights that child sexual offenders have deficiencies in various aspects of their lives, it is also important to look at child sexual offender's areas of competency in their offending. A script arranges one's knowledge about how to perform in everyday life and assists offenders with the automatic processing of offense-related information and decision-making. Crime scripts include instructions about how to execute certain actions, the order of how the actions should be carried out, and the probable consequences of a particular action. Specifically, child sexual offender scripts may contain information surrounding how to choose victims, groom victims, plan an offense, carry out an offense, attain victim compliance, deal with victim resistance, and avoid detection. There are also interconnected cognitive scripts on their past offenses and victims, which can facilitate future planning and execution.

- The internal and external constraints that shape crime scripts are referred to as choice-structuring properties and denote the choices and actions taken by the offender to commit a crime. Similar to other crimes, child sexual offenses are subject to specific choice-structuring properties. For instance, not only does the offense need to occur in an isolated place but the place needs to remain isolated for long enough so the offender can experience sexual gratification.

- For more than a decade, the threat of online child predators has been prominent in media stories, research, and preventative efforts. As of 2015, there were almost 850,000 registered online sexual offenders in the United States. There are a number of types of online offenders, including contact-driven offenders (groom online for the purpose of offline sexual contact), fantasy-driven offenders (solely to keep the relationship online), and child pornographers (download, collect, and disseminate child pornography). Other offenders also use the Internet to network with individuals who hold similar sexual interests in children (such as pedophile organizations).

- Some differences exist between online child predators and in-person child sexual offenders. Online predators are generally better educated, have higher levels of intelligence, and have no prior criminal history, in comparison with contact child sexual offenders.

QUESTIONS

1. What are some other common misconceptions that the public may hold surrounding child sexual offenders?
2. Why are female child sexual offenders viewed differently than male child sexual offenders? How could society overcome its hesitancy to the idea that females are capable of sexually abusing children?
3. What are cognitive distortions and what role do they play in sexual offending?
4. What is "grooming"? Why do offenders "groom" their victims?
5. What is the best way to prevent online child predators from soliciting children?

6. What are some new Internet sites and smartphone apps that may make children more susceptible to online child predators?
7. Leclerc et al. (2011) proposed an empirically based script model in child sexual offending in which the offense occurs across two phases and eight steps. Describe the eight steps and the two separate phases of the offense, according to this model.
8. Explain the pathways model of child sexual offending.
9. Describe the precondition model of child sexual offending.
10. What role do attachment theories play in explaining child sexual offending?

REFERENCES

Abel, G., Becker, J., & Cunningham-Rathner, J. (1984). Complications, consent, and cognitions in sex between children and adults. *International Journal of Law and Psychiatry*, 7, 89–103. http://dx.doi.org/10.1016/0160-2527(84)90008-6.

Ainsworth, M., & Bowlby, J. (1991). An ethological approach to personality development. *American Psychologist*, 46, 333–341. http://dx.doi.org/10.1037//0003-066x.46.4.333.

American Psychiatric Association. (2013). *Diagnostic and statistics manual of mental disorders* (5th ed.). Arlington, VA: American Psychiatric Publishing.

Australian Bureau of Statistics. (2005). *Personal safety survey Australia. (4906.0)*. Retrieved from: http://www.abs.gov.au/AUSSTATS/abs@.nsf/Lookup/4906.0Main+Features12012?OpenDocument.

Aydin, B., Akbas, S., Turla, A., Dundar, C., Yuce, M., & Karabekiroglu, K. (2015). Child sexual abuse in Turkey: an analysis of 1002 cases. *Journal of Forensic Sciences*, 60, 61–65. http://dx.doi.org/10.1111/1556-4029.12566.

Beauregard, E., Leclerc, B., & Lussier, P. (2012). Decision making in the crime commission process: comparing rapists, child molesters, and victim-crossover sex offenders. *Criminal Justice and Behavior*, 39, 1275–1295. http://dx.doi.org/10.1177/0093854812453120.

Beech, A. R., Bartels, R. M., & Dixon, L. (2013). Assessment and treatment of distorted schemas in sexual offenders. *Trauma, Violence & Abuse*, 14, 54–66. http://dx.doi.org/10.1177/1524838012463970.

Black, P., Wollis, M., Woodworth, M., & Hancock, J. (2015). A linguistic analysis of grooming strategies of online child sex offenders: implications for our understanding of predatory sexual behavior in an increasingly computer-mediated world. *Child Abuse & Neglect*, 44, 140–149. http://dx.doi.org/10.1016/j.chiabu.2014.12.004.

Bourke, P., Ward, T., & Rose, C. (2012). Expertise and sexual offending: a preliminary empirical model. *Journal of Interpersonal Violence*, 27, 2391–2414. http://dx.doi.org/10.1177/0886260511433513.

Bowlby, J. (1973). *Separation*. New York: Basic Books.

Briggs, P., Simon, W., & Simonsen, S. (2011). An exploratory study of internet-initiated sexual offenses and the chat room sex offender: has the internet enabled a new typology of sex offender? *Sexual Abuse: A Journal of Research and Treatment*, 23, 72–91. http://dx.doi.org/10.1177/1079063210384275.

Burke, A., Sowerbutts, S., Blundell, B., & Sherry, M. (2002). Child pornography and the internet: policing and treatment issues. *Psychiatry, Psychology and Law*, 9, 79–84. http://dx.doi.org/10.1375/132187102760196925.

Cornish, D. (1994). The procedural analysis of offending and its relevance for situational prevention. In R. V. Clarke (Ed.), *Crime prevention studies* (pp. 3151–3196). New York: Criminal Justice Press.

Cornish, D., & Clarke, R. (1987). Understanding crime displacement: an application of rational choice theory. *Criminology*, *25*, 933–948. http://dx.doi.org/10.1111/j.1745-9125.1987.tb00826.x.

Cortoni, F., & Hanson, R. (2005). *A review of the recidivism rates of adult female sexual offenders*. Ottawa, Ontario: Research Branch, Correctional Service of Canada.

Daigneault, I., Hébert, M., & McDuff, P. (2009). Men's and women's childhood sexual abuse and victimization in adult partner relationships: a study of risk factors. *Child Abuse & Neglect*, *33*, 638–647. http://dx.doi.org/10.1016/j.chiabu.2009.04.003.

Feelgood, S., & Hoyer, J. (2008). Child molester or paedophile? Sociolegal versus psychopathological classification of sexual offenders against children. *Journal of Sexual Aggression*, *14*, 33–43. http://dx.doi.org/10.1080/13552600802133860.

Finkelhor, D. (1984). *Child sexual abuse*. New York: Free Press.

Finkelhor, D., Ormrod, R., Turner, H., & Hamby, S. (2005). The victimization of children and youth: a comprehensive, national survey. *Child Maltreatment*, *10*, 5–25. http://dx.doi.org/10.1177/1077559504271287.

Fortune, C., Bourke, P., & Ward, T. (2015). Expertise and child sex offenders. *Aggression and Violent Behavior*, *20*, 33–41. http://dx.doi.org/10.1016/j.avb.2014.12.005.

Geddes, R., Tyson, G., & McGreal, S. (2013). Gender bias in the education system: perceptions of teacher–student sexual relationships. *Psychiatry, Psychology and Law*, *20*, 608–618. http://dx.doi.org/10.1080/13218719.2012.728428.

Grattagliano, I., Owens, J., Morton, R., Campobasso, C., Carabellese, F., & Catanesi, R. (2012). Female sexual offenders: five Italian case studies. *Aggression and Violent Behavior*, *17*, 180–187. http://dx.doi.org/10.1016/j.avb.2012.01.001.

Hall, G., & Hirschman, R. (1992). Sexual aggression against children: a conceptual perspective of etiology. *Criminal Justice and Behavior*, *19*, 8–23. http://dx.doi.org/10.1177/0093854892019001003.

Harris, D. (2010). Theories of female sexual offending. In T. A. Gannon, & F. Cortoni (Eds.), *Female sexual offenders: Theory, assessment, & practice* (pp. 31–52). .United Kingdom: Wiley-Blackwell.

Kwako, L., Noll, J., Putnam, F., & Trickett, P. (2010). Childhood sexual abuse and attachment: an intergenerational perspective. *Clinical Child Psychology and Psychiatry*, *15*, 407–422. http://dx.doi.org/10.1177/1359104510367590.

Leclerc, B., Wortley, R., & Smallbone, S. (2011). Getting into the script of adult child sex offenders and mapping out situational prevention measures. *Journal of Research in Crime and Delinquency*, *48*, 209–237. http://dx.doi.org/10.1177/0022427810391540.

Lewis, C., & Stanley, C. (2000). Women accused of sexual offenses. *Behavioral Sciences & the Law*, *18*, 73–81. http://dx.doi.org/10.1002/(sici)1099-0798(200001/02)18:1<73::aid-bsl378>3.0.co;2-#.

Maniglio, R. (2010). Child sexual abuse in the etiology of depression: a systematic review of reviews. *Depression and Anxiety*, *27*, 631–642. http://dx.doi.org/10.1002/da.20687.

Marcum, C. (2007). Interpreting the intentions of internet predators: an examination of online predatory behavior. *Journal of Child Sexual Abuse*, *16*, 99–114. http://dx.doi.org/10.1300/j070v16n04_06.

Marshall, W. (1989). Intimacy, loneliness and sexual offenders. *Behaviour Research and Therapy*, *27*, 491–504. http://dx.doi.org/10.1016/0005-7967(89)90083-1.

Marshall, W. (1993). The role of attachments, intimacy, and loneliness in the etiology and maintenance of sexual offending. *Sexual and Marital Therapy*, 8, 109–121. http://dx.doi. org/10.1080/02674659308408187.

Matthews, R., Matthews, J., & Speltz, K. (1989). *Female sexual offenders: An exploratory study*. Vermont: Safer Society Press.

McKillop, N., Smallbone, S., Wortley, R., & Andjic, I. (2012). Offenders' attachment and sexual abuse onset: a test of theoretical propositions. *Sexual Abuse: A Journal of Research and Treatment*, 24, 591–610. http://dx.doi.org/10.1177/1079063212445571.

Nathan, P., & Ward, T. (2002). Female sex offenders: clinical and demographic features. *Journal of Sexual Aggression*, 8, 5–21. http://dx.doi.org/10.1080/13552600208413329.

National Center for Missing and Exploited Children. (2015). *Registered sex offenders in the United States*. Retrieved from: http://www.missingkids.com/en_US/documents/Sex_Offenders_ Map.pdf.

Ó Ciardha, C., & Ward, T. (2012). Theories of cognitive distortions in sexual offending: what the current research tells us. *Trauma, Violence & Abuse*, 14, 5–21. http://dx.doi. org/10.1177/1524838012467856.

O'Connell, R. (2003). *A typology of cybersexploitation and online grooming practices*. Retrieved from: http://image.guardian.co.uk/sys-files/Society/documents/2003/07/24/ Netpaedoreport.pdf.

Proulx, J., Ouimet, M., & Lachaîne, N. (1995). Criminologie de l'acte et pédophilie [Criminology of actions and pedophilia]. *Revue Internationale de Criminologie et de Police Technique*, 48, 294–310.

Richards, K. (2011). *Misperceptions about child sex offenders*. Canberra: Australian Institute of Criminology (AIC). http://www.aic.gov.au/media_library/publications/tandi_pdf/ tandi429.pdf.

Robertiello, G., & Terry, K. (2007). Can we profile sex offenders? A review of sex offender typologies. *Aggression and Violent Behavior*, 12, 508–518. http://dx.doi.org/10.1016/j. avb.2007.02.010.

Salter, D., McMillan, D., Richards, M., Talbot, T., Hodges, J., Bentovim, A., et al. (2003). Development of sexually abusive behaviour in sexually victimised males: a longitudinal study. *Lancet*, 361, 471–476. http://dx.doi.org/10.1016/s0140-6736(03)12466-x.

Seto, M., Wood, J., Babchishin, K., & Flynn, S. (2012). Online solicitation offenders are different from child pornography offenders and lower risk contact sexual offenders. *Law and Human Behavior*, 36, 320–330. http://dx.doi.org/10.1037/h0093925.

Simons, D. (2007). Understanding victimization among sexual abusers. In D. Prescott (Ed.), *Knowledge & practice: Challenges in the treatment and supervision of sexual abusers* (pp. 56–90). Oklahoma: Wood 'N' Barnes Publishing.

Simons, D., Wurtele, S., & Durham, R. (2008). Developmental experiences of child sexual abusers and rapists. *Child Abuse & Neglect*, 32, 549–560. http://dx.doi.org/10.1016/j. chiabu.2007.03.027.

Sinnamon, G. C. B. (2015). Psychopathology and criminal behavior. In W. Petherick (Ed.), *Applied crime analysis: A social science approach to understanding crime, criminals, and victims* (pp. 208–252). Boston, MA: Anderson Publishing.

Stinson, J., Sales, B., & Becker, J. (2008). *Sex offending*. Washington, DC: American Psychological Association.

Syed, F., & Williams, S. (1996). *Case studies of female sex offenders in the Correctional Service of Canada*. Retrieved from: http://www.publicsafety.gc.ca/lbrr/archives/hv%20 8738%20s9%201996-eng.pdf.

Tedeschi, J. T., & Felson, R. B. (1994). *Violence, aggression, and coercive actions*. Washington, DC: American Psychological Association.

Ward, T. (1999). Competency and deficit models in the understanding and treatment of sexual offenders. *The Journal of Sex Research, 36*, 298–305. http://dx.doi.org/10.1080/00224499909552000.

Ward, T. (2000). Sexual offenders' cognitive distortions as implicit theories. *Aggression and Violent Behavior, 5*, 491–507. http://dx.doi.org/10.1016/s1359-1789(98)00036-6.

Ward, T., Gannon, T., & Keown, K. (2006). Beliefs, values, and action: the judgment model of cognitive distortions in sexual offenders. *Aggression and Violent Behavior, 11*, 323–340. http://dx.doi.org/10.1016/j.avb.2005.10.003.

Ward, T., & Hudson, S. (2011). Finkelhor's precondition model of child sexual abuse: a critique. *Psychology, Crime & Law, 7*, 291–307. http://dx.doi.org/10.1080/10683160108401799.

Ward, T., Hudson, S., Johnston, L., & Marshall, W. L. (1997). Cognitive distortions in sex offenders: an integrative review. *Clinical Psychology Review, 17*, 479–507. http://dx.doi.org/10.1016/s0272-7358(97)81034-3.

Ward, T., Hudson, S., Marshall, W., & Siegert, R. (1995). Attachment style and intimacy deficits in sexual offenders: a theoretical framework. *Sexual Abuse: A Journal of Research and Treatment, 7*, 317–335. http://dx.doi.org/10.1007/bf02256835.

Ward, T., & Keenan, T. (1999). Child molesters' implicit theories. *Journal of Interpersonal Violence, 14*, 821–838. http://dx.doi.org/10.1177/088626099014008003.

Ward, T., & Siegert, R. (2002). Toward a comprehensive theory of child sexual abuse: a theory knitting perspective. *Psychology, Crime & Law, 8*, 319–351. http://dx.doi.org/10.1080/10683160208401823.

Wolak, J., & Finkelhor, D. (2013). Are crimes by online predators different from crimes by sex offenders who know youth in-person? *The Journal of Adolescent Health, 53*, 736–741. http://dx.doi.org/10.1016/j.jadohealth.2013.06.010.

Wolak, J., Finkelhor, D., & Mitchell, K. (2004). Internet-initiated sex crimes against minors: implications for prevention based on findings from a national study. *The Journal of Adolescent Health, 35*, 424.e11–424.e20. http://dx.doi.org/10.1016/j.jadohealth.2004.05.006.

The Psychology of Adult Sexual Grooming: Sinnamon's Seven-Stage Model of Adult Sexual Grooming

16

Grant Sinnamon

Bond University, Gold Cosat, QLD, Australia; Bela Menso Brain and Behaviour Centre,
Varsity Lakes, QLD, Australia

CHAPTER OUTLINE

The Psychology of Criminal and Antisocial Behavior. http://dx.doi.org/10.1016/B978-0-12-809287-3.00016-X

INTRODUCTION

There are several proposed models of grooming that are posited to apply to both child and adult sexual grooming. In this chapter, the author proposes an adult model of sexual grooming that, while possibly having some application in the description of child sexual grooming, has been developed to explain the specific character of predatory sexual behavior involving the targeting of vulnerable adults, the engagement in the preparatory processes characterized as grooming, and the instigation and maintenance of sexually exploitative and abusive relationships with adult victims by sexual predators.

While the character of adult grooming is well understood, the prevalence and offense statistics surrounding adult sexual grooming and the consequent abuse and exploitation remains elusive. This is primarily due to what are believed to be extremely low rates of reporting by victims, and the challenge to differentiate what associated behaviors are actually illegal as opposed to unethical or immoral. Indeed, when it comes to child sexual grooming and abuse, any behavior that involves sexual interaction with a minor is readily identifiable as illegal and can be treated as such by the justice system. However, the process of dealing with predatory sexual behavior against adults can be far more difficult to identify and prosecute. For the eventual victim, the initial stages of grooming typically involve substantial emotionally and/or physically rewarding experiences at the hands of the perpetrator. Later in the process, as the manipulation increases and the exploitation commences, a predator's behavior may or may not cross the line between exploitation and abuse. While both are deviant, reprehensible, unconscionable, and never acceptable, the ability to distinguish between them is, in reality, extremely difficult.

ADULT SEXUAL ABUSE: THE STATISTICS

Across Australasia, North America, and Europe, it has been estimated that only 4–8% of adults who are abused or exploited as a result of sexual grooming behaviors come forward and report their abuse (www.rainn.org). This statistic comes largely from research conducted into grooming and abuse conducted at the hands of perpetrators in the helping professions, and therefore may not be readily generalizable to the broader population of victims. According to the Rape, Abuse, and Incest National Network (RAINN) in the United States, a number of reasons have been provided by victims for not coming forward including shame and guilt; fear of their abuser; fear of hurting family, friends, or other elements of their social community (e.g., church congregation, sporting club, school community); fear of not being believed or of being blamed; the stigma associated with sexual abuse; not knowing whom to turn to; feeling of being isolated (a tactic of the abuser is often to isolate the victim from their social supports); not feeling emotionally and psychologically capable of "dealing" with the fallout that they perceived would come with reporting the abuse; and not realizing they had been a victim until a substantial period of time had elapsed after the experience (www.rainn.org). The lack of reporting makes any broad examination of the prevalence difficult and speculative at best.

In general, the lifetime incidence of sexual abuse of women over the age of 15 years is disturbingly high. In Australia, the Personal Safety Survey results for 2012 indicated that almost 1:5 women aged 18 years or over had experienced sexual assault since the age of 15, and that almost 90% of these women knew their perpetrator (Australian Bureau of Statistics, 2012). In the United States, the estimated percentage of women who have experienced sexual assault is similar, with about 75% of assaults involving a perpetrator known to the victim (Kilpatrick, Resnick, Ruggiero, Conoscenti, & McCauley, 2007; Truman, 2011). The reported incidence of male sexual assault is much lower at approximately 4% of the adult population experiencing sexual assault after the age of 15 years in Australia. However, the rates of perpetrators who are known to the victim remain high at around 75% (Australian Bureau of Statistics, 2012). Once again, statistics from the United States are very similar with an estimated 3% of adult men having been a victim of sexual assault with around 75% of perpetrators known to their victims (Truman, 2011). While these statistics do not report on grooming, they do show high rates of sexual assault in adults and, in particular, high rates of acquaintance perpetration.

WHAT IS GROOMING?

The word *grooming* has a variety of meanings. In the context of this chapter, to groom or the process of grooming, refers to an act of preparation. In this context, the online *Oxford Dictionary* defines grooming as "preparing or training (someone) for a particular purpose or activity". Grooming is synonymous with terms such as preparing, priming, making ready, conditioning, tailoring, coaching, training, instructing, tutoring, drilling, teaching, educating, and schooling. In this way, this meaning is not unique to sexual predation or sexual abuse, but rather can be applied in any situation in which an individual prepares another for a specific purpose. It may be a positive process, for example, a young executive may be groomed for leadership, or a young athlete may be groomed for the professional ranks. However, grooming is not always motivated by a desire to prepare the person being groomed for positive opportunity. Grooming is often used as a means to prepare an individual or to place an individual into a position in which they are unwittingly subjected to abusive and/or exploitative behavior. It is an insidious form of predatory behavior that is a characteristic practice of con artists, sexual abusers, and antisocial and narcissistic personality types as a means to target and manipulate vulnerable people, and may be motivated by a pursuit of power, revenge, financial gain, or sexual gratification. Sexual, elder, and financial abuse; extortion; human trafficking; and slavery (including sex slavery), are several examples of the unsavory consequences of objectionable grooming endeavors. The challenge with "grooming" behaviors is that, at least in the early stages of the process, the actions undertaken in a honorable versus nefarious interaction may be indistinguishable. This is because exploitative grooming often takes the shape of a deliberate process of creating a strong, positively reinforced relationship, in which trust is garnered and intimate interactions are normalized.

WHAT IS SEXUAL GROOMING?

Sexual grooming is the process of deliberately establishing a connection with an individual in order to prepare that person for sexual exploitation and/or abuse. Sexual predators are often very considered in their approach to their selection of, and the tactics they employ to engage with, both the abuse environment and their intended victim. This deliberate consideration and associated behavior is the grooming process. Offenders have consistently stated that they identify and target vulnerable individuals and systematically set out to ingratiate themselves into the person's life. Establishing trust with the target and their family and social network, normalizing intimate interactions, blurring the lines of what is and is not appropriate behavior, desensitizing their victim to the warning signs of abuse or exploitation, and creating a psychologically, socially, emotionally, and often physically reinforcing experience as an integral component to these processes are all a part of the systematic preparation of a victim. As abusive interactions are slowly introduced into the relationship, the victim, while feeling some surprise or discomfort, is generally desensitized and habituated to the intimacy, such that the intensification of sexual contact does not elevate the victim's threat response sufficiently to instigate defensive behaviors. Further habituation can then result in increased acceptance of the abuse. Grooming is an effective tool for a sexual predator as it creates a space in which the grooming process and often the abuse itself, at least initially, may be identified by the victim as a positive experience. Later, confusion, guilt, fear, or some other overt or implied threat by the abuser are consistently reported by victims as factors that acted to prevent them from reporting the abuse.

WHAT IS "ADULT GROOMING"?

The vast majority of the extant literature on grooming is focused on child sexual abuse and exploitation. However, personal and environmental grooming can and frequently does occur in the course of sexual exploitation and abuse of adults. Adult sexual grooming is analogous to child sexual grooming, and can be defined as any situation in which an adult is primed to permit themselves to be abused and/or exploited for sexual gratification of another. The grooming process used by sexual predators on children and adults is essentially the same, focusing on emotional and psychological manipulation tactics.

THE GROOMING PROCESS

Generally speaking, adults have a greater potential than children to make use of their own experiences, the experiences of others, personal cognizance, and to reach out to any number of familial, social, and professional supports for advice and assistance. Therefore, in preparing adults for sexual exploitation, grooming the victim and the victim's environment are both essential components of the preparatory sexual predator's tactics, and the perpetrator's behaviors manifest within the grooming process include the deliberate manipulation of both areas.

Grooming may involve weeks, months, even years of preabuse preparation. The grooming process generally progresses through a series of stages during which the sexual predator uses a number of specific techniques to mask their intentions and prime their target for abuse. Often these two objectives—masking and priming—involve the same behaviors and are aimed at both the individual target as well as the target's social environment. Many sexual predators ingratiate themselves with the social environment, establishing themselves as a trustworthy, dependable, upstanding person in the community, who is never suspected of being an offender because they are "just too nice." They are seen as the helpful neighbor, the caring professional, the dedicated teacher or coach, and the devoted minister, counselor, or other form of "spiritual" advisor. This is a very powerful and effective tactic as it embeds an offender into the community, removes suspicion, provides a ready excuse for personal contact with victims, breaks down barriers, and can provide secondary rewards for the narcissistic or antisocial personality type who craves adoration (narcissistic personality) or receives perverse pleasure in successfully deceiving those around them (antisocial personality). It is these characteristics that result in people dropping their guard and allowing an increased amount of intimate contact to occur.

The predator's conscious efforts to ingratiate themselves to both the target as well as their family and social environment means that the victim will often also lose their external monitors and/or access to their usual "sounding boards." Given that the perpetrator is often an influential person in the victim's life, they may also lose access to the advisory role that they had come to fill, further isolating the victim from a supportive place to "check in" and obtain feedback about the escalation of intimacy and the appropriateness of these behaviors. In cases of sexual abuse where grooming is a feature, it is important to note that, in the vast majority of cases that are not undertaken solely within the domain of cyberspace, perpetrators are well known to the victim's family and social network. The sexual predator's ability to insert themselves into the victim's life is based on the use of charm, ingratiation, and manipulation, as a deliberate and calculated tactic. Victims and perpetrators alike report that a sexual predator's presentation as sincere, open, truthful, and "likable" are a primary factor in their ability to break down barriers and get close to their target without arousing suspicion in either the target or their family and social network. These tactics used by sexual predators fool many people and are often so effective that, even when the sexual abuse is brought to light, many of the victim's family and friends will not believe that the perpetrator is capable of such acts. In many cases families, congregations, schools, clubs, and whole communities have been torn apart by the division caused by the belief by some and disbelief of others.

WHO GROOMS THEIR VICTIMS: CHARACTERISTICS OF THE SEXUAL PREDATOR

The predator that uses grooming in the pursuit of their adult victims can possess numerous variations in personal characteristics. There are, however, several common traits that can usually be identified as a part of the personality characteristics of this type of sexual predator. Predatory sex offenders are characteristically motivated by a desire to maintain or restore their self-esteem through the manipulation and control of others, and by the prospect of excitement and the opportunity to deviously exhibit their dominance and superiority (Petherick & Sinnamon, 2013). Using the personality disorder pathology types as a stereotypical template for deviant personality characteristics, these primary traits are endemic in the narcissistic and the antisocial personality types, respectively. While other personality types may be manipulative and devious in various elements of their behavior, they are, generally speaking, not as likely to become sexual predators as are these two personality types.

The Narcissistic Sexual Predator

The narcissistic sexual offender uses sexual predation and gratification as an external source of restoration and/or maintenance of their amplified self-esteem needs. This fits with the assertive-oriented typology of perpetrators and victims proposed by Petherick and Sinnamon (2013). Ultimately, this type of predator is likely to have either a high, but fragile, or a low self-esteem. Compensatory behaviors aimed at dominating others and being the center of attention are sexually channeled into the predation and exploitation of others. The narcissistic belief that they are better than others, and therefore that their needs and desires are ultimately more deserving of fulfillment, are not necessarily supported by their low or high-fragile self-esteem, and this incongruence fuels their motivation and behavior. Fantasies about power, success, and their own attractiveness and value to others blur reality and exaggerations about personal achievement, success, and talent may be made. The individual may increasingly seek out praise and admiration from others, placing themselves in positions where these rewards are readily available. Sexual predation occurs when these fantasies and exaggerations are sexualized by the narcissist. In this way the need for praise and admiration are sexualized and the drive for recognition and dominance are synthesized into sexually oriented objectives. The narcissistic predator will thrive on the elements of the grooming process that involve fulfilling the needs of the victim and receiving the accolades, acceptance, and adoration of the victim and their social network. These actions provide the narcissist with the artificial restoration of self-esteem that is a fundamental requirement of their personality type. In the sexual relationship, the narcissist may attempt to genuinely provide mutual sexual gratification to the victim as a means of receiving further confirmation of their supe-riority and prowess.

However, if the narcissistic personality is underpinned by an unarticulated anger, as is common in narcissistic personality disorder, there may be a component of the sexual predation and exploitation in which the predator is motivated by the need to emotionally dominate and humiliate the victim in some sexualized manner. This is usually due to a retaliatory motivation on the part of the predator whereby they believe that they are owed more than they have received from either society at large or an individual or group more specifically. In this instance, the victim may be selected in part as a proxy for those whom the predator is angry with and seeks retribution (Petherick & Sinnamon, 2013). When this occurs, it is not enough that the predator should receive sexual gratification from the exploitation, but that the interaction also provides the predator with the opportunity to restore their own self-esteem through deliberately dominating the victim during their sexual encounters in a manner that is degrading and contrary for the victim. For example, if the victim is shy, the narcissistic predator may coerce them into performing solo sexual acts while being watched. This retaliatory motivation is often incongruent with the narcissist's need for adora-tion and the sexual relationship may be typified by inconsistent sexual behaviors by the predator toward the victim, creating significant confusion.

The Antisocial Sexual Predator

The antisocial sexual predator lacks any empathy for their victims and is focused entirely on successfully obtaining their own objectives. According to Petherick and Sinnamon (2013), this is consistent with the excitation-oriented perpetrator typol-ogy in which the pleasure and pain of others is secondary to their own desires and sexual gratification. The antisocial personality type will thrive on the elements of the grooming process that involve pretense and deception. These actions provide the antisocial predator with a sense of domination of others and an opportunity for them to exercise their devious superiority, and to exhibit their contempt for others and to show the manner in which all others are no more than playthings to be toyed with at the predator's discretion. Of course this display is for the benefit of no one but the predator as they are unlikely to share their devious plans with another, unless as a further means of dominance and manipulation for the achievement of yet more personally rewarding objectives.

Personal Power Characteristics of the Sexual Predator

All factors associated with the grooming, exploitation, and abuse undertaken by the sexual predator are motivated by a desire to exert power over another. The extent to which the predator is able to wield power over the victim and their environment is dependent on several personal characteristics of the predator: notoriety, charisma, social status, personal standing, and the predator's willingness and ability to translate the potential power they have from these factors into action. Ultimately using per-sonal power to exploit the vulnerable comes down to the ability to exert control. For the predator, power will be used either through covert manipulation via personality and circumstantial factors that influence the relational dynamics or through overt coercion using fear and intimidation.

Manipulation involves numerous tactics that seek to subvert the victim's own moral, ethical, and social compass in favor of accepting the predator's objectives as appropriate, legitimate, and even desirable aims. Fear and intimidation may occur through physical coercion or through despotic means. Physical coercion is a more intimate means of the exercise of power in which the predator directly engages the victim with physical methods of enforcing compliance, control, and relationship maintenance. Domestic violence is an example of this form of predatory control.

Alternatively, despotic tactics are a more tyrannical means of exercising power by the predator. In the exercise of despotic power, the predator exerts their power onto the environmental factors surrounding the victim in order to isolate the victim, enforce compliance, and control and maintain the progress of the predator's plan and/or the continuity of the sexual relationship once it is instigated. Turning the victim's social group into the predator's own allies; preventing the victim from accessing other individuals or services that could support them or advocate on their behalf; withholding resources, finances, transportation, social connectivity, medicines, or other items; and establishing the victim in a particular light so that others will interpret their claims or behaviors in a manner favorable to the predator, are all examples of the despotic use of power. Physical and despotic power take away the victim's resolve and force compliance. The victim will often feel that they cannot get out of the situation and therefore feel that going along is the lesser of two evils. Fear of the consequences of not complying outweigh the distasteful actions and guilt or humiliation of acquiescence.

Notoriety: (Celebrity)

Positive notoriety provides immediate acceptance, trust, and affiliation, as people like to associate with success, fame, and celebrity. People feel special when they are associating with celebrities or individuals of note. Additionally, celebrities are stereotyped as often being "quirky" or weird and so people will often ignore, minimize, and forgive the transgressions of celebrities. This is done either due to an error of attribution in which victims and their peers interpret the behaviors as "eccentric" or "harmless misunderstanding," or they will ignore or permit the behavior in order to maintain access of association with the famous person because of the "importance by association" that they receive. The power of notoriety is a characteristic in predators who are musicians, actors, television personalities, sports stars, or other cultural personalities who are well known to the wider public. The power of notoriety may also be wielded by individuals who are well known within a specific sphere and therefore they have celebrity status to a specific subcultural group. For example, a scientist may be a celebrity to a specific group of students and academics within their own discipline and so may wield power of notoriety if they target victims that come from within this same environment.

Charisma: (Charm)

Charismatic individuals have been responsible for some of history's greatest calamities. This is because charisma is attractive and acts like a magnet to people who are looking for guidance and are therefore open to manipulation by such people. Adolf Hitler, Idi Amin, Pol Pot, Napoleon Bonaparte, Benito Mussolini, Joseph Stalin, Al Capone, Ted Bundy, Charles Manson—these individuals were all charismatic and this trait enabled them to lead people into major chaos and turmoil. Of course charisma can also be a trait used by positive leaders and history has many examples such as Theodore Roosevelt, Winston Churchill, George Patton, Charles de Gaulle, John F. Kennedy, Nelson Mandela, Boadicea, Eva Peron, Joan of Arc, Martin Luther King Jr, and this list could go on. However, in the hands of a predator, charisma is a tool used with devastating effect to amplify personal power and manipulate victims and their environment. The charismatic predator exhibits warmth, friendliness, exceptional communication skills, and a "presence" that commands attention. They are usually full of charm and wit, and, in short, present themselves in a manner that is very likable. Charisma tends to engender trust, affiliation, and acceptance as a matter of course, and therefore people want to be around them and will find it hard to believe that such a "great person" could ever do anything unsavory.

Social Status: (Social Position, Including Political Power)

Notoriety and charisma are made more powerful when the predator combines these traits with the added power of a well-respected and trusted social position in the community. There are certain positions in society that, by virtue of their role and responsibilities, tend receive a level of inherent trust, authority, and/or respect by the community. These positions include the helping professions, allied health, medicine, education, clergy, coaches, charity workers, politicians, law enforcement, and employers. While the vast majority of people in these positions are honorable, dedicated individuals, if they are able, predators will select these positions as a way of deflecting suspicion, and in order to establish themselves into a position that results in a greater power differential between them and the victim. The former is obtained due to the communal belief in the inherent "goodness" of the position (doctor, minister, psychologist, coach), while the latter is derived from the authority and respect bestowed on the position by others. Social status provides significant power to the predator as a person who holds a position of authority and respect will generally receive acceptance, trust, and affiliation automatically, will often be given the benefit of the doubt when called out for their actions, and it is a very intimidating prospect to call out and accuse these people of inappropriate behaviors due to the power differential and the fear of potential retribution.

Personal Standing: (Personal Position, Including Fiscal Power)

While social status provides power through the virtue of the position held, the personal standing of the predator provides power based on their personal achievements or the ability they have to provide benefit to others. If the predator is able to demonstrate an active concern for their community, and in particular the most vulnerable in the community, the result is increased trust, acceptance, and affiliation both with those they help and with the wider community. Power may also come from the predator placing themselves into a position where they control or manage the flow of some benefit to the vulnerable, for example, working for an organization that provides emergency relief, food, health care, or some other necessity. Nongovernmental organizations, charities, philanthropic causes, and advocacy services may all appeal to the predator as a means of establishing themselves with personal standing in the community. These organizational types, and the personal standing the predator is able to receive through this environment, may also provide access to victims who are at the extreme end of vulnerability. Establishing a relationship with a victim and then using their position to control the victim is a common tactic used by sexual predators. Fear of losing access to services, assistance, resources, or other necessities can be a powerful motivator for a victim to remain in an abusive relationship with a perpetrator.

PREPARING THE VICTIM: GROOMING THE ADULT VICTIM

Once a victim is targeted, the predator sets out to make themselves, and the opportunity for any relationship between the predator and intended victim, both attractive and desirable. As power and control are as strong a motivator as sexual gratification, the predator will identify and target vulnerable individuals in the hope of using their vulnerabilities to manipulate and control the target, and maneuver the relationship toward an ultimately sexually exploitative liaison. This fills the power, control, and sexual gratification needs of the predator. However, the cultivation of any relationship necessarily involves the fulfillment of needs in both parties. The grooming process is an effective method of preparing individuals for exploitation and abuse precisely because the early stages of the process provides the victim with strong elements of reward. This is because the predator is adept at identifying potential victims (targets) who have needs or wants that make them vulnerable to anyone who can exploit them. An adult who is targeted by a sexual predator may have psychoemotional, physical, or financial needs or wants that make them vulnerable to exploitation.

Psychoemotional Vulnerabilities

Psychoemotional vulnerabilities stem from the mental and emotional characteristics of the victim, and can be broken down further into factors relating to desire, avoidance, and self-value.

Desire

As human beings we have the ability to look around and acknowledge that things could be different, for better or worse. For some who perceive they have less of a desired item, their circumstances collude with this realization to generate a longing for something more. Desire combined with a perception of a lack of means to obtain the object, position, or state that is desired makes an individual vulnerable to the ministrations of anyone who comes forward providing, or offering to provide, access to that which is desired. Desire may be derived from wanting to escape an existing negative environment, or from a desire for more, even though current circumstances may already be quite favorable. Desire may also be emotional or physical. An individual may desire emotional connection and companionship, they may desire physical affection, or they may desire other material objects such as nice clothes and personal jewelry. Whatever the desire, if an individual lacks the capacity or willingness to obtain it through their own endeavors, they become vulnerable to the manipulations of others who see this desire as a vulnerability to be exploited.

Avoidance

When faced with regular negative experience, emotional expression, or other undesirable factors, individuals may use avoidance as a coping mechanism. Individuals who do not want to face current circumstances may seek ways to avoid them. This may be avoiding anxiety by avoiding people, places, or specific situations that provoke fear; it may be other issues such as having to work, live with a relative, take on the care responsibilities of another, or be cared for by a relative in the face of a loss of independence. Predators who identify this vulnerability may use the provisions of a means of escape as a way of garnering favor with the target, gaining trust, and establishing their credentials as "a true friend."

Self-value

Low self-esteem, self-worth, and self-efficacy are amongst the most vulnerable psychoemotional traits open to exploitation by sexual predators. Individuals with low levels of self-value are vulnerable to the actions of anyone who is able to provide a sense of value to them. If a predator helps the target to feel good about themselves, then that will go a long way toward enabling the predator to manipulate the target into increasingly greater levels of sexual behavior over time. This vulnerability can make the target highly susceptible to losing themselves and becoming codependent on the predator who will often manipulate the target into a position of complete reliance and servitude. This is similar to the manner in which a charismatic leader may manipulate a congregation in a cult. Eventually the target becomes the victim and gets to a point where they wrap their sense of self up within the relationship with the predator and become increasingly willing to do whatever is asked of them in return for edification from the predator. This vulnerability is particularly enticing to the narcissistic predator who establishes the victim as a "worshipper" of sorts, thus fulfilling the narcissistic sexual predator's needs for adoration, power, control, and sexual gratification.

Physical Vulnerabilities

The notion of physical vulnerabilities may apply to any number of factors that relate to perceived or real vulnerabilities associated with a victim's physicality. Age, size, disability, and cultural factors all come under this heading.

Age

A predator may use age differential as a vulnerability factor if the victim perceives their difference in age to that of the predator to be a factor that in some way gives the predator power over the victim. If a victim is much younger than the predator and the victim identifies this difference as giving the predator some right of control, bestowed wisdom, or inherent trust, then the predator will make use of this vulnerability and exploit it to achieve their own objectives. The predator might use this age differential to fulfill a parental figure, mentor role, or advisory role for the victim. The victim may feel special that such a wise and "respected" person has taken the time to take them under their wing. Alternatively, the predator may be much younger than the victim. A younger predator may manipulate the older victim's ego by deferring to their wisdom, experience, or social position, and the older victim may be flattered by the attentions of a younger person. In both circumstances, the predator is able to manipulate the victim by using the victim's age-related insecurities against them.

Physical Size
Physical size, like age, can be used as a differential in both directions. A larger victim may be vulnerable to the insecurities about their weight. Alternatively, a smaller victim may be intimidated by a larger predator or be given a sense of security and protection if the predator acts as a guardian. Again, either way, the skilled predator identifies victims whose vulnerabilities match some need or want that they have the means to fulfill.

Disability/Physical Capacity
Both the physically and intellectually disabled are common targets for sexual predators. For a number of reasons these disabilities make the victim highly susceptible to the manipulation of predators. A physical disability may make an individual vulnerable either due to incapacity to defend against sexual advances or the psychoemotional elements associated with having a disability, such as social isolation, smaller opportunities to develop social and sexual relationships, and the potential for self-esteem and self-worth challenges. An intellectual disability may increase vulnerability due to the potential for reduced capacity to identify the manipulations of a predator.

Cultural Factors
Numerous cultural factors can create vulnerabilities that the predator is able to use to manipulate and exploit a victim. A new migrant is vulnerable as they may not have established social supports and are often reliant on advocates to assist them to navigate their new environment. Predators are able to insert themselves into this role and become an indispensable part of the victim's life. If the victim does not speak the dominant language, they are further disadvantaged. The predator may fulfill the need of interpreter for the victim thereby establishing themselves as the "gateway" for information and access to other assistance. Language and culture are, in themselves, strong social isolators for migrants. The predator can use these factors to keep the victim isolated and ignorant. Moreover, if the migrant is a female who has arrived from a country characterized by paternalistic cultural attitudes and customs, then they may readily succumb to a dominant "helpful" male predator who uses these

factors to reinforce and normalize their exploitative actions. The predator may also use fear as a control mechanism by using overt and/or veiled threats of deportation or other sanctions if the victim does not acquiesce.

Similarly, religion is a cultural factor well known to be used by predators to manipulate their victims. Submission to authority, gender-based roles, rights, and responsibilities, and fear of consequences if these religious "rules" are not adhered to, are powerful mechanisms that predators use to manipulate, exploit, and control their victims. Once the abuse has commenced, these same factors can be used to instill fear into the victim as a means of maintaining the relationship and ensuring silence. A victim may fear being judged by others within the religious group, being ostracized from the congregation or other religious social network, and may feel extreme shame and guilt over the sexual acts they have committed with the predator, seeing themselves as sinful and deviant. These are all factors the predator is able to reinforce in order to control the victim.

Within these religious or spiritual settings, if the predator is an authority figure they may claim divine insight and tell the victim that "God" has decreed they couple, or that it is a spiritual "duty" in some way. Cult leaders and other religious authority figures have consistently used this form of claim as a means to obtain compliance in their victims. In these circumstances guilt, shame, and fear are powerful motivators to ensure the victim remains compliant. Conversely, victims may also "buy in" to the predator's claims of divine insight, and feel that they have been "chosen" by God to fill an important role for the predator/leader. This sense of being special can go a long way to obtaining willing compliance in victims, sometimes for substantially extended periods of time.

Financial Vulnerabilities

Financial factors can create substantial vulnerabilities that are able to be exploited by a sexual predator. Having financial challenges can create immense pressure on individuals. The predator is able to exploit this vulnerability by fulfilling a financial need such as paying an overdue account or other financial obligations. Money and financial security has been established in society as a panacea, and we therefore tend to place significant weight on those who obtain it or who are willing to assist us to obtain it. Predators are able to use this to gain trust and credibility very quickly with their victims. If this simple meeting of a financial need is coupled with an element of additional material "gifting" such as expensive dinners, gifts of jewelry, or trips to desirable locations, then this trust and credibility is increased further. The victim may get used to these experiences, and as they are normalized and habituated to the lifestyle, they can be equally normalized and habituated to increasingly sexually exploitative interaction with the individual providing these things. Once conditioned to having greater financial security, the fear of losing it and returning to "the bad old days" becomes a strong mechanism for control and compliance.

Alternatively, an individual who finds themselves with financial resources but lacks experience in how to manage their money, or is not comfortable mixing within a changed social environment, can also become ready prey to a predator. Examples of this scenario may be recently divorced or widowed individuals who receive a substantial financial windfall. A predator may present themselves as a helpful advisor or social guide to assist the victim to navigate their newfound circumstances. Relief at receiving assistance, and gratitude for acceptance within a new social environment, can quickly instill trust and credibility to the predator. Additional emotional support provided to the victim in the wake of recent divorce or death of a spouse, parent, or other close relative increases the predator's credentials and the victim's sense of obligation.

PREPARING THE SPACE: GROOMING THE ADULT VICTIM'S ENVIRONMENT

Preparing the space around the victim so that he or she will support, endorse, or at least not actively hinder, the predator's plans is as essential to the adult sexual grooming process as it is to grooming children for sexual abuse. In some respects, it may be even more important given that adults tend to have a greater capacity for self-propelled interaction with a wider social context, coupled with a greater capacity for experience analysis and reflective cognition. These factors, at least in theory, provide an adult with a greater capacity to identify the manipulations of a predator, to have others around them identify the predator's actions as irregular, and to seek assistance. For the predator, the greater their reach into the social and familial environment of their intended victim, the more influence they will have, and therefore, the greater the chance that they will be able to successfully groom the victim and their environment, instigate a sexually exploitative relationship, and maintain the liaison over time. In this way, the greater the intended victim's social affiliation and the wider their social network, the less vulnerable they are to the ministrations and manipulations of the sexual predator. Conversely, the greater the social isolation and the smaller or more restricted the diversity of the intended victim's social network, the greater their vulnerability to sexual predation.

The predator has three primary goals when grooming the intended victim's environment: insert, credential, and deflect.

Insert

The first objective of the sexual predator is to insert themselves into the victim's social affiliations. A predator needs prey, and the first step in the environmental process is for the predator to enter the intended victim's social space. The predator sets out to affiliate with the victim's social network and family. By joining social groups, claiming interest in similar activities, and engaging in social activities with the victim's family and social network, the predator begins to habituate the victim and the victim's supports to the predator's presence.

Credential

The second objective of the sexual predator is to credential themselves in the eyes of the intended victim's social network. In this way the predator sets out to establish trust and credibility with those most likely to foil the predator's plans, and who will be potential unwitting allies during the grooming and exploitation process. This involves the predator manipulating the perceptions of the victim's family and social network so that they see the predator as not just an acceptable, but a desirable and valued, member of the victim's social group. Exaggerating connections; feigning shared interests, values, attitudes, and beliefs; pretending to buy into and promote group goals and objectives; taking on leadership responsibilities; and providing otherwise unavailable resources or support are all tactics the predator uses to establish their credentials with the victim's environment. Ultimately the predator seeks to establish the group as an unwitting support for their own agenda by having them welcome the predator's presence and condone and encourage the relationship (whatever it may be presented as) between the predator and victim. When a predator credentials themselves well, the victim's own environment will act as support and catalyst for the progression of the predator's plans, and ultimately will continue to act as an enabler and maintainer for the predator's sexual exploitation and abuse of the victim. Strong credentials are also important to ensure that the victim's social network accepts, supports, and facilitates the victim's progressive withdrawal from various interactions as the predator gradually isolates them from assistance.

Deflect

The final objective of the sexual predator in the environmental grooming process is to deflect attention, perspective, and suspicion in a manner that protects them from close scrutiny by the victim's social network. This essentially involves the predator redirecting the attentions of the victim's social network in a manner that alters their view from potentially seeing the predator's actions as manipulative, exploitative, and maleficent, to interpreting them as munificent, magnanimous, and benevolent. Establishing credible rationale for various actions, and using their established trust and credibility to frame behaviors in a positive and benign light, creates a perspective through which the predator's actions are interpreted in a way that garners belief in the predator's "genuine" care and concern. As a result, any suspect behavior is met with a "benefit-of-the-doubt" attitude that inherently disbelieves in the possibility of wrongdoing by the predator.

STAGES OF THE GROOMING PROCESS

There are a number of proposed models of the grooming process. While the models differ in the number of stages and the descriptions they use for various components of the process, all models agree that the grooming process involves a gradual, stepped, and calculated progression that entraps adults in a relationship that allows the perpetrator to engage them in an inappropriate, exploitative, and abusive sexual relationship. Fig. 16.1 shows the model of adult sexual grooming proposed by the author.

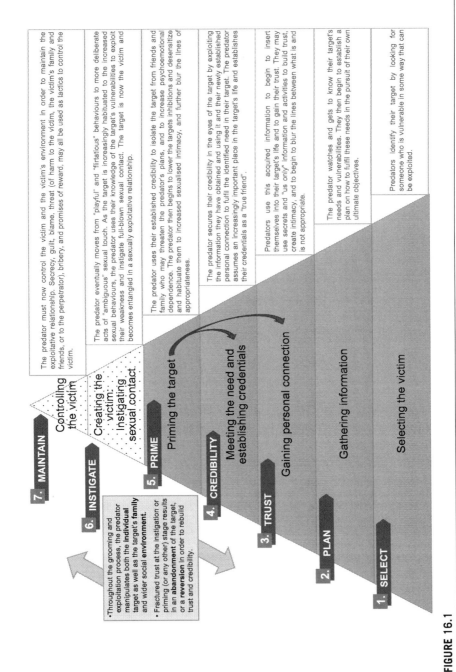

FIGURE 16.1

Sinnamon's Seven-Stage Model of Adult Sexual Grooming.

SINNAMON'S SEVEN-STAGE MODEL OF ADULT SEXUAL GROOMING

Sinnamon's model of adult sexual grooming, published here for the first time, proposes that the grooming and exploitation process can be categorized in seven stages. The first five stages involve the grooming tactics engaged by predators to prepare their targets for sexual contact. The final two stages describe the exploitation phase in which the perpetrator instigates and works to maintain the sexual predation.

Stage One: Selecting the Victim

Predators, irrespective of their end game, are exceptionally good at identifying the weak members of the herd. That is to say, predators can identify those individuals who have, for whatever reason, some kind of vulnerability that will make them more susceptible to their ministrations and manipulations. This is certainly true in nature and so it is in the human jungle. In the first stage of the grooming and sexual exploitation of adult victims, the sexual predator seeks out both a suitable environment and a suitable target. It is the environment that is usually the initial focus. Predators will be drawn to an environment in which there are likely ample targets as well as the opportunity to "hunt and catch" those that are targeted. Given that sexual predators who pursue adult victims are commonly characterized by narcissistic and antisocial personality types, environments in which they can also receive adoration, respect, and be seen as upstanding members of the community are commonly selected. For the narcissist, this environment provides an opportunity for strong reinforcement of their need for others to see them in a positive light. For the antisocial personality, this environment provides them with the challenge of deception and gives them the feelings of power and superiority they seek.

The selection of a "hunting ground" will often take the predator into the helping professions and other spaces in which they can use a position of power and trust to gain access to vulnerable targets. The clergy is one such example and has received much attention for this in recent years. Other "helping" professions such as counseling, social work, psychology, and other medical or allied health professions are also common. Teaching, coaching, and carer roles have also shown to be favored environments for sexual predators. The specific nature of a predator's predilections will then determine the more specific character of their preferred hunting ground. An environment that is generally seen as safe and nurturing presents the predator with potential targets who, by the fact that they are within this space, may have several layers of "armor" already removed. In this way, the predator is more readily able to identify, access, and exploit whatever individual vulnerabilities a specific target may have.

Predators identify their individual target by looking for those who are vulnerable in some way that the predator can exploit. Individuals who have low self-esteem, poor self-confidence, or feelings of inadequacy; who are isolated in some way (physically or emotionally); who are characteristically inclined toward codependence; or who may have been primed by previous experience such as childhood abuse or other psychological trauma are often identified by predators as potential targets. These vulnerable individuals often turn to their pastor, a counselor, or other health professional to seek assistance for these vulnerabilities, and, if positioned within this space, the predator is able to readily identify their target and be in a position to move seamlessly into the second stage of the grooming process, which is to gather information.

In the early stages of the grooming process, the inherent trust given to individuals in the helping professions or other positions of authority and power means that it can be very difficult for a target or their social supports to perceive the behavior of a sexual predator as anything other than genuine care and concern. For this reason, many professional codes of conduct explicitly prohibit sexual relationships between patient/client and the professional as they argue that true consent to sexual interaction by the patient/client is impossible due to the inherent power imbalance between the two parties. Similarly, ethical standards of educational institutions, sporting organizations, and other groups in which there is an imbalance in the power relationship often prohibit or place very strict guidelines around sexual relationships between different groups within the setting—for example, teachers and students, coaches and athletes, managers and employees, professional athletes and staff or members of the cheerleading squad, and so on.

Stage Two: Gathering Information

Once a predator has selected a target, the next stage in the grooming process is to get to know the target personally, gather information about the target, and specifically, to gather information about their target's needs and vulnerabilities. With this information in hand, the predator then sets out a plan as to how they can exploit the identified vulnerabilities by "helping" the target to fulfill their needs, all the while in the pursuit of the predator's own nefarious objectives. If the predator has established themselves in a position of trust, they will use this position to find out as much as they can about the target and to increasingly insert themselves into the target's environment. They may already have an inroad into this space via their position, for example, as a member of the ministry team at the target's church, as a coach or other "helper" or support within the target's social, educational, or professional environment, or as a colleague, superior, or advisor in the target's place of employment. The careful selection of the "hunting ground" and a calculated process of preparing or grooming the environment generally means that the perpetrator moves within this space without generating suspicion and is therefore able to mix readily with the target, their family, and their friends and associates. This further enables the predator to gather information and observe the target without provoking qualms from the target or other would be protectors. For the narcissistic predator, this stage provides an opportunity to also feed their need for approval and admiration from others as they set out to present themselves as a caring and genuine individual who is concerned for the welfare of another. For the antisocial predator type, this stage is a game-like endeavor in which they identify their actions as analogous to a spy or an otherwise undercover "agent," and are able to revel in their own clever devious and deceptive behaviors.

Environmentally, this stage involves the predator seeking out, and ingratiating and credentialing themselves to the target's support network, and where appropriate to the plan and the circumstances, befriending them. This allows the predator to further position themselves to gather valuable information about the target, gain acceptance from the target's family and peers, and commence the process of desensitizing the target's potential protectors and supports to their increased presence.

From a victim interaction perspective, the predator cautiously begins to increase contact with the target. Feigning care and concern, offering to assist with simple tasks, and engaging in increased conversation are all a part of the process aimed to provide opportunity to gather information, identify vulnerabilities, and to commence the process of disarming the target.

Stage Three: Gaining Personal Connection

Once predators have obtained sufficient information so as to have insight into their target's vulnerabilities, and have created a plan to exploit those vulnerabilities, the next stage in the grooming process is to work on furthering the strength of their personal connection with the target. Personally, the acquired information is used to help further insert the predator into the target's life, to deepen the "friendship," and to gain their trust. They may use secrets and "us only" information and activities to build trust, create intimacy, and to begin to blur the lines between what is and is not appropriate. Secrets and "special" moments are a way for the predator to normalize the target to not disclose the activities they share and to positively reinforce the excitation and elements of fear felt by the target when their interactions begin to stretch the boundaries.

Environmentally, the predator will seek to make themselves increasingly seen as "the great guy/gal," the "true friend," or the dedicated and caring professional, in the eyes of the targets friends and family. This further disarms and distances the target's confederates, and increases the target's isolation and reliance on the perpetrator. Often, those friends and family that the target would generally be able to count on as their strongest supports and protectors are unwittingly enlisted by the perpetrator. These friends and family will encourage the target to spend more time with the perpetrator or to "open up" and trust them. In these situations, even if the target has some misgivings about the intentions of the predator, their vulnerabilities will generally result in them placing more credence in the judgments of their peers and family than in their own concerns. Predators may be so adept at this manipulation that they will be able to get the target's friends and families to take an active role in developing the relationship by facilitating the contact between the predator and target and/or giving the target some "tough love" by removing some supports in order to "force" the target to lean more readily toward accepting the ministrations of the predator. In the postexploitation environment, this component of the process adds a significant weight to the feelings of anger and betrayal that the target has, as well as to the feelings of shame, guilt, and anger experienced by those friends and family of the target who come to believe that they are a victim of exploitation and abuse. Remember that, in many cases, a considerable number of those in the target's network will not accept that the perpetrator has engaged in any wrongdoing and will side with the predator and blame the victim for both the liaison as well as for any potential adverse fallout that the accusation of wrongdoing causes.

Stage Four: Meeting the Need and Establishing Credentials

In this stage of the grooming and exploitation process, the predator secures their credibility in the eyes of the target by exploiting the information they have obtained and using it and their newly established personal connection to fulfill the identified need in their target. In this way the predator assumes an increasingly important place in the target's life and establishes their credentials as a "true friend." This goes a long way to allaying any concerns or misgivings that the target may have had, and the target may even chastise themselves for having these feelings. Often any sense of apprehension that may have lingered in the target will be removed, and the fact that they had the feelings at all will create a sense of guilt that may result in a desire to "make it up" to the predator, producing personal devotion and feelings of indebtedness. These feelings collude with the target's vulnerabilities to produce an increasing loss of self in favor of amplified codependence and desire to "repay" the predator.

Environmentally, by fulfilling a need in the target, the perpetrator further ingratiates themselves to the target's friends and family. If the target is an overly needy individual and the predator is fulfilling this need, then friends and family may find themselves relieved that they do not have to invest as much time and energy into the target. If the target has some form of physical reduction in capacity that requires support and the predator fulfills this need, then the friends and family of the target may, once again, appreciate and come to rely on the release from obligation that the predator has provided them. This is also true if the predator has stepped in and provided financial support to the target. The predator may pay an overdue utilities bill or purchase a nice gift for/on behalf of the target. If, on the other hand, the predator has fulfilled a need through a counseling or advisory role, then the friends and family may see some psychoemotional improvement in the target that they attribute to the dedication and assistance provided by the predator. This further reinforces the predator's credentials in the eyes of the target's social network. This same result may be seen if the predator has taken on a spiritual advisor role. In cases where the predator is a member of the clergy or affiliated spiritual role, the benefits seen by others within the target's network may extend to other individuals, such as in the case that the predator is the minister at the family's church. When the predator has established themselves as a pivotal member of a small community of any kind, this is often the case.

This stage is the lynchpin for the predator's plan. If the predator is able to reach and successfully achieve this stage, the increased access and "room to maneuver" that they gain for themselves makes it highly unlikely that they will be "called out" for the escalated and increasingly sexualized behaviors that are a feature priming the target—the final preparatory stage in the grooming process. Indeed, when a predator is "called out" for their behaviors in the final stage of grooming, it is usually a result of new information or a new perspective from an "outsider" or a peer or family member who visits or returns to the environment without having been manipulated or habituated by the predator's prior ministrations.

Stage Five: Priming the Target

The priming stage is the final stage of the grooming process before the predator moves to instigate full sexual contact with their target. In this stage, the predator uses their established credibility to increase the target's psychoemotional dependence, and to further isolate the target from any friends and family who are still seen as potential threat to the perpetrator's plans. The perpetrator's actions toward the target are aimed at lowering inhibitions, and desensitizing and habituating the target to increased sexualized intimacy. Interactions increasingly blur the lines of what is and is not appropriate, and break down the final barriers of resistance held by the target. The introduction of sexual behaviors has been introduced over time in a gradual and deliberate manner. Up to this point some nonsexual touching, dirty jokes, conversations (including "secrets" and "don't tell anyone else" disclosures) about sex, and some flirting and innuendo are likely to have been used to slowly habituate and disinhibit the victim to sexualized interactions. The predator may have engaged the target in several reciprocal conversations that make disclosures of a sexual nature to the target in order to get them to reveal information about their own sexuality and sexual experiences. These intimate conversations are then used to build the sexualized interactions over time.

During the priming stage, there is an escalation by the predator of the sexualization of the discourse, and this is accompanied by increased sexualized behavioral content. The predator may select movies to watch together that contain increased sexual content and use this situation to shape the target's arousal conditioning to situations in which the predator is present and in close proximity. The predator may use the film content as an opportunity to start to press the target for greater details about their sex lives or previous sexual experiences, or they may push the target to share their sexual fantasies. They may start to linger in the kiss or embrace hello or goodbye, increase the incidence and intimacy of touching, and begin to create opportunities for increased sexual exposure and time alone that can be increasingly sexualized. For example, they may wait for the target to arrive at their home before taking a shower and leave the door open to the bathroom or walk out in a towel or other state of semiundress, or they may suggest excursions to more isolated swimming locations and "playfully" suggest they swim without their bathing suits on. In this way the predator pushes the boundaries of their sexual behaviors with the target, all the while ensuring that any actions can be interpreted ambiguously and explained away as "misunderstanding" in the event they are called out.

If they are not called out and the priming is successful, then the predator will continue to escalate their behaviors and push the boundaries of sexualized interactions with the target. As boundaries are stretched, the predator continues to push toward greater and greater intimacy in their interactions with the target. At each successful pushing of a boundary, the skilled predator will consolidate their gains and allow the target to assimilate this new "norm" into their perceptions of the character of the relationship. Small steps and patient consolidation of gains are the hallmark of this kind of sexual predator. Once again, this process allows the predator to shape the target's sexual conditioning by manipulating situations that provide opportunity for the target to become excited and sexually aroused while in the predator's company.

During this stage, targets and their family or peers may question some of the behaviors and wonder at the predator's motivations or intentions. However, the skilled predator will navigate this and placate any concerns with a reiteration of their genuine affection and concern for the target and a desire that they only want what is in the target's best interests. Intimations of hurt at having their actions "misinterpreted," or reminders about how they have "done so much to help" the target, can prey on the target's vulnerabilities and further erode any remaining resistance. The predator, when faced with this scenario, may also resort to veiled threats to further erode resistance. If the target has become codependent in some physical, emotional, or financial manner, then they may be further controlled and coerced through a veiled threat of removal of the predator's friendship, assistance, or resources. When this occurs, the victim may decide that the predator's behaviors, though somewhat disquieting, are worth putting up with due to the higher price of losing whatever benefits, real or perceived, they receive through the relationship. Coercion or fear-based submission may be blatant or it may be subtle, but either way it is an effective tool used by predators when priming their targets for exploitation and abuse. In this way, targets can be readily guided and conditioned to accept behaviors from the predator and to engage in behaviors themselves that they would have previously considered inappropriate or outright unacceptable. It is a short step from this point for the predator to instigate a full-blown sexual liaison.

Environmentally, the predator continues to reinforce their position as the caring friend or dedicated professional, and shore up their position within the target's social and/or support network. Having gained acceptance from the target's environment, during the priming stage, the predator's aim is to shore up this acceptance and to reciprocally provide assurance to any would-be foils that there are no disreputable motives behind their actions, or indeed any nefarious behaviors occurring between the predator and the target. The ultimate aim during this stage is to generate an environmental position that is disbelieving of any suggestion of maleficence or intent to maleficence, and thereby secure ongoing access to the target. This serves to establish the target's social network as confederates of the predator, and as the relationship continues to be reinforced and encouraged by the target's family and peers, the target loses any opportunity to escape.

Stage Six: Creating the Victim: Instigating Sexual Contact

In stage six, the predator moves to initiate more intense sexual engagement. Once the predator feels the target is adequately primed, and that the level of trust and emotional dependence is sufficient, increasingly overt sexualized interactions are introduced. As the interactions become overtly sexualized, the target becomes the victim. The crossover from priming to initiating full-blown sexual exploitation is usually a carefully orchestrated seduction by the predator, however, to the target this will often look and feel like a spontaneous event that escalates from an otherwise "innocuous" interaction into an explicitly sexual encounter. The skilled predator will use an already established routine or previously undertaken activity as the foundation for the first sexual encounter. Typical scenarios may include a picnic to an isolated location at which they previously swam together naked, or a movie night together that has previously included mutual massages and movies with some element of erotic content. Events such as these can be sexually intensified through increased visually and kinesthetically stimulating elements. While swimming, the predator can orchestrate greater opportunity for the target to see them naked, to get closer while swimming to include greater touch, and to escalate the level of excitement and arousal through "playfully" daring the target to engage in some form of "juvenile" sexual behavior such as flashing genitalia or posing nude out of the water. Similarly, at an event such as a home movie night the predator may manipulate increased intimacy in the seating, and increased touch during any sexual content in the film. Initially, sexual content in films being watched is not likely to contain hardcore pornography but rather is likely to be more romantic or "arthouse" in nature. At the juncture of priming and instigating the sexual exploitation, the predator may, after watching a film together with some element of sexual content, suggest that they watch something a little more "adventurous." Introducing more hardcore pornographic content is then used as a means of further escalating arousal and providing a scenario in which moving into a sexual encounter will appear as a smoother, natural, and spontaneous transition that is undertaken with mutual consent.

Given the diversity that can characterize human interaction, any number of scenarios may be used by the predator to initiate the sexual relationship, the common point being that, generally speaking, the predator will use an established routine or previous experience as the platform, and will orchestrate the interaction so as to make it appear spontaneous and mutually consensual.

Environmentally there may be different scenarios in which the exploitative relationship is undertaken. The predator may, in certain circumstances, establish themselves as a legitimate partner of the target (now victim). They do not need to hide the relationship but rather work to place themselves into a position where the family and friends of the victim see them as an ideal choice of romantic partner. Alternatively, the predator may be in a position where, for whatever reason, they must keep the liaison secret. This may be true if the predator or the victim is already married, if the two have a professional relationship, or the predator is in another role such as the victim's clergy, teacher, or coach.

Stage Seven: Controlling the Victim

Stage seven involves the predator working to control the victim and the victim's environment in order to maintain the exploitative relationship. Secrecy, guilt, blame, threat (of harm to the victim, the victim's family and friends, or to the perpetrator), bribery, and promises of reward may all be used as tactics to control the victim. Generally speaking, the victim is controlled through negatively valenced emotional motivations, even when promises of reward and bribery through benefits such as financial gain or material objects are involved. Using the victim's identified vulnerabilities, the predator will control the victim through fear and guilt, and/or by the predator generating a sense of helplessness, isolation, and despair in the victim. These emotional outcomes from the escalation of the relationship from a "friendship" to a sexual liaison are usually far different from what was inherently "promised" in the initial grooming experiences. This betrayal is often cited by victims as a significant basis of the psychological trauma caused by the abusive experience, and is commonly among the most enduring and difficult to treat psychological sequelae.

Guilt and fear are powerful behavior controls, whether internally generated by the victim's own vulnerabilities and realizations of the true nature of the relationship or whether externally cultivated by the predator as a means of control. Victims come to realize that they are being exploited and are often overcome by the feelings of shame, humiliation, and embarrassment that come with the realization of having been manipulated and used. Moreover, predators will often escalate the sexual activities to include increasingly deviant or humiliating (to the victim) encounters. This is a common element of the power and control personal motivations of the narcissistic and antisocial personality types who engage in this form of predatory behavior. The realization of having been exploited sexually in this way can generate strong emotions of guilt and shame, particularly in those who are already emotionally vulnerable. The predator understands this and uses it to control the victim by reinforcing the belief that the victim really wanted the sexual experiences and that if others "really knew what they were like" that they would judge them and reject them as being perverted or otherwise deviant in some way. The predator may use this to further isolate the victim and create greater dependence by suggesting that only the predator really understands the victim and that only the predator doesn't judge the victim and accepts them despite their depravities. In this way the predator encourages and increases the fear and guilt in the victim in order to maintain the relationship and keep control.

This serves to increase the isolation of the victim, increase the victim's reliance on the predator, and to exacerbate the victim's sense of self-loathing, all of which further limits the victim's access to help. Reducing the victim's escape options results in helplessness, hopelessness, and ultimately despair. Perpetrators will reinforce this point to the victim, and the victim comes to believe that there are no options for them other than to remain in the relationship, or that any alternative will result in a far worse scenario for the victim and/or their loved ones.

Environmentally, the predator will seek to control the perceptions of the victim's social network and to limit contact with situations and individuals who may be harder to control and therefore pose a risk to the predator. By controlling the access to the environment and by maintaining the positive perceptions (about the predator) of those within the victim's social environment, the predator works to ensure continued access to the victim and to fulfill secondary motivations. For example, the narcissistic predator does this to also obtain ongoing adoration and approval from others, while the antisocial predator receives rewards from the ongoing successful deception of others. While the sexual exploitation of the victim is the ultimate source power and reward for the sexual predator, the characteristics of their personality type also gain substantial reward from these secondary sources of power and reward. These secondary sources of reward should not be taken lightly and can be very helpful in differentiating individuals who enter a person's life and are motivated by genuine care and concern, as opposed to those with more nefarious intentions. Indeed, early detection of sexual grooming for malicious intent rarely appears any different from genuine care and concern, therefore other potential indicators are an important element to early detection of potential maleficence.

FRACTURED PLANS: WHEN THE GROOMING PROCESS FALTERS

As adults generally have a greater potential to identify and halt the predator from progressing through the grooming process, a sexual predator who engages with adult victims will likely have their plans fractured regularly. A fracture may occur at any stage but is most likely to take place during the priming or instigation stage of the process when the sexualization of the interactions is intensified and the relationship change is greatest. Of these, the priming stage is probably the highest risk as, if the predator successfully primes their victim, then the transition to a full-blown sexual liaison is often seamless. Indeed, victims will commonly reflect that they could not determine exactly when the sexual component of the relationship commenced but they could pinpoint when the sexual behaviors escalated, for example, the first time the predator walked out naked or brushed up against the victim with an erection.

A fracture may occur in number of ways. The victim may self-identify inappropriate behaviors by the predator, or a friend or family member may identify "strange" or "unusual" behavior. The "fracture" occurs as a result of the damage to the trust the victim and/or others in the victim's environment have in the predator. As a result, the predator losses credibility. When this happens the predator cannot progress and has two options: abandon the target and start again with someone new; or revert back to earlier stages of the plan in order to rebuild trust and credibility with the target and/or their family and friends. Depending on the secondary personality factors of the predator, and the circumstances of the fracture, they may appear contrite and apologetic, or they may present as indignant and hurt that their actions have been "misinterpreted" or "misrepresented." Either reaction by the predator provides them with a platform to either cut and run or try to rebuild the relationship. If a predator has spent considerable time establishing themselves in a position of trust that provides ready access to victims, they may be reluctant to risk discovery for a single victim. The predator may decide it is better to claim there has been a "misunderstanding" and then remove themselves from the situation to avoid further scrutiny. Alternatively, the predator may choose to loop back to the earlier stages of the grooming process and attempt to reestablish the trust and credibility they lost as a result of the fracture. While this option may be challenging, if the predator has invested significant time and other resources in grooming the target, then they may feel that they are too committed to the plan to abandon it.

CONCLUSIONS

The grooming of adults for exploitation by sexual predators is more common than is generally considered. The process is similar to that followed by sexual predators who groom children, however, due to the different personal and environmental circumstances of adults compared to children, there are also some basic differences. Grooming involves the premeditated, ordered, and stepped manipulation of the intended victim, their family, and the intended victim's wider social network in order to pave the way for the sexual exploitation of the intended victim. The grooming process occurs in a seamless progression in which the predator's trustworthiness and credibility is established with the intended victim and their environment. Once the predator is seen as a "true friend" and a trustworthy, credible, and valued member of the victim's social network, the predator incrementally sets out to normalize intimacy with the victim and sexually disinhibit the victim so that the increasingly sexual contact does not threaten the victim but rather primes them for a full-blown sexual liaison. Finally, the predator instigates an exploitative sexual relationship with the victim and works to control the victim and maintain the ongoing sexual contact. At any time, the process may fracture and the predator may lose the trust and credibility they have built up. In this event, the predator will either choose to abandon their plans and move on to select a new target or they may choose to revert to an earlier stage of the grooming process and attempt to rebuild the trust and credibility they have lost.

SUMMARY

- Sexual grooming is the process of deliberately establishing a connection with an individual in order to prepare that person for sexual exploitation and/or abuse. Sexual predators are often very considered in their approach to their selection of, and the tactics they employ to engage with, both the abuse environment and their intended victim.
- Adult sexual grooming is analogous to child sexual grooming and can be defined as any situation in which an adult is primed to permit themselves to be abused and/or exploited for sexual gratification of another. The grooming process used by sexual predators on children and adults is essentially the same, focusing on emotional and psychological manipulation tactics.
- Generally speaking, adults have a greater potential than children to make use of their own experiences, the experiences of others, personal cognizance, and to reach out to any number of familial, social, and professional supports for advice and assistance. Therefore, in preparing adults for sexual exploitation, grooming the victim and the victim's environment are both essential components of the preparatory sexual predator's tactics, and the perpetrator's behaviors manifest within the grooming process include the deliberate manipulation of both areas.

- Predatory sex offenders are characteristically motivated by a desire to maintain or restore their self-esteem through the manipulation and control of others, and by the prospect of excitement and the opportunity to deviously exhibit their dominance and superiority (Petherick & Sinnamon, 2013). These primary traits are endemic in the narcissistic and the antisocial personality types. The narcissistic sexual offender uses sexual predation and gratification as an external source of restoration and/or maintenance of their amplified self-esteem needs. This fits with the assertive-oriented typology of perpetrators and victims proposed by Petherick and Sinnamon (2013).
- The antisocial sexual predator lacks any empathy for their victims and is focused entirely on successfully obtaining their own objectives. According to Petherick and Sinnamon (2013), this is consistent with the excitation-oriented perpetrator typology in which the pleasure and pain of others is secondary to their own desires and sexual gratification.
- All factors associated with the grooming, exploitation, and abuse undertaken by the sexual predator are motivated by a desire to exert power over another. The extent to which the predator is able to wield power over the victim and their environment is dependent on several personal characteristics of the predator: notoriety, charisma, social status, personal standing, and the predator's willingness and ability to translate the potential power that they have from these factors into action. Ultimately using personal power to exploit the vulnerable comes down to the ability to exert control. For the predator, power will be used either through covert manipulation via personality and circumstantial factors that influence the relational dynamics or through overt coercion using fear and intimidation.
- Once a victim is targeted, the predator sets out to make themselves, and the opportunity for any relationship between the predator and intended victim, both attractive and desirable. As power and control are as strong a motivator as sexual gratification, the predator will identify and target vulnerable individuals in the hope of using their vulnerabilities to manipulate and control the target, and maneuver the relationship toward an ultimately sexually exploitative liaison. This fills the power, control, and sexual gratification needs of the predator.
- An adult who is targeted by a sexual predator may have psychoemotional, physical, or financial needs or wants that make them vulnerable to exploitation.
- Psychoemotional vulnerabilities stem from the mental and emotional characteristics of the victim, and can be broken down further into factors relating to desire, avoidance, and self-value.
- The notion of physical vulnerabilities may apply to any number of factors that relate to perceived or real vulnerabilities associated with a victim's physicality. Age, size, disability, and cultural factors all come under this heading.

- Financial factors can create substantial vulnerabilities that are able to be exploited by a sexual predator. Having financial challenges can create immense pressure on individuals. The predator is able to exploit this vulnerability by fulfilling a financial need such as paying an overdue account or other financial obligation. Once conditioned to having greater financial security, the fear of losing it and returning to "the bad old days" becomes a strong mechanism for control and compliance.
- Preparing the space around the victim so that it will support, endorse, or at least not actively hinder the predator's plans is essential to the adult sexual grooming process. Adults tend to have a greater capacity for self-propelled interaction with a wider social context, coupled with a greater capacity for experience analysis and reflective cognition. These factors, at least in theory, provide an adult with a greater capacity to identify the manipulations of a predator, to have others around them identify the predator's actions as irregular, and to seek assistance. The greater the intended victim's social affiliation and the wider their social network, the less vulnerable they are to the ministrations and manipulations of the sexual predator. Conversely, the greater the social isolation and the smaller or more restricted the diversity of the intended victim's social network, the greater their vulnerability to sexual predation.
- The predator has three primary goals when grooming the intended victim's environment: insert, credential, and deflect.
- There are a number of proposed models of the grooming process. While the models differ in the number of stages and the descriptions that they use for various components of the process, all models agree that the grooming process involves a gradual, stepped, calculated progression that entraps adults in a relationship that allows the perpetrator to engage them in an inappropriate, exploitative, and abusive sexual relationship.
- Sinnamon's model of adult sexual grooming, published here for the first time, proposes that the grooming and exploitation process can be categorized into seven stages. The first five stages involve the grooming tactics engaged by predators to prepare their targets for sexual contact. The final two stages describe the exploitation phase in which the perpetrator instigates and works to maintain the sexual predation.
- The seven stages of the grooming process are: (1) selecting the victim; (2) gathering information; (3) gaining personal connection; (4) meeting the need and establishing credentials; (5) priming the target; (6) creating the victim: instigating the sexual contact; and (7) controlling the victim.
- As adults generally have a greater potential to identify and halt the predator from progressing through the grooming process, a sexual predator who engages with adult victims will likely have their plans fractured regularly. A fracture may occur at any stage but is most likely to take place during the priming or instigation stage of the process when the sexualization of the interactions is intensified and the relationship change is greatest. A fracture may occur in a number of ways. The victim may self-identify inappropriate behaviors by the

predator, or a friend or family member may identify "strange" or "unusual" behavior. The "fracture" occurs as a result of the damage to the trust the victim and/or others in the victim's environment, as in the predator. As a result, the predator losses credibility. When this happens, the predator cannot progress and has two options: abandon the target and start again with someone new; or revert back to earlier stages of the plan in order to rebuild trust and credibility with the target and/or their family and friends.

QUESTIONS

1. Define grooming, sexual grooming, adult sexual grooming; provide examples.
2. Describe the seven stages of Sinnamon's Seven-Stage Model of Adult Sexual Grooming.
3. What are the primary characteristics of the narcissistic sexual predator?
4. What are the primary characteristics of the antisocial sexual predator?
5. Describe the personal power characteristics of the sexual predator.
6. Describe the socioemotional vulnerabilities that attract a predator to a potential victim.
7. Describe the physical vulnerabilities that attract a sexual predator to a potential victim.
8. Describe the three stages of preparing the space that a sexual predator undertakes in the process of adult sexual grooming and exploitation.

REFERENCES

Australian Bureau of Statistics. (2012). *Personal safety, Australia, 2012*. Doc. Number: 4906.0. Canberra: Australian Bureau of Statistics.

Kilpatrick, D. G., Resnick, H. S., Ruggiero, K. J., Conoscenti, L. M., & McCauley, J. (2007). *Drug-facilitated, incapacitated, and forcible rape: A national study.*. Doc. Number: 219181. Washington, DC: U.S. Department of Justice.

Petherick, W., & Sinnamon, G. (2013). Motivations: offender and victim perspectives. In *Profiling and serial crime: Theoretical and practical issues* (3rd.ed.) (pp. 393–430).

Truman, J. I. (2011). *National crime victimization survey 2010*. Washington, DC: U.S. Department of Justice, Office of Justice Programs, Bureau of Justice Statistics.

Searching for the Spectrum of the Querulous

17

Grant Lester
Victorian Institute of Forensic Medicine, Southbank Victoria, Australia

CHAPTER OUTLINE

Partial Insanity is a phenomenon so remarkable, that the more we observe it, the more are we astonished, that a man who feels, reasons and acts like the rest of the world, should feel, reason and act no more like other men upon a single point.

Jean-Etienne Esquirol (1845)

Between June 1926 and August 1929, Rupert Frederick Millane issued 56 legal proceedings against the Shire of Heidelberg, or its servants, agents, or members of the Shire Council. During the same period, 60 other proceedings were instituted by Millane in the Melbourne Court of Petty Sessions against the Shire of Heidelberg, the Corporations of Melbourne, the proprietors of leading daily newspapers, and others. So much administrative and court time was being wasted by these frivolous actions that the government considered it had no option but to intervene.

Freckleton (1988)

In response to Rupert Millane, the Vexatious Actions Act (1929) Victoria was born and Victoria created its first "vexatious litigant," that is, an individual who due to their history of instituting persistent and vexatious legal proceedings is barred from commencing any further legal proceeding without the permission of the courts (Lester & Smith, 2006).

These individuals, driven by beliefs of injustice, persistently petition courts and usually enjoin ever-increasing numbers of people and organizations in their legal battles. Often other aspects of their life are damaged in this crusade for justice, and they are at times incarcerated for threats and insults or actual violence including sexual assault or murder. Incarceration, either psychiatric or penal, will often only feed their sense of grievance and injustice (van der Heydt, 1952). Suicide is not uncommon.

For example, there was the celebrated German case of Max Freiherr von Hausen, who prior to his suicide in 1920 had filed 152 criminal charges over the years. Out of these, 78 were against judges for perversion of justice and 22 against witnesses for perjury. He himself was involved in 48 cases, where he had been accused of grievous bodily harm, insult, menace, and resisting arrest. He was involved in 304 civil proceedings and appealed over 300 times. His grandiose motivation was highlighted by the form and content of his suicide note that read (von Dietrich, 1968):

…von Hausen aimed throughout his whole life to be of value to his country. But because of his ineffably severe destiny, his life was wiped away without success.

Protection from such querulous (from the Latin *queri* to complain) behavior has been incorporated in legal systems dating back to the Prussian legal code of 1793 (Caduff, 1995). However, by the mid-1800s in Europe these individuals were more likely to have been involuntarily incarcerated in lunatic asylums than in prisons. Their inclusion under the rubric of "querulous paranoia" marked them as the property of psychiatrists, and this ownership has waxed and waned over the last 140 years.

THE QUERULOUS SPECTRUM

In the public domain, however, the term *querulous* is used to describe both behavior and the collective noun for individuals manifesting that behavior. The behavior at its simplest is an individual's heightened tendency to find fault and grievance in life and to air their dissatisfaction recurrently. Such querulousness can vary both in degree and duration having been either present as a personality trait persisting throughout the individual's life or having arisen anew at a certain period of their life.

In psychiatric and psychological domains, it is the morbidly querulous that have been the focus of attention. This is the group of individuals whose querulous behavior evolves over time, accruing increasing losses and negative consequences for themselves or others.

There is a significant but aging body of research into the diagnosis of querulous paranoia, with little recent research. From the late 1800s, derived from the fusion of the concepts of partial insanity or monomania and paranoia, it was believed to be a discrete entity in which a single pathological preoccupation with a loss or injustice develops in an otherwise sound mind. There is complaint to authorities and courts and a gradual but increasing network of grievances with those same authorities and courts.

Reviewing the psychiatric research into querulous paranoia, it appears this has been bedeviled by its reliance on the shifting concept of paranoia and its relationship with schizophrenia, arguments over the course and phenomenology of schizophrenia, and the quicksand issue of defining normal beliefs, delusional beliefs, and the intervening spectrum. It would seem almost unnecessary to state that there had been at best only an evolving consensus as to the defining phenomenology of this group.

In particular, it is evident that conceptually and diagnostically the research into the querulous has floated along with the historical tides that at first molded and then by the 1970s finally eroded and washed away the concept of paranoia and the diagnostic entity known as querulous paranoia.

Some clinicians and writers such as Thomas Szasz would welcome its demise. He wrote that the tools and methods of psychiatry, labeling and classification, are perfectly suited for social as much as medical functions (Szasz, 1974, chap. 2):

> *To classify another person's behaviour is usually a means of constraining him. This is particularly true of psychiatric classification, whose traditional aim has been to legitimise the social controls placed on the so-called mental patients.*

Equally, others such as Bloch and Reddaway have documented that in Soviet Russia psychiatry was used to stifle dissent. In most cases the dissenters were charged for criminal acts and then in the pretrial period assessed by Soviet psychiatrists. They would be diagnosed with a mental illness and hence found by the courts to be not guilty of the charge by virtue of mental illness. They were then incarcerated in forensic hospitals, languishing hidden from prying eyes and medicated heavily (Bloch & Reddaway, 1977, chap. 7).

Dissidents treated in this way ranged from the human rights activist Vladimir Bukovsky, to Svetlana Schramko who sent complaints to various bodies about pollution caused by a fiber plant, through to Viktoria Smirnova who on being refused permission to emigrate to Israel began writing letters to the United Nations. She was told (Bloch & Reedaway, 1977, chap. 9):

> *Stop writing letters to the UN and no one will put you in the mad house.*

The practice had reached such an extent that a psychiatrist reportedly told a dissident that his disease was dissent and as soon as he renounced his opinions and adopted correct ones he would be discharged (Bloch & Reddaway, 1977).

Equally, we must not be lulled into the false security of associating psychiatric abuse with totalitarian regimes. As Thomas Szasz and Michel Foucault note, European and American psychiatry over the last 300 years have at times used social undesirability and impoverishment as the criteria for involuntary incarceration in institutions (Szasz, 1974).

However, more recent research has shown that individuals exhibiting patterns of persistent long-term self-destructive complaint and litigation still haunt the ombudsmans' offices, tribunals, and courts. Of most concern, they are committing acts of aggression toward themselves and on those they perceive as having actively persecuted them, or even just having failed them (Lester, Wilson, Griffin, & Mullen, 2004).

It is essential therefore to any understanding of today's phenomenon of persistent complaint to acquaint ourselves with the nearly century and a half of psychiatric research into the understanding of paranoia and delusions.

PARANOIA

The history of paranoia mirrors the development of psychiatry in Western Europe over the last 2000 years. The words *paranoia* and *paranoid* are now part of the common language, focusing on misbeliefs, usually of a persecutory flavor. Yet this meaning is a mere shadow of its rich heritage in the history of psychiatry.

The term *paranoia* originates in the Greek language and was used as we might use *crazy* or *out of his mind*. Hippocrates used it to describe the delirium of high fever, and other writers used it to describe senile deterioration. Its medical use then disappeared from the literature (Lewis, 1970).

It was only in the 18th century that the term was revived. It regained significance because of the attempt by alienists to investigate insanity and to break it into classifiable component parts. Francois Boissier de Sauvages, in 1763, resurrected the term and used it to describe the nonfebrile forms of dementia. Its scope was broadened in 1772 by the German R. A. Vogel to include mania and melancholia and as such referred to an entity whose main features were impaired judgment and affect without fever or hallucinations. It foreshadowed the concept of "partial insanity" and highlighted the focus on misbeliefs or delusions (Lewis, 1970).

The term languished until Johan Heinroth in 1818 used it in his classificatory system. Heinroth basically classified mental disorders into disorders of temperament, intellect, or will. He classified the paranoias as disorders of the intellect and used *paranoia* synonymously with the German term *Verruchtheit* (Emanuel Kant was the first to give *Verruchtheit* a scientific sense: "the loss of common sense and the resulting logical willfulness") (Schifferdecker, 1995, p. 233).

Heinroth described both as:

> *Unfreedom of spirit with exaltation of the faculty of thought: perversion of concepts but undisturbed perceptions.*

Heinroth had a religio-biological outlook and viewed passion, vice, and delusion as three stages in a progressive disorder. This was a traditional view of insanity as disorder of spirit and soul and hence psychogenic in origin (Schifferdecker, 1995, p. 236). However, his view of insanity was swept away by a wave of biologism in the mid- to late 1800s in Germany, which emphasized the organicity of the insanities.

In the early to mid-1800s, contemporaneously with Heinroth, the Frenchman Jean-Etienne Esquirol, a student of Phillipe Pinel, built on his master's descriptions of partial mental disorders (partial insanity)—partial in the sense that only one or a few mental faculties, and not the entire mind, are affected (Bloch & Reddaway, 1977). Esquirol emphasized the "passions" as the cause of mental disorder and stated that:

> *A subject is mad or delirious when his thoughts, judgements and decisions are determined by passions, or can no longer be controlled by will.*

Esquirol first proposed the term *monomania* in 1810. The syndrome was characterized by an *idee fixe*, which was a single pathological preoccupation in an otherwise sound mind. He felt the abnormality could be understood as a "logical" consequence of a single false principle (Berrios & Porter, 1995, p. 361).

He described their outcomes as generally benign but with relapses, and a subgroup of people who progressively deteriorated. It is interesting to note that Esquirol's concept of monomanias was popular with his peers and supported with much enthusiasm not least because it vastly increased psychiatric involvement in the legal system as definers of sanity and criminal responsibility.

Von Krafft-Ebbing

It is the fusion of Heinroth's concept of paranoia and Esquirol's concept of monomania that enables Von Krafft-Ebbing to define paranoia as a systematized delusional disorder. He emphasized that the disorder was of organic origin, occurring "exclusively in tainted individuals" and classified paranoia amongst the "psychic degenerations" (Berrios & Porter, 1995, p. 363).

The chief characteristic was a single delusion, which became systematized and methodical. He recorded that persecutory delusions were most common, noting that judgment and reason are in general intact, the intellect undamaged, and neither the psychomotor nor emotional spheres were perturbed. He stated (Krafft-Ebbing, 1905, p. 369),

> *That on superficial observation, one is struck by the clearness and logic of such patients*

and that they appeared to be reasoning correctly from false premises. Von Krafft-Ebbing found hallucinations to be quite common, also noting that the development of the disorder reflects the affected individuals underlying personality (Krafft-Ebbing, 1905, p. 382):

> *An originally suspicious, retiring, solitary individual one day becomes persecuted; a rough, irritable, egotistic person, defective in his notions of justice becomes a querulous paranoiac…*

While emphasizing that paranoia was essentially a constitutional disorder he notes that:

> *The development of the disease is ordinarily gradual, growing, so to speak, out of the abnormal personality.*

He felt that the delusions were most often persecutory, the course always chronic, though they had remissions with insight (Gelder, Gath, & Mayou, 1993, p. 363).

With his interest in forensic psychiatry and subscription to Morelian degenerative theory, he collected a series of patients who persistently indulged in a series of complaints and claims lodged against authorities (Shorter, 1997, p. 95). Krafft-Ebbing was one of the first to study the querulous and believed they formed a separate subdivision in the paranoia group, called *paranoia querulentium*. Their main unifying features were the behavioral descriptors of persistent claiming of injustice, petitioning of the authorities, and associated persistent litigious behavior (Shorter, 1997, p. 338). He described them as having specific premorbid character traits, with gradually evolving and developing delusional beliefs. There were commonly accompanying hallucinations. Their reason and intellect remained intact through the course of the illness, which was a chronic one of remissions and relapses, though there generally was no progressive deterioration of faculties of reason or intellect (Berrios & Porter, 1995, p. 364).

Karl Ludwig Kahlbaum (1828–99) used cause, course, duration, and outcome to create a new taxonomy of mental illness. Paranoia described those cases whose symptoms were primarily delusions of persecution and grandeur and which followed a persistent and chronic course. They were believed to have an organic etiology. This taxonomy was later used by Emil Kraepelin as the basis for his work, however, he felt that course and outcome were of overriding importance in classification.

Emil Kraepelin

In 1896 Emil Kraepelin initially felt that paranoia (progressive systematized insanity), while separate from dementia praecox, was nonetheless an endogenous disease process developing on "a defective constitutional basis." It was a stable, nondeteriorating, monodelusional system, often with ideas of reference and over self-appreciation. It was without clouding of consciousness, disorder of form of thought, will, or conduct. Hallucinations might be present. Kraepelin separated querulous paranoia from other types of paranoia mainly because their psychogenic flavor was more distinct than in other types of paranoia (Kraepelin, 1910). Even in the 1890s he felt that some querulous represented a separate group of purely psychogenic origin.

By 1912, he had refined his view on paranoia to exclude those with a deteriorating course and those with hallucinations (which became the paraphrenias). He now believed that all the paranoias were uncommon and of psychogenic origin, i.e., they were "abnormal developments in a psychopathic (my addition–vulnerable personality) disposition under the influences of ordinary life" (Berrios & Porter, 1995, p. 366).

Sigmund Freud's contribution to the development of paranoia was mixed. His work on Schreber in 1911, addressing the essential question of the relationship between paranoia and the personality of the sufferer, is felt to have significantly influenced other workers such as Bleuler and Kretschmer. This is despite the evidence that Schreber's diagnosis was more likely to be schizophrenia than paranoia (Lewis, 1970).

Eugen Bleuler in his 1920 manual, with his emphasis on cross-sectional symptomatology and underlying psychological mechanisms, broadened the concept of schizophrenia. This resulted in all forms of paranoid psychosis (with the exception of paranoia) being included in the diagnosis of schizophrenia. With some reservations he agreed with Kraepelin that the paranoias were "a psycopathic form of reaction" (Bleuler, 1924; Kendler, 1981; Schifferdecker, 1995).

Ernst Kretschmer (1888–1964) was at odds with Kraepelin's emphasis on course and outcome and Bleuler's inclusive concept of schizophrenia. He believed, as did Bleuler, that the underlying psychopathology provided essential criteria for classification but felt that in many cases of paranoid psychosis the development of the delusions was comprehensible from a psychological perspective. Kretschmer, building on his 1927 work, *The Sensitive Delusion of Reference*, tried to create a classificatory system that could demonstrate how a particular psychosis may arise as a "reaction" in a particular type of character (personality). In a sense he attempted to correlate psycopathic types with their psychic reaction to experience (Schneider, 1958; Themes and Variations in European Psychiatry, 1974, chap. 8). Thus he believed that those forms of paranoid psychoses with understandable delusions were not disease processes but were developments in an abnormal personality subjected to a specific kind of stress. For the stress to be pathogenic it must be specific for a particular personality's vulnerabilities (Berrios & Porter, 1995, p. 366).

Emil Kraepelin, and in particular Ernst Kretschmer, were influenced by the work of Karl Jaspers. He described mental disorders as being of three types. These were his reactions, developments, and processes. Distinguishing between the psychologically understandable delusional states and those un-understandable delusional states, he emphasized that the un-understandable must arise from an organic "process" (Jaspers, 1963).

Kolle (1931) reanalyzed a large series of Kraepelin's patients with the diagnosis of either paranoia or paraphrenia and concluded that, based on the results of family studies and course, that most had a mild form of schizophrenia. In his study of the group of querulous paranoias he came to the conclusion that the majority were what he described as the "neurotic quarrellers," who were psychopathic not psychotic, with the remainder suffering from schizophrenia (Kendler, 1981; Kolle, 1931).

The French

Charles Laseque first described persecutory delusions in 1852. However, it was Benedict Morel's description in 1853 of a psychosis found in the young and that he labeled *demence precoce* that has had a profound effect on French psychiatric classifications. From this time the French used *irreversible deterioration* to separate dementia precoce from the delusional disorders in which it does not occur. This created a large group of delusional states, which were viewed as distinct from dementia praecox or schizophrenia.

Equally influential was Morel's 1856 *Treatise on Degeneracies*, which introduced hereditary constitution as a principle of classification. Built on by Valentin Magnan, mental disorders were divided into those that could be developed by "sound stock" and those that could be developed by "degenerates" (Pichot, 1982).

The term paranoia was never widely used in France, however, the disorders of chronic delusions with a nondeteriorating course were initially called "the chronic delusions of degenerates." A similar disorder but with a more severe course occurred in "sound stock" and was called "chronic delusional state of systematic evolution." The dilemmas of incorporating a Kraepelinian nomenclature into the French system were such that by World War I the concept of hereditary constitution had all but died out in French psychiatry and the above-noted disorders were merged and then subdivided based upon symptomatology, or what the French describe as "delusional mechanisms."

In 1909 Serieux and Capgras described a group of nonhallucinatory chronic delusional states with coherent delusions, which developed gradually in vulnerable individuals and did not lead to dementia (Pichot, 1982). They corresponded to Kraepelin's paranoia group of 1912. Termed "chronic interpretive psychosis" they were a systematized psychosis feeding on delusional interpretations, and at their core was (Pichot, 1982, p. 478):

> *False reasoning originating in the misinterpretation of correctly perceived fact or facts, to which logical but erroneous inferences lend misconstrued subjective meaning consonant with personal inclinations, sentiments, and preoccupations.*

A subgroup was called "vindictive delusional states" in which a single, relentless and patently pathological thought or thought complex, intensified by opposition, subdues and dominates all other mental activity. This group is similar to Kraepelin's querulous paranoia.

G. de Clerambault, in the 1930s, similarly described a subdivision based on sentiment or passion-driven misinterpretations. These were single, permanent, and unshakeable but erroneous convictions of either conjugal or erotic structure, e.g., she is unfaithful to me or she loves me. He believed other interpretive delusions, e.g., persecutory and grandiose, developed insidiously, with suspicion, doubt, and mystery slowly crystallizing into delusion. Conversely, he felt that those who developed delusions of passion had reactions that were "hypersthenic" and "expansive" (as per Kretschmer), i.e., the delusions of passion developed suddenly with ideas fully formed, with immediate sense of purpose and goal driven activity of almost hypomanic ferocity. De Clerambault's distinctions remained firmly entrenched in the French classificatory system up into the 1980s, and his model has remained of value to those who have subsequently performed research into morbid jealousy, erotomania, and querulousness (Mullen, 1997; Pichot, 1982).

Post World War II

Kurt Schneider in 1949 stated that the paranoias were only a peripheral form of schizophrenia (Themes and Variations in European Psychiatry, 1974, chap. 2). In the ninth edition of his work *The Psychopathic Personalities* (where psychopathic is taken to mean the subgroup of abnormal personalities who either suffer personally because of their own abnormality or make the community suffer because of it), Schneider is at pains to point out that paranoia does not exist. Instead, taking the querulent as an example, he believes they fall into either the schizophrenic group or into a group of "reactive paranoid developments" (Schneider, 1958, p. 100). The latter develop in either a "hyperthymic" or "fanatic psychopathology."

The American Psychiatric Association's Statistical Manuals from the first in 1918 until the seventh in 1945 followed Kraepelin's classifications. However, in the first edition of the *Diagnostic and Statistical Manual* (DSM) in 1952 it was evident that Bleuler's influence was paramount with the term schizophrenia adopted and the point specifically made that deterioration only occurred in some cases of schizophrenia (Kendler, 1981). Paranoia along with "paranoid state" was present under the term "paranoid reactions," and defined as persistent delusions of persecutory or grandiose type normally without hallucinations or intellectual deterioration (Kendler, 1980, 1981).

Bleuler's influence along with the restrictive content of delusions described by the American Psychiatric Association's Statistical Manuals limited the diagnosis of paranoia and the concept went into decline from the 1950s to the 1970s. However, research by Winokur (1977), Kendler (1980), Munro (1982, 1987), and others helped revive the concept. Paranoia became what first Winokur and then Kendler described as "delusional disorder." Kendler felt it important to separate delusional disorder with hallucinations from delusional disorder without hallucinations, which he termed "simple delusional disorder." Kendler's work supported the view that simple delusional disorder was sustainable as a separate disorder from schizophrenia and mood disorders (Kendler, 1980; Kendler, Gruenberg, & Strauss, 1981; Winokur, 1977).

ICD9 of 1978 described paranoia as a gradually developing systematized delusions without hallucinations or schizophrenic type of disordered thinking. No comment regarding etiology is made. In DSM-III (1980) "paranoia" was classified under "paranoid disorder" and the delusions were either persecutory or delusional jealousy, and again hallucinations could be present but not prominent. There is no deterioration of intellect.

ICD10 (1992) includes paranoia within "persistent delusional disorders" and allows hallucinations if only occasional or transitory auditory type. The delusions may be variable in content, but are persistent and possibly lifelong. No mention of course or deterioration is mentioned.

In DSM-IV paranoia is no longer mentioned and delusional disorder takes the place of paranoid disorder. The delusions must be nonbizarre and tactile and olfactory hallucinations may be present. This remains unchanged in either DSM-IV-TR or DSM-V.

DELUSIONS

The presence of delusions has historically been the hallmark of insanity, and yet delusions have been defined in a number of ways, and as yet no agreement has been reached on their nature or origins (Berrios, 1991; Butler & Braff, 1991; Roberts, 1992).

There have been investigators who have disagreed that they even are a form of belief but in fact are (Berrios, 1991):

> *Empty speech acts, whose informational content refers to neither world nor self. They are not the symbolic expression of anything. Its contents is but a random fragment of information 'trapped' in the very moment the delusion becomes crystallised.*

Many researchers, however, remained wedded to the general concept of delusions as beliefs (Garety & Hemsley, 1994; Jaspers, 1963; Sedler, 1995).

Karl Jaspers

In particular, Jaspers has been influential in defining the essence of delusional beliefs. He acknowledged the Kantian theory that all experience or knowledge entails both an incoming sensation (content) and an organizing concept (form). This formed the origin of the concept of form and content within his *General Psychopathology* (Jaspers, 1963; Walker, 1991).

Jaspers describes four forms of belief: normal beliefs, overvalued ideas, delusion-like beliefs, and primary delusions.

One can understand the evolution of normal, and overvalued, ideas from the personality and its life events. One can understand the delusion-like idea from the personality, life events and from some other psychopathological experience, but the primary delusion is something new, irreducible, and nonunderstandable. For Jaspers the major distinction is between primary delusions and the rest rather than between delusions (primary and secondary) and the rest.

Primary Delusion

Jaspers believes that delusions are always manifest as judgments and therefore arise in the process of thinking and judging. To this extent, pathologically falsified judgements are termed delusions (Walker, 1991).

Jaspers felt that the external characteristics of primary delusions are held with an extraordinary conviction with an incomparable subjective certainty, that there is an imperviousness to other experiences and to compelling counterargument and that their content is impossible. However, these are just the external characteristics, and Jaspers states clearly that they fail to account for the essential differences between the delusion and other forms of belief (Jaspers, 1963, p. 99).

Jaspers felt that delusions were the result of a specific abnormal process whose basis was unknown but that involved a radical transformation in the way meaning became attached to events. So for Jaspers the essential criterion distinguishing between the different forms of belief lie not in their conviction and certainty, not in their incorrigibility, and not in their impossible content but in their origins.

The essential distinguishing factor within the four forms of belief is the concept of understanding. Jaspers's sense of (*verstehen*) understanding was the psychiatrist's empathic access to the other person's subjective experience using the analogy of his own experience. In his view it is the psychologically irreducible and "un-understandable" nature of primary delusions that separate them from other delusional forms. They are unmediated by thought, and importantly there is an implied change in their personality. Jaspers describes personality as (Jaspers, 1963, p. 428),

> The term we give to the individually differing and characteristic totality of understandable connections in any one psychic life.

A primary delusion intrusively creates a new meaning in that "totality of understandable connections" and hence distorts this totality. In the primary delusional category were delusional atmosphere (delusional mood), delusional perceptions, delusional ideas, and delusional awareness (Sedler, 1995; Walker, 1991).

Von Krafft-Ebbing and initially Kraepelin both viewed the morbidly querulous as having delusions. Kraepelin later believed that they were not delusions at all, falling more into the overvalued idea type.

Normal Belief

Normal beliefs are understandable because of their origins in the personality's shared beliefs and meanings; they are incorrigible because of the social cohesion and shared values of the group.

Delusion-like Idea and the Overvalued Idea

Delusion-like ideas meet the external criteria for delusions but they can be traced to preceding psychopathological experiences such as hallucinations, morbid affects, fears, or primary delusions. Given these, they can be seen to fit into a web of meaningful connections.

Jaspers describes overvalued ideas as isolated beliefs accompanied by a strong affective response that take precedence over all other mental activity and maintain this indefinitely. Overvalued ideas are understandable because of their origins in the strong effect of the particular personality and its situation; they are incorrigible because, although often idiosyncratic and false, they have the force of highly charged and compelling insights. Their qualities are similar to passionate political or religious beliefs and differ only in degree (Walker, 1991). Jaspers (1963, p. 599) made little or no practical distinction between delusion-like ideas and overvalued ideas and at times uses them interchangeably in his writings. Jaspers included the beliefs of the morbidly querulous as overvalued ideas.

C. Wernicke

It was Wernicke who first defined the overvalued idea as a solitary belief that comes to determine an individual's actions to a morbid degree, yet remains able to be considered justified and a normal expression of the individual's nature. He felt they tended to develop in predisposed personalities and often dated from experiences that at the time aroused strong feelings, and in fact he felt that overvalued ideas were memories of some affect-charged experience or series of experiences (Schneider, 1958, p. 97, Wernicke, 1900). Wernicke felt that the overvalued idea could progress to full psychosis or was occasionally a manifestation of melancholia or general paralysis (Mc Kenna, 1984).

Wernicke distinguished overvalued ideas from obsessions by observing that they were never felt to be senseless by the sufferer. He included the morbidly querulous in the overvalued ideas group.

Fish notes that in the patient with an overvalued idea it is invariably acted upon, determinedly and repeatedly, whereas in the patient with delusions there is often a discrepancy between the degree of conviction and the extent to which the belief directed action (Hamilton, 1974). In contrast Bleuler (1924), took the view that action on a delusion is largely a consequence of the associated affectivity (Wessely et al., 1993).

In McKenna's 1984 review of disorders with overvalued ideas (Mc Kenna, 1984), he includes the querulous paranoid state as the standard clinical example of the overvalued idea. Referring to Jaspers he emphasizes the abnormal premorbid personality, the initial slight or injustice, and the persistent claiming behavior without deterioration. McKenna states that the central belief "lacks a specific delusional quality" and "the accompanying misinterpretations also seem uncritical more than delusional." However, he also notes that researchers have found some cases to progress to psychosis as well as some cases commencing with psychosis (Mc Kenna, 1984, p. 580).

THE SPECTRUM OF QUERULENCE

The German E. Berrios writes of the classificatory drive, which appeared in Western Society during the 17th and 18th centuries. Alienists were not immune to this movement, and by the 19th century vigorous debates were being held about the validity of various psychiatric classificatory systems, for example, those based on phenomenology versus those based on etiology (Berrios, 1999). It was at this time that the initial studies of the querulous were born.

Various psychiatric researchers have attempted to describe and categorize the querulous. They were influenced by their guiding psychiatric paradigms and by a significant selection bias in the querulous patients they examined, for the querulous do not voluntarily seek out psychiatric care. In fact, it is society, through its courts and other authorities, who refer the querulous patients to psychiatric professionals. As a result, researchers, particularly early researchers such as Krafft-Ebbing and Kraepelin, studied those querulous who had been referred to them by the courts or other authorities for involuntary incarceration and observation. They were therefore usually selected not only because of their particularly persistent and annoying level of querulousness but also because of their level of dangerousness.

Krafft-Ebbing took an etiological approach, believing the querulous to have an organic psychosis, which always developed in "tainted" individuals (Gelder et al., 1993, p. 363).

Kraepelin believed that querulous behavior could occur in nonpsychotic individuals who were: "Very perverse, quarrelsome and under some circumstances simply weak minded people…" (Kraepelin, 1904, p. 150).

The remaining querulous suffered from a disease process. He believed this group to be a heterogeneous mix of psychotic disorders. With the concept of partial insanity or paranoia firmly in mind, he initially separated them into those with dementia praecox and those with a subgroup of paranoia, which he called the querulous paranoias. Eventually by 1912 Kraepelin's prodigious struggles to categorize and subcategorize the querulous had resulted in the querulous being separated into the discrete entities of schizophrenia, paraphrenia, querulous paranoia, and the others (querulous personalities, weak minded, etc.).

However, he could not maintain his belief in the organic psychosis concept for the querulous paranoias, for they had misbeliefs uncharacteristic of the primary delusion. The misbeliefs were ordinary and followed understandably from their underlying personality and overlaid life experiences. Exhausted, he finally relented and redefined querulous paranoia as a disorder of abnormal developments in a psychopathic disposition under the influences of ordinary life. It appears he believed their misbeliefs to have the form of overvalued ideas.

By this stage he believed those with querulous paranoia to have experienced an event that led to the development of an ever-steepening spiral of grievance. There were delusions of grievance with an underlying strong over self-appreciation. There should be no evidence of thought disorder, emotional blunting, or hallucinations. The course was chronic and fluctuating with periods of quiescence and relapse. He remained clear in his mind that those with querulous paranoia had deviated clearly from the groups with disordered personalities or, as he described, the "perverse, quarrelsome and weak minded" querulous (Lewis, 1970; Munro, 1982; Schifferdecker, 1995).

It was this final position of Emil Kraepelin, along with his belief in the discrete entities, that has been most influential on subsequent researchers into querulousness. Kraepelin's student Kurt Kolle reviewed Kraepelin's querulous paranoiacs and believed most of them not to have paranoia but to be *neurotic quarrelers* who shared the grandiosity and desired goal of the paranoias (Bleuler, 1924, p. 88). However, subsequent researchers continued to search for the discrete entity, querulous paranoia. They hoped it could be isolated and studied as it came to be believed that their misbeliefs took the form of overvalued ideas, which could be distinguished from primary and secondary delusions as well as from normal beliefs.

Karl Jaspers's writings on the division of mental disorders have influenced researchers from Kretschmer and van der Heydt through to Mullen and Caduff. Jaspers wrote of mental disorders as processes, developments, or reactions (Jaspers, 1963; Mullen, 1997).

A morbid reaction is a response to a precipitating event in which the intensity and content of the provoking event makes understandable the emergence of the disorder. Temporally there is a close link between the event, and the reaction, which should decline when the provoking event ceases.

A developmental disorder arose from the interaction of a provoking event and a specific personality structure. The evolution of the disorder is not necessarily connected to the course of the provoking situation. Ernst Kretschmer attempted to both categorize and explain the etiology of the querulous paranoias by their underlying personality structures (Themes and Variations in European Psychiatry, 1974, chap. 8). Kurt Schneider (1958), who referred to the querulous in his work on psychopathic personalities, believed them to be either a development from psychopathic personalities or to suffer from schizophrenia.

Later still, the researcher A. van der Heydt (1952) who had a series of 34 querulous patients, tried a diagnostic and descriptive categorization:

1. **Normal**–seeker of justice, with no disturbance of personality or psychosis. It is a reaction to injustice suffered. When the injustice is remedied, the querulousness disappears.
2. **Opportunistic**–seeker of personal advantage. Personality disordered with antisocial traits whose querulousness is in order to gain financial compensation, business advantage, or avoidance of punishment.
3. **Justice**–seeker of justice for justice's sake. It initially may have appeared to be as in Group 1, however it spirals into a series of complaints. They produce large volumes of written complaints, counter accusations, and justifications. These become increasingly vituperative and insulting. Lasting many years, it increasingly involves previously uninvolved entities, and their struggle often loses contact with the original injustice. Their life focus is on seeking justice and other areas of their life are neglected.

4. **Conjugal**–personality disordered with the overwhelming need to be right. Triggered by marital disharmony and associated legal proceedings.
5. **Irritable and peevish personality disorder**–chronically quarrelsome with an overwhelming need to be right. They have always fought against everyone and everything. These rarely go to court and do not produce the volume of written material.
6. **Secondary to psychosis**–the querulousness occurs with an endogenous psychosis (either affective or schizophrenic). Resolution of the psychosis leads to resolution of the querulousness (van der Heydt, 1952).

Van der Heydt (1952) went some way to further describe the spectrum of the querulous. He remained firmly Kraepelinian in his adherence to the entity querulous paranoia at whose heart lay the overvalued idea. He believed Group 3 represented the querulous paranoias. He believed their neurotic symptoms were so closely connected to their character that it is reasonable to speak of it as a "character neurosis." He describes Group 3 as the "genuine querulent." He is possibly referring to Recke's genuine querulent whose querulousness arises from an innate tendency to querulousness, which is triggered by "real" injustice (Caduff, 1995). Later researchers such as von Dietrich (1973) and Caduff (1995), perhaps unwilling to further muddy the water, have used von der Heydt's categorizations in their research (von Dietrich, 1968; Caduff, 1995). The difficulties in sustaining separate categories for the querulous have led some researchers, such as Rowlands (1988) (who interviewed a group of vexatious litigants), into quite confusing positions. In his work he states that:

> The psycopathology of the symptoms merge, and it is difficult to separate overvalued ideas from delusions,

while curiously attempting to separate the querulous into the categories of:

- Querulous paranoia, i.e., as per Kraepelin's abnormal development in a psychopathic disposition
- Paranoia, i.e., as we would understand delusional disorder
- Paranoid personalities
- Schizophrenia

Thus he attempts to separate paranoia from querulous paranoia, a feat that not even Kraepelin at his most optimistic attempted and a position unsupported by the accompanying case histories (Rowlands, 1988).

Mullen, writing on the pathologies of passion, believes that combining some of the characteristics of Jaspers's reactive and developmental mental disorders best fits the development of this group of the querulous. The individuals have personality vulnerabilities or disorder, which have been sensitized to specific stressors by past experience. They are then serendipitously exposed to those specific stressors, which then provoke a response. However, the response, while understandable in quality, is exaggerated both psychologically and behaviorally. The evolution of this reaction continues to be influenced by environmental factors such as the reception of their complaints. Mullen (1991) espouses a continuity of querulousness without multiple discrete entities.

Evidence, of the difficulty of characterizing and defining querulous paranoia as well as of evolving classificatory systems is the profusion of terms found in the psychiatric literature. They range from paranoia querulentium (Krafft-Ebbing) (Kraepelin, 1910), querulous paranoia and querulent paranoia (Kraepelin) (Schifferdecker, 1995), querulent paranoid (Freckleton, 1988), paranoia querulans (ICD10), querulous paranoid state (Rowlands, 1988), litigious paranoia, litigious paranoid (Cameron, 1959), litigious delusional states (Mullen & Pathe, 1994), justice seeker (van der Heydt, 1952), querulous syndrome (Rowlands, 1988), morbid querulousness (Mullen, 1991), delusional disorder; persecutory type (DSMIV) through to the compulsively querulous (Caduff, 1995).

THE RESEARCH

Definition
The most prosaic yet useful definition of the morbidly querulous is an individual who embarks on a persistent quest for restitution for real or imaginary wrongs through complaint, claims, petitioning of authorities and sometimes litigation, with resulting negative impact on their personal, interpersonal, and social functioning.

Diagnostic Criteria
- Persistent, relentless petitioning of governmental and nongovernmental agencies and or the courts, with evidence of contagion, i.e., spread of foci of grievance.
- Beliefs of having suffered loss or injustice that dominate the mental life. The beliefs have been of at least six months duration.
- The resulting behavior is directed to attainment of compensation, vindication, and vengeance, and stay of persecution.

For a significant portion of the time, since the onset of the behavior, one or more major areas of functioning, such as financial management, work, or interpersonal relations, are markedly below the level achieved prior to the onset. Further, there has been significant disturbance and distress caused to other targeted individuals, organizations, or their representatives.

Types
Primary: Querulousness is the only significant phenomena. There is no evidence for schizophrenia or mood disorder. Nor is there evidence that the querulousness is due to the direct physiological effects of a substance (e.g., a drug of abuse or medication) or a general medical condition.

Secondary: The criteria for schizophrenia or mood disorder have been met or the querulousness is due to the direct physiological effects of a substance (e.g., a drug of abuse or medication) or a general medical condition.

Epidemiology

Incidence

Most if not all researchers have been attempting to isolate and describe the primary type of morbid querulousness (PMQ). However, their research methods and inclusion criteria vary considerably, and so the various rates found must be viewed with reservations.

It is important to state that there has been no attempt to assess a population incidence of PMQ.

I will commence with the group of researchers who retrospectively assessed case records of all admitted patients to a psychiatric institution. As a percentage of all admitted patients, we have a rate of querulous paranoia ranging from Winokur, 0.02% (in this study paranoia had a rate of 0.1%), Kolle who assessed the records of all the 30,000 admissions to Kraepelin's clinics and found 13 with a diagnosis of querulous paranoia, a rate of 0.04%, through to Johansen (1964) who found a rate of 0.9% for querulous paranoia (paranoia had a rate of 6% in this study) (Johanson, 1964; Kolle, 1931; Winokur, 1977).

Another group of researchers assessed the case histories of patients with functional psychoses only, and so as a percentage of admitted patients with functional psychoses the rate of querulous paranoia ranged from Caduff, 0.15%, and Refsum, 0.2% (paranoia had a rate of 3.5%), through to Astrup, 0.7% (Astrup, 1984; Caduff, 1995; Refsum, 1983).

The only prospective study was that of Pang, Ungvari, Lum, Lai, and Leung (1996) who found that of 1551 referrals to the psychiatric outpatient clinic in Hong Kong (over 1 year) 0.2% had querulous paranoia.

In reviewing the overall results, it is evident that the Scandinavians had high rates of both paranoia and querulous paranoia. This may be explained by their emphasis on a deteriorating course to diagnose schizophrenia. As a result, schizophrenia was not diagnosed despite the patient having emotional blunting, thought disturbance, and/or auditory or somatic hallucinations. This skews the number who are diagnosed with paranoiac psychoses and paranoia. This gives a significantly wider range of phenomenology in the patient groups of the Scandinavians in general, and Refsum (1983) in particular, and puts them at odds with most of the other researchers.

If we focus on the researchers who exclude patients with emotional blunting, thought disorder, and hallucinations, we are left with a range of rates for PMQ of 0.02% (Winokur)→0.04% (Kolle, 1931) of all hospitalized patients, 0.15% (Caduff, 1995) of hospitalized psychotic patients, and 0.2% (Pang et al., 1996) of outpatients.

Age

There is surprising unanimity in the research findings that the majority developed their querulousness in their thirties and forties and fifties. The findings of Astrup and others showed that there was often a significant period of time between onset and first presentation; 70% had a period of 1–5 years of disorder prior to presentation, and 30% had a period of 5–10 years of symptoms prior to first presentation (Astrup, 1984).

Sex

The initial studies by Krafft-Ebbing, Kraepelin, and Kolle demonstrated that 70–80% of the querulous were men. This was on an involuntary and often forensic population. Van der Heydt and Caduff have supported these figures (Caduff, 1995; Heydt van der, 1952; Kraepelin, 1904; Krafft-Ebbing, 1905; Kolle, 1931).

Astrup (1984) found that 50% were male, while Johansen found over 60% were male. Johanson's (1964) patients were voluntary and nonforensic.

Premorbid Functioning

The major studies of Kolle, van der Heydt, and Caduff paint a picture of competent individuals. Typically, the elder child of middle-class parents, they had a good education and middle- to upper-class employment levels. Winokur found 76% to have had a satisfactory work history (Caduff, 1995; van der Heydt, 1952; Kolle, 1931; Winokur, 1977).

Kolle (1931) found that 63% were married, 16% divorced, and 16% had never married. Astrup (1984) found a lower level of marriage with 33% married, 18% divorced, and 45% never married.

Premorbid Personality

Beginning with Krafft-Ebbing's "a rough, irritable, egotistic person, defective in his notions of justice," the researchers have some consistency in the described personality types most prone to the querulous development (Berrios & Porter, 1995, p. 364).

Kolle found there to be three main premorbid personality types. These he described as:

Hyperthymic (39%) as per Kurt Schneider's "hyperthymic psychopath" who are energetic, busy, restless, irritable, have a sense of humor and are sociable but have inflated self-esteem and are sensitive to slights. Kurt Schneider himself called them pseudoquerulents because though they tend to quarrel and complain, they are easily assuaged (Kolle, 1931; Schneider, 1958).
Fanatic (12%) again as per Kurt Schneider's "fanatic psychopath," who are holders of overvalued ideas that are held assertively and combatively (Kolle, 1931; Schneider, 1958). Tenacious and uninhibitedly aggressive they are *always right* and stubborn. They may exhibit eccentricities of manner, behavior, dress, or speech. As per Kretschmer, they have a tender vulnerable core of buried inferiority feelings and when struck by loss they form an "expansive reaction," being energetic, arrogant and self-assured (Themes and Variations in European Psychiatry, 1974, chap. 8).

Defiant (27%) These individuals are "against the grain" people who are rebel-lious, have great difficulty with authority of any type and have histories of parental conflict (Kolle, 1931).

Van der Heydt (1952) and Caduff (1995) support this finding though Caduff using van der Heydt's classification described the "genuinely" querulous of Group 3 to be mainly hyperthymic.

Astrup (1984) and Refsum (1983) describe 75% as having "self-assertive person-alities" and that over 30% had a premorbid criminal history.

Winokur (1977) found that patients were not generally fussy or rigid but had been chronically jealous and suspicious (66%) and embittered (45%).

Ricardo Pons (1987) describes them as having overly sensitive and mistrustful personalities, best summed up by the Spanish saying as "those who look for noon at 2 p.m."

Dietrich found them to have premorbid personalities of mainly paranoid type, with hidden hostility, over reaction to threat, and sensitivity about their competence. A history of dysfunctional relationships highlights their difficulty in empathizing with others and hence their inability to value societal interests compared to their own. They are suspicious, prone to misunderstandings and wrong conclusions. Their sensitivity and insecurity require rigid defenses, which preclude weakness, mistake, or failure on their part (von Dietrich, 1968).

Pang et al. and Ungvari describe premorbid inflexibility, difficulty with intimacy, assertiveness with hypersensitivity to criticism, and distrust (Mullen & Pathe, 1994; Pang et al., 1996; Ungvari, Pang, & Wong, 1997; Ungvari, 1995).

Johanson (1964) felt that premorbidly they had high self-esteem.

In summary, the querulous tend to be ambitious, self-assertive, and egotistical with high but fragile self-esteem. They may be irritable and antiauthoritarian, and their relationships are marked by lack of empathy, distance, and at times conflict.

Precipitating (Key) Experience

The original researchers such as Emil Kraepelin were impressed by the understand-able quality of the development when seen as a product of the underlying personality and a key or precipitating event. Kretschmer viewed querulous paranoia as a "key reaction" in that only a specific key event or experience for a given personality is able to unlock its development (Themes and Variations in European Psychiatry, 1974, chap. 8). Kolle found that there was a high level of identifiable significant events pre-ceding the querulousness. In all cases the onset was preceded by a severe disturbance of living conditions, and in particular he found that 60% had a preceding stressful court case and 31% had been dismissed from work (Kolle, 1931). This has been supported by van der Heydt and Caduff who in particular found a high level of legal problems preceding overt querulousness by a period of years. Other researchers have had more mixed results. Astrup (1984) found 81% had an identifiable stressor prior to the onset and of these 27% had an episode labeled "acute mental trauma". He was concerned that in 18% no acute event or stressor could be identified.

Johanson (1964) was able to identify a significant "environmental stressor" in 50%.

Overall, the process is one of slowly developing querulous behavior commencing with an event most often legal in nature. There is no support for de Clerambault's beliefs that delusions of passion develop suddenly and fully formed (Themes and Variations in European Psychiatry, 1974, chap. 15).

Etiology

From the earliest research of von Krafft-Ebbing there was a belief that, though the expression of the illness was seen clearly to develop from premorbid personality and their experienced life events, they all had the underlying etiology of organic brain disease.

Kraepelin commenced his studies of this group with the belief that they were all caused by a disease process as found in dementia praecox. However, a significant number lacked the symptoms, course, or family history of dementia praecox or manic depressive disorder. So that the "understandability" of their beliefs (given his knowledge of their personality and the precipitating events) eventually led him to conclude that this group were morbid reactions in pathological personalities (Lewis, 1970; Kraepelin, 1904).

Equally, when Kolle reviewed the group of querulous he felt they fell clearly into two groups. The first were a group with a primary "neurotic presentation in a disordered personality," i.e., psychopathology (Kolle, 1931). The second group were secondary to a "process," i.e., paraphrenia or schizophrenia. This split has been supported by the vast majority of subsequent researchers.

Psychodynamic Theory

Von Dietrich (1968) describes the development of the querulous as a staged process.

Early Childhood influences In particular, he describes a self-fulfilling aspect, i.e., a querulent has a temperament that differentiates him from others and hence is at risk of disturbed emotional attachments. Freud believes the conflict is with the same gender parent and occurs between the ages of 3–5 years. The child is frightened and tormented by a hostile, sadistic, distant, or absent relationship with the carer and environment. This is supported by van der Heydt's (1952) and Pang et al.'s (1996) observation of their harsh and emotionally cold families. Von Dietrich states that they develop a sadistic super ego, which impairs their identification with their same sex parent and disturbs their healthy ego development. Their early life is marked by rebellion against father and authorities. In adult life, the stressful "key events" cause regression, bringing the primitive, sadistic super ego to the fore. This super ego is feared; hence it is projected onto outside figures, which are perceived as attacking and condemning (Caduff, 1995).

Key Events. Freudian dynamics describe the querulent as having a developed Oedipus complex driven by the conflict with the father and will therefore react abnormally toward any restrictions of the male status symbols such as prestige, position, power, property, and rights. Account must be made of the age of onset, which is at 40–60 years, a time of reevaluation of goals and perhaps the need to accept nonaccomplishment and to face mortality and loss of power in the future. As von Dietrich states,

> To start to hate for ever, the chances for love must appear to be disappearing.

Threats to status, lack of promotion, the humiliation of defeat or failure are all blows to a sensitive, overcompensated, and defended self-esteem (von Dietrich, 1968).

Cognitive Theory

Cognitive theories of paranoia are built around the concept of self, and the issues of threat and defense of self. In particular, it is proposed that paranoia is a defense against low self-esteem (Chadwick, Birchwood, & Trower, 1996, p. 135). This theory connects to the "self-serving bias," which notes that people have a tendency to blame someone else for their shortcomings, which enables us to feel indignant and angry rather than low and deficient (Beck, 1976; Chadwick, Birchwood, & Trower, 1996, p. 160).

Bentall et al. have shown that the self-serving bias is exaggerated in paranoia, and that those with paranoia typically display high self-esteem while having depressive self-schema (Trower, Casey, & Dryden, 1988). He believes that at the heart of the paranoid defense is an exaggeration of the ordinary tendency to reject responsibility for negative events. This exaggerated self-serving bias attempts to limit the discrepancy between the ideal and actual selves.

Others feel that paranoia is like a form of angry attributional style, i.e., individuals perceive interpersonal negative evaluation and construe it as being unjust, and they reject the criticism and condemn the persecutor (Chadwick, Birchwood, & Trower, 1996, p. 137).

Chadwick and Trower believe there are two types of paranoia:

Poor Me (Persecution)—blame others, see others as bad, see themselves as victims
Bad Me (Punishment)—blame themselves, see themselves as bad, hence others justifiably punish them

They adhere to a theory of self in which a fundamental human passion is the construction of self and that the self is a constantly constructed entity and never secure (Chadwick, Birchwood, & Trower, 1996).

There are three necessary and sufficient conditions for the construction of self, namely:

An objective self—this is the product, i.e., the most familiar aspect of self, the observed, behavioral, public self. It is the self-presentation behavior of an individual.

A subjective self—this is the self as agent, i.e., the one who chooses the actions and monitors them and feedback from others; has the power of action and the cognitive processes of observing, inferring, evaluating, etc.

An other–this is the other person who acts as observer.

The construction of self may be conceptualized as a series of stages. First, it begins with self-presentation behaviors for others, i.e., the attempt to control images of self before the audience. Second is the perceived, anticipated, or imagined evaluation by others of the self so presented. The third stage may be either evaluation of self by self-consequent upon the other's evaluation or it might be the evaluation of the other by self.

There are two major forms of threat to the construction of self:

The Alienated Self in which the *other* (parent) is excessively present and intrusive. The other controls and may in fact construct the objective self. Hence the objective self feels imposed, almost alien to the subjective self. He feels overwhelmed by the other and he seeks to escape the entrapment. The self is experienced as flawed, bad. He fears being controlled and interprets others as powerful and himself as weak. This is exemplified by the Bad Me paranoid.

The Insecure Self in which the subjective self is able to produce self-representations but the other is neglectful, absent, and therefore the objective self cannot be produced. This failure is experienced as abandonment, emptiness, insignificance, and worthlessness and emotionally as depressive ennui or anguish.

The subjective self, having total freedom, produces the fantasy self and searches for the other to objectify this fantasy or desired self. His despair is to be ignored or rejected and hence to feel the existential nothingness. He responds with a defense of narcissistic rage. The Poor Me paranoid exemplifies the trait of the insecure self. Parenting that is psychologically unavailable, uncaring, neglectful, and with inconsistent affection may be associated with this group.

The Poor Me type is motivated by the need to defend against a sense of being ignored, neglected, and insignificant, or rejected with associated feelings of emptiness and despair. This is highlighted by their delusional reconstruction where the persecutor's (who normally is either unaware of, or gives no thought to them) every action is aimed in some way at them (Chadwick, Birchwood, & Trower, 1996, chap. 7).

Social Factors

Mary Douglas, an anthropologist describes changes in attribution of blame associated with tribal and preindustrial societies versus the industrial and postindustrial society. She states that tribal and preindustrial cultures thought in terms of danger to the community. Attribution of causation of calamities was to supernatural causes. The blame was on the individual sufferer who had in some way broken a taboo or sinned. The responsibility for the disturbance of the community remained with the individual.

In industrial and postindustrial societies there has been a marked change. The term *risk*, first used in the 17th century, was a neutral calculation of probability simply taking account of losses and gains. Its use developed in tandem with technology and industry and was embraced by both as a theoretical base for decision-making. In turn it became part of political and social language. Significantly, risk was tied to the newly arrived and ever-expanding industry. In the face of this expanding industrial system, risk transformed into a synonym for loss and danger losing by the wayside the positive gain aspects. Thus risk became part of the system and risk had transformed into the danger presented by the community/system to the individual. Hence blame for negative occurrences was now attributed to the system, i.e., externalized. Each individual becomes a potential victim (Bental & Kinderman, 1994).

Max Scheler in his essay on compensation neurosis spoke of the social and psychic contagiousness of suffering and the power of the prospect of benefit. By this he was describing the fact that community "attitudes" become reified in the psyche of the individual. This occurs in all but to an even greater extent in those with existing predispositions. While he was addressing illness and "hysterical" predispositions, I feel it is evident that community attitudes on victimhood could easily interact with those who possess predispositions to querulousness.

Charles Dickens in his novel *Bleak House* describes the pathology of a legal system, which is voracious, encouraging and then feeding on the litigiousness of individuals. There is no research that has attempted to correlate rates of morbid querulousness with legal systems. It is self-evident that in certain societies litigation is more prominent, e.g., the United States. While in the United States there is a long tradition of using litigation to bring about social change, there is significant concern by social researchers that the adversarial system is shaping and distorting expectations and interpersonal communications (Scheler, 1984, chap. 5).

Caduff in his discussion of the history of querulousness cites Venzlaff who states that querulousness is the product of a complicated form of law, a jungle of official regulation, which is not easily seen through or understood at first glance. He thought that the reason why the study of querulousness had begun and thrived in Germany, Switzerland, and France was because of their codified legal system. Caduff then makes the point that though there was a word for querulousness in the German (*Querulanz*), French (*Persecutes Possesifs*) and Italian (*Prozessomania*) languages, there was not one initially in the English language. He quotes Mayer Gross who felt that this was due to the less-codified legal system of the English (Caduff, 1995).

Pang has noted the relative absence of the querulous paranoia diagnosis in China. He feels it may possibly be related to sociocultural factors. He states that in Confucianism (Pang et al., 1996),

> *Filial piety requires unquestioning obedience to parental authority and emphasis on duties and obligations. The collectivist culture places personal need below country, society and family; thus individual rights are often sacrificed for the sake of a higher cause.*

This either is not conducive to the development of or suppresses the manifestation of querulousness.

QUERULOUS BEHAVIOR IN THE 21ST CENTURY

The most obvious external defining characteristic of the morbidly querulous is not their belief of having been wronged or their pursuit of redress. For this is common to all of those we know of as complainants. Neither is it simply persistence of complaint, as this is in common to those complainants we would describe as "social activists."

To distinguish the morbidly querulous complainant from their normal counterpart it is essential to weigh a number of qualities, of which the most significant are:

- Proportionality (e.g., lack of balance between effort in all its modalities and potential loss or gain).
- Focus (e.g., number of additional grievances accrued during progress of seeking redress for complaint).
- Valuation (e.g., degree of importance ascribed to "perfect" resolution).
- Victimization (e.g., degree to which the complaint had developed into a grievance and other past grievances are "bundled" with the current and the degree of personalization attributed to the grievance).
- Vindication (degree to which resolution becomes imbued with qualities that will validate their past life and its failures).

It is important to emphasize at the outset that querulousness as with any behavior may be produced by a variety of factors interacting in a complex manner and its consequences are similarly various (Lester et al., 2004; Mullen, Lester, Litigants, & Persistent, 2006).

Society evolved from using criminal legal proceedings, e.g., United Kingdom, barratry to then procedural impediments (vexatious litigant legislation) and psychiatry in Europe but to procedural impediments alone in the United Kingdom, United States, Australia, Canada.

The signs and symptoms of querulence have been richly described over the last 140 years. These are much more accessible than the various theoretical constructs deemed to underlie the syndrome at various periods over the last one to two centuries and in various countries, primarily Germany, France, and Russia/Soviet Union.

Relatively recent research into the signs both early and late of the development of querulence has occurred in limited amounts in English language research. Freckleton in 1988 wrote from personal experience as police ombudsman on the characteristics of unreasonable complainants. Rowland's 1988 reviewed a number of vexatious litigants in the United Kingdom from a psychiatric perspective. In 2004 Lester et al. conducted research with a group of Australian ombudsman offices exploring the differences between "unusually persistent complainants" and a control group.

In 2013 Skilling et al. reviewed clients of the Scottish police complaints commissioner attempting to assess three groups, a normal control, a persistent group, and a querulent group where due to confidentiality issues, experienced complaint handlers were tasked with the work of separating out the persistent from the querulent based on duration, complexity, and use of complaints handling resources (Skilling et al., 2015).

B. Levy, in his impressive review of the history of the European querulent and the vexatious, criticized English-speaking psychiatry for not taking charge and management of this group and hence allowing them to fall into the clutches of the law (vexatious litigant legislation), which he posited was ill equipped to manage them. However, as can be seen by the evolution of querulous paranoia, being a psychiatric conceptualization, it requires a societal acceptance of the role for psychiatry in managing persistent complainants and litigants (Levy, 2014).

However, since the 1960s the idea of management of the querulent by psychiatry in English-speaking countries has met resistance in multiple forms and shapes. Not the least of which were the proponents of the idea, exemplified by the claim by Szasz (1974), that psychiatry is prone to pathologizing normal or abnormal behaviors either with benign or malign intent. S. Smith in his work on vexatious litigants hypothesized that, in particular in Australia, there is a belief that the abnormally persistent litigants or complainants are the "mavericks" of society. Hence, given our convict roots and place of refuge for Irish refugees from British government mistreatment, this view is that the maverick is a potent symbol of the freedom enjoyed by Australians from government injustice. Therefore, any attack or pathologizing of these litigants may be seen as an attack on the freedoms of the majority (Smith, 2009). This is strongly echoed in the United States. Ironically, it is the very abuse of these freedoms that separates out this group from the majority.

In Victoria, Australia, the Parliament of Victoria formed a Law Reform Committee to review the Vexatious Litigants Act passed in 1928. Evidence was gained from disparate sources such as the Law Institute, the Victorian Institute of Forensic Mental Health, Human Rights Commission, ombudsman's offices, and community legal centers.

The evidence highlighted the divide between what would be seen as the psychiatric perspective on persistent complaint and litigation and the sociopolitical perspective.

The evidence of Mullen and Lester was that the phenomenon of the vexatious litigant was partly overlain onto the psychiatric discourse of querulous paranoia or morbid complaint. They also stated that there was a spectrum of morbid complainants and that while not all "vexatious litigants" were part of the spectrum, they strongly emphasized that those along the querulent spectrum were poorly served by vexatious litigant legislation. Society was equally poorly served. They proposed that mandatory psychiatric evaluation should be included within any changes made to vexatious litigant legislation.

The sociopolitical perspective hinged on the persistent complainant as misunderstood or badly treated or supported citizen who could be brought back to normality through improvement of legal support and services or through the various existing mechanisms by which courts may curtail or prevent unwarranted litigation.

For a range of historical and political reasons, the Law Reform Committee were of a mind to be particularly cognizant of the dangers of pathologizing and hence limiting the rights of the vexatious litigant through introducing any form of mandatory psychiatric evaluation. Rather they opted for the status quo with the request for further research to be performed both within psychiatry and within the justice system (Parliament of Victoria, 2008).

Our research in 2004 with a range of Victorian ombudsman offices has shown that the querulent as vexatious litigant is a tiny percentage of the spectrum of abnormally persistent complaint. Various ombudsmen have estimated that those exhibiting some form or degree of querulous behavior make up 5–6% of their clients with the number of those displaying the full range of querulous behaviors being about 0.1–0.2% of their clients. They estimated that this 0.1–0.2% of their clients took up to 15–20% of their time (Lester et al., 2004).

The number of litigants made vexatious litigants each year is tiny. The number of individuals showing varying degrees of querulousness is large, and the majority either do not journey into the courts or if they do are not made vexatious litigants. So the vexatious litigant is simply the tip of the iceberg when it comes to societal impact of the unreasonable complaint and litigant behavior. In fact, it is at the level of ombudsman office or tribunal rather than the courts proper that early intervention may be of most use.

It was from this understanding that ombudsman's offices worldwide have been exploring how to best manage those with a persisting pattern of complaint behavior.

In Australia this commenced in 2006 with a consortium of all Australia's state ombudsman offices including the Commonwealth Ombudsman. To prevent stigmatization of individuals, they avoided the terms *querulous* or *vexatious*, instead utilizing the term that was being more broadly used in English speaking countries, that of *unreasonable complainant*. However, to focus on the practical, they recognized they could not contain an individual but could modify their behaviors as experienced by the offices, and hence they focused on managing unreasonable complaint behavior. Building on the experience of complaints managers as well as recent psychiatric research, they developed a manual for the best practices management of unreasonable complaint behavior in 2007, and this has been updated at regular intervals (Ombudsman, 2012).

Psychiatry still does play a small role in the management of the querulous. Unfortunately, the literature and my own experience show that the querulous never present to psychiatry or psychology voluntarily as they lack insight into their contribution to the devastation occurring in their lives. It is only when they have criminally offended (usually through the uttering of threats of harm to complaints management staff, legal counsel, or judges, or more seriously the destruction of property, sieges, assault, kidnapping, or murder of the above) that they come into contact with psychiatry. Then it is mainly for assessment and only for the more serious offending, management.

If evaluated by experienced forensic psychiatrists or psychologists, they are likely to be recognized as existing within this querulous spectrum and depending on other phenomena may be diagnosed with either delusional disorder or schizophrenia. The experience of the Victorian Institute of Forensic Mental Health has been with those who have either been imprisoned or released into the community on a community-based order, which requires them to cooperate with psychiatric evaluation and therapy. In prison, if assessed as suffering from a psychotic disorder, therapy may be commenced in prison clinics or in rarer cases, in hospital if transferred to our medium secure forensic hospital, Thomas Embling Hospital.

The most effective treatment regime is low-dose atypical antipsychotic medication in combination with cognitive behavioral therapy aimed at challenging and evaluating their overvalued ideas. This combination has been most successfully used on those who have been transferred to hospital, as involuntary treatment is mandated. Of those cases managed in the community or in prison where they are not compelled to commence medication, it has limited value due to their rejection of any, as they see, aspersion, that their cause is not just and righteous bur rather pathological to some degree or other. However, similar to the successful uptake of drug rehabilitation, it is often when the sufferer feels they have "hit rock bottom" and have nothing more to lose that they are most accessible for the psychiatrist or psychologist. This time is crucial in their lives as if they do not receive therapy; early 20th century research found that over a quarter will take their own lives (Kolle, 1931).

CONCLUSIONS

The querulent, vexatious, or unreasonable complainant presents an interesting study of offender as victim of their own behaviors. However, it is essential that the other victims in their sagas not be forgotten.

The first of the victim groups, the most obvious, are those against whom the grievances are initially aimed. For while there are increasing avenues for community conflicts to be mediated before reaching even panels, boards, or tribunals, the querulent will not accept any but their own, often inflated and growing demands before being satisfied. Hence, a high proportion of the querulent march resolutely and repetitively into the courts. It is for this victim group that flexible and useable vexatious litigant legislation could act as their primary protector (Lester, 2005).

The second, less obvious are those individuals tasked with mediating and or expediting resolution of complaint and litigation in our society. These range from case officers, managers, complaints managers, mediators, board or tribunal members, legal counsel, court staff ranging from the judges through to the staff manning their registry offices.

Over the last 15–20 years of investigating the phenomenon of querulousness, training and workshopping with complaint managers and ombudsmen staff, I have come to know that the majority of trauma to those working with the querulous is psychological trauma, for physical violence is relatively rare. The psychological trauma is derived from a range of behaviors of the querulent—from the exposure to recurrent displays of emotional lability, recurrent use of covert or overt threatening behavior through to stalking behavior. It is pertinent to acknowledge that the most obvious behavior of the querulent is the least recognized as traumatizing those who work with them, that is, the power of complaint itself.

To be the focus of "a complaint" has multiple negative effects upon the receiver, and in the case where the complaints are aimed at the individual currently managing the complaints, it also has significant effects on that individual's management of the complaint.

Complaint may cause self-doubt in the individual, may create fears of organizational or legal censure. These responses often create the environment where the querulent's inflated expectations and demands are not immediately challenged; the querulent's established pattern of unwarranted emotional lability, threats, and aggressive behavior are tolerated rather than appropriately reviewed and curtailed; where there is delay in the communication of investigation results if contrary to the demands of the querulent; and where the querulent is given greater access to reviews and secondary assessments within the organization than is required. This contributes to the unusually prolonged management times we found in our 2004 research and may contribute to the very entitlement and inflated value that the querulous attribute to their complaint (Lester et al., 2004). Because of these issues we have focused our further research on the management of unreasonable complaint behavior within government and corporate structures in the hope of both reducing trauma to those tasked with managing the querulent as well improving communication of realistic goals and expectations to the querulent with a view to minimizing the amount of their life energy they devote to any particular complaint.

Finally, recognition should be given to a third group of victims, the family members of the querulent. Historical research has found that only about 50% of the querulent manage to accrue a "life partner" and that of those who did have such a partner a significant percentage were in the throes of relationship difficulties at the time of the onset of their querulence. Those surviving relationships are most commonly sacrificed on the pyre of the querulent's burning drive to achieve "justice" and leave spouses and children perplexed as to why this husband and father who felt, reasoned, and acted like the rest of the world, should feel, reason, and act no more like other men upon a single point.

SUMMARY

- The term *querulous* is used to describe both behavior and the collective noun for individuals manifesting that behavior. The behavior at its simplest is an individual's heightened tendency to find fault and grievance in life and to air their dissatisfaction recurrently. Such querulousness can vary both in degree and duration having been either present as a personality trait persisting throughout the individual's life or having arisen anew at a certain period of their life.
- In psychiatric and psychological domains, it is the morbidly querulous who have been the focus of attention. This is the group of individuals whose querulous behavior evolves over time accruing increasing losses and negative consequences for themselves or others.
- There is a significant but aging body of research into the diagnosis of querulous paranoia, with little recent research. From the late 1800s, derived from the

fusion of the concepts of partial insanity or monomania and paranoia, it was believed to be a discrete entity in which a single pathological preoccupation with a loss or injustice develops in an otherwise sound mind. There is complaint to authorities and courts and a gradual but increasing network of grievances with those same authorities and courts.

- The history of paranoia mirrors the development of psychiatry in Western Europe over the last 2000 years. The words *paranoia* and *paranoid* are now part of the common tongue, focusing on misbeliefs, usually of a persecutory flavor. Yet this meaning is a mere shadow of its rich heritage in the history of psychiatry.
- The term *paranoia* originates in the Greek language and was used as we might use crazy or out of his mind. Hippocrates used it to describe the delirium of high fever, and other writers used it to describe senile deterioration. Its medical use then disappeared from the literature.
- In 1896 Emil Kraepelin initially felt that paranoia (progressive systematized insanity), while separate from dementia praecox, was nonetheless an endogenous disease process developing on "a defective constitutional basis." It was a stable, nondeteriorating, monodelusional system, often with ideas of reference and over self-appreciation. It was without clouding of consciousness, disorder of form of thought, will, or conduct. Hallucinations might be present. Kraepelin separated querulous paranoia from other types of paranoia mainly because its psychogenic flavor was more distinct than in other types of paranoia. Even in the 1890s he felt that some querulous represented a separate group of purely psychogenic origin.
- The presence of delusions has historically been the hallmark of insanity, and yet delusions have been defined in a number of ways, and as yet no agreement has been reached on their nature or origins. There have been investigators who have disagreed that they are even a form of belief but are rather empty acts of speech, with content that has no reference point in reality of the world or of the self.
- Various psychiatric researchers have attempted to describe and categorize the querulous. They were influenced by their guiding psychiatric paradigms and by a significant selection bias in the querulous patients they examined, for the querulous do not voluntarily seek out psychiatric care. In fact, it is society, through its courts and other authorities, who refer the querulous patients to psychiatric professionals. As a result, researchers, particularly early researchers such as Krafft-Ebbing and Kraepelin, studied those querulous who had been referred to them by the courts or other authorities for involuntary incarceration and observation. They were therefore usually selected not only because of their particularly persistent and annoying level of querulousness but also because of their level of dangerousness.
- Evidence of the difficulty of characterizing and defining querulous paranoia as well as of evolving classificatory systems is the profusion of terms found in the psychiatric literature. They range from paranoia querulentium (Krafft-Ebbing), querulous paranoia and querulent paranoia (Kraepelin), querulent paranoid, paranoia querulans, querulous paranoid state, litigious paranoia, litigious

paranoid, litigious delusional states, justice seeker, querulous syndrome, morbid querulousness, delusional disorder, and persecutory type through to the compulsively querulous.

- The most prosaic yet useful definition of the morbidly querulous is an individual who embarks on a persistent quest for restitution for real or imaginary wrongs through complaint, claims, petitioning of authorities and sometimes litigation, with resulting negative impact on their personal, interpersonal, and social functioning.

- Diagnostic criteria: (1) Persistent, relentless petitioning of governmental and nongovernmental agencies and or the courts, with evidence of contagion, i.e., spread of foci of grievance; (2) Beliefs of having suffered loss or injustice that dominates the mental life. The beliefs have been of at least 6 months duration; (3) The resulting behavior is directed to attainment of compensation, vindication and vengeance, and stay of persecution.

  - For a significant portion of the time, since the onset of the behavior, one or more major areas of functioning such as financial management, work, or interpersonal relations are markedly below the level achieved prior to the onset. Further, there has been significant disturbance and distress caused to other targeted individuals, organizations, or their representatives.

  - **Types:** *Primary*: Querulousness is the only significant phenomena. There is no evidence for schizophrenia or mood disorder. Nor is there evidence that the querulousness is due to the direct physiological effects of a substance (e.g., a drug of abuse or medication) or a general medical condition. *Secondary*: The criteria for schizophrenia or mood disorder have been met or the querulousness is due to the direct physiological effects of a substance (e.g., a drug of abuse or medication) or a general medical condition.

- Many researchers have attempted to isolate and describe the primary type of morbid querulousness (PMQ). However, their research methods and inclusion criteria vary considerably, and so the various prevalence rates found in the literature must be viewed with some skepticism.

- Rates of PMQ appear to fall between 0.02% and 0.7% of inpatient psychiatric populations; the majority develop their querulousness in their thirties through to their fifties; approximately 70% have symptoms for up to 5 years and 30% for between 5 and 10 years, before presenting to a professional; and up to 80% of sufferers are male.

- The most obvious external defining characteristic of the morbidly querulous is not their belief of having been wronged or their pursuit of redress. To distinguish the morbidly querulous complainant from their normal counterpart it is essential to weigh a number of qualities, of which the most significant are: (1) Proportionality (e.g., lack of balance between effort in all its modalities and potential loss or gain); (2) Focus (e.g., number of additional grievances accrued during progress of seeking redress for complaint); (3) Valuation (e.g., degree of importance ascribed to "perfect" resolution); (4) Victimization (e.g., degree to which the complaint had developed into a grievance and other past grievances are "bundled" with the current and the degree of personalization attributed to the grievance); and (5) Vindication (degree to which resolution becomes imbued with qualities that will validate their past life and its failures).

- The querulent, vexatious, or unreasonable complainant presents an interesting study of offender as victim of their own behaviors. However, it is essential that the other victims in their sagas not be forgotten.

QUESTIONS

1. What is querulence?
2. What is paranoia and why is it of concern in querulence?
3. What are delusions and why are they an issue within querulence discourse?
4. What are the contemporary diagnostic criteria for querulence?
5. Describe the history of querulence.
6. Describe querulence from a psychodynamic theory perspective.
7. Describe querulence from a cognitive theory perspective.
8. Discuss the social factors of issue in querulence and its development in individuals.
9. In contemporary querulence theory: To distinguish the morbidly querulous complainant from their normal counterpart, what factors should you consider?
10. What is known about the prevalence and epidemiology of querulance?

REFERENCES

Astrup, C. (1984). Querulent paranoia: a follow up. *Neuropsychobiology, 11*, 149–154.

Beck, A. T. (1976). *Cognitive theory and the emotional disorders.* New York: International University Press.

Bental, R., & Kinderman, P. (1994). Cognitive processes and delusional beliefs: attributions and the self. *Behaviour Research and Therapy, 32*, 331–341.

Berrios, G., & Porter, R. (1995). *A history of clinical psychiatry.* New York: New York University Press.

Berrios, G. E. (1991). Delusions as "wrong beliefs": a conceptual history. *British Journal of Psychiatry, 159*(Suppl. 14), 6–13.

Berrios, G. E. (1999). Classifications in psychiatry: a conceptual history. *Australian New Zealand Journal Psychiatry, 33*, 145–160.

Bleuler, E. (1924). *Textbook of psychiatry (trans. A.A.Brill).* New York: Macmillan.

Bloch, S., & Reddaway, P. (1977). *Russia's Political Hospitals: The abuse of psychiatry in Soviet Russia.* London: Victor Gollanz Ltd.

Butler, R. W., & Braff, D. L. (1991). Delusions: a review and integration. *Schizophrenia Bulletin, 17*, 633–647.

Caduff, F. (1995). Querulanz-ein verschwindendes psychopatholgisches Verhaltensmuster? *Fortschritte der Neurologie-Psychiatrie, 63*, 504–510.

Cameron, N. (1959). Paranoid conditions and paranoia. In S. Arietti (Ed.), *American handbook of psychiatry.*

Chadwick, P., Birchwood, M., & Trower, P. (1996). *Cognitive therapy for delusions, voices and paranoia.* Chichester: John Wiley and Sons.

von Dietrich, H. (14 June, 1968). Jahrgang. *Der querulant Munchener Medizinische Wochenschrift* (110. , 1445–1450.

Douglas, M. (1992). *Risk and blame essays in cultural theory*. London: Routledge, part 1: Chapters1, 2 ,3.

Esquirol, J.E. (1995). Mental maladies: a treatise on insanity (trans E. K. Hunt) 1845 cited by. In G. Berrios, & R. Porter (Eds.), *A history of clinical psychiatry* (p. 361). New York: New York University Press.

Freckleton, I. (1988). Querulent paranoia and the vexatious complainant. *International Journal of Law and Psychiatry*, *11*, 127–143.

Garety, P. A., & Hemsley, D. R. (1994). *Delusions: investigations into the psychology of delusional reasoning*. Oxford: Oxford University Press.

Gelder, M., Gath, D., & Mayou, R. (1993). *Oxford textbook of psychiatry* (2nd ed.). Oxford: Oxford University Press.

Hamilton, M. (1974). *Fish's clinical psycopathology*. Bristol: John Wright.

van der Heydt, A. (1952). *Querulatoische Entwicklungen*. Marhold: Halle a. S.

Hirsch, S., & Shepherd, M. (Eds.). (1974). *Themes and variations in European psychiatry: An Anthology*. Bristol: John Wright and Sons. Ch 2 K. Schneider., Ch. 8 E. Kretschmer., Ch. 15 H. Baruk.

Jaspers, K. (1963). *General psycopathology*. 1923 (trans. J.Hoenig and M.W.Hamilton). Manchester: Manchester University Press.

Johanson, E. (1964). Mild paranoia. *Acta Psychiatrica Scandinavica*, *40*(Suppl. 177), 171–174.

Kendler, K., Gruenberg, A., & Strauss, J. (1981). An independent analysis of the Copenhagen sample of the danish adoption study of schizophrenia. September *Archives of General Psychiatry*, *38*, 985–987.

Kendler, K. S. (June 1980). The nosological validity of paranoia (simple delusional disorder). *Archives of General Psychiatry*, *37*, 699–706.

Kendler, K. S. (1981). Nosology of paranoid schizophrenia and other paranoid psychoses. *Schizophrenia Bulletin*, *7*(4), 594–610.

Kolle, K. (1931). *Uber Querulanten. Archiv fur Psychiatrie und Nervenkrankheiten*. Berlin: Verrlag von Julius Springer.

Kraepelin, E. (1904). *Lectures in clinical psychiatry* (Trans. ed. Johnstone T). London: Bailliere, Tindall and Cox.

Kraepelin, E. (1910). *Psychiatrie* (8th Aufl.). Leipzig: Barth.

Krafft-Ebbing, R. (1905). *Text book of insanity: Based on clinical observations. For practitioners and students of medicine* (Trans. Charles Chaddock, MD). Philadelphia: F.A. Davis Company.

Lester, G., & Smith, S. (2006). Inventor, rascal, crank or querulent? Australia's vexatious litigant sanction 75 years on. *Psychiatry Psychology Law*, *13*(1), 1–27.

Lester, G. (April 2005). The vexatious litigant. *Judicial Officer's Bulletin*, *17*(3), 17–19.

Lester, G., Wilson, B., Griffin, L., & Mullen, P. (2004). Unusually persistent complainants. *The British Journal of Psychiatry*, *184*, 352–356.

Levy, B. (2014). From paranoia querulans to vexatious litigants: a short study of madness between psychiatry and law. Part 1 and 2. *History of Psychiatry*, *25*(3), 299–316.

Lewis, A. (1970). Paranoia and paranoid: a historical perspective. *Psychological Medicine*, *1*, 2–12.

Mc Kenna, P. J. (1984). Disorders with overvalued ideas. *British Journal of Psychiatry*, *145*, 579–585.

Mullen, P. (1991). Jealousy: the pathology of passion. *British Journal of Psychiatry*, *158*, 593–601.

Mullen, P. (1997). In D. Bhugra, & A. Munro (Eds.), *Disorders of passion in troublesome disguises: Under diagnosed psychiatric syndromes*. London: Blackwell Science, pp. 102–103.

Mullen, P., & Lester, G. (2006). Vexatious litigants and unusually persistent complainants: from querulous paranoia to querulous behaviour. *Behavioral Sciences & the Law*, *24*, 333–349.

Mullen, P., & Pathe, M. (1994). The pathological extensions of love. *British Journal of Psychiatry*, *165*, 614–623.

Munro, A. (1982). Paranoia revisited. *British Journal of Psychiatry*, *141*, 344–349.

Munro, A. (1987). Paranoid delusional disorders: DSM-III-R and beyond. *Comprehensive Psychiatry*, *28*(1), 35–39.

Ombudsman, N. S. W. (2012). *Managing unreasonable complainant conduct manual*. www.ombo.nsw.gov.au/publications.

Pang, A., Ungvari, G., Lum, F., Lai, K., & Leung, C. (1996). Querulous paranoia in Chinese patients: a cultural paradox. *Australian and New Zealand Journal of Psychiatry*, *30*, 463–466.

Parliament of Victoria, Law Reform Committee. (2008). *Inquiry into vexatious litigants*. http://trove.nla.gov.au/version/33394365.

Pichot, P. (1982). The diagnosis and classification of mental disorders in French speaking countries: background, current views and comparison with other nomenclatures. *Psychological Medicine*, *12*, 475–492.

Pons, R. (1987). Delires querulents. seance du *Societe Medico-Psychologique*, 23–24 Octobre, 104–108.

Refsum, H. E. (1983). Paranoiac psychoses: a follow up. *Neuropsychobiology*, *10*, 75–82.

Roberts, G. (1992). The origins of delusion. *British Journal of Psychiatry*, *161*, 293–308.

Rowlands, M. W. (1988). Psychiatric and legal aspects of persistent litigation. *British Journal of Psychiatry*, *153*, 317–323.

Scheler, M. (1984). The psychology of so called compensation hysteria and the real battle against illness. (trans. E. Vacek). *Journal of Phenomenological Psychology*, *15*(2), 125–143.

Schifferdecker, M. (1995). The origins of the concept of paranoia. *The Psychiatric Clinics of North America*, *18*(2), 231–249.

Schneider, K. (1958). *Psycopathic personalities* trans. MW Hamilton (9th ed.). London: Cassell.

Sedler, M. J. (June 1995). Understanding delusions. *The Psychiatric Clinics of North America*, *18*(2), 251–265.

Shorter, E. A. (1997). *History of psychiatry*. New York: John Wiley and Sons.

Skilling, G., et al. (2015). *Unusually persistent complainants against the police in Scotland*. www.forensicnetwork.scot.nhs.uk.

Smith, S. (2009). *Maverick litigants*. Maverick Publications.

Szasz, T. S. (1974). *Ideology and insanity: Essays on the psychiatric dehumanisation of man*. Middlesex: Penguin Books.

Trower, P., Casey, A., & Dryden, W. (1988). *Cognitive behavioural counselling in action*. London: Sage.

Ungvari, G. (1995). Delusional disorder, litigious type. *Clinical Gerontologist*, *16*(2), 71–73.

Ungvari, G. S., Pang, A., & Wong, C. (1997). Querulous behaviour. *Medicine Science and Law, 37*(3), 265–270.

Walker, C. (1991). Delusions: what did Jaspers really say. *British Journal of Psychiatry, 159*(Suppl. 14), 94–103.

Wernicke, C. (1900). *Grundiss der Psychiatrie*. Leipzig: Verlag von Georg Thiem.

Wessely, S., Buchanan, A., Reed, J., Cutting, B., Garety, P., & Taylor, P. (1993). Acting on Delusions. I: Prevalence. *British Journal of Psychiatry, 163*, 69–76.

Winokur, G. (1977). Delusional disorder (paranoia). *Comprehensive Psychiatry, 18*(6), 511–521.

A Multidisciplinary Approach to Understanding Internet Love Scams: Implications for Law Enforcement

Majeed Khader, Poh Shu Yun

Nanyang Technological University, Singapore

CHAPTER OUTLINE

In recent years, the frequency of reported Internet love frauds has escalated with the normalization of technology. Perpetrators typically join online dating websites and generate fake profiles, using them as guises to select and subsequently defraud their victims (Australian Competition and Consumer Commission, 2012). In a national-scale study led by Professor Monica Whitty of Leicester University, who has devoted keen research toward unraveling the Internet love scam, it was reported that Internet love scams affected up to 230,000 individuals in Britain alone between 2011 and 2012, with monetary losses in the range of £50–£800,000 (Whitty & Buchanan, 2012a). In Canada, the Internet love scam is found to be the most frequently reported crime, amounting to at least $17 million in monetary losses in 2012 (Foote, 2013).

The Psychology of Criminal and Antisocial Behavior. http://dx.doi.org/10.1016/B978-0-12-809287-3.00018-3

In the following year, a single retired Canadian woman lost upwards of $1.3 million to a man she met through a dating Web service (Quinn, 2013). Furthermore, in 2013, a reported AU$25.3 million was lost to approximately 3000 Australian victims of Internet love scams (Starr, 2014). The US Federal Bureau of Investigation (FBI) (2013a) has also published a report detailing 6000 victims, and a combined loss of $81 million to perpetrators of Internet love scams in 2013. Apart from visible monetary losses, victims also suffer the hidden emotional loss of a relationship when the scam is revealed (Whitty, 2012a; Whitty & Buchanan, 2012b). In light of the latter, many Internet love scam cases go unreported. Victims typically experience a host of negative emotions, including a fear of public embarrassment, which may consequently deter them from making a report (Barwick, 2012; Davenport, 2010). According to an assertion by the Canadian Anti-Fraud Centre, only 5% of Internet love scam victims make official reports after the scam has come to light (as cited in Verstraten, 2013). This, in turn, has serious implications concerning the reality of the incidence of Internet love scams around the world.

Internet love scams may be understood as a type of organized crime that is conducted over cyberspace (Foote, 2013). It may be seen as a crime that involves a planned violation of the law through trickery in attempts to acquire monetary profit from selected victims (Kranacher, 2010). Given the cyber nature of Internet love scams, perpetrators are reported to utilize online dating services as their main gateway to connect with a pool of potential victims (Bindley, 2012; Home Affairs Committee, 2013). Other common methods of connection include the use of informal chat rooms and various social networking sites (Pearson, 2014; Whitty & Buchanan, 2012c).

The first step in the perpetrators' modus operandi is to create false identities on online dating services or social media, each tailored to attract specific types of victim profiles (Whitty, in press). The next step involves contacting potential victims. Once an emotional connection is established with selected victims, perpetrators encourage victims to privatize communications by using chat or email functions that are not hosted by the original dating websites or social networking sites (Metropolitan Police Service, 2013; Whitty & Buchanan, 2012a). Once an exclusive communication channel is constructed, perpetrators gradually increase intimacy in the relationship over time. Trust is consequently built to the point where perpetrators believe that their victims will comply with financial requests. This process varies with victims, ranging from a few weeks to months, or even to years (Teller Vision, 2010; Whitty, 2012b).

There are a few variations as to how perpetrators make victims part with their money. The most common variation is the "story method," where perpetrators claim that they want to have a face-to-face meeting with their victims but do not possess enough currency to fund their trips due to unexpected circumstances. These circumstances may be administrative, medical-related, and/or family disaster stories (Whitty, 2012b). One other variant is that perpetrators are themselves detained at checkpoints into the country but do not have enough currency upon their persons to seek release (Bliss, 2011; Fong, 2011). Another variant of this story is that the perpetrator encourages victims to invest in fake organizations or come on board a false business venture, both of which are recognized as "get-rich-quick" scams (Home Affairs Committee, 2013; Singapore Police Force, 2012a). Under the guise of these stories, perpetrators would then request monetary support from their victims.

Internet love scam perpetrators also employ parcel love scams or sex video blackmail as alternate methods of cheating their victims of money (Camoens, 2014; Whitty & Buchanan, 2012c). Using the parcel love scam method, perpetrators lead victims to believe that a parcel of romantic memorabilia has been sent to them from outside the country. This parcel is then purportedly detained at Customs, upon which the perpetrator would contact the victim for money to secure its clearance (Royal Malaysia Police, 2014).

In the "sex video" blackmailing method, victims are led to perform sexual acts during an online video chat session with the perpetrator, during which they are filmed without their knowledge. Subsequently, victims would be threatened with exposure unless they paid up (Singapore Police Force, 2012b; Whitty & Buchanan, 2012b).

A MULTIDISCIPLINARY APPROACH

For the purpose of understanding Internet love scams as a general crime in itself, a nomothetic crime type profile structure is employed. In the subsequent section, a review of relevant research findings pertaining to Internet love scams was conducted using the recommended CLIP profiling approach, employed by the Singapore Home Team Behavioural Sciences Centre. The CLIP analysis (Khader et al., 2012) is a framework where (C) refers to criminalistics and forensic science, (L) refers to legal and local issues, (I) refers to investigative and operational considerations, and (P) refers to psychological and/or behavioral sciences considerations. This chapter later introduces and examines a selected localized Internet love scam case study, before concluding with recommendations for crime prevention, criminal investigation, interview, and rehabilitation. The CLIP analysis is employed in this chapter mainly for its scientific and multidisciplinary perspective on crime. Notably, CLIP examines and distills pertinent information from empirical research. Using this information, behavioral possibilities associated with specific crimes are generated. This consequently provides an informed structure for appropriate application in relevant areas of crime prevention, investigation, interview, and rehabilitation.

CRIMINALISTICS AND FORENSIC SCIENCE CONSIDERATIONS

Generally, criminalistics and forensic science can be understood as the systematic examination of relevant physical evidence in crime detection in accordance with a country's criminal and civil laws (Saferstein, 2006). In the context of Internet love scams, where crime is perpetuated mainly through cyberspace, it is notably challenging to establish the primary crime scene. This is because perpetrators may commit the crime repeatedly in various physical locations, and from various virtual platforms in cyberspace (Association of Chief Police Officers, 2011). Perpetrators also typically operate in different locations from the victims, which could possibly contribute to negating a relationship between both parties without proper physical evidence (Casey, 2011).

For the crime of Internet love scams, computer forensic evidence recovery is crucial in establishing a relationship between perpetrator and victim that incriminates the perpetrator. With reference to Ashcroft (2001), circumstantial forensic evidence may take the form of various electronic correspondence, such as email messages, phone call records, online chat records and/or private messages on online dating services, and social networking platforms addressed to the victim by the perpetrator. A matched comparison of bank details and financial movement records provided by the victim and those recovered in possession of the perpetrator count as relevant forensic evidence (Kranacher, 2010). Other incriminating evidence may include electronic records of compromising images and videos of victims recorded and used by the perpetrator for blackmail purposes (Association of Chief Police Officers, 2011).

Moreover, forensic evidence pointing to the perpetrator's modus operandi may include possession of stolen or doctored images of unidentified and attractive individuals used to establish fake online identities (Whitty & Buchanan, 2012b), perpetrator-created templates for filling out dating profiles, as well as digital email and message archives of premeditated responses to the victim by the perpetrator (Camoens, 2014; Foote, 2013). Additional potential forensic evidence includes digital spreadsheets detailing victim identities and transfer details of funds, as well as Internet browser bookmarks of commonly accessed social networking platforms and online dating services (Gubanov, 2012; Marrington, Baggili, Ismail & Kaf, 2012).

LEGAL CONSIDERATIONS

There are several laws in existence to combat the crime of Internet love scams, both in international and local settings. According to legislation in the United Kingdom (2006), under the Fraud Act, purposeful fraud, or dishonestly making a false representation with an intention to obtain a gain for self, or another, or to cause a loss to another or expose another to the risk of loss is considered an offense punishable by an imprisonment term of up to 10 years, or a fine, or both (United Kingdom Legislation, 2006). Further, Internet love scam perpetrators found in possession of articles used to conduct fraud are also liable to an imprisonment term of up to 5 years, a fine, or both (United Kingdom Legislation, 2006). A person found guilty of performing blackmail in the United Kingdom is also liable to an imprisonment term of up to 14 years (United Kingdom Legislation, 1968). By the same token, according to the Criminal Code of Canada, fraud by deceit, whether or not property, money, or goods were obtained, and whether the crime was committed under false pretenses or not, a person found guilty of this offense is liable to an imprisonment term of up to 14 years (Department of Justice, 2014).

In the United States, according to their judicial code, a person found guilty of committing the offense of fraud or a swindle is liable to a punishment of an imprisonment term of up to 20 years, a fine, or both (Legal Information Institute, 2008). Further, should a person be found guilty of blackmail in the United States, he or she is also liable to an imprisonment term of up to 3 years, or a fine, or both (Legal Information Institute, 1994). Pertaining to Australia, according to the Criminal Code Amendment Act, obtaining property or a financial advantage by deceptive means is punishable by an imprisonment term of up to 10 years (Division 134) (Commonwealth of Australia, 2000). Moreover, according to the Crimes Act 1958, a person found guilty of possessing intent to cause loss to another, with a gain for self, or another, and in making unwarranted menacing demands against others is said to be engaging in blackmail, of which crime is punishable by imprisonment of up to 15 years in Australia (Section 87) (Australasian Legal Information Institute, n.d.). The Australian government also runs an official scam news website known as SCAMwatch. Australian citizens are encouraged to subscribe to the site's updates on scam developments to stay aware of the new scam methods, as well as access previous reports and tips from scam victims (Australian Competition and Consumer Commission, 2012).

Alternatively, in the Singapore context, according to the Penal Code of Singapore (2008), an Internet love scam can be seen as a premeditated crime of cheating (Section 415) and/or cheating by personation (Section 416) that is punishable by imprisonment up to 3 years, or subject to a fine, or both (Section 417), and by imprisonment up to 5 years, or subject to a fine, or both (Section 419), respectively. Given that the objective of Internet love scam perpetrators is to obtain money from victims, this particular crime may alternatively be considered as cheating and dishonestly inducing a delivery of property that is punishable by imprisonment up to 10 years and a fine (Section 420). In cases where perpetrators encourage victims to fund false investment schemes only to convert the money into dishonest or personal use may also qualify as a criminal breach of trust (Section 405) punishable by imprisonment up to 7 years, or subject to a fine, or both (Section 406).

There are also laws that account for blackmail methods employed by perpetrators during Internet love scams. Blackmail involves purposeful recording of compromising images and videos of victims, with the intent of subsequently threatening victims for money. This is considered extortion (Section 383) and/or putting a person in fear of harm in order to commit extortion (Section 385). In addition, recording of compromising media of victims with ill intent and possessing knowledge that said media will harm victims' reputations qualifies as defamation (Section 499) punishable by imprisonment up to 2 years, or subject to a fine, or both (Section 500). Should perpetrators print and/or burn the compromising videos and images onto compact discs, it may constitute an act of printing or engraving matter known to be defamatory, punishable by imprisonment up to 2 years, or subject to a fine, or both (Section 501). In addition, concerning cybercrime legislation in Singapore, there exists the Computer Misuse and Cybersecurity Act (CMCA), first introduced in 1993 (Urbas, 2008). According to Chapter 4 of the CMCA (2007), concerning Internet love scams, use of a computer—based on the CMCA's definition—to intentionally commit an offense involving property, fraud, or dishonesty is punishable by imprisonment for at least 2 years. Moreover, individuals guilty of dishonest use of computing devices are also liable to a fine of up to S$50,000 or to an imprisonment term up to 10 years, or both.

INVESTIGATIVE AND OPERATIONAL CONSIDERATIONS

According to Kranacher (2010), who is a certified fraud examiner, to ascertain the fact that a scam has occurred, investigators are typically required to establish a time-line for its occurrence. Key details that need to be uncovered include the process of deception, attempts at concealing the crime, and the benefits to the perpetrator (Kranacher, 2010). As Internet love scams are predominantly an organized document-reliant crime (Kiernan, 2005), forensic recovery may furnish adequate physical evidence of the cheating process, especially evidence of prior planning (mens rea) and the victim grooming process (Rege, 2009). With reference to Ashcroft (2001), evidence of concealment may take the form of encrypted, altered, or compressed digital files. Perpetrators may also deliberately misname digital files or attempt to destroy and/or hide incriminating documentation on electronic storage devices separate from their main computer terminals or on online storage services (Ashcroft, 2001). Finally, benefits to the perpetrator may be accounted for through credits and/or expenditures that do not match reported incomes, as well as suspicious or missing bank deposits (Kranacher, 2010).

In the course of establishing the timeline, witness statements may also be taken. These include statements from the victims, which can be used to corroborate the physical evidence (University of Illinois Chicago, 2009). In the context of Internet love scams, where victims are emotionally exploited, it is useful to note that victims may not wish to give a statement due to fears of appearing foolish (Kiernan, 2005). Anticipating this issue may prove helpful in structuring questions during the interview to reassure the victim.

In the event that perpetrators of Internet love scams are caught, effective interviewing can result in admission evidence that can subsequently be used to prosecute the case. Effective interviews are typically planned before the interview session, where selected interviewers are knowledgeable of the investigative work of the case (American Institute of Certified Public Accountants, n.d.). As Internet love scams often comprise organized work units (Steyerl, 2011), multiple offenders may be apprehended. It is recommended to interview each offender in ascending order of probable culpability should multiple offenders be involved in a single case. This is done so that the investigator is able to gather as much useful information as possible by the time the main perpetrator is interviewed (Kranacher, 2010).

PSYCHOLOGICAL AND BEHAVIORAL SCIENCES CONSIDERATIONS

Where crime is concerned, psychology and behavioral sciences are applied to get a better understanding of perpetrators through their criminal behaviors. Such information has proven helpful in a number of applied settings such as criminal investigation and crime prevention (FBI, n.d.).

In the context of Internet love scams, the key motive of perpetrators is to obtain money from their victims (Steyerl, 2011; Whitty, in press; Zuckoff, 2006). Discounting the duration of the grooming process, Internet love scams are highly lucrative, providing perpetrators with large sums of money in a relatively short period of time. It is cost-effective, as perpetrators only need basic computer literacy, access to a computing device, and an Internet connection to lure potential victims (Home Affairs Committee, 2013; Rege, 2009). Understandably, the use of false identities also encumbers potential arrests (Channel News Asia, 2011). In light of this, aside from larger organized criminal units, individuals and smaller groups may also successfully perpetrate Internet love scams due to the perceived rewards, minimal risks, and easy accessibility to victims (Bjelopera & Finklea, 2012).

With reference to Alderman (2014), Internet love scam perpetrators generally target their victims in the time periods leading up to widely celebrated occasions in the year. These include festivities such as the Christmas season, Valentine's Day, as well as personal birthdays, as it is during these periods that love scam victims are believed to be most emotionally vulnerable (Burnett, 2013; FBI, 2014). Perpetrators are also reported to target individuals who profess their grief online after experiencing divorce or loss of a loved one (Malcolm, 2013). Anticipating when Internet love scam perpetrators are highly likely to strike may help the relevant authorities in planning for crime awareness and prevention to achieve maximum effectiveness.

According to Etter (2001), the Internet has a disinhibiting effect upon online scam criminals. This is largely accounted for by the dissociative anonymity that comes with most online activity (Suler, 2004). Taken together, operating over the Internet offers love scam perpetrators the opportunity to disown their criminal actions and to distance themselves from the reality of harm committed against victims (DiNapoli, n.d.). Alternatively, to justify their immoral behavior, perpetrators may engage in rationalization and convince themselves that their victims deserved to be tricked, or that an exchange of resources hurts neither party (Dixon, 2005; Rege, 2009). Perpetrators may also have the belief that they are utilizing their victims' money for a good purpose, or have the perception that scamming is common practice (Kranacher, 2010). Knowledge of these possible thought processes and rationalizations may aid criminal investigators in obtaining confessions from Internet love scam perpetrators during interview.

BEHAVIORAL CHARACTERISTICS PERTAINING TO INTERNET LOVE SCAM

PERPETRATOR PROFILE

Both men and women may be perpetrators of Internet love scams as the desire for an intimate partner is not exclusive to a single gender (Borders, 2014; Romance Scams, n.d.). The ability to use false credentials on online dating services also allows perpetrators to assume gender identities not corresponding with their own (Bartlett & Miller, 2011; Herring & Martinson, 2004). Also, it is possible that men and women may pair up to form scam groups to effectively con victims of both genders (Rege, 2009; Steyerl, 2011) since in general women are suggested to be more adept than men at emotion-related communication online (Thelwall, Wilkinson & Uppal, 2010), whereas men are more likely to be assertive and open to risk-taking than women (as cited in Schmitt, Realo, Voracek, & Allik, 2008).

Furthermore, as long as the potential perpetrator possesses basic computer literacy and access to computing devices and an Internet connection, perpetrating the fraud is easy to do. This is independent of perpetrator age or nationality (Herald Scotland, 2014; Rege, 2009; Romance Scams, n.d; Uwujaren, 2014).

Given that Web love scams are committed primarily over the Internet with minimal face-to-face interactions (Whitty, in press), perpetrators would typically be connected with users over large portions of their day (Rege, 2009). This process is thus different from face-to-face relationships in that the former may be more intense. In addition, technological advancement has allowed the average individual to access mobile connectivity easily today and from Internet service providers such as Internet cafés (Dixon, 2005; Lanford & Lanford, n.d.; Olukoya, 2002).

VICTIM PROFILE

In general, Internet love scam victims comprise both men and women of all types of backgrounds, ages, and income levels, with some victim profiles being more vulnerable than others (Borders, 2014; Metropolitan Police Service, 2013; Rege, 2009). It is a common misconception that intelligent individuals are less likely to be victims, but in the context of Internet love scams, intellect and level of education are factors independent of victim susceptibility as perpetrators strike using sentimentality and emotional techniques (Dartis, 2013; Munton & McLeod, 2011; Whitty & Buchanan, 2012b).

Internet love scam perpetrators exploit the human need for love and attachment for monetary gains (Munton & McLeod, 2011). Hence, individuals who are generally unable to fulfill this need in a satisfactory manner may become vulnerable. Therefore, individuals who are living alone (Span, 2012), who report pervasive loneliness (Bindley, 2012), stress and/or an emotional loss (Weisbaum, 2014), who have a history of abusive relationships, and a tendency to idealize their intimate partners may be more likely to be victimized (Whitty & Buchanan, 2012b). Such individuals who engage in online dating typically experience "optimism bias," a form of denial that gives them a false sense of security against being duped (Munton & McLeod, 2011).

To illustrate, Bindley (2012), a news reporter for the *Huffington Post*, reported that Jodi Bourgeois, an American woman who had experienced divorce, fell victim to an Internet love scammer shortly after separating from her husband. Jodi, who did not have children, later accessed a Web dating service and was approached by a widower who identified himself as Greg. Over the span of a week, Jodi was charmed by words of affirmation and romance over the Internet sent to her from Greg, and within a month, she was discussing a marriage to him and becoming a mother to his son. Despite her requests to do so, Greg put off a physical meeting with Jodi and eventually began asking her for money. Jodi later admitted that by coming out of her divorce childless, she was propelled into the relationship by a desire to be a wife and mother. This supports Whitty and Buchanan's (2012b) findings that victims are typically highly motivated to fall in love at the beginning of the scam, increasing their vulnerability.

Furthermore, Colin Woodcock, a senior investigator with the Serious Organized Crime Agency, in the United Kingdom, reported that victims desperate to be loved would agree to do almost anything for someone paying them the attention, and that these victims may not be ready to believe that this attention is not genuine (as cited in Jones & Hill, 2011).

Other victim types include individuals who participate in online sexual activity. Dating Web services not only bring people together in a romantic fashion but also serve as a platform for people to meet others based on shared interests and sometimes also in engaging in sexual activities (Demasi, 2011). Online sexual activity is generally attractive to individuals as it is affordable and easily accessed with a relative degree of anonymity (as cited in Cooper, Mansson, Daneback, Tikkanen & Ross, 2003). Consequently, these individuals may be vulnerable to the "sex video" blackmail variant of the Internet love scam.

To illustrate, Scottish Television (2013) reported a case of sex video blackmail involving a 17-year-old Scottish male victim who subsequently committed suicide after experiencing overwhelming fear of exposure. Daniel Parry befriended a girl he believed was the same age as him, and both began a relationship over Skype during which he was led to a state of undress and unknowingly filmed. The "girl" he befriended later attempted to blackmail Daniel by threatening to expose him to his friends and family if he did not furnish the money demanded. While this is not a typical love scam case, it illustrates the process of deceit that may also occur in Internet love scam situations.

RECOMMENDATIONS
CRIME PREVENTION STRATEGIES

Making buyers beware: For successful perpetration of the scam, consent on the victim's part is necessary (Economic and Social Research Council, 2013) and this implies that victims need to be involved with the preventive effort. According to the Legal Information Institute (n.d.), this implicates a doctrine of caveat emptor, a Latin phrase that translates to "let the buyer beware." This doctrine places the responsibility upon a buyer to examine a set of property and acknowledge its conditions before purchase. Applying this particular legal policy to Internet love scams, the UK Metropolitan Police Service notes that potential victims of Internet love scams have the responsibility to exercise vigilance in their own participation in a Web-based con to avoid falling for the scam (as cited in Independent Television, 2012).

Encouraging more reporting: Internet love scams are typically underreported (Rege, 2009), which may hint at a higher prevalence of Internet love scam victims than is currently represented in official statistics. According to a survey conducted by Whitty and Buchanan (2012a, 2012b, 2012c) that involved over 2000 British citizens, 52% had heard of an Internet love scam and 2% personally knew a victim of this scam. Therefore, it is recognized that raising Internet love scam awareness and educating Internet users in exercising personal vigilance online are both key in crime prevention over a long-term period (Munton & McLeod, 2011; Trevathan & Myers, 2012). Hopefully, such strategies may increase the likelihood of victims reporting their victimization process so that more victims can come forward.

Developing checklists: As part of their prevention measures, the FBI (2012) released a checklist for citizens to use in assessing whether their online dates are scammers. This checklist includes warning citizens that scammers typically request a change in communicative platforms than the previously established channels, profess feelings of love within a short period of cross communication, and that they may send glamourized profile pictures to victims. Scammers may also claim to be traveling or working overseas, may fail to make good on their promises for physical dates due to a variety of disastrous personal events, and may request monetary transfers (FBI, 2012). Further, American and Canadian victims are encouraged to file a report with the Internet Crime Complaint Center (IC3) and the Canadian Anti-Fraud Centre, respectively, both of which are accredited with the government to allow the authorities to examine commonalities between complaints, which could aid in identifying the perpetrators (Canadian Resource Centre for Victims of Crime, 2014; FBI, 2012). In addition, both the FBI and the Competition Bureau Canada urge their citizens to utilize nationally reputable dating websites, and to check website addresses carefully to avoid falling victim to illegitimate sites set up by perpetrators (Pearson, 2014).

Scam Watch websites: The Commonwealth of Australia has released a series of Internet love scam crime prevention strategies to the public via their official SCAMwatch website. The listed warning signs of Internet love scam victimization are similar to those previously released by the FBI in 2012. In addition to the earlier mentioned red flags, the Australian government encourages citizens to talk to an independent friend, relative, or authorized agency before following through with any money transfers, limit the amount of personal information posted to social networking sites, and to always consider the possibility of being targeted for scams (SCAMwatch, 2014). These above-mentioned Internet love scam advisories are also shared by the City of London Police and the UK National Fraud Intelligence Bureau on their official Action Fraud website (Action Fraud, n.d.).

Crime Prevention Events: To raise awareness regarding the prevalence of Internet love scams, Australian law enforcement agencies utilized the National Cyber Security Awareness Week, and the Think Fraud! Global Day of Action, to come together with the local community, relevant industry partners, and cooperative international organizations to jointly educate citizens on how to protect themselves from becoming a victim of Internet-based crimes (SCAMwatch, 2011, 2010). Further, in their bid to deter perpetrators, the Sentencing Council for England and Wales passed tougher sentencing laws for scam perpetrators, of which legal punishment is not only dependent on monetary losses but on the psychological and emotional extent of a scam's impact on victims as well (cited in Action Fraud, 2014).

According to the National Cyber Security Alliance (2014), which collaborates with the US Department of Homeland Security, Americans are educated concerning the safe use of the Internet during the month of October each year during the National Cyber Security Awareness Month. This event brings together relevant communities and organizations, including the FBI, and educates Americans through traditional media, social media, poster events, and other programs that aim to increase citizen awareness regarding cybercrime (FBI, 2013a, 2013b; National Cyber Security Alliance, 2014).

In Canada, apart from events held during their Fraud Awareness Month (Saskatchewan Association of Chiefs of Police, n.d.), seminars led by crime authorities and local police expounding upon scam victims' experiences are also organized to raise awareness and educate citizens regarding the perils of online dating (as cited in Pearson, 2014).

In Asian settings such as Singapore, the Singapore Police Force has released a series of posters concerning Internet love scams and sex video blackmail scams to the public (Singapore Police Force, 2014). Similar to that of its international counterparts, Internet love scam advisories have also been made available on the Singapore Police Force's official website (Singapore Police Force, 2013), including advisories such as making a police report should anyone attempt an extortion, make requests for money, or claim he or she is in some kind of trouble abroad and urgently requires monetary assistance.

Dating websites: The Ministry of Social and Family Development in Singapore details a registry of accredited dating agencies (MSF, 2011). To minimize the possibility of victimization, individuals should be encouraged to utilize accredited dating agencies (Hendricks, 2014). Further, dating services that encourage face-to-face interactions between matched clients, and that collect feedback from clients, are also preferable compared to those whose main form of communication between individuals is electronic messaging (LunchActually, 2014). Such agency practices encourage client accountability and personal security, minimizing the risk of becoming an Internet love scam victim (Newcomb, 2012).

INVESTIGATIVE AND INTERVIEWING RECOMMENDATIONS

Embarrassment: It is helpful for investigators to anticipate aversion on the victims' part to give statements as they may be embarrassed by their situation, and they may experience psychologically traumatizing hurt as a result of being suddenly abandoned by a person who had lied about their affection toward them (Whitty, 2012b). According to a large-scale survey conducted by Whitty and Buchanan (2012a) into the aspects of these scams, all victims reported experiencing negative emotional impacts regardless of whether they lost money, and further, some victims reported feelings of being "mentally raped" after discovering the truth. Jenny, an Internet love scam victim, reported that she felt "very tragic," "stupid," and "ashamed" after uncovering the scam (Wahlquist, 2014).

Suicide: Some studies reported that Internet love scam victims might attempt suicide (Whitty, 2012a). According to Brooke (2010), Philip Hunt, a 58-year-old English male Internet love scam victim committed suicide by lying across the tracks before a train arrived, killing him. Hunt was reported to be facing heavy debt and feeling "cold, lonely and depressed" from being swindled online. Moreover, others may experience these negative emotions so acutely that they choose not to involve the police (Jones & Hill, 2011). To illustrate, when interviewed, Pat said, "you don't want to talk to anybody about it, because you feel so stupid" (Jordan, 2014). It was suggested that the extent of distress is dependent on the individual involved, the amount of time spent corresponding with the perpetrator, and the degree of betrayal experienced (Christensen, 2013).

Concept of losing face: Sometimes the uncovering of a scam by a victim results in "losing face," which is defined as a predominant way of self-evaluation by individuals based on other people's impressions of them (Kim & Cohen, 2010). Previous research has found that situations resulting in a loss of face are perceived to be socially catastrophic for individuals belonging to a collectivist society where social evaluation plays a crucial role in moderating one's self-esteem, identity, and acceptance by the society (Australian Federal Police, 2014; Triandis & Suh, 2002; Wong & Tsai, 2007). Victims report feeling foolish after uncovering the con (Christensen, 2014), and may express fear of negative judgment from others (Astbury, 2013; Special Broadcasting Service, 2014). To illustrate, according to a news report by Saarinen (2013), the family members of a female scam victim labeled her as "stupid" after discovering that she was scammed by a fraudulent online date. Furthermore, in a survey conducted by the Dutch Fraud Help Desk (2013), it was found that 33% of over 1000 respondents believed victims of online dating fraud to be "very naive." According to the UK National Fraud Authority, this potential loss of face may act as a major deterrent and thus discourages victims from making police reports or engaging in police interviews.

Denial: In addition, Jones and Hill (2011) report that some victims do not get over the con despite uncovering the scam. One such victim is Debbie Day, as reported in Anchondo (2013). Day refused to believe that the man she met over the Internet was a scammer, and kept at the relationship "on the off chance that he's real." Further, she stated that if she could come up with the money he is asking for, she would consider sending it to him. Furthermore, women who have uncovered the scam may also be drawn back into it when, during confrontation, the perpetrator insists that he still loves them despite being a con man (Rege, 2009; Whitty, in press). In other reports, victims admit to retaining the false profile pictures and other images that the Internet love scam perpetrator sent them despite knowing that they were false or stolen images (9 News, 2013).

A victim explains on Romancescam.org (2011) that because of the strong association she has drawn between the pictures the con man sent her and the person who communicated with her over the course of the scam, it is difficult to accept the reality of the man being a swindler. She said, "I could accept that I lost money, I could accept that I was fooled, but I can't accept that the guy I spoke to for months, laughed with, played scrabble with, argued with, fell in love with did not exist." It is suggested that these victim behaviors may stem from the reluctance to let go of a promised future with the con man (Quinn, 2013), and/or, according to Professor Monica Whitty, an unwillingness to relinquish the therapeutic effects the online relationship has on the negative living circumstances of victimized individuals (as cited in Walker, 2011). To illustrate the latter, when interviewed, an Internet love scam victim reported to the Columbia Broadcasting System that "I was so empty inside. I was so desperate to find somebody that really cared about me" (Smith, 2012).

Taken together, all the factors mentioned herein suggest serious interviewing implications for investigators and law enforcement officers when dealing with victims of Internet love scams. It was noted in research by Whitty and Buchanan (2012a, 2012b, 2012c) that there was a need for law enforcement to ease the scam reporting process in a way that alleviates the distress of the victim (Economic and Social Research Council, 2013). One recommended approach was to identify Internet love scam casualties as "vulnerable" victims (Whitty & Buchanan, 2012a, 2012b, 2012c). This involves the providence of aid and support from relevant health care professionals, especially when the victim's family and other social supports are unavailable (Whitty & Buchanan, 2012a, 2012b, 2012c), and the adoption of a more sympathetic and sensitive approach by authorities to victims during interviews (Button, Lewis & Tapley, n.d.).

Hence, establishing a certain degree of rapport may help to address potential feelings of reluctance on the part of the victim during the course of the interview (Laforest, Belley, Lavertue, Maurice & Rainville, 2009). Subsequently, it is recommended that interviewers begin with broad, open-ended questions, allowing victims to speak freely at their own pace with minimal prompts. Notably, clear questions beginning with either how, where, when, who, what, or why help investigators facilitate a smooth progression of the interview (Laforest et al., 2009). In addition, it is imperative that active listening and observation skills are exercised during the course of the interview to determine accuracy of victim statements in terms of actual speech, vocal inflection, and body language (American Institute of Certified Public Accountants, n.d.).

To conclude the interview, it is recommended to review the statement given and allow the victim some time to ask questions. Investigator details should be made available to the victims in the event that victims require assistance or information pertaining to their report. In addition, together with appreciation of the victim's participation, a brief outline of follow-up actions should be conveyed to manage victim expectations (Laforest et al., 2009; Zulawski & Sturman, 2013).

It is recommended for suspects to be interviewed according to the cognitive techniques laid down by the police-preferred PEACE model of interviewing, where (P) refers to preparation and planning, (E) refers to engage and explain, (A) refers to account, (C) refers to closure, and (E) refers to evaluation (International Competition Network, 2008). According to the PEACE model, a narrative is obtained from the suspect using one of four recommended cognitive interviewing techniques inclusive of the Report Everything (RE), Context Reinstatement (CR), Reverse Order (RO), and Change Perspective (CP) techniques. Interviewers speaking to victims should endeavor to acquaint themselves with the PEACE approach to interviewing.

SUMMARY

- Internet love scams may be understood as a type of organized crime that is conducted over cyberspace. It may be seen as a crime that involves a planned violation of the law through trickery in attempts to acquire monetary profit from selected victims. Many Internet love scam cases go unreported. Victims typically experience a host of negative emotions, including a fear of public embarrassment, which may consequently deter them from making a report.
- Given the cyber nature of Internet love scams, perpetrators are reported to utilize online dating services as their main gateway to connect with a pool of potential victims. Other common methods of connection include the use of informal chat rooms and various social networking sites.
- The first step in the perpetrators' modus operandi is to create false identities on online dating services or social media, each tailored to attract specific types of victim profiles. The next step involves contacting potential victims. Once an emotional connection is established with selected victims, perpetrators encourage victims to privatize communications by using chat or email functions that are not hosted by the original dating websites or social networking sites. Once an exclusive communication channel is constructed, perpetrators gradually increase intimacy in the relationship over time. Trust is consequently built to the point where perpetrators believe that their victims will comply with financial requests. This process varies with victims, ranging between a few weeks to months, or even to years.
- Internet love scam perpetrators also employ parcel love scams or sex video blackmail as alternate methods of cheating their victims of money. Using the parcel love scam method, perpetrators lead victims to believe that a parcel of romantic memorabilia has been sent to them from outside the country. This parcel is then purportedly detained at Customs, upon which the perpetrator would contact the victim for money to secure its clearance. In the "sex video" blackmailing method, victims are led to perform sexual acts during an online video chat session with the perpetrator, during which they are filmed without their knowledge. Subsequently, victims would be threatened with exposure unless they paid up.
- The CLIP analysis is a framework where (C) refers to criminalistics and forensic science, (L) refers to legal and local issues, (I) refers to investigative and

operational considerations, and (P) refers to psychological and/or behavioral sciences considerations.

- The CLIP analysis is employed for its scientific and multidisciplinary perspective on crime. Notably, CLIP examines and distills pertinent information from empirical research. Using this information, behavioral possibilities associated with specific crimes are generated. This consequently provides an informed structure for appropriate application in relevant areas of crime prevention, investigation, interview, and rehabilitation.

- Generally, criminalistics and forensic science can be understood as the systematic examination of relevant physical evidence in crime detection in accordance with a country's criminal and civil laws. In the context of Internet love scams, where crime is perpetuated mainly through cyberspace, it is notably challenging to establish the primary crime scene. This is because perpetrators may commit the crime repeatedly in various physical locations, and from various virtual platforms in cyberspace. Perpetrators also typically operate in different locations from the victims, which could possibly contribute to negating a relationship between both parties without proper physical evidence.

- There are several laws in existence to combat the crime of Internet love scams, both in international and local settings. There are also laws that account for blackmail methods employed by perpetrators during Internet love scams. Blackmail involves purposeful recording of compromising images and videos of victims, with the intention of subsequently threatening victims for money. In addition, recording of compromising media of victims with ill intent and possessing knowledge that said media will harm victims' reputations qualifies as defamation.

- To ascertain the fact that a scam has occurred, investigators are typically required to establish a timeline for its occurrence. Key details that need to be uncovered include the process of deception, attempts at concealing the crime, and the benefits to the perpetrator. As Internet love scams are predominantly an organized document-reliant crime, forensic recovery may furnish adequate physical evidence of the cheating process, especially evidence of prior planning (mens rea) and the victim grooming process.

- In the event that perpetrators of Internet love scams are caught, effective interviewing can result in admission evidence that can subsequently be used to prosecute the case. Effective interviews are typically planned before the interview session, where selected interviewers are knowledgeable of the investigative work of the case. As Internet love scams often comprise organized work units, multiple offenders may be apprehended. It is recommended to interview each offender in ascending order of probable culpability should multiple offenders be involved in a single case. This is done so that the investigator is able to gather as much useful information as possible by the time the main perpetrator is interviewed.

- Where crime is concerned, psychology and behavioral sciences are applied to get a better understanding of perpetrators through their criminal behaviors. Such information has proven helpful in a number of applied settings such as criminal investigation and crime prevention.

- In the context of Internet love scams, the key motive of perpetrators is to obtain money from their victims. Discounting the duration of the grooming process, Internet love scams are highly lucrative, providing perpetrators with large sums of money in a relatively short period of time. It is cost-effective, as perpetrators only need basic computer literacy, access to a computing device, and an Internet connection to lure potential victims.
- Internet love scam perpetrators generally target their victims leading up to widely celebrated occasions in the year. These include festivities such as the Christmas season, Valentine's Day, as well as personal birthdays, as it is during these periods that love scam victims are believed to be most emotionally vulnerable.
- Perpetrators are also reported to target individuals who profess their grief online after experiencing divorce or loss of a loved one.
- Anticipating when Internet love scam perpetrators are highly likely to strike may help the relevant authorities in planning for crime awareness and prevention to achieve maximum effectiveness.
- Both men and women may be perpetrators of Internet love scams as the desire for an intimate partner is not exclusive to a single gender. The ability to use false credentials on online dating services also allows perpetrators to assume gender identities not corresponding with their own. Men and women also commonly pair up to form scam groups to effectively con victims of both genders. In general women are suggested to be more adept than men at emotion-related communication online, whereas men are more likely to be assertive and open to risk-taking than women.
- In general, Internet love scam victims comprise both men and women of all types of backgrounds, ages, and income levels. Internet love scam perpetrators exploit the human need for love and attachment for monetary gains. Hence, individuals who are generally unable to fulfill this need in a satisfactory manner may become vulnerable. Therefore, individuals who are living alone, who report pervasive loneliness, stress and/or an emotional loss, who have a history of abusive relationships, and a tendency to idealize their intimate partners, may be more likely to be victimized. Such individuals who engage in online dating typically experience "optimism bias," a form of denial that gives them a false sense of security against being duped.
- Other victim types include individuals who participate in online sexual activity. Dating Web services not only bring people together in a romantic fashion but also serve as a platform for people to meet others based on shared interests and sometimes also in engaging in sexual activities. Online sexual activity is generally attractive to individuals as it is affordable and easily accessed with a relative degree of anonymity. Consequently, these individuals may be vulnerable to the "sex video" blackmail variant of the Internet love scam.
- It is recommended that crime prevention strategies include:

- Making buyers aware: The successful perpetration of the scam requires victim consent, and therefore awareness of the risk of being scammed needs to be an element of the preventive effort.
- Encourage more reporting: Internet love scams are typically underreported, which may hint at a higher prevalence of Internet love scam victims than is currently represented in official statistics.
- Develop checklists: As part of the prevention effort, a checklist for citizens to use in assessing whether their online dates are scammers would be of immense benefit. The checklist should include warning citizens that scammers typically request a change in communication platforms, profess feelings of love within a short period of cross communication, and often may send glamorized profile pictures to victims. Scammers may also claim to be traveling or working overseas, may fail to make good on their promises for physical dates due to a variety of disastrous personal events, and will ultimately request monetary transfers.
- Scam watch websites: The Commonwealth of Australia has released a series of Internet love scam crime prevention strategies to the public via their official SCAMwatch Website. In addition to the earlier mentioned red flags, the Australian government encourages citizens to talk to an independent friend, relative, or authorized agency before following through with any money transfers, limit the amount of personal information posted to social networking sites, and to always consider the possibility of being targeted for scams.
- Crime prevention events: To raise awareness regarding the prevalence of Internet love scams, Australian law enforcement agencies utilize the National Cyber Security Awareness Week, and the Think Fraud! Global Day of Action, to come together with the local community, relevant industry partners, and cooperative international organizations to jointly educate citizens on how to protect themselves from becoming a victim of Internet-based crimes.
- Register of accredited dating websites: To minimize the possibility of victimization, individuals should be encouraged to utilize accredited dating agencies.
- Embarrassment: It is helpful for investigators to anticipate aversion on the victims' part to give statements as they may be embarrassed by their situation, and may experience psychologically traumatizing hurt as a result of being suddenly abandoned by a person who had lied about their affection toward them.
- Suicide: Some studies reported that Internet love scam victims might attempt suicide.
- Concept of losing face: Sometimes the uncovering of a scam by a victim results in "losing face," which is defined as a predominant way of self-evaluation by individuals based on other people's impressions of them.
- Denial: Some victims do not get over the con despite uncovering the scam and will deny that it ever happened.

QUESTIONS

1. What is an Internet love scam?
2. What are the typical motivations of a love scam perpetrator?
3. Describe the profile characteristics of a love scam perpetrator.
4. Describe the typical profile characteristics of a love scam victim.
5. What makes an individual vulnerable to a potential love scam?
6. Describe the types of love scams that are commonly utilized by perpetrators.
7. Where do perpetrators usually identify their targets?
8. Describe CLIP and the four components of the model.
9. There are 10 recommendations for love scam prevention discussed in the chapter. Describe the six preventative measures that government agencies can provide.
10. There are 10 recommendations for love scam prevention discussed in the chapter. Describe the four personal victim characteristics that agencies should be aware of in order to assist with preventing and investigating love scams.

REFERENCES

9 News. (2013). *Blog: My relationship with an online scam artist.* Retrieved May 20, 2014, from 9 News: http://www.9news.com/story/news/local/investigations/2014/02/26/1861200/.

Action Fraud. (2014). *Tougher sentencing laws for fraudsters targeting vulnerable victims.* Retrieved May 17, 2014, from Action Fraud: http://www.actionfraud.police.uk/ tougher-sentencing-laws-for-fraudsters-targeting-vulnerable-victims-may14.

Action Fraud. (n.d.). *Action Fraud | Report fraud and Internet crime.* Retrieved May 17, 2014, from Action Fraud: http://www.actionfraud.police.uk/home.

Alderman, J. (2014). *Don't fall for Valentine's Day scams.* Retrieved March 23, 2014, from Huffington Post: http://www.huffingtonpost.com/jason-alderman/dont-fall-for-valentines_b_4778141.html.

American Institute of Certified Public Accountants. (n.d.). *Conducting effective interviews.* Retrieved March 15, 2014, from the American Institute of Certified Public Accountants, Forensic and Valuation Services Section: http://www.aicpa.org/InterestAreas/Forensic AndValuation/Resources/PractAidsGuidance/DownloadableDocuments/10834-378_ interview%20whiite%20paper-FINAL-v1.pdf.

Anchondo, J. (2013). *Local woman likely victim of online 'romance scam'.* Retrieved May 18, 2014, from the Tribune Broadcasting Company, FOX59 News: http://fox59. com/2013/05/27/local-woman-likely-victim-of-online-romance-scam/#axzz32jqgpnoi.

Ashcroft, J. (2001). *Electronic crime scene investigation: A guide for first responders.* Retrieved March 10, 2014, from National Criminal Justice Reference Service: https:// www.ncjrs.gov/pdffiles1/nij/187736.pdf.

Association of Chief Police Officers. (2011). *ACPO managers guide: Good practice and advice guide for managers of e-crime investigation.* Retrieved May 15, 2014, from Association of Chief Police Officers: http://www.acpo.police.uk/documents/crime/2011/ 201103CRIECI14.pdf.

Astbury, S. (2013). *Internet romance scam victims fight for self-respect.* Retrieved May 20, 2014, from Gulf Times: http://www.gulf-times.com/technology/233/details/349012/ internet-romance-scam-victims-fight-for-self-respect.

Australasian Legal Information Institute. (n.d.). *Crimes Act 1958 – Sect 87*. Retrieved May 15, 2014, from Australasian Legal Information Institute (AustLII): http://www.austlii.edu.au/au/legis/vic/consol_act/ca195882/s87.html.

Australian Competition and Consumer Commission. (2012). *The little black book of scams*. Retrieved May 13, 2014, from Australian Competition and Consumer Commission: http://www.accc.gov.au/system/files/Little%20Black%20Book%20of%20Scams%20-%20Pocket-sized%20guide.pdf.

Australian Federal Police. (2014). *Asian culture and crime trends*. Retrieved May 20, 2014, from the Commonwealth of Australia, Australian Federal Police: http://www.afp.gov.au/media-centre/publications/platypus/previous-editions/1998/march-1998/asian.aspx.

Bartlett, J., & Miller, C. (2011). *Truth, lies and the Internet: A report into young people's digital fluency*. Retrieved March 23, 2014, from Demos: http://www.demos.co.uk/files/Truth_-_web.pdf.

Barwick, H. (2012). *AusCERT 2012: Fear of ridicule causing online scams to go unreported*. Retrieved March 4, 2014, from ComputerWorld: http://www.computerworld.com.au/article/424861/auscert_2012_fear_ridicule_causing_online_scams_go_unreported_/.

Bindley, K. (2012). *Online romance scams: Digital lotharios take to the web*. Retrieved May 14, 2014, from the Huffington Post, Women: http://www.huffingtonpost.com/2012/07/02/romantic-predators-take-to-the-web_n_1610395.html?utm_hp_ref=women&ir=Women.

Bjelopera, J. P., & Finklea, K. M. (2012). *Organized crime: An evolving challenge for U.S. law enforcement*. Retrieved March 23, 2014, from Federation of American Scientists: http://www.fas.org/sgp/crs/misc/R41547.pdf.

Bliss, G. (2011). *Commentary: Fraud facts: Love hurts… especially when fraud is involved*. New York: Rochester: The Daily Record (Retrieved from Regional Business News database).

Borders, J. (2014). *Scammers will 'go after anyone, regardless of age, gender or income'*. Retrieved March 23, 2014, from West Virginia: http://www.timeswv.com/business/x1984789719/Scammers-will-go-after-anyone-regardless-of-age-gender-or-income.

Brooke, C. (2010). *Lonely divorcee kills himself after falling for 82,000 Internet dating con*. Retrieved May 20, 2014, from the Daily Mail Online: http://www.dailymail.co.uk/news/article-1247774/Divorcees-train-suicide-82-000-internet-date.html.

Burnett, R. (2013). *'Romance scams' jump each year as Valentine's Day approaches*. Retrieved March 23, 2014, from Orlando Sentinel: http://articles.orlandosentinel.com/2013-02-12/business/os-florida-romance-scams-valentines-day-20130212_1_romance-scams-moneygram-kim-garner.

Button, M., Lewis, C., & Tapley, J. (n.d.). *Fraud typologies and victims of fraud*. Retrieved May 20, 2014, from the United Kingdom National Fraud Authority: https://www.gov.uk/government/uploads/system/uploads/attachment_data/file/118469/fraud-typologies.pdf.

Camoens, A. (2014). *Scammers learn 'language of love'*. Retrieved May 15, 2014, from The Star Online: http://www.thestar.com.my/News/Nation/2014/02/23/Scammers-learn-language-of-love/.

Canadian Resource Centre for Victims of Crime. (2014). *Romance fraud/scams*. Retrieved May 18, 2014, from Canadian Resource Centre for Victims of Crime: http://crcvc.ca/2014/03/24/romance-fraudscams/.

Casey, E. (2011). Investigative reconstruction with digital evidence. In E. Casey (Ed.), *Digital evidence and computer crime: Forensic science, computers and the Internet* Retrieved March 10, 2014, (from Google Books).

Channel News Asia. (2011). *Watch out for the 'online boyfriend'*. Retrieved March 23, 2014, from Xin MSN News: http://news.xin.msn.com/en/singapore/article.aspx?cp-documentid=4713009.

Christensen, D. A. (2013). *Victims of dating scams – Psychological and emotional trauma.* Retrieved May 18, 2014, from Hoax Slayer: http://www.hoax-slayer.com/dating-scam-victim-trauma.shtml.

Christensen, D. A. (2014). *Jill's story – Romance, fraud and money laundering scam.* Retrieved May 20, 2014, from Hoax Slayer: http://www.hoax-slayer.com/jill-story.shtml.

Commonwealth of Australia. (2000). *Criminal Code Amendment (Theft, fraud, bribery and related offences) Act 2000.* Retrieved May 15, 2014, from Commonwealth of Australia: http://www.comlaw.gov.au/Details/C2004A00730.

Cooper, A., Mansson, S., Daneback, K., Tikkanen, R., & Ross, M. W. (2003). Predicting the future of Internet sex: online sexual activities in Sweden. *Journal of Sexual and Relationship Therapy*, *18*(3), 277–291. 15 pp. Retrieved March 23, 2014, from: http://www.hawaii.edu/hivandaids/Predicting_the_Future_of_Internet_Sex__Online_Sexual_Activities_in_Sweden.pdf.

Dartis, M. (2013). *W5 investigates scams that prey on those seeking online romance.* Retrieved May 13, 2014, from Canadian Television Network: http://www.ctvnews.ca/w5/w5-investigates-scams-that-prey-on-those-seeking-online-romance-1.1567247.

Davenport, J. (December 1, 2010). Briton is kidnapped in online 'romance fraud'. *Evening Standard*, 5 1 pp. (Retrieved from Regional Business News database).

Demasi, S. (2011). Shopping for love: online dating and the making of a cyber culture of romance. In S. Seidman, N. Fischer, & C. Meeks (Eds.), *Introducing the new sexuality studies* (2nd ed.) (pp. 206–214). London: Routledge (Retrieved from Google Books).

Department of Justice. (2014). *Criminal code, fraud.* Retrieved May 15, 2014, from Government of Canada, Justice Laws Website: http://laws-lois.justice.gc.ca/eng/acts/c-46/page-183.html#h-105.

DiNapoli, T.P. (n.d.). *Red flags for fraud.* Retrieved March 23, 2014, from New York State Office of the State Comptroller: http://www.osc.state.ny.us/localgov/pubs/red_flags_fraud.pdf.

Dixon, R. (2005). *Nigerian cyber scammers*, 7125847. Retrieved March 23, 2014, from Los Angeles Times: http://www.latimes.com/la-fg-scammers20oct20.story#axzz2wz08m9ZU.

Dutch Fraud Help Desk. (2013). *Dating fraud victims are not stupid of naïve.* Retrieved May 20, 2014, from Dutch National Anti-Fraud Helpline, Fraud Help Desk: http://www.fraudhelpdesk.org/newsitem/dating_fraud_victims_are_not_stupid_or_na_ve.

Economic and Social Research Council. (2013). *Romantic delusions allow online dating scams to flourish.* Retrieved May 17, 2014, from the Economic and Social Research Council: http://www.esrc.ac.uk/news-and-events/press-releases/25035/Romantic_delusions_allow_online_dating_scams_to_flourish.aspx.

Etter, B. (2001). *The challenge of the forensic investigation of computer crime.* Retrieved May 15, 2014, from Australian Federal Police: http://www.afp.gov.au/~/media/afp/pdf/c/comp-crim.ashx.

Federal Bureau of Investigation. (2012). *Beware of online dating scams.* Retrieved May 20, 2014, from Federal Bureau of Investigation: http://www.fbi.gov/news/stories/2012/february/dating-scams_021412.

Federal Bureau of Investigation. (2013a). *2013 Internet crime report.* Retrieved May 13, 2014, from Federal Bureau of Investigation, Internet Crime Complaint Center (IC3): http://www.ic3.gov/media/annualreport/2013_IC3Report.pdf.

Federal Bureau of Investigation. (2013b). *National cyber security awareness month 2013.* Retrieved May 17, 2014, from Federal Bureau of Investigation, News Blog: http://www.fbi.gov/news/news_blog/national-cyber-security-awareness-month-2013.

Federal Bureau of Investigation. (2014). *Looking for love? Beware of online dating scams.* Retrieved May 17, 2014, from Federal Bureau of Investigation, Press Releases: http://www.fbi.gov/sandiego/press-releases/2014/looking-for-love-beware-of-online-dating-scams.

Federal Bureau of Investigation. (n.d.). *Fraud target: Senior citizens.* Retrieved May 20, 2014, from the Federal Bureau of Investigation: http://www.fbi.gov/scams-safety/fraud/seniors/seniors.

Fong, T. (2011). *Watch out for the online 'boyfriend', resurgence in love scams, police warn.* Retrieved March 6, 2014, from Singapore Association of Social Workers: http://www.sasw.org.sg/public/documents/1603HNP016.pdf.

Foote, A. (2013). *Online dating most popular fraud target in Canada.* Retrieved May 13, 2014, from Canadian Broadcasting Corporation News: http://www.cbc.ca/news/canada/ottawa/online-dating-most-popular-fraud-target-in-canada-1.1333506.

Gubanov, Y. (2012). *Retrieving digital evidence: Methods, techniques, and issues: Part 1.* Retrieved May 14, 2014, from Digital Forensic Investigator News: http://www.dfinews.com/articles/2012/05/retrieving-digital-evidence-methods-techniques-and-issues-part-1.

Hendricks, D. (2014). *Background checks increasingly common in online dating.* Retrieved March 26, 2014, from Tech Cocktail: http://tech.co/background-checks-increasingly-common-online-dating-2014-01.

Herald Scotland. (2014). *Student jailed for three years after six lonely women scammed out of £186,000.* Retrieved March 23, 2014, from Herald Scotland: http://www.heraldscotland.com/news/home-news/student-jailed-for-three-years-after-six-lonely-women-scammed-out-of-186000.1393859910.

Herring, S. C., & Martinson, A. (2004). Assessing gender authenticity in computer-mediated language use: evidence from an identity game. *Journal of Language and Social Psychology*, *23*, 424–446. 23 pp. http://dx.doi.org/10.1177/0261927X04269586.

Home Affairs Committee. (2013). *E-crime.* Retrieved May 14, 2014, from United Kingdom Parliament: http://www.publications.parliament.uk/pa/cm201314/cmselect/cmhaff/70/70.pdf.

Independent Television. (2012). *Met advises vigilance after romance scam convictions.* Retrieved May 17, 2014, from United Kingdom Independent Television, News: http://www.itv.com/news/london/2012-10-25/met-advises-vigilance-after-romance-scam-convictions/.

International Competition Network. (2008). *Anti-cartel enforcement manual.* Retrieved March 26, 2014, from International Competition Network: http://www.internationalcompetitionnetwork.org/uploads/library/doc345.pdf.

Jones, L. A., & Hill, E. (2011). *Rom scam: How African fraudsters now make £80million a year ripping off women (and a few men) so desperate for love they'll believe anything.* Retrieved May 17, 2014, from the Daily Mail Online: http://www.dailymail.co.uk/news/article-1354155/African-fraudsters-make-80m-year-ripping-women-desperate-love.html.

Jordan, M. (2014). *Users of online dating sites fall victim to fraud.* Retrieved May 18, 2014, from the Wall Street Journal, News: http://online.wsj.com/news/articles/SB10001424052702304851104579363024081588350.

Khader, M., Ang, J., Diong, S. M., Poh, L. L., Toh, S. M., Jayagowry, A., et al. (2012). Police psychology in Singapore: the red dot experience. *Journal of Police and Criminal Psychology*, *27*(1), 24–32.

Kiernan, P. (2005). *Fraud investigation and prosecution in the United Kingdom.* Retrieved March 15, 2014, from United Nations Asia and Far East Institute for the Prevention of Crime and Treatment of Offenders (UNAFEI), Resource Material Series No. 66: http://www.unafei.or.jp/english/pdf/RS_No66/No66_13VE_Kiernan2.pdf.

Kim, Y. H., & Cohen, D. (2010). Information, perspective, and judgments about the self in face and dignity cultures. *Personality & Social Psychology Bulletin*, *36*(4), 537–550. http://dx.doi.org/10.1177/0146167210362398. Retrieved May 18, 2014, from Yonsei University, Seoul: http://web.yonsei.ac.kr/younghoonkim/PSPB%20(2010).pdf.

Kranacher, M. J. (2010). *Introduction to fraud examination and financial forensics*. Retrieved March 15, 2014, from Professional Bookshop Limited: http://www.pbookshop.com/media/filetype/b/i/1346318907.pdf.

Laforest, J., Belley, C., Lavertue, R., Maurice, P., & Rainville, M. (2009). *Guide to organizing semi-structured interviews with key informant*. Retrieved March 26, 2014, from the Centre Québécois de Resources en Promotion de la Sécurité et en Prévention de la Criminalité (CRPSPC): http://www.crpspc.qc.ca/Guide_entretien_versionWEB_eng.pdf.

Lanford, A., & Lanford, J. (n.d.). *Top 10 work at home and home based business scams*. Retrieved March 23, 2014, from Internet ScamBusters: http://www.scambusters.org/work-at-home.html.

Legal Information Institute. (1994). *18 U.S. Code § 880 – Receiving the proceeds of extortion | LII/legal information Institute*. Retrieved May 15, 2014, from Cornell University Law School, Legal Information Institute: http://www.law.cornell.edu/uscode/text/18/880.

Legal Information Institute. (2008). *18 U.S. Code § 1341 – Frauds and swindles | LII/legal information Institute*. Retrieved May 15, 2014, from Cornell University Law School, Legal Information Institute: http://www.law.cornell.edu/uscode/text/18/1341.

Legal Information Institute. (n.d.). *Caveat emptor | Wex legal dictionary/Encyclopedia | LII/Legal Information Institute*. Retrieved May 20, 2014, from Cornell University Law School, Legal Information Institute: http://www.law.cornell.edu/wex/caveat_emptor.

LunchActually. (2014). *LunchActually*. Retrieved March 26, 2014, from Dating Agencies | Online Dating – LunchActually Singapore | LunchActually Singapore, Malaysia, and Hong Kong: http://www.lunchactually.com/dating-agencies/.

Malcolm, H. (2013). Romance scams are in bloom. 1/2 pp. *USA Today, Money*, 01b (Retrieved from MAS Ultra – School Edition database).

Marrington, A., Baggili, I., Ismail, T. A., & Kaf, A. A. (2012). *Portable web browser forensics: A forensic examination of the privacy benefits of portable web browsers*. Retrieved May 15, 2014, from Academia: http://www.academia.edu/attachments/32329024/download_file?st=MTQwMDUxNDYxMCwyMjAuMjU1LjEuMTQ1&ct=MTQwMDUxNDYxMg%3D%3D.

Metropolitan Police Service. (2013). *The little book of big scams* (2nd ed.). Retrieved March 24, 2013, from the Metropolitan Police Service, Mayor's Office for Policing and Crime and the Crown: http://www.met.police.uk/docs/little_book_scam.pdf.

Ministry of Social and Family Development. (2011). *Registry of dating agencies*. Retrieved March 24, 2014, from Registry of Dating Agencies – Ministry of Social and Family Development: http://app.msf.gov.sg/Policies/DatingIndustryServices/RegistryofDatingAgencies.aspx.

Munton, J., & McLeod, J. (2011). *The con: How scams work, why you're vulnerable, and how to protect yourself*. Lanham: North America: Rowman & Littlefield Publishers. Retrieved March 23, 2014, (from Google Books).

National Cyber Security Alliance. (2014). *About | Staysafeonline.org*. Retrieved May 17, 2014, from National Cyber Security Alliance, Stay Safe Online: http://www.staysafeonline.org/ncsam/about.

Newcomb, T. (2012). *Major online dating sites to start background checks on users.* Retrieved March 26, 2014, from TIME: http://newsfeed.time.com/2012/03/21/major-online-dating-sites-to-start-background-checks-on-users/.

Olukoya, S. (2002). *Nigeria grapples with e-mail scams.* Retrieved March 23, 2014, from BBC News: http://news.bbc.co.uk/2/hi/africa/1944801.stm.

Pearson, M. (2014). *Victims speak out about romance scams.* Retrieved May 20, 2014, from Ottawa Citizen, News: http://www.ottawacitizen.com/life/Victims+speak+about+romance+scams/9587599/story.html.

Quinn, J. (2013). *Online dating relationship ends badly, $1.3M later.* Retrieved May 13, 2014, from Toronto Star Newspapers, Investigations: http://www.thestar.com/news/investigations/2013/11/30/online_dating_relationship_ends_badly_13m_later.html.

Rege, A. (2009). What's love got to do with it? Exploring online dating scams and identity fraud. *International Journal of Cyber Criminology*, *3*(2), 494–512. 19 pp. Retrieved March 14, 2014, from: http://www.cybercrimejournal.com/AunshullJCCJuly2009.pdf.

Romance Scam. (2011). *Romance scams. Why is he still doing it? Why can't he be caught?.* Retrieved May 18, 2014, from Romance Scam, Forum: http://www.romancescam.com/forum/viewtopic.php?f=22&t=68683.

Romance Scams. (n.d.). *About romance scammers.* Retrieved March 23, 2014, from Romance Scams, the Official Romance Scams Website: http://romancescams.org/AboutRomance Scammers.html.

Royal Malaysia Police. (2014). *Parcel scams.* Retrieved May 13, 2014, from Commercial Crime Investigation Department, Royal Malaysia Police: http://www.ccid.my/en/crimes/parcel_scam.

Saarinen, J. (2013). *Love in the time of online scams.* Retrieved May 20, 2014, from Next Media, itNews for Australian Business: http://www.itnews.com.au/News/344310. ,love-in-the-time-of-online-scams.aspx.

Saferstein, R. (2006). *Criminalistics: An introduction to forensic science* (9th ed.). Upper Saddle River, New Jersey: Pearson Prentice Hall.

Saskatchewan Association of Chiefs of Police. (n.d.). *SK Association of Chiefs of Police: Fraud Awareness.* Retrieved May 18, 2014, from Saskatchewan Association of Chiefs of Police: http://www.sacp.ca/fraudawareness/.

SCAMwatch. (2010). *Think fraud! Global day of action 1 June.* Retrieved May 17, 2014, from the Australian Competition & Consumer Commission, SCAMwatch: http://www.scamwatch.gov.au/content/index.phtml/itemId/789075.

SCAMwatch. (2011). *National cyber security awareness week 2011 – 30 May to 3 June 2011.* Retrieved May 17, 2014, from the Australian Competition & Consumer Commission, SCAMwatch: http://www.scamwatch.gov.au/content/index.phtml/itemId/844296.

SCAMwatch. (2014). *Dating and romance scams.* Retrieved May 17, 2014, from the Australian Competition & Consumer Commission, SCAMwatch: http://www.scamwatch.gov.au/content/index.phtml/tag/DatingRomanceScams.

Schmitt, D. P., Realo, A., Voracek, M., & Allik, J. (2008). Why can't a man be more like a woman? Sex differences in big five personality traits across 55 cultures. *Journal of Personality and Social Psychology*, *94*(1), 168–182. 15 pp. Retrieved March 23, 2014, from: http://www.researchgate.net/publication/5671655_Why_can't_a_man_be_more_like_a_woman_Sex_differences_in_Big_Five_personality_traits_across_55_cultures/file/79e414f996c9590d9b.pdf.

Scottish Television. (2013). *Teenage boy 'killed himself over online chat blackmail threats'*. Retrieved May 18, 2014, from Scottish Television, News: http://news.stv.tv/east-central/236217-fife-teenage-boy-killed-himself-over-online-blackmail-threats/.

Singapore Police Force. (2012a). *Police bust 'internet love scam' ring that extorted over S$100,000 from victims*. Retrieved March 6, 2014, from the Singapore Police Force | Media Releases: http://www.spf.gov.sg/mic/2012/02/20120228_internet_love.html.

Singapore Police Force. (2012b). *Key crime concerns*. Retrieved March 6, 2014, from the Singapore Police Force: http://www.spf.gov.sg/stats/stats2011_key_crime_concern.htm.

Singapore Police Force. (2013). *Scam through social networking website*. Retrieved March 23, 2014, from the Singapore Police Force: http://www.spf.gov.sg/mic/2013/11/20131111_others_scam.html.

Singapore Police Force. (2014). *Singapore Police Force crime prevention posters index*. Retrieved March 23, 2014, from the Singapore Police Force: http://www.spf.gov.sg/crimeprevention/posters_index.htm.

Smith, L. (2012). *Romance scam continues to grow online*. Retrieved May 18, 2014, from Columbia Broadcasting System, Denver: http://denver.cbslocal.com/2012/09/25/romance-scam-continues-to-grow-online/.

Span, P. (2012). *Prime targets for scam artists*. Retrieved March 23, 2014, from The New York Times: http://newoldage.blogs.nytimes.com/2012/04/20/prime-targets-for-scam-artists/?_php=true&_type=blogs&_r=0.

Special Broadcasting Service. (2014). *Comment: The high price I paid for online dating*. Retrieved May 20, 2014, from Special Broadcasting Service, News: http://www.sbs.com.au/news/article/2014/04/01/comment-high-price-i-paid-online-dating.

Starr, M. (2014). *Australians lost $25m to romance scams in 2013*. Retrieved May 13, 2014, from Computer Network, News (CNET): http://www.cnet.com/news/australians-lost-25m-to-romance-scams-in-2013/.

Steyerl, H. (2011). Epistolary affect and romance scams: letter from an unknown woman. *October, 138*, 57–69. 13 pp. Retrieved from Academic Search Premier database:.

Suler, J. (2004). The online disinhibit ion effect. *Journal of Cyberpsychology and Behaviour, 7*(3), 321–326. Retrieved May 15, 2014, from: http://www.samblackman.org/Articles/Suler.pdf.

Teller Vision. (June 2010). *The "sweetheart scam" cons those looking for love. Teller Vision (1394)*, 7. 1/3pp. Retrieved from Business Source Premier database.

Thelwall, M., Wilkinson, D., & Uppal, S. (2010). Data mining emotion in social network communication: gender differences in MySpace. *Journal of the American Society for Information Science and Technology, 21*(1), 190–199. 10 pp. Retrieved March 23, 2014, from: http://www.researchgate.net/publication/220433642_Data_mining_emotion_in_social_network_communication_Gender_differences_in_MySpace/file/d912f513452806ccb3.pdf.

Trevathan, J., & Myers, T. (2012). Anti-social networking? *World Academy of Science, Engineering and Technology, 6*(12), 127–135. 9 pp. Retrieved March 24, 2014 from World Academy of Science, Engineering and Technology: http://waset.org/publications/2207/Anti-Social-Networking.

Triandis, H. C., & Suh, E. M. (2002). Cultural influences on personality. *Annual Review of Psychology, 53*, 133–160. Retrieved May 18, 2014, from Yonsei University, Seoul: http://web.yonsei.ac.kr/suh/file/Cultural%20influences%20on%20personality.pdf.

United Kingdom Legislation. (1968). *Theft act 1968, section 21*. Retrieved May 15, 2014, from United Kingdom Legislation: http://www.legislation.gov.uk/ukpga/1968/60/section/21.

United Kingdom Legislation. (2006). *Fraud act 2006, Sections; 1, 2 & 6*. Retrieved May 15, 2014, from United Kingdom Legislation: http://www.legislation.gov.uk/ukpga/2006/35/section/2.

University of Illinois Chicago. (2009). *Fraud investigation I, II & III*. Retrieved March 15, 2014, from University of Illinois, Chicago: http://www.uic.edu/classes/actg/actg537/ClassNotes/FE13.Fraud.Investigation%20I,II_III%20.4.14.09.pdf.

Urbas, G. (2008). *An overview of cybercrime legislation and cases in Singapore*. Retrieved March 23, 2014, from National University of Singapore, Law: https://law.nus.edu.sg/asli/pdf/WPS001.pdf.

Uwujaren, W. (2014). *EFCC press release: EFCC arrests 4 undergraduates, 3 others for internet scam*. Retrieved March 23, 2014, from Sahara Reporters: http://saharareporters.com/press-release/efcc-press-release-efcc-arrests-4-undergraduates-3-others-internet-scam.

Verstraten, K. (2013). *Online romance turns sour as Victoria victim loses $88,000 in scam*. Retrieved May 13, 2014, from The Globe and Mail: http://www.theglobeandmail.com/news/british-columbia/online-romance-turns-sour-as-victoria-victim-loses-88000-in-scam/article15515522/.

Wahlquist, C. (2014). *WA woman 'lost hundreds of thousands' to online romance scam – But got some back*. Retrieved May 18, 2014, from Perth Now, News: http://www.perthnow.com.au/news/western-australia/wa-woman-lost-hundreds-of-thousands-to-online-romance-scam-but-got-some-back/story-fnhocxo3-1226872433513.

Walker, P. (2011). *Online dating scam dupes 200,000 study finds*. Retrieved May 13, 2014, from The Guardian: http://www.theguardian.com/lifeandstyle/2011/sep/28/online-dating-scams-study.

Weisbaum, H. (2014). *Lonely, stressed? You're more likely to be victim of online fraud*. Retrieved March 23, 2014, from Daily Finance: http://www.dailyfinance.com/2014/03/06/lonely-stressed-more-likely-victim-online-frau/.

Whitty, M. (2012a). *Online losers in love*. Retrieved May 18, 2014, from Society Now Summer 2012, Issue 13: http://www.esrc.ac.uk/_images/Society_Now_13_tcm8-21683.pdf.

Whitty, M. (2012b). *True romance?*. Retrieved March 4, 2014, from the University of Leicester: http://www2.le.ac.uk/departments/media/people/monica-whitty/True%20Romance_Whitty.pdf.

Whitty, M. (in press). *Anatomy of the online dating romance scam*. Retrieved March 6, 2014, from the University of Leicester: http://www2.le.ac.uk/departments/media/people/monica-whitty/Anatomy%20of%20the%20romance%20scam_Whitty_Security%20Journal.pdf.

Whitty, M., & Buchanan, T. (2012a). The online romance scam: a serious cybercrime. *Journal of Cyberpsychology, Behaviour and Social Networking*, *15*(3), 181–183. http://dx.doi.org/10.1089/cyber.2011.0352 3 pp.

Whitty, M., & Buchanan, T. (2012b). *The psychology of the online dating romance scam*. Retrieved March 14, 2014, from the University of Leicester: http://www2.le.ac.uk/departments/media/people/monica-whitty/Whitty_romance_scam_report.pdf.

Whitty, M., & Buchanan, T. (2012c). *An examination of the online romance scam*. Retrieved May 15, 2014, from the Economic and Social Research Council: http://www.esrc.ac.uk/my-esrc/grants/RES-000-22-4022/outputs/Download/e2a39cf6-892e-4af3-9c62-8f65db041c1b.

Wong, Y., & Tsai, J. (2007). Cultural models of shame and guilt. In J. L. Tracy, R. W. Robin, & J. P. Tangney (Eds.), *The self-conscious emotions: Theory and research* (pp. 209–223). New York: Guilford Press. Retrieved May 20, 2014, from Stanford University, Department of Psychology: http://www-psych.stanford.edu/~tsailab/PDF/yw07sce.pdf.

Zuckoff, M. (2006). *The perfect mark*. Retrieved March 23, 2014, from Both Favourites: http://www.bothfavorites.com/blog/wp-content/uploads/The_Perfect_Mark.pdf.

Zulawski, D. E., & Sturman, S. G. (2013). *PEACE 2013*. Retrieved March 26, 2014, from Wicklander-Zulawski & Associates, Inc: http://www.w-z.com/blog/wp-content/uploads/2012/12/LP-Mag-Nov-Dec-12.pdf.

Firesetters: A Review of Theory, Facts, and Treatment

19

Therese Ellis-Smith

Bond University, Gold Coast, QLD, Australia

CHAPTER OUTLINE

The impact of deliberately lit property fires and bushfires on communities can be devastating, and it may take many years for the financial and psychological effects to subside. Those who engage in deliberate firesetting are often complex individuals with a diverse set of treatment or intervention needs, warranting a targeted approach that ameliorates their risk of further offending. This chapter will provide a broad introduction to the theories developed to explain deliberate firesetting and some of the common traits attributed to arsonists, in addition to a summary of key treatment targets identified as contributing to reduced recidivism. It is beyond the scope of this chapter to provide a comprehensive overview of all aspects associated with the study of firesetting, as this complex behavior is multidimensional, and those who engage in it, are often very complicated.

The term *arson* is a legal term used to define a statutory offense, and *arsonist* refers to an individual who has been convicted of that offense. *Firesetting*, on the other hand, is the term used to describe the behavior of deliberately setting a fire, irrespective of whether such action results in charges being laid or convictions being incurred. This chapter will therefore use the term *firesetter*. First, in order to

The Psychology of Criminal and Antisocial Behavior. http://dx.doi.org/10.1016/B978-0-12-809287-3.00019-5

introduce the reader to the impact of arson, the following section provides a brief outline of the costs associated with firesetting and its prevalence in Australia, the United States, and the United Kingdom.

COSTS

It is difficult to accurately estimate the cost of deliberate firesetting, especially when fire-service preventative actions, police investigations, insurance claims and postfire land management costs are considered. The estimated costs due to losses from fire number in the tens of billions of dollars globally, or approximately 1% of global gross domestic product per annum (The Geneva Association, 2014). As Wickramasekera, Wright, Elsey, Murray, and Tebeuf (2015) note, calculating the full cost of any type of crime can be difficult due to the often limited availability of outcome data. In many instances deliberate firesetting results in unknown long-term consequences associated with the rebuilding of lives and businesses, and the actual costs are immeasurable. Despite these actuarial anomalies, estimates have put the annual economic impact of deliberate firesetting in the United Kingdom to be in the vicinity of B£2.3 (Department for Communities & Local Government, 2011), in Australia between B$1.6 (Rollings, 2008) and B$2.3 in 2011 (Smith, Jorna, Sweeney, & Fuller, 2014), and in the United States at B$1.3 (Evarts, 2012). As many of the costs associated with loss of life and personal property cannot be ascertained, these estimates are likely to be conservative and under-represent the full costs borne by a community from both bushfires and deliberate property fires.

It is argued that fires that have been deliberately lit are likely to cause far more damage, and therefore be more costly, than those fires that result from accidental ignition (Fire Protection Association, 2010). This is because deliberately lit fires may be:

- lit using multiple points of ignition
- lit at vulnerable points in a building
- assisted by the use of flammable liquids or other accelerants, and therefore spread quickly
- started at a time when there will be a delay in the fire being discovered (such as when the premises are unattended or only partially occupied)
- assisted by compromising fire protection measures in a building (for example, fire doors may be wedged open to help a fire develop and spread throughout the property), or by the sabotage of automatic fire protection measures (such as by isolating a sprinkler system or automatic fire detection installation)
- represent an attempt to destroy evidence of another crime

The costs associated with preventative efforts generally, and those specifically targeting known firesetters, must also be factored into an overall assessment of the cost of deliberate firesetting in a community. In Australia, police in some jurisdictions actively monitor known firesetters, particularly during peak fire risk periods, by going to their homes to warn them that they are being observed, and by maintaining a vigilant watch over areas frequented by deliberate bushfire arsonists (South Australia Police, 2015). The financial outlay for these preventative measures must therefore be added to the overall estimate of the cost of arson (Ducat & Ogloff, 2011).

PREVALENCE AND CLEARANCE RATES

Across Australia fire services respond to thousands of incidents in relation to fires and explosions each year, and in New South Wales alone, state fire services responded to 21,793 incidents during the 2014–15 year (Fire and Rescue, New South Wales, 2014). In terms of the number of bushfires occurring in Australia, it is estimated that Australian fire services attend between 46,000 and 62,000 bushfires each year (Australian Institute of Criminology, 2009) and some estimates suggest that of these, up to 50% are suspicious or confirmed to have been deliberately lit (Bryant, 2008). The recording of fire incidents and the eventual identification of the causes of these incidents, be they accidental, deliberate, or unknown, is confounded by the different methods and definitions used by policing and fire service agencies. For instance, UK fire services recorded 68,400 instances of suspected or deliberate firesetting across England during 2014–15 (Fire & Rescue Statistical Release, 2015), while police estimates of fires are much lower at 20,576 over the same period (Office for National Statistics, 2015).

It is not unusual for only a proportion of suspected deliberate fires attended to by fire service agencies to be later classified as arson offenses by policing agencies, as the latter agency must prove intention or recklessness. Early indications that a fire was set deliberately or following a reckless act may not always result in a conviction, and it may be a lengthy period before a fire is recorded as deliberate, if at all. This interferes with prevalence analyses that rely on the identification of a crime within a specific time period. Certain arson offenses, which may take several years to be prosecuted, are likely to be counted as "suspicious" until such time as a successful prosecution is achieved.

Another problem associated with the identification of the true number of arson offenses is the generally low clearance rates, following police investigations (Dickens & Sugarman, 2012). Unfortunately, those who set bushfires in particular evade justice, with a majority of offenders responsible for a setting a bushfire neither caught nor convicted (Willis, 2004). Clear-up rates for arson offenses in Australia are consistently low, for instance in Queensland there were 1021 confirmed arson offenses in 2015 (Queensland Police Service, 2016), and of these only 227 or 22% were solved by the end of the year. Similarly, in Victoria, of the 2818 arson offenses recorded in 2013–14, only 549 or 19.5% were cleared by the end of that year (Victoria Police, 2014).

Arson clearance rates reported by policing agencies are also historically low across international jurisdictions. For instance, in the United Kingdom 69% of all arson investigations during 2014–15 were closed without the identification of suspects (Home Office, 2015). In the United States the clearance rates for arson offenses are also low, and are reported to be 18.8% for the 2011 calendar year and 21% in 2013 (Uniform Crime Reports, Federal Bureau of Investigations, 2011, 2013). Willis (2004) outlines some of the reasons for poor clearance rates including a loss of evidence in the fire, lengthy delays while the cause of the fire is investigated, and the often randomness of some deliberately lit fires with few links to possible suspects. It is important to recognize that the reliability and comparability of these rates depends on all law enforcement agencies reporting accurately and similarly, and there exist opportunities for variations in classification, as well as misreporting, that may render these rates inaccurate.

Firesetting has challenged policy makers, researchers, psychologists, and criminologists for many years, and a body of literature has amassed that is focused on the identification of etiology and contributing factors, common motivations, and specific treatment targets for this behavior. Single-factor theories of firesetting, such as social learning theory (Bandura, 1976) and psychoanalytical theory (Freud, 1932), have contributed to the development of an array of multifactorial theories. This next section traverses these developments in the pursuit of a theoretical understanding of firesetting behavior that not only classifies firesetters into meaningful typologies but also informs treatment targets and management strategies.

EXPLANATORY THEORIES

A variety of suggestions have emerged from the criminology and psychology literature as to the correlates of firesetting behaviors, including the notion that indicators of social disorder, such as broken windows in public buildings, contribute to firesetting (Thomas & Butry, 2011). Other classifications and typologies focus on an inductive understanding of the behavior according to its motivation (Lewis & Yarnell, 1951; Inciardi, 1970; Prins, 1994; Rix, 1994) or a deductive approach based on offense and offender variables (Canter & Fritzon, 1998). One of the first multifactor theories developed to explain firesetting was Fineman's (1980) dynamic-behavioral theory. This theory suggests that firesetting behavior results from historical social learning influences, and identifies specific variables such as childhood experiences, environmental factors, and proximal cognitions that contribute to the development and maintenance of firesetting behavior.

Fineman (1980) proposed that firesetting results from historical factors such as social disadvantage or social ineffectiveness, coupled with previous or existing environmental reinforcers such as fire fascination or favorable childhood experiences of fire, following a range of proximal situational environmental factors including crime scene features, impulsivity, or permission-giving cognitions (Gannon, Ó Ciardha, Doley, & Alleyne, 2012). Dynamic-behavioral theory introduced a sequence of factors that both led to, and reinforced the maintenance of, firesetting behaviors, and pioneered the identification of individual treatment targets for firesetters. While this theory is considered to have sound clinical utility (Gannon & Pina, 2010), it is limited by its inability to explain recidivist firesetting (Doley, 2009). Moreover, Fineman's theory lacks specific reference to cultural factors that may contribute to firesetting, and focuses on developmental factors that are likely to be more pertinent to firesetting in children, as opposed to adult-onset firesetting (Tyler et al., 2014).

More recently, Jackson, Glass, and Hope (1987) explain firesetting in terms of the principles of functional analysis theory. Their theory seeks to explain firesetting by distinguishing those factors that reinforce the behavior, such as power and acceptance from peers, an increase in attention, and enhanced self-esteem. By identifying antecedents and consequences that facilitate and maintain firesetting, Jackson et al. (1987) hypothesize that these reinforcers (power, influence, attention, and acceptance from peers) specifically contribute to the development and maintenance of firesetting behavior in children. Functional analysis theory is consistent with findings that identified young firesetters as having poor social skills, experiences of isolation and depression, and according to Gannon and Pina (2010) represents a theory with strong unifying power as it is able to account for other theoretical perspectives and findings from various studies. This theory also assists clinicians in developing appropriate treatment given its multifactorial basis, and as such, it offers sound clinical utility. Several authors, however, have argued that this theory lacks explanatory depth when compared to Fineman's model (Fritzon, 2012; Gannon & Pina, 2010) as it neglects proximal cognitions, or those thoughts that immediately precede the firesetting behavior, and does not explain the mechanisms associated with desistence (Gannon & Pina, 2010).

Another perspective on firesetting takes quite a different approach. Rather than emphasizing etiological or developmental factors as the previous two models have, the action systems model developed by Canter and Fritzon (1998) focuses on the motivation for firesetting behavior based on inferred offender and crime scenes characteristics. It classifies firesetting according to the target of the fire and specifically addresses firesetter cognitions or inferred motives, and then plots these along two axes relating to the arson target (either an object or a person) and the arson objective (either expressive or instrumental) (Fritzon, 2012). The action systems model identifies four types of firesetting behavior summarized following.

Classification	Description
Instrumental person	Firesetting that targets known others for the purpose of revenge or following a dispute, often conducted after the firesetter has made previous threats.
Instrumental object	Opportunistic firesetting often conducted in groups, and in conjunction with other crimes such as break and enter.
Expressive person	Firesetting aimed at restoring emotional well-being or to alleviate distress by gaining the attention of others, often identified as a cry for help.
Expressive object	Firesetting that usually targets public buildings, often repeatedly, after an emotionally challenging event, to attract fire service responses.

This classification system has since been replicated with adult prisoners in the United Kingdom (Almond, Duggan, Shine, & Canter, 2005) and also applied to an Australian sample of arsonists (Fritzon, Doley, & Clark, 2013). It has been well received particularly because of its utility in assisting the investigative processes by profiling the firesetter likely responsible for the fire. Some criticism has focused on its lack of clinical utility for treatment planning (Gannon & Pina, 2010; Dickens & Sugarman, 2012), however, it can be argued that its identification of proximal factors contributing to motivation lays the foundation for the recognition of initial treatment targets.

In response to some of the criticisms of current theories or typologies explaining firesetting, the Multi-Trajectory Theory of Adult Firesetting (M-TTAF) has been developed as an integrated and unifying theory, accounting for the etiology and the motivation for adult firesetting, as well as identifying treatment targets (Gannon et al., 2012). It also references a range of factors that have been neglected in other theories, such as cultural factors. Early childhood factors, biological factors, social learning factors, and contextual factors, such as critical life events or precipitating events, are also identified. Psychological vulnerabilities, such as fire interest, offense supportive attitudes, emotional regulation issues, and communication problems, also contribute to a holistic case formulation designed to inform treatment targets. By combining etiological factors, cultural factors, and proximal motivation, the M-TTAF (Gannon et al., 2012) advances previous theories and typologies or classification systems that have offered a less complex approach to this complex behavior. It also focuses on the identification of cognitions contributing to both the development and the maintenance of firesetting behavior. These offense-supportive cognitions, or implicit theories, are defined as beliefs that allow the firesetter to interpret various events or situations that allow them to offend (Ward, 2000), and may even guide them to situations that reinforce their erroneous beliefs about the world (Plaks, Grant, & Dweck, 2005).

Offense-supportive cognitions are relevant to both the development of firesetting and the maintenance of the behavior, and five implicit theories for firesetters are offered by Gannon et al. (2012). These can be summarized as the "dangerous world implicit theory" or a belief that the world is a hostile place and others cannot be trusted. Also, the "normalization of violence implicit theory" is held by those who believe that violence is normal and acceptable. Additionally, the "fire as a powerful tool belief" is often represented in a sense of entitlement to use fire to send a powerful message. A fourth implicit theory is the belief that "fire is fascinating and exciting" despite being potentially dangerous, and lastly there is the belief that "fire is controllable" or can be controlled as others will respond before it gets out of control.

Finally, the M-TTAF identifies five pathways to the development of firesetting behavior, or trajectories, which are based on empirical evidence, clinical practice, and accepted typological classifications commonly observed in adult firesetters (Gannon et al., 2012). The five trajectories are summarized as follows:

- Antisocial cognition – This trajectory refers to firesetting behavior that is predominantly related to antisocial cognitions, scripts, and values. These cognitions are thought to be generally criminal in nature, and such individuals are unlikely to have intense fire interest or fascination. Fires may be lit to avoid detection, hide evidence, or in conjunction with the commission of other crimes.

- Grievance – This trajectory relates to firesetters whose predominant risk factors are aggression, anger, and hostility. These individuals are likely to see fire as a means to send an authoritative message, and their motivation is likely to be around revenge or retribution rather than intense fire interest or fascination. They are likely to experience anger and ruminate over perceived slights or hold negative attributions toward others who become the object of their firesetting.
- Fire interest – This trajectory refers to firesetters who demonstrate elevated levels of fire interest. Individuals in this trajectory may view fire as pleasurable and hold fire supportive attitudes that have developed through social learning, classical conditioning, and cultural forces. They are not likely to hold general criminal attitudes. A diagnosis of pyromania is not required, however, firesetters following this trajectory are likely to have developed an entrenched coping script, particularly in times of stress or anxiety.
- Emotionally expressive/need for recognition – This trajectory encapsulates firesetters who have poor communication and social skills, low self-regulation, and problem-solving deficits. These firesetters are likely to be unassertive and lack intimacy in their relationships. When these individuals face proximal triggers that place stress on coping resources, they may act impulsively and use fire to communicate their frustration. Firesetters within this trajectory may also use fire for self-harm or suicide as a means of communication or to release negative affect and pain. A subset of firesetters within this trajectory are those possessing a high need for recognition, and this group is likely to use fire to communicate their need for social relevance.
- Multifaceted – The final trajectory refers to firesetters who hold elevated fire interest and offense supportive attitudes. The main difference between this trajectory and the fire interest trajectory is the presence of antisocial cognitions and other risk factors (self-regulation issues and communication deficits). This trajectory includes firesetters who have developed complex and serious problems across a variety of risk factors associated with firesetting, such as inappropriate fire scripts or a fixated interest in fire.

As the act of setting fire to an object may require little planning or preparation, firesetting is often opportunistic and unsophisticated, and can occur in the heat of an argument or when emotional regulation fails. Firesetting in this instance is likely to be "expressive" or a means of communicating emotions such as frustration, anger, or boredom. Instrumental firesetting, on the other hand, occurs for a specific purpose or targets a particular person or business, often in the context of committing insurance fraud or to conceal another crime. Willis (2004) identifies some of the common expressive and instrumental motivations for firesetting to include:

- **Instrumental:** financial gain, including insurance fraud; to conceal another crime or eliminate evidence of another crime; and gang-related vandalism or in conjunction with property crime, often influenced by peer group pressure.

- **Expressive:** revenge, perhaps against an employer, ex-partner, or institution; excitement/thrill seeking or relief from boredom; and attention seeking, or to gain recognition and "hero status."

FIRESETTER PROFILES

Consistent with these differing explanations as to how firesetting behaviors are established, or the various models focused on understanding the motivations for firesetting, the profile of a typical arsonist, whether adult or child, has also been debated in the literature (Ducat & Ogloff, 2011). Researchers suggest that deliberate firesetters are more likely to be male, who experienced problems in school, are socially isolated and unassertive, from an impoverished family, unmarried, with low intelligence, and who are also likely to have had a substance abuse history and committed previous property offenses (Bennett & Davis, 2016; Chaplin & Henry, 2016; Doley, Fineman, Fritzon, Dolan, & McEwan, 2011; Gannon & Pina, 2010; McEwan & Ducat, 2016; Tyler et al., 2014). In addition, poor self-esteem, high levels of impulsivity, and a history of low tolerance to frustration have also been identified in firesetters (Gannon & Pina, 2010), as have features of antisocial personality disorder (Blanco et al., 2010; Geller, 1987). High rates of major mental illness in firesetters, including schizophrenia and major depression, are also indicated (Harris & Rice, 1996), however, some early studies tended to look for firesetting in samples of psychiatric patients, rather than investigate the presence of mental illness in general samples of firesetters, and this may skew findings.

Deliberate firesetting amongst children and juveniles is not uncommon with an estimated 45% of all arson arrests in the United States being persons aged under 18 years of age (Lambie, Ioane, & Randell, 2016). A distinction must be drawn between those whose firesetting is accidental or while playing with matches or lighters and those whose firesetting is malicious or undertaken for destructive purposes. Accidental and "match-play" fires set by children are common according to the authoritative US Fire Administration (US Fire Administration, 2012), and across the United States, fires started by children playing accounted for an average of 56,300 fires or $286 million in direct property damage per year between 2005 and 2009. Of these, younger children were more likely to set fires in homes, while older children and teenagers were more likely to set fires outside, and males were more likely to engage in fire-play than females. In these circumstances, the children are unlikely to be prosecuted, although they may be referred for education/intervention to modify their play activities and address any attraction to match-play.

On the other hand, those who set fires for malicious or deliberate purposes may also demonstrate additional antisocial behaviors, such that firesetting is often just one of a suite of rebellious or harmful behaviors employed (Ducat & Ogloff, 2011). The incidence of self-harming behavior and substance use is also high in this group when compared to young people who do not engage in firesetting (Lambie et al., 2016). Other risk factors include a history of trauma, stressful life events, and family dysfunction, and diagnoses of conduct disorder or attention deficit hyperactivity disorder (Lambie et al., 2016). In terms of typologies for juvenile firesetters, an early classification developed by Kolko (2002) comprised four categories to describe the relationship between background factors and motivation, as follows:

Curiosity firesetter: this group is usually very young, firesetting is experimental, and there is an absence of wider psychopathology or family dysfunction.
Cry-for-help firesetter: this group will often show early behavior problems, engage in firesetting behavior largely for attention, and the behavior occurs within a dysfunctional or stressful environment.
Delinquent firesetter: firesetting is usually present by adolescence, and this group exhibits the greatest deviance and behavioral dysfunction.
Severely Disturbed: this group is rare, and firesetting is comorbid with a wide range of other pathologies, where there are early signs of behavior resulting from individual pathology.

More recently, Stadolnik (2016) describes the expansion of typologies for juvenile firesetters to include motivations such as "anger and revenge, sadness and loss, complex curiosity, self-soothing, thrill seeking, and maladaptive coping and thought disordered" thereby recognizing some of the many facets associated with this behavior (p. 245). Lambie and Randall (2011) caution the overuse of firesetter typologies and profiles given they are often not empirically derived and are unlikely to fully capture the complexity of the behavior, nor the evolution of some factors associated with firesetting over a lifetime. Despite this concern, typologies and profiles have been shown to inform investigations and assist the identification of common treatment targets designed to impact on recidivism.

PROGRAMS DESIGNED TO REDUCE RECIDIVISM

High rates of recidivism, particularly in juveniles, have been established, with some studies showing up to 60% of juveniles aged 6–13 years who have engaged in deliberate firesetting do so again (Kolko, Day, Bridge, & Kazdin, 2001). In a 2009 study Dickens et al. (2009) found that in a sample of 167 adult arsonists referred for forensic psychiatric evaluation, 49% had set fires on more than one occasion. Other researchers, such as Ducat and Ogloff (2011), suggest at least 30% of convicted arsonists will commit subsequent acts of arson. Such high levels of recidivism and associated costs have led to the development of offense specific education and treatment programs for firesetters, often facilitated by clinicians in conjunction with fire service personnel. Residential treatment programs for adjudicated juvenile firesetters and correctional treatment for adult firesetters have been operating in the United States for many years (Stadolnik, 2016), while in Australia, the emphasis has largely been on preventative programs and the education of children identified as at risk of setting fires (Muller & Stebbins, 2007).

Treatment programs target a range of criminogenic needs and factors associated with firesetting and usually include a component on fire safety education and the recognition of the often unintended consequences of firesetting. Most programs employ a cognitive behavioral approach to challenge cognitive distortions and build capacity in problem solving, communication, self-regulation, and relapse prevention (Gannon & Pina, 2010; Gannon et al., 2015), in addition to addressing a range of problems associated with self-esteem, social competence, and goal setting, amongst others. The current approach of addressing generic deficits is the first generation of firesetter treatment, and as these programs are evaluated and treatment gains are measured longitudinally, it is likely we will see increased psychological sophistication that facilitates a range of structured, yet individualized, responses to firesetting emerge.

The first Australian community-based treatment program to knit current firesetter theory with individualized modules has only recently commenced at the Australian Centre for Arson Research and Treatment (ACART) at Bond University. The ACART Firesetter Treatment Program is comprised of seven modules and caters to firesetters aged 14 years or older. It is delivered on an individual basis by a specialist clinician, who administers a range of preprogram assessments. These assessments contribute to the development of a client's case formulation, and the program content is then tailored to address the identified treatment targets. The program, which is being piloted at this time, is based on the M-TTAF (Gannon et al., 2012) and incorporates materials developed to reflect the strength-based principles of the Good Lives Model (Ward & Stewart, 2003). It also recognizes the value of developing a strong therapeutic alliance between the client and the clinician as emphasized in the Multi-Factor Offender Readiness Model (Ward, Day, Howells, & Birgden, 2004). Extensions of this program to allow for group-based delivery, as well as an open-group format, will likely see the utility of this program enhanced for institutional implementation.

FUTURE DIRECTIONS IN FIRESETTER RESEARCH

This chapter has taken an introductory approach to several key issues associated with deliberate firesetting, such as the various theoretical explanations, recent prevalence, and costs associated with the behavior, as well as programmatic and treatment targets designed to address recidivism. As the research community continues to generate knowledge of the etiological and contributing factors, motivations, and offender characteristics associated with firesetting, it is likely that many of the gaps in our understanding of firesetting will be eliminated. As yet little is known of the relationship between culture or a person's ethnic background and their firesetting propensity or the maintenance of the behavior, and further research in this area will inform the treatment of ethnic minorities, including Indigenous peoples. Similarly, knowledge of which factors influence desistence in those using fire for expressive purposes as opposed to an instrumental motivation is lacking. As the identification of firesetting scripts, thinking errors, and new risk assessments emerge in the literature, research efforts are likely to become increasingly specialized and offender specific, leading to individualized treatment approaches. A focus on understanding the differences and similarities across not only age and culture, but also gender and location-specific proximal factors, will also ensure treatment efforts evolve to meet the increasingly challenging presentations seen in custody and clinical settings.

SUMMARY

- The impact of deliberately lit property fires and bushfires on communities can be devastating, and it may take many years for the financial and psychological effects to subside. Those who engage in deliberate firesetting are often complex individuals with a diverse set of treatment or intervention needs, warranting a targeted approach that ameliorates their risk of further offending.
- The term *arson* is a legal term used to define a statutory offense, and *arsonist* refers to an individual who has been convicted of that offense. *Firesetting*, on the other hand, is the term used to describe the behavior of deliberately setting a fire, irrespective of whether such action results in charges being laid or convictions being incurred.
- It is difficult to accurately estimate the cost of deliberate firesetting, especially when fire-service preventative actions, police investigations, insurance claims, and postfire land management costs are considered. The estimated costs due to losses from fire number in the tens of billions globally, or approximately 1% of global gross domestic product per annum.
- It is argued that fires that have been deliberately lit are likely to cause far more damage, and therefore be more costly, than those fires that result from accidental ignition (Fire Protection Association, 2010). This is because deliberately lit fires may be: (1) lit using multiple points of ignition; (2) lit at vulnerable points in a building; (3) assisted by the use of flammable liquids or other accelerants, and therefore spread quickly; (4) started at a time when there will be a delay in the fire being discovered (such as when the premises are unattended or only partially occupied); (5) assisted by compromising fire protection measures in a building (for example, fire doors may be wedged open to help a fire develop and spread throughout the property), or by the sabotage of automatic fire protection measures (such as by isolating a sprinkler system or automatic fire detection installation); and (6) represent an attempt to destroy evidence of another crime.
- In terms of the number of bushfires occurring in Australia, it is estimated that Australian fire services attend between 46,000 and 62,000 bushfires each year, and some estimates suggest that of these, up to 50% are suspicious or confirmed to have been deliberately lit.
- A variety of suggestions have emerged from the criminology and psychology literature as to the correlates of firesetting behaviors, including the notion that

indicators of social disorder, such as broken windows in public buildings, contribute to firesetting.

- Other classifications and typologies focus on an inductive understanding of the behavior according to its motivation, or a deductive approach based on offense and offender variables.

- One of the first multifactor theories developed to explain firesetting was Fineman's (1980) dynamic-behavioral theory. This theory suggests that firesetting behavior results from historical social learning influences, and identifies specific variables such as childhood experiences, environmental factors, and proximal cognitions that contribute to the development and maintenance of firesetting behavior.

- More recently, Jackson, Glass, and Hope (1987) explain firesetting in terms of the principles of functional analysis theory. Their theory seeks to explain firesetting by distinguishing those factors that reinforce the behavior, such as power and acceptance from peers, an increase in attention, and enhanced self-esteem. By identifying antecedents and consequences that facilitate and maintain firesetting, Jackson et al. (1987) hypothesize that these reinforcers (power, influence, attention, and acceptance from peers) specifically contribute to the development and maintenance of firesetting behavior in children.

- The action systems model developed by Canter and Fritzon (1998) focuses on the motivation for firesetting behavior based on inferred offender and crime scene characteristics. It classifies firesetting according to the target of the fire and specifically addresses firesetter cognitions or inferred motives, and then plots these along two axes relating to the arson target (either an object or a person) and the arson objective (either expressive or instrumental). The action systems model identifies four types of firesetting behavior: (1) instrumental person; (2) instrumental object; (3) expressive person; and (4) expressive object.

- Multi-Trajectory Theory of Adult Firesetting (M-TTAF) has been developed as an integrated and unifying theory, accounting for the etiology and the motivation for adult firesetting, as well as identifying treatment targets (Gannon et al., 2012). Early childhood factors, biological factors, social learning factors, and contextual factors, such as critical life events or precipitating events, are identified. Psychological vulnerabilities, such as fire interest, offense supportive attitudes, emotional regulation issues, and communication problems, also contribute to a holistic case formulation designed to inform treatment targets.

- M-TTAF identifies five pathways to the development of firesetting behavior: (1) antisocial cognition; (2) grievance; (3) fire interest; (4) emotionally expressive/need for recognition; (5) multifaceted.

- Instrumental motivations for firesetting include: financial gain, including insurance fraud; to conceal another crime or eliminate evidence of another crime; and gang-related vandalism or in conjunction with property crime, often influenced by peer group pressure.

- Expressive motivations for firesetting include: revenge, perhaps against an employer, ex-partner or institution; excitement/thrill seeking or relief from boredom; and attention seeking, or to gain recognition and "hero status."
- Researchers suggest that deliberate firesetters are more likely to be male, who experienced problems in school, are socially isolated and unassertive, from an impoverished family, unmarried, with low intelligence, who are also likely to have had a substance abuse history and committed previous property offenses. In addition, poor self-esteem, high levels of impulsivity and a history of low tolerance to frustration, features of antisocial personality disorder, and high rates of major mental illness such as schizophrenia and major depression, are also indicated.
- Deliberate firesetting amongst children and juveniles is not uncommon with an estimated 45% of all arson arrests in the United States being aged under 18 years of age.
- In terms of typologies for juvenile firesetters, an early classification developed by Kolko (2002) comprised four categories to describe the relationship between background factors and motivation: (1) Curiosity firesetter; (2) Cry-for-help firesetter; (3) Delinquent firesetter; and (4) Severely disturbed. More recently, Stadolnik (2016) describes the expansion of typologies for juvenile firesetters to include motivations such as: (1) anger and revenge; (2) sadness and loss; (3) complex curiosity; (4) self-soothing; (5) thrill seeking; (6) maladaptive coping; and (7) thought disordered.
- Treatment programs target a range of criminogenic needs and factors associated with firesetting and usually include a component on fire safety education and the recognition of the often unintended consequences of firesetting. Most programs employ a cognitive behavioral approach to challenge cognitive distortions and build capacity in problem solving, communication, self-regulation, and relapse prevention.
- The ACART Firesetter Treatment Program is comprised of seven modules and caters to firesetters aged 14 years or older. It is delivered on an individual basis by a specialist clinician, who administers a range of preprogram and postprogram assessments. These assessments contribute to the development of a client's case formulation, and the program content is then tailored to address the identified treatment targets.

QUESTIONS

1. Define the terms *arson* and *firesetting*. How are they similar and how do they differ?
2. Why are deliberately lit fires thought to cause more damage than accidental or naturally occurring fires? Discuss all six reasons given in the chapter.
3. Describe Fineman's dynamic-behavioral theory of firesetting.
4. Describe the functional analysis theory of firesetting.

5. What is the action systems model of firesetting?
6. M-TTAF, is an integrated or "unifying" theory. What is it, and what are the five essential components of the theory?
7. What are the instrumental and expressive motivations for setting?
8. Describe Kolko's four categories for describing the prelateship between background and motivation of child firesetters.
9. Stadolnik extended Kolko's four categories: What are the "expansion typologies" proposed by him?
10. Outline the core elements of current psychological intervention for firesetting.

REFERENCES

Almond, L., Duggan, L., Shine, J., & Canter, D. (2005). Test of the action system model in an incarcerated population. *Psychology, Crime and Law, 11*(1), 1–15. http://dx.doi.org/10.10 80/1068316031009634287.

Australian Institute of Criminology. (2009). *Bushfire arson bulletin no 59*. Canberra: Bushfire Cooperative Research Centre. Retrieved from http://www.aic.gov.au/publications/ current%20series/bfab/41–60/bfab059.html.

Bandura, A. (1976). Self-reinforcement: theoretical and methodological considerations. *Behaviourism, 4*, 135–155.

Bennett, D., & Davis, M. R. (2016). Risk assessment of parolees. In R. M. Doley, G. L. Dickens, & T. A. Gannon (Eds.), *The psychology of arson* (pp. 184–197). London: Routledge.

Blanco, C., Alegria, A. A., Petry, N. M., Grant, G. E., Simpson, H. B., Liu, S. M., et al. (2010). Prevalence and correlates of fire-setting in the United States: results from the national Epidemiologic Survey on Alcohol and Related Conditions (NESARC). *Journal of Clinical Psychiatry, 71*(9), 1218–1225.

Bryant, C. (2008). *Understanding bushfires: Trends in deliberate vegetation fires in Australia. Technical and background paper Series, 27.* Canberra: Australian Institute of Criminology.

Canter, D., & Fritzon, K. (1998). Differentiating arsonists: a model of firesetting actions and characteristics. *Legal and Criminological Psychology, 3*, 73–96.

Chaplin, E., & Henry, J. (2016). Assessment and treatment of deliberate firesetters with intellectual disability. In R. M. Doley, G. L. Dickens, & T. A. Gannon (Eds.), *The psychology of arson* (pp. 55–67). London: Routledge.

Department for Communities and Local Government. (2011). *The economic cost of fire: Estimates for 2008* (London).

Dickens, G., & Sugarman, P. (2012). Differentiating firesetters: lessons from the literature on motivations and dangerousness. In G. L. Dickens, P. A. Sugarman, & T. A. Gannon (Eds.), *Firesetting and mental health: Theory, research and practice* (pp. 48–68). London: Royal College of Psychiatrists.

Dickens, G., Sugarman, P., Edgar, S., Hofberg, K., Tewari, S., & Ahmad, F. (2009). Recidivism and dangerousness in arsonists. *The Journal of Forensic Psychiatry and Psychology, 20*, 621–639.

Doley, R., Fineman, K., Fritzon, K., Dolan, M., & McEwan, T. E. (2011). Risk factors for recidivistic arson in adult offenders. *Psychiatry, Psychology and Law, 18*, 409–423.

Doley, R. M. (2009). *A snapshot of serial arson in Australia*. Köln, Germany: Lambert Academic Publishing.

Ducat, L., & Ogloff, J. R. P. (2011). Understanding and preventing bushfire-setting: a psychological perspective. *Psychiatry, Psychology and Law*, *18*(3), 341–356.

Evarts, B. (2012). *Intentional fires*. Quincy, MA: National Fire Protection Association, Fire Analysis and Research Division.

Fineman, K. R. (1980). Firesetting in childhood and adolescence. *Psychiatric Clinics of North America*, *3*, 483–499.

Fire & Rescue Statistical Release. (2015). *Fire statistics monitor: England April 2014 to March 2015*. London: Department for Communities and Local Government.

Fire and Rescue, New South Wales. (2014). *Annual Report*. Retrieved from http://www.fire.nsw.gov.au/page.php?id=453.

Fire Protection Association. (2010). *Risk control – Arson prevention: The protection of premises from deliberate fire raising*. RC48, Version 01, London.

Freud, S. (1932). The acquisition of power over fire. *International Journal of Psychoanalysis*, *13*, 405–410.

Fritzon, K. (2012). Theories on arson: the action systems model. In G. L. Dickens, P. A. Sugarman, & T. A. Gannon (Eds.), *Firesetting and mental health: Theory, research and practice*. London: The Royal College of Psychiatrists.

Fritzon, K., Doley, R., & Clark, F. (2013). What works in reducing arson-related offending. In L. A. Craig, L. Dixon, & T. A. Gannon (Eds.), *What works in offender rehabiliation: An evidence-based approach to assessment and treatment* (pp. 255–270). Chichester, England: Wiley-Blackwell.

Gannon, T. A., Alleyne, E., Butler, H., Danby, H., Kapoor, A., Lovell, T., et al. (2015). Specialist group therapy for psychological factors associated with firesetting: evidence of a treatment effect from a non-randomized trial with male prisoners. *Behaviour Research and Therapy*, *73*, 42–51.

Gannon, T. A., Ó Ciardha, C., Doley, R. M., & Alleyne, E. (2012). The multi-trajectory theory of adult firesetting. *Aggression and Violent Behaviour*, *17*, 107–121.

Gannon, T. A., & Pina, A. (2010). Firesetting: psychopathology, theory and treatment. *Aggression and Violent Behavior*, *15*, 224–238.

Geller, J. L. (1987). Fire-setting in an adult psychiatric population. *Hospital and Community Psychiatry*, *38*, 501–506.

Harris, G. T., & Rice, M. E. (1996). A typology of mentally disordered fire-setters. *Journal of Inter-Personal Violence*, *11*, 351–363.

Home Office. (2015). *Crimes outcomes in England and Wales 2014/15* (London).

Inciardi, J. (1970). The adult firesetter. *Criminology*, *8*, 145–155.

Jackson, H., Glass, C., & Hope, S. (1987). A functional analysis of recidivistic arson. *British Journal of Clinical Psychology*, *26*, 175–185.

Kolko, D. J. (2002). *Handbook on firesetting in children and youth*. California: Academic Press.

Kolko, D. J., Day, B. T., Bridge, J. A., & Kazdin, A. E. (2001). Two-year prediction of children's firesetting in clinically referred and nonreferred samples. *Journal of Child Psychology and Psychiatry*, *42*(3), 371–380.

Lambie, I., Ioane, J., & Randell, I. (2016). Understanding child and adolescent firesetting. In R. M. Doley, G. L. Dickens, & T. A. Gannon (Eds.), *The psychology of arson* (pp. 20–28). London: Routledge.

Lambie, I. & Randall, I. (2011). Creating a firestorm: a review of children who deliberately light fires. *Clinical Psychology Review*, *31*, 307–327.

Lewis, N. O., & Yarnell, H. (1951). Pathological firesetting (pyromania). *Nervous and mental disease monograph* (82). Nicholasville, Kentucky: Coolidge Foundation.

McEwan, T., & Ducat, L. (2016). The role of mental disorder in firesetting behaviour. In R. M. Doley, G. L. Dickens, & T. A. Gannon (Eds.), *The psychology of arson* (pp. 211–227). London: Routledge.

Muller, D. A., & Stebbins, A. (2007). Juvenile arson intervention programs in Australia. *Trends & issues in crime and criminal justice* (335). Australian Institute of Criminology.

Office for National Statistics. (2015). *Crime in England and Wales, year ending June 2015* (Statistical Bulletin. London).

Plaks, J. E., Grant, H., & Dweck, C. S. (2005). Violations of implicit theories and the sense of prediction and control: implications for motivated person perception. *Journal of Personality and Social Psychology*, *88*(2), 245–262. http://dx.doi.org/10.1037/0022-3514.88.2.245.

Prins, H. (1994). *Fire raising: Its motivation and management*. London: Routledge.

Queensland Police Service. (2016). *QPS Crime Map*. Retrieved from https://www.police.qld.gov.au/forms/crimestatsdesktop.asp.

Rix, K. J. (1994). A psychiatric study of adult arsonists. *Medicine, Science and Law*, *34*, 21–34.

Rollings, K. (2008). *Counting the costs of crime in Australia: A 2005 update*. Canberra, Australia: Australian Institute of Criminology.

Smith, R. G., Jorna, P., Sweeney, J., & Fuller, G. (2014). *Counting the costs of crime in Australia: A 2011 estimate*. Research and Public Policy Series.129. Canberra: Australian Institute of Criminology.

South Australia Police. (2015). *Bushfires start when we stop paying attention*. Retrieved from https://www.police.sa.gov.au/sa-police-news-assets/traffic/bushfires-start-when-we-stop-paying-attention.

Stadolnik, R. (2016). Promising practice in the development of assessment and treatment models for juvenile firesetting/arson. In R. M. Doley, G. L. Dickens, & T. A. Gannon (Eds.), *The psychology of arson* (pp. 243–259). London: Routledge.

The Geneva Association. (April 2014). *Fire and climate risk* World fire statistics No 29. Retrieved from https://www.genevaassociation.org/media/874729/ga2014-wfs29.pdf.

Thomas, D. S., & Butry, D. T. (2011). Enticing arsonists with broken windows and social disorder. *Fire Technology*, *47*, 255–273.

Tyler, N., Gannon, T. A., Lockerbie, L., King, T., Dickens, G. L., & De Burca, C. (2014). A firesetting offense chain for mentally disordered offenders. *Criminal Justice and Behavior*, *41*, 512–530.

Uniform crime reports. (2011). *Federal Bureau of Investigation*. United States Department of Justice. Retrieved from https://www.fbi.gov/about-us/cjis/ucr/ucr.

Uniform crime reports. (2013). *Federal Bureau of Investigation*. United States Department of Justice. Retrieved from https://www.fbi.gov/about-us/cjis/ucr/ucr.

US Fire Administration. (2012). *Prevent youth firesetting. National Arson Awareness Week Media Kit, May 6–12*.

Victoria Police. (2014). *Annual report 2013–2014*. Melbourne.

Ward, T. (2000). Sexual offenders' cognitive distortions as implicit theories. *Aggression and Violent Behaviour*, *5*(95), 491–507. http://dx.doi.org/10.1016/5/359-1789(98)00036-6.

Ward, T., & Stewart, C. A. (2003). The treatment of sex offenders: risk management and good lives. *Professional Psychology: Research and Practice*, *34*(4), 353.

Ward, T., Day, A., Howells, K. & Birgden, A. (2004). The multifactor offender readiness model. *Aggression and Violent Behavior*, *9*(6), 645–673.

Wickramasekera, N., Wright, N., Elsey, H., Murray, J., & Tubeuf, S. (2015). Cost of crime: a systematic review. *Journal of Criminal Justice*, *43*(3), 218–228.

Willis, M. (2004). *Bushfire arson: A review of the literature*. Research and Public Policy Series, No 61. Canberra, ACT: Australian Institute of Criminology.

Cults

20

Wayne Petherick

Bond University, Gold Coast, QLD, Australia

CHAPTER OUTLINE

INTRODUCTION

Cults are a universal phenomenon and can likely be found in some form in every country around the world. Haworth (1997) suggests that there are 500 cult groups operating in the United Kingdom and other parts of Europe, meaning that on a per capita basis, the breadth and depth of cults is the same as in the United States. Langone (undated) suggests that cult educational organizations have compiled lists of more than 2000 groups with perhaps 1000 of these groups actually meeting the criteria of cults. Furthermore, as an indication of their global nature, he suggests that grassroots cult educational organizations exist in more than 15 countries (with these organizations arising to deal with the problems presented by cults).[1]

---

[1] Research into this topic showed that we know far from enough regarding cults in general and individual groups specifically. As a result, some information about the cults used herein is drawn from media and Internet sources. Every attempt has been made to establish the validity of the included information.

The Psychology of Criminal and Antisocial Behavior. http://dx.doi.org/10.1016/B978-0-12-809287-3.00020-1

The emergence of many cult groups suggests that an examination of the problem is warranted to identify the religious, cultural, psychological, and social milieu of cult groups including their leaders and members. Any understanding of cult groups we currently have has come largely from the mainstream media and a number of high profile groups over the years. This would include, but is in no way limited to, the Branch Davidians in Waco, Texas[2], Aum Shinrikyo in Tokyo, Japan, and Jim Jones in French Guyana (the People's Temple). These depictions are not necessarily helpful in understanding the cult, however, and may give a skewed perception of what a cult involves, the leaders, the members, recruiting practices, and general dynamics.

This chapter will provide an overview of the features of cults, as well as case studies from around the world. Throughout, a number of examples will be used to highlight certain points, including the global nature of the problem, and the behavior or various organizations from the United States to Australia to Russia and Uganda.

WHAT IS A CULT?

Like other social constructs, definitions of cults are many and varied. Some actually define what a cult is, while others adopt a more behavioral classification identifying those features that may be observed within cults. These definitions are usually relative to one's occupation (i.e., law enforcement), religious philosophy (one common definition is that a cult is a religion outside of mainstream or orthodox religions), or research orientation (such as academic research attempting to identify cult features), among others.

Tapper (2005) agrees, suggesting that the term *cult* is a controversial word used differently dependent on perspective. It is also suggested that, in North America, information about cults comes from three broadly defined approaches (Tapper, 2005, p. 1):

- Some religious conservatives, in accordance with their own doctrine, define cults as religions that deviate from orthodox scriptural truth as they define it.
- Sociologists and academic theologians study cults—a word they find pejorative—as normal vehicles of social change found in all cultures. They feel that people are dangerously quick to brand and persecute innocent groups whose only crime is being different.
- Those most critical of cults—often former cult members, their families, and mental health workers who treat them—focus not on the beliefs of any group but on specific behaviors they feel violate human rights.

---

[2] This author is not entirely convinced that the Branch Davidians were a cult in the typical use of the word. There is no doubt that their behavior was unusual or "deviant" to those on the outside, but this departure from the norm doesn't necessarily meet the requirements for a group to be labeled as a cult. They are included herein because of their depiction in general forums and the media.

But this is far from a definition. Instead, these points provide the variety of ways through which cults can be identified, and through which a definition may be constructed.

Coming from an investigative perspective, Bennett and Hess (2001, p. 478) define a cult as "a system of religious beliefs and rituals. It also refers to those who practice such beliefs." This definition is far from helpful because one common discussion in the literature is how a cult differs from a religion, so grouping the two together would seem to be inappropriate. This definition also does nothing in helping us to understand the difference between a cult and a religion.

Haworth (1997) offers a definition of a cult that is also based the presence of certain characteristics. The implication is that if a group has these features then they can be labeled as a cult. These features are:

1. uses psychological coercion to recruit members, indoctrinate members, and retain members
2. forms an elitist totalitarian society
3. its founder is self-appointed, charismatic, dogmatic, messianic, and lacks accountability
4. there is a belief that "the end justifies the means"
5. accumulated wealth does not benefit society

Langone (Undated, p. 1) provides the following exhaustive definition of a cult:

Cult: a group or movement exhibiting a great or excessive devotion or dedication to some person, idea, or thing, and employing unethically manipulative techniques of persuasion and control designed to advance the goals of the group's leaders, to the actual or possible detriment of members, their families, or the community. Unethically manipulative techniques of persuasion and control include but are not limited to: isolation from former friends and family, use of special methods to heighten suggestibility and subservience, powerful group pressures, information management, suspension of individuality or critical judgment, promotion of total dependency on the group and fear of leaving it, etc.

It should be noted that not all cult groups are religious or hang the group's identity on religious ideation. However, because this chapter is not concerned with Elvis cults or other fanatical music groupies, political cults, or cults of celebrity, we will focus exclusively on groups with religion as the central focus of their activities. Therefore, for this chapter, a cult will be defined as "an organization that employs coercive indoctrination techniques to recruit members into a rigid framework of religious or pseudo religious ideation." This would differ from a sect, which is typically a splinter group from a mainstream religion, and which does not typically use coercive mind control techniques to bind their members (Haworth, 1997).

Now that we have a working definition of a cult, we can turn to an examination of cult characteristics.

Tapper (2005, p. 2) provides the following five characteristics, noting that most or all may be present in extreme degrees:

- A rigid belief system that cannot be questioned;
- A charismatic, authoritarian leader who claims to have a new truth or vision and who exercises considerable control over the members;
- Isolation from nonmembers and families of origin, imposed by lifestyle, communal living, or the group's belief that contact with nonmembers is detrimental;
- A high-demand schedule with much time spent in group-centered activities, such as meditation and chanting, fund-raising, proselytizing, and religious study; extreme peer pressure urges conformity, and nonconformists may be shunned or expelled;
- Deceptive recruitment tactics; extreme emotional manipulation of members; privileges granted to the leader, but denied to its members; and the expectation that members relinquish all financial assets to the group.

While the previous criteria are useful, the gold standard for identifying a group as cultic is provided by Robert Lifton based on his examination of thought reform in the mid-1900s (see Lifton, 1969). Lifton suggests that a cult can be identified through comparing the characteristics in the checklist with their behavior (Aron, 1999). There are eight psychological themes against which an environment may be judged (Lifton, 1969), which is the source of the following information unless otherwise stated.

MILIEU CONTROL

This relates to the control of human communication within the group. If this is intense, it becomes an attempt to control information within the group, dictating what a person sees, hears, reads, and writes. This is done so as to alienate members from the outside world and to prevent them from hearing negative press about the leader(s) or the group as a whole. As an example (Eckel, 2008):

> Seven women who had holed up in a cave for months other members of a Russian cult awaiting the end of the world emerged Friday night and were being treated by emergency workers, regional officials said.

> More than two dozen others remained behind but were expected to come out as early as Saturday, the governor's office said.

> About 35 members of the Christian cult entered the cave near the village of Nikolskoye, 400 miles southeast of Moscow, in early November to await the end of the world, which they expected in May. They threatened to detonate gas canisters if police tried to remove them by force.

> The vice governor of the Penza region, Oleg Melnichenko, said in televised comments that the seven women came out voluntarily, carrying satchels with their belongings. He said the cult leader, the self- declared prophet Pyotr Kuznetsov, was brought from a local psychiatric hospital to help persuade the women to leave.

He said the women walked on their own nearly a mile to a prayer house, where emergency workers were talking with them, the RIA-Novosti news agency reported.

...

Kuznetsov has been charged with setting up a religious organization associated with violence. Earlier this week, officials said they had seized literature that included what appeared to be extremist rhetoric. He has been confined to a psychiatric hospital since November.

An engineer from a devout family, Kuznetsov, who goes by the title of Father Pyotr, declared himself a prophet several years ago. He left his family and established the True Russian Orthodox Church and recruited followers in Russia and Belarus.

He reportedly told followers that, in the afterlife, they would judge whether others deserved heaven or hell.

Followers were not allowed to watch television, listen to the radio or handle money, Russian media reported.

MYSTICAL MANIPULATION

Specific patterns of behavior and emotion are manipulated in such a way that they appear to have happened spontaneously though they are actually well orchestrated by the leader. This adds to their power and mystique, in that they can seemingly pluck something from nothing (also referred to as planned spontaneity for the seeming ability to produce something almost on a whim). Group members are also left to feel like they are in control of their own membership or destiny, though in reality they have little power over their own behavior.

For example, during communes at Jonestown in the French Guyana, Jim Jones would have cult members spend days secretly preparing feasts. These were then produced to members of the group, appearing out of nowhere at the clap of his hands, as if by magic. This reinforced Jones's status as a leader with god-like abilities.

THE DEMAND FOR PURITY

The world is viewed in binary terms: individuals are either pure or they are impure. Things are considered pure when they are in line with or conform to the direction of the group, so impurity would be anything that is not in line with this. Purity is promoted as being absolutely attainable, but absolute purity rarely is and the resulting dissonance produces guilt. The group provides relief from this guilt, which binds members more closely to it.

Because the view of the world is absolute, purity creates an environment in which the end justifies the means, with deception and lying being acceptable if they serve the aim of the cult (Aron, 1999). In the furtherance of group aims, the leader may even dictate who is allowed to associate with whom and under what conditions. Matthews (2008) provides this report about Jim Jones of the Peoples Temple:

He also used a 'divide and conquer' method among his followers.

'What Jones did was try to break all ties that were not to him,' said former believer Vernon Gosney. 'Transfer all that loyalty, all that bonding to him. And so families were broken apart. Relationships were divided.'

Such divisions caused family members to spy and report on one another, or friends to turn in friends for various transgressions.

Jones furthered the poisonous atmosphere among his followers by encouraging physical fighting to either solve problems or administer punishment. Audiotapes of such sessions reveal Jones laughing, apparently entertained.

Jones' mastery of the spoken word also enabled his many sexual exploits with both female and male followers. Jones deftly justified his actions to his followers by saying that what he did to them was actually for their own benefit, or the benefit of making the church a stronger, tighter-knit organization.

CONFESSION

Confession requires that group members admit to everything about their past and present behavior (Aron, 1999), and it is through this confession that purity is achieved. According to Lifton (1981), confession contains mixtures of revelation and concealment, and while individuals are told that their confessions will set them free, these confessions essentially bind them to the group. Any concerns or lack of faith expressed by the member may be met with reminders about their past indiscretions, and how, if they chose to leave the group, past confidences cannot be assured. Snow (2003, p. 156) provides the following:

Confession and criticism are a large part of the methodology of cult conversion. Cult members are made to confess over and over the sinfulness of their lives before joining the cult, and they therefore begin to see everything and everyone they dealt with before coming to the cult as sinful. After enough confession, a cult member feels completely unworthy, and consequently is much less likely to believe that he or she has the right to question or criticize cult leaders or the cult ideology. In addition, a large part of this ceremony involves being criticized, often brutally, by other cult members, usually for having questions or some type of independent thought. New members soon learn that the best way to avoid confession and criticism is to accept the cult ideology without question, and to never say anything critical of the cult ideology or the cult leaders.

SACRED SCIENCE

Cult leaders often claim to have special scientific insight into problems that are relevant to all of mankind. Anyone who disagrees with this viewpoint is not only immoral but unscientific (Aron, 1999), and any questioning of basic assumptions is prohibited (Lifton, 1969). Ironically, the leader's claims are baseless and largely nonscientific, and any criticism of members for the doubts they express are highly hypocritical. The following news article highlights claims made by an Australian cult leader more recently jailed for child sexual offenses (Webber, 2005):

As a prophet of the End Times, William Kamm often preached about God's fiery judgment and the world's imminent damnation.

Today, a district court judge laid out the future for the 55-year-old known as The Little Pebble—five years jail as punishment for molesting a 15-year-old girl from his flock.

If Kamm does his penance right, he might just impress the parole board and work his way out of purgatory in three-and-a-half years.

Kamm founded The Order of Saint Charbel, an off-shoot of the Catholic church, about 20 years ago at Cambewarra, near Nowra, on the NSW south coast.

He was highly esteemed as a holy man who interceded with the Virgin Mary and had also declared himself to be 'the last pope' who was waiting to ascend the papacy.

Many followers fell away from The Little Pebble in protest when he claimed to receive new revelations from heaven that he should head a "royal house" of 12 queens and 72 princesses to bear him children in a new holy era.

But others remained loyal and believed his assurances that the conceptions would result from a holy hug and not from sex.

But a NSW District Court jury decided on July 8 that his embraces with a 15-year-old girl were sexual to the point of breast fondling; his kisses were performed with his tongue and on one occasion he parked his car on a public street and masturbated her in broad daylight.

The subsequent charges of aggravated sexual intercourse and four counts of aggravated indecent assault were dated between July and November 1993—when Kamm was almost three times his victim's age.

The offences happened 12 years ago—and another world away.

Kamm's Order of St Charbel, based on 'holy grounds' amid bushland, was to be an idyllic refuge from a troubled world.

Prosecutor Richard Herps opened the case by tabling more than a dozen highly sexualized letters written by Kamm to his new queen.

'Do you ever think about us making love, do you ever desire it,' he wrote on July 14.

Kamm told the girl a few months later that she could sleep with him because 'heaven has already said yes to me', even though she was still below the legal age of consent.

'So we can make love any time but you can not fall pregnant yet ... I know how to make love to you without you falling pregnant', he wrote.

The girl had a diary in which she would write petitions to the Virgin Mary, and the inspired answers—written by the Little Pebble's hand—reinforced his beckoning for a deeper intimacy.

'You have permission for an intimate union with your husband at any time but remember, be discreet,' a reply from 'Mary' said.

Defence barrister Greg Stanton produced a collection of letters during a grueling cross-examination to show the girl had also written flowery love letters to Kamm—before and after the assaults happened.

Kamm has made various failed predictions about the end of the world—predictions which he now describes as 'delayed'.

The Catholic Church denounced Kamm and outlawed the order in 2002 after Rome endorsed an investigation which found his teachings were 'false, harmful and contrary to those of the Catholic Church'.

The denouncements continued today, as Judge John Williams described Kamm's assaults against the girl as 'an inexcusable and gross breach of trust'.

'I am concerned there is a significant risk of reoffending,' he said during the sentencing.

Foreshadowing a difficult reception in prison, Judge Williams said: 'He will probably spend most of his sentence on protection'.

Kamm's legal team is appealing against the conviction and sentence.

A spokesman for the Order would not comment.

Kamm's other claims to sacred knowledge include there being a comet inside the tail of the Hale–Bopp comet set to destroy the earth, and multiple warnings about the dangers of digital watches.

Apart from the deceptive nature of sacred science (claims are essentially unprovable or untestable ideas about the way of the world), some are outright dangerous. For instance, at least one member of the Breatharian group died as a result of claims that humans can exist on air alone; no food or other nourishment is typically allowed (Klotz, 1999):

A man who believed people could live on air alone has been jailed for six years for killing a fasting woman for whom he and his wife delayed getting medical aid.

Jim Vadim Pesnak, 60, and his wife Eugenia Pesnak, 63, both of Beckwith Street, Ormiston, Bayside Brisbane had pleaded not guilty to the manslaughter of Lani Marcia Roslyn Morris, 53, between June 12 and July 2 last year.

A Supreme Court jury took only three hours to convict them of manslaughter last week.

Today, Justice Margaret Wilson sentenced Pesnak to six years in prison and his wife to three years, both with no recommendation for early parole.

'Mr Pesnak, your recklessness was of a high order,' Justice Wilson told him.

'Mrs Pesnak, not only did you make no endeavor to dissuade your husband from that course of conduct, you actively assisted him.

'It is important that other members of the community be deterred from dangerous, cruel and inhumane conduct, albeit in the pursuit of spiritual beliefs,' Justice Wilson added.

The couple's defence counsel Kelly Macgroarty had asked for significantly lower sentences, suspended after four months for Mr Pesnak and wholly suspended for his wife.

The Pesnaks are followers of the breatharian philosophy which has as its central tenet that an energy force known as 'prana' pervades the atmosphere and therefore humans do not need food to survive and can live on air alone.

Ms Morris, a mother of nine, travelled from her Melbourne home to undertake the 21-day 'spiritual cleansing' initiation process into breatharianism.

The process involved seven days without any nourishment at all, including water, and then a further 14 days on orange juice.

After a week, the 53-year-old appeared to be paralyzed down one side, could not talk, was vomiting a black tar-like substance and eventually was so ill she had trouble breathing.

On day 11, Mr Pesnak went to the lengths of forcing a crude tube down her throat to help her breathe, and only hours later did he call an ambulance.

The Pesnaks gave interviews to police in which they maintained they believed Ms Morris was undergoing a 'spiritual blockage', and was not in danger physically.

She died on July 1 after being admitted to the Mater Hospital's intensive care unit and being placed on life support.

Ms Morris had suffered a stroke from severe dehydration, was in a coma, had renal failure, gangrenous feet and breathing problems.

Justice Wilson said the Pesnaks were entitled to their spiritual beliefs, and their sincerity was not questioned.

'However, the death of Ms Morris demonstrates just how dangerous this 21-day process was and how misguided you were about the nature of its spiritual character,' she told them.

The couple, married for 34 years, have four adult children who are all working in professions and do not share their parents' breatharian philosophy.

Mr Pesnak is a retired electrical engineer and his wife a retired tax agent.

Both their families migrated as refugees from post-war Europe after being displaced and exploited by the German and Russian armies.

His family was Estonian, and hers was Polish, and both still follow the Russian Orthodox faith.

The couple have spent the past seven days in custody.

Under the sentences imposed, Mr Pesnak will have to serve a further three years jail before being considered for parole and his wife 18 months.

LOADING THE LANGUAGE

Many groups adopt idiosyncratic clichés and expressions (Aron, 1999). This further serves to separate out the group and its members from the rest of society, creating a feeling of belonging. Words in everyday use take on a different meaning within the group, becoming group words or phrases (Lifton, 1969). Lifton (1981, p. 2) provides the following:

> *The term loading the language refers to literalism and a tendency to deify words or images. A simplified, cliché-ridden language can exert enormous psychological force reducing every issue in a complicated life to a single set of slogans that are said to embody the truth as a totality.*

DOCTRINE OVER PERSON

Doctrine over person requires the cult member to disregard their own experience and reality in favor of that of the cult (Aron, 1999). This doctrine is invoked when the members sense a conflict between what they are experiencing and what group doctrine says they should experience (Lifton, 1996). When serious doubt arises, members begin to question their continuing membership to the group, and perhaps even plan to leave. It is at this point that the group may turn to destructive behaviors.

The following example highlights the problems that may arise when members begin to doubt their association and the group's philosophies. This and other examples throughout this chapter also highlight the global nature of the cult problem (Associated Press, 2000):

> *The unfulfilled prophecy of a Christian doomsday sect cost the faith of loyal followers, and perhaps their lives, as they started to challenge the cult's leaders, a surviving 17-year-old cult member said.*

> *Peter Ahimbisibwe's allegation came Sunday as dignitaries joined residents of Kanungu and nearby villages in southwestern Uganda. They condemned the deaths of 924 members of the reclusive sect who authorities say were killed by their leaders.*

> *Until Sunday, no sect member, past or present, had confirmed the common belief here: The failure of the world to end Dec. 31 led members to demand belongings they had surrendered to join the Movement for the Restoration of the Ten Commandments of God—a challenge that allegedly led to retaliation by sect leaders.*

A March 17 blaze inside the chapel of the sect's secretive compound in Kanungu burned 530 sect members alive. Authorities initially termed the deaths a mass suicide, but the discovery of the bodies of six slain men in a compound latrine soon shifted that assessment to murder.

Since then, mass graves at three other compounds linked to the cult have yielded 388 more bodies, many stabbed and strangled. The pungent scent of rotting bodies emanating Sunday from a latrine in the main Kanungu compound suggested the toll could still rise.

Monday, police investigators were headed to a fifth sect site to search for more bodies and clues.

The site was just outside the capital, Kampala, far from the southwestern villages of the other sect bases. Police spokesman Assuman Mugenyi said the site was a home used by cult followers.

Also Monday, mental-health officials in Kampala were putting together a crisis intervention team to travel to the sect's home of Kanungu, James Walugembe of the Mental Health Ministry said.

'Nothing like this has ever happened before,' Walugembe said. 'People are shattered, really shattered.'

Ahimbisibwe, whose mother and sister died in the fire two weeks ago, said sect members began pressing Credonia Mwerinde, a movement founder who was known as 'The Programmer,' about the fate of their property during worship services.

'The people who sold their property would inquire one-by-one. Whoever would inquire would disappear,' Ahimbisibwe told reporters in Kanungu on Sunday for a government-convened prayer service for the victims.

Ahimbisibwe survived March 17 only because he became hungry during what would be the last of the sect's frequent fasts, and slipped away to eat at his father's house, he said.

Ahimbisibwe also said he saw a man carrying a hammer and nails early March 17. It is partly this testimony, authorities say, that has persuaded them that windows and doors were blocked to prevent sect members from leaving the chapel before the flames erupted—or fleeing afterward.

Sect members were 'always preparing' to go to another world, Ahimbisibwe said. But when they entered the chapel that morning for prayers dressed in the sect's uniform of green-and-white robes, they had no idea of what was about to happen, he said.

Meanwhile, thousands of townspeople gathered on a hilltop soccer field Sunday to mourn the neighbors they barely knew.

Ugandan Vice President Speciosa Kazibwe called the architects of the deadliest cult tragedy in modern history 'diabolic, malevolent criminals masquerading as holy and religious people.'

During the memorial service, Kazibwe acknowledged the failure of the country's police and intelligence agencies to expose sect.

'Through deception and conspiracy, these criminals outwitted the security network (and) exploited the ignorance and illiteracy of thousands,' she said, adding that the government planned to convene an interagency group to study the country's cults.

DISPENSING OF EXISTENCE

The cult views outsiders as not wholly people, who are missing some aspect of their life that cult members have, but these others do not (Lifton, 1969). Because of the absolutist view that the cult is good, those not in the cult are seen as the epitome of evil. The only hope, therefore, is for outsiders to come to the group and be 'saved.' Once this happens, confession inevitably ensues, and the individual becomes bound to the group.

Because life is a gift from God (or whatever or whoever the group worships), any attempt to leave the cult will strip the individual of the gift. This could come in the form of thoughts about their own mortality should they leave, or it could come in other forms, such as a female cult member's doubt about their ability to conceive should they depart the group. Aron (1999, p. 18) states that "a former member of the Moonies in Melbourne sought counseling with me over a fear that because she had left the group she would not become pregnant. It took several years before she overcame her fear."

And it is not just the fear of what might happen to oneself through mystical or supernatural forces should the cult be left behind that may play a role in whether one stays or goes. Many cult groups around the world have openly threatened members who would leave with harm to themselves or their families, and some have even carried out those threats. The Aum Shinrikyo cult in Japan, under the auspices of Shoko Asahara, is one such example (from Akimoto, 2006, p. 4):

According to Tokyo District Prosecutors Office, the indicted facts for Asahara number 17 cases, and most of them are murders. Among them the most tragic one is the murder of Lawyer Tsutsumi Sakamoto, his wife and their 2-year-old infant son on 4 November 1989. Sakamoto was a consultant for the Aum Victims Group, formed by parents of believers who had rejected all communication with their families. He had been quick to perceive the truth about the wily Asahara and his cult and was preparing to accuse Asahara and his cult. Asahara considered the lawyer as an obstacle to his plans and resolved a 'poa' (a Sanskrit word meaning 'do away with') him. The murder of the lawyer and his family was allegedly committed by six of Asahara's followers. The victims' corpses were later carried to a remote mountain area and were discarded separately. Antecedent to this murder, in February 1989, a believer who wanted to defect was murdered and his body burned in a heating furnace. Besides these cases, many other similar murders were committed by the followers under the command of Asahara. Those murders were lynching persons who were regarded as the obstacle or the betrayer by Asahara.

Beyond the fear of existing cult members about their leaving and what may happen as a result, prospective members may also be drawn into a psychological state of uncertainty and doubt if they *do not* join a group. If we adopt a more global perspective on membership, this may also help explain why people are drawn into membership in the first place. The following is from Salvatore (1987):

Seventy-four-year-old Catherine, recently widowed, joined a religious group at a neighbor's urging in the hope of learning how to prepare her soul for death. Over time, Catherine's daughter Susan noticed that her usually healthy mother was losing weight and was tired and withdrawn.

After nine months, Catherine abruptly decided to move to the group's headquarters in a neighboring state. She liquidated all her assets, removed her daughter's name from their joint bank account and withdrew thousands of dollars of her life savings. But the day before Catherine was scheduled to join the group, Susan had to rush her mother, hysterical and incoherent, to the hospital. Doctors confirmed she had suffered a severe nervous breakdown.

For most people the word 'cult' conjures up '60s images of college students wearing flowing robes, chanting rhythmically and spouting Eastern philosophy. But today's realistic young people may be more concerned with career planning and money than mysticism.

'As a result, cults have had to turn to new, more susceptible groups,' said Herbert Rosedale, a New York lawyer who works for no fee to help those who feel a cult has victimized them.

In fact, recent developments have changed cults—about 3000 groups nationwide with between 3 million and 8 million followers—in important ways. Cults today are expanding their membership through a new pool of recruits: the elderly, the middle-aged and churchgoing Christians.

...

Those ripest for cult recruitment, said Marcia Rudin, a leading authority on cults, are people 'in a period of transition that makes them vulnerable.' As a result, said Reginald Alev, information officer and former executive of Cult Awareness Network (CAN) in Chicago, 'It's common for the elderly to be recruited after the death of a spouse.'

Not only does this loss make the elderly emotionally vulnerable, it also stirs up a profound fear of their own death. That fear, critics say, is exploited by cults.

'Literally millions of dollars,' said Philip Abramowitz, director of the Task Force on Missionaries and Cults of the Jewish Community Relations Council of New York, 'are given to cults by people who are told they will be taught to communicate with those they leave behind when they die.'

Loneliness is also a problem for the old, one that cults take advantage of, critics say. 'The elderly are neglected in our society,' said Abramowitz. 'They want someone to listen to their problems and be sympathetic.'

Cult members know this and do much of their recruiting in hospitals and nursing homes or, said Abramowitz, 'pose as cleaning- or cooking-service workers or offer to do shopping, gardening or provide transportation to doctors' appointments.'

Experts say the elderly are being targeted today for two reasons: There are more of them and they have more money. Currently, those over 65—women in particular—represent the fastest-growing segment of our population. And senior citizens have had a lifetime to accumulate assets.

'Cults go where the money is,' Alev said.

Rudin said groups that have aimed intense recruitment efforts directly at the elderly include the Church Universal and Triumphant; the Rev. Sun Myung Moon's Unification Church, which has an Orange Blossom Corps specifically for outreach to seniors; the Divine Light Mission; the Way International, whose older members belong to its Sunset Corps; the Tony and Susan Alamo Foundation, and the Walk. Visits to some of these groups' meditation programs are offered as recreational outings by some unsuspecting senior-citizen centers.

The middle-aged, especially middle-aged women, are primarily responsible for the popularity of the New Age movement—components of which, some say, represent a new kind of cult. Made chic in large part because of actress Shirley MacLaine's best seller and miniseries Out on a Limb, New Age blends Eastern and Western thought and encompasses self-help groups, healing crystals, reincarnation and channeling (communicating with spirits through a medium).

CAN says the New Age phenomenon, particularly channeling, shares characteristics with destructive cults.

…

Part of the reason for this growth may be demographics. New Age has attracted the majority of its adherents from aging baby boomers—a group second only to the elderly in population growth.

Some New Agers, said Alev, are children of the '60s who still have not found the answers they have been looking for. Others, added Rudin, 'are now realizing that although they have become prosperous, material happiness is not enough.'

...

Young or old, victims of cults looking for compensation often find themselves unwittingly challenging First Amendment protections of freedom of religion. To avoid such a legal quagmire, anti-cult activists have sought to distinguish legitimate freedom of speech from destructive cult behavior, which they argue ought not be protected.

Michael Langone, director of research for the American Family Foundation, a research and educational organization in Massachusetts, said a destructive cult is defined as 'a group that manipulates and exploits its members, dictates how they should think and act, claims an exalted status that sets it in opposition to mainline society, and utilizes mind-control techniques to recruit prospects and make its members subservient.'

Such mind control was used in the case of Catherine. Catherine's daughter later discovered her mother was targeted for recruitment by a 'friendly' neighbor who moved in with her, ostensibly to help out. The woman, herself a mental hostage of the group, kept Catherine on a diet heavy in starches, which made her sluggish and weak.

She deprived Catherine of sleep and forced her to copy by hand reams of incoherent prose, which made Catherine highly suggestible. In addition, Catherine, as with members of many cults, was told that worldly harm and eternal damnation would befall her and her family if she tried to break free.

...

There is life after cults. Today Catherine lives in a senior-citizen community where she is active and happy, after going for counseling with a group that specialized in the problems of those leaving cults.

'My mother is still not as healthy as she was before,' said her daughter. 'But we're not wasting time looking back. We have a lot of life to catch up on.'

WHAT IS THE ATTRACTION TO CULTS?

The last part of this chapter will cover in brief the reasons why a person might join a cult or be attracted to their ideology. The intent is not to provide a full psychological, social, and emotional review of the state of a prospective cult member at any point in time, rather to the canvass the broad issues relating to cult attraction. A number of examples will be provided to highlight key points.

Given the previous discussion on the thought reform techniques used and their destructive nature, the obvious question is, why someone would join a cult in the first place? This question becomes more pertinent when one considers the extensive amount of media exposure cults receive, especially when they clash with outside agencies (law enforcement as in the case of the Branch Davidians, and the government as in the case of the People's Temple).

It would be all too easy to suggest that the typical cult member is a psychologically unstable and socially maladjusted individual who may also be possessed of lower intelligence as well as being a social isolate. This propensity to write off cult members is likely a psychological defense mechanism not unlike that employed in other realms: if we can accept or believe that "others" (cult members, victims of crime, offenders) are unlike "us" (normal, well-adjusted, and law-abiding citizens) we are protected from the thought that we could somehow suffer the same fate as they have.

However, research and anecdotal experience of those who work with ex-cult members has in fact shown that many of them are remarkably well adjusted, educated, and successful. Haworth (1997, p. 1) has the following to say on the matter:

There are many myths associated with an understanding of the general cult phenomenon today. One popular notion suggests that to become a member of a cult you have to be experiencing a personal problem. This school of thought further postulates that the prospective cult member must be a lost, searching soul with no faith, who may be unstable and suffer from low self-esteem. It continues with the idea that he is likely to be an uneducated teenager, who may have a history of mental illness and/or joined the cult in order to fill a void in his life. The reality is vastly different.

By far the majority of people who are recruited into cults are in fact normal and healthy. They usually come from economically advantaged family backgrounds, have average to above average intelligence and are well educated, idealistic people, with no prior history of mental illness. Their spiritual perspectives vary greatly. Some have a strong faith and some do not.

People of all ages are influenced and many are professionals. It appears that anyone can be recruited. For rather than joining a cult they are actively recruited. No one wakes up in the morning and says 'it's about time I got involved in a cult' and goes out looking for one. Instead they become unwitting victims of deception and subtle techniques of psychological manipulation.

Raphael Aron, an Australian cult exit counselor also provides some insight on the matter (1999, p. 20–21):

Although everyone is vulnerable to the influences of cults, there appears to be particular situations which lend themselves to cult involvement. Low points, at which time life becomes more difficult, illness, death of a loved one and times of crisis or soul searching—all these create opportunities for cult groups to offer assistance in the form of counseling, accommodation, and even shelter. An unhappy relationship, conflict at home, communication problems, unemployment and financial difficulty can also create a sense of vulnerability. Failure, a loss of self-esteem and a sense of hopelessness further weaken resistance to outside influences, whether positive or counter-productive.

Times of spiritual turmoil, feelings of rejection by one's chosen church and a need to find deeper meaning in life can also direct the searching individual to other alternatives, whose attraction is magnified as a result of these circumstances. Family situations which have never been resolved and conflicts regarding identity can help create the climate in which the helping hand of the cult is welcome.

Although the above situations may set the scene for cult involvement, it is wrong to assume that stable relationships, steady employment and a high self-esteem will guarantee insulation from the cult experience. They do provide a healthier anchor, however, with strong ties which, in turn, will serve as some counterbalance to the opportunities offered by the cult.

Because all of the just-discussed life circumstances are common and quite universal, in fact they are all part of the human condition, it would be flippant to suggest that anyone suffering any or all of the above is more at risk of the lure of cult groups. Other environmental factors are undoubtedly at play such as an individual's social support including friends and family, their willingness to ask for help during periods of turmoil, and any other coping mechanisms they may bring to bear in times of duress or angst. However, as noted in the extract by Aron, they do provide the context during which recruitment is made easier. There can be no doubt though that social, psychological, cultural, racial, financial, and interpersonal barriers play a role, whether in the weak of spirit or the strong.

Further insight into why someone would join a cult can be garnered through an examination of the cult leaders themselves. Ironically, the perception of the cult leader by members and initiates may indeed play a part, even when the leader is themselves paranoid or suffering from other clinical conditions. Any associated ramblings may be explained by the group executive as a special insight or some shedding of the worldly body as the cult boss ascends to a higher level of knowledge. And cult leaders who have become psychotic or deranged in other ways are not special or rare. In fact, for many people this may be their draw—they seem to possess special insight or power, though the reality is that in some cases their visions may simply be the psychotic ramblings of an individual who is fast losing touch with reality. The following from Ross (2006) is an example of this:

Chizuo Matsumoto, also known as 'Shoko Asahara' led his followers to a day of reckoning, but it wasn't the one he predicted, instead it was the beginning of the end for him and the cult he created called 'Aum Supreme Truth.'

Asahara was sentenced to death in February 2004 for the poison gas attack he ordered in Tokyo, which claimed of lives of twelve people and injured 5500. Including the murder of a lawyer and his family and other related crimes, 27 lives were lost in the wake of Matsumoto's madness.

Japanese justice moves slowly and after 11 years and with all his appeals exhausted the cult leader may soon be executed by hanging on the gallows.

In the past decade Aum has disintegrated and splintered into factions as its founder, who was once regarded as divine, lapsed into silence. Today the man that once ruled the sect like a king languishes in a jail cell alone wearing diapers, apparently unwilling or unable to communicate or even use a toilet.

One of the guru's lieutenants also convicted of cult crimes and sentenced to death says that Matsumoto might remain a symbol to some of his remaining followers after his death.

'If Matsumoto is to be executed without testifying, he will become a martyr,' Kenichi Hirose, 41 wrote in a letter, reports Yomiuri Shimbun.

'If Matsumoto is going to have his death sentence finalized without testifying, fails to atone for his actions and maintains a barrier of self-containment, I've nothing to say to him,' Hirose also said.

Throughout the years since his arrest the once talkative guru has been mute. He did not speak coherently during his court trial, though at times he has demonstrated the ability to masturbate in front of his jailers.

Regardless of whether Matsumoto is faking, or has unraveled without the power he once held, the murderous cult leader will not be protected by an insanity defense.

Tokyo High Court on Monday rejected an objection filed by his lawyers and nothing remains between the heinous cult leader and the hangman.

Many cultists then are, or at least have been in the past, stable, intelligent, professional people who are simply searching for something that they feel is missing from their lives. This may lead them, as with the elderly discussed previously who fear death, to seek out some form of enlightenment or salvation, with the cult and its biblical philosophies providing such an outlet. An example of this is Heaven's Gate, where followers of Marshall Applewhite committed suicide in San Diego nearly two decades ago, believing they were transcending their earthly bodies to take their place in the universe on a spaceship. This from Carlin (1997):

The 39 cultists who 'shed their containers', or committed mass suicide, in San Diego last week already seemed to have divested themselves of many of the trappings of humanity. The first police on the scene thought they were all youngish men, because of their shaved hair and uniform clothing; it turned out that more than half were women, and mostly well into their 40s and 50s. Several of the men, it also emerged, had been castrated.

Yet however outlandish their exit may appear, the only surprise is that it does not happen more often. If you consider that 222 million Americans, or 87 per cent of the population, believe they will go to heaven; that 125 million believe in the existence of UFOs; and that 200,000 believe they have been abducted by aliens—then the decision by 39 people to hitch a ride to eternity on a passing spaceship does not seem as strange as all that.

Indeed, as the millennium approaches and more people begin dwelling on last things as the Internet broadens its proselytizing scope, mass suicides may become increasingly common. The prophets of doom who populate the Internet have a captive audience in the lonely souls who spend their days trawling through cyberspace in search of love and companionship, a sense of belonging and community they hunger for in 'meatspace' but cannot find.

The cultists who ceremonially quaffed hemlock at the luxury mansion in Rancho Santa Fe last week all belonged to that misfit tribe who roam the Internet to escape the void of their inadequacy. 'Heaven's Gate' was the name of the website the 39 called home. Where 'Heaven's Gate' came from there is plenty more. Home pages abound blending technological virtuosity with atavistic warnings that 'the Day of Tribulation' is nigh.

It is the age of the computer, but the message the terrorized faithful heard as the year 1000 approached has not changed. Then, as now, visions of comets and other celestial disorders presaged the destruction of the world; then, as now, close readings of the Psalms and Revelations taught that 'the End of Age' had arrived.

A website titled 'Apocalyptic Signs in the Heavens', one randomly selected among many in the same vein, combines numerological readings of the scriptures with a study of the chaotic motions in the heavens to argue that 'the countdown' has begun, that '1997 should be considered the final warning before the Tribulation'.

…

And then, as if the Biblical evidence were not convincing enough, we are told that there have been three eclipses in the past year, followed now by the comet Halle–Bopp, which is traversing the heavens from Sagittarius to Orion. 'According to the Talmudic sages,' our omnivorous webmaster informs us, 'a comet crossing Orion signifies the destruction of the earth.'

…

The danger with all these ravings is that some people will take the lunatic premises postulated on the Web to their terrible logical conclusions. Such was the case, a court in Colorado will contend tomorrow, with Timothy McVeigh, the man charged with the Oklahoma bombing—the Net is also the main instrument of propaganda for the far-right militias, who call on their followers to take up arms in defense of the republic against the dark forces advocating 'one-world government'.

The Heaven's Gate cult expressed the most refined distillation of all the millennial mania out there. People of powerful technological competence, computer programmers all, they drew from Biblical, extra-terrestrial and astral myths to create a life-denying theology whose only end was suicide.

Their rejection of the world led them to devise an idiosyncratic vocabulary where people became 'vehicles' or 'containers'; Jesus Christ, 'the Captain'; life-after-death, 'the Next Level'. Marshall Herff Applewhite, the founder of the cult and one of the 39 who died, wrote this impassive commentary on the death in 1985 of his companion, Bonnie Lu Nettles: 'She separated from her borrowed container and returned to the Next Level.'

Cybermonks and nuns who all dressed in black and wore their hair close-cropped, they shunned sexual activity, fearing it would contaminate the purity of their immortal souls. Thus in their writings did they express disdain for 'vehicular gratification' and 'mammalian behavior' and, thus, did the male members of the cult banish the temptations of the flesh forever by having their testicles surgically removed. The coroner at San Diego said most of the men whose bodies he had inspected were eunuchs.

From voluntary castration to suicide is not, perhaps, a difficult step to take. A more impressive act of will was displayed by two of the women in the group who killed themselves in the full knowledge that they were leaving behind children, one of them a baby seven months old.

All of which suggests these people once led ordinary lives, though we know nothing about them as yet save for Applewhite, whose father was a Presbyterian minister and who himself trained for the church before switching his attention to music. In 1969 he obtained a master's degree in music at the University of Colorado before moving to Houston, where he sang with the Grand Opera as well as teaching at the University of St Thomas.

The Washington Post reported yesterday that Applewhite went into a psychiatric hospital in the early 1970s and asked to be cured of homosexual impulses after an affair with a male student led to his dismissal from the university. It was during his hospital stay that he met a nurse, Bonnie Lu Trusdale Nettles, a mother of four and a part-time professional astrologer.

The Heaven's Gate site describes their meeting thus: 'In the early 1970s, two members of the Kingdom of Heaven (or what some might call two aliens from space) incarnated into two unsuspecting humans in Houston... They consciously recognized that they were sent from space to do a task that had something to do with the Bible.'

They began their task by opening a bookshop called the Christian Arts Center that sold information on metaphysics, astrology and theosophy. Applying their minds to this eclectic reading matter they began formulating a set of beliefs whose consummation came with the arrival of the comet and the UFO spotted trailing in its wake. 'We fully desire, expect and look forward to boarding a spacecraft from the Next Level very soon,' reads one of the last entries in the cult's website. 'Halle–Bopp's approach is the 'marker' we've been waiting for.'

And then with clinical efficiency they supped together from their poisoned chalices, lay face up on their bunk beds and covered their heads with purple Easter veils. But, for all the cold clarity of purpose they espoused, they betrayed their confused humanity with two pathetic touches. They packed their belongings neatly in canvas bags next to each of their bunks and made a point of slipping their passports into their shirt pockets. Just in case there was immigration control at the Pearly Gates, and their souls in paradise might need the gratification of a change of clothes.

CONCLUSIONS

A cult is an organized group that uses techniques of thought reform to recruit and indoctrinate members into what is usually a rigid set of beliefs, often revolving around religious ideology or philosophy. Some cults also have apocalyptic visions of the end of time, with followers committing ritual suicide at a predetermined point in time (and those who choose not to commit suicide may indeed be killed by other members). These groups who identify an end of time are known as millenarian. Cult groups are largely identified by the presence or absence of a number of characteristics, with the most common characteristics provided by Lifton, based on his study of thought reform techniques. These would include milieu control, mystical manipulation, and the demand for purity, among others.

Despite some popular depictions of cult members as psychologically unstable or immature individuals, many are stable, mature, and professional people who likely suffer a period of turmoil or instability and seek out some form of belonging. The cult is the perfect vehicle through which this belonging can be achieved, though once indoctrinated, a number of techniques serve to bind the members to the group. As a result, they may believe they are free to come and go as they please, though the reality is that they have far less autonomy.

SUMMARY

- Cults can be found across the globe in virtually all countries.
- Our understanding of cults as informed by systematic research is not fully developed.
- A cult is defined differently by different groups. Law enforcement will define a cult differently to religious groups, and this may be different from definitions from social and other sciences. One of the best definitions of a cult is provided by Haworth (1997) who states that a cult uses psychological coercion to control members, forms a totalitarian society, the founder is usually self-appointed, they believe that the end justifies the means, and they do not generally benefit society.
- Robert Lifton of John Jay College in the United States studied Nazi doctors during World War II and provides a checklist of characteristics that can identify a cult. There are eight characteristics in the checklist, and the behaviors of the group are compared to this list. The more characteristics the group has, the more destructive they are deemed to be.
- Milieu control involves the total control of communication within the group. The cult may prevent members from talking to nonmembers, or reduce or eliminate access or exposure to media sources such as television, newspapers, radio, or the Internet. This is done so as to prevent the members from being exposed to negative press about the leader or the group as a whole.
- Mystical manipulation involves patterns of behavior and emotion that are manipulated so it appears that they were spontaneous despite being orchestrated by the group.

- The demand for purity imparts a view of the world that exists in a binary state. Things are considered good or evil depending on how they align with the philosophies of the group. A behavior such as lying is seen as good if it is perpetrated against outsiders but bad if perpetrated against other members or the group.
- Confession involves the admission of past sins and behaviors with the stated goal of purging sin and wrongdoing. However, these admissions can be used at a later point against the penitent should they try to leave or threaten the group.
- Sacred science occurs when the leader class has special or unique insight into a phenomenon or problem. These claims are usually baseless, nonscientific, and may be of the type that are easy to disprove.
- Loading the language refers to the adoption of a special language or communication style within the group. This serves to isolate group members from the general community (and vice versa) in such a way that intergroup communication becomes difficult if not impossible.
- For doctrine over person, individual members are required to dispense with their own experience and adopt the reality provided by the group. This helps to remove any dissonance the individual may have over what they believe, and what the group would have them believe.
- The final characteristic, dispensing of existence, views nonmembers as being only partly whole, or as missing something vital in their life. Life is viewed as a gift from God, and so individuals who try to leave the group may fear that their life will be spontaneously extinguished, or a woman may be concerned about her ability to reproduce should she leave.
- While there is a tendency to believe that cult members must lack intelligence, be psychologically unstable, or socially maladjusted, this is not necessarily the case. Just as with many aspects of the human condition, there are a number of factors that contribute to someone joining a cult. This could include any range of vulnerabilities, such as a recent loss or other life struggles. For some, they will join the cult because it provides something that they believe will fill a void in their life.

QUESTIONS

1. Definitions of a cult vary according to who is providing the definition. True or false?
2. Litton developed his checklist of cults that has how many characteristics?
    a. 4
    b. 5
    c. 6
    d. 7
    e. 8

3. What are the three broadly defined approaches identified by Tapper (2005) in developing information about cults?
4. The characteristic of a cult that relates to the control of communication within the group is known as:
    a. Doctrine over person
    b. Milieu control
    c. Communication override
    d. Sacred science
    e. None of the above
5. Mystical manipulation is also known as:
    a. Planned spontaneity
    b. Sacred science
    c. Milieu control
    d. Dispensing of existence
    e. Loading the language
6. Some groups adopt idiosyncratic clichés and expressions. This is done to further bind the members to the group. True or false?
7. What are some of the reasons why people join cults?
8. It could be said that cult members are all of lower intelligence or gullible. True or false?

REFERENCES

Akimoto, H. (2006). The Aum Cult leader Asahara's mental deviation and its social relations. *Psychiatric and Clinical Neurosciences, 60*(1), 3–8.

Aron, R. (1999). *Cults: Too good to be true*. Pymble: Harper Collins Publishers.

Associated Press. (April 3, 2000). *Failed prophecy shook faith, cult survivor says*. Deseret News.

Bennett, W., & Hess, K. (2001). *Criminal investigation* (6th ed.). Belmont: Wadsworth Thompson.

Carlin, J. (March 1997). Who's next through heaven's gate? *The Independent, 30*. Available from http://www.independent.co.uk/news/world/whos-next-through-heavens-gate-1275859.html.

Eckel, M. (March 28, 2008). *7 Russian cult members emerge from cave*. Associated Press.

Haworth, I. (1997). *Caring for cult victims*. Carer and Counselor, Summer.

Klotz, S. (November 1999). *Breatharians jailed six, three years over death*. Australian Associated Press.

Langone, M.D. *Cults: Questions and answers*. (undated). Available from http://www.csj.org/studyindex/studycult/cultqa.htm.

Lifton, R. J. (1969). *Thought reform: The psychology of totalism*. New York: W. W. Norton & Co.

Lifton, R. J. (February, 1981). Cult formation. *The Harvard mental Health Letter*.

Lifton, R. J. (1996). *The nazi doctors: medical killing and the psychology of genocide*. New York: Basic Books.

Matthews, D. M. (November 13, 2008). *Jim Jone' followers enthralled by his skills as a speaker*. CNN.

Ross, R. (2006). *Heinous cult leader will be hung*. Cult News. Available from http://www.cultnews.com/?cat=14.

Salvatore, D. (September 27, 1987). Soul searching: cults targeting an older pool of recruits. *Ladies Home Journal, Chicago Sun Times*.

Snow, R. L. (2003). *Deadly cults: The crimes of the true believers*. Westport: Praeger Publishers.

Tapper, A. (September 2005). *The impact of cults on health*. Nursing Spectrum.

Webber, G. (October 2005). In *NSW: Judge punishes doomsday prophet* (Vol. 14). Australian Associated Press.

Index

'*Note*: Page numbers followed by "f" indicate figures, "t" indicate tables and "b" indicate boxes.'

A

Made in the USA
San Bernardino, CA
22 December 2019